Human Rights, Digital Society and the Law

The internet has created a formidable challenge for human rights law and practice worldwide. International scholarly and policy-oriented communities have so far established a consensus regarding only one main aspect – human rights in the internet are the same as offline. There are emerging and ongoing debates regarding not only the standards and methods to be used for achieving the "sameness" of rights online, but also whether "classical" human rights as we know them are contested by the online environment. The internet itself, in view of its cross-border nature and its ability to affect various areas of law, requires adopting an internationally oriented approach and a perspective strongly focused on social sciences. In particular, the rise of the internet, enhanced also by the influence of new technologies such as algorithms and intelligent artificial systems, has influenced individuals' civil, political and social rights not only in the digital world, but also in the atomic realm. As the coming of the internet calls into question well-established legal categories, a broader perspective than the domestic one is necessary to investigate this phenomenon.

This book explores the main fundamental issues and practical dimensions related to the safeguarding of human rights in the internet, which are at the focus of current academic debates. It provides a comprehensive analysis with a forward-looking perspective of bringing order into the somewhat chaotic online dimension of human rights. It addresses the matter of private digital censorship, the apparent inefficiency of existing judicial systems to react to human rights violations online, the uncertainty of liability for online human rights violations, whether the concern with personal data protection overshadows multiple other human rights issues online and will be of value to those interested in human rights law and legal regulation of the internet.

Mart Susi is Professor of Human Rights Law at Tallinn University, Estonia.

Routledge Research in Human Rights Law

Socio-Economic Rights in Emerging Free Markets
Comparative Insights from India and China
Surya Deva

Comparative Executive Clemency
The Prerogative of Mercy in the Commonwealth
Andrew Novak

Social and Economic Rights in Theory and Practice
A Critical Assessment
Helena Alviar Garcia, Karl Klare and Lucy A. Williams

Challenging Territoriality in Human Rights Law
Building Blocks for a Plural and Diverse Duty-Bearer Regime
Wouter Vandenhole

Care, Migration and Human Rights
Law and Practice
Siobhán Mullally

China's Human Rights Lawyers
Advocacy and Resistance
Eva Pils

Indigenous Peoples, Title to Territory, Rights and Resources
The Transformative Role of Free Prior and Informed Consent
Cathal M. Doyle

Civil and Political Rights in Japan
A Tribute to Sir Nigel Rodley
Edited by Saul J. Takahashi

Human Rights, Digital Society and the Law
A Research Companion
Edited by Mart Susi

For more information about this series, please visit: www.routledge.com/Routledge-Research-in-Human-Rights-Law/book-series/HUMRIGHTSLAW

Human Rights, Digital Society and the Law

A Research Companion

Edited by Mart Susi

Routledge
Taylor & Francis Group
LONDON AND NEW YORK

First published 2019 by Routledge

2 Park Square, Milton Park, Abingdon, Oxon, OX14 4RN
605 Third Avenue, New York, NY 10017

Routledge is an imprint of the Taylor & Francis Group, an informa business

First issued in paperback 2020

British Library Cataloguing-in-Publication Data
A catalogue record for this book is available from the British Library

Library of Congress Cataloging-in-Publication Data
Names: Susi, Mart, 1965- author.
Title: Human rights, digital society, and the law : a research companion / Mart Susi.
Description: Abingdon, Oxon [UK] ; New York, NY : Routledge, 2019. |
Includes bibliographical references and index.
Identifiers: LCCN 2019004034 | ISBN 9781138493063 (hardback) |
ISBN 9781351025386 (ebook)
Subjects: LCSH: Right to Internet access. | Human rights. | Internet—Access control—Law and legislation. | Data protection—Law and legislation. |
Internet—Political aspects. | Freedom of information.
Classification: LCC K3240 .S855 2019 | DDC 341.4/833—dc23
LC record available at https://lccn.loc.gov/2019004034

ISBN: 978-1-138-49306-3 (hbk)
ISBN: 978-0-367-72787-1 (pbk)

Typeset in Bembo
by Apex CoVantage LLC

To Mari-Ann – my wonderful wife and best friend

Contents

Notes on contributors x

PART I
Introduction 1

Human rights in the digital domain – the idea of non-coherence theory 3
MART SUSI

PART II
Right to the internet and rights inside the internet – theoretical dimension 13

1 **The sameness of human rights online and offline** 15
MILOON KOTHARI

2 **Right of access to the internet – global approaches** 31
CAROLINA AGUERRE

3 **The right to privacy: The end of Privacy Fatalism** 44
JONATHON PENNEY

4 **Freedom of expression online** 58
MATTHIAS C. KETTEMANN AND WOLFGANG BENEDEK

5 **The digital disruption of human rights foundations** 75
HIN-YAN LIU

PART III
Legislation, judicial and stakeholder practices – practical dimension 87

6 **The main challenges related to protecting human rights in the internet** 89
CHANGROK SOH, DANIEL CONNOLLY AND SEUNGHYUN NAM

7 **Liability regimes for online human rights violations** 103
STEN SCHAUMBURG-MÜLLER

8 **Multistakeholderism – meaning and implications** 117
JOANNA KULESZA

9 **Judicial balancing of human rights online** 132
ORESTE POLLICINO AND OLEG SOLDATOV

10 **The role and practices of online stakeholders** 148
THOMAS WISCHMEYER

11 **The jurisprudence of the ECJ and ECtHR regarding data protection in the internet** 163
CARSTEN M. WULFF

12 **The Internet Balancing Formula** 178
MART SUSI

PART IV
Specific issues related to human rights and the internet 195

13 **Human rights and the right to be forgotten** 197
UGO PAGALLO AND MASSIMO DURANTE

14 **Finding a judicial definition of journalism: a challenging exercise in the digital age** 209
ELLEN HOVLID

15 **Combating hate speech online** 225
JUKKA VILJANEN

16 **European copyright and human rights in the digital sphere** 239
CHRISTINA ANGELOPOULOS

17 Digital security and human rights: a plea for counter-infringement measures 259
MIREILLE HILDEBRANDT

PART V
Data protection issues 271

18 The challenge of personal data protection in the digital era and global responses 273
ALEXANDROS VARVERIS AND FERENIKI PANAGOPOULOU

19 Data protection in the private sector: convergence or localisation of rights and expectations? 286
W. SCOTT BLACKMER

20 The protection of personal data in a digital society: the role of the GDPR 303
TIINA PAJUSTE

PART VI
Global perspective 317

21 Africa, the internet and human rights 319
CH POWELL AND TOBIAS SCHONWETTER

22 The approach of North American courts towards the internet 337
DAVID P. STEWART

23 Asian human rights law, jurisprudence and practices toward the internet 354
SATOSHI YOKODAIDO

24 Latin American human rights law jurisprudence and practices towards the internet 371
OSCAR RAÚL PUCCINELLI

25 The Russian perspective on human rights protection online 384
DMITRY DEDOV

Index 397

Contributors

Editor

Mart Susi is a Professor of Human Rights Law and Head of Legal Studies at Tallinn University. He has been leading several international research and development projects (EU Commission-funded Horizon 2020 project "Hurmur" and Nordic Council of Ministers-funded project "Law and Media Network"). He has authored several monographs and more than 50 articles. Currently, he is editing several books on the topics of new media, and human rights and the digital society. Susi has recently introduced and is developing the concept of the Internet Balancing Formula.

Contributors

Carolina Aguerre Principal Researcher at Centro de Tecnología y Sociedad, University of San Andrés

Christina Angelopoulos Lecturer in Intellectual Property Law, University of Cambridge

Wolfgang Benedek Professor of International Law at the Karl Franzens University of Graz

W. Scott Blackmer Professor from Practice, Georgetown University Law Center

Daniel Connolly Research Professor, Korea University

Dmitry Dedov Judge at the European Court of Human Rights

Massimo Durante Professor of Jurisprudence, University of Turin

Mireille Hildebrandt Research Professor on Interfacing Law and Technology Vrije Universiteit Brussel and Chair of Smart Environments, Data Protection and the Rule of Law, Institute of Computing and Information Sciences (iCIS) Radboud University Nijmegen

Ellen Hovlid Associate Professor, Volda University College

Matthias C. Kettemann Head of Research, Leibniz Institute for Media Research, Hans-Bredlow-Institut, Hamburg and Associated Researcher, Alexander von Humboldt Institute for Internet and Society, Berlin

Miloon Kothari Former Special Rapporteur on Adequate Housing, UN Human Rights Council; Senior Advisor, MIT Displacement Research Action Network (DRAN)

Joanna Kulesza Professor of international law and Internet governance, University of Lodz

Hin-Yan Liu Associate Professor, Faculty of Law, Copenhagen University

Seunghyun Nam Research Professor, Korea University

Ugo Pagallo Professor of Jurisprudence, University of Turin

Tiina Pajuste Lecturer at Tallinn University

Fereniki Panagopoulou, Assistant Professor, Department of Public Administration, Panteion University

Jonathon Penney Assistant Professor of Law; Director, Law and Technology Institute, Schulich School of Law, Dalhousie University

Oreste Pollicino Full Professor of Law at Bocconi University, Italy

CH Powell Senior Lecturer, University of Cape Town

Oscar Raúl Puccinelli Judge at the Commercial Appeals Court and Professor of Constitutional Law and Human Rights, Rosario National University

Sten Schaumburg-Müller Professor at the Law Department of the University of Southern Denmark

Tobias Schonwetter Director of Intellectual Property Unit, University of Cape Town

Changrok Soh Professor of Korea University Graduate School of International Studies and member of the Advisory Committee of UN Human Rights Council (UN HRC)

Oleg Soldatov PhD Student, Bocconi University

David P. Stewart Professor from Practice, Georgetown University Law Center

Alexandros Varveris Special Laboratory Educational Staff, Law and Informatics Laboratory, University of Athens

Jukka Viljanen Associate Professor, Tampere University

Thomas Wischmeyer Professor of Law, Bielefeld University

Carsten M. Wulff PhD Student, Tallinn University

Satoshi Yokodaido Associate Professor, Keio Law School

Part I

Introduction

Human rights in the digital domain – the idea of non-coherence theory

Mart Susi

The principal matter that all the chapters in this volume more or less directly or indirectly address – either in relation to a specific human rights topic or in reference to a specific region – is whether human rights law as we know it from the offline world exists also in the digital domain. The idea of the sameness of human rights online and offline[1] may seem at first glance *conditio sine qua non* based on common sense, yet it implies that not only human rights norms from the offline dimension, but more broadly the whole human rights framework is transposed from the offline to the online sphere. This implication can be explained either using "ordinary" language or conceptually. By the "ordinary" meaning of human rights I have in mind what rights we have, how we can enforce these rights and what happens if someone interferes with our enjoyment of our human rights. This is mapped at the conceptual or scientific landscape of human rights as the aspects, first, of the origin and meaning of human rights norms, including human rights theory, and second, of the implementation of human rights claims, including who has obligations corresponding to these rights, and third, of remedies against human rights violations. In relation to all three aspects there are concerns about whether the human rights digital framework simply mirrors the non-digital or whether the offline image becomes distorted once online. The actual question that emerges is not whether the image is somewhat distorted – we all know that it is – but whether the distortion is of such a degree that it amounts to what one would call a paradigmatic shift. The chapters in the present volume constitute sufficient scholarly evidence to present these concerns in a holistic manner. In the offline dimension, human rights norms, the practice of their implementation and the remedies form a coherent system, where the various parts are interconnected and the functioning of each part critically depends on the functioning and predictability of the other parts. A paradigmatic shift in the human rights framework in the offline-online divide means that the coherent offline system becomes dysfunctional online. Or rather, the question arises of whether we are using conceptual tools originating from the offline human rights discourse which may not be suitable for the online human rights

1 The idea of the sameness of offline and online rights is the main overarching concept in current internet-related legislation, policies and debates, and is rarely challenged. It originates from the 2012 United Nations Human Rights Council resolution on 'the promotion, protection and enjoyment of human rights on the internet'. This resolution affirms that the same rights that people have offline must also be protected online, in particular freedom of expression, which is applicable regardless of frontiers and through any media of one's choice, in accordance with article 19 of the Universal Declaration of Human Rights and the International Covenant on Civil and Political Rights – see UN General Assembly Resolution A/HRC/20/L.13 on the promotion, protection and enjoyment of human rights on the internet. Retrieved from http://www.un.am/res/Human%20Rights/GA%20resolution%20on%20internet%20as%20the%20human%20right%202012_eng.pdf (accessed 29.03.2019).

environment. This may mean that the principles of legal certainty, foreseeability and predictability, which are all features of constitutional democracy, are not applicable in the online domain.

To illustrate this for the offline dimension of human rights (human rights as we know it), if Archibald wishes to write an article for a newspaper, suggesting that Mathilda as his supervisor has created an environment of harassment in the workplace, then both can realise their rights through the established human rights system. Archibald can claim that he only implements his right to freedom of expression, whereas Mathilda can claim that this intrudes on her privacy and reputation. Both Archibald and Mathilda know that their rights are relative and in principle deserve the same protection. Both can turn to a court which has to explain which right merits more protection given the circumstances. When the court is not sure whether the lawmaker intended to protect one's workplace reputation at the same level as one's reputation as a private person, then the court can turn to the *travaux preparatoires* from civil liability law. The court can impose a prohibition against the publication until the case is resolved. Should Mathilda win the case, the article will never be published, if the interim measure was applied. If the article is published, and five years later Mathilda wishes to apply for a new job, the employer is not likely to find out about the allegation of harassment. Archibald may also apply for a new position in five years and the future employer is not likely to obtain information that he has once been a whistleblower against a previous employer. This image becomes distorted online.

The first concern related to the distortion is about the challenges originating from the digital domain towards the offline human rights deontological architecture; that is, the meaning of human rights norms, the origin of the standards for their realisation, and the interrelationships and theoretical considerations which are intrinsic to such architecture. Is there evidence to suggest that the meaning and scope of concrete human rights as formulated and accepted in the offline (physical) world is changing in the online world? My response to this question is that such evidence exists. Not only is this related to human rights norms, but also to human rights doctrinal matters. The deontological character of human rights online is different from deontological character of human rights offline.

Regarding human rights norms, we can see that their meaning changes once transposed into the digital domain. Penney argues that technology has not only lead to the birth of the modern meaning of privacy, but also to its mortal twin – the phenomenon of privacy fatalism.[2] From the other side of the coin, Pollicino and Soldatov suggest that the world wide web is threatening the meaning of the freedom of expression.[3] We are also witnessing the emergence of internet-specific human rights. Angelopoulos raises the question of the nature of copyright and its relationship with other interests, a question that has emerged due to the development of digital technology.[4] She asks whether copyright is a new human right and if it is, how are its clashes with other rights to be resolved? Pagallo and Durante propose that the reason for the articulation of the new human rights for the protection of personal data is because of the need to complement the canonical protection

2 Jonathan Penney (2019) The Right to Privacy: The End of Privacy Fatalism. In: Mart Susi (Ed.), *Human Rights, Digital Society and the Law*. London: Routledge, 45.

3 Oreste Pollicino and Oleg Soldatov (2019) Judicial balancing of human rights online. In: Mart Susi (Ed.), *Human Rights, Digital Society and the Law*. London: Routledge, 144–145.

4 Christina Angelopoulos (2019) European copyright and human rights in the digital sphere. In: Mart Susi (Ed.), *Human Rights, Digital Society and the Law*. London: Routledge, 257.

of privacy in the online domain.[5] A related debate is whether the right to erasure, or de-listing, should be conceived as a new human right. Taken separately, it may not be sufficient in the context of the emergence of internet-specific human rights and the change in the scope of traditional human rights to speak of a paradigmatic change in the human rights framework caused by the internet. But in conjunction with other changes, let us explore this further.

Internet-specific human rights standards in the digital domain originate directly from the service providers themselves – powerful online companies create the standards for their own usage. This is exactly what Kulesza means when she writes about the changing norm-making paradigm[6] regarding how and by whom normative and procedural standards are formulated. Despite the developing international – political, judicial and academic – consensus that both vertical and horizontal mechanisms have an important role to play in internet governance,[7] the concept of the dual nature of human rights governance online remains rhetorical and illusory because there is no evidence that these governance models can operate in concert. Rather, the chapters in the present collection demonstrate the opposite – a perpetual dichotomy, where the vertical model assumes that the offline human rights framework is transposable to the online sphere, and the horizontal model assumes that it is not. International soft law instruments suggest that governments should adopt regulations outlining the terms of service for online companies and call for these companies to publish their own standards for content moderation. Such legislation and standards need to meet the criteria of transparency, accessibility and foreseeability. We are witnessing that the legislation adopted usually applies only to hate speech and leaves the matter of legally acceptable online user-generated content at the mercy of service providers. In recent years, the main global social media actors have published community standards regarding their anticipated actions towards online content.[8] The focus of these standards is against hate speech and/or clearly illegal content, but there are also guidelines for when legal content affecting someone's privacy can be removed or blocked. These standards neither refer to the international normative human rights architecture, nor do they address the matter of the sameness of online and offline rights. When YouTube writes in its standards that it "reserves the right to make the final determination of whether a violation of its privacy guidelines has occurred", this reflects the doctrine of law as practice. We may use terms like *Lex Facebook, Lex Twitter*, etc., which means that the origin of digital human rights law has, strictly speaking, a private character.

We also see that the principles of transparency, accessibility and foreseeability lose their overarching functionality in regard to human rights online; that is, these principles are not usable for conceptualising human rights online. The image of human rights online can be painted according to how and why these principles are not applicable. Transparency offline means that individuals can understand why certain outcomes regarding their ability

5 Ugo Pagallo and Massimo Durante. Human rights and the right to be forgotten. In: Mart Susi (Ed.), *Human Rights, Digital Society and the Law*. London: Routledge, 197.

6 Joanna Kulesza (2019) Multistakeholderism – meaning and implications. In: Mart Susi (Ed.), *Human Rights, Digital Society and the Law*. London: Routledge, 130.

7 See Council of Europe Committee of Ministers Recommendation CM/Rec (2018)2 to the member States on the roles and responsibilities of internet intermediaries.

8 See Facebook community standards www.facebook.com/communitystandards/ (accessed 20.10.2018), see YouTube community standards www.youtube.com/intl/eng/yt/about/policies/#community-guidelines (accessed 20.10.2018), and see Twitter community standards https://help.twitter.com/en/rules-and-policies/hateful conduct-policy (accessed 20.10.2018).

to realise human rights are achieved, usually by reading a court judgment or some other articulated document related to their individual situation. The concern about the lack of transparency when online companies access user-generated content is evident from many chapters in the present volume that touch upon this matter. Transparency regarding individual human rights protection is replaced by statistical data regarding the outcomes of the assessment of similar online conflicts of rights or values. Accessibility relates to both access to regulative principles, which is positive law, and remedies in the event of an alleged violation. We are used to having easy access to legal norms which tell us what consequences we can expect as a result of our behaviour. When it comes to the protection of rights online, we are not sure where we can find the applicable regulation, if it exists at all. Regarding remedies offline we know at least in principle where to find the protection of one's rights when a violation is claimed. Since the matter of remedies against online human rights violations remains at the stage of contestation, it is often not clear which remedies are available if there is an online violation – either judicial or via the platform itself and what is the appropriate procedure to follow.

The offline human rights framework is partially based on the assumption that rights such as the freedom of expression and the right to privacy deserve equal protection – both are relative, and which right prevails in a concrete situation is resolved on a case-by-case basis applying consensual standards. Elsewhere, I have argued that the doctrine of sameness – leading to the understanding that the freedom of expression and the right to privacy online are of equal importance and deserve equal protection – remains at the stage of contestation in the digital domain.[9] This contestation in itself does not lead to rejecting balancing as the process of online content assessment, since the initial weight of the rights to be balanced changes the scales, but not the process. The balancing paradigm has therefore undergone a shift in the online dimension, where the consensual idea of the equal weight of the right to privacy vis-à-vis freedom of expression is replaced by a practice-dependent weight assigned to these rights by the online stakeholders. This situation is characteristic of a utilitarian or relative understanding of human rights. It is appropriate to speak about balancing within the meaning of particular online portals, such as Facebook or Twitter or Google. The balancing paradigm in the online dimension is characterised by fragmentation and proliferation. The idea of the sameness of online and offline human rights is based on the perspective of the universality of these rights, but the currently developing online balancing paradigm rests on the utilitarian perspective. This situation is against the principle of foreseeability.

Many human rights doctrinal understandings change in the digital domain. Hovlid writes that digitalisation challenges the boundaries of journalism and has created the term "citizen journalism".[10] Because of the digitalisation of media, the functional approach is now to replace the former professional or institutional understanding of who is a journalist.[11] Liu points out that digitalisation poses orthodox concerns to privacy, due process

9 See: Mart Susi (2019) Balancing fundamental rights in the internet – proportionality paradigm and private online capabilities. In: Massimo La Torre, Mart Susi, Leone Niglia (Eds.), *The Quest for Rights: Ideal and Normative Dimensions of Law*. Elgar Publishing, forthcoming 2019.

10 Ellen Hovlid (2019) Finding a judicial definition of journalism: a challenging exercise in the digital age. In: Mart Susi (Ed.), *Human Rights, Digital Society and the Law*. London: Routledge, 209.

11 Ibid. As the author writes, it is problematic to justify journalistic privileges if these are granted to too many people.

and freedom of expression.[12] Hildebrandt points out that the matter of online security raises the novel question of whether fundamental rights and security are at the same level, expressing her view that their relationship is more complicated, as one may be conditional on the other.[13] Hildebrandt asks whether this means that the balancing paradigm involving just two factors has become non-applicable in at least some online conflict areas.

An attentive reader will surely note the rhetorical intensity in the discourse in this volume about human rights in the digital space. Kulesza uses the expression "dramatically" with reference to the law-making power shifting away from governments. Liu writes about the digital disruption of human rights foundations.[14] Pagallo and Durante use the term "digital revolution" when writing about the impact of digitalisation upon human rights.[15] They also refer to crucial democratic concerns about the private bureaucracies which Google and Facebook have created.[16] Penney uses the expression privacy fatalism[17] and refers to privacy as being on death row.[18] Viljanen writes about the need for vigilant measures on all levels to protect democracies and the rule of law online, primarily due to threats originating from the spread of hate speech.[19] Although the strong rhetorical component in human rights discourse may "pollute" the scientific and impartial exploration of substance, it nevertheless points to the challenge towards the coherence of some fundamental elements in the target context, which is the human rights online architecture.

The second concern is related to the implementation of human rights entitlements in the digital domain. New obligations that emerge from the digital domain to the legislators and challenges that emerge to the courts[20] call for "shared" responsibility over human rights protection online. A new specific term – multistakeholderism[21] – has been proposed regarding the process whereby states "share" some of their obligations towards human rights protection with private actors; that is, the states shift their positive duties to private entities.[22] This process involves not only the shift of obligations to protect human rights, but also entails the shift of the standard-setting away from the states and international public community to global private communities. Pagallo and Durante point out, in this respect, that companies that began as technology companies soon discover not only that they are media companies but that they are also governance structures facing concerns as to the enforcement of human rights.[23] The danger, following the "traditional" approach

12 Hin-Yan Liu (2019) The digital disruption of human rights foundations. In: Mart Susi (Ed.), *Human Rights, Digital Society and the Law*. London: Routledge, 75.

13 Mireille Hildebrandt (2019) Digital security and human rights: a plea for counter-infrigement measures. In: Mart Susi (Ed.), *Human Rights, Digital Society and the Law*. London: Routledge, 266.

14 Liu (2019), 75.

15 Pagallo and Durante (2019), 197.

16 Ibid. 200.

17 Penney (2019), 45.

18 Ibid.

19 Jukka Viljanen (2019) Combating hate speech online. In: Mart Susi (Ed.), *Human Rights, Digital Society and the Law*. London: Routledge, 237.

20 Angelopoulos (2019), 258.

21 Multistakeholderism is a distributed policy-making model based on the voluntary cooperation of key actors, usually identified as: the state, business and civil society, operating "in their respective roles", through "rough consensus and running code". This approach, although neither new nor unique to cyberspace, significantly differs from national law-making or international norm development, both traditionally dominated by states. See: Kulesza (2019), 117.

22 Kulesza (2019), 118.

23 Pagallo and Durante (2019), 200.

to human rights protection, is, as formulated by Pajuste, that for some data controllers the risk assessments may end up being just about following formal procedures for the sake of it, instead of engaging in a meaningful way with the risks and the impact of their data processing activities.[24] This concern is also related to novel threats that originate from the internet. As Soh, Connoly and Nam have suggested, there are three types of threats to human rights in the internet. The first is the threat that governments pose to their own citizens. The second is the broad spectrum of bottom-up danger emanating from individuals and non-state groups. The third consists of threats from beyond the state posed by individuals, organised groups and foreign governments.[25] All these threats are specific to the digital domain. Wischmeyer has observed that all over the globe intermediaries are struggling against what they frame as an overly zealous regulatory state and what regulators conceptualise as necessary and proportionate measures to bring the political, economic and social powers of intermediaries in line with public interests such as security, privacy, consumer protection and the respect for the fundamental rights of those affected by liability exemptions; for example, the victims of online hate speech.[26] This struggle represents the incompatibility of two divergent perspectives: the perspective that human rights online need to mirror human rights offline, and another perspective resting on the practical realisation that they cannot.

The third concern is related to the responses to human rights violations, which is tied to the matter of liability. Schaumburg-Müller's entire chapter speaks about the jurisdictional issues of liability online, which are profoundly different from traditional approaches.[27] Wischmeyer points to the ongoing debate where intermediaries are increasingly often described as quasi-public entities for the online world which must be held to the same standards of transparency, rights protection and legitimacy as state actors.[28] If the responses to human rights violations were to be predominantly offline in nature, then this would automatically mean their ineffectiveness, since information online can cause potential harm within minutes, but offline reactions would take months or years. If on the other hand the responses or remedies were predominantly of an online nature, this means that the fundamental assumption that there needs to exist a judicial solution for each human rights violation is abandoned.

The discipline of digital human rights needs to accept that the coherent framework of human rights offline is non-transposable to online in practice and non-justifiable theoretically. The digital domain compromises not only some elements of the offline human rights framework sporadically, but all of its main elements. This does not mean abandoning the framework, but a change in the meaning and scope of offline human rights to a greater or lesser degree, leading to inter-relational and functional changes between elements of the offline human rights framework once online. The theoretical foundations for human rights from the offline world become non-applicable or significantly changed

24 Tiina Pajuste (2019) The protection of personal data in a digital society: the role of the GDPR. In: Mart Susi (Ed.), *Human Rights, Digital Society and the Law*. London: Routledge, 307.

25 Changrok Soh, Daniel Connolly and Seunghyun Nam (2019) The main challenges related to protecting human rights in the internet. In: Mart Susi (Ed.), *Human Rights, Digital Society and the Law*. London: Routledge, chapter 6, 100–101.

26 Thomas Wischmeyer (2019) The role and practices of online stakeholders. In: Mart Susi (Ed.), *Human Rights, Digital Society and the Law*. London: Routledge, 149.

27 Sten Schaumburg-Müller (2019) Liability regimes for online human rights violations. In: Mart Susi (Ed.), *Human Rights, Digital Society and the Law*. London: Routledge.

28 Wischmeyer (2019), 149.

in the online domain. The essential definition of human rights as entitlements against governments is evaporating online. Dworkin's[29] thesis that an individual's rights exist outside of positive or written law may still hold, yet these rights obtain a dual nature as claims are made simultaneously against governments and private online entities. Radbruch's understanding that the principles of purposiveness, justice and legal certainty[30] as antinomies that direct the operation of the law is a framework which seems entirely non-applicable for human rights law online, since these principles representing constitutional democracy are replaced by the principles of economic efficiency and/or the realisation of business or social or political goals. Alexy's thesis[31] that the propositions about the intensity of interference and degrees of importance lend themselves to a rational justification becomes meaningless online due to the inability of online service providers to provide argumentative decisions when assessing online content. Alston's idea that human rights and development work in tandem[32] is rejected by the fragmentation of the online human rights landscape and preponderance of economic power held by online service providers. The idea of this tandem rests on the assumption that human rights are a tool to foster some social value or cause or serve to promote the interests of some vulnerable group – but the online service providers have not demonstrated the linkage of human rights to such values online, nor is there an element of vulnerability associated with them. Much more could be said about all these theoretical considerations, but the brief introduction has to suffice here.

The digital dimension of human rights can be described via a novel principle that I term the variance principle, which says that this dimension is characterised by a consistent condition of unpredictability and lack of clarity on whether human rights norms, their realisation, related obligations, and remedies against violations as established in the offline world continue to exist online undistorted or, if distorted, what are the degree and consequences of such distortion, or whether they are replaced by online-specific elements. The variance principle claims that ontic and epistemic aspects of human rights from the offline domain may be at variance with these aspects in the online sphere. It is perhaps more accurate to state that offline norms and principles may apply sporadically, but there exists no predictability about the circumstances under which they apply and exactly how. In some instances they may apply, such as in relation to some concrete online service providers, or in some countries, or regarding some specific rights – and in other instances they may not.[33] The variance principle leads to the non-coherence theory of digital human rights, which claims that human rights law and its application online is

29 R. Dworkin (1977) *Taking Rights Seriously*. Harvard: Harvard University Press.

30 G. Radbruch (1950) Legal Philosophy. In: E. Lask and C. Wilk (Eds.), *The Legal Philosophies of Lask, Radbruch and Dabin*. Cambridge: Harvard University Press.

31 R. Alexy, *A Theory of Constitutional Rights*, 82–84; see also R. Alexy (1989) *A Theory of Legal Argumentation* (first publ. 1978), trans. Ruth Adler and Neil MacCormick. Oxford: Clarendon Press, 212–220.

32 P. Alston (2005) Ships Passing in the Night: The Current State of the Human Rights and Development Debate Seen through the Lens of the Millennium Development Goals. *Human Rights Quarterly*, Vol. 27, No. 3, 755–829.

33 See for example similar propositions from the present collection. Schaumburg-Müller writing: "I am not arguing that life online and offline is always completely the same and ought to be regulated in precisely the same manner in all details. What I am arguing is that they are not fundamentally different either" (Schaumberg-Müller, 2019, 111), or Kulesza writing: "Does the internet's transboundary nature, scale, speed of communication, automation, interconnectivity and invisibility change the way in which we view and protect fundamental rights (privacy, data protection, non-discrimination, due process, presumption of innocence and free speech)? Are human rights online exactly the same as offline or are they modified by the internet-specific circumstances, possibly impacting their very core?" (Kulesza, 2019, 129).

characterised by a decrease in transparency, legal certainty and foreseeability. An extreme decrease in these principles means that the online sphere of human rights is characterised by non-transparency instead of transparency, legal uncertainty instead of certainty, non-foreseeability instead of foreseeability and secrecy instead of accessibility. Human rights exist online in a non-coherent system characterised by the fragmentation of human rights normative sources and interpretation through discursive practice, a multitude of actors with changing roles, novel compliance mechanisms or their overall absence, and the systemic dependence on the capabilities of online stakeholders for the protection of human rights, and the systemic susceptibility to utilitarian considerations which are non-resilient to time; that is, considerations which may change swiftly in time at will, like the goals related to the protection of national security or economic interests. This introductory chapter to the present volume simply introduces the idea of such non-coherence theory and leaves it open for further articulation in subsequent collective research and debates. Such research will have to respond to the question of whether the usage of human rights language in the digital domain reflects the import of ideas and values from offline to online, or whether human rights online can be justified as an integral part of the universal human rights framework. Should the latter be accurate, then the non-coherence theory of human rights online merely characterises the process of the contestation of traditional human rights norms, instruments, actors and processes, and the practical utility of this theory should wither once the online human rights framework becomes coherent. Should, on the other hand, the former be accurate, then the idea of the universality of human rights as a practical maxim needs to be rejected.

Against this background it is time to ask whether the doctrine of the sameness of online and offline human rights is justifiable, or whether it is time to recognise it as illusory. Perhaps the most unexpected common feature of the chapters in the present volume to me as the editor was the unconditional "underwriting" of the proposition of the sameness of online and offline human rights by the majority of the authors. There seems an overwhelming acceptance of this proposition,[34] although its justification has not been properly articulated and debated. The fact that this proposition remains uncontested by the majority of the authors here suffices to verify my point. Were it otherwise, then we could note the existence of the debate around the proposition of sameness. But there is no such debate. Perhaps in the absence of online-specific constitutional regulation and comprehensive international legal instruments, the idea of the sameness of offline and online human rights is an open door offering easy access. The ease of accepting, uncontested, the idea of the sameness of rights is evident across different continents. In Latin America, the scarceness of cyberspace law leads in general terms to the acceptance of the sameness principle for offline and online.[35] In North America, the existing constitutional principles imply the "sameness of rights" doctrine.[36] More could be said about the contexts where

34 See for example twhe reflection of this proposition in national politics – Dmitry Dedov in his article about the internet and Russia has referred to the views of Mikhail Fedotov, Chairman of the Presidential Council for Human Rights, that the same safeguards should apply both offline and online – see: Dmitry Dedov (2019) The Russian perspective on human rights protection online. In: Mart Susi (Ed.), *Human Rights, Digital Society and the Law*. London: Routledge, 10.

35 Oscar Raul Puccinelli (2019) Latin American human rights law jurisprudence and practices towards the internet. In: Mart Susi (Ed.), *Human Rights, Digital Society and the Law*. London: Routledge, 371.

36 David Stewart (2019) The approach of North American courts towards the internet. In: Mart Susi (Ed.), *Human Rights, Digital Society and the Law*. London: Routledge, 337.

the sameness of online and offline rights is implied. Against the non-coherence theory of digital human rights, the sameness proposition cannot be justified. Acceptance of such non-justifiability has deep consequences. It seems to me, that the idea of the sameness of online and offline human rights is the last stand for the universalist perspective and if abandoned, leads swiftly to the realisation of a paradigmatic change in the human rights online dimension from the offline dimension.

Part II

Right to the internet and rights inside the internet – theoretical dimension

1 The sameness of human rights online and offline

Miloon Kothari

The use of information and communication technologies (ICT) has had significant impact in the economic, social, cultural and political development of societies and nations. The significance of online communication through the internet, mobile telephony and other means of communication facilitated by technology has been recognised as a determining factor in the realisation of a range of human rights. The worldwide web, based on the internet, has increasingly emerged as an indispensable tool for all citizens to receive information, voice opinions and coordinate action. In Jeremy Rifkin's words, "The so-called 'digital revolution' has changed the way we think in terms of information, education, and communication. The invention of mainstream Internet has created a new community that exists without borders, irrespective of time differences and spatial divides".[1] The new digital communication technologies are reconfiguring human rights practices across the board, including the key practices of preventing human rights violations, fact-finding cases of violations, and advocating for the amelioration of individual cases as well as for the promotion of a broader culture of human rights.[2] As a globally interconnected network of networks, the internet is helping to break down geographical, economic and cultural barriers to communication. In doing so, the internet is strengthening freedom of expression as a foundation for realising other fundamental rights and freedoms, including those to education, association, democracy and human development.[3] These very human rights are, however, also threatened through the limitations and abuse of the internet as discussed in this chapter.

J. Coccoli has argued that, for instance, innovative forms of communication have provided numerous possibilities for the effective implementation of the right to freedom of expression. Similarly, this has facilitated immediate benefits with regard to a range of other human rights, such as the right to education by ensuring wider access to knowledge.[4] Therefore, non-discriminatory access to information for all individuals both online

1 Jeremy Rifkin (2000) *The Age of Access: The New Culture of Hyper capitalism, Where All of Life is a Paid-For Experience.* New York: J.P. Tarcher/Putnam, 8, 14.

2 Sameer Padania and others (2011) *Cameras Everywhere: Current Challenges and Opportunities at the Intersection of Human Rights, Video and Technology*. Brooklyn, NY: Witness, www.ohchr.org/Documents/Issues/Opinion/Communications/Witness_1.pdf

3 Freedom of Expression and the Internet (May 2011) Report from Regional Consultation Meetings Convened by the Demos Institute Lisa Horner Global Dialogue, 1, www.global-dialogue.eu/sites/global-dialogue.clients.homemadedigital.com/files/Freedom_of_Expression_and_the_Internet.pdf

4 J. Coccoli (2017) The Challenges of New Technologies in the Implementation of Human Rights: an Analysis of Some Critical Issues in the Digital Era. *Peace Human Rights Governance*, Vol. 1, No. 2, 225, http://phrg.padovauniversitypress.it/system/files/papers/2017_2_4.pdf

and offline must be ensured and protected. Non-discrimination refers to a foundational human rights standard that stipulates that "everyone is entitled to enjoy human rights and freedoms, without distinction of any kind, such as race, colour, sex, language, religion, political or other opinion, national or social origin, property, birth or other status".[5] In recent years, there have been attempts by governments all across the world to either regulate or restrict these spaces, with implications for human rights and freedoms, particularly the freedom of expression, public assembly, conscience and thought. Cases documented in recent years have shown

> how technology has been used for surveillance and censorship by states around the world, and points to weaknesses in existing national legal standards. Cases have also shown how illegal surveillance undermines not only privacy rights, but has also been used to carry out further violations of human rights in the physical world.[6]

Online threats to rights such as the freedom of expression can have far more serious offline repercussions to human rights defenders and citizens given the enhanced potential for surveillance and locating actors using digital methods.[7] Therefore, the issue of the protection of citizens' rights – both online and offline – has been at the forefront of debates related to the internet. With the increasing convergence between the digital and physical spaces, there is a growing need to understand whether the two realms are different or have similarities or sameness in terms of their impact on the way individuals and groups are able to organise actions to defend and promote their human rights. Undoubtedly, the internet as a communication tool has given people and civil society a new space to articulate their demands for inclusive and open societies where their civil and political rights as well as economic, social and cultural rights are respected and protected. Even then, crucial gaps still exist between the two spaces given the existing disparities at economic, social and political levels all over the world. As argued by the former United Nations High Commissioner for Human Rights, Mary Robinson,

> the internet has enabled an explosion of information and expression worldwide, and while I am sceptical about claims that Twitter and Facebook 'caused' events like the Arab Awakening, it is evident that social media was an indispensable tool in the dissemination of uncensored information and the coordination of public protests in the region.[8]

5 As articulated in a number of human rights instruments. For a useful discussion on this topic see: Eva Maria Lassen (Ed.), Monika Mayrhofer, Peter Vedel Kessing, Hans-Otto Sano, Daniel García San José, Rikke Frank Jørgensen (2017) *Factors Which Enable or Hinder the Protection of Human Rights*. Copenhagen: The Danish Institute for Human Rights, 148, www.humanrights.dk/sites/humanrights.dk/files/media/dokumenter/udgivelser/research/frame/frame_-_factors_which_enable_or_hinder_the_protection_of_human_rights.pdf

6 Tamy Guberek and Romesh Silva (2014) "Human Rights and Technology": Mapping the Landscape to Support Grant Making. *A Report by Partners for Human Rights PRIMA Information, Methodology and Analysis*, 15, www.fordfoundation.org/media/2541/prima-hr-tech-report.pdf

7 Gaia Marcus, Human Rights and the New(ish) Digital Paradigm, 37, http://sas-space.sas.ac.uk/6205/1/06marcus.pdf

8 Protecting fundamental freedoms, online and offline, Opinion Mary Robinson, 10 December 2012, https://theelders.org/article/protecting-fundamental-freedoms-online-and-offline

Online and offline world: conceptual framework

From a human rights perspective, it is assumed that the advent of the internet and subsequent creation of online spaces has created a new domain in which groups, communities and civil society actors organise their social and political actions to achieve specific goals. The formation of collective identity and the very location of their collective actions raises the critical issue of collective identity and whether it exists only in its online avatar or if it has a complementary non-virtual character. It has been extremely difficult to rigorously address questions comparing these two worlds – online and offline spheres – and the repercussions of technology usages on society – positive or negative, intended or unintended.

For the purpose of this chapter, the offline sphere refers to a group of people who share social interaction and have some common relations between themselves and the other members of the group and share an area or physical space for at least some of the time. The online sphere is understood to consist of a group of people who interact socially and have shared purposes such as interests, needs, information exchanges or services and computer systems to mediate social interaction to facilitate opinions and a plan of action for a certain common purpose.[9]

Scholars like Paul Verschueren have put forward arguments around the significance attached to technological changes in western discourses. Accordingly, technologies are treated both negatively as a threat to contemporary ways of being, known as the dystopian way and positively as a liberating force known as the utopian way. According to Paul Verschueren, for scholars supporting utopian views, the internet was seen as offering more freedom and more equality with the assumption that civil society in the virtual space would reclaim powers held by the state in the geographical space. Advocates of dystopian views critiqued the idea of techno-liberation. They suggested that virtual communities and computer-mediated communication contribute to isolation, to a decrease of human interdependence, to the decline of local communities in the physical world, and to the commodification of social behaviour.[10]

More often there are views depicting the online space or cyberspace as an unprecedented development in the field of information and communication technologies, and the enhanced ability of the internet to create new spaces is seen as the most definitive answer to the question of how to put theories of participatory and engaged politics into practice because of its vast potential to connect people in an interactive medium.[11] Some describe virtual and physical spaces and activism as complementary to each other. The argument is that online activism complements but cannot be a substitute for the traditional forms of activism and advocacy. Therefore, online and offline worlds are viewed as two distinct realms. However, online activism such as mass email action alerts are criticised and termed as "slacktivism" or "clicktivism" by observers and intellectuals. They argue that mass emails are functionally equivalent to the photocopied and faxed petitions and postcards of

9 Yeslam Al-Saggaf and Mohamed M. Begg (2004) Online Each Communities versus Offline Communities in the Arab/Muslim World. *School of Information Studies, Info, Comm & Ethics in Society*, Vol. 2, 43, http://citeseerx.ist.psu.edu/viewdoc/download?doi=10.1.1.565.4092&rep=rep1&type=pdf

10 Ibid., 170.

11 Trevor G. Smith (2015) Theorizing an Online Politics: How the Internet is Reconfiguring Political Space, Subjectivity, Participation, and Conflict. A thesis submitted in partial fulfilment of the requirements for the degree in Doctor of Philosophy, the University of Western Ontario, 11, https://ir.lib.uwo.ca/cgi/viewcontent.cgi?article=4477&context=etd

"offline" activism and represent a difference-of-degree rather than a difference-in-kind. Online actions are usually considered the same kinds of low-quality, high-volume actions. They further note that the lowered transaction costs of the medium produce a novel form of activism that carries with it hidden costs and dangers for the public sphere.[12]

Christine Abdalla Mikhaeil has argued in her research into the similarities and differences between the online and the offline worlds that

> the denial of status of real to the online world is a damageable false assumption. Such an assumption has led to talk about 'slacktivism' as not real activism, when cyber-activism should have been put into perspective with physical world activism. Instead, digital and physical worlds are enmeshed to constitute the real. It is the conjunction of online and offline efforts that made its impact in events such as the uprisings in the Arab world.[13]

Michael Haagensen further notes that

> there is a need in the IS literature to contextualize the online world and articulate it with societal consequences. Online and offline are treated as two conceptual devices and experiential modes. The concept of offline only exists in mirror of the online. Therefore, these two concepts are inextricable.[14]

Journalist and social commentator Evgeny Morozov has argued in his book "The Net Delusion: The Dark Side of Internet Freedom" that interaction in the online space is invisible and different from traditional forms of the offline space.

> It is on this register that the internet often troubles people, as its difference can be seen as either threatening, or as a new target for anti-political attitudes that can win favour when it seems like the argument against politics is aimed at a new technology instead of the concept of a political realm itself. It is on this issue that many critics of the potential of the online political space are eager to point out that online activities are either less real, not serious enough, or fundamentally disconnected from the offline political space to have any serious political potential.[15]

Trevor G. Smith recognises the future potential of the internet in creating a superior political realm by transcending the limitations that exist in the offline space.

> In considering the possibilities of the internet, it will become apparent that online space may actually serve to create a superior version of the political realm due to the ease through which the constraints which limit offline space may be overcome.

12 David Karpf (2010) Online Political Mobilization from the Advocacy Group's Perspective: Looking Beyond Clicktivism. *Policy & Internet*, Vol. 2, 7–41.

13 Christine Abdalla Mikhaeil (2017) Integrating Online-Offline Interactions to Explain Societal Challenges. A Dissertation Submitted in Partial Fulfilment of the Requirements for the Degree of Doctor of Philosophy in the Robinson College of Business, Georgia State University, 51 https://scholarworks.gsu.edu/cgi/viewcontent.cgi?article=1068&context=cis_diss

14 Ibid., 54.

15 Explanation in Smith, 66.

> Online space operates in a way that can facilitate more inclusion and participation by moving beyond the model of meeting in person in a limited space with a limited amount of time.[16]

The issues surrounding the online and offline spaces have important social and economic implications, as the group or community interaction at social and political levels makes its profound impact on the formation of opinions, political participation and collective action.

The UN framework: human rights – online and offline

Human rights and fundamental freedoms are applicable both to offline and online spheres. Before examining the existing gaps between the two spaces, it is pertinent to note here that as a consequence of the rising awareness about the human rights implications of the internet and other types of information and communication technologies at the global level, there have been attempts by international legal instruments to adopt internet-related resolutions and reports. The key objective was to ensure that all human rights are upheld in a world where boundaries between the digital and physical space are increasingly blurred. However, there is no unanimously agreed human rights perspective to recognise the principles of the indivisibility and interdependence of human rights in the physical and the digital spaces. It has been argued by some that international human rights protocols only guarantee such freedom in the physical world or offline spaces because "human rights have primarily been framed around an international system of nation-states (e.g. UN member states), and therefore bounded within the physical space. Core official institutions for the protection of human rights are also geographically defined around systems in physical space".[17] These instruments did not specify the operational scope of this offline status extending to cover online status in upcoming future technological developments. As argued by Tamy Guberek and Romesh Silva, the networked digital sphere introduced a whole new dimension of space within which individuals meet, interact, exchange ideas, engage speech and expression by others, and organise content and people, and within which rights need to be defended.[18] Therefore, a mere exclusion of "virtual space" in the text of law is not sufficient grounds to invalidate the obligations of state parties to protect freedoms and liberties in online spaces.[19] Sustained international efforts have resulted in the development of new principles after redefining the existing human rights framework to reflect new technology and changing norms specific to the online or digital space. Subsequently, several UN resolutions and reports have recognised internet governance as a human rights issue and explicitly framed a set of rules which guide the standard practices to be applied by the state parties in respecting the rights of people in the online world in the same way as they are applied to the offline world. In this context, digital rights, or

16 See Smith, 60.

17 Tamy Guberek and Romesh Silva (August 2014) "Human Rights and Technology": Mapping the Landscape to Support Grantmaking. A Report by Partners for Human Rights PRIMA Information, Methodology and Analysis, 9, www.fordfoundation.org/media/2541/prima-hr-tech-report.pdf

18 Ibid., 9.

19 Ordeals in 'The Long Walk to Freedom': The State of Internet Governance inn Zimbabwe. Zimbabwe Democracy Institute & Media Centre, Harare Zimbabwe, November 2017 Report, 3, http://kubatana.net/wp-content/uploads/2017/12/zdi_media_centre_state_internet_freedom_1712.pdf

internet rights, are considered an extension of human rights in the offline world as recognised, protected and promoted by international laws and conventions.[20]

The first UN Human Rights Council resolution on the impact of the internet on human rights was adopted in October 2009. In September 2011, the UN Human Rights Committee (HR Committee), the treaty monitoring body for the International Covenant on Civil and Political Rights (ICCPR), issued General Comment No. 34 which constitutes an authoritative interpretation of the minimum standards guaranteed by Article 19 of the ICCPR. "Importantly, General Comment No.34 states that Article 19 of the ICCPR protects all forms of expression and the means of their dissemination, including all forms of electronic and internet-based modes of expression. In other words, the protection of freedom of expression applies online in the same way as it applies offline".[21]

Internet-related potentials and challenges have also increasingly been addressed by UN special procedures. The UN Special Rapporteur on the Promotion and Protection of the Right to Freedom of Opinion and Expression, Frank La Rue, in his ground-breaking report on freedom of expression online developed a framework to assess freedom of expression (legal frameworks) and identified obstacles on the internet, including the arbitrary filtering or blocking of content, the criminalisation of legitimate expressions, blocking websites or filtering websites, cyberattacks, privacy and data protection, and internet access. In his report to the General Assembly on 16 May 2011 he stated that

> The Internet is one of the most powerful instruments of the 21st century for increasing transparency in the conduct of the powerful access to information, and for facilitating active citizen participation in building democratic societies. Indeed, the recent wave of demonstrations in countries across the Middle East and North African region has shown the key role that the Internet can play in mobilising the population to call for justice, equality, accountability and better respect for human rights. As such, facilitating access to the Internet for all individuals, with as little restriction to online content as possible, should be a priority for all States.[22]

Blocking access to the internet, regardless of the justification provided, is considered a violation of Article 19 of the ICCPR, which states that, "Everyone shall have the right to freedom of expression; this right shall include freedom to seek, receive and impart information and ideas of all kinds, regardless of frontiers, either orally, in writing or in print, in the form of art, or through any other media of his choice".[23]

The UNHRC held its first discussion on freedom of expression on the internet in 2012 following the report of the UN Special Rapporteur, Frank La Rue, on freedom of opinion and expression in 2011. In 2012, the UNHRC adopted a landmark resolution on "the promotion, protection and enjoyment of human rights on the Internet". This

20 Marwa Fatafta, Internet Freedoms in Palestine: Mapping of Digital Rights Violations and Threats. 7amleh Arab Center for Social Media Advancement and the Association for Progressive Communications (APC), 4, http://7amleh.org/wp-content/uploads/2018/01/7amleh_Internet_Freedoms_in_Palestine.pdf

21 Freedom of expression and ICTs: Overview of International Standards, 2013, 6, www.article19.org/data/files/medialibrary/37380/FoE-and-ICTs.pdf

22 Report of the Special Rapporteur on the promotion and protection of the right to freedom of opinion and expression, Frank La Rue, Human Rights Council, Seventeenth session, Agenda item 3, 16 May 2011, 4, https://undocs.org/en/A/17/27

23 International Covenant on Civil and Political Rights, www.ohchr.org/en/professionalinterest/pages/ccpr.aspx

resolution affirmed that the same rights that people have offline must also be protected online, in particular freedom of expression, which is applicable regardless of frontiers and through any media of one's choice, in accordance with Article 19 of the Universal Declaration of Human Rights and the International Covenant on Civil and Political Rights[24] The important link between the internet and human rights has been reiterated by the UN in its further resolutions in 2014 and 2016, and the HRC and UN General Assembly Resolutions on the right to privacy in the digital age have also expanded on this fundamental principle.[25]

Digital divide: accessibility and human rights

One of the positions taken by a number of scholars is that the difference between basic liberties and internet liberties in terms of "offline" or "online" statuses is rather simple. It means the practice and enjoyment of the former, online. The legal and moral grounds from which these liberties emanate are the same; what differs is the space from which humanity claims those liberties.[26] In this context, the critical gaps in the realisation of freedom of expression and other human rights through the use of information and communication technologies online and in offline contexts acquire significance as they are inextricably linked to the issue of universal access to the internet across the world. The debate has largely centred on the relationship between human rights and new technologies and the legal sanctions of the right of access to the internet.

Considering the significant impact of internet access on human rights, however, raises the issue as to whether access to the internet should be considered a human right in itself rather than a medium through which rights can be realised. Vinton Cerf, an expert on internet governance and an opponent of the right to internet access, argued in a New York Times opinion piece that "technology is an enabler of rights, not a right itself" by maintaining that it would be wrong to declare the internet a human right. The internet as just another tool that can be used for both good and bad purposes. For him, a human right involves something essential for the achievement of a meaningful life. "There is a high bar for something to be considered a human right. Loosely put, it must be among the things we as humans need in order to lead healthy, meaningful lives, like freedom from torture or freedom of conscience. It is a mistake to place any technology in this exalted category"[27]

Scholar Giorgi Chitidze[28] has argued that the use of the internet as a tool of free expression remains largely ineffective if universal access to the online space is not guaranteed. In the present context, universal access to the internet is not recognised as an independent legal right. It has been further argued that universal access is not even recognised as a part of other rights such as freedom of expression, and therefore places no obligation on state parties to ensure such access to the internet for all users. The proposed linkage is relevant

24 UN General Assembly Resolution A/HRC/20/L.13 on the promotion, protection and enjoyment of human rights on the Internet, www.ohchr.org/Documents/HRBodies/HRCouncil/.../A.HRC.20.L.13_en.doc

25 See A/HRC/RES/28/16, A/RES/68/167, and A/RES/69/166.

26 *Supra* note 2, 2.

27 Op-Ed by Vint Cerf published in the *New York Times* on 4 January 2012, www.nytimes.com/2012/01/05/opinion/internet-access-is-not-a-human-right.html

28 Giorgi Chitidze (2015) Human Rights Online: Redefining the Concept of Freedom of Expression in the Digital Age. A dissertation submitted in partial fulfilment for the degree: Master in Human Rights Policy and Practice School of Global Studies, University of Gothenburg, https://munin.uit.no/bitstream/handle/10037/8240/thesis.pdf?sequence=2

in the context of social, economic and cultural rights, which the state parties have agreed and are obliged to respect and protect with available economic resources within national boundaries. A clear example of this is the International Covenant on Economic, Social and Cultural Rights. In particular, Article 2 of the mentioned Covenant states:

> each State Party to the present Covenant undertakes to take steps, individually and through international assistance and co-operation, especially economic and technical, to the maximum of its available resources, with a view to achieving progressively the full realisation of the rights recognised in the present Covenant by all appropriate means, including particularly the adoption of legislative measures.[29]

Lack of universal access to communication technology such as the internet has created a phenomenon globally known as the digital divide – unequal access to digital information and communication technologies. "The digital divide is defined as an unequal environment created by the division of people falling in two extreme categories based on the ones that have access to digital technologies and the ones that don't".[30] The digital divide in turn reinforces social, economic and other disparities among large sections of society affecting the economy, education and information access. "The digital divide exists between those in cities and those in rural areas. It also exists between the educated and the uneducated, between economic classes, and between the more and less industrially developed nations".[31] It is primarily wealthy people and developed countries that can afford the diffusion of new information technologies. The cost of newly adopted technologies and poor technological infrastructure combined with economic and power disparities across the world exclude the poor and people living in certain geographic areas from accessing the online space, which has been regarded as deeply problematic from a human rights perspective. This discrepancy explains the line of differentiation that exists between the people using the online space and people who are not digitally connected or are limited to the offline space in the realisation of their human rights.

A study conducted by Chinn and Fairlie on the computer and internet digital divide among 161 countries, with available data for the years between 1999 and 2001 from various reliable sources, shows, "that the digital divide is a growing gap between the rich and poor because only 6% of the world's population have used the internet out of which 85% to 90% of these people are from industrial economies where 90% of all internet hosts are located".[32]

According to Eileen Donahoe of Human Rights Watch,

> globally, nearly six out of ten people are not connected to the Internet. Even more stark is the fact that roughly 65 percent of people in the developing world do not

29 Ibid., 21.

30 Osama Manzar and Shivani Lal, Digital Rights and Digital Divide, Lack of Internet Access Undermines Freedom of Speech and Expression, www.commoncause.in/publication_details.php?id=503

31 Dr. Parthasarathy Bhattacharya, *The Digital Divide*. New Delhi (2014): The Energy Research Institute, http://epgp.inflibnet.ac.in/epgpdata/uploads/epgp_content/library_and_information_science/knowledge_society/04._the_digital_divide/et/4304_et_et.pdf

32 Tanveer Zia, Yeslam Al-Saggaf, Md Zahidul Islam, Lihong Zheng, and John Weckert, The Digital Divide in Asia: Cases from Yemen, Bangladesh, Pakistan and China. Charles Sturt University, Australia, https://pdfs.semanticscholar.org/e40f/13a256070c951ace975ba8956553f99806ec.pdf

yet use the Internet. And women generally have less access to the Internet (another expression of gender inequality), as do people living in rural areas.[33]

Experts suggest that in Asia-Pacific countries like India and China, an estimated 2 to 4 billion people have no internet access, comprising over half of the world's disconnected populace. Despite the widely reported phenomenal growth in information and communications technology (ICT), a 2016 report by the United Nations Economic and Social Commission for Asia and the Pacific (ESCAP) on the State of ICT in Asia and the Pacific found that the gap between advanced and developing countries in fixed broadband access is indeed widening. The report found that in 2015, less than 2% of the population had adopted fixed broadband in as many as 20 countries in Asia and the Pacific, widening the digital divide between high-income and low-income countries at an alarming speed.[34]

According to a report released at the India Mobile Congress 2017, while overall internet penetration in India is 33%, it is only 16% in rural areas.[35] Internet usage is largely concentrated in metro cities and the non-metro or rural areas have internet penetration levels lower than the national average. Almost 70% of total internet users are from the top seven cities: Mumbai, Delhi, Bangalore, Hyderabad, Chennai, Kolkata and Pune, and only 30% are from all the other areas together.[36] According to a survey by the Digital Human rights Empowerment Foundation, New Delhi of 600 individuals living in rural regions of India, "Internet penetration in rural India is limited to 7%, and women internet users in the country are just 17%". The study found that 37% of users are aware of government regulation or monitoring of content.[37]

The World Bank's World Development Report ranked Pakistan among the five least-connected countries globally. According to their 2016 report, titled "Digital Dividends", 165 million people or 83% of the population (200 million) were found to be offline in the country and only 17% of the 200 million population were connected. The report puts Pakistan among other South Asian and Sub-Saharan African nations that have the lowest internet adoption rate, between 0 and 19%.[38] Although internet usage in Pakistan has grown rapidly, 90% of the users nonetheless live in the three major cities; Karachi, Lahore and Islamabad, which is only 12% of the population; the remaining 88% has no or very little internet access. The digital divide in Pakistan is due to several factors such as unequal geographic dispersion, sector absorption, connectivity infrastructure, affordability, government policies and regulatory control. In Bangladesh, access to computers and the internet is very limited. The poor economic condition of Bangladesh is one of the

33 Eileen Donahoe, Director of Global Affairs (2016) Digital Disruption of Human Rights, Part 2, Just Security, 25 March, www.justsecurity.org/30225/digital-disruption-human-rights/

34 State of ICT in Asia and the Pacific 2016: Uncovering the Widening Broadband Divide, REPORT from UN Economic and Social Commission for Asia and the Pacific (19 August 2016), https://reliefweb.int/report/world/state-ict-asia-and-pacific-2016-uncovering-widening-broadband-divide

35 Budget 2018 Reinforces Focus On Improving Internet Penetration In Rural India, IT NEXT, February 2018, www.itnext.in/article/2018/02/01/budget-2018-reinforces-focus-improving-internet-penetration-rural-india

36 Dr. Kawaljeet Kaur and Jaswinder Singh (2016) ICT Diffusion and Digital Divide in India: Implications for Economic Policies. *Pacific Business Review International*, Vol. 1, No. 2, 4, www.pbr.co.in/July2016/1.pdf

37 Ritu Srivastava and Joao Pessoa (2015) Understanding Freedom of Expression Online and Offline (3 December), www.apc.org/en/blog/understanding-freedom-expression-online-and-offline

38 Farooq Baloch (2016) Largest Offline Populations: India Tops List, Pakistan Fourth, Says World Bank Report. *The Express Tribune* (15 January), https://tribune.com.pk/story/1027657/largest-offline-populations-india-tops-list-pakistan-fourth-says-world-bank-report/

major factors for the existing digital divide. Only 12 out of every thousand people own a computer and 3 out of every thousand people have access to the internet. Almost 80% of the ISPs are located in the capital city Dhaka, whereas around 80% of the population live in rural areas.[39]

Human rights online and offline

Tools of repression

Despite the enormous potential and benefits of ICT in the realisation of a range of human rights in the online space, it is at the same time clear that the increasing practice of restrictions on ICT, and the harsh treatment of human rights activists who use the internet, results in multi-faceted violations of human rights in practice on the ground. Steven Feldstein opines that from a human rights perspective "Instead of treating offline and online activity as separate and distinct, advocates should follow what authoritarian governments already recognise and challenge: that there is no meaningful distinction between the two, and therefore they deserve the same protections".[40]

Some scholars maintain that as with offline forms of violence and intimidation, governments seem most likely to resort to other sophisticated measures like cyberattacks when their power is threatened by mass actions in the physical sphere. The Arab Spring is one such example, which has been marked by a series of revolutionary anti-government protests and demonstrations beginning from Tunisia and spreading to parts of North Africa and the Middle East. The "victory" of the Tunisians led to the eruption of a wave of protests successively in Egypt, Jordan, Algeria, Yemen, Bahrain, Libya, Morocco and Syria. The outcome of the mass protests in Egypt and Tunisia forced other governments in the region to resort to more aggressive crackdowns to crush any signs of dissent and revolt. Access to social media platforms like Twitter, Facebook and YouTube used as a tool for mobilisation by human rights activists were disrupted for a long time following the 2016 coup attempt in Turkey. State authorities from Egypt to Iran shut down all internet services in response to internal unrest.

The State of Internet Freedom in East Africa 2015 report, released in September 2015, found a pattern of laws being passed that "threaten the right to freedom of expression, both online and offline". There is a growing consensus among civil society activists that censorship and abuses online are often linked to broader attacks on human rights and civil liberties. In Uganda, the crackdown on online dissidents comes off the back of new legislation restricting freedom of expression and assembly. The Non-governmental Organisations bill passed in 2015, allows the government to shut down organisations that engage in acts "prejudicial to the interests of Uganda and the dignity of the people of Uganda".[41]

Observers have reservations about the potential of digital communication as a robust tool for political action in the physical realm. They are concerned that the battle to control the internet may ultimately harm democratisation and open access, and enable repression

39 See *supra* note 12.

40 Steven Feldstein (2018) Hybrid Repression Online and Offline in China: Foretelling the Human Rights Struggle to Come. Power 3.0: Understanding Modern Authoritarian Influence (25 January 2018), www.power3point0.org/2018/01/25/hybrid-repression-online-and-offline-in-china-foretelling-the-human-rights-struggle-to-come/

41 Clair MacDougall (2016) Death Threats and Repressive Regimes: The Activists Fighting For Online Freedom in Africa 23 October 2016, www.wired.co.uk/article/african-governments-repress-online-expression

and control. Evgeny Morozov points out in his book "The Net Delusion: The Dark Side of Internet Freedom", that the same tools that can spark a revolution can also be used to suppress one.[42] According to Coccoli, multi-faceted dangers include censorship across large populations or entire networks, content filtering and/or blocking, identification of activists and critics, disconnection of access to technologies, and leaks of user information as some of the threats that can affect freedom of expression, and the criminalisation of legitimate expression followed by the adoption of restrictive legislation to justify such measures represent the catastrophic culmination of these practices.[43] Very often both state and non-state perpetrators are directly involved in violating human rights both online and offline. As noted by the UN Special Rapporteur on freedom of opinion and expression, David Kaye, in his first report to the Human Rights Council, "We live in a world in which mass and targeted surveillance, digital attacks on individuals and civil society, harassment of members of vulnerable groups, and a wide variety of digital opinion and expression result in serious repercussions, including detention, physical attacks, and even killings".[44]

Kelly McKone et al. found that activists involved in human rights practices face new threats to safety and security. It is impossible to completely mitigate them, working either on- or offline. Technological advances in surveillance capabilities often create a development response from freedom-of-expression technologists to overcome the new surveillance.[45] Alba Mohedano Roldán conducted a comparative analysis of the use of the internet for online action and offline action by social movements from the perspective of the capacity and propensity of states for repression in democratic as well as non-democratic systems, taking Venezuela and Spain as case studies. The study reached certain conclusions and suggested that

> the level of repression in non-democracies means that costs of offline action are higher than in democracies. However, the online action costs are relatively low for movements in both systems. Consequently, the differential between online and offline costs is higher in non-democracies. In this sense, the Internet offers a more significant opportunity for movements in those regimes, although online monitoring and censorship can distort this similarity. The use of the net for mobilisation generally implies the existence of an offline action. Higher costs due to repression and lower incentives are expected in non-democracies compared to democracies.[46]

Anita Rosemary Gohdes has argued in her research that the choice of internet control affects the type and scale of state-sanctioned violence used against perceived domestic threats. Where states have chosen to visibly respond to critical domestic threats through a

42 John Wihbey, Digital Activism and Organizing: Research Review and Reading List, https://journalistsresource.org/studies/politics/citizen-action/digital-activism-organizing-theory-research-review-reading-list

43 See Coccoli, 229.

44 Human rights, encryption and anonymity in a digital age, www.ohchr.org/EN/NewsEvents/Pages/HRencryptionanonymityinadigitalage.aspx

45 Kelly McKone, Maria J. Stephan, and Noel Dickover (2015) Using Technology in Nonviolent Activism against Repression. Special Report 357, United States Institute of Peace, 2, www.usip.org/sites/default/files/SR357-Using-Technology-in-Nonviolent-Activism-against-Repression.pdf

46 Alba Mohedano Roldán, Political Regimes and the Use of the Internet by Social Movements. CIS Working Paper No. 79, University of Zurich www.ethz.ch/content/dam/ethz/special-interest/gess/cis/cis-dam/Research/Working_Papers/WP_2013/2013_WP79_MohedanoRoldan2.pdf

demonstration of control in the form of censorship, they will also be more likely to visibly demonstrate their authority through a heightened use of violent repression.[47]

Steven Feldstein has coined the term "hybrid repression" to denote the blending of offline and online repressive tactics developed and used by authoritarian regimes to crush any group or organisation demanding promotion and protection of human rights. According to him, there is no meaningful difference between the two actions; the first is physically breaking into the offices of a human rights organisation and stealing confidential records and the second using intrusion software to seize a private membership list from an opposition political party. According to him the first action is prohibited under international human rights law, but the latter activity is generally permissible. The hybrid tactics are the result of gaps in the protection mechanism, which are utilised to violate human rights in both the online and offline spaces. Steven Feldstein presents the case of the uneasy relationship between the ethnic Uyghur population and the Chinese government in Xinjiang province, which faces harsh crackdowns due to opposition to government actions and policies in the province.

> Even by historical standards, the latest government crackdown – led by Communist Party Secretary Chen Quanguo – has been particularly brutal and widespread. Tactics span the range from enforcing the involuntary collection of DNA samples and bio-data to imposing mandatory satellite GPS tracking of vehicles, monitoring text messages and social media posts for unfavourable content, and ordering the mass surrender of passports to local authorities.[48]

According to a report by the Uyghur Human Rights Project, "since 9/11, China has in particular manipulated the "Global War on Terror" to validate this repression of Uyghur human rights".[49] A report documented by the UHRP in 2014 says there is "limited space afforded [to] Uyghurs to discuss economic, social and cultural issues online. There is a pattern of the systemic denial of the freedom of expression and association all underpinned by a labyrinth of national and local regulations. Furthermore, in an environment where one internet footprint could land them in jail, Uyghurs tended to heavily self-censor".[50]

Besides the strict enforcement of unrestrained control measures on freedom of expression and an endless chain of surveillance, new advanced technologies are used by the Chinese regime to maintain authoritative control over the lives of ethnic Uyghurs, which blur the lines between offline and online repression. The project report states:

> The government has ordered many Xinjiang residents, particularly ethnic Uyghurs, to hand in their passports and request permission for any travel abroad. In certain parts of Xinjiang, government authorities require all vehicles to install GPS tracking devices, so that at any given moment security forces can locate a specific vehicle. In

47 Anita Rosemary Gohdes (2014) *Repression in the Digital Age: Communication Technology and the Politics of State Violence*. Universität Mannheim, 4, https://ub-madoc.bib.uni-mannheim.de/37902/1/Gohdes_Anita_Doktorarbeit_Mar2015.pdf

48 Feldstein.

49 Legitimizing Repression: China's "War on Terror" Under Xi Jinping and State Policy in East Turkestan. A Report by the Uyghur Human Rights Project, Washington, DC, 48, http://docs.uyghuramerican.org/pdf/Legitimizing Repression.pdf

50 Ibid., 51.

> Xinjiang, this is part of the everyday reality. Until recently, it seemed implausible that a government would systematically survey messages posted by ordinary citizens to private social media groups and impose long jail sentences for questionable content. In today's China, this has become normalized.[51]

New communication technologies and in particular the digital media has posed new challenges to the practice of human rights. A careful examination of the nature and scale of restrictions and violations of human rights in both online and offline spheres shows that both realms receive similar treatment in both democratic and authoritarian regimes. Allison Pytlak and Brandon Valeriano aptly describe in the case ofVenezuela that "Cyber repression in Venezuela takes two forms – digital actions that shutdown online spaces for freedom of expression, and offline punishment, including physical violence. Digital repression is easy when control of online systems is held by the state, a continuation of the idea that a strong state maintains a monopoly on violence".[52]

According to a report by the US Council of Foreign Relations: "For Tibetans, digital repression is a continuation of the offline policy to which they have become accustomed. Activists are shrivelled and attacked online, even after they have left the country. Within China, Tibetan cultural goods, such as educational books featured on the iTunes store, are blocked. Self-censorship, both online and off, has become a way of life for many Tibetans".[53] The findings of a report by the University of California, San Diego, 2016 suggests that although activist use of social media tools did play an important role in the 2011 protests in the Middle East and North Africa (MENA region), most of the work to mobilise, organise and manage the protests occurred offline and was led by formal NGOs and their staff working with individual activists affiliated with informal organisations and identity groups. Offline community organising techniques – spreading information via direct face-to-face contact, text messages, or phone calls and sharing resources and determining strategy in the offices of registered NGOs – drove mobilisation and information dissemination through social media like Facebook, YouTube and Twitter, once the protests were underway.[54]

Anita R Gohdes examined the reported daily incidences of fatal regime violence between March 2011 and September 2013 in Syria collected by human rights groups and concluded that network disruptions or shutting down internet and cell phone services in the country formed a part of the Syrian regime's coercive response strategy, which was used to commit more large-scale acts of violence against the civilian population. The increase in documented violence indicates that "the Syrian regime conducted the type of atrocious campaigns against both rebel fighters and non-combatants that assumes anyone not showing explicit support as being opposed to them. The explicit focus of these disruptions was or might have been used to attack as many civilians as possible. Empirically, a

51 Ibid.

52 Allison Pytlak and Brandon Valeriano (September, 2017) The Frontlines of Cyber Repression: The Venezuelan Digital Caudillo, https://niskanencenter.org/blog/frontlines-cyber-repression-venezuelan-digital-caudillo/

53 The Future of Digital Repression (2013) Centre for Preventive Action, Council of Foreign Relations, Washington, DC (16 May), www.cfr.org/content/publications/.../Future_of_Digital_Repression_Report_6-613.pdf

54 James Fowler and Zachary Steinert-Threlkeld (2016) Online and Offline Activism in Egypt and Bahrain: Research and Innovation Grants Working Papers Series, USAID in partnership with the Institute of International Education, University of California, San Diego (29 April), www.usaid.gov/sites/default/files/documents/1866/Online%20and%20Offline%20Activism%20in%20Egypt%20and%20Bahrain1.pdf

significant increase of possibly unobserved violence that only occurred during the internet shut downs, therefore indicate a higher proportion of civilians killed in the physical realm".[55]

The preceding analysis makes it clear that despite optimism and excitement over the potential of technological advances to improve human rights advocacy and action, there are rising concerns over the repressive potential of technological tools enabling governments across the world to violate and trample human rights in both online and offline spheres. The threats to human rights due to rapid technological changes are real and perceived as a negative side-effect of otherwise extraordinary positive developments. Proposing, therefore, the idea of a continued division between the efforts to defend human rights in the physical and digital spheres may prove to be counter-productive. As an example, we can refer to the collective scholarly analysis of online and offline mass mobilisation in the context of the Arab Spring and its aftermath. The scholars conclude that, in this context, it is increasingly difficult to separate the two spheres, as the two reinforced each other in both positive and negative dimensions.

It is clear from the preceding overview of the issues related to the human rights implications of the internet, that the global human rights community must take online repression as seriously as it takes offline repression.

The question of sameness

The ICCPR General Comment 34 to Article 19 looks carefully at the obligations of the state parties in the protection of the right to freedom of expression over the internet. Paragraph 15 says

> States parties should take account of the extent to which developments in information and communication technologies, such as the internet and mobile based electronic information dissemination systems, have substantially changed communication practices around the world. There is now a global network for exchanging ideas and opinions that does not necessarily rely on the traditional mass media intermediaries. States parties should take all necessary steps to foster the independence of these new media and to ensure access of individuals thereto.[56]

It has been unequivocally argued that scope and extension of the right to freedom of expression was not confined to suit the required standards of any particular medium or technology. The right to freedom of expression over the internet whether it is exercised online or offline is an internationally protected right to which almost all countries of the world have committed themselves.[57] The sameness of human rights practice online or offline is reaffirmed by the fact that access to the internet is

55 Anita R. Gohdes (2014) Pulling the Plug: Network Disruptions and Violence in Civil Conflict, University of Mannheim, 6 August, 14, www.anitagohdes.net/uploads/2/7/2/3/27235401/gohdes_synetworkaug14.pdf

56 United Nations CCPR/C/GC/34, Human Rights Committee, 102nd session, 11–29 July 2011, General comment No. 34, Article 19: Freedoms of opinion and expression, 4, http://www2.ohchr.org/english/bodies/hrc/docs/gc34.pdf

57 Freedom of expression and ICTs: Overview of international standards, ARTICLE 19, Free Word Centre 60 Farringdon Road, London, EC1R 3GA, United Kingdom, 2013, 3, www.article19.org/data/files/medialibrary/37380/FoE-and-ICTs.pdf

considered a crucial part of human rights that already exist, particularly freedom of expression. In May 2011, the UN Special Rapporteur, Frank La Rue emphasised that Article 19 was drafted with foresight to include and to accommodate future technological developments. Hence, the framework of international human rights law remains relevant today and equally applicable to new communication technologies such as the internet.[58]

This perspective clearly indicates that access to the internet for all practical purposes remains inseparable from the rights themselves. This was also recognised by the 2011 Joint Declaration of four special mandates on freedom of expression,[59] which stressed that giving effect to the right to freedom of expression imposes an obligation on States to promote universal access to the internet. In June 2016, the UN took internet access a step further and declared that it considers the internet to be a human right. Paragraph 12 of the Oral revision calls upon all states to consider formulating, through transparent and inclusive processes with all stakeholders, and adopting national internet-related public policies that have the objective of universal access and enjoyment of human rights at their core.[60]

Access to the internet as a new human right

The question of universal access to the internet is inextricably connected with the practice of human rights online as well as offline. In that respect, any restriction or disruption in access becomes vital to the practice and protection of human rights online. Advocates of the internet and many countries contend that internet access in general should be recognised as a basic human right. The UN Human Rights Council adopted a resolution[61] in 2016 which was widely interpreted as an affirmation of access to the internet as a basic human right. Many western countries such as Finland, Estonia, France and Greece have recognised this and call internet access a human right. Opponents of this right propose that the usefulness of the internet cannot be overstated but it should not be obligatory on the part of the state to provide access to every citizen. As already discussed in this chapter, Vincent Cerf argued that "technology (the internet) can be an enabler of rights, not a right itself".[62]

Disapproving this view, Scott Edwards of Amnesty International USA responded by pointing out that the right to access the internet is inseparable from other rights like the rights to freedom of assembly and association and the right to expression. Jesse Tomalty endorses this point of view and writes, "in view of the tremendous importance of the internet it seems reasonable to hold that to prevent someone from accessing the internet is to deprive her of adequate opportunities to exercise her freedom of expression and association".[63] Scott Edwards further argues that communication technologies have

58 Ibid., 7.

59 International Mechanisms for Promoting Freedom of Expression, Joint Declaration on Freedom of Expression and the Internet www.osce.org/fom/78309?download=true

60 Op. cit., 1. United Nations A/HRC/32/L.20.

61 A/HRC/32/L.20. Adopted on 27 June 2016.

62 Op-Ed by Vint Cerf published in the *New York Times* on 4 January 2012, www.nytimes.com/2012/01/05/opinion/internet-access-is-not-a-human-right.html

63 Jesse Tomalty (2017) Is There A Human Right To Internet Access?, https://philosophynow.org/issues/118/Is_There_A_Human_Right_To_Internet_Access

become indispensable for the protection of the human rights of the world's most marginalised communities in the past few decades. He says

> Indeed, loss of access in places from Sub-Saharan Africa to the most impoverished communities here in the US, could mean an immediate threat to lives and livelihoods. And the increasing necessity of internet access for the world's most impoverished as it relates to health, education, employment, the arts, gender equality – all things we have the right to enjoy means that Information Technologies (yes, the internet) are inseparable from the rights themselves.[64]

The viewpoint from developing countries supports a comprehensive human rights-based approach in providing and expanding access to the internet in which access to internet-based services to people who cannot afford them is given precedence over the restriction and disruption of internet services for current users. Supporters of this approach draw a distinction between negative and positive rights, which assumes significance in relation to developing countries like India. In an opinion piece the author argues

> Negative rights are intrinsic to us as human beings and the Constitution merely guarantees the protection of such rights. The Constitution usually curtails the power of government or other entities in performing certain actions which violate the negative rights of the individual. A positive right, on the other hand, enables the holder of the right to claim a good or a service against the state or someone else. When legislated, positive rights become justiciable and enable the citizens to demand better services from their governments.[65]

Therefore, they argue that besides the uncontested usefulness of the internet, governments should take every possible policy measure to bridge the digital divide among its citizens and to enable them all to enjoy every human right. The internet has fast been emerging as a fundamental method of communication and connection, which has allowed new ways for people to demand and defend human rights. Therefore, recognising access as a right by identifying and addressing key areas of concern such as a regulatory framework for the internet will be an important step towards making it available to as many people as possible.

64 Scott Edwards (2012) Is Internet Access A Human Right?, blog.amnestyusa.org (10 January), https://blog.amnestyusa.org/middle-east/is-internet-access-a-human-right/

65 "Why the "'right to the Internet'" is a bad idea", www.livemint.com/Opinion/yoyNyx6EsVQZpNHtv2qKlM/Why-the-right-to-Internet-is-a-bad-idea.html

2 Right of access to the internet – global approaches

Carolina Aguerre

Introduction

The discussion of whether internet access should be deemed a human right touches upon one of the most contested aspects about the epistemic quality of rights and human rights since the second half of the twentieth century. Access to the internet was proclaimed a human right in a United Nations Human Rights Council resolution in 2016, following a decade-long trend where several UN declarations had progressively developed the relationship between access to the internet, the exercise of human rights and the equal status of online and offline human rights

This chapter examines the underlying debate related with human rights and the singular features of the internet as a general-purpose technology. It dwells upon the different approaches to internet access and its contemporary threats, to frame the characteristics of the rights at stake when approaching access to the internet from a global perspective. Finally, it addresses some national approaches to contextualise the implementation of this issue.

Contextualising the "policy" debate

The relationship between internet access and human rights is not a new discussion in policy and development forums. The internet is a multi-purpose technology based on transmission protocols that are based on code[1] and have enabled the connection of different devices and networks over the course of its nearly half a century of existence.[2]

Yet, it was distinctively in 2003 with the beginning of the World Summit on Information Society (WSIS), when the connection between the Internet, Information and Communication Technologies (ICTs) and the perspective of human rights and development became clear to many governments and civil society organisations that had not been directly involved with the original development of internet protocols. The WSIS Declaration of Principles in 2003 makes specific reference to the importance of the right to freedom of expression in the "Information Society" in stating:

> 4. We reaffirm, as an essential foundation of the Information Society, and as outlined in Article 19 of the Universal Declaration of Human Rights, that everyone has the right to freedom of opinion and expression; that this right includes freedom to hold

1 L. B. Solum (2008) Models of Internet Governance. Illinois Public Law Research Paper No. 07–25, http://ssrn.com/abstract=1136825 (accessed 22.10.2018).

2 Janet Abbatte (2000) *Inventing the Internet*. Cambridge: MIT Press.

> opinions without interference and to seek, receive and impart information and ideas through any media and regardless of frontiers. Communication is a fundamental social process, a basic human need and the foundation of all social organization. It is central to the Information Society. Everyone, everywhere should have the opportunity to participate and no one should be excluded from the benefits the Information Society offers.[3]

Two years later, the explicit reference of the Universal Declaration of Human Rights and particularly the provisions concerning freedom of expression were reaffirmed in the Tunis Agenda for the Information Society in its paragraph:

> 42. We reaffirm our commitment to the freedom to seek, receive, impart and use information, in particular, for the creation, accumulation and dissemination of knowledge. We affirm that measures undertaken to ensure Internet stability and security, to fight cybercrime and to counter spam, must protect and respect the provisions for privacy and freedom of expression as contained in the relevant parts of the Universal Declaration of Human Rights and the Geneva Declaration of Principles.[4]

In the context of the Millennium Development Goals, the impact of ICTs was becoming more evident in the promotion of human welfare. In a global order that was being founded in knowledge and information, production, storage, dissemination and retrieval were becoming more critical. Information flows should consequently be guaranteed and one of the primary justifications came from the right to freedom of expression.

From the standpoint of international law, the Tunis Agenda is a consensus statement that was adopted without proceeding to a formal vote; the only requirement was not voicing a formal objection.[5] "The Tunis Agenda encompasses authoritative decision-making standards involving global governance that require closeness with the principles enshrined in the Universal Declaration of Human Rights".[6] But, this adoption of the Universal Declaration of Human Rights of 1948 as a foundation for the Tunis Agenda provides a shaky ground for the discussion of human rights and internet access because in many parts the first equates human rights with natural rights.[7]

In 2011, the United Nations Special Rapporteur on the promotion and protection of the right to freedom of opinion and expression, Frank La Rue, submitted a report to the UN Human Rights Council that makes eighty-eight recommendations on the promotion and protection of the right to freedom of expression online.[8] This report underlines

3 World Summit on the Information Society (2003) www.itu.int/net/wsis/docs/geneva/official/dop.html (accessed 22.10.2018).

4 World Summit on the Information Society (2005) Tunis Agenda. www.itu.int/net/wsis/docs2/tunis/off/6rev1.html (accessed 22.10.2018).

5 The General Assembly endorsed the Tunis Agenda for the Information Society in its resolution 60/252 titled "World Summit on the Information Society".

6 Roy Balleste (2012) Rising Toward Apotheosis: The Deconstruction of the WSIS Tunis Agenda for the Information Society. *Pittsburgh Journal of Technology Law & Policy*, Vol. 12, 153.

7 Charles Beitz (2003) What Human Rights Mean. *Daedalus*, Vol. 132, No. 1, *On International Justice*, 36–46

8 Report of the Special Rapporteur on the promotion and protection of the right to freedom of opinion and expression, Frank La Rue (2011) http://www2.ohchr.org/english/bodies/hrcouncil/docs/17session/A.HRC.17.27_en.pdf (accessed 22.10.2018)

two dimensions of internet access: access to content and access to physical infrastructure (centred in its recommendations 60 to 66). Although most of the report is centered in the problematic nature of the difficulties encountered in the content dimension of access (blocking, shutdowns to censor the internet for political and/or economic reasons, intellectual property provisions, cybersecurity attacks and the like), the material access to the physical infrastructure is underscored mentioning the countries where internet access is enshrined as a right (Estonia, Costa Rica, Finland, France[9]).

On 26 June 2016, fifty-two countries endorsed a draft resolution by the United Nations Human Rights Council in an addition to Article 19,[10] in its Section 32 that reads in its title "The promotion, protection and enjoyment of human rights on the Internet". It includes fifteen recommendations to cover the rights of those who are already using the internet, but also advocates for those who are excluded and the most affected by the digital divide, focusing on women, girls and people with disabilities. It also invokes several aspects related with the background for these recommendations[11] and the implications for three rights that are directly related with internet access in this document: freedom of expression, privacy and the right to education. Recommendation five states:

> Affirms also the importance of applying a comprehensive human rights-based approach in providing and in expanding access to Internet and requests all States to make efforts to bridge the many forms of digital divides;[12]

This assertion reinforces a claim found in other parts of this document whereby the justification of a comprehensive human rights approach provides a framework to address the "many forms" of the digital divide. While neither this, nor the UN Special Rapporteur's document of 2011 ascertained that internet access *is* a human right, both are explicit of how internet access *enables* the exercise of other human rights. Since WSIS, the context for justification of internet access had been refined from one where freedom of expression was one of the main rights which it enabled, to one where economic, social and political

9 Recommendation 65 states: *In some economically developed States, Internet access has been recognized as a right. For example, the parliament of Estonia passed legislation in 2000 declaring Internet access a basic human right.52 The constitutional council of France effectively declared Internet access a fundamental right in 2009, and the constitutional court of Costa Rica reached a similar decision in 2010.53 Going a step further, Finland passed a decree in 2009 stating that every Internet connection needs to have a speed of at least one Megabit per second (broadband level).* Ibid.

10 Article 19, Universal Declaration of Human Rights: *Everyone has the right to freedom of opinion and expression; this right includes freedom to hold opinions without interference and to seek, receive and impart information and ideas through any media and regardless of frontiers.* Retrieved from: www.un.org/en/universal-declaration-human-rights/ (accessed 22.10.2018).

11 The recommendation provides a clear background of previous resolutions that have been considered: *Recalling all relevant resolutions of the Commission on Human Rights and the Human Rights Council on the right to freedom of opinion and expression, in particular Council resolution 20/8 of 5 July 2012 and 26/13 of 26 June 2014, on the promotion, protection, and enjoyment of human rights on the Internet, as well as resolutions 12/16 of 2 October 2009, on freedom of opinion and expression, 28/16 of 24 March 2015, on the right to privacy in the digital age, and 23/2 of 13 June 2013, on the role of freedom of opinion and expression in women's empowerment, and 31/7 of 23 March 2016, on the rights of the child: information and communications technologies and child sexual exploitation, and also recalling General Assembly resolutions 68/167 of 18 December 2013 and 69/166 of 18 December 2014, on the right to privacy in the digital age, 70/184 of 22 December 2015, on information and communications technologies for development, and 70/125 of 16 December 2015, containing the outcome document of the high-level meeting of the General Assembly on the overall review of the implementation of the outcomes of the World Summit on the Information Society,* Res. 32/13, 26 June 2016, www.ohchr.org/EN/HRBodies/HRC/RegularSessions/Session32/Pages/32RegularSession.aspx (accessed 22.10.2018).

12 Ibid.

rights were more clearly defined with the Special Rapporteur's recommendation in 2011 and the addition of Section 32 to Article 19. The increased trend of national internet shutdowns was a strong driving force for the resolution by the UNGA in 2016,[13] where not only was free speech and free press undermined, but the exercise of political and economic rights is also undermined by restricting access to this technology. Finally, in the 32nd session of the Human Rights Council, Agenda Item 3, set forward the recommendation titled "The promotion, protection and enjoyment of human rights on the Internet" that has become the latest milestone in the discussion about the status of the internet for the exercise of human rights, as well as the idea that online human rights deserve equal protection as those of the offline world.

Conceptualising access to the internet

This section of the chapter explores the different dimensions of access. One theoretical discussion that frames access rights to the internet questions its nature as that of a public good. Economic definitions of public goods include requirements that it be *non-excludable*, in that it is a good that cannot be withheld from any individual, and that it be *non-rivalrous*, meaning that its use by some does not preclude its use by others.[14]

This is a feature also shared with information goods,[15] which in an increasingly digital world implies most forms of cultural and economic production. Strictly speaking, the internet does not meet the requirements of a public good. The fact that half of the world still does not have internet access and that technically internet access can be shut down for whole countries as shown in recent examples,[16] evinces its exclusionary capacity.[17] The internet relies on infrastructure that is not available for every citizen, as is the case with breathing air, and it is possible to discriminate its access, as opposed to the luminous emissions from a lighthouse.

> The attraction of a notion of public goods no longer confined within national boundaries – from trade and environmental protection to climate change and security – is not fundamentally different from its attraction at a national level. For public goods provide presumptively politically non-contentious and morally unobjectionable reasons for common action on common problems, whether these sound at the national or at the global level, or, indeed, at any level in between.[18]

13 Darrell West (2016) Internet Shutdowns Cost Countries $2.4 Billion Last Year. Brookings Institute, www.brookings.edu/wp-content/uploads/2016/10/intenet-shutdowns-v-3.pdf (accessed 22.10.2018).

14 E. Ostrom (2011) Background on the Institutional Analysis and Development Framework. *The Policy Studies Journal*, Vol. 39, No. 1, 7–28.

15 C. Shapiro and H. Varian (1999) *Information Rules. A Strategic Guide to the Network Economy*. Boston: Harvard Business School Press.

16 *Countries that shut down the Internet in all or parts of the country in 2016 include Bahrain, Ethiopia, Pakistan, Iraq, Turkey, and Malaysia*. (5). Jonathan L. Zittrain, Robert Faris, Helmi Noman et al. The Shifting Landscape of Global Internet Censorship *Berkman Klein Center Research Publication No. 2017-4 Harvard Public Law Working Paper No. 17-38*, https://cyber.harvard.edu/publications/2017/06/GlobalInternetCensorship (accessed 22.10.2018).

17 A. Doria (2015) Draft. Human Rights Protocol Considerations Research Group. IETF, https://tools.ietf.org/html/draft-doria-hrpc-proposal-00 (accessed 22.10.2018).

18 Neil Walker (2015) Human Rights and Global Public Goods: The Sound of One Hand Clapping. *Indiana Journal of Global Legal Studies* (July 21) Forthcoming; Edinburgh School of Law Research Paper No. 2015/21, 5. SSRN: https://ssrn.com/abstract=2633446 (accessed 22.10.2018).

To understand the limitations of conceptualising internet access as global public good and its relationship with a rights scheme, in the following subsection the work will address the main contemporary threats and challenges to internet access from a global perspective.

Threats and challenges of internet access

The starting point of the current challenges to attain global internet access for all citizens is related with the deployment of networks, both fixed and mobile. Mobile networks and phones have enabled access to the internet to millions, particularly in developing regions, thus reducing the access gap from an infrastructure perspective.[19]

A controversial issue about this approach is that evidence has sustained that internet access from a mobile phone is less enabling for the improvement of digital skills and overall development opportunities than when accessed from a computer. This is not trivial when analysing internet access from a rights perspective, since how a right is grounded is essential for its implementation. In addition, the physical access dimension leads to the analysis of whether the internet is a utility; many discussions surrounding this issue have claimed it is a public good, to differentiate it from other utilities, as discussed briefly in the previous section.

Related policy discussions include the notion of universal service, understood as the principle that all citizens should be provided with a range of basic but good quality services at affordable prices so that they are able to participate fully in society.[20] In the case of the internet, universal access also refers to the provisions of services on a shared basis (community telecentres, etc.), alternative business models and digital literacy programs.[21] When access to a public utility becomes enshrined by a government, legal protection ensures to guarantee equitable access to that good or service, which increases its interpretation as a civil right. Although many countries have set provisions for universal access to telecommunications facilities through instruments such as access funds, the problem is far from bridged.[22]

But access to the internet is not only threatened ex ante by the lack of possibilities to connect or to engage with content. It is also endangered by a range of practices embarked by governments and the private sector,[23] related with blocking and filtering content for commercial or political reasons. There are hundreds of such examples in both democratic and authoritarian regimes.[24] Typically, blocking and filtering content for political motives

19 ITU (2018) *World Telecommunication Facts and Figures*, www.itu.int/en/ITU-D/Statistics/Pages/facts/default.aspx (accessed 27.03.2019).

20 European Parliamentary Research Service. Ron Davies (2016) *Broadband as a Universal Service*, www.europarl.europa.eu/RegData/etudes/BRIE/2016/581977/EPRS_BRI(2016)581977_EN.pdf (accessed 22.10.2018).

21 M. Aledhari, N. Aneja, A.K. Bashir, R. Bennett et al. (2018) Options and Challenges in Providing Universal Access. Internet Initiative, IEEE, https://bit.ly/2DyX5vl (accessed 22.10.2018).

22 D. Thakur and L. Potter (2018) *Universal Service and Access Funds: An Untapped Resource to Close the Gender Digital Divide.* Washington, DC: Web Foundation, https://bit.ly/2FOgLfu (accessed 22.10.2018).

23 With respect to the activities of the private sector and their role in the information society, it is necessary to underscore the report by the UN Rapporteur for Freedom of Expression's 2016 report for the UN Human Rights Council which on the role of the private sector in the digital age. "The contemporary exercise of freedom of opinion and expression owes much of its strength to private industry, which wields enormous power over digital space, acting as a gateway for information and an intermediary for expression."

24 Jonathan L. Zittrain, Robert Faris, Helmi Noman et al. The Shifting Landscape of Global Internet Censorship *Berkman Klein Center Research Publication No. 2017-4 / Harvard Public Law Working Paper No. 17-38*, https://cyber.harvard.edu/publications/2017/06/GlobalInternetCensorship (accessed 22.10.2018).

are more subtle approaches than the internet shutdowns mentioned earlier.[25] Internet platforms' interference on user-generated-content and takedown procedures (even when they infringe their own terms of service, mostly related with compliance with intellectual property rights) is increasingly typified as restrictions on freedom of expression and private sector censorship in many democratic countries.[26]

The network neutrality principle has been particularly relevant in framing internet access discussions both from a public good and a human rights perspective.[27]

> The basic principle behind a network antidiscrimination regime is to give users the right to use non-harmful network attachments or applications, and give innovators the corresponding freedom to supply them. Such a regime avoids some of the costs of structural regulation by allowing for efficient vertical integration so long as the rights granted to the users of the network are not compromised.[28]

Net neutrality provisions are enablers for content access and as such become key instruments for rights attributed to the publication, search and retrieval of information in the online environment. From a user's perspective, net neutrality has been a central issue in internet governance for the last decade with diverse approaches in different contexts. While the United States had supported the net neutrality principle under the "common carrier regulation" approach until recently, close to the idea of a public utility, at the end of 2017 the FCC[29] established preemptive measures to categorise it as "information services", which is less regulated. These moves have spurred the debate at a global level. In Europe on the other hand, the regulation of net neutrality has been labelled as "a major achievement for the Digital Single Market in 2016. It creates the individual and enforceable right for end-users in the EU to access and distribute internet content and services of their choice".[30] The regulation also enshrines the principle of non-discriminatory traffic management. In many countries in Latin America there are no specific net neutrality provisions, but zero-rating practices for mobile content are extended, as well as in Asia.[31]

Technological developments help reframe the conditions and provisions of public goods.[32] The internet is a general-purpose technology, like semiconductors, electrical motors and the steam engine. These technologies enable the work of computers, heaters, medical equipment, transport devices, which in turn promote development and improved

25 R. Deibert, J. Palfrey, R. Rohozinski and Jonathan Zittrain (Eds.) (2010) *Access Controlled: The Shaping of Power, Rights, and Rule in Cyberspace*. Cambridge: The MIT Press.

26 L. Belli, and N. Zingales (2017) Platform Regulation. Dynamic Coalition on Platform Responsibility (DCPR). IGF. Retrieved from: Dynamic Coalition on Platform Responsibility (DCPR), www.intgovforum.org/multilingual/index.php?q=filedepot_download/4905/1172 (accessed 22.10.2018).

27 Johannes M. Bauer and Jonathan A. Obar (2014) Reconciling Political and Economic Goals in the Net Neutrality Debate (January 1, 2014). *The Information Society*, Vol. 30, 1–19. Available at SSRN: https://ssrn.com/abstract=2910104 (accessed 22.10.2018).

28 Tim Wu (2003) Network Neutrality, Broadband Discrimination. *Journal on Telecommunication and High Tech Law*, Vol. 2.

29 Federal Communications Commission, www.fcc.gov/restoring-internet-freedom (accessed 22.10.2018).

30 Open Internet (2018), https://ec.europa.eu/digital-single-market/en/open-internet-net-neutrality (accessed 22.10.2018).

31 The relationship between net-neutrality and zero-rating practices has been well developed by several authors. A recent study documents the relationship between both practices. ARCEP (2018) www.arcep.fr/uploads/tx_gspublication/report-state-internet-2018_conf050618-ENG.pdf (accessed 22.10.2018).

32 R. Coase (1974) The Lighthouse in Economics. *Journal of Law and Economics*, Vol. 17, No. 2, 357–376.

life standards. Access to semiconductor technology has not been debated as a human right, but electricity and the internet have been discussed through this lens. The internet connects an increasing number of devices, people and applications that *enable* them to communicate faster, more efficiently and access more content, thus promoting the exercise of rights such as freedom of expression, freedom of association, and access to knowledge, among many others. In the last decades, both technologies have experienced the push to be considered a public good and in many discussions, justifying it as a human right.

While this last section of the chapter has explored the challenges that internet access faces from a public goods perspective, the human rights arguments about internet access are challenged from the different theoretical approaches that will be discussed in the next section. Access to public goods acts as a normative approach that frames many human rights. Nevertheless, it is important to underscore that the perspectives of public goods and human rights provides two registers of political thought. If combined they contribute a general answer to the challenge of how to work out and how to operationalise global ethics of collective social responsibility, as carriers of ideas of global justice and global governance,[33,34] as well as within the jurisdiction of the state, as the net neutrality approach has shown. Yet, each perspective offers different and complementary views. A key aspect to reconcile the contributions of both involves striking a productive balance of political authority and political morality for the accomplishment of public goods provision on human rights grounds, since both suffer from the same ambiguity when projected from the jurisdiction of states to the global order. Political authority has a firmer grounding in national jurisdiction, and even though public goods and human rights have difficulties in being established even at this level, the international order supposes far greater obstacles, considering the diffuse nature of authority and enforcement, as well as a greater uncertainty and relativity of the ethical principles that underpin them.

A network of rights: approaches to the human rights debate

The rights dimension to internet access addresses in full the discussion about the definition of rights and particularly the conceptualisation and justification of human rights in the twenty-first century. Since the UN uptake of the discussion of access to the internet as an essential enabler for the exercise of several human rights, as mentioned in the first section of this work, the issue has taken a hold in the public agenda. The following section will address the complexity of this case from different philosophical, political and legal traditions. This will enable the reader to frame this topic with theoretical foundations. The last part will discuss some of the national approaches that have a rights-based approach to internet access.

Treaties, movements and alternative instruments

The increasingly influential discourse of the international human rights regime, which implies that the international community must develop legal principles and implement rules to regulate the conduct of governments with respect to their own citizens and

33 Walker.

34 Augenstein (2015) To Whom It May Concern: International Human Rights Law and Global Public Goods. *Indiana Journal of Global Legal Studies.*

residents,[35] is at the core of the different measures related with internet access and human rights. The Universal Declaration of Human Rights (UDHR), as the founding document of contemporary human rights doctrine, has been noted to be vague in its theoretical foundations. To achieve a common understanding for its general approval in the post Second World War context it had to trade off clarity of the underlying philosophical principles that sustain it.[36] The level of abstraction of many of the articles contained in this document have implied that much further work is needed to interpret and implement them in specific environments.

For some authors[37] the UDHR and the widespread view of human rights of the twentieth century conflates human rights with natural rights. This is particularly problematic as it evinces a lack of clarity not only on the foundations of these rights, but also on how to make them effective and enforceable. As some[38] have commented, the rights inflation culture obscures the characteristics of rights, which is also tied with an instrumental usage of international human rights treaties as facades of political correction, but with no correlation as to the enforcement of those rights in many jurisdictions. This has led to questioning of these instruments and points at the ambiguous relationship between international legal regimes and national jurisdictions.

One proposed remedy to treaty inflation is provided by a *welfarist* alternative to the international legal regime of human rights. According to Posner, in the absence of a philosophical justification, states never agreed on what rights are human rights, what human rights to give priority, what resources should be allocated in order to correct human rights violations and on what level of human rights. However, the welfare of individuals is indeed a matter of moral concern. The author argues that treaties, instead of specifying the obligations of governments in terms of respect for specific rights, whether negative or positive, should ask states to increase general welfare. This relative approach to human rights equates human rights with law, rather than as an ethical horizon. Although it is out of scope for this work to address in depth Posner's claim about the creation of an alternative *welfarist* treaty, which would not require states to carry out specific behaviours to increase welfare, but rather let them experiment and take advantage of their own resources, this approach resonates with the discussion about internet access, as it is especially prone to specific national arrangements, considering their resources and capabilities.

The preceding perspective contrasts with that of other scholars. Kathryn Sikkink,[39,40] with a constructivist approach to human rights, imbues the debate about their validity in the promotion of general welfare and global social justice, not only by using treaties as instruments, but also relying on activism and social movements. This perspective is particularly germane with the human rights advocacy networks around internet governance. These have managed to infuse originally technical discussions with a rights dimension

35 Jean L. Cohen (2008) Rethinking Human Rights, Democracy, and Sovereignty in the Age of Globalization. *Source: Political Theory*, Vol. 36, No. 4, 578–606.

36 Beitz (2003); Mary Ann Glendon (2001) *A World Made New: Eleanor Roosevelt and the Universal Declaration of Human Rights*. New York: Random House Trade.

37 M. Cranston (1983) Are there Any Human Rights? *Daedalus*, Vol. 112, No. 4, Human Rights (Fall, 1983), 1–17.

38 E. Posner (2008) Human Welfare, Not Human Rights. *Columbia Law Review*, Vol. 108, No. 7, 1758–1801.

39 Kathryn Sikkink (2002) Transnational Advocacy Networks and the Social Construction of Legal Rules. In: Yves Dezalay and Bryant Garth (Eds.), *Global Prescriptions: The Production, Exportation, and Importation of a New Legal Orthodoxy*. Ann Arbor: University of Michigan Press, 37–64.

40 Kathryn Sikkink (2017) *Evidence for Hope*. Making Human Rights Work in the XXI Century. Princeton University Press.

that has provided a foundation for the principles and debates that have ensued since the Tunis Agenda.

Although none of the existing human rights treaties contemplate a self-standing right of internet access,[41] treaties are still a sought-for instrument by policymakers and scholars in the internet policy environment. At a national level, a constitutional right to access the internet is emerging thanks to interpretations of freedom of expression as the most relevant parameter.[42]

Humanist and political approaches

The political view of human rights shares the concern of establishing stronger theoretical foundations for human rights. "In scope and detail, international human rights are not very much more minimal than those proposed in many contemporary theories of social justice".[43] Beitz has emphasised the distinctive *political* function of human rights. Advocates of the political view have tended toward fidelity to existing human rights practices, and to rights minimalism, given the need to find common ground among the variety of political responses to human rights ideas in different national contexts. But because the political view construes human rights as dependent upon political institutions and practices, it is unlikely to satisfy those attracted to human rights precisely because of their independence from particular political practices,[44] as proponents of the naturalist perspective would consider.

To bridge the gap between these different approaches, the analysis proposed by Gilabert on complementary possibilities between the political (practical) perspective and the humanist perspective provides a relevant point to understand the relationship between both traditions and how it touches upon crucial dimensions related with the provision of the right to internet access. According to the political perspective, human rights constitute demands that individuals have towards institutions, particularly modern states, by virtue of their interests within the contexts that include them. On the other hand, the humanist or naturalist perspective holds that human rights conform demands of individuals towards other individuals by virtue of their characteristic interests of their common human condition. According to Gilabert,[45] both theories, originally contrary, are complementary, and both are necessary to achieve a satisfactory explanation of the contemporary practice of human rights.

The humanist perspective holds that there are a series of abstract rights that are demanded by individuals versus other individuals on the basis of their common human condition, not their membership in any institution. The political perspective justifies the idea that human rights are and should be demanded in practice through the identification of specific rights with institutional frameworks. The author mentions five analytical dimensions and reasons to justify the relationship between the two perspectives that

41 Stephen Tully (2014) A Human Right to Access the Internet – Problems and Prospects. *Human Rights Law Review*, Vol. 14, No. 2, 175–196.

42 Tommaso E. Frosini (2013) Access to Internet as a Fundamental Right. *Italian Journal of Public Law*, Vol. 5, No. 2, 226–234.

43 Beitz, 29.

44 Tim Dare (2017) What Human Rights Are. *Philosophy Now*, https://philosophynow.org/issues/118/What_Are_Human_Rights (accessed 22.10.2018).

45 P. Gilabert (2011) Humanist and Political Perspectives on Human Rights. *Political Theory*, Vol. 39, No. 4, 439–467.

include institutions as cross-cutting enablers and deterrents for the conceptions and applications of human rights.[46] Therefore, a humanist position is fundamental to recognise the meaning of institutions, to grant a framework to their form and impact, and to explain why their creation and transformation are necessary. Political reasoning, in order to be normatively plausible, must be based on humanist considerations. That is why the political approach should not be analysed independently of the humanist perspective.

Amartya Sen[47] provides a humanist perspective to the debate that has changed the notion of development by including human rights and freedoms as central component of this issue. From a different disciplinary background than authors cited previously with an international law and philosophy of law background, he also argues to develop a theory of human rights. For Sen, human rights can be seen as ethical pretensions and, although they can inspire legislation, this is a later fact and not a constitutive feature of human rights. On the other hand, the importance of human rights lies in the meaning of the freedoms that are the object of these rights. These freedoms, in order to be the foundations of human rights, must satisfy conditions of special importance and social influence. Likewise, human rights generate reasons for action in those agents who are in a position to help promote and safeguard underlying freedoms. On the other hand, human rights can be implemented through legislation or through other means, such as public recognition, monitoring or public agitation. Essentially, a theory of human rights cannot be confined to the legal model. Sen's approach is different from other political views of human rights as he is interested not only in the conceptual clarity but also in the richness of the practice which is vital to understand their theoretical foundations. His ideas of alternatives other than legal instruments for the development of a theory on human rights, as well as the need to include institutional dimensions of the contexts where those rights should be enhanced, is germane to the discussion about the different applications of the rights of internet access in different settings, as the chapter will explore in the next section.

The idea that human rights and development should work in tandem is also part of the tradition of Alston's proposal.[48] Rather than human rights and development goals moving in parallel tracks, yet heading towards the same destinations, the human rights agenda should engage more fully in the development debate without being overly prescriptive. This recommendation is particularly central to internet access approaches, considering the wide range of levels of access and implications contained in them.

46 First, the content: institutional structures are not instrumental only to violate or protect human rights, but also generate specific social relationships and, therefore, specific rights. Second, there is the issue of consistency with practice and justification. In this regard, Gilabert argues that the vision on human rights related to institutions is consistent with current legal and political practice. Third, self-determination and diversity refer to the fact that when there are institutions that incorporate forms of political self-determination, there are agents that can identify the priority of rights according to historical circumstances and autonomously define the specific implementation. Fourth refers to the correlative duties: robust institutions help to identify routinely who has the responsibility to do what and for whom, which is fundamental to grant duties correlative to human rights that are perfect. Even when the duties are imperfect, it is more appropriate to consider institutions as the main responsible entity for those duties and, in addition, allows a more flexible allocation of responsibility. Finally, regarding feasibility, the author considers that robust institutions increase the viability of compliance with human rights, and make human rights demands more realistic and relevant in practice. Ibid.

47 A. Sen (2004) Elements of a Theory of Human Rights. *Philosophy and Public Affairs*, Vol. 32, 4; Research Library Core, 315.

48 Philip Alston (2005) Ships Passing in the Night: The Current State of the Human Rights and Development Debate Seen through the Lens of the Millennium Development Goals. *Human Rights Quarterly*, Vol. 27, No. 3, 755–829.

A somewhat different yet complementary perspective is provided by Dworkin's[49] thesis that individual's rights exist outside of written law. Dworkin provides a comprehensive perspective about fundamental rights, like freedom of expression, which, "*are supposed to represent rights against the Government in the strong sense; that is the point of the boast that our legal system respects the fundamental rights of the citizen*".[50] This approach of rights (as trumps) is a vital component for the debate about whether human rights in the online world are the same as in the offline one. This is a discussion since the early days of the internet but it has been endorsed and framed by the United Nations' Human Rights Council in 2016:

1. Affirms that the same rights that people have offline must also be protected online, in particular freedom of expression, which is applicable regardless of frontiers and through any media of one's choice, in accordance with articles 19 of the Universal Declaration of Human Rights and the International Covenant on Civil and Political Rights.[51]

Freedom of expression is a fundamental right that entwines rights' theories and approaches from the analogue age fully into the realm of the digital environment that encompasses the internet and its access. From a development perspective it becomes an essential human right in the context of the digital informational era.

National applications of the right of internet access

Over the last decade, some states have announced their views with regards to internet acces as a human right. Following the line of the political perspective of human rights described before, these rights have taken a distinctive turn which tends to match their institutions as well as the capacity of citizens and stakeholders to mobilise and campaign for the different types of rights that are at stake with internet access. These states have worked with their own legal, political and economic backgrounds, as well as with legacy technologies and institutions that mould how internet access is conceptualised in each context. Some countries have declared these to be rights before the discussions with the United Nations' Human Rights Council and General Assembly resolutions in the post-WSIS environment.

> For example, the parliament of Estonia passed legislation in 2000 declaring Internet access a basic human right. The constitutional council of France effectively declared Internet access a fundamental right in 2009, and the constitutional court of Costa Rica reached a similar decision in 2010. Going a step further, Finland passed a decree in 2009 stating that every Internet connection needs to have a speed of at least one Megabit per second.
>
> *(broadband level)*[52,53]

49 R. Dworkin (1977) *Taking Rights Seriously*. Harvard: Harvard University Press.

50 Ibid., 191, emphasis added.

51 United Nations General Assembly, Human Rights Council, 32nd session, 27 June 2016.

52 United Nations Human Rights Office of the High Commissioner. Contributions by the Office of the High Commissioner for Human Rights to UNESCO's Comprehensive Study on Internet-related Issues. November 2014, www.unesco.org/new/fileadmin/MULTIMEDIA/HQ/CI/CI/pdf/Events/netconference_march2015_submissions/E/response_from_ohchr_office_of_the_high_commissioner_for_.pdf (accessed 22.10.2018).

53 This list is not comprehensive of all the States that have decreed access to the Internet as a human right. Other countries include Greece and Spain, www.diplomacy.edu/blog/right-access-internet-countries-and-laws-proclaim-it (accessed 22.10.2018).

There is a wide variety of countries and experiences from the evidence collected by the United Nations on these schemes, but they do share one characteristic and that is that these states are to a large extent committed to democratic values and the respect for human rights, in both the physical and the Content sphere. Yet, the way internet access was conceived, framed and achieved in these experiences varies significantly and this chapter will briefly examine two of them: Estonia and Costa Rica.

Estonia is considered one of the first countries where internet access became a human right in February 2000 by the *Riigikogu* (Parliament). This recognition as a human right and not just a legal right underscores Dworkin's view of the first to exist outside the written law,[54] and that is not confined to a legal model, as characterised by Amartya. It is relevant to contextualise that access to telecommunications services in the decade of the 1990s in the country was still very precarious, but rather than relying on building legacy infrastructure, the government stimulated the development of IP networks to bring connectivity to the whole territory. The Telecommunications Act of 2000 added internet access to its universal service list: The set of telecommunications services specified in subsection (1) of this section comprises: 2) internet service which universally available to all subscribers regardless of their geographical location, at a uniform price.[55]

Wireless access to the internet is guaranteed in schools, public buildings and government offices, to the point where it is getting practically impossible to be out of reach of a hotspot. Yet, this contemplates only the infrastructure dimension of access: Estonia has embraced a strategy where access to the internet is considered an essential component for everyday life, for interactions with government and all types of organisations (health, finance, education, businesses) which increases welfare and a full exercise of social and economic rights which drive the current growth of Estonia.[56] But most fundamentally, access to the internet is considered a vital component for the exercise of freedom of expression,[57] access to information and as an instrument to hold government accountable to its citizens, highly valued after becoming a democratic and independent state in 1991 after the collapse of the Soviet Union.[58]

Costa Rica presents a different approach. The *Sala Constitucional* (Constitutional Court) decided in 2010 that the government's delay in opening the telecoms market to competition was tantamount to a breach of fundamental freedoms, including freedom of choice for consumers, the right of access to ICTs and the right to equality and eradication of the digital divide.[59] It was initially presented as a legal protection appeal by a citizen in a rural area against the telecommunications company of Costa Rica (ICE) which had been until recently a monopolistic service for communications in the country. This judgement triggered a fast revision of the national telecommunications development plans, since the country had not enacted any provision for universal access of the service. Essentially, this constitutional court decision has triggered an expansion of internet access and the

54 George Letsas (2015) Dworkin on Human Rights. *Jurisprudence*, Vol. 6, No. 2, 327–340.

55 Estonia. Telecommunications Act Adopted. IRIS 2000–5:14/21 http://merlin.obs.coe.int/iris/2000/5/article21.en.html (accessed 22.10.2018).

56 ICT related activities in Estonia account for 20% of its GDP. Source: Estonian Ministry of Foreign Affairs. Retrieved from: https://vm.ee/en/estonian-economy-overview (accessed 27.03.2019).

57 Estonia scored one of the highest marks in the Freedom on the Net 2016 report, Freedom House. Available at: https://freedomhouse.org/report/freedom-net/2016/estonia (accessed 22.10.2018).

58 Frosini.

59 S. Borg Psaila (2007) Right to Access the Internet: The Countries and the Laws that Proclaim it. Diplo Foundation, www.diplomacy.edu/blog/right-access-internet-countries-and-laws-proclaim-it (accessed 22.10.2018).

country now presents one of the better served profiles in the region. The freedoms that are object to the right of access emerged forcefully in the court decision and sustain the argument as an enabler of rights.[60]

Both examples underscore the inevitable relationship between fundamental human rights from a humanist viewpoint, as well as the political conditions that generate the frameworks for the enactment of the rights in the digital age and how both the humanist and the political perspectives can be used to assess this issue. The case of Estonia is highly relevant to illustrate an enactment of human rights that is not only subject to legal instruments, but on institutional and political approaches that ground these measures, following Dworkin's perspective on a comprehensive approach about human rights. The case of Costa Rica differs with that of Estonia in that the conception of the right to access is more aligned with a political tradition of human rights.

The internet as a new frontier for social struggles

Is it accurate to assess the UN resolution of July 2016 that internet access became a human right? This resolution has made information technologies inseparable from the rights themselves. But the idea that states should be providing internet access to its citizens is only a good intention, since this would entail obligations to provide infrastructure which is not yet accomplishable in many jurisdictions, as the UN Rapporteur on Freedom of Expression has stated.[61]

Assessing the different dimensions comprised by internet access: to the network, devices, content and the different threats and opportunities contained in these three levels, the right of access emerges more forcefully for the layer of content, which, due to its relative immateriality compared to the rest, is clearly more connected to an intangible ethical and moral dimension. This does imply that internet access at the network level should be deemed irrelevant. Yet, for analytical clarity, a large portion of the debate related with scepticism towards the idea of internet access as a human right is derived from the evidence of the past with utilities that have not yet been able to be administered to the local populations, in both developing and developed contexts. There is little room for contestation after this resolution at a global level that the same rights that have been enshrined for the offline world should not be incorporated into the online one. As the internet has become a new terrain of social struggles[62] and new manifestations of digital and physical divides, to be offline is to be silenced.

60 V. Cerf (2012) Internet Access Is Not a Human Right, 4 January 2012, www.nytimes.com/2012/01/05/opinion/internet-access-is-not-a-human-right.html (accessed 22.10.2018).

61 David Kaye (2017) Internet Access Is Now a Basic Human Right: Part 1 – Chips with Everything Tech Podcast. *The Guardian,* www.theguardian.com/technology/audio/2016/jul/29/internet-access-human-right-tech-podcast (accessed 22.10.2018).

62 Daniel Joyce (2015) Internet Freedom and Human Rights. *European Journal of International Law,* Vol. 26, No. 2 (1 May), https://academic.oup.com/ejil/article/26/2/493/423010 (accessed 22.10.2018).

3 The right to privacy

The end of Privacy Fatalism

Jonathon Penney[1]

Introduction

The right to privacy, more than a century after its prominent articulation by Warren and Brandeis,[2] appears more important and relevant today than ever: governments and businesses around the world are engaged in internet tracking and profiling;[3] the amount of data online is growing exponentially and is already measured in exabytes;[4] and new forms of sophisticated detection and surveillance, powered by artificial intelligence (AI), machine learning, and Big Data analytics, pose serious new threats to our privacy and civil liberties, online and off.[5] And yet, privacy itself is constantly and regularly declared dead.[6]

1 Penney is Research Fellow, The Citizen Lab, University of Toronto; Research Associate, Princeton Center for Information Technology Policy; Research Associate, Civil Servant Project, MIT Media Lab; Director, Law and Technology Institute, Schulich School of Law, Dalhousie University.

2 Samuel D. Warren and Louis D. Brandeis (1890) The Right to Privacy. *Harvard Law Review*, 4, 193.

3 Jonathon Penney (2015), ' The Cycles of Global Telecommunication Censorship and Surveillance',. *(2015) 36 University of Pennsylvania Journal of International Law, U. Pa. J. Int'l L.*Vol. 36, 693, 693–694, available at https://papers.ssrn.com/sol3/papers.cfm?abstract_id=2398491 (last accessed 23.10.Oct 23 2018); Dustin Volz (2015), ' Global Internet Surveillance, Censorship on Rise: Report' (October 28, 2015). Reuters (October 28, 2015), available at www.reuters.com/article/us-cybersecurity-report-idUSKCN0SM1M220151028 (last accessed Oct 23.10. 2018).

4 V. Boehme-Neßler (2016), 'Privacy: A Matter of Democracy. Why Democracy Needs Privacy and Data Protection'. (2016) 6 *International Data Privacy Law*, Vol. 6, 222, 222; C. Kuner (2013), *Transborder Data Flow Regulation and Data Privacy Law*. Oxford: (Oxford University Press, 2013).

5 Woodrow Hartzog, Gregory Conti, John Nelson, and Lisa Shay (2015) Inefficiently Automated Law Enforcement. *Michigan State Law Review*, Vol. 1763, 1765; Lisa Shay, Woodrow Hartzog, John Nelson, Dominic Larkin, and Gregory Conti (2016) Confronting Automated Law Enforcement. In: Ryan Calo, Michael Froomkin, and Ian Kerr (Eds.), *Robot Law*. Elgar, 235, 270; Primavera De Filippi and Samer Hassan (2016) Blockchain Technology as a Regulatory Technology: From Code Is Law to Law Is Code. *First Monday* (4 December), Vol. 21, No. 12, http://firstmonday.org/ojs/index.php/fm/article/view/7113 (accessed Oct 23 2018); Frank Pasquale and Glyn Cashwell (2018) Prediction, Persuasion, and the Jurisprudence of Behaviourism. University of Toronto Law Journal, Vol. 68, 63, at Frank Pasquale (2015) *The Black Box Society: The Secret Algorithms that Control Money and Information*. Cambridge, MA: Harvard College. Niva Elkin-Koren and Michael Gal (forthcoming 2018) The Chilling Effect of Governance by Data on Data Markets. *University of Chicago Law Review*, Vol. 68, 1, at 4; M. Ryan Calo (2011) Robots and Privacy. In: Patrick Lin, George Bekey, and Keith Abney (Eds.), *Robot Ethics: The Ethical and Social Implications of Robotics*. Cambridge, MA: MIT Press.

6 In 2018 alone, there are countless examples. See e.g., Christopher Mims (2018) Privacy Is Dead. Here's What Comes Next. *Wall Street Journal* (6 May), www.wsj.com/articles/privacy-is-dead-heres-what-comes-next-1525608001 (accessed 23.10.2018); Adrian Tan (2018) Privacy Is Dead. *The Business Times* (9 June), www.businesstimes.com.sg/opinion/privacy-is-dead (accessed 23.10.2018); Keith Bonnell (2018) Privacy Is Dead and We All Helped Kill It. *Ottawa Citizen* (2 April); Cameron F. Kerry (2018) Why Protecting Privacy Is a Losing Game Today – and How to Change the Game. *Brookings Institute Report* (12 July), www.brookings.edu/research/why-protecting-privacy-is-a-losing-game-today-and-how-to-change-the-game/ (accessed 23.10.2018).

This is important, for what good is a *right* to privacy if it is a right to something that no longer exists or will soon cease to be so? Indeed, there is perhaps no other right that is so often and so casually declared deceased.[7]

This grand and seeming perpetual tradition of declaring the death of privacy – or as I like to call it Privacy Fatalism[8] – is at least half a century old and possibly as old as privacy itself.[9] Given the great length of this tradition it is no surprise that others have noticed it,[10] but as Peters and John recently note, few have attempted to theorise or explain its origins and persistence through time.[11] This chapter not only offers some reasons for Privacy Fatalism in research and scholarship, including conceptual, empirical and technological challenges to privacy and its legal protection, but also argues that important new legal, theoretical and empirical developments around privacy – and frameworks protecting internationally – may mean that this great tradition of Privacy Fatalism may soon itself come to a fatal end. And understanding the *reasons* for Privacy Fatalism, and its own end, provides important context not just to better understand the right to privacy – especially in online and similar technological contexts – but also its future, which may not be as dark as most privacy prognosticators would suggest.

In the next section, I argue that Privacy Fatalism is best understood as a product of three factors complicating privacy and legal rights to it: First, the emergence of new technologies and new data practices that threaten privacy, or at least certain understandings of it; second, persistent conceptual, theoretical and normative problems, rendering rights to privacy less effective in addressing real privacy challenges; and third, lack of systematic study, leading to empirical scepticism. However, in the following section, entitled "The origins of privacy fatalism", I argue that recent developments may mean these factors will be less important going forward, spelling a possible end to Privacy Fatalism. Among those developments is (a) emerging new empirical insights as to the impacts and harms of privacy right violations; (b) new openness among courts in both the US and Europe to privacy and surveillance harm claims; and, most importantly, (c) a convergence of the American and European privacy traditions leading to new and innovative positive protections for privacy, reputation and data protection like the GDPR and the RTBF. I end with a brief conclusion.

7 Stan Karas (2002) Privacy, Identity, Databases. *American University Law Review*, Vol. 52, 393 at 405n58 (noting that privacy has been declared dead more often than rock n' roll); Bart van der Sloot (2016) The Individual in the Big Data Era: Moving towards an Agent-Based Privacy Paradigm. In: Bart van der Sloot, Dennis Broeders and Erik Schrijvers (Eds.), *Exploring the Boundaries of Big Data*. Amsterdam: Amsterdam University Press, 177 (noting privacy has been declared dead since its been conceived); Neil Richards (2015) Four Myths of Privacy. In Austin Sarat (Ed.), *A World Without Privacy: What the Law Can and Should Do* 1. Cambridge: CUP, 1–2, https://papers.ssrn.com/sol3/papers.cfm?abstract_id=2427808 (accessed 23.10.2018); Kerry (2018); Nicholas A. John and Benjamin Peters (2017) Why Privacy Keeps Dying: The Trouble with Talk about the End of Privacy. *Information, Communication, & Society*, Vol. 20, No. 2, 284 at 285–287 (noting the tradition of privacy "endism").

8 I use the term in the sense that those who declare the "death" of privacy are often fatalistic – that the arrival of a certain technology inevitably will bring about privacy's end.

9 van der Sloot 177; John and Peters 286.

10 John and Peters 285.

11 Ibid.

The origins of privacy fatalism

Privacy Fatalism is a persistent contemporary phenomenon.[12] As Neil Richards notes, the last twenty years has seen "innumerable books" with titles, in various ways, declaring privacy is "dead" or "dying".[13] And even the most casually privacy-interested reader is likely familiar with the now infamous quote by Sun Microsystems' CEO Scott McNealy: "you have zero privacy . . . get over it".[14] Though that quote often is misattributed to Mark Zuckerberg, the Facebook CEO has his own infamous quotes on privacy, declaring in 2010 that "privacy is no longer a social norm".[15]

Yet, this contemporary trend has older roots. Though privacy interests are likely ancient,[16] modern notions of privacy are most often traced to Warren and Brandeis's seminal 1890 article entitled "The Right to Privacy".[17] But if that article marked the birth of modern privacy, it had a relatively short life. The death of privacy would be declared only decades later, starting a tradition of Privacy Fatalism that persists to the present.[18] Why? There are a plethora of reasons for this fascination with privacy's death, a comprehensive study of which would take us beyond the scope of this chapter. Nevertheless, I do want to set out what I think to be among the central factors in this persistent privacy tradition: technological challenges; theoretical and conceptual complications; and a lack of empirical substantiation of 1the impact and harms of privacy violations. Each is elaborated in this section.

New technology and data challenges

By far the most important factor contributing to Privacy Fatalism is technology. More specifically, the emergence of new technologies that are so invasive, intrusive, or otherwise negatively impacting privacy rights, interests, or social norms, that they pose an existential threat to privacy, with its death now upon us or imminent.[19] The central role of technology, in fact, can be seen not only with the birth of modern privacy rights itself, but also the beginnings of its mortal twin – Privacy Fatalism.

New technological concerns, for instance, were a key driver behind Warren and Brandeis's seminal 1890 article. The late nineteenth century, the context in which Warren and Brandeis wrote, saw the emergence of new media technologies were having a significant impact on the private lives of the population.[20] Among those technological innovations were mass printing technologies – like the rotary press, linotype and automatic folder – which made newspapers longer and brought them to a greater number of people.[21] Moreover, the wireless telegraph, and new camera/film technologies that allowed

12 See Mims (2018); Tan (2018); Bonnell (2018); Kerry (2018).

13 Richards 2.

14 Kerry 5.

15 Bobbie Johnson (2010) Privacy No Longer a Social Norm, Facebook Founder Says. *The Guardian* (11 Jan), www.theguardian.com/technology/2010/jan/11/facebook-privacy (accessed 23.10. 2018).

16 Barrington Moore (1984) *Privacy: Studies in Social and Cultural History*. New York: M.E. Sharpe, 123 (discussing privacy in ancient Greece). See also Jonathon Penney (2008) Privacy and the New Virtualism. *Yale Journal of Law and Technology*, Vol. 10, 194, at 219.

17 Karas 403; John and Peters 286; Richards 2.

18 Karas 403; John and Peterst 286; Richards 2.

19 Richards 5; John and Peters 288–289.

20 Richards 3–4; John and Peters 286.

21 David J. Seipp (1978) *The Right to Privacy in American History*. Cambridge, MA: Harvard, 66–67.

for new forms of surveillance, observation and mass information sharing, all raised new privacy concerns, especially for elites dealing with gossip and rumour in the news and press industry.[22] "The telegraph and the innumerable newspapers" noted one commentator in the 1870s, "have made the world one enormous ear of Dionysius – a perpetual whispering gallery".[23] Thus, Warren and Brandeis likewise lamented and strongly critiqued "the press", which was "overstepping in every direction" beyond common decency and engaging in "vicious" and "unseemly" gossip.[24] The growing "newspaper enterprise" driven by new technologies like "instantaneous photographs" were, they argued, invading the "sacred precincts of private and domestic life".[25] Hence, they would argue for a new legal right to privacy – essentially a "right to be let alone" to address these new technological challenges to privacy and private life.[26]

One additional dynamic in this technological factor is the fusion of state power, resources, and reach with these new technologies as well as new forms of data, raising new invasions into the privacy of a wider cross-section of citizens. This was also true in the nineteenth century. Part of the reason why the legal right fashioned by Warren and Brandeis has been deemed a "luxury" of the wealthy and a product of elite concern with a democratic press publicising their lives,[27] was that its influence at the time can be attributed, at least in part, to the fact that it was soon after tested in courts by wealthy and high-profile citizens in a range of widely publicised cases.[28] In 1893, for instance, relatives of the late Mary Hamilton Schuyler – a well-known philanthropist in her lifetime – brought a lawsuit, based in part on the legal right to privacy, to prevent a women's association from erecting a statue in her honour at the Chicago World Fair.[29]

But this is not the full story either. The broader population also had new privacy concerns, but those were more tied to the state and invasive new forms of data and information gathering and retention employed by government. The late nineteenth century saw many significant societal changes – urbanisation, immigration and a growing state bureaucracy aiming to track, probe and politicise these societal changes, with the federal government's national census being the primary concern.[30] Since its establishment in the late eighteenth century, the national consensus had grown in terms of the scope and level of detail it collected and retained about citizens.[31] Additionally, new electronic tabulation technologies (to "read" hole punched cards) were introduced in the 1890 census, allowing faster and more efficient processing at scale.[32] Another central concern was government access to citizen communications through the increasingly global telegraph system, which became the topic of domestic and international attention.[33] These wider public concerns

22 Seipp 67; John and Peters 286; Richards 3–4, 6–7.

23 Seipp 67.

24 Warren and Brandeis 196; Seipp 66–67. See also Dorothy J. Glancy (1979) Invention of the Right to Privacy. *Arizona* Law Review, Vol. 21, 1.

25 Warren and Brandeis, 195.

26 Ibid.; Seipp 85.

27 Richards 4 citing Lawrence Friedman; Seipp 86.

28 Seipp 75.

29 Wilbur Larremore (1912) The Law of Privacy. *Columbia Law Review*, Vol. 12, 693; Seipp 75.

30 Seipp 2.

31 Seipp 42–53. See also Priscilla M. Regan (1995) *Legislative Privacy: Technology, Social Values, and Public Policy*. UNC, 46.

32 Seipp 53–54.

33 Ibid., 30–42. See also Penney 109–127.

also helped entrench Warren and Brandeis' notion of modern privacy rights in both public imagination and the law.

So, new technologies and data gathering led to the birth of modern privacy rights. But they also, it would turn out, foster the first laments for privacy's deaths. By the 1960s, a new "privacy panic" captured public attention in the US – the emergence of new electronic data banks that allowed for the collection and storage of significant new forms of data.[34] Not surprisingly, it was also in this period that the first examples of Privacy Fatalism appeared. In 1969, Jerry Rosenberg in his widely cited book *Death of Privacy*, argued that with "the advance of technology, centralized data accumulation becomes easier, the reward for intrusion is increased, and control shifts to still fewer people".[35] This was also the period that Alan Westin would publish his seminal work *Freedom and Privacy*. Rosenberg's work, which was among a range of prominent privacy works in this period – including Alan Westin's famous work *Freedom and Technology* published in 1967 – all focused on new technology and associated data practices and the threats and challenges to privacy, particularly the development of new computing and databasing technologies.[36] And as these technologies continued to develop in subsequent years – in terms of sophistication, power and level of deployment throughout society – laments about the death of privacy would continue. Hence, famed Canadian media philosopher Marshall McLuhan would similarly declare in 1981 that "electronic banking" would be the "death of privacy".[37]

Today, Privacy Fatalism retains these intellectual origins focused on technology and data practices – the only change is the technology and data practices at issue. The internet's emergence in the late 1990s would lead computer scientist Simson Garfinkel and legal scholar Michael Froomkin to both declare, independently, the "Death of Privacy" in 2000.[38] And the rise of social networks in the mid-2000s prompted the aforementioned privacy death announcements from the "captains of industry" like McNealy, Mark Zuckerberg, and Google CEO Eric Schmidt,[39] as well as similar declarations from legal scholars[40] and popular writers.[41]

More recently, with online connectivity, social sharing, ubiquitous handheld computing, and the Internet of Things now facts of everyday life, it is primarily Big Data, driven by sophisticated data analytics, and propelled by emerging technologies like artificial intelligence, machine learning, and automation, fuelling the latest Privacy Fatalism. The death or "end" of privacy, and the role of Big Data, is well documented in popular media today,[42]

34 Richards 4; Regan 13.

35 Jerry Rosenberg (1969) *The Death of Privacy*. New York: Random House, 1; Regan 13.

36 Regan 13–14.

37 M. McLuhan and B. Powers (1981) Electronic Banking and the Death of Privacy. *Journal of Communication*, Vol. 31, 164.

38 A. Michael Froomkin (2000) The Death of Privacy? *Stanford Law Review*, Vol. 52, 1461; Simson Garfinkel (2000) *Database Nation: The Death of Privacy*. O'Reilly, 2000.

39 John and Peters 285; Richards 2–3.

40 E.g., Daniel Solove (2008) The End of Privacy? *Scientific American*, Vol. 299, No. 3, 100; Jed Rubenfeld (2008) The End of Privacy. *Stanford Law Review*, Vol. 61, 101.

41 Judith Timson (2009) Forget Tiger's Privacy. What about Yours? *The Globe and Mail* (7 December), www.theglobeandmail.com/life/forget-tigers-privacy-what-about-yours/article793560/ (accessed 23.10.2018); Kathy Sherian, A Tale of Two Booms. *The Irish Times* (30 November), www.irishtimes.com/life-and-style/people/a-tale-of-two-booms-1.781182 (accessed 23.10.2018); C. J. Sykes (1999) *The End of Privacy*. New York: St. Martin's Press, 1999; R. Whitaker, *The End of Privacy: How Total Surveillance Is Becoming a Reality*. New York: New Press, 1999.

42 See e.g., Euronews (2014) Big Brother, Big Data, and the Death of Privacy in the Digital Age. *Euronews* (1 June); Alex Preston (2014) The Death of Privacy. *The Guardian* (3 August), www.theguardian.com/world/2014/aug/03/

as well as research and scholarship.[43] And as with earlier times – including the nineteenth century – these privacy concerns are magnified by the state and corporate actors employing new technologies and data practices. These public concerns are thanks in part to widespread coverage of the Snowden revelations about sophisticated mass online and telecommunications surveillance being conducted by governments, as well as the Facebook/Cambridge Analytica scandal.[44] These high-profile stories, detailing data-driven surveillance and other privacy-invasive state and corporate practices, no doubt shape perceptions about privacy and challenges to its future.

In short, the continual emergence of new technologies and data practices are a key factor in privacy's seemingly never-ending dying, from the early twentieth century to the present. But it is not the only contributing factor.

Theoretical and conceptual challenges

Another central factor is that privacy has had enduring theoretical, conceptual, and definitional complications and problems. A key part of the challenge, as John and Peters have noted, is the enduring influence of Warren and Brandeis, at least within the American privacy tradition, who defined the modern right to privacy in their famous 1890 piece in negative terms.[45] That is, they defined the right to privacy as essentially the right to solitude, to be left alone, and to not have information and gossip to be spread, shared and publicised about private individuals.[46] Thus, Richards points out, if we define privacy as "the scope of information we can keep completely secret or unknown" then certainly that form of privacy is "shrinking" – or dying – due to new technological realities and, as well, new forms of data being generated and stored about us and our activities both online and off.[47] So, the solution would seem to be simple: re-define privacy, to wrest control of privacy discourse from Warren and Brandeis' conceptualisation, with the end of their negative approach is also the end of Privacy Fatalism, right? Not so fast.

---

internet-death-privacy-google-facebook-alex-preston (accessed 23.10.2018). See also Mims (2018); Tan (2018); Bonnell (2018); Kerry (2018).

43 See e.g., Martin Enserink and Gilbert Chin (2015) The End of Privacy. *Science,* 30 January, 347, 490; Ira S. Rubinstein (2013) Big Data: The End of Privacy or a New Beginning? *International Data Privacy,* Vol. 3, 74. Lori Andrews (2013) *Know Who You Are and I Saw What You Did: Social Networks and the Death of Privacy.* New York: Free Press; Bruce Boyden (2013) Regulating the End of Privacy. *University of Chicago Law Review Forum,* Vol. 1, 173.

44 Dennis Broeders, Erik Schrijvers, Bart Van der Sloot, Rosamundevan Brakel, Jostade Hoog, and Ernst Hirsch Ballin (2017) Big Data and Security Policies: Towards a Framework for Regulating the Phases of Analytics and ZUse of Big Data. *Computer Law & Security, Review,* Vol. 33, No. 3, 309 at 315; Nathaniel Fruchter, Michael Specter, and Ben Yuan (2018) Facebook/Cambridge Analytica: Privacy Lessons and a Way Forward. *MIT Internet Policy Research Initiative* (20 March), https://internetpolicy.mit.edu/blog-2018-fb-cambridgeanalytica/ (accessed 23.10.2018); Julie Beck (2018) People Are Changing the Way They Use Social Media. *The Atlantic* (7 June), www.theatlantic.com/technology/archive/2018/06/did-cambridge-analytica-actually-change-facebook-users-behavior/562154/ (accessed 23.10.2018); Ellen Daniel (2018) Five Years On, What has Changed since the Edward Snowden Scandal? *The Verdict* (8 June), www.verdict.co.uk/snowden-scandal-five-years-gdpr/ (accessed 23.10.2018); FDR Group & PEN American Center (2015) *Global Chilling: The Impact of Mass Surveillance on International Writers,* www.pen.org/sites/default/files/globalchilling_2015.pdf (accessed 23.10.2018); Margot Kaminski (2018) Toward Defining Privacy Expectations in An Age of Oversharing. *The Economist* (16 August), available at www.economist.com/open-future/2018/08/16/toward-defining-privacy-expectations-in-an-age-of-oversharing (accessed 23.10.2018).

45 John and Peters 293–294. See also Richards 6–7.

46 John and Peters 293–294.

47 Richards 7.

This task has turned out to be easier said than done, for with each new technology and emerging data practice, privacy has been re-defined, extended and further elaborated. The result is that today, defining and conceptualising privacy has become a fraught and increasingly complex and complicated task,[48] often divided up and segmented into numerous categories. Jerry Kang, for instance, divides privacy up into three "clusters": physical or "spatial" privacy; decisional privacy; and informational privacy.[49] Anita Allen offers four basic types: physical, decisional, proprietary and informational.[50] Richards, more recently, rather than defining privacy as falling into categorical "types", instead argues privacy is best understood as falling into four categories of *legal rules* including those involving (a) invasions into protected spaces, relationships, or decisions, (b) collection of information, (c) use of information and (d) disclosure of information.[51] Daniel Solove offers an even more elaborate and complicated taxonomy of privacy-related activities, including information collection, processing, dissemination and invasion, among many others.[52]

These definitional and conceptual complications have led leading privacy scholar Solove to declare privacy to be "in disarray".[53] But these complications with privacy were around long before Solove made this observation, tracking the very technological developments and challenges discussed earlier. In 1971, Arthur Miller lamented that the concept of privacy was "vague".[54] Just over a decade later in 1984, after reviewing the privacy field, Judith Thomas declared that nobody appeared "to have any very clear idea what [privacy] is".[55] In the following decade, Julie Innis would argue that theoretical discussions on privacy were in "chaos",[56] while others lament it as "chameleon-like"[57] with a "vine-like existence".[58] In 2006, Solove argues that privacy appeared to be about "everything" and therefore about "nothing".[59]

These complications, no doubt, have contributed to the contemporary problem of Privacy Fatalism. If privacy itself is too complicated, fragmented and complex to for even experts to define, how useful is it in understanding new challenges posed by technology and data practices? And what good would a legal right to this overly "vague", even "chaotic" concept be in protecting people's interests? In this light, it is easier to see how someone might declare privacy dead, over, or imminently perishing. Solove, himself a leading privacy scholar, has even cited these conceptual concerns in pushing others to

48 Elbert Lin (2002) Prioritizing Privacy: A Constitutional Response to the Internet. *Berkeley Technology Law Journal*, Vol. 17, 1088, at 1093 ("Defining informational privacy is a dizzying endeavor."); Jerry Kang (1998) Information Privacy in Cyberspace Transactions. *Stanford Law Review*, Vol. 50, 1193, at 1202 ("Privacy is a chameleon that shifts meaning depending on context").

49 See Kang 1202–1203.

50 See, *e.g.*, Anita L. Allen-Castellitto (2001) The Origins and Growth of U.S. Privacy Law. *Practicing Law Institute/Patents*, Vol. 632, 9, at 16 (dividing privacy up into physical, territorial, decisional, informational).

51 Richards 7.

52 Daniel J. Solove (2006) A Taxonomy of Privacy. *University of Pennsylvania Law Review*, Vol. 154, 477 at 489.

53 Solove 477.

54 Arthur R. Miller (1971) *The Assault on Privacy: Computers, Data Banks, and Dossiers*. Ann Arbor, MI: University of Michigan Press, 25.

55 Judith Jarvis Thomas (1984) The Right to Privacy. In: Ferdinand David Schloeman (Ed.), *Philosophical Dimensions of Privacy: An Anthology*. CAMBRIDGE: CUP, 272.

56 Julie C. Inness (1992) *Privacy, Intimacy, and Isolation*. New York: Oxford University Press, 3.

57 Lillian R. BeVier (1995) Information About Individuals in the Hands of Government: Some Reflections on Mechanisms for Privacy Protection. William & Mary Bill of Rights Journal, Vol. 4, 455 at 458.

58 Ken Gormley (1992) One Hundred Years of Privacy. *Wisconsin Law Review*, Vol. 154, 1335 at 1340.

59 Solove 479.

abandon the vague term of privacy, and instead focus on a cataloguing privacy-related activities.[60] John and Peters similarly suggest a link between these conceptual fragmentations in privacy and declarations about privacy's limits or end.[61] As does Juan D.Velásquez who recently noted that embracing a privacy concept in disarray is tantamount to conceding that "that privacy itself in a technological environment is totally dead".[62]

Empirical challenges and legal scepticism

Another factor contributing to ongoing declarations as to privacy's death is enduring challenges in substantiating privacy harms and injuries, and the resulting legal scepticism. Like the concept of privacy itself, privacy harms have likewise proven difficult to conceptualise, quantify, measure and document.[63] And due to these challenges, and privacy harm's unique nature, courts and legal scholars have long evinced scepticism about such privacy harms.[64] This scepticism has also compounded the problem with courts often requiring higher standards of evidence to prove such harms compared to other areas of the law.[65]

A quintessential example of this, in both the US and Europe, has been empirically demonstrating the harms associated with forms of state and corporate surveillance, including the idea of "chilling effects", that is, that surveillance would chill or deter a person from speaking, seeking out information, or exercising other basic rights and freedoms.[66] As with privacy harms more generally, chilling effects are notoriously difficult to prove and empirically document,[67] which has contributed to long-term scepticism among lawyers, judges, scholars and researchers as to their existence, scope and actual impact beyond nuisance or triviality.[68] One part of the challenge is the challenge in designing research to empirically substantiate or explore chill – how does one prove a counterfactual state of affairs; that a person would have said something or done something but for awareness of

60 Ibid., 481–483.

61 John and Peters 293–294. See also Richards 6–7.

62 Juan D.Velásquez (2013) Web Mining and Privacy Concerns: Some Important Legal Issues to be Consider before Applying any Data and Information Extraction Technique in Web-based Environments. *Expert Systems with Applications* Vol. 40, No. 13, 5228.

63 M. Ryan Calo (2011) The Boundaries of Privacy Harm. *Indiana Law Journal*,Vol. 86, 1131 at 1132; Daniel J. Solove (2013) Introduction: Privacy Self-Management and the Consent Dilemma. *Harvard Law Review*,Vol. 126, 1879 at 1891 ("many privacy harms are cumulative in nature: people may agree to many forms of data collection, use, and disclosure over a long period of time, and the harmful effects may only emerge from the downstream uses of the combination of the data".); Lexi Rubow (2014) Standing in the Way of Privacy Protections: The Argument for a Relaxed Article III Standing Requirement for Constitutional and Statutory Cause of Action. *Berkeley Technology Law Journal*, Vol. 29, 1007 (noting that difficulties in proving privacy harms often means privacy claims fail on standing grounds).

64 Calo (2011) 1132.

65 Ryan Calo (2014) Privacy Harm Exceptionalism. *Colorado Technology Law Journal*, Vol. 12, No. 2, 361.

66 Jonathon Penney (2016) Chilling Effects: Online Surveillance and Wikipedia Use. Berkeley Technology Law Journal,Vol. 31, 117.

67 Frederik J. Zuiderveen Borgesius, Sanne Kruikemeier, Sophie C. Boerman, and Natali Helberger (2017) Tracking Walls, Take-It-or-Leave-It Choices, the GDPR, and the ePrivacy Regulation. *European Data Protection Law Review*, Vol. 3, 353, at 364; Penney (2016), 123.

68 Leslie Kendrick (2013) Speech, Intent, and the Chilling Effect. *William & Mary Law Review*, Vol. 54, 1633, at 1657; Penney (2016), 120–121; David Alan Sklansky (2014) Too Much Information: How Not to Think about Privacy and the Fourth Amendment. *California Law Review*, Vol. 102, 1069, at 1094–1100.

government surveillance?[69] These challenges have led courts, in both the US and Europe, to be reluctant to recognise legal claims founded on chilling effect harms. US courts often dismiss such claims as "subjective", "self-inflicted", or too "speculative" for legal recognition or judicial enforcement.[70] Similarly, courts in Europe, though willing to recognise chilling effect claims,[71] have often framed them narrowly as "hypothetical", "in abstracto", "a priori", or "minimal" harms or claims.[72] These challenges in conceptualising and proving privacy harms, as well as the enduring legal and judicial scepticism, is another key factor in Privacy Fatalism.

The end of privacy fatalism?

The last section mapped out a number of historical and contemporary challenges to central dimensions of privacy – technological, conceptual/theoretical, and empirical. Each of these challenges, I argued, contributes to the ongoing and persistent contemporary phenomena of Privacy Fatalism.[73] However, there are a number of recent and important trends in privacy, and legal rights to its protection, that I believe may mean that this seemingly ceaseless tradition is not so ceaseless and enduring; it may itself have an end in sight.

The convergence of American and European privacy concerns

The most significant change in recent years has been what I call the convergence of the American and European privacy concerns. The American tradition, as earlier noted, has long been deeply influenced by Warren and Brandeis' conceptualising of the right to privacy.[74] They defined the right to privacy in negative terms – the right to solitude, to be left alone, and to not have information and gossip to be spread, shared and publicised about private individuals.[75] The fact that this "negative" conceptualisation – defining privacy as right to be free from the interferences of others – captured the imagination of both the American public and legal academy is no surprise. Warren and Brandeis' work was influenced by, and reflected, a broader American culture, and legal culture, centred on notions of liberty.[76] The American privacy legal tradition has thus emphasised notions of liberty, and the need for the law to protect places of solitude like the sanctity of the home from invasions, particularly by the state.[77]

69 Penney 122–123.

70 See, for example, *Clapper v. Amnesty Int'l*, 568 U.S. 398 (2013); *Laird v. Tatum*, 408 U.S. 1 (1972); Penney (2016), 165–168; Perri Pierluigi and David Thaw (2017) Ancient Worries and Modern Fears: Different Roots and Common Effects of U.S. and E.U. Privacy Regulation. *Connecticut Law Review*, Vol. 49, 1621, at 1634.

71 An example is the well-known *Digital Rights Ireland* case where the CJEU struck down the data retention directive, and in the process appeared to acknowledge how privacy-related chilling effects may impact other fundamental rights: EU Court of Justice, Digital Rights Ireland, C-293/12 and C-594/12, ECLI:EU:C:2014:238, para. 28, 37. See also Pierluigi and Thaw 1634.

72 van der Sloot 19; van der Sloot 182.

73 See Mims (2018); Tan (2018); Bonnell (2018); Kerry (2018).

74 John and Peters 293–294. See also Richards 6–7.

75 John and Peters 293–294.

76 James Q. Whitman (2004) The Two Western Cultures of Privacy: Dignity versus Liberty. *Yale Law Journal*, Vol. 113, 1151; Robert C. Post (2001) Three Concepts of Privacy *Georgetown Law Journal*, Vol. 89, 2087; Pierluigi Perri and David Thaw (2017) Ancient Worries and Modern Fears: Different Roots and Common Effects of U.S. and E.U. Privacy Regulation *Connecticut Law Review*, Vol. 49, 1621.

77 Perri and Thaw 1645–1646; Whitman 1161–1162.

By contrast, the European privacy tradition has been largely centred on the importance of personal dignity.[78] With this focus, the European tradition has been more concerned about respect, reputation and notions of privacy in public, as well as privacy violations by businesses and other private sector actors.[79] Elaborate and expansive European data protection regulations are an excellent example of the difference between American and European privacy traditions.[80] These data protection laws – which largely empower people with legal rights to control information about themselves in public and in the possession of others – reflect notions of "informational self-determination" famously articulated by Germany's Federal Constitutional Court (BVerfGE) in its 1983 census decision.[81] The US has no central data protection framework and instead endures with a patchwork of federal, state and constitutional law for privacy protection.[82]

These two privacy traditions have, in the past, often been defined as a means to illustrate differences in laws and to explain privacy conflicts and clashes between the two continents.[83] However, there is good reason to believe that recently there has slowly but surely been a convergence on key privacy concerns, and as a result, broader approaches.

First is a growing recognition among US legal scholars and regulators as to the limitations of the American conceptualisation and approach to privacy in narrow, negative terms. The aforementioned conceptual and theoretical complications exemplify this recognition and the need to re-think the nature, scope and focus of privacy rights. In doing so, American scholars have increasingly looked to the European privacy tradition for new privacy approaches. Richards, for instance, admits that if American privacy scholars were to start "from scratch" it would probably make sense to use the European term of "data protection" rather than privacy.[84] Joe Reidenberg, another prominent American privacy scholar, argues that elements of European and US privacy and surveillance law has "reached a turning point for the future of information privacy online", and draws on European rules for the collection and retention of data.[85] And Kenneth Bamberger and Deirdre Mulligan herald a "new American story", wherein US regulators have drawn on European data protection regulators and processes to address new privacy challenges.[86]

Second, there has been increasing acknowledgement, in both the US and Europe, as to shared privacy commitments and concerns. One area this is apparent in is shared concerns about private sector privacy violations. Faced with the common challenge posed to privacy and data protection by the internet and associated digital technologies, experts and regulators on both sides are recognising the need to overhaul the regulation of corporate treatment of information privacy.[87] In Europe, this has taken the form of the formulation

78 Perri and Thaw 1646; Whitman 1161.

79 Perri and Thaw 1625; Whitman 1161.

80 Perri and Thaw 1625; Whitman 1161.

81 Joris van Hoboken (2016) From Collection to Use in Privacy Regulation? A Forward-looking Comparison of European and US Frameworks for Personal Data Processing. In: Bart van der Sloot, Dennis Broeders and Erik Schrijvers (Eds.), *Exploring the Boundaries of Big Data*. Amsterdam: Amsterdam University Press, 231, 243.

82 Perri and Thaw 1644.

83 Ibid., 1623.

84 Richards 12.

85 Joel R. Reidenberg (2014) The Data Surveillance State in the United States and Europe. *Wake Forest Law Review*, Vol. 49, 583 at 583–584.

86 Kenneth A. Bamberger and Deirdre K. Mulligan (2013) Privacy in Europe: Initial Data on Governance Choices and Corporate Practices. *George Washington Law Review*, Vol. 81, 1521; Richards 12.

87 Bamberger and Mulligan 1532–1533.

and enactment of the new General Data Protection Regulation,[88] an ambitious, complex and contentious new data protection law designed to "fit" the challenges of the "digital age".[89] In the US context, as Bamberger and Mulligan document, this has taken the form of, among other things, how important US regulators like the Federal Trade Commission have recently taken on new bold new roles more akin to European data protection regulators; something previously foreign to the American privacy tradition.[90] Another area where is there is convergence is on shared concerns about the harms and impact of online surveillance.[91] Perri and Thaw, for instance, recently argue that a shared concern about "chilling effects" due to surveillance, particularly online, can form the basis of a common approach to addressing the issue.[92]

A final area of convergence is notions of data expiry and forgetting to preserve privacy and reputation over the long term. In Europe, this has taken the form of the contentious "right to be forgotten" (RTBF), first recognised by the European Union Court of Justice in the *Google Spain* case and later codified in the GDPR.[93] The right provides for erasure or deletion of previously collected personal data as a means to ensure people's reputations are not adversely impacted by such data indefinitely.[94] However, a key part of the contentious debate is that critics argue that the RTBF itself will adversely impact freedom of expression and access to information. Reflecting the traditional transatlantic divide, many of these criticisms have come from US scholars.[95] Nevertheless, due to widespread public support – 88% of Americans support such a right – US policymakers and regulators appear increasingly open to the idea, with the New York State Assembly tabling legislation to enact a RTBF at the state level.[96]

Fully detailing this convergence would take us beyond the scope of this chapter, but it can be seen in other areas as well. For example, in 2015 a group of American and European privacy experts drafted a report entitled "Privacy Bridges – EU and US Privacy Experts in Search of Transatlantic Privacy Solution", detailing ten substantial areas or "bridges" for

88 Regulation (EU) 2016/679 of the European Parliament and of the Council of 27 April 2016 on the Protection of Natural Persons with Regard to the Processing of Personal Data and on the Free Movement of Such Data, and Repealing Directive 95/46/EC [2016] OJ L 119/1.

89 Andrew D Selbst and Julia Powles (2017) Meaningful Information and the Right to Explanation. *International Data Privacy Law*, Vol. 7, No. 4, 233; Paul de Hert and Vagelis Papakonstantinou (2016) The New General Data Protection Regulation: Still a Sound System for the Protection of Individuals? *Computer Law & Security Review*, Vol. 32, No. 2, 179; Lilian Mitrou (2017) The General Data Protection Regulation: A Law for the Digital Age? In T.E. Synodinou, P. Jougleux, C. Markou, and T. Prastitou (Eds.), *EU Internet Law*. New York: Springer; Dennis Broeders, Erik Schrijvers, Bart van der Sloot, Rosamundevan Brakel, Jostade Hoog, and Ernst Hirsch Ballin (2017) Big Data and Security Policies: Towards a Framework for Regulating the Phases of Analytics and Use of Big Data. *Computer Law & Security Review*, Vol. 33, No. 3, 309; Eugenia Politou, Efthimios Alepis, and Constantinos Patsakis (2018) Forgetting Personal Data and Revoking Consent under the GDPR: Challenges and Proposed Solutions. *Journal of Cybersecurity*, Vol. 20, No. 1, 1, at 1; Paul de Hert and Michal Czerniawski (2016) Expanding the European Data Protection Scope Beyond Territory: Article 3 of the General Data Protection Regulation in Its Wider Context. *International Data Privacy Law*, Vol. 6, No. 3, 230.

90 Kenneth A. Bamberger and Deirdre K. Mulligan (2013) Privacy in Europe: Initial Data on Governance Choices and Corporate Practices. *George Washington Law Review*, Vol. 81, 1521; Richards 12.

91 Perri and Thaw 1625; Whitman 1161.

92 Perri and Thaw 1623.

93 Politou et al. 9.

94 Ibid., 9.

95 See for example Jeff Rosen (2011) The Right to be Forgotten. *Standford Law Review Online* 64; Politou et al. 11–12.

96 Rebecca Heilweil (2018) How Close Is An American Right-To-Be-Forgotten? *Forbes* (4 Mar), www.forbes.com/sites/rebeccaheilweil1/2018/03/04/how-close-is-an-american-right-to-be-forgotten/#a649f14626ef (accessed 23.10.2018).

stronger cooperation on privacy and data protection. The convergence is also apparent in American companies willingly complying with the requirements of the GDPR, with Mark Zuckerberg, for example, claiming Facebook always "shared the values" embodied in the GDPR and that the platform would implement its requirements "globally".[97] With a shift to more shared transatlantic and international approaches, and US abandonment of a narrow negative conceptualisation, these developments may mean privacy has new life (and thus, far less declarations of its death).

New empirical evidence of privacy harms

A second important development may also address empirical challenges and enduring legal and judicial scepticism. As noted earlier, privacy harms are notoriously difficult to prove and empirically document – this is especially the case with chilling effects.[98] This has contributed to long-term scepticism among lawyers, judges, scholars and researchers as to their existence, scope and actual impact beyond nuisance or triviality.[99] This scepticism is compounded by the fact that far less work has been done to document chilling effects associated with private sector data practices.[100]

However, new empirical research, drawing on innovative methods and new data sets, is emerging to help address these empirical challenges. A number of very recent empirical studies on privacy and regulatory chilling effects, for instance, offer new insights and a sound empirical foundation for privacy claims based on harms like chilling effects and similar impacts.[101] These works include, for example, experimental studies demonstrating how social network users, when made aware of online surveillance, were chilled from freely expressing political opinions.[102] Another empirical study documents how both government and private sector surveillance can have a chilling effect on range of online

97 Perri and Thaw 1623.

98 Frederik J. Zuiderveen Borgesius, Sanne Kruikemeier, Sophie C. Boerman, and Natali Helberger (2017) Tracking Walls, Take-It-or-Leave-It Choices, the GDPR, and the ePrivacy Regulation. *European Data Protection Law Review,* Vol. 3, 353, 364; Penney (2016), 123.

99 Leslie Kendrick (2013) Speech, Intent, and the Chilling Effect. *William & Mary Law Review,* Vol. 54, 1633, at 1657; Penney (2016), 120–121; David Alan Sklansky (2014) Too Much Information: How Not to Think about Privacy and the Fourth Amendmen. *California Law Review,* Vol. 102, 1069, at 1094–1100.

100 Borgesius et al. 12.

101 For instance, the massive collection of information about people's online activities may cause chilling effects: people adapt their behaviour if they know their activities may be tracked: Jonathon Penney (2017) Internet Surveillance, Regulation, and Chilling Effects Online: A Comparative Case Study. *Internet Policy Review,* Vol. 6, No. 2, https://papers.ssrn.com/sol3/papers.cfm?abstract_id=2959611 (accessed 23.10.2018). For other recent research on chilling effects, see Alex Marthews and Catherine Tucker (2017) Government Surveillance and Internet Search Behavior. In David Gray et al. (Eds.), *Cambridge University Handbook on Surveillance Law.* CUP, forthcoming 2017; Jonathon Penney (2016) Chilling Effects: Online Surveillance and Wikipedia Use. Berkeley Technology *Law Journal,* Vol. 31, 117; Elizabeth Stoycheff (2016) Under Surveillance: Examining Facebook's Spiral of Silence Effects in the Wake of NSA Internet Monitoring. *Journalism and Mass Communication,* Vol. 93, No. 2, 296; Karin Wahl-Jorgensen, Lucy K. Bennett, and Jonathan Cable (2017) Surveillance Normalization and Critique: News Coverage and Journalists' Discourses around the Snowden Revelations. *Digital Journalism,* Vol. 5, No. 3, 386; Lina Dencik and Jonathan Cable (2017) The Advent of Surveillance Realism: Public Opinion and Activist Responses to the Snowden Leaks. *International Journal of Communication,* Vol. 11, 763; Paul Lashmar (2017) No More Sources? The Impact of Snowden's Revelations on Journalists and their Confidential Sources. *Journalism Practice,* Vol. 11, No. 6, 665; Kelly D. Martin, Abhishek Borah, and Robert W. Palmatier (2017) Data Privacy: Effects on Customer and Firm Performance. *Journal of Marketing,* Vol. 81, No. 1, 36; S. Barocas and A. Selbst (forthcoming) Big Data's Disparate Impact. *California Law Review* Vol. 104, 671. 1–60.

102 Stoycheff 296.

activities – including speech, search, sharing – while also raising privacy concerns more generally.[103] These new empirical insights should lead not to more declarations of privacy's death but means to advance more expansive protections for privacy online.

New judicial openness to privacy and surveillance harms

Despite historical scepticism, courts in both Europe and the US appear increasingly open to legal claims based on privacy and surveillance-related harms. Beyond the common challenges to privacy and data online, these developments have no doubt also been influenced by greater public awareness thanks to high-profile international privacy incidents like the Snowden disclosures about online and telecommunications surveillance and the Cambridge Analytica/Facebook scandal.

European Courts, despite historical reluctance to recognise privacy harms and chilling effects in certain contexts, have demonstrated a greater willingness to embrace such claims in a number of recent high-profile cases. These include the transformative European Union Court of Justice decision in *Google Spain* recognising a limited right to be forgotten in 2014;[104] the European Court of Justice's decision striking down the Safe Harbour Principles in 2015;[105] and the very recent decision of the European Court of Human Rights finding that the mass online surveillance practices of the United Kingdom's Government Communications Headquarters (GCHQ), the UK's signal intelligence agency, violated privacy and did not include sufficient safeguards for surveillance harms.[106] US courts have not showed the same embrace, but there are indications that American courts, too, may be more open to these privacy and surveillance claims, with the Fourth Circuit Court of Appeal recently allowing a lawsuit brought by the American Civil Liberties Association against the US government for privacy harms to due surveillance to proceed, overturning a lower court ruling dismissing it full.[107]

Conclusion

Privacy Fatalism has been one of privacy's great traditions in modern times,[108] with "innumerable books" in the last decades declaring privacy is "dead" or "dying".[109] Understanding the reasons for Privacy Fatalism – including ever-emerging new technologies; conceptual and theoretical problems; and lack of empirical substantiation – provide a broader context

103 Penney (2017).

104 Politou et al. 9.

105 Judgment in Case C-362/14 *Maximillian Schrems v. Data Protection Commissioner.* The Court of Justice declares that the Commission's US Safe Harbour Decision is "invalid" (press release). Court of Justice of the European Union. 6 October 2015, 3.

106 Owen Bowcott (2018) GCHQ Data Collection Regime Violated Human Rights, Court Rules. *The Guardian* (13 September), www.theguardian.com/uk-news/2018/sep/13/gchq-data-collection-violated-human-rights-strasbourg-court-rules (accessed 23.10.2018).

107 Jordan Brunner, Quinta Jurecic, Yishai Schwartz (2017) The Fourth Circuit Remands Wikimedia's Suit Against the NSA Back to District Court. *Lawfare Blog* (26 May), www.lawfareblog.com/fourth-circuit-remands-wikimedias-suit-against-nsa-back-district-court (accessed 23.10.2018); Lily Hay Newman (2018) The ACLU's Biggest Roadblock to Fighting Mass Surveillance. *Wired Magazine* (29 June), www.wired.com/story/wikimedia-nsa-surveillance-privacy-lawsuit/ (accessed 23.10.2018).

108 See Mims (2018); Tan (2018); Bonnell (2018); Kerry (2018).

109 Richards 2.

to persistent challenges in legal and policy efforts to protect privacy, particularly rights to privacy in digital contexts. This chapter has also argued that Privacy Fatalism's days may be numbered due to emerging new empirical evidence for privacy harms; less judicial scepticism, and a convergence of American and European privacy concerns. Privacy Fatalism about privacy undercuts good faith efforts to protect privacy, and whether this great privacy tradition itself is dying for the reasons I have set out here, wider appreciation of the historical contingency of the factors underlying it, is a step in the right direction.

4 Freedom of expression online

Matthias C. Kettemann and Wolfgang Benedek

Introduction

The protection of internet freedom and freedom of expression, as a key element of it, is challenging: "Declines outnumber gains for the eighth consecutive year. Out of the 65 countries assessed in Freedom on the Net, 26 experienced deterioration in Internet freedom". The key findings of the annual *Freedom of the Net* report by the NGO Freedom House for 2018 give little room to celebrate: "Citing fake news, governments curbed online dissent: At least 17 countries approved or proposed laws that would restrict online media in the name of fighting "fake news" and online manipulation".[1] Even democracies are at risk, as they introduce "overreaching restrictions on freedom of expression" and outsource "key censorship decisions to ill-equipped and often opaque tech companies".[2]

Protection of freedom of expression online is essential: offline just as online. In one of its fundamental cases on the role of Article 10 in online environments, the 2015 *Cengiz and Others* case, the Strasbourg judges confirmed that

> the Internet has now become one of the principal means by which individuals exercise their right to freedom to receive and impart information and ideas, providing as it does essential tools for participation in activities and discussions concerning political issues and issues of general interest.[3]

Just as freedom of expression in all its forms is widely considered the right essential to meaningful internet use,[4] the evolution of the internet has become determinative for our communicative relations. The Court again in *Cengiz*: "user-generated expressive activity on the internet provides an unprecedented platform for the exercise of freedom of expression."[5]

The internet today has become, as UN Special Rapporteur on Freedom of Expression, Frank La Rue, put in his 2011 report, a "vital communications medium which

1 Freedom House (2018) Freedom of the Net 2018: The Rise of Digital Authoritarianism, October 2018, https://freedomhouse.org/report/freedom-net/freedom-net-2018

2 Ibid., 11.

3 ECtHR, *Cengiz and Others v. Turkey*, judgment of 1 December 2015, § 49.

4 Cf. Human Rights Council Resolution 20/8, The promotion, protection and enjoyment of human rights on the Internet, 5 July 2012, para. 1: "[The Human Rights Council] [a]ffirms that the same rights that people have offline must also be protected online, *in particular freedom of expression*, which is applicable regardless of frontiers and through any media of one's choice, in accordance with Articles 19 of the Universal Declaration of Human Rights and the International Covenant on Civil and Political Rights" (emphasis added). Biannual resolution with the same content followed.

5 ECtHR, *Cengiz and Others v. Turkey*, judgment of 1 December 2015, § 52.

individuals can use to exercise their right to freedom of expression, or the right to seek, receive and impart information and ideas of all kinds, regardless of frontiers".[6] Unlike any other medium in history, "the Internet allows individuals to communicate instantaneously and inexpensively, and it has had a dramatic impact on the way information and ideas are shared and accessed".[7]

In this contribution we will first define the scope of freedom of expression online and discuss its evolution, legal basis and the case law of the European Court of Human Rights. The section allows us to clarify the extent to which freedom of expression and connected rights are protected on the internet and what limits exist. We will then discuss how standard-setting activites by institutions such as the Council of Europe are normatively important for the development of the obligations of states and other actors regarding freedom of expression. In the next section we will expose selected normative challenges of protecting freedom of expression. These are both institutional (such as the obligations structure of human rights commitments) and related to policing online content (intermediary liability exemptions). Finally, we develop some conclusions.[8]

Scope of freedom of expression (online)

Development

New opportunities for freedom of expression have been a major promise of the internet since its conception. The World Summit on the Information Society (WSIS) in its Geneva Declaration of Principles of 2003[9] and the Tunis Agenda of 2005 reaffirm the commitment to freedom of expression, which according to Article 19 of the Universal Declaration on Human Rights (UDHR) of 1948 includes the freedom "to seek, receive and impart information and ideas through any media and regardless of frontiers". The internet has opened new dimensions of freedom of expression and information, for example for bloggers, electronic media platforms, web pages, exchanges of views on social media and also citizen journalists. However, while the WSIS was mainly concerned with providing more people with access to the internet, today we are struggling with an increasing trend towards restricting freedom of expression and information on the internet.

More and more states, but also private companies use filtering and blocking technologies, bloggers and citizen journalists are persecuted and the internet is utilised to collect information on its users like through tools of facial recognition and tracking in China. Search engines show clients what they consider relevant for the user, leaving them in so-called "filter bubbles". The respective algorithms remain a business secret. Artificial intelligence selects what users can see. But misuse of the internet comes also from its users in the form of hate speech and fake news, of images of child abuse and terrorist propaganda.

6 Special Rapporteur on the promotion and protection of the right to freedom of opinion and expression, Frank La Rue, Promotion and protection of the right to freedom of opinion and expression, UN Doc. A/66/290 of 10 August 2011, www.ohchr.org/Documents/Issues/Opinion/A.66.290.pdf, para. 10.

7 Ibid.

8 This contribution draws from previous work of the authors, including Kettemann (2019) *The Normative Order of the Internet* (to be published) and Benedek and Kettemann (2013) *Freedom of Expression on the Internet*. Strasbourg: Council of Europe Publishing.

9 See World Summit on the Information Society, Geneva Declaration of Principles, Building the Information Society: A Global Challenge in the New Millenium, Document, UN-Doc. WSIS-03/GENEVA/DOC/4-E of 12 December 2003, para. 4 and Tunis Agenda for the Information Society, WSIS-05/TUNIS/DOC/6(REV.1)-E, para. 42.

The internet can be used to realise human rights and to endanger them. This raises the responsibility of the gatekeepers, of intermediaries, but also of everyone using the internet.

Legal basis

Freedom of expression is one of the key civil and political rights. In the 18th and 19th centuries freedom of expression was fought for by philosophers and economists such as Voltaire (1694–1778) and John Stuart Mill (1806–1873) as key to a liberal society and to development as a concept freeing societies from corruption. (The idea of "sunlight" being "the best disinfectant" thus has long roots.) The First Amendment to the US Constitution of 1791 adopted a wide approach to freedom of expression (and the Supreme Court has been extending the reach of the First Amendment ever since) and President Roosevelt included it in 1941 in his four freedoms to guide the post-war order.

Today a key international legal basis for freedom of expression is Article 19 of the Universal Declaration of Human Rights:

> Everyone has the right to freedom of opinion and expression; this right includes the freedom to hold opinions without interference and to seek, receive and impart information and ideas through any means and regardless of frontiers.

Even though the UDHR is based on a non-binding resolution of the General Assembly, it is by now largely considered to reflect customary law. In addition, in 1976 the International Covenant on Civil and Political Rights (ICCPR) was adopted, which in its Article 19 reiterates the text of the Universal Declaration and then clarifies (in para. 2) that

> shall have the right to freedom of expression; this right shall include freedom to seek, receive and impart information and ideas of all kinds, regardless of frontiers, either orally, in writing or in print, in the form of art, or through any other media of his choice.

Accordingly, the right goes beyond the freedom of the press and the freedom of the media to include individual expression in the widest sense. However, the right is not absolute or without limits. Under certain clearly defined conditions it can be restricted. No restrictions, however, can be applied to freedom of opinion, which in the ICCPR has been separated from the freedom of expression in Article 19 (1). Freedom of opinion is an absolute right, which shall never be restricted.

In the latest 2018 resolution on human rights on the internet (passed biannually since 2012), the Human Rights Council affirmed, with references to Articles 19 of the UDHR and the ICCPR, the special role of freedom of expression online: "the same rights that people have offline must also be protected online, in particular freedom of expression, which is applicable regardless of frontiers and through any media of one's choice".[10]

The protection of freedom of expression under regional human rights law is similar. Article 10 (1) of the ECHR enshrines "the right to freedom of expression. This right

10 UN Human Rights Council Resolution 38/7, The promotion, protection and enjoyment of human rights on the Internet, UN Doc. A/HRC/RES/38/7 of 5 July 2018.

shall include the freedom to hold opinions and to receive and impart information and ideas without interference by public authority and regardless of frontiers". Note the reference to the non-interference "by public authority": states are obliged to protect freedom of expression both as a free-standing right and as an essential "enabler" of other rights through the internet. As former UN Special Rapporteur for Freedom of Expression, Frank La Rue, wrote, "by acting as a catalyst for individuals to exercise their right to freedom of opinion and expression, the internet also facilitates the realisation of a range of other human rights".[11]

Article 19 (2) of the ICCPR guarantees interconnection technologies with its reference to the protection of expression by "any . . . media of [one's] choice". If the internet does not function, most "media" will cease to work as well. [12] This point is well made also by the Human Rights Committee, which, in the most recent General Comment on Art. 19 ICCPR, recalls the technological premises of the internet's communication function: "[a]ny restrictions on the operation of websites, blogs or any other Internet-based, electronic or other such information dissemination system, including systems to support such communication, such as Internet service providers or search engines, are only permissible to the extent that they are compatible with paragraph 3".[13] Interfering with ISPs thus amounts to interfering with the right to privacy.

The jurisprudence of the European Court of Human Rights helps understand how freedom of expression, as enshrined in the ECHR, can be considered to indirectly protect the integrity of the internet. According to established case law, freedom of expression can be considered "one of the essential foundations for a democratic society and one of the basic conditions for its progress and for each individual's self-fulfillment".[14] The Strasbourg Court interprets the Convention "in the light of present-day conditions",[15] taking into account the specific nature of the internet, as a "modern means of imparting information",[16] in particular because of the greater impact, accessibility, durability and asynchronicity of information on the internet. [17]

There are several neighbouring rights which are closely related to the freedom of expression, like freedom of assembly and of association, freedom of thought, conscience and religion and the right to education as well as academic freedoms. The Committee of Ministers of the Council of Europe has adopted a recommendation on freedom of assembly and association on the internet, based on a pertinent report by experts, highlighting the role of the internet in this respect, but also challenges ranging from urban violence to the

11 Report of the Special Rapporteur on the promotion and protection of the right to freedom of opinion and expression, UN Doc. A/HRC/17/27 of 16 May 2011, paras. 22 and 23. But the internet also brings about new challenges to these same human rights.

12 Molly K. Land (2013) Toward an International Law of the Internet. *Harvard International Law Journal*, Vol. 54, 393–458.

13 Cf. Human Rights Committee, General Comment No. 34, Art. 19 ICCPR, UN Doc. CCPR/C/GC/34 of 12 September 2011, para. 43.

14 E.g. ECtHR, *Stoll v. Switzerland, judgment of* 10 December 2007, Application No. 69698/01, para. 104 with further references.

15 Ibid., para. 101.

16 ECtHR, *Mouvement Raëlien Suisse v. Switzerland*, judgment of 13 January 2011, Application No. 16354/06, para. 54 as endorsed by the Great Chamber judgment in para. 40.

17 Nina Vajic and Panayotis Voyatzis (2012) The Internet and Freedom of Expression: A "brave new world" and the European Court of Human Rights' Evolving Case Law. In Josep Casadevall et al. (Eds.), *Freedom of Expression. Essays in Honour of Nicolas Bratza*. Osterwijk: Wolf, 391–420 (395 and 399).

prosecution of online activities and concluding that restrictions of access to the internet targeting the right to assembly on the internet also affect the freedom of expression and usually lack proportionality.

Freedom of expression and democracy are closely related. According to the European Court of Human Rights, "freedom of expression constitutes one of the essential foundations of a democratic society".[18] Independent and critical reporting by journalists is not sufficiently protected on the national level, which affects the quality of democracy.[19] Accordingly there is a need for a stronger monitoring system.[20]

Case law of the European Court of Human Rights

The ECtHR committed itself to interpreting the ECHR in the light of present-day conditions, taking into account the specific nature of the internet as a "modern means of imparting information".[21] However, because of the wider reach of the internet special care is required as the internet has "the ability to magnify the impact of problematic speech".[22] Accordingly, the ECtHR held that the impact of information is multiplied when it is displayed in public with a reference to the address of a website accessible to everyone through the internet.[23] The Court also highlighted the distinctness of the internet from printed media because of its capacity to store and transmit information, which increases the risk of harm to the enjoyment of other human rights, in particular the right to private life.[24]

The online freedom like its offline version consists basically of two main components, the freedom to express and impart and the freedom to receive information and ideas. The freedom of information includes the right to receive content produced by any media or the right of access to such content. The Court thus emphasised "the right of the public to be properly informed on matters of public interest".[25]

Freedom of expression and information online presupposes the availability of access to the internet, which therefore can be considered as a right on its own.[26] The ECtHR has recognised that "the Internet plays an important role in enhancing the public's access to news and facilitating the dissemination of information in general".[27] Already in *Yildirim*, the Court found that the complete blocking of access to Google sites constituted an unjustified (disproportionate) restriction of internet access.[28] In *Cengiz*, the Strasbourg

18 ECtHR, *Lingens v. Austria*, judgment of 8 July 1986, Application No. 9815/82.

19 Dirk Vorhoof, The Right to Freedom of Expression and Information under the European Human Rights System: Towards a more Transparent Democratic Society, EUI Working papers RSCAS 2014/12, http://cadmus.eui.eu/handle/1814/29871

20 Just see Jan Malinowski (2014) Monitoring Freedom of Expression in Council of Europe Member States: Only Desirable or also Unavoidable? In Benedek et al. (Eds.), *European Yearbook on Human Rights 2014*. Vienna: NWV, 311–332.

21 European Court of Human Rights, Research Division (2015) Internet: Case-law of the European Court of Human Rights, June 2015.

22 Vajic and Voyatzis 395, 399.

23 ECtHR, *Mouvement Raëlien Suisse v. Switzerland*, judgment of 13 January 2011, Application No. 16354/06, para. 54.

24 ECtHR, *Editorial Board of Pravoye Delo and Shteckel v. Ukraine* (5 May 2011), Application No. 33014/05, para. 63.

25 ECtHR, *Sunday Times v. United Kingdom* (26 April 1979), Application No. 6538/74.

26 Benedek and Kettemann 41, 75.

27 ECtHR, *Cengiz and Others v. Turkey*, judgment of 1 December 2015, § 49.

28 ECtHR, *Yıldırım v. Turkey*, judgment of 18 December 2012, Application No. 3111/10.

judges confirmed that a wholesale blocking of access to YouTube had been a violation of Article 10.

Access to the internet is a functional precondition for exercising freedom of expression (on the internet). The Parliamentary Assembly of the Council of Europe called for a right to internet access, according to which "everyone shall have the right to Internet access as an essential requirement for exercising rights under the European Convention on Human Rights".[29] On the global level the rapporteurs on freedom of expression of the human rights protection mechanism stated in their annual joint declaration already in 2011 that freedom of expression "imposes an obligation on states to promote universal access to the Internet".[30]

There is actually a dual right to internet access, which is crucial for human rights protection: access to internet content (threatened, inter alia, by filtering) and access to the internet per se (threatened, inter alia, by underdeployment of ICTs). Physical access to the internet and access to content on the internet are both necessary to ensure freedom of expression online.[31] Having the infrastructure (cables, computers, routers) necessary to access the internet in place is not enough. The right to internet access includes access to content "without any restrictions except in a few limited cases permitted under international human rights law".[32]

A limited right to access to the internet has also been confirmed by the ECtHR in two prisoner cases: in *Kalda v. Estonia*, the Court found a violation of Article 10 because the authorities had denied a prisoner access to three internet websites containing *legal* information relevant to prepare his defence. The judges found there was no general duty to grant prisoners access to the internet, but if states provide access, they can not arbitrarily withhold access to specific sites containing legal information.[33] In *Jankovskis v. Lithuania* a prisoner complained that he had not been given access to the website of the Ministry of Education and Science after the Ministry had answered his written request for educational information with a reference to its website. The Court found a violation of Article 10 as the interference by the Lithuanian authorities was not necessary in a democratic society. It once more observed that the internet played an important role in people's everyday lives, also because certain information was exclusively available on the internet.[34]

The exercise of freedom of expression using the internet needs clear rules, which take the specificities of the internet into account. Regarding online journalism, the ECtHR requested a "sufficient domestic legal framework on how to use information obtained from the Internet", the absence of which hinders the ability of the press to exercise its vital function as a public watchdog.[35] From this follows a positive obligation to create an appropriate domestic regulatory framework to ensure freedom of expression on the internet, in particular of journalists. However, with regard to publication on the internet, the "duties and responsibilities" referred to in Article 19 (2) need to be

29 Council of Europe, Parliamentary Assembly, The Right to Internet Access, Resolution 1987 (2014).

30 International Mechanisms for Promoting Freedom of Expression, Joint Declaration on Freedom of Expression and the Internet (2011), www.osce.org/fom/78309?download=true, para. 6 (a).

31 Cf. Report of the Special Rapporteur on the promotion and protection of the right to freedom of opinion and expression, Frank La Rue, UN Doc. A/HRC/17/27 of 16 May 2011, para. 3 (and chapters IV (access to content) and V (availability of infrastructure) of the report).

32 Ibid., para. 3.

33 ECtHR, *Kalda v. Estonia,* judgment of 19 January 2016, Application No. 17429/10.

34 ECtHR, *Jankovskis v. Lithuania*, judgment of 17 January 2017, Application No. 21575/08, 2017.

35 ECtHR, *Editorial Board of Pravoye Delo and Shteckel v. Ukraine* (5 May 2011), Application No. 33014/05, para. 64.

reinforced. In the context of responsible journalism, the ECtHR emphasises that "in a world in which the individual is confronted with vast quantities of information circulated via traditional and electronic media . . . monitoring compliance with journalistic ethics takes an added importance."[36] In another case it stated that the specific responsibility of journalists also applies to the publication of information on the internet, like public internet forums.[37]

This principle is also relevant with regard to the increasing problem of fake news.[38] The publication of false information on the internet is not protected by the ECHR.[39] In such cases the Court may resort to Article 17. In the case of xenophobic remarks of a politician on his website the Court found that there was a pressing social need to protect the rights of the immigrant community. Incitement to racial discrimination and hatred could not be excused by the passions evoked by an electoral process.[40]

The freedom of expression has also to be balanced with other human rights as in particular the right to respect for private and family life. Particular protection is provided to minors.[41] Private persons enjoy higher protection than politicians. If the information does not come within the scope of any public or political debate on a matter of general importance,[42] even information already available on the internet may be restricted from reproduction as the protection of private life prevails over the sole purpose of satisfying the curiosity of a particular readership.[43]

Limitations of freedom of expression online

Principles

Freedom (of expression) on the internet also has its negative aspects: hate speech, glorification of terrorism, promotion of genocide and sexual exploitation of children are present online. These four categories of "speech" are prohibited by international law and all states are obliged to criminalise them. The majority of online expression, however, is less clear-cut. As the Council of Europe Recommendation on internet intermediaries puts it,

> the rise of the Internet and related technological developments have created substantial challenges for the maintenance of public order and national security, for crime prevention and law enforcement, and for the protection of the rights of others". Especially within social networks "targeted disinformation campaigns, designed specifically to sow mistrust and confusion and to sharpen existing divisions in society, may also have destabilising effects on democratic processes.

36 ECtHR, *Stoll v. Switzerland, judgment of 10* December 2007, Application No. 69698/01, para. 104.

37 ECtHR, *Fatullayev v. Azerbaijan* (22 April 2010), Application No. 40984/07, para. 94.

38 European Parliament, Final Report of the High Level Expert Group on Fake News and Online Disinformation, 12 March 2018, https://ec.europa.eu/digital-single-market/en/news/final-report-high-level-expert-group-fake-news-and-online-disinformation

39 ECtHR, *Schuman v. Poland*, 3 June 2014, Application No. 52517/13.

40 ECtHR, *Féret v. Belgium* (16 July 2009), Application No. 15615/07.

41 ECtHR, *K.U. v. Finland*, judgment of 2 December 2008, Application No. 2872/02.

42 ECtHR, *Editions Plon v. France* (18 May 2004), Application No. 58148/00.

43 ECtHR, *Ovchinnikov v. Russia* (16 December 2010), Application No. 24061/04, para. 50.

Freedom of expression, different from freedom of opinion, is not an absolute right. Pursuant to Article 10 (2) ECHR

> the exercise of these freedoms, since it carries with it duties and responsibilities, may be subject to such formalities, conditions, restrictions or penalties as are prescribed by law and are necessary in a democratic society, in the interests of national security, territorial integrity or public safety, for the prevention of disorder or crime, for the protection of health or morals, for the protection of the reputation or rights of others, for preventing the disclosure of information received in confidence, or for maintaining the authority and impartiality of the judiciary.

Freedom of expression can thus be restricted. In international human rights law, the conditions can be found in Article 19 (3) ICCPR. Any restriction of online content needs to follow a three-part cumulative test, i.e. the restriction must be provided by law, it must be based on the purposes foreseen by Article 19 (3) ICCPR (or Article 10 (2) ECHR) and must be necessary and proportionate with regard to the aim pursued.

The most elaborate doctrine of legitimate restrictions or interferences has been developed in the decade-long pre-internet jurisprudence of the ECtHR. As the Strasbourg court has confirmed passim in *Yildirim* and *Cengiz*, *t*he principles for restrictions offline also apply online. In determining what is "necessary in a democratic society", the Court uses a test looking at the concept of "pressing social needs". The objective of the Strasbourg court is a pluralist society governed by democratic means, to which pluralist media have an important contribution to make. The limitations are to be considered as exceptions for which the least restrictive form of interference is to be chosen, which requires the application of the principle of proportionality. Depending on the existence of a more or less consistent European practice, but also other factors, the Court applies the doctrine of *margin of appreciation* according to which the interfering country has more or less leeway to restrict the right.

Practice

In the first of a series of cases against Turkey's blocking of internet platforms, *Yıldırım v. Turkey* (2012), the Court confirmed that publishing information online constitutes a means of exercising freedom of expression,[44] and that the public had a right, under Article 10, to receive it.[45] In particular, the court held that state measures stopping access to specific sites engaged the responsibility of the state under Article 10.[46]

In the 2015 *Cengiz and Others v. Turkey* judgment, the Court went further and clearly committed to the importance of the internet as a forum for freedom of expression (which, again, presupposes its integrity). The Court's reasoning for rejecting a Turkish ban ofYouTube on the application of three academics underlined the importance of the internet: "[T]he Internet has now become one of the principal means by which individuals exercise their right to freedom to receive and impart information and ideas, providing as it does essential tools for participation in activities and discussions concerning

44 ECtHR, *Yıldırım v. Turkey*, judgment of 18 December 2012, Application No. 3111/10, para. 49.

45 Ibid., para. 50.

46 Ibid., para. 53, with reference to *Vereinigung demokratischer Soldaten Österreichs et Gubi v. Austria*, judgment of 19 December 1994, para. 27.

political issues and issues of general interest". The internet as a whole has thus become an important means to exercise freedom of expression. Specific sites, especially "[u]ser-generated expressive activity on the Internet[,] provides an unprecedented platform for the exercise of freedom of expression". This also applies to consuming news and disseminating information: "in the light of [the Internet's] accessibility and its capacity to store and communicate vast amounts of information, [it] plays an important role in enhancing the public's access to news and facilitating the dissemination of information in general".[47]

In *Stoll* the Court held that where the freedom of the press was at stake, the authorities have only a limited margin of appreciation to claim a pressing social need.[48] The main ground or value for limitations in practice is the protection of the reputation or rights of others. Among them the respect for private life and the protection of minors have given ground for several internet cases.[49] For the protection of minors also the protection of health and morals and the prevention of crime can play a role.[50]

According to Article 19 UDHR, freedom of expression can be exercised by any means, which includes artistic, cultural or satirical expression. This is also true for Article 10 ECHR.[51] However, there might be a need to balance this expression with the right to reputation as part of the right to private life and with the right to freedom of religion.

Standard-setting

Most major international institutions and organisations that deal with human rights have developed normative instruments regarding freedom of expression online. The European Commission, for instance, has adopted the EU Human Rights Guidelines on Freedom of Expression Online and Offline.[52] Within Europe, the Council of Europe is most active in terms of standard-setting.[53]

The 2018 Council of Europe Recommendation on the roles and responsibilities of internet intermediaries underlined the importance of freedom of expression on the internet and of the internet for freedom of expression: by "enhancing the public's ability to seek, receive and impart information without interference and regardless of frontiers, the Internet plays a particularly important role with respect to the right to freedom of expression".[54]

47 ECtHR, *Cengiz and Others v. Turkey*, judgment of 1 December 2015, applications nos. 48226/10 and 14027/11, paras. 49 and 52.

48 ECtHR, *Stoll v. Switzerland, judgment of 10* December 2007, Application No. 69698/01, para. 105.

49 ECtHR, *K.U. v. Finland*, judgment of 2 December 2008, Application No. 2872/02.

50 ECtHR, *Mouvement Raëlien Suisse v. Switzerland*, judgment of 13 January 2011, Application No. 16354/06, para.72.

51 Benedek and Kettemann 33.

52 Council of the European Union (2014) EU Human Rights Guidelines on Freedom of Expression Online and Offline, Brussels 12 May 2014.

53 Benedek and Kettemann (2013). See also Council of Europe, Internet Governance Standard Setting, www.coe.int/en/web/freedom-expression/internet-standard-setting

54 Recommendation CM/Rec(2018)2 of the Committee of Ministers to member States on the roles and responsibilities of Internet intermediaries, adopted by the Committee of Ministers on 7 March 2018 at the 1309th meeting of the Ministers' Deputies, 2.

Further recommendations of the Council of Europe were dedicated to internet freedom,[55] network neutrality,[56] transboundary flow of information on the internet,[57] human rights for internet users,[58] and human rights issues with regard to search engines[59] and providers of social networking services.[60]

Freedom of expression also includes expression under anonymity, which is controversial with some governments which want to have a stricter control of expression on the internet. While anonymous defamation or stalking clearly is unlawful, writing under pseudonyms has a long history offline and also is used online for different reasons, not at least in order to express criticism under repressive regimes. One special case is "whistleblowing", which is in the public interest, but the author fears silencing reactions. The Parliamentary Assembly of the Council of Europe (PACE) in 2010 adopted a resolution for the protection of whistle-blowers in view of their contribution to the fight against corruption.[61] According to a report of the UN Special Rapporteur on Freedom of Opinion and Expression to the UN Human Rights Council, the right to anonymity and to encryption needs to be respected and shall only be restricted under certain conditions.[62] Although there might be good reasons to introduce real-name policies (it tends to increase the quality of discourse and decrease personal attacks), there is the danger of a "chilling effect" of the prohibition of anonymity.

Selected normative challenges of protecting freedom of expression online

Positive and negative obligations of states

As states have the primary responsibility and ultimate obligation to protect human rights and fundamental freedoms in the digital environment, all regulatory frameworks they introduce, including self- or co-regulatory approaches, have to include effective oversight mechanisms and be accompanied by appropriate redress opportunities.[63]

55 Council of Europe, Recommendation CM/Rec(2016)5 of the Committee of Ministers to member States on Internet freedom.

56 Council of Europe, Recommendation CM/Rec(2016)1 of the Committee of Ministers to member States on protecting and promoting the right to freedom of expression and the right to private life with regard to network neutrality.

57 Council of Europe, Recommendation CM/Rec(2015)6 of the Committee of Ministers to member States on the free, transboundary flow of information on the Internet.

58 Council of Europe, Recommendation CM/Rec(2014)6 of the Committee of Ministers to member States on a Guide to human rights for Internet users.

59 Council of Europe, Recommendation CM/Rec(2012)3 of the Committee of Ministers to member States on the protection of human rights with regard to search engines.

60 Council of Europe, Recommendation CM/Rec(2012)4 of the Committee of Ministers to member States on the protection of human rights with regard to social networking services.

61 Council of Europe, Parliamentary Assembly (PACE), Resolution 1729 (2010).

62 UN Special Rapporteur on Freedom of Opinion and Expression (2015), David Kaye, Report on encryption, anonymity and the human rights framework, UN Doc. A/HRC/29/32 of 22 May 2015.

63 Council of Europe, Recommendation CM/Rec(2018)2 of the Committee of Ministers to member states on the roles and responsibilities of internet intermediaries (2018) ('Recommendation on internet intermediaries'), para. 1.1.3.

States are, of course, not the only actors in ensuring human rights online. As the 2018 Recommendation of the Council of Europe on internet intermediaries notes, a

> wide, diverse and rapidly evolving range of players, commonly referred to as "Internet intermediaries", facilitate interactions on the Internet between natural and legal persons by offering and performing a variety of functions and services. Some connect users to the Internet, enable the processing of information and data, or host web-based services, including for user-generated content. Others aggregate information and enable searches; they give access to, host and index content and services designed and/or operated by third parties.

Internet intermediaries have duties under international and national law. In line with the UN Guiding Principles on Business and Human Rights and the "Protect, Respect and Remedy" Framework, intermediaries should respect the human rights of their users and affected parties in all their actions. This includes the responsibility to act in compliance with applicable laws and regulatory frameworks. Internet intermediaries also develop their own rules, usually in form of terms of service or community standards that often contain content-restriction policies. This responsibility to respect within their activities all internationally recognised human rights, in line with the United Nations Guiding Principles on Business and Human Rights, exists independently of the states' ability or willingness to fulfil their own human rights obligations.[64]

States have also misused intermediaries in the past to introduce filters and enforce laws that violate international human rights commitments. Therefore, as the Recommendation notes, any norms applicable to internet intermediaries, regardless of their objective or scope of application, "should effectively safeguard human rights and fundamental freedoms, as enshrined in the European Convention on Human Rights, and should maintain adequate guarantees against arbitrary application in practice".[65]

It should be noted that member states do not only have the negative obligation to refrain from violating the right to freedom of expression and other human rights in the digital environment. As the Recommendation confirms,

> they also have a positive obligation to protect human rights and to create a safe and enabling environment for everyone to participate in public debate and to express opinions and ideas without fear, including those that offend, shock or disturb state officials or any sector of the population.

This positive obligation to ensure to all citizens on a state's territory or under its control all applicable rights and freedoms encompasses the obligation to ensure that private companies comply with relevant human rights guarantees.

Global intermediaries and national laws

A specificity of the internet is the role of the private sector. The vast majority of communicative spaces on the internet are privately held and owned. This is due to the powerful

64 Ibid., para. 2.1.1.

65 Ibid., preambular para. 6.

role of intermediaries, companies that enable our online activity. As the Council of Europe Recommendation on roles and responsibilities of internet intermediaries describes them,

> [they] facilitate interactions between natural and legal persons on the Internet by offering and performing a variety of functions and services. Some connect users to the Internet, enable the processing of information and data, or host web-based services, including for user-generated content. Others aggregate information and enable searches, and give access to, host and index content and services designed and/or operated by third parties. Some facilitate the sale of goods and services, including audio-visual services, and enable other commercial transactions, including payments.[66]

These intermediaries, including social media companies, have become important normative actors by controlling the private spaces in which communication takes place. Globally, by the end of 2017, Facebook had reached two billion active monthly users, YouTube 1.5 billion, WhatsApp 1.2 billion, WeChat 889 million, Instagram 700 million and Twitter 330 million.[67] The number of domain name registrations in all Top Level Domains surpassed 330 million with 130 million alone in .com, 145 million in country-coded Top Level Domains and 21 million in more recently developed new generic Top Level Domains.[68] The numbers hint at the importance of developing a normative order of the internet.

Network effects and mergers have led to the domination of the market by a relatively small number of key intermediaries, including Silicon Valley's "AMAFAGs" (Apple, Microsoft, Amazon, Facebook and Alphabet's Google) and the Chinese BATs (Baidu, Alibaba and Tencent).[69] As the 2018 Recommendation warned, these few companies have growing power: "[the] power of such intermediaries as protagonists of online expression makes it imperative to clarify their role and impact on human rights as well as their corresponding duties and responsibilities, including as regards the risk of misuse by criminals of the intermediary's services and infrastructure".[70]

Due to the multi-layered nature of the regulatory framework governing services provided by or through intermediaries, their regulation is challenging. As they operate in many countries and data streams, especially for cloud-based services, and often cross many countries and jurisdictions, different and conflicting laws may apply.[71] This is exacerbated by, as the 2018 Council of Europe recommendation identified, "the global nature of the internet networks and services, by the diversity of intermediaries, by the volume of Internet communication, and by the speed at which it is produced and processed".[72]

66 Recommendation on Internet intermediaries, preambular para. 6.

67 Robert H. Zakon, Hobbes' Internet Timeline 10.2, www.zakon.org/robert/Internet/timeline

68 Ibid.

69 Wolfgang Kleinwächter (2018) Internet Governance Outlook 2018: Preparing for Cyberwar or Promoting Cyber Détente?, CircleID (6 January), www.circleid.com/posts/20180106_Internet_governance_outlook_ 2018 _preparing_for_cyberwar_or

70 Council of Europe, Recommendation on Internet intermediaries, preambular para. 11.

71 Ibid., para. 6.

72 Ibid., preambular para. 9.

Intermediaries are subjected to national judgments and laws. Consider the German *Netzwerkdurchsetzungsgesetz*[73] to increase enforcement of national speech-related provisions in social networks, which has, however, been received critically.[74]

There is substantial literature on the duties of private entities in international law, especially with regard to the duties of transnational corporations.[75] Much of it is applicable to internet standard-setters, but also to internet content companies, such as search engine providers and social networking services.[76] A key notion is that the corporate responsibility of companies does not diminish state obligations. The *United Nations Guiding Principles on Business and Human Rights* (*"Ruggie Principles"*) establish, *first*, a state duty to protect human rights, *second*, a corporate responsibility to respect human rights and, *third*, a right to access to remedies for victims of business-related abuses.[77] The corporate responsibility encompasses a responsibility to avoid violations and to address negative human rights impacts directly linked to the operations and committed through business relationships, including formal and informal agreements – including thus non-commercial relationships of internet exchange points and server administrators.

Similarly, the Council of Europe, in two recommendations for search engine companies and social network services, first addresses member states, reminding them to develop and promote, in consultation with the private sector and civil society, strategies to protect freedom of expression and other human rights.

Following the UN Guiding Principles on Business and Human Rights, intermediaries have an independent obligation to respect human rights, a "corporate responsibility to protect" that is independent of the state's duty to safeguard human rights. Companies comply with these obligations for example through transparency reports, increased control of subcontractors along the supply chain and Human Rights Impact Assessments.[78] There are also a number of human rights-focused initiatives that technology companies take part in, such as the Global Network Initiative.[79] Members commit themselves to

73 Gesetz zur Verbesserung der Rechtsdurchsetzung in sozialen Netzwerken (Netzwerkdurchsetzungsgesetz – NetzDG), Federal Gazette 2017 Part I No. 61, 7 September 2017.

74 Georg Nolte (2017) Hate-Speech, Fake-News, das »Netzwerkdurchsetzungsgesetz« und Vielfaltsicherung durch Suchmaschinen. *ZUM*, 552; Fiete Kalscheuer (2017) Christian Hornung: Das Netzwerkdurchsetzungsgesetz – Ein verfassungswidriger Schnellschuss. *NVwZ*, Vol. 1721, Nikolaus Guggenberger (2017) Das Netzwerkdurchsetzungsgesetz in der Anwendung. *NJW*, 2577.

75 Especially after the adoption of the UN Guiding Principles on Business and Human Rights. See Radu Mares (Ed.), *The UN Guiding Principles on Business and Human Rights. Foundations and Implementation*. Leiden: Nijhoff, 2011; and, for a comprehensive analysis, Wesley Cragg (Ed.) (2012) *Business and Human Rights*. Cheltenham: Edward Elgar. For the international trade dimension relevant for aspects of ICTs, see Alistair M. Macleod, Human rights and international trade: normative underpinnings, in ibid., 179–196.

76 Council of Europe, Committee of Ministers (4 April 2012), Recommendation CM/Rec(2012)3 on the protection of human rights with regard to search engines and Recommendation CM/Rec(2012)4 on the protection of human rights with regard to social networking services.

77 See the "Ruggie Principles": Report of the Special Representative of the Secretary-General on the issue of human rights and transnational corporations and other business enterprises, John Ruggie, Guiding Principles on Business and Human Rights: Implementing the United Nations "Protect, Respect and Remedy" Framework, UN Doc. A/HRC/17/31 of 21 March 2011.

78 Report of the Special Representative of the Secretary-General on the issue of human rights and transnational corporations and other business enterprises, John Ruggie, Guiding Principles on Business and Human Rights: Implementing the United Nations "Protect, Respect and Remedy" Framework, UN Doc. A/HRC/17/31 of 21 March 2011.

79 Global Network Initiative (GNI), Principles on Freedom of Expression and Privacy, www.globalnetworkinitiative.org/principles/index.php.

self-developed (but human rights-based) principles and seek to improve their performance through an Accountability, Policy and Learning Framework.[80]

The fundamental friction here lies in the diverging interests between intermediaries and states. Intermediaries, especially the providers of social networking services, prefer a liberal approach to content – the content's attractiveness being commensurate with its diversity. States, however, are obliged to ensure protection of human rights (from the prohibition of violent hate speech to that of the sexual exploitation of minors). In some cases – as in the case of copyright infringement – takedowns usually follow a stakeholder/rightsholder request ("notice and takedown").

In other cases, intermediaries may also be required to take initiative in order to counteract the spread of illegal content. Here it is up to the intermediaries themselves (at least on a first decision-making level) to balance between rights while facing a dilemma: erasing too much may make the service less attractive; deleting too little may make it unattractive as well, make companies liable for hate speech and might make states pass laws impacting negatively the business models of intermediaries, such as the German *Network Enforcement Act* of 2018.[81]

Intermediary liability exemptions

In principle, Article 14 of the E-Commerce Directive[82] provides strong protection for information society services through whose platforms users make content publicly available. Member States may only hold a provider responsible for content stored in the user order when he "actually has knowledge of the illegal activity or information" or "the illegal activity . . . is evident".[83] However, a general search obligation amounting to prior censorship would be contrary to European law (Article 15 (1) of the E-Commerce Directive and the jurisprudence of the CJEU, especially *SABAM v. Netlog NV*).[84] Demanding a preemptive filtering system would alter the network's functionality and violate freedom of expression. In *Delfi v. Estonia*, the ECtHR decided that, with regard to the rights and interests of others and to society as a whole, state parties were allowed under certain conditions to hold intermediaries (in this case an internet news portal) liable and demand a certain form of de facto live screening of content to filter for obvious cases of illegality.[85]

The *Delfi* conditions include that a commercial news portal is at issue; that the company did not immediately delete the incriminated comments (the company did so up to six weeks after their publication); that comments were clearly illegal by being, for instance, qualified "hate speech"; and that the portal allowed the authors to remain anonymous. However, under the Strasbourg intermediary liability regime, intermediaries fulfil the

80 GNI, Accountability, Policy and Learning Framework, February 2015, https://globalnetworkinitiative.org/content/accountability-policy-and-learning-framework, including common discussions on the results of accountability review within the framework of the stakeholder-led Telecommunications Industry Dialogue, www.telecomindustrydialogue.org

81 Georg Nolte (2017) Hate-Speech, Fake-News, das »Netzwerkdurchsetzungsgesetz« und Vielfaltsicherung durch Suchmaschinen. *ZUM*, 552.

82 Directive 2000/31/EC of the European Parliament and of the Council of 8 June 2000 on certain legal aspects of information society services, in particular electronic commerce, in the Internal Market ('Directive on electronic commerce'). *OJ L* 178, 17.7.2000, 1–16.

83 Ibid., Article 14.

84 CJEU, *SABAM v. Netlog NV* (16 February 2012), C-360/10.

85 ECtHR, *Delfi* AS *v. Estonia* (16 June 2015), Application No. 64569/09.

role of assessing, prima facie, whether a post is merely offensive (and then waiting for a "notice" or deleting on their own volition) or "in itself" already illegal (and to be deleted immediately). In *MTE and Index.hu ZRT v. Hungary* (2016), the ECtHR qualified its approach, emphasising that the "notice-and-takedown" procedures remained legitimate and sufficient unless the comments themselves were clearly unlawful.[86]

In *Pihl v. Sweden* (2017)[87] concerning comments made on the blog of an individual, the Court limited oversight duties of platform providers by noting that not only the nature of the statement and the context but the size (here: small) and (non-)commercial nature of the platform were important elements in deciding upon the possibility of direct liability of the actual author and the (financial) consequences of the national decision on removal or non-removal of contents.

We know from the case law that the ECtHR generally gives freedom of expression a very high priority. Under established case law of the European Court of Human Rights, "freedom of expression constitutes one of the essential foundations for a democratic society and one of the basic conditions for its progress and for each individual's self-fulfilment".[88] Under the ECtHR, even opinions that can "offend, shock or disturb"[89] are protected. In the cases *Yıldırım v. Turkey*[90] and *Cengiz and Others v. Turkey*[91] this approach was applied to the internet.

On the other hand, freedom of expression does not extend to statements and representations prohibited under international law. These include calls for genocide, terrorism, serious discrimination in the form of violent hate speech and sexual exploitation of minors. Here intermediaries are obliged to become active on their own with the deletion of corresponding content under the ECtHR's *Delfi* jurisprudence.[92]

National laws that in effect provide for de facto filtering duties ex ante to stop the reappearance of "copies" of the incriminated content are in violation of the liability exemptions for host providers contained under the E-Commerce Directive.[93] In an Austrian case, the CJEU has been asked to clarify what constitutes a copy and whether internet platforms must ensure that the same or effectively similar content is not uploaded.[94]

The prohibition on national laws providing for general monitoring sits uneasily with the 2018 Recommendation by the European Commission on measures to effectively

86 ECtHR, *MTE and Index.hu* ZRT v. Hungary (2 February 2016), Application No. 22947/13.

87 ECtHR (3rd section), *Pihl v. Sweden* (7 February 2017), Application No. 74742/14.

88 ECtHR, *Stoll v. Switzerland* (10 December 2007), Application No. 69698/01., para. 101.

89 ECtHR, *Handyside v. UK* (7 December 1976), Application No. 5493/72, para. 49.

90 ECtHR, *Yıldırım v. Turkey* (18 December 2012), Application No. 3111/10.

91 ECtHR, *Cengiz and Others v. Turkey*, judgment of 1 December 2015, applications nos. 48226/10 and 14027/11.

92 ECtHR, *Delfi* AS *v. Estonia* (16 June 2015), Application No. 64569/09.

93 Cf. CJEU, *McFadden vs. Sony* (15 September 2016), C-484/14 (duties of access providers); CJEU, *SABAM v. Netlog NV* (16 February 2012), C-360/10 and *Scarlet v. SABAM* (24 November 2011) (no general monitoring duties for providers), C-70/10 and *L'Oréal/ebay* (12 July 2011), C-324/09 (some preventive duties for "non-active" providers do not violate EU law).

94 OGH, 6Ob116/17b, 25 October 2017, K&R 2018,144 – Miese Volksverräterin II: The questions run as folllows: "1. Is it contrary to Article 15 [E-Commerce Directive] to order a host provider, which has not immediately removed unlawful information, not only to remove this illegal information within the meaning of Article 14 (1) (a) of the Directive, but also other information identical in terms of its wording [wortgleich]: a. worldwide? b. in the respective Member State? c. of the respective user worldwide? d. of the respective user in the respective Member State? 2. As far as question 1 was answered in the negative: Does this also apply to the information identical in terms of the content [sinngleich]? 3. Does this also apply to information identical in terms of content [sinngleich] as soon as the operator becomes aware of this fact?"

tackle illegal content online.[95] It suggests to states that encourage hosting service providers to take "proportionate and specific proactive measures in respect of illegal content". If these measures are automated (as they would have to be), they need to be "proportionate and subject to effective and appropriate safeguards". These safeguards should ensure that filtering and takedown decisions are "accurate and well-founded" and that human oversight and verifications are present and "detailed assessment of the relevant context" is performed.[96] This seems unlikely to be respected in light of the number of removal decisions that are handled by platforms.

Conclusion

The internet has become a vital medium of communication that mediates much of our lived experience and through which individuals exercise their human rights, especially through the enabling right to freedom of expression, including the right to seek, receive and impart information and ideas of all kind, regardless of frontiers. The internet as a "principal means" (*Yıldırım*) to exercise freedom of expression and the latter right as an "essential foundation for a democratic society and one of the basic conditions for its progress" (*Stoll*) are closely connected.

Para. 1 of the Human Rights Council Resolution on the promotion, protection and enjoyment of human rights on the internet (2018) affirms that "the same rights that people have offline must also be protected online, in particular freedom of expression, which is applicable regardless of frontiers and through any media of one's choice". The primary normative objects here are the rights which are applicable online just as offline. But indirectly, the internet's intangible dimension of offering a space for the exercise of these rights is protected as well. The internet's integrity is a structural condition of the exercise of human rights, which are both challenged by technology[97] and realised through it.

Protecting the internet in both its dimensions – kinetic and non-kinetic, including a protective normative framework – lies in the common interest of all states. Its functioning is precondition for the exercise of freedom of expression, the key enabling right of the information society, by any media of one's choice and independent of borders.

The European Court of Human Rights has developed a substantial and robust jurisprudence on freedom of expression. Even if an expression should "offend, shock or disturb"[98], it is protected. Transferred into the internet age by the *Yıldırım*[99] and *Cengiz*[100] cases (access to the internet as the principal means to exercise freedom of expression must be ensured, restrictions must be proportionate), the principle remains applicable today.

The internet, as we have argued, is also a place of violations of rights, a place that is misused to radicalise people and to spread hateful speech. Therefore, freedom of expression does not extend to statements and representations prohibited under international law. These include calls for genocide, terrorism, serious discrimination in the form of violent

95 European Commission Recommendation of 1 March 2018 on measures to effectively tackle illegal content online (C(2018) 1177 final), http://ec.europa.eu/newsroom/dae/document.cfm?doc_id=50095, para. 19.

96 Ibid.

97 Cf. Giovanni Sartor (2017) Human Rights and Information Technologies. In Roger Brownsword, Eloise Scotford and Karen Yeung (Eds.), *Oxford Handbook of Law, Regulation, and Technology*. Oxford: OUP, 424–450.

98 ECtHR, *Handyside v. UK* (7 December 1976), Application No. 5493/72, para. 49.

99 ECtHR, *Yıldırım v. Turkey* (18 December 2012), Application No. 3111/10.

100 ECtHR, *Cengiz and Others v. Turkey*, judgment of 1 December 2015, applications nos. 48226/10 and 14027/11.

hate speech and sexual exploitation of minors. Just as states, intermediaries are obliged to become active on their own to delete such content under the ECtHR's *Delfi* jurisprudence.[101] With regard to most other content, however, intermediary liability exemptions have proven an important tool to enhance freedom of expression.

States have a duty to protect their citizens with regard to the internet (and regarding their online activities, including the exercise of freedom of expression). In so doing, they are obliged to protect them from the activities of third parties as well, be they other individuals or companies. Tech companies, too, including social networking platforms, have a corporate social responsibility to respect human rights within their sphere of influence, which – on the internet – is growing rapidly as the majority of relevant communicative acts takes place in private spaces. The special role of intermediaries is another challenge for regulating the internet. As the majority of online spaces lies in private hands, it is private law that prima facie frames many norm conflicts online. When states react belatedly through laws or judgments, these may lead to over-blocking or legal conflicts between competing jurisdictions.[102]

As the *Freedom of the Net 2018* report by Freedom House posits, "[f]or democracy to thrive, citizens must have freedom of expression and access to a public forum that allows rational discourse".[103] As this contribution has shown, freedom of expression on the internet even extends to certain kinds of *irrational* discourse, to shocking, offending and disturbing content. After all, content that everyone agrees with hardly needs protection. Without doubt, however, the internet fulfils a key function as a public forum for freedom of expression to be realised. Freedom of expression, as part of internet freedom, needs to be secured against the "rise of digital authoritarianism". This is, as both the *Freedom of the Net 2018* report and we conclude, "fundamental to protecting democracy".[104]

101 ECtHR, *Delfi* AS *v. Estonia* (16 June 2015), Application No. 64569/09.

102 See the evolution of the "right to be forgotten": Years of uncertainty followed the CJEU judgment in *Google Spain and Google* (2014). They culminated in a 19 July 2017 referral decision by the French Conseil d'État, of its case *Google Inc.*, n° 399922, to the CJEU to clarify the geographical reach of its 2014 ruling (de-listing globally or only within the EU). The right to erasure ("right to be forgotten") can now be found in Article 17 GDPR.

103 Freedom House, Freedom of the Net 2018: The Rise of Digital Authoritarianism October 2018, https://freedomhouse.org/report/freedom-net/freedom-net-2018, 14.

104 Ibid., 32.

5 The digital disruption of human rights foundations

Hin-Yan Liu[1]

Introduction

Contemporary discourses have largely compartmentalised the human rights challenges posed by digitalisation and the internet as impinging upon the right to privacy,[2] or asserted that the freedom of expression must be preserved and defended online.[3] Thus, digitalisation and the internet are primarily perceived as information and communication media which pose human rights questions in relation to the freedoms elaborated within Articles 17 and 19 of the ICCPR.[4] Given the emphasis of human rights law upon state action or omission and notions of victimhood,[5] these types of direct challenges clearly occupy the foreground. But without diminishing the seriousness of the challenges posed to the protection of these discrete enumerated rights, this chapter explores some of the more foundational questions exposed by digitalisation and the internet upon the edifice of human rights itself.

This departure is justified because digitalisation and the internet have far more pervasive effects that perturb the broader social equilibria within which human rights frameworks are embedded. While much of the discourse on the human rights issues of the digital age is introspectively assessing the impact of the technology upon the protection of discrete rights, digital technologies are disrupting large swathes of society and the economy that have significant, yet indirect, impact upon human rights law. In this vein, the transnational nature of the internet, the digitalisation and hence traceability of everything, and the privatisation of governance have been highlighted as conceptual challenges to the universal human rights framework.[6] The disruptive impact of digital technologies also threatens the practical enjoyment of human rights in the real world by exacerbating global inequality, facilitating political repression, and opening new vulnerabilities for abuses.[7] Such lines

1 Associate Professor, Centre for International Law, Conflict and Crisis, and Coordinator, Artificial Intelligence and Legal Disruption Research Group, Faculty of Law, University of Copenhagen. Email: hin-yan.liu@jur.ku.dk

2 United Nations General Assembly (2014) The Right to Privacy in the Digital Age, 21 January 2014. A/RES/68/167.

3 United Nations Human Rights Council (2016) The Promotion, Protection and Enjoyment of Human Rights on the Internet, 27 June 2016. A/HRC/32/L.20.

4 United Nations General Assembly (1966) International Covenant on Civil and Political Rights, 16 December 1966. 2200A (XXI).

5 For example, see Article 34 of the European Convention on Human Rights, and the categories of direct victim, indirect victim and potential victim. See generally, Antônio Augusto Cançado Trindade (2011) *Access of Individuals to International Justice*. Oxford: Oxford University Press, 125–127.

6 Eileen Donahoe (2016) So Software Has Eaten the World: What Does It Mean for Human Rights, Security & Governance?, *Just Security* (18 March), www.justsecurity.org/30046/software-eaten-world-human-rights-security-governance/ (accessed 17.4.2018).

7 Eileen Donahoe (2016) Digital Disruption of Human Rights. *Just Security* (25 March) www.justsecurity.org/30225/digital-disruption-human-rights/ (accessed 17.4.2018).

of enquiry pursue human rights challenges indirectly and tangentially: digital technologies do not necessarily raise human rights questions as their most compelling problems, but their impact upon the enjoyment of human rights are more subtle and pervasive. In other words, the human rights impact of digital technologies may be both secondary and second-order. Thus, the result is that other technological features attract the limelight, and that much of the incursion of digital technologies upon human rights are overlooked and perhaps unintended consequences that are not related in neat and causally connected fashion. The looming threat of this type of shock to the foundations of the human rights law framework is exacerbated by the fact that these are not first and foremost questions of human rights. While this appears tautological, the difficulty enunciated by the societal disruption of digital technologies is such that it would be insufficient to deploy human rights mechanisms to confront them: a problem itself confounded because human rights have largely crowded out competing frameworks for understanding harms.[8]

Instead, this chapter occupies different vantage points to gain alternative perspectives upon the same underlying digital technologies and the capacities that these technologies enable. These perspectives underscore the internet as a *system*, as a *network*, and as a *distributor and dissipater*. The hope is that foregrounding particular features or characteristics of digital technologies and the internet will reveal different ways that the protection and enjoyment of human rights are being disrupted, thus paving the way for framing appropriate solutions.

Digitalisation and human rights from the systems perspective

A holistic approach to digitalisation, information and communications technologies would suggest the prospect for systems behaviour. After all, the internet is inherently an interconnected network that serves a purpose and which maintains an equilibrium over time, so the "system-ness" of digital technologies and the capabilities that it enable seem to be core features of this group of technologies.[9] To clarify, "a system is an interconnected set of elements that is coherently organised in a way that achieves something",[10] and what is pertinent for our purposes is that the behaviour of the system is an intrinsic property:

> A system is a set of things . . . interconnected in such a way that they produce their own pattern of behaviour over time. . . . The system, to a large extent, causes its own behaviour! An outside event may unleash that behaviour, but the same outside event applied to a different system is likely to produce a different result.[11]

This perspective suggests that incursions made into the realm of human rights by digital technologies may neither be intended, foreseen, or indeed foreseeable,[12] and that such incursions may be system behaviours as opposed to the actions or omissions of an agent. Both these observations make it extremely difficult to invoke the concept of human

8 'As a dominant and fashionable vocabulary for thinking about emancipation, human rights crowds out other ways of understanding harm and recompense', David Kennedy (2005) *The Dark Sides of Virtue: Reassessing International Humanitarianism*. Princeton: Princeton University Press, 9.

9 Note also that systems can be nested in other systems, and that the purposes at various levels are able to compete and conflict against each other, Donella H. Meadows (2008) *Thinking in Systems: A Primer*. White River Junction, VT: Chelsea Green Publishing, 15–16.

10 Ibid., 11.

11 Ibid., 2.

12 'In fact, one of the most frustrating aspects of systems is that the purposes of subunits may add up to an overall behavior that no one wants', Ibid., 15.

rights, let alone claim their breach. This is because, from a legally doctrinal point of view, there must be direct causal connection between the actions or omissions of a state or its agents and the concrete enumerated right possessed by an individual for the human rights system itself to become engaged.

First, foreseeability and predictability are key criteria relevant even for the enlarged conceptions of victimhood that have developed in human rights jurisprudence.[13] Even for the seminal cases which expanded the notion of victimhood under the jurisprudence of the European Court of Human Rights during the 1970s and 1980s, the notion of potential victim remain anchored in the legalised threats hanging over an individual's enjoyment of enumerated human rights. Finally, it should be noted that the jurisprudence underpinning potential victimhood have clear origins – a threatening law on the books – as to the source of the potential violation, which no longer holds with the impact of digital technologies on the enjoyment of human rights.

Second, if the impugned behaviour is an expression of system behaviour, rather than state action or omission,[14] then that behaviour appears to be removed beyond the realm of legal human rights protections. This is because part of the justification of human rights law as a mechanism to hold state power to account dissipates with the prospect for human rights violations to be "merely" the outcomes of system behaviours. Furthermore, the access to justice dimension that human rights law serves also becomes neutralised because a finding of a violation would not readily lead to reparations for the victims nor rectification of those violations for the future. In short, the causally- and agent-oriented nature of human rights law mean that it is largely toothless in the face of unforeseeable system "violations".

Another way of phrasing this is to ask what the meaning of human rights is, if human rights violations are relegated to the mere outcomes of systems behaviour. Recourse to the vocabulary of natural disaster and acts of God come close to the outcomes of system behaviours: events that remain outside of the capacity of human understanding and ability to influence. In such contexts, human beings are reduced to patients who must suffer the ill-effects without the ability to challenge or remedy the treatment. But with such externalisation of treatment comes the neutralisation of the very meaning of human rights itself because such treatment is rendered beyond the sphere of rights and responsibilities.

Human rights violations as normal accidents?

Viewing the human rights challenge of digital technologies from a systems perspective also raises the spectre of human rights violations as "normal" accidents, which are a small and exceptional class of technologically induced accident.[15] Thus, systems with potential

13 See the cases that are authority for laws that violate an individual's human rights by virtue of their being on the books, irrespective of their actual implementation or application to an individual, Trindade 127–129.

14 Unless the state itself is also considered as a system, which in reality is perhaps a closer analogy, rather than the contemporary approach of treating the state as an actor. Such a shift might close the gap between systems theory and human rights law. In this respect, it is worth noting that systems can be nested within other systems, Meadows 15–16.

15 Normal accident theory has been applied to understand a range of catastrophic technological failures. The essential claim is that accidents are unavoidable – and hence become normal – where systems are complex, tightly coupled, possess multiple objectives, and are embedded within competitive environments. Charles Perrow (2011) *Normal Accidents: Living with High Risk Technologies*. Princeton: Princeton University Press. For the application of normal accident theory to the governance of artificial intelligence, see Matthijs Michiel Maas (2018) Regulating for "Normal AI Accidents" – Operational Lessons for the Responsible Governance of AI Deployment. *Association for the Advancement of Artificial Intelligence*.

human rights impacts that also possess the underlying features of normal accidents may generate human rights violations as a natural matter of course.[16] In other words, a direct analogy would place breaches of human rights on par with spectacular normal accidents such as Three Mile Island, Challenger and Fukushima.[17] This direct comparison would transform the "risk" from orthodox accidents to risks in terms of human rights breaches. If such a comparison with normal accidents stands, breaches of human rights are endemic within complex, tightly coupled systems that possess competing objectives and which are deployed in competitive settings. Cyberwarfare might provide an example, insofar as technological or organisational vulnerabilities allow for vulnerabilities that result in the compromise or deprivation of basic services that are considered as core human rights, such as to health, water or food.[18]

The normal accident theory remains, however, focused upon discrete catastrophic events suggesting that alleged human rights violations that arise as a result would have a relatively discrete and singular origin. It may furthermore be possible to extend human rights violations beyond "spectacular" normal accidents by drawing an analogy with our recent typology of "boring" apocalypses.[19] The focus of normal accidents remains on the dramatic, but perhaps that is only where failure modes are the most visible. Thus, this focus on spectacular normal accidents need not constrain its application to the idea of human rights violations as a feature, rather than a bug, of technological systems enabled by digital technologies. Removing the threshold of spectacular catastrophe suggests that lower level normal accidents might be much more routine, but which largely evade detection and analysis.[20] If human rights violations inhabit this space of lower-threshold higher-regularity normal accidents, it would seem that normal accidents with human rights implications become more ordinary and mundane. Taken together, a third category of human rights-relevant activity might be described. In addition to intentional or active violations and negligent, reckless or otherwise omission-based passive violations, this third category encompasses human rights violations as attractors in a dynamical system. This third category hints at the possibility that a system may be predisposed towards certain value-states and that such attractors may map onto the sphere of outcomes that have traditionally been articulated in human rights language. In other words, it is possible that a system might lean towards breaches of human rights by its very nature or as a result of its particular configuration.

16 Perrow himself discusses what an accident is, and provides a typology of victimhood focusing on third-party innocent bystander victims and fourth-party foetuses and future generation victims, Perrow 62–71. Such a treatment demonstrates the difficulty of applying human rights law to such normal system accidents, since victimhood in law is generally not so accommodating.

17 Ibid., 15–31.

18 These examples deploy social and economic positive rights, which may be conceptually further from the core civil and political negative rights that are often discussed in the context of digital technologies and human rights. But this very much illustrates the point in that traditional human rights approaches fail to capture the multi-faceted challenges posed by digitalisation.

19 Hin-Yan Liu, Kristian Cedervall Lauta and Matthijs Michiel Maas (2018) Governing Boring Apocalypses: A New Typology of Existential Vulnerabilities and Exposures for Existential Risk Research. *Futures*, Vol. 102, 6–19.

20 This is analogous to claims that, because accidental nuclear wars have not occurred, that the danger of nuclear weapons accidents are minimal, Scott D. Sagan (1993) *The Limitations of Safety: Organizations, Accidents and Nuclear Weapons*. Princeton: Princeton University Press, ch 1. As Sagan himself recognised, the counterargument would be that, given the patterned flaws or structured vulnerabilities, such dynamical systems have failure as attractors. The mere insistence that such an accident has not occurred can then be answered by the success of local patches and serendipity.

This is important in the context of digital technologies because of the types of fixes that are implemented when human wrongs occur. Take, for example, Google Photo's tagging of black people as "gorillas" in 2015: more than two years later, the company has still evaded implementing a more lasting and systemic solution, opting instead to erase gorillas and some other primates from its lexicon.[21] This obviously superficial solution at the point of expression does nothing to rectify the underlying data set or the black box learning algorithms that arrived at such a conclusion. Digital technologies in this context exhibit a predisposition towards discriminatory effects:[22] this predisposition continues to lurk within the underlying data and data-processing mechanisms even as explicit wrongs that emerge are merely patched over.

Taken together, a systems perspective of digital technologies and their impact upon human rights suggest that infringements on fundamental protections might be expressions of system behaviours and normal accidents, placing such infractions beyond the realm and remedy of human rights law. But the digitalisation potentially provides more pernicious wrongs in laying the foundation or infrastructure that prejudices towards infringements against human rights or makes their occurrence more probable. This last point can be explored from the perspective of digital technologies forming networks in the next section.

Digital networks and the aggregation of human wrongs

Digital technologies enable rapid interaction and continuous communication that form the foundations of digital networks exemplified by the world wide web. The network perspective foregrounds two forms of human rights disruption: the patterned and cumulative incursions in human rights-relevant arenas; and the formal "horizontal" equality of the nodes in that network that diffuse the necessary "vertical" hierarchical relations that human rights law requires. The latter observation is discussed as digital diagonality through the lens of distribution and decentralisation in the third section of this chapter.

Human rights law requires an infringement to pass beyond a threshold of severity before a claim will be considered before a court or tribunal, thereby presenting a barrier against violations which occur through an incremental process. Where human rights law requires a significant single-origin action or omission that is causally connected to the alleged infringement, digital technologies enable a series or complex of more minor incidents to be structured in such a way as to amount to a more major interference. In the parlance of risk studies, a human rights "risk" is conflated largely with a human rights "hazard" that narrows consideration to one-hit knock-out interferences that pass

21 Furthermore, "A Google spokesperson confirmed that "gorilla" was censored from searches and image tags after the 2015 incident, and that "chimp", "chimpanzee", and "monkey" are also blocked today". Tom Simonite (2018) When It Comes to Gorillas, Google Photos Remains Blind. *WIRED,* www.wired.com/story/when-it-comes-to-gorillas-google-photos-remains-blind/ (accessed 3.5.2018). This solution has also been deployed by other services encountering similar problems, Alex Hern (2018) Google's Solution to Accidental Algorithmic Racism: Ban Gorillas. *The Guardian* (12 January) www.theguardian.com/technology/2018/jan/12/google-racism-ban-gorilla-black-people (accessed 3.5.2018).

22 It is important to note that such biases are often picked up from algorithmic inferences from collated human behaviours, Hannah Devlin (2017) AI Programs Exhibit Racial and Gender Biases, Research Reveals. *The Guardian* (13 April) www.theguardian.com/technology/2017/apr/13/ai-programs-exhibit-racist-and-sexist-biases-research-reveals (accessed 3.5.2018).

the threshold for a violation.[23] Yet, a network enables patterned accretion of outcomes that, when taken as a whole, exhibit greater impact than an examination of the sum of the parts would suggest. Thus, the problem is akin to the structured accumulation of smaller wrongs, each of which would individually fail to surpass the threshold required to register as a human rights-relevant event. This argument is akin to the idea of structural discrimination that interconnected autonomous vehicle networks are likely to exhibit, through minor and subtle biases that lean in the same direction, if direct interventions to the contrary are not implemented.[24] Furthermore, there are cycling or recursive effects at play here: for example, getting turned down for a credit application may reduce your score in other systems, making it less probable in being able to secure an insurance policy, which in turn makes success less likely for a desirable professional position. Such vicious cycles may be precipitated by relatively minor and arbitrary trigger conditions.

A different way of phrasing this is that human rights procedures only filter out larger wrongs that are above a certain magnitude, reflecting the severity appropriate to the seriousness of human rights violations. What happens, however, if the smaller interferences that are not strained out by this filter pass through it and are thus not considered as human rights violations, but which afterwards coalesce into a mass that would not have been able to pass through the gaps in that filter in the first place? In other words, human rights law mechanisms that filter for severity at a single point will remain oblivious to the aggregation of more minor wrongs that lean consistently in the same direction.

Yet another way of approaching this idea is that human rights violations can be framed as a probabilistic function: that there is a given probability that a given system will impact upon an enumerated right of a particular individual. Such probabilities remain relatively constant regardless of whether a human rights violation actually materialises or becomes registered. That an individual's human rights are threatened probabilistically is akin to the expansion of victim status, discussed previously, where a discriminatory law on the books can underpin potential victimhood even if that law is not implemented. The difference in the digital context, however, is that the looming stochastic threats to human rights are not explicit and overt as with archaic legislation. The difficulty in detecting such probabilistic impacts upon one's rights posed through network effects constitutes a significant barrier to challenging and changing statistical infringements upon an individual's human rights.

Digital technologies may be especially prone to this consistent leaning or the structured accumulation of minor biases. This is because it provides the stable infrastructural basis in the form of big data which exhibits disparate impacts.[25] In other words, digital technologies allow for the coding, accumulation, retention and propagation of the biases inherited from previous decision-makers. Furthermore, the aggregation facilitated by networked digital technologies connects hitherto distinct and isolated areas which allow for these

23 The risk calculus is as follows: Risk = Hazard * Vulnerability * Exposure. See Liu et al. (2018).

24 Hin-Yan Liu (2018) Three Types of Structural Discrimination Introduced by Autonomous Vehicles. *UC Davis Law Review Online*, 149–180, available at https://lawreview.law.ucdavis.edu/online/vol51/51-online-Liu.pdf; Hin-Yan Liu (2017) Irresponsibilities, Inequalities and Injustice for Autonomous Vehicles. *Ethics and Information Technology*, Vol. 19, 193; Hin-Yan Liu (2016) Structural Discrimination and Autonomous Vehicles: Immunity Devices, Trump Cards and Crash Optimisation. In Johanna Seibt, Marco Nørskov and Søren Schack Andersen (Eds.), *What Social Robots Can and Should Do*. Amsterdam, The Netherlands: IOS Press.

25 Solon Barocas and Andrew D. Selbst (2016) Big Data's Disparate Impact. *California Law Review*, Vol. 104, 671; Karen Yeung (2018) Algorithmic Regulation: A Critical Interrogation. *Regulation & Governance*, Vol. 12, 505–523; Anthony Danna and Oscar H. Gandy (2002) All That Glitters Is Not Gold: Digging Beneath the Surface of Data Mining. *Journal of Business Ethics*, Vol. 40, 373.

disparate impacts to accumulate in ways that were not possible prior to the interconnectivity enabled by digitalisation.

From the perspective of the individual, the networked nature of databases can become a pernicious problem that places them in algorithmic prisons.[26] These are not literal prisons depriving individuals of liberty and which can be challenged through *habeas corpus*: rather these are algorithmic gatekeepers that influence access to important opportunities and services such as jobs, credit and insurance. While credit scores and other metrics have obviously influenced access to credit, for instance, these metrics have not hitherto been so networked and thus pervasive. An important factor is that it is no longer clear who is presenting these barriers and what behavioural aspects erected these obstacles.[27] Furthermore, there are again the cycling or recursive effects mentioned previously, which in the contextual framework of algorithmic prisons, can become especially problematic.

Indeed, the metaphor of a prison is perhaps overly monolithic since this suggests that there is a single authoritative jailor to be appealed to or challenged. Instead, this aggregation connects many hitherto disparate factors, temporarily uniting them to have the effect of jailing an individual by constraining her liberty and access to opportunities. A different way of putting this is that the algorithmic prison comprises of separate bars which are put in place by different databases: each one, taken individually, may be only a minor nuisance or a temporary inconvenience and be circumvented with some effort. The cumulative effect of these individual bars, taken together, is sufficient to frame a lasting cage.

This presents three human rights-relevant problems for the individual: first, that a whack-a-mole approach to perceived violations cannot provide a lasting remedy; second, that the same underlying data profile might underlie a range of different effects detrimental to individual freedom or well-being; and third that the data is often collected and retained by private entities that do not have direct human rights obligations.

Taking these in turn, the first issue is the absence of a feedback mechanism between the finding of a human rights violation and the prospect of a lasting remedy. Even if the contours of the algorithmic prison can be described and challenged as interfering with an enumerated right, any prescribed remedy will not affect the underlying data profile that was the source of that (and most likely other future) human rights infractions. Hence, wielding human rights law against the constraining forces of networked data can provide little more than a temporary and superficial salve to the latest infraction.

The second issue is very much the reverse side of the same coin: that networked digital technologies are robust and resilient to change. Even with the right to be forgotten and the required purging of data, it remains difficult to confirm compliance given the volume and pace of data collection.[28] Furthermore, data profiles can be reconstructed from data points held in other databases or can be points of convergence. Not only does tackling the outcomes as they emerge become a fruitless strategy, but even earnest attempts to alter the core data profile may be difficult to effect. This is not only because digitalisation provides the basis for near costless deposition of data, but also near costless duplication. This means that even if a human rights challenge to the manifest outcomes of a data profile were

26 Bill Davidow (2014) Welcome to Algorithmic Prison. *The Atlantic,* www.theatlantic.com/technology/archive/2014/02/welcome-to-algorithmic-prison/283985/ (accessed 26.4.2018).

27 'Even if an algorithmic prisoner knows he is in a prison, he may not know who his jailer is. . . . A prisoner might not have any idea as to what type of behavior got him sentenced to a jail term'. Ibid.

28 The right to be forgotten can also be readily circumvented by relocation to jurisdictions that adopt a more laissez-faire attitude.

successfully upheld, and the remedy required systematic eradication of the basis of data profile that gave rise to that infraction, in practical terms that data profile will persist in the network (in the form of duplications, earlier copies, or from convergent data profiles gathered by other entities on the same individual). This robustness underpinned by networked digital technologies ultimately requires a more systemic and continuous onslaught to remove. Human rights law mechanisms, however, provide only piecemeal, unsustained and isolated objections that will be unable to dislodge these disparate impacts arising from networked digital technologies.

Finally, there is the private dimension of data and digital networks: often it is private firms that collect and collate the relevant data that generate algorithmic prisons. This is further exacerbated by the fact that the walls of these algorithmic prisons are often built by other private entities, be these employers, creditors, or insurers. With no legal obligation beyond perhaps merely respecting human rights,[29] the absence of state power or state action makes it difficult to articulate these influences as human rights questions in the first place. A different way of putting this is that, in addition to the digital disruption of human rights, there are the familiar problems produced by private action that remove the immediacy of human rights obligations. Then, to top this all off, the digital network conforms to no jurisdictional boundaries making it even more unclear as to where any such claim might be made. This last observation is more readily apparent if the distributive and decentralising aspects of digitalisation are foregrounded.

Digital decentralisation: the diagonality of human rights obligations

Digital technologies have a flattening role, exemplified in the surveillance shift from Big Brother to Big Other,[30] and "in the complex personal data ecosystem that now exists, it is practically impossible for individuals to provide meaningful, voluntary consent to the sharing and processing activities which algorithmic regulation entails".[31] As digital technologies magnify the reach and impact of private organisations, the law, and especially human rights law, still treat these practically powerful companies formally as private entities.

Beyond exacerbating the public-private divide as it relates to human rights obligations, digitalisation also distributes decision-making authority by interjecting digitalised data-driven processes.[32] Even advisor and recommender style systems, however, can cause problems for human rights procedures for two converging reasons. First, there is the legitimating impetus of digitalisation providing the backdrop of better and more efficient performance.[33] This shifts the norm towards the deployment of algorithmic systems in a way that requires justification to opt out. Second, human agents or organisations might be relegated to bearing

29 John Gerard Ruggie (2013) *Just Business: Multinational Corporations and Human Rights*. W. W. Norton & Company.

30 Shoshana Zuboff (2015) Big Other: Surveillance Capitalism and the Prospects of an Information Civilization. *Journal of Information Technology*, Vol. 30, 75.

31 Yeung 10.

32 Many 'concerns can be avoided if algorithmic systems are configured as recommender systems . . . rather than automated sanctioning systems', Ibid. 12.

33 See for example the contrasting opinions in the context of safety and autonomous vehicles, Aarian Marshall (2017) To Save Lives, Deploy Self-Driving Cars as Soon as You Can. *WIRED*, www.wired.com/story/self-driving-cars-rand-report/ (accessed 28.3.2018); Peter Hancock (2018) Are Autonomous Cars Really Safer Than Human Drivers? *The Conversation*, http://theconversation.com/are-autonomous-cars-really-safer-than-human-drivers-90202 (accessed 28.3.2018).

the brunt of accountability where human-technological assemblages go wrong.[34] This dispersal of decision-making echoes the claim made earlier about the meaning of a human rights violation that arises as an emergent outcome of complex interactions in a system. In other words, this dispersal of decision-making has decentralised the source of a human rights violation and thus obscured its author. Indeed, in holding up a mirror to examine the processes underlying a human rights violation, it may have knock-on effects that demonstrate a general lack of intentional authorship in human rights violations.[35]

The challenge is more than that introduced by mere horizontality, and is not easily remedied through positive obligations imposed upon the state.[36] Rather, decision-making authority persists such that power asymmetry invokes the idea of human rights, but that authority is no longer centralised in a way that is identifiable, and more importantly, challengeable. And the core challenge enabled by digitalisation is not one of horizontality in its orthodox sense, since a form of horizontality is introduced that maintains an asymmetry of power and the possibility of resistance. In other words, it is no longer a situation of orthogonal relations of verticality and horizontality reflecting state power and authority, but instead a *diagonality*, whereby nominally equal entities nevertheless exercise structural power and authority over those with the same nominal legal status. Such diagonal relations are necessarily difficult to contemplate through the lens of human rights law. The refusal or inability to do so, however, will leave unexamined and unchallenged the impact of decentralisation and dispersal enabled by digitalisation.

From one vantage point, digitalisation does not introduce new challenges because private corporations have been accruing wealth and power.[37] Digitalisation merely magnifies corporate power, extending and cementing the trends towards hegemony. From the perspective of digital technologies being distributors and dissipaters, however, a fundamental challenge to human rights protections emerges. As the law treats the corporation as a legal person,[38] the causal chain in any alleged human rights violation remains relatively clear and straightforward since the corporation as a distinct and independent entity is the source of the alleged human rights interference. That the law in its contemporary form largely insulates the corporation from human rights liabilities, so to speak, is a conceptually simple obstacle that is theoretically capable of being overturned. The distributing and dissipating functions facilitated by digital technologies, however, present a different layer of fundamental human rights challenges by breaking this neat causal chain. This compounds the formal legal difficulty of holding corporations to account for

34 M. C. Elish (2016) Moral Crumple Zones: Cautionary Tales in Human-Robot Interaction. *WeRobot 2016*; Wendell Wallach and Colin Allen (2008) *Moral Machines: Teaching Robots Right from Wrong*. Oxford: Oxford University Press.

35 The dilution of authorship resembles Arendt's famous observation on the banality of evil, Hannah Arendt (1994) *Eichmann in Jerusalem: A Report on the Banality of Evil*. Penguin.

36 This is most obviously because of the trans-jurisdictional nature of digital technology and its impacts, but also because it is not easy to define precisely what it is that the state has a positive obligation to providing or ensuring that would be legally actionable.

37 See for example the spectacular power wielded by the charter corporations, Nick Robins (2006) *The Corporation That Changed the World: How the East India Company Shaped the Modern Multinational*. London: Pluto Press. Indeed, such is the power of the corporation that it can be analogised with God, with corporate law serving as the system of mythology surrounding it. In this sense, corporate law serves the purposes of mediation and legitimation: 'The corporation is essentially a magical and mysterious entity that smooths over the contradictions in our culture and makes inequities seem natural'. Douglas Litowitz (2005) The Corporation as God. *The Journal of Corporate Law*, Vol. 30, 501.

38 *Santa Clara County v. Southern Pacific Railroad* (1886) 118 US 394 (US Supreme Court); *Salomon v. A Salomon* (1897) [1897] AC 22 (UK House of Lords).

human rights with the difficulty of dissipating the sources (the dilution of sources might even render these as just influencing factors) that lead to human rights infractions.

The compounding challenges to human rights posed by digitalisation would suggest that the orthogonal relations that have characterised human rights law must also be supplemented by diagonal obligations that recognise the practical and substantive power differentials rather than merely the legal form that an entity adopts. Yet, this diagonality will merely assuage a prior challenge because it only causally connects the corporation as a source of human rights-relevant activity. Where the sources or influencing factors that precede an outcome are dispersed or dissipated, as made possible by digitalisation, the question of causation itself becomes the core issue that conflicts with the very notion of human rights.

Concluding thoughts: digital infrastructure facilitating human rights disruption

This chapter has highlighted the disruption wrought by digital technologies to the very foundations of human rights. This was made possible by adopting three perspectives that digital technologies enable or facilitate, that are markedly different from the challenges illuminated by a more myopic focus on digitalisation itself. The following table summarises these fundamental challenges posed by digital technologies from these different perspectives.

Table 5.1 Fundamental challenges posed by digital technologies

	Effect	*Human Rights Challenges*
System	- Unintentional, unforeseen and unforeseeable behaviours. - Attractor or equilibrium states. - "Normal" accidents.	- Removal of outcomes from human rights scrutiny. - Systemic violations: system configuration may naturally predispose towards violations. - Neutralising the meaning and stigma of human rights violations. - A small subset of unavoidable violations.
Network	- Relatively minor, but patterned, structured, aggregated, or cumulative effects. - Duplication and replication of databases, convergence of data points. - Stochastic or probabilistic impacts.	- Private actors as a source or influencing factor of violations. - Cycling or recursive effects leading to vicious cycles. - Algorithmic prisons leading to structured denial of services and opportunities. - Causality focus problematic for probabilistic impacts.
Distributor/ Dissipater	- Blurs causation. - Exacerbates power differentials.	- Private actors as a source of violations. - Obscure sources and influencing factors of violations. - Compounds extant challenges of corporate human rights liabilities.

Networked digital communications technology has been claimed to give rise to or enable "a new system of social ordering known as algorithmic regulation".[39] Thus, the digitalisation impulse lays the infrastructure necessary for further forms of human rights

39 Yeung.

disruption that has been variously termed algorithmic regulation[40] or algocracy[41]. While digitalisation in itself does not present these threats, it lays the infrastructure that facilitates these developments. The difficulty of deploying human rights and other legal tools to confront the challenges posed by digital technologies is thus that it is not an action or omission, nor an agent or patient, that is the source of the problem. Instead, digitalisation provides the base conditions which are particularly difficult to engage with legally. Accustomed to interacting with actors and actions, law and regulation remains largely blind to the preconditions – the stage where the play is enacted out.[42]

The infrastructural perspective derives ready analogies with architectural modes of regulation[43] and architectural exclusion.[44] These analogies point to other types of difficulties: first, if digitalisation is akin to architectural or code modalities of regulation, then law is relegated to a parallel modality of regulation.[45] But what this means is that it is the combined effects of these different regulatory modalities which give rise to the regulation of behaviour as a whole, with the effect that the law is not supreme or capable of overriding other effects as legal doctrine would seem to suggest. Second, if the infrastructural perspective is analogous to architectural exclusion, a large initial hurdle is the presumption that artefacts[46] and architecture[47] are neutral. These presumptions undergird the received notion that the infrastructural level is not an appropriate level for regulatory interventions. This translates in the digitalisation context to immunising the infrastructural predispositions from regulatory scrutiny. While the focus upon actors and actions is consistent with legal doctrine and provides the continuity of the legal perspective, it overlooks the possibility that the digitalisation will create or facilitate winners and losers under this new system of social ordering.

Looking towards the horizon, digital technologies may impose impacts upon human rights protections in a more prospective manner. Big data facilitates the profiling of individuals and thus imposes subtle constraints upon personal freedom, as discussed earlier.[48] First, there is the collective judgement objection, that these constraints are imposed through a collective manner. Specific data points in an individual profile are statistically correlated with certain behaviours or outcomes of a larger group which shares those particular data points. Digitalisation thus allows collective probabilities to be transformed into predicted actions for the individual. Second, there is the prospective curtailment of opportunities and possibilities which are a long way from the retrospective nature of human rights violations that requires that the alleged breach had already occurred in the past. It is simply not possible to deploy human rights law to the possibility of probable future breaches.[49]

40 Ibid.

41 John Danaher (2016) The Threat of Algocracy: Reality, Resistance and Accommodation. *Philosophy & Technology*, Vol. 29, 245.

42 Langdon Winner (1980) Do Artifacts Have Politics? *Daedalus*, Vol. 109, 121.

43 Lawrence Lessig (1999) The Law of the Horse: What Cyber Law Might Teach. *Harvard Law Review*, Vol. 113, 501.

44 Sarah Schindler (2014) Architectural Exclusion: Discrimination and Segregation Through Physical Design of the Built Environment. *Yale Law Journal*, Vol. 124, 1836.

45 Lessig identifies law, social norms, market and architecture as modalities of regulation, Lawrence Lessig (1998) The New Chicago School. *The Journal of Legal Studies*, Vol. 27, 661.

46 But see, Winner 1980.

47 Schindler 2014.

48 Davidow 2014.

49 Beyond those where anachronistic laws hold the prospect for discriminatory impact if enforced, as discussed previously.

This prospective dimension also creates difficulties to contain the possibilities of social manipulation and control engendered by digital technologies. The contemporary developments of China's Social Credit System[50] exemplify the disjuncture between technological realities and human rights law. The social credit system operates largely to restrict or facilitate access to desirable goods and services, and as such these are in the realm of social and economic positive rights (freedom to) that are notoriously difficult to enforce. Contemporary human rights law is much better at addressing civil and political negative rights (freedom from) that are oriented against preventing mistreatment. Compounding these matters further is the fact that the goods and services sought are often not considered within the substantive ambit of existing human rights and are also offered or provided by private actors. Thus, contemporary human rights jurisprudence is badly aligned towards attaining better standards or conditions in the context of social credit systems.

Social credit systems also manipulate individual behaviour, and perhaps individual identity, in the quest for a higher score. On its face, the individual engages with these systems in a voluntary and consensual manner that fails entirely to engage human rights law. But the effect is much more pernicious than mere nudging[51] because it complements a choice architecture with real, significant and consistent consequences. In doing so, such systems mould compliant and malleable individuals in a way that cannot readily be confronted with the paradigm of conflictual and coerced compliance that undergirds contemporary human rights protections. In this way, social credit systems many constitute yet another regulatory modality that runs in parallel to law,[52] that limit the regulatory potential played by law. Insofar as human rights *law* has crowded out other forms of understanding harm,[53] it also curtails the efficacy of human rights as a tool to push back against undue influence.

Digitalisation essentially provides the infrastructural basis for power, coercion, manipulation to flow. As long as the aim of human rights is oriented towards stemming such excesses, it has a role to play in the implementation and deployment of digital technologies. But, as the different challenges made visible from the system, network and distributor or dissipater perspectives make clear, there is significant work that needs to be done before human rights law mechanisms will be fit for purpose.

50 Rachel Botsman (2017) Big Data Meets Big Brother as China Moves to Rate Its Citizens. *WIRED*, www.wired.co.uk/article/chinese-government-social-credit-score-privacy-invasion (accessed 3.4.2018); Mara Hvistendahl (2017) Inside China's Vast New Experiment in Social Ranking. *WIRED*, www.wired.com/story/age-of-social-credit/ (accessed 3.4.2018); Simina Mistreanu (2018) Life Inside China's Social Credit Laboratory. *Foreign Policy*, https://foreignpolicy.com/2018/04/03/life-inside-chinas-social-credit-laboratory/ (accessed 26.4.2018). See also, Rogier Creemers (2018) China's Social Credit System: An Evolving Practice of Control (9 May). Available at SSRN: https://papers.ssrn.com/sol3/papers.cfm?abstract_id=3175792

51 Richard H. Thaler and Cass R. Sunstein (2008) *Nudge: Improving Decisions about Health, Wealth, and Happiness*. New Haven, CT: Yale University Press; Cass R. Sunstein (2015) The Ethics of Nudging. *Yale Journal on Regulation*, Vol. 32, 413; Cass R. Sunstein (2016) *The Ethics of Influence: Government in the Age of Behavioral Science*. Cambridge: Cambridge University Press.

52 Social credit systems may also constitute elaborate and explicated forms of the social norm regulatory modality.

53 Kennedy 2005.

Part III

Legislation, judicial and stakeholder practices – practical dimension

6 The main challenges related to protecting human rights in the internet

Changrok Soh, Daniel Connolly and Seunghyun Nam

It is easy to forget the optimism of the 1990s, when the young technology known as the internet was celebrated for transforming human rights advocacy by making it easier to gather, process and disseminate information across borders.[1] As Canada's former Minister of Foreign Affairs, Lloyd Axworthy enthused, "the mouse is mightier than the missile".[2] Published in 1996 by John Perry Barlow, one of the founders of the Electronic Frontier Foundation, the *Declaration of Cyberspace Independence* provocatively asserted that state attempts to control information flows were doomed to failure, even characterising the internet as "a virus of liberty".[3] Fast-forward nearly two decades, however, and this optimism has been tempered by a creeping suspicion that human rights violators are more internet savvy than anyone could have expected. A growing list of developments such as the Snowden revelations, China's Golden Shield project, the rise of monopolistic social media companies, and internet shutdowns in scores of countries around the world have all contributed to a growing awareness that the internet is also a unique threat. Adding to the challenge, the governance of the internet's physical and digital infrastructure remains complex and poorly understood by non-specialists.[4]

This chapter surveys the main challenges to protecting human rights in the internet and illustrates them with the case of South Korea, one of the earliest internet nations.[5] A prosperous democratic country with some of the world's highest rates of internet and smart phone use, South Korea showcases some of the traditional challenges to human rights in the internet but also emerging issues. These threats can be conceptualised as coming from three distinct directions, each of which involves different types of actors and evokes a range of theoretical and legal issues.

1 Jamie Frederic Metzl (1996) Information Technology and Human Rights. *Human Rights Quarterly* Vol. 18, No. 4 (November), 705–746, https://muse.jhu.edu/article/13554.

2 Lloyd Axworthy (2000) The Mouse Is Mightier than the Sword. In Steven Hick, Edward F. Halpin, and Eric Hoskins (Eds.), *Human Rights and the Internet*. New York: St. Martin's Press, 20.

3 John Perry Barlow (2016) A Declaration of the Independence of Cyberspace. Electronic Frontier Foundation, 20 January 2016, www.eff.org/cyberspace-independence.

4 Laura DeNardis (2014) *The Global War for Internet Governance*. New Haven: Yale University Press.

5 K. Chon et al. (2013) A History of Computer Networking and the Internet in Korea. *IEEE Communications Magazine*, Vol. 51, No. 2 (February), 10–15, https://doi.org/10.1109/MCOM.2013.6461175.

Above

This refers to heavy-handed regulation of the internet by the government, including activities such as blocking websites, internet shutdowns, mass surveillance, and the manipulation and/or coercion of users. Today it may also include government-sponsored malware attacks and deliberate backdoors in commercial software.

Below

This refers to the misuse of the internet by non-state actors or individuals to disseminate hatred, violate privacy, or conduct criminal activity. This can be conducted horizontally, such as hate crimes against other individuals or groups, or vertically against the state as in the case of terrorism.

Beyond

This refers to online activities that originate from beyond the state's borders and violate the human rights of its citizens. This covers a broad spectrum of activities such as phishing attacks conducted by foreigners, violations of user rights by foreign companies, or even state-sponsored cyberattacks.

The following sections will examine the dynamics of each challenge in detail, illustrate them with recent developments in South Korea, and situate them in broader theoretical context. Protecting human rights on the internet will require comprehensive solutions and close cooperation among multiple stakeholders. Moreover, tackling this issue is more urgent than ever because our digital and physical worlds are fusing together in unprecedented ways due to new technologies.[6] The interdependence of our offline and online rights is a major problem for the human rights community, which must respond to digitalisation at a theoretical and practical level, but is also an opportunity to holistically integrate our protection frameworks so as to encompass all spheres of human activity and experience. Identifying the key threats to our rights in the internet will be the first step in this process.

Challenges from above

In the early days of the internet, governments were often caught flatfooted by the new technology. States that subsidised the spread of the internet paradoxically increased the visibility of their own human rights violations, a situation that one activist characterised as a "honeymoon of ignorance".[7] However, since the 1990s, the growing economic and security importance of the internet has encouraged national authorities to assume more control over digital spaces.[8]

Traditionally, these top-down violations of privacy and the right to expression in the internet by state actors, such as intelligence agencies and police forces, have been the central concern of human rights defenders. Although the securitisation of the internet during the War on Terror has raised the salience of this issue, it is important to note that

6 Klaus Schwab (2016) *The Fourth Industrial Revolution*. Geneva: The World Economic Forum.

7 Wayne Sharpe (2000) Rebel Internet: Human Rights and the New Technology. In: Steven Hick, Edward F Halpin and Eric Hoskins (Ed.), *Human Rights and the Internet*. New York: St. Martin's Press, 49.

8 Chris C. Demchak and Peter J. Dombrowski (2014) Rise of a Cybered Westphalian Age: The Coming Decades. In Maximilian Mayer, Mariana Carpes, and Ruth Knoblich, Global Power Shift (Eds.), *The Global Politics of Science and Technology – Vol. 1* Springer Berlin Heidelberg, 91–113, https://doi.org/10.1007/978-3-642-55007-2_5

the mass surveillance of global communications by powerful states pre-dated the World Trade Center attacks.[9] Broadly, these top-down violations of human rights on the internet are principally justified by security concerns or public morality.

With increasing threats from state-sponsored and independent actors such as terrorist groups, more governments are responding with new cyber security laws. Japan enacted one of the earliest, the Cyber Security Basic Act & Information Processing Promotion Act in November 2014, in order to boost response from national and local authorities to cybersecurity threats and enhance cooperation between the private sector and government.[10] The US also enacted the Cybersecurity Act of 2015, which came into effect in December 2018, providing a framework for information sharing between and among the public and private sectors and authorising certain authorities to monitor certain information systems.[11] Similarly, in August 2016, new EU-wide cybersecurity laws came into effect and member states were required to transpose these laws into national law.[12] Under this framework, the EU Agency for Network and Information Security (ENISA) plays a key role in providing support to member states, EU institutions and businesses, and implementing the EU certification framework to increase trust and security in products and services.[13] Later in June 2017, China also adopted a new Cybersecurity law.[14]

Based on these global trends, the Republic of Korea similarly found a need to strengthen its regulations on cyber security threats, particularly after various cyberattacks that occurred since the early 2000s including the Internet Crisis in 2003, the DDoS Incident in 2009, the Nyonghyub telegraph shutdown in 2011 and the Korea Hydro & Nuclear Power Co., LTD shutdown incident in 2014, and the hacking of the Military Data Integration Center in 2016.[15] As such, since 2000, legislators have discussed the possibility of enacting the "Prevention of Cyber Terror Act" to respond to potential cyber terrorist attacks, similar to cyber security laws enacted by the US, EU, Japan and China. In addition, the government has also been concerned with digital threats to public morality. Thus, in 2011, the government began to implement a controversial online game shutdown policy, which is also referred to as the "Cinderella law", from 12:00 a.m. to 6:00 a.m. to prevent internet game addiction among young Korean adolescents.[16]

Yet, liberal opposition parties have largely resisted such efforts due to concerns over possible risks of infringing the human rights of Korean and foreign nationals. With regard to the "Prevention of Cyber Terror Act", opposition groups were mostly concerned about possible abuse of power by Korea's national intelligence agencies.[17] In fact, Korea has

9 Nicky Hager (1996) *Secret Power*. Nelson, New Zealand: Craig Potton.

10 Sayuri Umeda (2014) Japan: Cybersecurity Basic Act Adopted. *Global Legal Monitor*, 10 December, www.loc.gov/law/foreign-news/article/japan-cybersecurity-basic-act-adopted/.

11 *U.S. Cybersecurity Act of 2015*, Public Law 114–113; *U.S. STAT* 129 (December 18, 2015): 2242.

12 Government Europa (2018) European Commission Welcomes New EU-wide Cybersecurity Laws. May 4, www.governmenteuropa.eu/new-eu-wide-cybersecurity-laws/87138/

13 Cybersecurity. European Commission, https://ec.europa.eu/digital-single-market/en/cyber-security accessed (21.5.2018); The EU Cybersecurity Certification Framework. European Commission, https://ec.europa.eu/digital-single-market/en/eu-cybersecurity-certification-framework (accessed 21.5.2018).

14 Jack Wagner (2017) China's Cybersecurity Law: What You need to Know. *The Diplomat* (June 01), https://thediplomat.com/2017/06/chinas-cybersecurity-law-what-you-need-to-know/

15 Whasun Jho and Woong Kwon (2017) Cyber-security Governance in South Korea and the United States: A Comparison of Securitization of Cyber-threat. *Information Society & Media* Vol. 18, No. 2, 97–120.

16 Jiyeon Lee (2011) South Korea Pulls Plug on Late-night Adolescent Online Gamers. *Digital Biz, CNN*, 22 November, https://edition.cnn.com/2011/11/22/world/asia/south-korea-gaming

17 Young-Bub Kweon (2013) A Study on Countermeasures with Criminal Law against Terrorism- focusing on Proposed Legislative Bills through Comparative Legal Studies. *Human Rights and Justice*, Vol. 436, 88–108.

had a long history of surveillance by the government under the "National Security Act" which was adopted in 1948 "to secure the security of the State and the subsistence and freedom of nationals, by regulating any anticipated activities compromising the safety of the State".[18] Based on these terms, this law has been widely applied to punish those who are in favour of the North Korean regime or communism.[19] But due to its arbitrary application, liberal groups and certain civil society groups such as Amnesty International and Human Rights Watch have called upon legislators to repeal this law as it violates rights of individuals to exercise their right to freedom of expression, opinion and association.[20] For example, mere possession of books that contain views similar to the North Korean regime can lead to imprisonment up to seven years.[21] This issue was eventually taken to the Supreme Court in a case concerning sentencing of student activists and a landmark decision was concluded which reaffirmed the constitutionality of the National Security Law because possibilities remain for North Korea to directly or indirectly overthrow the system of South Korea.[22]

The constitutionality of the online shutdown law, which was implemented in the name of public morality, was also debated in the Constitutional Court of Korea. Human rights activists complained that this law posed possible violations of the right to happiness, parents' right to decide upon their children's education and the rights and freedom of expression of internet providers.[23] Despite resistance from the game industry and human rights activists, however, in September 2015, the Court concluded that the "shutdown law" was constitutional because "in light of high popularity, addictiveness of online games and juveniles' overindulgence in it, such a law is necessary to ensure the sound development of juveniles".[24] Nonetheless, more recent studies have shown that this law has not been effective in reducing the internet use of adolescents and question whether this law is necessary at all.[25] Thus, certain legislators are calling for a bill to scrap the shutdown law altogether.[26]

Given such history, liberal opposition groups have strongly resisted adoption of additional laws that provide more authority to the government in attaining private information of individuals on the grounds of national security. The "Act on Anti-Terrorism for the Protection of Citizens and Public Security" was promulgated on 3 March 2016 by the National Assembly, but this bill also faced fierce opposition through a nine-day filibuster

18 National Security Act, Act No. 13722, 06. Jan, 2016, Amendment by Other Act, National Law Information Center, www.law.go.kr/LSW/eng/engLsSc.do?menuId=1&query=national+security+act&x=0&y=0#liBgcolor16

19 Ibid.

20 Human Rights Watch (2015) South Korea: Cold War Relic Law Criminalizes Criticism. (28 May), www.hrw.org/news/2015/05/28/south-korea-cold-war-relic-law-criminalizes-criticism; Amnesty International (2015) South Korea: National Security Law Continues to Restrict Freedom of Expression. Public Statement, Index: ASA 25/001/2015, January 20, www.amnesty.org/download/Documents/212000/asa250012015en.pdf

21 Human Rights Watch (2015).

22 Jeon Soo-yong (2004) Supreme Court Upholds National Security Law. *The Chosun Ilbo*, 2 September, http://english.chosun.com/site/data/html_dir/2004/09/02/2004090261020.html

23 Yoon Sung-won (2017) Lawmaker Urges Scrap of "Forced Game Shutdown Law". *The Korea Times*, 23 November, www.koreatimes.co.kr/www/tech/2017/11/134_239703.html

24 Yoo Sun Chung (2015) Analysis of "Shutdown Law" Precedent – Case No.: 2011Hun-Ma659, 2011Hun-Ma683, *Lex Korea*, 28 September, http://lexkorea.org/?p=331

25 Jihyun Choi, Hyunseok Cho, Seungmin Lee, Juyeong Kim, Eun-Chel Park (2018) Effect of the Online Game Shutdown Policy on Internet Use, Internet Addiction, and Sleeping Hours in Korean Adolescents. *Journal of Adolescent Health*, Vol. 62, No. 5(May), 548–555, http://lexkorea.org/?p=331

26 Sung-won (2017).

from liberal groups such as the Min-ju party and human rights activists.[27] Concerns over possible human rights abuse were particularly acute during Park Geun-hye's administration. Government monitoring was traditionally limited to public safety and other national security issues including pro-North Korean activities, but surveillance by the government began to spread to other political purposes.[28] For example, allegations begun to surface that the National Intelligence Service (NIS) participated in monitoring of internet discussions of opposition groups ahead of former President Park's December 2012 election.[29] The NIS was also involved in obtaining warrants to oversee chats on Kakao Talk, which is the top mobile messaging application.[30] After these cases were addressed to the public, former N.I.S. chief, Won Sei-hoon was eventually punished for ordering this online campaign to support the election of President Park.[31] Freedom House also downgraded South Korea's press freedoms as only "partly free" in 2014 after this case was reported.[32]

To sum up, Korea continues to search for the right balance between the protection of cyberspace for national security and the protection of individual rights. Articles 17 and 18 of South Korea's Constitution clearly prohibit invasion of privacy, but Article 37, paragraph 2 of the Constitution provides that freedoms and rights of citizens may be restricted for the purposes of "national security, the maintenance of law and order or for public welfare". The extent to which the government should be allowed to invade the lives of Korean people is still not clear, but it is certain that the Korean people still do not have complete trust towards the government as a result of increasing reports of surveillance of the public, forcing some Koreans to digitally migrate to foreign messenger apps with tighter security such as Telegram.[33] In addition to monitoring and mass surveillance, the Korean government also censors and blocks certain information. For instance, the government blocked North Korean and some pro-North Korea websites, even when they were internationally based.[34] The public also cannot access the official newspaper of the ruling Workers' Party (Rodong Sinmun) and Korean Central News Agency (KCNA), which are two of the most important sources of information.[35]

Other countries are facing similar challenges. After adoption of the Cybersecurity Law in China, Human Rights Watch raised concerns over its new law because it is strengthening

27 Jack Kim and Dahee Kim (2016) Record-breaking South Korea Filibuster Over "Terror" Law Ends on Ninth Day. *Reuters*, ed. Clarence Fernandez, 2 March, www.reuters.com/article/us-southkorea-politics-filibuster-idUSKCN0W41BX

28 Se-Woong Koo (2015) South Korea's Invasion of Privacy. *The New York Times*, 2 April, www.nytimes.com/2015/04/03/opinion/south-koreas-invasion-of-privacy.html

29 Ibid.

30 Ibid.

31 Choe Sang-Hun (2017) Former South Korean Spy Chief Sentenced for Trying to Sway Election. *The New York Times*, 30 August, www.nytimes.com/2017/08/30/world/asia/south-korea-spy-chief-sentenced.html

32 Se-Woong Koo (2015); Freedom House (2014) *Freedom in the World 2014* (Washington, DC: Freedom House).

33 Sohee Kim (2014), Messaging App Telegram Launches Korean Version to Cash in on Privacy Fears. *Reuters*, ed. Tony Munroe and Miral Fahmy (7 October), www.reuters.com/article/us-southkorea-apps-telegram/messaging-app-telegram-launches-korean-version-to-cash-in-on-privacy-fears-idUSKCN0HW0RR20141007

34 Philip Iglauer (2015) North-South Tension Causes Internet Censorship in Korea: Is it Justified? *ZDNet*, 27 August 2015, www.zdnet.com/article/north-south-tension-causes-internet-censorship-in-korea-is-it-justified/.

35 Choe Sang-Hun (2017) In Reporting on North Korea, Tech Helps Break Through Secrecy. *The New York Times*, 5 July, www.nytimes.com/2017/07/05/technology/personaltech/in-reporting-on-north-korea-tech-helps-break-through-secrecy.html?utm_content=buffer536e9&utm_medium=social&utm_source=twitter.com&utm_campaign=buffer

censorship, surveillance and other controls over the internet.[36] More specifically, this new law requires companies to censor "prohibited" information and restrict online anonymity, to monitor and report to the government "network security incidents", and further allows the government to implement large-scale network shutdowns when there are "major security incidents".[37] On the other hand, in the US, civil liberties groups have campaigned aggressively against the Cybersecurity Information Sharing Act due to potential infringement of Americans' privacy.[38] Such concerns have heightened after former NSA contractor Edward Snowden revealed US government surveillance activities, and Americans continue to debate the extent to which government surveillance should be justified.[39] The EU Parliamentary Assembly of the Council of Europe also addressed similar concerns by reporting that surveillance practices conducted by the US and their partners in certain Council of Europe member states, including the United Kingdom, endanger the right to privacy, freedom of information and expression and the rights to a fair trial.[40]

Challenges from below

Horizontal violations of human rights on the internet are an emerging issue around the world. In Korea it often takes the form of cyberbullying, which has resulted in numerous celebrity suicides. In 2008, for example, a popular Korean actress, Choi Jin Sil, committed suicide because of rumours and insulting comments from aggressive netizens.[41] Other celebrities have been slandered and the victims of fake news, leading them to sue cyberbullies in court.[42] As these cases illustrate, the internet is frequently used by non-state actors and individuals to violate human rights in ways that are uniquely different from top-down threats. This goes beyond cyberbullying to include various forms of cyberstalking, revenge pornography, and identity theft. This also includes the misuse or illegal collection of personal data from domestic companies or non-state organisations. Traditional human rights activism, which has focused on state violations, has only haltingly responded to the new threat posed by these horizontal actors.

Nevertheless, the solution seems straightforward. States have the responsibility to protect the human rights of their citizens and this includes when they are online. Traditional law and order approaches should be sufficient to solve this problem. However, this issue

36 *Human Rights Watch* (2016) China: Abusive Cybersecurity Law Set to be Passed, Law Strangles Online Freedom, Anonymity. 6 November, www.hrw.org/news/2016/11/06/china-abusive-cybersecurity-law-set-be-passed

37 Ibid.

38 Andrea Peterson (2015) Senate Passes Cybersecurity Information Sharing Bill Despite Privacy Fears. *The Washington Post*, 27 October, www.washingtonpost.com/news/the-switch/wp/2015/10/27/senate-passes-controversial-cybersecurity-information-sharing-legislation/

39 *BBC News* (2014) Edward Snowden: Leaks that Exposed US Spy Programme. January 17, 2014, www.bbc.com/news/world-us-canada-23123964.; Lee Rainie and Mary Madden (2015) Americans' Views on Government Surveillance Programs. *Pew Research Center*, 16 March, www.pewinternet.org/2015/03/16/americans-views-on-government-surveillance-programs/

40 Pieter Omtzigt, Netherlands, Group of the European People's Party, Committee on Legal Affairs and Human Rights (2015) Mass Surveillance. Parliamentary Assembly, Council of Europe; Luke Harding (205) Mass Surveillance Is Fundamental Threat to Human Rights, says European Report. *The Guardian*, 25 January 2015, www.theguardian.com/world/2015/jan/26/mass-surveillance-threat-human-rights-council-europe

41 Choe Sang-Hun (2008) South Korea Links Web Slander to Celebrity Suicides. *The New York Times*, 12 October 2008, www.nytimes.com/2008/10/12/technology/12iht-kstar.3.16877845.html

42 Outraged Stars to Fight Cyber Bullies. *The Korea Times*, 13 January 2016, www.koreatimes.co.kr/www/news/culture/2016/01/201_195178.html

is far more complicated in practice. Strengthening state capacity in digital spaces – such as the cybersecurity laws described in the previous section – invariably exacerbates concerns that these powers will be abused. In the case of Korea, for example, the requirement for real-name registration was first created as a response to cyberbullying and preventing internet users from hiding behind false IDs in 2007.[43] Portal operators were required to record the real IDs of users and were obliged to hand over this personal information when victims wanted to sue the attackers for libel or invasion of privacy.[44] But this law was challenged by the Constitutional Court of Korea for violations of freedom of expression, right of self-determination on private information and freedom of the press.[45] More specifically, the court ruled that Article 44–5 of the Act on Promotion of Information and Communications Network Utilisation and Information Protection was unconstitutional because it was an excessive restraint and other less restrictive ways could be utilised to protect individuals from cyberthreats.[46]

The perceived trade-off between the provision of cyber security by the state and the privacy of individuals becomes particularly salient in debates surrounding the issue of encryption and the use of tools to protect anonymity, such as onion routing, which are often blamed for facilitating criminal activities. States see these technologies as security threats rather than human rights protections.[47] On the other hand, David Kaye, the special rapporteur on the promotion and protection of the right to freedom of opinion and expression, has argued for the use of encryption and online anonymity to be expanded because it protects people from unlawful and arbitrary state interference.[48]

The issue of encryption has been most widely debated in the US with increasing reports of the US government being involved in the collection of phone records.[49] As an increasing number of criminal cases require access to electronic devices, the US government has been collecting phone records, but tech companies are strengthening their encryption products and services to protect the privacy of individuals and user data from hackers. As a result, the US government has openly accused tech companies in Silicon Valley of weakening security with strong encryption services. The case was most contentiously debated when the FBI requested Apple for access to an iPhone in order to find

43 South Korea Enforces New Law to Curb Cyber Bullying. *The Sydney Morning Herald*, June 28, 2007, www.smh.com.au/news/Technology/South-Korea-enforces-new-law-to-curb-cyber-bullying/2007/06/28/1182624070701.html

44 Ibid.

45 Identify Verification System on Internet, Global Freedom of Expression, Columbia University, https://globalfreedomofexpression.columbia.edu/cases/internet-identity-verification-system/

46 Ibid.

47 Daniel Moore and Thomas Rid (2016) Cryptopolitik and the Darknet. *Survival*, Vol. 58, No. 1 (2 January), 7–38, https://doi.org/10.1080/00396338.2016.1142085; Michael Chertoff (2017) A Public Policy Perspective of the Dark Web. *Journal of Cyber Policy*, Vol. 2, No. 1, 26–38, https://doi.org/10.1080/23738871.2017.1298643

48 UN Human Rights Council (2015) *Report of the Special Rapporteur on the Promotion and Protection of the Right to Freedom of Opinion and Expression, David Kaye*, A/HRC/29/32.

49 Dustin Volz (2018) Spy Agency NSA Triples Collection of U.S. Phone Records: Official Report. *Reuters* (5 May), www.reuters.com/article/us-usa-cyber-surveillance/spy-agency-nsa-triples-collection-of-u-s-phone-records-official-report-idUSKBN1I52FR; *BBC News* (2014); Charlie Savage (2018) N.S.A. Triples Collection of Data from U.S. Phone Companies. *The New York Times* (May 4), www.nytimes.com/2018/05/04/us/politics/nsa-surveillance-2017-annual-report.html; Harold Abelson et al. (2015) Keys under Doormats: Mandating Insecurity by Requiring Government Access to all Data and Communications. Computer Science and Artificial Intelligence Laboratory Technical Report, MIT-CSAIL-TR-2015–026, 6 July, http://dspace.mit.edu/bitstream/handle/1721.1/97690/MIT-CSAIL-TR-2015-026.pdf?sequence=8

information about the shooter in the San Bernardino attacks.[50] The case went to court, but it was eventually dropped because Apple was able to unlock the phone through a third-party.[51]

Similar cases have been reported in South Korea. It has been widely reported that the country's three main telecommunications companies – KT, SK Telecom and LG Uplus have been providing subscriber information to law-enforcement agencies when a request is made without any warrant or notification to customers.[52] In fact, from 2013 to 2016, there were 1,045,107 cases of provision of subscriber's information per year, which is 20% of the total population.[53] In 2016, big controversies were brought up when a hot-line between the police and telecommunication companies was revealed which was used for requesting and sharing unauthorised information.[54] The Korean government is also reported to have requested information from Naver, one of the leading search engines. In 2015, 223,940 personal accounts had been turned over to the authorities and this is an increase from previous years. In 2012, it was reported that 169,669 accounts had been submitted.[55]

Ultimately, there appear to be two solutions to criminality on the internet. The first is an expansion of law-enforcement powers, the solution being adopted in Korea and elsewhere, which raises new concerns about top-down human rights violations. The other option is to embrace privacy by design and anonymity by design, even if it means that some social ills may be aggravated in the process. Yet, it needs to be emphasised that technology alone cannot safeguard privacy. For example, unbreakable encryption will simply incentivise governments' use of more aggressive methods that can bypass encryption, such as malware tools designed to hijack citizens' devices.[56] This suggests that protecting the right to privacy requires a political and social consensus, forged at the national and international levels, regarding the appropriate balance between security and privacy. Who do we fear more? Our own state or hackers?

Challenges from beyond

This section will focus on the human rights challenge posed by the activities of foreign companies, states and non-state actors. Digital threats from beyond the state are an extension of the challenges discussed so far. However, the fact that they are occurring across

50 Arjun Kharpal (2016) Apple vs. FBI: All You Need to Know. *CNBC*, 29 March, www.cnbc.com/2016/03/29/apple-vs-fbi-all-you-need-to-know.html.; Spencer Ackerman and Sam Thielman (2016) FBI Director Admits Apple Encryption Case Could Set Legal Precedent. *The Guardian*, 25 February, www.theguardian.com/technology/2016/feb/25/fbi-director-james-comey-apple-encryption-case-legal-precedent

51 Kharpal (2016).

52 Se-Woong Koo (2015).

53 Korea Internet Transparency Reporting Team et al. (2017) Korea Internet Transparency Report 2017. (October), http://transparency.kr/wp-content/uploads/2017/10/Korea-Internet-Transparency-Report-2017.pdf

54 Tae Hun Kim (2016) Three Telecommunication Companies Provided Customer Information to Police and Prosecution Service through Hotline. *Hankyung Business Magazine*, 23 March 2016, http://magazine.hankyung.com/business/apps/news?popup=0&nid=01&c1=1004&nkey=2016032301060000651&mode=sub_view; Jun-ho Bang (2016) More Fears about NIS Taking Personal Info of Politicians, Journalists and Regular Folks. *Hankyoreh*, 13 March, http://english.hani.co.kr/arti/english_edition/e_national/734638.html

55 Jae Seop Kim (2016) Naver, Increasingly Proved User's Information to Investigating Authorities. *Hankyoreh*, 26 January, www.hani.co.kr/arti/economy/it/727903.html

56 Ben Buchanan (2016) Cryptography and Sovereignty. *Survival*, Vol. 58, No. 5, (November), 114, https://doi.org/10.1080/00396338.2016.1231534

borders makes them qualitatively different. For example, North Korea's cyber force, estimated to range between 3,000 to 6,000 hackers, has systematically attacked South Korean institutions, media organisations and politicians for nearly a decade.[57] As if that were not bad enough, sloppy safeguards by the private sector have regularly left Korean consumers vulnerable to massive data leaks, such as the 2011 hack of a social media site and a search engine which compromised the data of 35 million users, over half of the country's population. This attack is believed to have been carried out by a Chinese hacker who then sold the data to Korean scammers and voice phishers.[58] As these examples indicate, attacks on human rights from beyond the state vastly complicate attempts to identify perpetrators and seek remedies.

The key players in safeguarding human rights in the internet at the global level are transnational internet intermediaries, especially social media networks, search engines, and hosting services. As Rossi points out, the effective global standards of internet privacy are not being set by states or supranational legal authorities like the European Union, but by these large intermediaries, such as Facebook and Google.[59] Interestingly, these companies portray themselves as human rights protectors but are often blind to the human rights implications of their own business models.[60] In fact, multinational social media companies exercise considerable power through their user policies and technical design decisions, both of which directly impact privacy rights and the right to freedom of expression.[61] More worrisome, internet intermediaries often take deliberate actions to further obfuscate their human rights obligations, such as Facebook's controversial move in 2018 to shift the responsibility for the privacy of 1.5 billion users from its headquarters in Ireland, which would fall under the protections of the EU's General Data Protection Regulation, to the US, where privacy laws are relatively weaker.[62] An important protection for victims of transnational technology companies is offered by the United Nations' *Guiding Principles on Business and Human Rights*, which stipulates that businesses have a responsibility to respect human rights by avoiding and mitigating violations and by providing access to remedies. However, it has been pointed out that these principles are non-binding and they were not designed with internet intermediaries in mind, which may limit their usefulness.[63]

This situation is further complicated by the symbiotic relationship between national intelligence agencies and large technology companies, which should be considered key

57 Emma Chanlett-Avery et al. (2017) *North Korean Cyber Capabilities: In Brief.* Washington, DC: Congressional Research Service, August 3, 2.

58 Sung-jin Yang (2011) 35m Cyworld, Nate Users' Information Hacked. *The Korea Herald* (July 28), www.koreaherald.com/view.php?ud=20110728000881

59 Agustín Rossi (2014) Internet Privacy: Who Sets the Global Standard? *The International Spectator*, Vol. 49, No. 1 (2 January), 65–80, https://doi.org/10.1080/03932729.2014.875823

60 Rikke Frank Jørgensen (2018) Framing Human Rights: Exploring Storytelling within Internet Companies. *Information, Communication & Society*, Vol. 21, No. 3 (March), 340–355, https://doi.org/10.1080/1369118X.2017.1289233

61 L. DeNardis and A. M. Hackl (2015) Internet Governance by Social Media Platforms. *Telecommunications Policy*, Vol. 39, No. 9, 761–770, https://doi.org/10.1016/j.telpol.2015.04.003

62 Alex Hern (2018) Facebook Moves 1.5bn Users out of Reach of New European Privacy Law. *The Guardian* (19 April), www.theguardian.com/technology/2018/apr/19/facebook-moves-15bn-users-out-of-reach-of-new-european-privacy-law

63 Yael Ronen (2015) Big Brother's Little Helpers: The Right to Privacy and the Responsibility of Internet Service Providers. *Utrecht Journal of International and European Law*, Vol. 31, 72–86; For more on the possible blind spots of this framework, see Sarah Joseph (2016) "Is Fox News a Breach of Human Rights?": The News Media's Immunity from the Guiding Principles on Business and Human Rights. *Business and Human Rights Journal*, Vol. 1, No. 2 (July), 229–253, https://doi.org/10.1017/bhj.2016.10

"locations of control" due to their possession of vast amounts of personal data.[64] A frequent complaint by larger internet intermediaries, which are spread out across multiple legal jurisdictions, is that there is no common regulatory framework for them to respond to state requests for information.[65] At other times, states have been guilty of covert operations aimed at subverting these companies, even when they are headquartered in allied countries. An infamous example of this was the theft of encryption keys, designed to safeguard the SIM cards used in cell phones, from Gemalto, a Dutch multinational, by the US National Security Agency (NSA) and the UK Government Communications Headquarters (GCHQ).[66]

Compared to many other countries, South Korea's ability to control and regulate the activities of foreign companies is relatively strong. South Korea's Personal Information Protection Act (PIPA), which came into force in 2012, creates a legal regime governing the export of consumers' data. It is celebrated as one of the strongest in the world, at least on paper.[67] The country has fought several battles with Google over the export of mapping data and levied a token fine on the company over the misuse of consumer's personal information in 2014.[68] This appears to indicate a strong willingness to protect individual rights by the South Korean government but in truth these strong domestic data regulations have a strong national security orientation – a shortcoming evident in the legislation of other countries as well.[69] Data localisation requirements have also been cited as being overt protectionist measures that favour domestic companies and erode the liberal trade order.[70] Finally, the South Korean government's strong protection of its citizens' data rights – from foreign interference – should be juxtaposed with its past record of attacks on the digital privacy of its own citizens.[71]

The final challenge is the growing development and use of cyberwarfare capabilities and the lack of international legal norms governing the use of these tools. Although the use of armed force is covered by international humanitarian law, there is no similar consensus regarding cyberattacks.[72] North Korea's cyber force, for example, is believed to have stolen at least 235 gigabytes of classified data from the South Korean government in

64 Arne Hintz (2014) Outsourcing Surveillance – Privatising Policy: Communications Regulation by Commercial Intermediaries. *Birkbeck Law Review*, Vol. 2, 359–360.

65 Dan Jerker B. Svantesson (2014) Between a Rock and a Hard Place – An International Law Perspective of the Difficult Position of Globally Active Internet Intermediaries. *Computer Law & Security Review*, Vol. 30, No. 4 (August), 348–356, https://doi.org/10.1016/j.clsr.2014.05.005

66 Maria Helen Murphy (2016) Technological Solutions to Privacy Questions: What Is the Role of Law? *Information & Communications Technology Law*, Vol. 25, No. 1, 26–27, https://doi.org/10.1080/13600834.2015.1134148

67 Haksoo Ko et al. (2017) Structure and Enforcement of Data Privacy Law in South Korea. *International Data Privacy Law*, Vol. 7, No. 2 (May), 100–114, https://doi.org/10.1093/idpl/ipx004

68 Young-won Kim (2014) Google Fined W210m for Data Gathering. *The Korea Herald* (28 January), www.koreaherald.com/view.php?ud=20140128001166

69 Ira S. Rubinstein, Gregory T. Nojeim and Ronald D. Lee (2014) Systematic Government Access to Personal Data: A Comparative Analysis. *International Data Privacy Law*, Vol. 4, No. 2, 96–119, https://doi.org/10.1093/idpl/ipu004

70 Chan-Mo Chung (2018) Data Localization: The Causes, Evolving International Regimes and Korean Practices. *Journal of World Trade*, Vol. 52, No. 2, 187–208.

71 For some examples, see Freedom House (2017) Freedom on the Net 2017 – South Korea, https://freedomhouse.org/sites/default/files/FOTN%202017_South%20Korea.pdf

72 Jody Prescott (2011) War by Analogy. *The RUSI Journal*, Vol. 156, No. 6, 32–39, https://doi.org/10.1080/03071847.2011.642683

2016, including US-ROK joint war plans.[73] While this could be interpreted as legitimate espionage in the interests of national security, North Korea's suspected complicity in the Wannacry ransomware attacks in May 2017, which affected users in over 100 countries, including the National Health Service in the UK, went unpunished even though it targeted civilians and non-military targets.[74] The secretive nature of these attacks makes it difficult to assign blame and seek remedy for human rights violations. Further complicating the issue of attribution are the presence of criminal organisations and terrorist groups that use commercial software and may even temporarily ally with state intelligence agencies – as in the case of Lazarus Group, which is believed to be cooperating with the North Korean government. Such foreign threats have justified the South Korean government's procurement and use of sophisticated foreign spyware, despite allegations that these tools may be used against its own population.[75]

The rise of hostile non-state groups on the internet has further exacerbated security concerns. If early surveillance regimes used the internet to track real-world threats, now the threats themselves are online. Jihadist groups such as Al-Qaida and ISIS have actively used the internet for recruitment, planning and operations.[76] This has given rise to the concept of cyberterrorism, a contested term which broadly refers to politically motivated attacks on information or information processes.[77] These new threats often push human rights farther down the agenda even as they encourage new forms of intergovernmental cooperation. The European Convention on Cybercrime, for example, broadly strengthens protections against non-state actors but does not employ a human rights approach, and by outsourcing surveillance and law enforcement-type activities across borders can even aggravate the risk of human rights violations by states and corporations.[78] This is seen by the tendency for cooperation between state intelligence agencies to circumvent each other's domestic laws and judicial review.[79] According to the UN Human Rights Council, "there is credible information to suggest that some Governments systematically have routed data collection and analytical tasks through jurisdictions with weaker safeguards for privacy".[80] Paradoxically, international cooperation is weakening human rights protections.

73 Choe Sang-Hun (2017) North Korean Hackers Stole U.S.-South Korean Military Plans, Lawmaker Says. *The New York Times* (20 October), www.nytimes.com/2017/10/10/world/asia/north-korea-hack-war-plans.html

74 Rash or Rational? North Korea and the Threat It Poses. House of Commons Defence Committee (5 April 2018), 18, 20.

75 Bill Marczak and Sarah McKune (2015) What We Know about the South Korea NIS's Use of Hacking Team's RCS. The Citizen Lab (August 9) https://citizenlab.ca/2015/08/what-we-know-about-the-south-korea-niss-use-of-hacking-teams-rcs/

76 Martin Rudner (2017) "Electronic Jihad": The Internet as Al Qaeda's Catalyst for Global Terror. *Studies in Conflict & Terrorism*, Vol. 40, No. 1, 10–23, https://doi.org/10.1080/1057610X.2016.1157403

77 For an early definition see Bill Nelson et al. (1999) *Cyberterror Prospects and Implications*. Monterey, CA: Center for the Study of Terrorism and Irregular Warfare, https://calhoun.nps.edu/handle/10945/27344; Also see Anna-Maria Talihärm (2010) Cyberterrorism: In Theory or in Practice? *Defence Against Terrorism Review*, Vol. 3, No. 2 (Fall), 59–74.

78 Judith Bessant (2012) Human Rights, the Law, Cyber-Security and Democracy: After the European Convention. *Australian Journal of Human Rights*, Vol. 18, No. 1 (1 April), 20, https://doi.org/10.1080/1323-238X.2012.11882096

79 Privacy International (2018) Secret Global Surveillance Networks: Intelligence Sharing Between Governments and the Need for Safeguards (London, UK, April 2018), https://privacyinternational.org/sites/default/files/2018-04/Secret%20Global%20Surveillance%20Networks%20report%20web%20%28200%29.pdf

80 UN Human Rights Council (2014) *The Right to Privacy in the Digital Age*, A/HRC/27/37, para. 30.

Conclusion

The primary challenge of safeguarding human rights on the internet is often considered to be striking a balance between security and privacy.[81] However, this chapter suggests that the real dilemma is how to reconcile legal, technical and political responses to three distinct types of threats to human rights in the internet. The first is the threat that governments pose to their own citizens. The second is the broad spectrum of bottom-up danger emanating from individuals and non-state groups. The third consists of threats from beyond the state posed by individuals, organised groups, and foreign governments. These threats are deeply interlinked and solutions that focus on one side of the puzzle will exacerbate other types of threats. Thus, new types of encryption to safeguard citizens' communications from the prying eyes of governments may end up empowering new forms of bottom-up criminal and terrorist activity. Conversely, the same spyware and malware that can thwart foreign attackers may become useful tools to track and eliminate domestic dissent. There are no easy answers to this three-sided dilemma.

In practice, though, governments around the world have preferred to focus on threats from beyond and below, resulting in a reassertion of state sovereignty over the internet. Cybersecurity concerns are increasingly used as a justification for strict regulatory regimes which place limits on citizens' freedom of expression and access to information.[82] This process, which is marked by data localisation requirements and heightened surveillance of online communications, is not only happening in China and Russia but also in the United States, the European Union, South Korea, and other countries, all of which are ostensibly worried about terrorist activity online. Looming above this all are structural shifts in internet governance and the rise of powerful technology companies that operate across borders and have a vested interest in collecting and using personal data to make a profit. Most discussions of human rights on the internet still focus on civil and political rights, but perhaps more basic questions of social and economic autonomy need to be raised. As Bernal reminds us, powerful companies such as Google and Apple are effectively dedicated to knowing "what someone is thinking".[83]

While internet regulations have increased on the domestic level, international human rights bodies have also worked to address cybersecurity threats based on a human rights approach considering its transnational nature. In particular, there is emphasis by human rights advocates for compliance of international human rights law both offline and online. The Human Rights Council (HRC) addressed human rights issues online in 2012 through a resolution on the promotion, protection and enjoyment of human rights on the internet, and in 2014 called for states to

> address security concerns on the Internet in accordance with their international human rights obligations to ensure protection of freedom of expression, freedom of association, privacy and other human rights online, including through national

81 Eloise F. Malone and Michael J. Malone (2013) The "Wicked Problem" of Cybersecurity Policy: Analysis of United States and Canadian Policy Response. *Canadian Foreign Policy Journal*, Vol. 19, No. 2, 158–177, https://doi.org/10.1080/11926422.2013.805152

82 Marietje Schaake and Mathias Vermeulen (2016) Towards a Values-Based European Foreign Policy to Cybersecurity. *Journal of Cyber Policy*, Vol. 1, No. 1 (2 January), 75–84, https://doi.org/10.1080/23738871.2016.1157617

83 Paul Bernal (2016) Data Gathering, Surveillance and Human Rights: Recasting the Debate. *Journal of Cyber Policy*, Vol. 1, No. 2 (2 July), 254–255, https://doi.org/10.1080/23738871.2016.1228990

democratic, transparent institutions, based on the rule of law, in a way that ensures freedom and security on the Internet.[84]

The UN General Assembly also affirmed both the right to privacy and the negative impact of surveillance and interception of communications on human rights in Resolution 68/167 in 2013.[85]

Other multistakeholder initiatives have made attempts to provide a set of principles for governing behaviour in cyberspace. For example, through the London Process or the Global Conference on Cyber Space which was established in 2011, hundreds of participants gather to discuss emerging issues and conclude with the Chair's statements.[86] In October 2013, the third conference was held in Seoul, providing the most important outcome which resulted in the Seoul Framework for Commitment to Open and Secure Cyberspace.[87] With 1600 delegates from eighty-seven countries, eighteen international and regional organisations as well as research centres and private enterprises, this conference was one of the largest conferences on cyberspace.[88] The framework essentially reaffirmed principles under international law, emphasising that the same rights that people have offline must also be protected online, particularly freedom of expression.[89] While these are all positive developments, these initiatives do not provide specific guidelines for states. Thus, more multistakeholder initiatives should aim to provide more specific guidelines and to enhance transparency in the system. For example, questions remain as to what extent states should be able to regulate the internet for purposes of cyber security when there are risks of violating human rights online. It is ultimately up to the state to decide, but governments are often not sufficiently aware of the human rights risks, and thus, more international guidelines should be developed for states in order to ensure they are able to identify the human rights risks involved in response to potential cyber security threats and to exercise preventive measures and effective responses in accordance with international human rights norms.

Finally, it needs to be emphasised that although this chapter focused mostly on the rights to privacy and freedom of expression, there is a broader spectrum of human rights threatened in the internet from above, below and beyond. As pointed out by the Human Rights Council, digital practices by state and non-state actors additionally impact the right to receive and impart information, freedom of assembly and association, and the

84 UN General Assembly (2012) *The Promotion, Protection and Enjoyment of Human Rights on the Internet.* Human Rights Council 20th Session, Agenda item 3, A/HRC/20/L. 13, 29 June, https://documents-dds-ny.un.org/doc/UNDOC/LTD/G12/147/10/PDF/G1214710.pdf?OpenElement; UN General Assembly (2014) *The Promotion, Protection and Enjoyment of Human Rights on the Internet.* Human Rights Council 26th Session, Agenda item 3, A/HRC/26/L.24, 20 June, https://documents-dds-ny.un.org/doc/UNDOC/LTD/G14/059/67/PDF/G1405967.pdf?OpenElement

85 UN General Assembly (2014) *Resolution adopted by the General Assembly on 18 December 2013: 68/167. The Right to Privacy in the Digital Age*, Sixty-eighth session, Agenda item 69(b), A/RES/68/167, 21 January, http://undocs.org/A/RES/68/167

86 Global Forum on Cyber Expertise (2018) Global Conference on Cyber Space, www.thegfce.com/about/gccs (accessed 23.5.2018).

87 Global Conference on Cyber Space (2018) Global Conference on CyberSpace 2013, www.gccs2015.com/seoul-17-18-october-2013 (accessed 23.5.2018).

88 Ibid.

89 Association for Progressive Communications (2015) What is the Global Conference on Cyberspace? FAQs on the GCCS, The Hague, 16–17 April 2015, www.apc.org/en/news/what-global-conference-cyberspace-faqs-gccs-hague-16-17-april-2015 (accessed 23.5.2018).

right of family life, among others.[90] Looking into the future, it is important to note that the boundary between online threats and offline threats is blurring. The rapid growth of the Internet of Things (IoT) and fusion of digital, material and biological spaces in the Fourth Industrial Revolution raise the possibility of state and non-state actors being able to violate physical integrity over the internet through the hacking of medical implants, critical infrastructure, autonomous cars, or various types of household appliances.[91] This close interlinkage between three different threats and the narrowing boundary between offline and online rights needs to be closely considered by the international community as it seeks to strengthen human rights protections in an era of deep technological transformation.

90 UN Human Rights Council, *The Right to Privacy in the Digital Age*, para. 14.

91 For scenarios involving cars, see L. Pan et al. (2017) Cyber Security Attacks to Modern Vehicular Systems. *Journal of Information Security and Applications*, Vol. 36, (October), 90–100, https://doi.org/10.1016/j.jisa.2017.08.005; Schwab 88.

7 Liability regimes for online human rights violations

Sten Schaumburg-Müller

Introduction: liability and liability regimes

Liability is an important part of human life and human interaction. In fact, we cannot comprehend human action if we do not think in terms of liability. If we cannot understand that a certain person is responsible for an act, we simply cannot understand human behaviour and we cannot make sense of the world inhabited by human beings. And similarly, if we cannot ascribe liability to the person – or perhaps reject liability for one reason or the other – we cannot have a system of workable human interaction. Acting seems to involve responsibility, and somehow human beings are bound to make up a system of workable liability.

However, it is not that easy. *Firstly*, there are conceptual problems. Am I responsible for having fallen ill? Perhaps I should not have been smoking heavily, or been on such a fat and sugary diet. Or perhaps it is even punishment for my sinful life, including my evil thoughts and the hidden desire for my neighbour's spouse. And should I also be liable and forfeit my right to free hospitalisation if I have been a heavy smoker, or pay a higher insurance premium for my bad habits? *Secondly*, there are political problems, so to speak, issues of interests. The tobacco industry has its interest, and so does the cancer patient and the tax payers. And as universal as the necessity of ascription of responsibility and liability appears, the propensity to reject one's liability appears similarly universal. In addition, the disclaiming of responsibility and liability often invokes more general and even (alleged) universal principles. *Thirdly*, there are problems of which law or which perception of responsibility prevails where and when. Even though the ascription of (legal) responsibility seems universal, the solutions are obviously not. Unborn children have been held liable for their forefathers' acts, rats and other animals were held liable in the Middle Ages, and as a point of departure companies cannot be held liable under criminal German law, just to mention a few examples that differ markedly from contemporary mainstream liability ascription.

The following may be illustrative. In Karen Blixen's *Out of Africa*, the author tells a story of a sad incident.[1] She does it in order to point out particularities in "African" thought, but I'd rather see it as an account of different liability regimes, the propensity to reject liability, and the legal mess of several liability regimes. Blixen had a coffee farm, and she had a number of people working for her. One of the tasks was to bring the coffee from the fields to the grinding mill, which was done by oxcarts driven by young males. The young females were fond of jumping on the carts when they were driven from the field.

1 Karen Blixen (1942) *Den afrikanske Farm*. København: Gyldendals Boghandel, 105ff. English title *Out of Africa*, translation by Blixen.

Blixen had this behaviour banned, perhaps because it could be dangerous, perhaps because it was a waste of time. Therefore, the girls used to leave the oxcart before getting near the mill. One day, a young girl who was jumping off from the cart fell so unfortunately that the wheel drove over her head and as a consequence, she died. The parents therefore came to claim compensation for their loss. Blixen rejected any liability, explaining to the reader that the African parents were unable to see that she had not committed any mistake and therefore was not responsible. Implicitly, the author assumed that "fault" constitutes a natural and necessary prerequisite for liability. However, as a goodwill payment she paid the equivalent to that of a sheep to the parents for their situation and their efforts. After the incident, some colonial policemen showed up, who according to Blixen brought more mess than solutions to the situation.

Here we have the ingredients: A situation which involves questions of responsibility and liability, and whose solution is not self-evident but involves conceptual issues as well as issues of differing interests. A rejection of liability with reference to alleged universal principles. And a mess of legal regimes, here including colonial law, African customary law and a perception of general principles of liability.

My point is, of course, that we have a similar situation in relation to online human rights violations. They involve questions of liability and responsibility, solutions involve conceptual issues as well as issues of interests, rejection of liability (e.g. by internet service providers) with implicit and dubious reference to general principles, and a mess of legal regimes, national law, international law, company law, perhaps even internet customary law etc.

The present chapter seeks to analyse the situation further. First, I sketch out the implicit construction of liability for human rights violations in the Universal Declaration of Human Rights. In the following sections, I shall take the European Human Rights Conventions as a point of departure, dealing with online private life violations, the opposing concepts of "anonymity" and "living together", and online freedom of speech violations. Finally, I sketch out some local problems and solutions.

Human rights violations: who is responsible?

In December 1948 the UN General Assembly adopted the Universal Declaration of Human Rights, a landmark in international human rights history.[2] In the preamble it spoke of "inherent dignity" and of "the equal and inalienable rights of all members of the human family", which according to the Declaration is the foundation of "freedom, justice and peace in the world", no less. In thirty succinct articles, the Declaration spells out the basic rights, covering basic civil, political, social, economic and cultural rights plus the right to a "social and international order", which evades the listed categories of rights, but is equally important, also and perhaps especially when it comes to digital society and the internet.

One major shortcoming of the Declaration, which was realised already at the time of the drafting, is the absence of any clear means of implementation. The Declaration vaguely speaks of "a pledge" which the member states have made for themselves, a pledge to "achieve . . . the promotion of universal respect for and observance of human rights and fundamental freedoms", and it also points out that "every individual and every organ of

2 Splendidly accounted for in Mary Ann Glendon (2002) *A World Made New*. New York: Random House.

society . . . shall strive . . . to promote respect for these rights and freedoms". The Declaration also emphasises that the "measures" to be taken – measures not being specified in any way – are not only needed at the national, but also at the international level.[3]

Thus, the Declaration gives us some hints as to the implementation: Member states, the UN, individual and "organs of society" all have a responsibility, at the national as well as the international level. What kind of responsibility for which kind of actors is not spelled out, nor is the relation between the national and the international levels.

Later developments have pulled in the direction of public international law. States have signed and ratified a range of human rights conventions, and thereby they have created international obligations in relation to the national legal order and they have created international organs such as human rights institutions, committees, commissions and courts. The UN, itself a creation of public international law, has also created various organs, such as the Human Rights Council. However, it is a point worth mentioning that the Declaration did not exclusively focus on public international law. Organs of society are pointed out as relevant actors with – undefined – human rights responsibilities. I take "organs" to encompass not only civil society organisations (NGOs), some of which has played a significant part in promoting human rights, but also companies and especially transnational companies (TNCs). The role of the latter in relation to human rights promotion is much less defined, at the international[4] as well as at the national level.[5]

In this regard, one could consider a possible "transnational" level beyond the national and international spheres. In public international law there is an easy distinction between the national (or domestic) level which is basically matters *within* the state, and the international level, matters *between* the states. Human rights institutions such as the Council of Europe and the European Court of Human Rights and the corresponding Inter-American and African institutions easily fall within the national/international frame. However, other relevant human rights issues do not. Climate problems, external repercussions of national decisions or acts, to some extent migration, and to a large extent the activities of TNCs, are not readily reducible to the national/international categorisation. Relevant for the present approach, the internet and the ensuing digital society/ies[6] clearly has transnational aspects besides and beyond the national and international aspects. The internet itself is a means of communication that does not easily fall into strict categories of national borders, it does not easily lend itself to national or international regulation, and its actors are more transnational than national or international. Tech giants such as Microsoft, Google and Facebook provide services to the global community (or perhaps rather: global communities), to a large extent without borders, and they do not easily fall under national or international regulations. The same goes for the more clandestine activities by internet trolls whose problematic activities are neither easily detected, nor easily targeted.

Returning to the Universal Declaration of Human Rights, I briefly showed the vagueness as to the implementation of the fundamental human rights and the important question of who is responsible for what. And despite the enormous development within

3 The Declaration makes sure to mention that the rights are not only for the people of the member states but also for "the peoples of territories under their jurisdiction". By 1948 a large part of the human population was still under colonial rule.

4 See e.g. Guiding Principles on Business and Human Rights. Implementing the United Nations, "Protect, Respect and Remedy" Framework. UN, 2011.

5 I have no proper research on this point, it is rather a qualified assumption.

6 It may be misleading to talk of one digital society.

international human rights law (and within a number of national human rights regimes), I contend that we presently are in a rather similar situation. Indeed, we do have a much more developed human rights law which deals with responsibility and liability, but it is by no means clear as to who holds which liability in relation to digital society phenomena, including online human rights violations. We still struggle with conceptual issues such as understanding the social media – are they like traditional media or mere internet service providers or something else? – and there are all sorts of interests involved, ranging from large companies who would rather keep their business model largely exempt from costly liabilities, internet activists who would rather claim freedom of speech than take responsibility for their (speech) acts, to internet trolls who may have a particular interest in stirring up trouble. And as for law, there are different and partly incommensurable liability regimes, ranging from all sorts of differing domestic law over public international law to transnational law, including the terms offered by large online companies, which mainly seeks to bypass non-US domestic law and keep liability at bay.

Online private life violations: who is responsible for what?

Private life is probably *the* human right most challenged by online activities. I use the term "private life" rather than "privacy", firstly because this is the wording of ECHR Art. 8. Secondly, the former Commission pointed out that "private life" is a broader and more encompassing term than "privacy",[7] and thirdly, I tend to conceive "privacy" as more of a tradeable commodity – e.g. you can trade your private data for access to various online services – whereas "private life" is a more basic right, necessary for the development of the personality,[8] and ultimately for democracy.[9]

Private life human rights protection covers a very large range of issues from public authorities' surveillance and use of personal data, access to knowledge of one's biological origin to expulsion issues and publication of threats, pictures, rumours and allegations. Indeed, the Court emphasises that "private life is a broad term not susceptible to exhaustive definition".[10] For the present purpose, dealing with online violations and liability regimes, I limit the presentation to non-state parties' online activities.

According to the case law of the European Human Rights Court, the member states do not only have negative obligations, implying that states should not intervene in anyone's private life except in circumstances provided for in Art. 8(2). The states also have positive obligations in order to secure that the right to private life is not interfered with by private actors, or rather that there are adequate legal measures available if such interference occurs.

In *X and Y v. the Netherlands* 26 March 1986, the Court held that it was a violation of Art. 8 not to have procedures in place which could secure criminal prosecution against a person charged with rape of a handicapped girl, and as early as 1979 the Court found Art. 8 to be violated because a married woman could not divorce her negligent and violent

7 *X v. Iceland*, the Commission 18 May 1976, appl. nr. 6825/74.

8 See e.g. *Hannover v. Germany (no.2)* 7 Feb 2012 GC, pr. 95; also *Paradiso & Campanelli* 24 Jan 2017 GC, pr. 160.

9 I base this on a reading of Jürgen Habermas, *Strukturwandel der Öffentlichkeit*, in which he shows that a well-functioning public sphere is a prerequisite for democracy. Perhaps less noticed, Habermas also shows that the development of a private sphere is as much a prerequisite for a well-functioning democracy. I elaborate on this in "Borgerlig privathed i en digitaliseret verden" [The Private Sphere in a Digitalized World], *Retfærd*, 2016, No. 1, 19–37.

10 *Barbulescu v. Romania* 5 Sept 2017 GC, para. 70.

husband, because divorce was only possible before a court of law and she could not afford the costs, cf. *Airey v. Ireland* 9 Oct 1979.[11]

Of course, criminalisation is not the only way for a member state to fulfil its positive obligations, and there is a margin of appreciation for the states to decide which measures are appropriate. Still, the Court emphasises that the measures taken must be proportionate in relation to the severity of the act, and if the relevant activities involve a most intimate aspect of private life, the margin is narrowed.[12]

In relation to online violations the following judgment may be illustrative:

> In *K.U. v. Finland* 2 Dec 2008 the Court found Art. 8 to be violated because at the time there was no legal remedy in place in Finland to have a person (or persons) identified who had uploaded defamatory content. The case was rather serious, as the relevant material was presented as if a boy, who was 12 years at the time and identified by name, was looking for homosexual relationships with experienced men. The Court notes that it is to no avail criminalizing an act if there are no ways to identify an alleged offender and bring him to justice, pr. 63. It follows, I contend, that for any violation of Art. 8, the state must provide for procedures enabling the offended to bring action – criminal or civil according to the seriousness of the action. If it is not practically possible to identity the actual offender – and of course there is no requirement under Art. 8 for the State to do the impossible[13] – one could argue that the state must provide for adequate measures for complicity. If, say, an online media allows for anonymous content, it may be necessary to be able to hold the media liable for the content. See further the discussion relating to *Delfi v. Estonia*.

Exactly which measures are taken and which procedures are put in place is to a large extent under the margin of appreciation of the state. In *Egill Einarsson v. Iceland* (no. 2) 17 July 2018, the central question was whether the declaration of an (unfounded) accusation to be "null and void" was sufficient or whether it was a violation of Art. 8 not to receive non-pecuniary damages and to be required to pay the costs. The Court found no violation of Art. 8 in this case. Obviously, there is still a question of proportionality, and the sanctions may be judged too lenient[14] or too harsh.[15] Also one may critically remark that costs in defamation cases – not sanctions but merely fees to the court, to lawyers etc. – may have a preventive character, which may in real life undermine the substantial rights.

In the otherwise well-known and much debated case of *von Hannover v. Germany* (no.1) 24 June 2004 there is an aspect which may be less known. One of the arguments for establishing a violation of Art. 8 was the fact that the complainant was under "continual harassment". Not only did the Court point out the relevance of private life protection even in public places, but it also emphasised the element of being under constant surveillance by paparazzi photographers which constituted a situation of continual harassment (pr. 59).

11 On this count it was a close 4–3 judgment. However, this does not seem to render to judgment less influential, see e.g. *Hämäläinen v. Finland* 16 July 2014 GC, pr. 63: "this obligation [i.e. a positive obligation under Art. 8] may involve the adoption of specific measures, including the provision of an effective and accessible means of protecting the right to respect for private life".

12 *Söderman v. Sweden* 12 Nov 2013 GC, pr. 79; See also *Mosley v. UK* 18 May 2011, 108–111.

13 *K.U. v. Finland* 2 Dec 2008, para. 28.

14 *Biriuk v. Lihuania* 25 Nov 2008.

15 E.g. *Tolstoy Miloslavski v. UK* 13 July 1995; *Steel & Morris v. UK* 25 Feb 2005.

This aspect may also be relevant in cases of online private life violations. It is one thing to have one's pictures taken when in a public place, even if it is embarrassing, but it is quite another to continuously have photographers ready at any time to take pictures and later have them published. Similarly, it is one thing to receive harsh and disparaging comments on a website thread, but it is quite another to receive this kind of unwanted attention on a continuous basis. If there are no national remedies for this kind of situation, which is likely to appear especially online, it may be an issue under Art. 8.

For the present purpose, *Delfi v. Estonia* 16 June 2015 GC, another well-known and much debated case, is interesting in two ways. *Firstly*, the Court emphasises that "the risk of harm posed by content and communications on the Internet to the exercise and enjoyment of human rights and freedoms, particularly the right to respect for private life, is certainly higher than that posed by the press", para. 133. This implies that the legal means which the member states are required to establish must be at least as efficient and accessible as the ones in relation to the press. And it implies that, even though the member states enjoy a certain margin of appreciation, it is not in good accordance with Art. 8 to have smooth complaint procedures when dealing with the traditional media and only cumbersome and expensive procedures when it comes to online violations.

Secondly, the outcome of *Delfi* emphasises the possibility of media liability. The question for the Court was to determine whether it was a violation of Art. 10 to sanction the media for racist remarks, made anonymously, appearing on the Delfi's website for 6 weeks and deleted as soon as the offended asked for it. There were many intervenients in favour of the media, and the judgment has been widely criticised. In contrast, I assert that it is a good and useful judgment. None of the intervenients take Art. 8 into consideration, and of course it is always easy to find a solution when half of the equation is left out. In its judgment, the Court assigns great weight to the following facts: the media in question produced income by the amount of comments, it was not a mere service provider but produced content itself and did in fact edit the comments, and the sanction was not severe. (para. 144, 145 and 160). The judgment, of course, does not imply that from now on, media are always liable for the content. In fact, the Court emphasises that the exact opposite is the case. Strict liability would be a violation of Art. 10.[16] The judgment is not in conflict with EU law, either. The E-commerce Directive,[17] Art.14 states that a mere host cannot be held liable unless there has been a notification of the content and the host proceeds by doing nothing. In *Delfi*, the media in fact took the contested content down immediately upon notice. However, in the preamble no. 42, the Directive states that "the exemptions from liability established in this Directive cover only cases where the activity . . . is of a mere technical, automatic and passive nature". In other words, the exclusion of liability under Art. 14 of the Directive only pertains to technical "hosts", not to more active agents. It is obvious that Delfi was providing more than technical assistance: The media was highly active, called for comments, earned income according to the number of comments, produced its own content and edited external content. Whether the fact that the media provides content on its own is crucial for the option of liability has

16 *Magyar TE v. Hungary* 2 Feb 2016; *Pihl v. Sweden* 9 March 2017 (decision).

17 Directive 2000/31/EC of the European Parliament and of the Council of 8 June 2000 on certain legal aspects of information society services, in particular electronic commerce, in the Internal Market ("Directive on electronic commerce").

not been decided by the judgment. I tend to be of the opinion that the mere fact of editing is sufficient to render Art. 14 of the Directive useless. Once an online media – it could be Facebook to mention an important actor – edits content on its own initiative, such as deleting or hiding nudity, it is no longer a mere technical provider, hence Art. 14 is not applicable, and hence it is up to the member states to provide liability which fulfils the requirements of ECHR Art. 10 *and* of Art. 8.

From this it does not follow that the online media must always be liable, but it does follow that rendering the media liable is not in itself a violation of ECHR Art. 10. And it also follows that it could very well constitute a violation of Art. 8 if no one can be held liable for online violations (see the preceding discussion in relation to positive obligation). If the offender is anonymous, or if the offender cannot be prosecuted according to national law, this may involve a violation of Art. 8.

Summing up Art. 8 does not involve larger questions as to the concept of "private life". But there are other pressing conceptual problems. One, obviously, is the understanding of intermediaries and the connected ascription of liability. The E-commerce Directive is not overly helpful, which is hardly surprising since it dates back to the year 2000, which in relation to the technology is a long time ago. However, it *is* sufficiently clear that monitoring and any kind of editing on the media's own initiative is not a mere technical activity but involves knowledge and control.[18]

It is also clear that there are large interests involved. To quote Marc Zuckerberg: "Governments sometimes order us to remove content they believe is illegal but doesn't violate our Community Standards. . . . We fight to protect our community from unnecessary or overreaching government intervention".[19] In other words, Facebook would rather not abide by democratically adopted laws – which may include company liability for content – but rather stick to their own rules without interference from governments, legislators, human rights courts or anyone else. In addition, the euphemism "community standard" is applied, thus attempting to hide the fact that the company is in charge – a kind of company sovereignty – not any other "community" participant.

This also highlights the issue of liability regimes. Facebook tries to uphold its own liability regime (no liability for the company) whereas other stakeholders such as the European Court of Human Rights mete out some responsibility to member states in order to guarantee private life vis-à-vis companies. It is questionable whether states live up to their responsibility and deliver a human-rights abiding liability regime in relation to online private life infringements.

Anonymity and living together

There is a widespread consensus that anonymity is a value and worth protecting. Since the Court also has decided that "living together" is an important value, entailing that a ban on face covering in public places is acceptable under Art. 8, it is worth considering how and whether the values of anonymity and of living together are reconcilable. How is it possible to guarantee anonymity and at the same time make sure that you know who you are dealing with when entering the public sphere?

18 Cf. the wording of preamble no. 42. Similarly, the prohibition of a general obligation to monitor content in Art. 15 of the Directive is irrelevant for actors who monitor and edit on their own initiative.

19 Mark Zuckerberg, 15 March 2015. The quote is no longer accessible.

In *Delfi v. Estonia* 16 June 2015 GC the Court has the following consideration with regards to anonymity:

> the Court is mindful of the interest of Internet users in not disclosing their identity.
>
> Anonymity has long been a means of avoiding reprisals or unwanted attention. As such, it is capable of promoting the free flow of ideas and information in an important manner, including, notably, on the Internet. At the same time, the Court does not lose sight of the ease, scope and speed of the dissemination of information on the Internet, and the persistence of the information once disclosed, which may considerably aggravate the effects of unlawful speech on the Internet compared to traditional media. (para. 147)

As is often the case, the Court adopts a balanced view, reiterated in para. 149: "anonymity on the Internet... (is) an important value, (but) must be balanced against other rights and interests". Anonymity is a value but carries its dangers as well. Still, some aspects ought to be added to the balance. Firstly, the desire to avoid reprisals and unwanted attention is ubiquitous in the way that it is a common human feature to shun responsibility. This goes for swindlers and fraudsters as well. Attention is unwanted, let alone reprisals. Admittedly – and importantly – internet users are not necessarily swindlers or fraudsters. But they may be, and this fact needs to be taken into consideration when doing the balancing exercise. This leads to the second point that while it is true that anonymity "is capable of promoting the free flow of ideas and information", it is likewise true that anonymity is capable of promoting the free flow of deliberate misinformation and of orchestrated attacks on persons, ideas and even institutions. In addition, online misinformation travels much faster than online information.[20]

Here *SAS v. France* 1 July 2014 GC seems to offer another approach. The case deals with another type of question, namely the French "burka ban", and the issue is primarily dealt with as an Art. 9 issue, i.e. the question of freedom of religion (para. 108). The Court finds that the ban is a restriction on freedom of religion as well as the right to private life, and as a consequence, the condition for the restriction of a right must be available. The Court rejects the presented suggestions that the ban could be necessary for protecting the equality of men and women and for protecting human dignity (paras 118–120). However, it accepts that the idea of "living together" could fall under the protection of the rights and freedom of others (paras. 121f).

> (The Court) can understand the view that individuals who are present in places open to all, may not wish to see practices or attitudes developing there, which would fundamentally call into question the possibility of open interpersonal relationships, which, by virtue of an established consensus, forms an indispensable element of community life within the society in question. (para. 122)

Thus, open interpersonal relationships are indispensable in places open to all, and this implies that anonymity can only be granted in closed fora, not in open online fora. The

20 S. Vosoughi, D. Roy and S. Aral (2018) The Spread of True and False News Online. *Science*, Vol. 359, 1146–1151.

"virtue of an established consensus" needs to be considered: Does this entail that when no consensus has been established, which is quite clearly the case relating to online communication, there is no need for open interpersonal relationships? This is untenable. The importance of open interpersonal relationships cannot relate solely on an established consensus, especially not in relation to relatively new phenomena where a consensus has had no chance of being established. Secondly, this would imply a fundamental difference between real life and online relations with the unacceptable legal consequence of treating personal relationships fundamentally different offline compared to online.

Online life is also community life, and there is also a need for "living together", implying i.e. that it must be possible to identify participants, especially, of course, if they are engaged in attacks on other individuals or engage in more anti-social activities such as hate speech, undermining democratic processes and the like. I am not arguing that life online and offline is always completely the same and ought to be regulated in precisely the same manner in all details. What I am arguing is that they are not fundamentally different either. If open interpersonal relationships are *indispensable* – and not only preferable – in places open to all, this must have repercussions also for interpersonal relationships online.

In the *SAS* case, the Court accepts "that the barrier raised against others by a veil concealing the face is perceived by the respondent State as breaching the right of others to live in a space of socialisation which makes living together easier" (para. 122). In other words, anonymity in itself may constitute a violation of the rights of others.

I therefore conclude that when entering into the public sphere – online or offline – the point of departure is openness, non-anonymity and transparency. This does not imply that the media must reject anonymous contributions. But it entails, I contend, only the following alternatives when a media or other intermediaries accept anonymity:

- Alternative One: On request, the identity must be revealed. (The nature of the request differs: for technical service providers only on court injunctions. For actively editing media on reasonably well-founded requests from the public).
- Alternative Two: The media – by law or by consent – takes on the liability for any illegal content, if it is not erased upon request.
- Alternative Three: As an exception, anonymity can be upheld, but only if the case at hand provides relevant reasons. This implies that reference to anonymity as a general value does not suffice. "Face" and open interpersonal relationships are equally important. It also implies that in some cases anonymity could overrule openness, perhaps in whistle-blower cases, and perhaps in cases which involve solidly based information on matters of public interest.

At any rate, Alternative Two needs to be considered. In the important case of *Jersild v. Denmark* 23 September 1994 the Court held that it is against Art. 10 to render the journalist (i.e. the media) liable for racist remarks. Here, however, the interviewees were not anonymous. If that had been the case, e.g. if their faces had been obscured, i.e. if the media had decided to bring the criminal remarks and at the same time hide the faces of the ones primarily responsible, liability for the media appears unproblematic, and no issue under Art. 10 would arise. Alternative Three is exceptional, thus rendering anonymity possible and at the same time keeping the standards of an open society with open interpersonal relationships, also online.

Online freedom of expression: what does it entail and who is responsible for obstacles?

Similar to Art. 8 and the concept of private life, freedom of expression in Art. 10 is broadly constructed. Firstly, Art. 10 covers not only the right to disseminate ideas – the Enlightenment version[21] – but also the right to receive them, and the right covers both ideas (opinions etc.) *and* information. Secondly, the idea of expression is broad. My favourite example is the disturbance of fox hunting.[22] The case, of course, is not about some persons who had lost their sense of direction and all of a sudden were in the midst of a fox hunt, disturbing the hunters. They were consciously making a statement against fox hunting and as such the situation falls under Art. 10.[23] The right to receive information and ideas obviously also pertains to online activities,[24] and for the present purpose, I limit the presentation to non-state parties' online activities.

As mentioned previously, the member states do not only have a negative obligation implying that states should not intervene in freedom of expression (broadly constructed) except in circumstances provided for in Art. 10(2). The states also have positive obligations in order to secure that the freedom is not interfered with by private actors, or rather that there are adequate legal measures available if such interference occurs. The most dramatic case is *Özgür Gündem v. Turkey* 16 March 2000 in which Turkey was held responsible for inaction in relation to numerous deadly and violent attacks on a newspaper's journalists, its offices, newspaper vendors etc. Obviously, a member state is not responsible for private parties' criminal actions, but not doing anything in order to protect individuals may in itself constitute a violation, including a violation of the freedom of expression.

In relation to possible online violations, they are much less dramatic than the *Özgür Gündem case*, but still important and worth considering. *Appleby et al v. UK* 6 May 2003 deals with good old analogue freedom of expression, but is illustrative because it involves a private property owner rejecting expressions on the premises of a centrally located shopping mall. Some of the applicants had set up their posters etc., but were sent away by security guards. Others had applied to the director for setting up stands with posters, leaflets, petition papers, but he refused access:

> The owner's stance on all political and religious issues, is one of strict neutrality and I am charged with applying this philosophy. I am therefore obliged to refuse permission for you to carry out a petition within the Galleries or the adjacent car parks.

Besides being an example of the tendency to refute responsibility – "I am obliged to" – it marks the importance of the decision of the property owner, and in fact the Court notices that the case involves rights under Art. 10 as well as under Protocol 1, Art. 1, which protects property rights. The Court states: "Where, however, the bar on access to property

21 See e.g. the French 1789 Declaration, Art. 11: "La libre communication des pensées et des opinions est un des droits les plus précieux de l'homme; tout citoyen peut donc parler, écrire, imprimer librement, sauf".

22 *Hashman & Harrup v. UK* 25 Nov 1999 GC, espec. pr. 28.

23 It is, of course, another issue to establish whether the interference with rights under Art. 10(1) is legitimate under Art. 10(2). In the fox hunting case, the Court found that it was not sufficiently "prescribed by law", and as a consequence there was a violation of Art. 10.

24 E.g. *Cengiz et al. v. Turkey* 1 Dec 2015.

has the effect of preventing any effective exercise of freedom of expression or it can be said that the essence of the right has been destroyed, the Court would not exclude that a positive obligation could arise for the state to protect the enjoyment of the Convention rights by regulating property rights" (para. 47). In other words, neither of the rights are absolute and the Court accepts regulation of property rights in order to protect freedom of speech. As always, the Court is preoccupied with the effectiveness of the protection of the right in question. And in the present case, some of the applicants were in fact allowed to stay in one of the supermarkets and on the gangways leading to the privately owned shopping mall, and they had been able to gather some 3,000 signatures. Consequently, the Court rejected any violation of Art. 10.

It may also be of interest that the applicants had claimed that the privately owned shopping mall located in the city centre was a "quasi-public place", and as a consequence, the running of such a place could not be left to the proprietor. As can be seen, the Court avoids getting into a discussion of this kind of politically contested concepts. Instead it focuses on the rights involved: Is the right to freedom of expression violated in this case? And the answer is no because the complainants were not barred from expressing their views. Still, the court leaves a door open: there could be cases in which effective protection of the freedom of expression would require state action to regulate private property.

For the present purpose, it is relevant to consider whether e.g. rejecting access to fora such as Facebook may constitute an obligation for a state to establish freedom of expression. Obviously, if access is denied because of illegal activities such as distributing child pornography, inciting to violence etc., this raises no question under Art. 10. But what about activities that are perfectly legal?

The Danish author, Peter Øvig Knudsen has written extensively on various historical issues, including a book *Hippie*[25] dealing with collective and hippie living in the late 1960s. The book featured nude pictures, illustrating the life of the "hippies". Postings of the photos on Facebook were banned, and according to the author's statement[26] he was told that if he continued to upload his pictures, his account would be closed. From a human rights perspective, this is relevant. And of course, for the author and other persons in a similar situation, the situation is serious. Facebook is an important means of communication, and being ex-communicated[27] may imply loss of means of communication, of audience, and hence of income and fame.

The question is whether (European) states have an obligation to secure access to a very central means of communication. Taking *Appleby* as a point of departure, it cannot be ruled out that state inaction vis-à-vis private companies' denying access may constitute a violation of Art. 10. However, it appears that there are still other means of communication and the Danish author would not be totally excluded from communicating with his audience without access to Facebook's services. After all, he published a book with no interferences. To my assessment, the situation does not (yet) imply juridically based obligation for state action.

The same result ensues if the situation is conceived of in terms of editorial discretion rather than property rights. In the decision *Melnychuk v. Ukraine* 5 July 2005 (decision),

25 Peter Øvrig Knudsen (2011, 2012) *Hippie 1* and *Hippie 2*. København: Gyldendals Boghandel respectively.

26 Facebookistan. Documentary, DR [Danish Broadcasting Company], 2015.

27 See previously for the Zuckerberg quote in which he refers to Facebook as a community.

the applicant complained that a newspaper did not want to accept his reply to a literary review. The Court notes

> that, as a general principle, newspapers and other privately owned media must be free to exercise editorial discretion in deciding whether to publish articles, comments and letters submitted by private individuals. However, there may be exceptional circumstances in which a newspaper may legitimately be required to publish, for example, a retraction, an apology or a judgment in a defamation case.
>
> ("The Law" section, para. 2)

In both cases, the Court emphasises the decision right by the editor and the proprietor respectively, but does not leave out that in exceptional cases the legal situation may be different. This implies that the member states must be aware of (exceptional) situations in which private actors effectively bar freedom of expression.

In my opinion, it is worth considering whether the present situation with very strong online actors is tenable in the long run. Private companies running freedom of speech as a private enterprise only under company rule raises questions of timely and adequate political, i.e. legislative and executive, response.

Concluding on Art. 10, there are no real conceptual problems in relation to the concept of freedom of speech. But there are conceptual problems in relation to i.e. understanding social media. And there are obviously interests involved, interests of property owners, of editors, of social media, social media users etc. And there are various liability regimes, a director being liable vis-à-vis the company, the company to its shareholders, and – not least – the state to its citizens, who should have effective protection of freedom of speech.

Local solutions, local problems: complicity, anonymity and jurisdiction

All states have to deal with the complicated issues of liability for online human rights violations, and there is not one single right way of doing it.[28] In this section, I briefly sketch out some Danish solutions, which may serve as an inspiration as to how to do it or how not to do it. I focus on complicity, anonymity and jurisdiction, which are all highly relevant concepts when it comes to online human rights liability.

As for *complicity* in criminal cases, the Danish penal code provides for a very broad approach: "The penalty provided for an offence applies to everybody who is complicit in the act by incitement or aiding and abetting", CC section 23.[29] Translation is not a straightforward activity, and I would prefer "by incitement, advice or deed", indicating that according to the wording everybody who is somehow involved in the act may be criminally liable. The important point is that the criminal provision is very broad, and

28 This principled statement relates to a large discussion as to the degree of universality of human rights. Presently it may suffice to refer to my position elaborated generally in, *Cuadernos constitucionales de la Cátedra Fadrique Furió Ceriol*, Nr. 62/63, 2011, 113–126, and for a similar position: Jack Donnelly (2007) The Relative Universality of Human Rights. *Human Rights Quarterly*, Vol. 29, 281–306.

29 Translated by: Anette Nørgaard Jappe and Karen Wolf-Frederiksen. Legal advisor: Lars Lindencrone Petersen. It should be mentioned that traditional media and many online media is out of reach of section 23. See the following section on anonymity.

the problem of cutting complicity to the proper size is left to the courts and indirectly to doctrine. In principle, this is unattractive to rule of law proponents, leaving the more exact limits for criminal liability open. The construction presupposes a large amount of trust in the courts. By and large, it works, and in fact the level of trust in Denmark is generally very high.[30] And interestingly, trust in judges is significantly higher than trust in politicians, i.e. members of the legislature and the upper strata of the government.[31]

On the downside, the position of the prosecution is somewhat worrying. In order to have a case tried before a court of law, the prosecution must take action. Firstly, political considerations may play a part. From a rule of law perspective, following the law is preferable. Secondly, biases are at play. Back in the 1970s, drunk driving was a rather large problem. But the prosecutors never thought of the idea of charging hosts with complicity even if they served large amounts of alcohol to persons who clearly were going to drive back home. In contradistinction, when it comes to violence, drugs etc. the prosecutors did not lack creativity in terms of activating section 23. The same critique could be directed at the lack of prosecution of the large online media. Recently, in the so-called umbrella case, more than a thousand youngsters were charged with child pornography, as they had shared videos of two 15-year old persons having sex. Apparently, the prosecution did not even think of the possibility of charging Facebook, who had knowledge of the sharing.

According to the Media Liability Act (MLA) *anonymity* is guaranteed (as the point of departure, there are always exceptions). However, there will always be someone to charge (criminally or by tort action). The liable person(s) is either the author, the editor-in-chief or both. The system functions well. If the author (which could be the journalist or the programme planner) decides to bring anonymous features, the author – and in some cases the editor – is liable for criminal content. This way of handling liability gives the media the right to decide *and* the corresponding liability for criminal or wrongful acts.

The downside is that not all types of media fall under this arrangement: Traditional media such as newspapers and broadcasting companies, based in Denmark, fall under the MLA. Online media can opt in – but only if they are based in Denmark and carry an edited content. This entails that non-national media cannot benefit from the MLA, neither can authors of books or other non-traditional media. Hence, the arrangement is probably against EU law as well as European human rights law.[32]

As for *jurisdiction*, section 9a of the Criminal Code provides that "(a)n offence relating to text, sound or image data, etc., made generally available in Denmark through the Internet or a similar system for dissemination of information by acts committed abroad is deemed to have been committed within the Danish state if the data is related specifically to Denmark". The last requirement is fulfilled e.g. if a person in a picture is located in Denmark and if the language is Danish. As for the law, this implies that the whereabouts of the server or the culprit is irrelevant, which is an advantage for the prosecution of online criminal acts. However, the practical implementation of the prosecution still presupposes

30 See e.g. Gert Tinggaard Svendsen (2012) *Tillid* [Trust]. Aarhus: Aarhus Universitets Forlag. (A small popular publication explaining the researcher's findings.)

31 Radius Kommunikation (2017) *Troværdighedsundersøgelsen* [Research in Trustworthiness]. Judges come in third only surpassed by midwives and nurses whereas politicians have a low score, lower than e.g. car dealers, https://radiuscph.dk/wp-content/uploads/2017/09/Trovaerdighedsundersoegelsen-2017-af-Radius.pdf (accessed 01.04.2019).

32 T o some extent, the courts may ease the problem. In 2016 a city court, referring to the ECHR Art. 10, granted rights to an author of a journalistic article rights as if under MLA.

smooth cooperation with foreign jurisdiction; and even for national prosecution, the prosecutors have been somewhat slow to pursue online human rights violations.

Conclusion

Liability is an important concept – and it is also complicated. How far the liability chain is reaching is not only a question of information and knowledge. Who did exactly what and when are important questions, but insufficient to answer questions of liability. Ascription of liability is also a matter of decision: who do we want to be liable for online human rights violations and under which circumstances? This is where interests come in. All sorts of diverging interests are involved, social media companies, states, NGOs, persons who want to make use of free speech, persons whose rights are violated online, politicians etc. To make matters even more complicated, different fora may decide differently, for good reasons or less convincingly. It is well known that US law generally protects freedom of expression stronger and the right to private life weaker compared to the European tradition including the ECHR. Therefore, the answer to the question as to who we want to be liable also depends on the "we". Different societies (in the broad sense of the term) may choose different solutions, be it as a result of thorough deliberations, of tradition, of interests or a mix. And because digital online expressions travel much faster and much easier across borders than the old days' offline analogue ones, problems of overlapping and intermixing jurisdictions become urgent. The present contribution cannot solve all the problems involved, but hopefully it has assisted in bringing some clarifications.

8 Multistakeholderism – meaning and implications

Joanna Kulesza

Introduction

Internet governance relies on multistakeholderism – a distributed policy-making model based on the voluntary cooperation of key actors, usually identified as: states, business and civil society, operating "in their respective roles"[1] through "rough consensus and running code".[2] This approach, although neither new nor unique to cyberspace, significantly differs from national law-making or international norm development, both traditionally dominated by states.[3] While the states play a key role in both of those scenarios, internet governance grants national governments and institutions only a complementary role in setting and enforcing "principles, norms, rules, decision making procedures and programs" for the global network.[4] While a similar supporting rather than leading role of the states can be witnessed in many other areas of international law and relations, including environmental protection, production of pharmaceuticals or banking to mention a few, where much is left to good business practice, civil society input and/or consumer choice, the interplay of governments, companies and individuals is nowhere more complex, abundant and transnational than online. This is likely due to three factors:

1 WSIS (2005) *Tunis Agenda for The Information Society*, www.itu.int/wsis/docs2/tunis/off/6rev1.html (accessed 16.07.2018).

2 The phrase is a shorthand allusion to the decision-making processes within the bottom-up models of governance, specific to the original technical communities behind the global network, with time adopted as the fundamental guideline for all internet governance related decision-making models. For the specific reference see: David Clark (1992) A Cloudy Crystal Ball – Visions of the Future. *Proceedings of the Twenty-Fourth Internet Engineering Task Force*, 539–543, July 1992, www.ietf.org/proceedings/24.pdf (accessed 16.07.2018); Erik Huizer, Stephen D. Crocker (1994) IETF Working Group Guidelines and Procedures. *RFC 1603*, March.

3 The current debate on norm development puts forever more emphasis on the role of non-state actors; for a general reference see Lan Cao (2016) *Culture in Law and Development: Nurturing Positive Change*. Oxford: Oxford University Press, 267 ff., discussing, among others, the New Haven School's inclusive approach to norm making. While this "inclusiveness" is true also for cyberspace, this author argues that similar processes have been present in various other areas of international law and policy making and as such are not unique to the internet.

4 William J. Drake (2009) Introduction: The Distributed Architecture of Network Global Governance. In: William J. Drake and Ernest J. Wilson (Eds.), *Governing Global Electronic Networks*. Cambridge, MA: MIT Press, 8–9.

1 The complexity and scale of online interactions, with 3.6 billion internet users worldwide in 2017;[5]
2 The global model for electronic commerce and the resulting dominance of a small number of US based companies (often referred to as "GAFA": Google, Amazon, Facebook and Apple); and
3 The gross value of the online market (estimated at 2.304 trillion USD in online transactions globally in 2017),[6] where the lines between roles the of individual stakeholders are nowhere more controversial and disputed than in the online environment.

While many still praise the network's unique governance model, viewing it as key to the internet's boom and rapid development since the early 1990s that led to shifts in the global economy and fundamental political changes across the world, the existing multistakeholder model is far from ideal. Not only does it fail to effectively identify the particular rights and obligations of individual actors – states, business and members of civil society, acting collectively or individually – but, most significantly at the time of the global war on terror and increasing terrorist uses of the network, it strongly disables state institutions in performing their original roles as lawmakers and enforcers.

Over centuries international law developed a relatively clear set of rights and obligations resting upon the state and, indirectly, on other actors in the form of, for example, international human rights law. Transferring those rights and obligations onto the multi-faceted, transnational cyberspace, governed by multistakeholder processes proves challenging. In particular, it is the link between the positive duties of states to diligently and actively prevent harm to individual rights and the obligations of private actors, such as transnational online platforms, that causes much controversy. Referring to Dworkin's "law as practice" doctrine, one might argue that the law is nothing but "an interpretative concept like courtesy",[7] allowing for flexible interpretations of well-established rules and processes. There might be a line to be drawn for human rights law, which at its core, when protecting an individual's life or emanations of one's dignity, leaves little room for interpretation. Much is being said about an alleged "lex Facebook" – a company policy that serves as a global law for billions of its users – particularly in light of the recent (2018) Cambridge Analytica scandal, disclosing ways to effectively influence individual political choices via personal data profiling with the use of advanced advertising algorithms.

A fundamental question that is being answered through everyday practice is one on the scope of human rights obligations directly applicable to private actors. Whereas traditionally – that is, before the age of globalisation – international obligations needed to be implemented in national law and only then became binding to private actors, there is more discussion on the direct applicability of human rights obligations to private parties.[8]

5 According to the International Telecommunications Union (ITU), www.itu.int/en/ITU-D/Statistics/Pages/stat/default.aspx (accessed 17.07.2018).

6 eMarketer, Worldwide Retail and Ecommerce Sales: eMarketer's Updated Forecast and New Mcommerce Estimates for 2016–2021, www.emarketer.com/Report/Worldwide-Retail-Ecommerce-Sales-eMarketers-Updated-Forecast-New-Mcommerce-Estimates-20162021/2002182 (accessed 17.07.2018).

7 Ronald Dworkin (1986) *Law's Empire*. Harvard: Harvard University Press, 87.

8 For a specific reference see: United Nations Guiding Principles on Business and Human Rights, 2011, also known as "Ruggie Principles" after their author, John Ruggie, United Nations Secretary-General's Special Representative for Business and Human Rights from 2005 untill 2011; The Guiding Principles on Business and Human Rights: Implementing the United Nations, "Protect, Respect and Remedy" Framework, UN Doc. A/HRC/17/31, 21 March 2011. The Principles refer to three basic tools aimed at ascertaining human rights enforcement vis-a-vis

Law-making power is dramatically shifting away from states, who are desperate to regain it at a time of political and economic insecurity. In their attempts to do so, either in the domain of online security or global trade, they must consider the specifics of the networks in terms of architecture, design and, most significantly, the particular traits of the current multistakeholder model of governance, as discussed in the following.

Multistakeholder governance

Governance – a term often used in reference to the unique internet ecosystem – is neither new nor unique to the global communication network. A recent comprehensive anthology by Levi Faur offers a versatile review of the rich array of contemporary policy areas subject to "governance". They range from state reform and its democratic institutions to international organisations, global economic relations, labour relations, public health management, banking, risk management and environmental protection.[9] In this context, Dutton refers to the internet and its governance as "a Fifth Estate" describing how the internet "is being used ... in ways that support social accountability across many sectors".[10] He refers to the power the internet holds over social relationships and political decisions, reflecting the eighteenth-century concept of the Fourth Estate created by the press, now, as he alleges, substituted by the unique impact the internet has on global society. While nearing "a fuzzy term (that) can be applied to almost anything and ... explains nothing",[11] Dutton's take on governance focuses on the actual challenge the internet poses to existing regulation mechanisms and reflects the versatility of its process and actors. Yet as Bygrave rightfully notes, the "nebulous and broad" concept of governance has been defined with other references like "processes influencing other actors" or "the sum of the many ways in which individuals and institutions public and private manage their common affairs".[12] While "governance" is often perceived as contrary to "government", Bygrave views it as one of many methods of regulation. He sides with a "decentered" definition of the latter, covering more than just the activities of governments and state actors.[13] Drake on the other hand offers an "action-oriented" approach to global governance, relying on its steering mechanisms or institutions rather than the actors behind them. He defines global governance as "the development and application of shared principles, norms, rules, decision-making procedures, and programs intended to shape actor's expectations and practices and to enhance their collective management capabilities in world affairs".[14] This

transnational companies. Those include states' obligation to protect human rights, corporate responsibility for their protection and the accessibility of a legal remedy for victims of abuses caused by companies. Contemporary international law does not permit putting international obligations directly onto private parties, therefore it is states who are obliged to assure that private companies operating under their jurisdiction, power or control meet human rights standards set by international law. For this author's attempt at answering the question see: Joanna Kulesza (2014) Protecting Human Rights Online – an Obligation of Due Diligence. *Jean Monnet Working Paper 24/14*, New York, https://jeanmonnetprogram.org/paper/protecting-human-rights-online-an-obligation-of-due-diligence/ (accessed 16.07.2018).

9 See generally: David Levi Faur (Ed.) (2012) *The Oxford Handbook of Governance*. Oxford: Oxford University Press.

10 William Dutton (2012) The Fifth Estate. In: David Levi Faur (Ed.), *The Oxford Handbook of Governance*. Oxford: Oxford University Press, 585.

11 Lee A. Bygrave (2015) *Internet Governance by Contract*. Oxford: Oxford University Press, 12 citing Jessop.

12 Ibid., 11–17.

13 Ibid., 13.

14 William J. Drake (2009) Introduction: The Distributed Architecture of Network Global Governance. In: William J. Drake and Ernest J. Wilson (Eds.), *Governing Global Electronic Networks*. Cambridge, MA: MIT Press, 8–9.

definition offers a good reflection of the complexity of actions and institutions behind contemporary global governance processes and seems best suited for the following discussion on internet governance.

Distributed governance operating on the basis of "rough consensus"[15] and different decision-making models inclusive of various groups of stakeholders are, as already said, not unique to the internet model. As noted by Weber and Weber, particular analogies are to be drawn with environmental law, where individual rights, including the right to information and freedom of speech, in particular the right to protest, are granted by international treaties, most notably by the Aarhus Convention.[16] The authors use this analogy to suggest a "Memorandum of Understanding" between internet governance bodies and civil society to ensure their equal participation in the existing governance model. Other popular analogies include references to international trade law where self-regulation, good business practice and political lobbying have always played a major role in shaping global and local policies.[17] Much like the much disputed lex Facebook, international companies, particularly within the banking sector, have long used their dominant position to influence policies and adapted to popular consumer demands even if there was no specific law requiring them to do so. Haufler refers to specific examples that include labour standards abroad, information privacy and environmental protection where the private sector takes the lead on policy making and leaves states to only later repeat those within local and international laws.[18] In addition, the international food safety regulations, most notably the Codex Alimentarius and its implementing norms within the World Health Organization (WHO), are often referred to as a case of "private law making".[19] As Henson and Humphrey note, these private standards have become a "prevalent part" of global food governance, relying on standards for food safety and quality developed by "private firms and standards setting coalitions, including companies and NGOs".[20] While developed by the Food and Agriculture Organization (FAO) and WHO, the document remains a classic example of soft law and although non-binding to states, serves as a set of globally adopted fundamental safety standards among food suppliers.

These bottom-up processes of international standard setting and law-making have not gone unnoticed by international law scholars, who have coined the term "Global Administrative Law" (GAL) to frame them.[21] While GAL remains disputed as to its methodology and application, it offers a comprehensive and insightful look at global governance. The authors see global governance processes aligned along five categories, all based on "global administrative regulation". Kingsbury, Krisch and Stewart include internet governance

15 Please see n. 2 *supra* for the references defining "rough consensus".

16 Rolf H. Weber, Romana Weber (2009) Inclusion of the Civil Society in the Governance of the Internet. Can Lessons Be Drawn from the Environmental Law Framework?, *Cri* Vol. 1, 9–15.

17 For a detailed discussion see generally: Virginia Haufler (2013) *A Public Role for the Private Sector: Industry Self-Regulation in a Global Economy.* Washington DC: Carnegie Endowment.

18 Haufler 31–100.

19 Spencer Henson and John Humphrey (2011) Codex Alimentarius and Private Standards. In B. M. J. van der Meulen (Ed.), *Private Food Law: Governing Food Chains Through Contracts Law, Self-regulation, Private Standards, Audits and Certification Schemes.* Wageningen, The Netherland: Wageningen Academic Publications, 149–174.

20 Ibid., 42.

21 For more details on this pioneering work see the resources available at NYU's Institute for International Law and Justice: www.iilj.org/gal/ (accessed 28.06.2018) and Benedict Kingsbury, Nico Krisch and Richard B. Stewart (2005) The Emergence of Global Administrative Law. *Law and Contemporary Problems,* Vol. 68, 15.

with its multistakeholder model as one of those key types, referred to as "Hybrid Administration". They view it as a "hybrid intergovernmental-private arrangement" and directly point to the Internet Corporation for Assigned Names and Numbers (ICANN), discussed further herein, as a unique example.[22]

All these perspectives on global governance provide a better understanding of and set the scene for the internet multistakeholder model, offering lessons and analogies to be applied to today's global network and the regime behind it. Yet before this is done, a look at the definition and meaning of "internet governance" is necessary.

Internet governance

The internet operates based on an intentionally decentralised design – to effectively defer threats to the network and its resources, there is no central point of control, which, when compromised, could disable the operation of the entire global web. This reflects the purpose of the original network design which was to create a global communication system resilient to an individual, likely nuclear, attack.[23] Its purpose was to protect data from being permanently erased from the system – a design that today poses understandable challenges to "the right to be forgotten", proposed for a network that was created to "remember". This decentralised design relied not only on a dispersed infrastructure (in terms of both local software and the network's backbone architecture) but also on a democratic, peer-to-peer model of cooperation and trust. All nodes on the network are of equal status and their efficient operation relies on trust in the other actors – trust has always been the oil of the global digital economy. This egalitarian dispersed model varied significantly from other governance models – whether public or private, networks and communities usually operate on authority, power and enforcement. Despite having neither, the internet still worked and its governance model quickly proved to be a key to its success.

What started off in 1969 as an exercise in US national security entered the global political discourse in 2003, when the International Telecommunications Union (ITU) member states realised what social, economic and political potential it held. The 2003 ITU World Summit on the Information Society (WSIS) was the first official, intergovernmental meeting to refer to the opportunities and challenges posed by the global network to international and domestic policies.[24] It called upon a Working Group on Internet Governance (WGIG) – a small group of professionals dealing with telecommunications and international relations designated by member states – to identify the initial challenges

22 The other four types include: (1) "International Administration" by formal international organisations, e.g. United Nations Security Council, (2) "Network Administration" relying on "collective action by transnational networks of cooperative arrangements between national regulatory officials" with the work of and round the Basel Committee and the banking sector, (3) "Distributed Administration" of national regulators implementing international "treaty, network, or other cooperative regimes", and (4) "Private Administration" by private bodies, such as the International Standardization Organization (ISO). Benedict Kingsbury et al. 20–23.

23 For a review of Internet's history and origins see: Roy Balleste (2015) *Internet Governance. Origins, Current Issues and Future Possibilities*. Lanham, MD: Rowman and Littlefield, 11–15.

24 Most notable documents developed in the original WSIS process include: WGIG (2005) Report of the Working Group on Internet Governance, www.wgig.org/docs/WGIGREPORT.pdf; WSIS (2003) *Declaration of Principles; Building the Information Society: A Global Challenge in the New Millennium*, www.itu.int/wsis/docs/geneva/official/dop.html; WSIS (2003) *Plan of Action*, www.itu.int/wsis/docs/geneva/official/poa.html; WSIS (2005) *Tunis Agenda for the Information Society*, www.itu.int/wsis/docs2/tunis/off/6rev1.html. (all accessed 16.07.2018).

and possible solutions posed to international policies by this global communication phenomenon. WGIG presented its Report in 2005 defining "Internet governance" as "the development and application by governments, the private sector and civil society, in their respective roles, of shared principles, norms, rules, decision-making procedures, and programmes that shape the evolution and use of the Internet", a definition later adopted by the WSIS within its 2005 "Tunis Agenda for the Information Society".[25]

This definition reflects the rich variety of standard-setting and decision-making bodies as well as processes crucial for the day-to-day operation of the global network. It also puts into words the basic principle of internet governance: the principle of multistakeholderism.[26] While multistakeholderism is a well-recognised term in international relations theory and practice, the official UN documents often refer to a "multistakeholder approach" to internet governance. The Tunis Agenda also emphasised the significance of the multistakeholder approach as a way to "improve the coordination of the activities of international and intergovernmental organisations and other institutions concerned with Internet Governance and the exchange of information among themselves".[27]

The principle of multistakeholder governance has also been recognised in the context of securing human rights online, as reflected in, for example, the Council of Europe (CoE) 2011 Declaration of the Committee of Ministers on internet governance principles, where the ministers refer to "multistakeholder governance".[28] The CoE recommends "the development and implementation of Internet governance arrangements" that ensure "in an open, transparent and accountable manner, the full participation of governments, the private sector, civil society, the technical community and users, taking into account their specific roles and responsibilities".[29] The document puts emphasis on both aspects of multistakeholder governance: equal representation from among all community sectors and all geographical regions. When referring to the integrity of the network, the CoE ministers point to "security, stability, robustness and resilience of the Internet" as "key objectives" of internet governance.[30] This aim is to be achieved through "national and international multistakeholder co-operation" for the purpose of preserving "the integrity and ongoing functioning of the Internet infrastructure, as well as users' trust and reliance on the Internet".

While internet governance principles are subject to policy recommendations and a wide selection of academic literature, thus far only one forum effectively serves as a testing bed for this novel bottom-up decision-making approach. ICANN, a California-based not for profit corporation, tasked with managing core internet resources and the community around it offer initial reflections on what this governance model has achieved and how it can be improved.[31]

25 Para. 34 of the WSIS Tunis Agenda, n 20, reads: "A working definition of Internet governance is the development and application by governments, the private sector and civil society, in their respective roles, of shared principles, norms, rules, decision-making procedures, and programmes that shape the evolution and use of the Internet".

26 For a discussion on other Internet governance principles see e.g.: J. Kulesza (2012) *International Internet Law*. New York: Routledge, 138–139.

27 WSIS Tunis Agenda, para. 37.

28 Council of Europe, Declaration by the Committee of Ministers on Internet governance principles, adopted on 21 September 2011.

29 Ibid.

30 Ibid.

31 Other multistakeholder platforms, such as the Internet Governance Forum (IGF) have no effective policy making powers.

ICANN as the current multistakeholderism paradigm

One of the reasons why ITU called upon the WSIS to look into internet governance and its processes was the monopoly the US government had over what grew to be the global network due to its historical design (an Advanced Research Projects Agency's research project). Once the US National Science Foundation, shepherd of the US academic network, allowed for its commercial use in the early 1990s, the commercial potential and rapid economic growth of the online market stunned White House officials. They attempted to resist the lobbying from both: local business and international governments, opting for a novel, non-commercial model of supervising critical technical resources of the network. A new, unique solution was offered in 1998 with the setting up of ICANN – a non-profit corporation operating from California.

As per ICANN Bylaws, its mission is to "ensure the stable and secure operation of the Internet's unique identifier systems".[32] In particular, ICANN:

1 Coordinates the allocation and assignment of names in the root zone of the Domain Name System ("DNS") and coordinates the development and implementation of policies concerning the registration of second-level domain names in generic top-level domains ("gTLDs");
2 Facilitates the coordination of the operation and evolution of the DNS root name server system; as well as
3 Coordinates the allocation and assignment at the top-most level of Internet Protocol numbers and Autonomous System numbers.[33]

ICANN offers "registration services and open access for global number registries", working closely with the Internet Engineering Task Force (IETF) and Regional Internet Registries (RIRs).[34] Its Bylaws explicitly state that "ICANN shall not act outside its Mission", as defined previously, and in particular it is not to "regulate (i.e. impose rules and restrictions on) services that use the Internet's unique identifiers or the content that such services carry or provide". It is characterised as holding no "governmentally authorized regulatory authority". Yet despite this, in the last twenty years, the corporation has become the stage for all internet governance-related debates and policy making. Although its primary legal obligation is towards its "contracted parties", operating through lengthy private contracts with registrars, its policies and guidelines have long become actual policy standards within the internet governance environment. ICANN is considered the living example of multistakeholder governance, with issues discussed ranging from intellectual property to human rights, and in particular privacy[35] and freedom of expression. A good representation of the complexity of internet governance-related issues that fall within the broad mandate of ICANN is the long-lasting dispute over the ".amazon" generic top-level domain (gTLD).

32 ICANN, Bylaws For Internet Corporation for Assigned Names And Numbers, a California Nonprofit Public-Benefit Corporation as amended 18 June 2018, www.icann.org/resources/pages/governance/bylaws-en/#article1, sec. 1.1.

33 ICANN, n 27, sec. 1.1.

34 Ibid.

35 The latest unveiling of ICANN's privacy and personal data protection struggle were the 2018 changes in its WHOIS database policy following the implementation of the EU General Data Protection Regulation (GDPR). For a recap of WHOIS history and the changes implemented following GDPR see: https://whois.icann.org/en/history-whois (accessed 17.07.2018).

Awarding the highly valuable and culturally onerous internet identifier to either a US-based company (Amazon) or a group of South American countries located within the region of the continent's largest river, led by Brazil, has been one of the more interesting public law issues of the last decade. It is within ICANN's multistakeholder forum that both Brazil and Amazon have approached all diplomatic and policy-making tools available to make sure the name, as used online, will be awarded to them. While the final decision is still pending, this example is a vivid representation of the breadth of the tasks that fall within the scope of "managing unique Internet identifiers" and a good representation of the complexity of multistakeholder policy making, where a continental leader (Brazil) faces an internet giant (Amazon) on equal footing.

ICANN's policy making is defined within its Bylaws. They reiterate ICANN's "Core Values" – what could be considered basic principles of multistakeholder policy making. They include a commitment to preserving "the operational stability, reliability, security, global interoperability, resilience, and openness of the DNS and the Internet" as well as the "maintenance of a single, interoperable Internet". In doing so ICANN relies on "open, transparent and bottom-up, multistakeholder policy development processes that are led by the private sector (including business stakeholders, civil society, the technical community, academia and end users), while duly taking into account the public policy advice of governments and public authorities". ICANN's "core values" provide more insight into how the multistakeholder process works in practice. The corporation and the community around it are to "seek input from the public, for whose benefit ICANN in all events shall act; promote well-informed decisions based on expert advice, and . . . ensure that those entities most affected can assist in the policy development process".[36]

Multistakeholderism also implies "consistent, neutral, objective and fair" decision-making based on "documented policies". All ICANN processes must remain non-discriminatory, make no "unjustified prejudicial distinction between or among different parties" with ICANN remaining "accountable to the Internet community through mechanisms defined in its Bylaws".[37] ICANN principles reflect the way the internet works and have been purposely formulated in a flexible manner, serving more as guidelines than strict norms. Effectively, their appropriate application depends directly on the nature of the situation in which they are to be used. Yet this complex, broad and vague formula makes ICANN a unique policy battle ground, often criticised for being subject to opaque lobbying efforts from domain name and IT businesses.[38] What adds to that argument is the significant economic power the California-based non-profit holds, with funds under management as per 30 June 2018 amounting to 443 million USD.[39]

Cybersecurity and human rights as challenges to the multistakeholder model

The twenty-first century saw the new face of international terrorism. The already ambiguous list of "asymmetric" threats to international peace and security – that is, those founded

36 ICANN, sec. 1.2.

37 Ibid.

38 For a comprehensive look at ICANN history and a critique of the multi-stakeholder model see: A. Michael Froomkin (2003) Habermas@discourse.net: Toward a Critical Theory of Cyberspace. *Harvard Law Review*, Vol. 116, 749.

39 ICANN's budget plan for 2018 available at: www.icann.org/en/system/files/files/adopted-opplan-budget-fy18-24jun17-en.pdf (accessed 17.07.2018), 31.

by private individuals such as terrorists or radical groups, possibly by states not capable of a "traditional armed attack conducted with the use of national military – was amended with the notions of "cyberthreats", "cyberterrorism" and "cyberwarfare", none of which can be clearly and reliably defined as per contemporary legal scholarship and international practice. Their general common trait is the use of the global computer network as tools for conducting attacks on national security and creating new threats to international peace.[40] The direct reference to the well-recognised, yet not uncontroversial, notions of terrorism and war show the scale of potential harm to domestic and international interests caused by cyberthreats.[41] The legal qualification of threats originating online has been subject to political and scholarly debate since the late 1990s, accompanying the slow rise of other internet governance-related debates on international agendas. One of the early scholarly attempts at a legal assessment of cyberthreats described cyberterrorism as the use of a digital system to commit an act punishable or prohibited by the UN anti-terrorist treaties.[42] With this UN reference, "cyberterrorism" could be defined as: "an intentional use or threat of use, without legally recognized authority, of violence, disruption or interference against cyber systems, when it is likely that such use would result in death or injury of a person or persons, substantial damage to physical property, civil disorder, or significant economic harm".[43]

The definition centres on a particular category of information systems, with reference to "critical infrastructure". It is because of the security of such systems that states need to take particular measures to protect international peace and prevent their damage, as critical infrastructures are forever more frequently operated online or at least equipped with an internet connection. The latter, a relatively new technical feature, can be considered their Achilles' heel. This particular risk of significant harm caused to states as well as international security with the use of the global network has been increasingly appearing on international diplomatic agendas. The international duty of states to prevent online-generated threats is being discussed in the context of international cooperation on law enforcement and can be enacted through a combination of various means, covering "all practicable measures" to prevent threatening conduct within or outside state territories as per the universal norms of jurisdiction. This can also be done through the exchange of information, coordination of administrative and other activities and introducing any other appropriate measures.[44]

These observations have been reflected in various policy documents. Arguably, the Council of Europe, with its 2011 Recommendation on the protection and promotion of the universality, integrity and openness of the internet, was the first international forum to recognise the role of human rights and cybersecurity due diligence in internet governance.[45] It has called upon states to cooperate with other stakeholders – business and civil

40 See generally: Sushil Jajodia (2011) *Moving Target Defense: Creating Asymmetric Uncertainty for Cyber Threats*. New York: Springer.

41 M. E. O'Connell (2012) Cyber Security without Cyber War. *JCSL*, Vol. 14, 189–190.

42 Stanford University (2000) *Draft International Convention to Enhance Protection from Cyber Crime and Terrorism*. http://iis-db.stanford.edu/pubs/11912/sofaergoodman.pdf (hereinafter: *Stanford Cybersecurity Draft*) (accessed 17.07.2018).

43 Ibid., Article 1.

44 Ibid.

45 Council of Europe, Recommendation CM/Rec(2011)8 of the Committee of Ministers to member states on the protection and promotion of the universality, integrity and openness of the Internet; 21 September 2011, pt. 1.3 (hereinafter cited as: *CoE, Recommendation CM/Rec(2011)8...*).

society – to identify and enforce all necessary measures "to prevent, manage and respond to significant transboundary disruptions to . . . the infrastructure of the Internet". This duty was to be enforced "within the limits of non-involvement in day-to-day technical and operational matters" as performed by private parties, such as internet service and content providers. The reference to "all relevant stakeholders" mirrors the multistakeholder principle. The recommendation goes on to identify a minimum standard of care in cases of maintaining risks and consequences of any "disruptions;" that is, negative consequences influencing "the stable and ongoing functioning of the network", resulting from "technical failures". It also emphasises the positive obligations of states when securing human rights online, requiring them to act with due care in preventing disruptive actions generated from within their jurisdictions. Similar language can be found in the long-awaited UN General Assembly Declaration on human rights online and in the work of the UN's Special Rapporteur on freedom of expression online.[46]

Second-order internet governance – lessons learned from multistakeholderism

When discussing governance and its evolution, Jessop argues new governance models are built upon the failures of old ones and describes the process as "second order governance".[47] This process brings with it a reordering of networks and improvement of communication modes, rooted in constitutional changes. While his argument is focused on states, the general lessons on governance seem to be applicable also to cyberspace with its multistakeholder model. The post-WSIS decade (2005–2015) has fuelled discussions on specifying the ambiguous notion of "internet governance", most significantly through defining the "respective roles" of states, business and civil society. Contemporary academic discourse seems to offer a few novel solutions to this challenge.[48]

Privatising internet governance

Some authors emphasised the role of private actors in national and international policy making. Bygrave rightfully notes that the whole ICANN ambience relies on private contracts between the Corporation and registries.[49] He takes this argument beyond this classical multistakeholder setting, arguing for private internet law-making as the lex-Facebook example proves. It is not through intergovernmental accord but simply through the power

46 UN Human Rights Council, Resolution on promotion, protection and enjoyment of human rights on the Internet, 5 July 2012, UN Doc. A/HRC/20/L.13; UN Human Rights Council, Promotion and protection of all human rights, civil, political, economic, social and cultural rights, including the right to development, Report of the Special Rapporteur on the promotion and protection of the right to freedom of opinion and expression, Frank La Rue, 17 April 2013, UN Doc A/HRC/23/40. See also UN Special Rapporteur on Freedom of Expression, Report of the Special Rapporteur to the General Assembly on the contemporary challenges to freedom of expression; 2016, UN Doc A/71/373, where the UN Special Rapporteur acknowledged the obligation of Internet service providers to verify state takedown requests and private complaints against applicable law.

47 Bob Jessop (2015) *The State: Past, Present, Future*. New York: John Wiley & Sons, 170.

48 For a comprehensive discussion on trends in internet governance discourse see generally: R. Radu, J. M. Chenou, R. H. Weber (Eds.) (2014) *The Evolution of Global Internet Governance: Principles and Policies in the Making*. New York: Springer Science & Business Media. For an analysis of different approaches to Internet governance see: D. Sylvan, *Global Internet Governance: Governance without Governors*. New York: Springer Science & Business Media, 23–37.

49 Bygrave 11–17.

of Facebook's terms of use that the largest "population" in the world is governed. The combined amount of Facebook users, bound by terms of service imposed by the internet giant, is larger than any national population (as per 2018). Bygrave sees the private contractual setting as a remedy to many of the current internet governance challenges, which include conflicts of jurisdiction and transnational law enforcement. This approach offers effective solutions to many of the internet's challenges: it reflects the actual practice with private law-making being a fact for all online platforms and the reference to private dispute resolution is indeed attractively simple and quick. The latter allows for the speedy resolution of disputes and abstracts from complex jurisdictional issues, with parties complying with one legal system, usually that of the service provider.[50] Yet on the sidelines of this policy trend there are increasing state efforts, rooted in the concept of sovereignty, to lead all internet-related policies, especially when it comes to securing state interests online. This trend is vividly present in the UN as well in within the EU, investing significant funds and efforts into its current cybersecurity policy.

Governing the internet as a public resource

The cybersecurity discourse seems to follow a contradictory argument, with increasing attention paid to the role of states in ensuring global peace and preventing cyber conflicts. Klimburg strongly opposes the tripartite multistakeholder model of power divided between states, business and civil society. He views the concept of multistakeholderism, as defined in the WSIS Agenda, as incomplete, with the ongoing debates offering many more shades of decision-making and a richer variety of actors than those defined within the WSIS agenda. More significantly, however, he views internet governance as ineffective and illegitimate in light of international relations history and tradition. When it comes to security, he argues, states must take the leading role, acting as the only international sovereigns.[51] Similarly, Broeders argues for the enhanced role of states in the multistakeholder discourse, identifying the "public core" of the internet as entailing an obligation of care resting upon states. This line of argumentation leads current Dutch international policy efforts on internet governance, focusing on the initial, technical, narrow perception of the term.[52] Broeders relies on the evolving two-tier approach to the notion of internet governance.[53] This distinction is fundamental to the concept of the "public core of the internet" and the policy proposal to consider it a "global good".[54] This follows a current trend in cybersecurity debates, focused on redefining internet governance to better reflect current policy needs. Many authors offer novel approaches to the distribution of competence among stakeholders. For example,

50 Although this might lead into consumer protection issues, as with e.g. existing EU legal framework, obliging business to comply with local consumer protection laws at the seat of the consumer.

51 Alexander Klimburg (2017) *The Darkening Web, The War for Cyberspace*. New York: Penguin, 301–357.

52 Dennis Broeders (2015) *The Public Core of the Internet*. Amsterdam: AUP; Laura DeNardis (2009) *Protocol Politics. The Globalisation of Internet Governance*. New York: MIT Press.

53 Broeders argues that the first layer of governance refers to the "Internet's infrastructure, i.e. the governance of the core infrastructure and protocols of the Internet". As he claims "it is this public core that drives the Internet's development", where "the collective infrastructure takes precedence in this form of governance". The second form of governance covers using the Internet's infrastructure, where the Internet "becomes a tool in the battle to control online content and behavior"; Broeders 10.

54 For a comprehensive analysis of policies and trends in governance of global public goods see also: N. Kirsch (2014) The Decay of Consent: International Law in an Age of Global Public Goods. *American Journal of International Law*, Vol. 108, 1–40.

Savage and McConnell recommend "simplifying internet governance (IG) by partitioning it into issues that can be addressed by existing international agencies and those that cannot".[55] They suggest modifying the way international agencies dealing with internet governance related issues operate so as to reflect the multistakeholder model specific to ICANN.

The international fora to be considered as possibly addressing the issues relevant to the internet's core are:

1 The ITU as an intergovernmental organisation within the ambit of the United Nations, which, despite having taken steps towards multistakeholderism, still lacks the recognition from civil society or business;
2 The Internet Governance Forum (IGF) – run under UN auspices for over a decade, the IGF was never designed to actively attend to pertinent policy issues or serve as a platform for diplomatic negotiations, and hence still enjoys little interest from states, perceived more as a talk shop formula for civil society; and
3 ICANN as the current paradigm of multistakeholderism, yet, unlike the ITU, ill-suited for binding intergovernmental negotiations.

Multistakeholderism and international public law

Numerous scholars, this one included, have called for linking internet governance with the framework of international human rights law. They view the network as a global enabler for free speech, right to assembly and other human rights, following the path set by media law, relying on freedom of expression guarantees as the baseline of state commitment to the free flow of information online. This line of argumentation has also been reflected in a series of international organisations' policy documents, such as the Council of Europe and the United Nations. The CoE skilfully linked cybersecurity and human rights obligations resting upon states, where it combined effective network resilience and international cooperation. With critical infrastructure relying heavily on online technologies, be it for the purpose of reporting, early warning or exchange of information, there can no longer be security without cybersecurity. Simultaneously, cybersecurity relies on the usual good security practice, inclusive of sector cooperation, early warning systems, case studies and benchmarking.

In the transboundary world of the internet era, cybersecurity is an international matter. International cooperation is "intrinsically related to" the decentralised and distributed nature of this unique medium. Significantly, since all actions "in one jurisdiction may affect the ability of users to have access to information on the Internet in another", the international no-harm principle needs to be recognised as the starting point of any cybersecurity cooperation. This is also a derivative of the general obligation of states to act in compliance with international law, ensuring that "their actions do not have an adverse transboundary impact". The CoE Committee of Ministers made a direct reference to the possible harmful effect that the activities taken in one location may have on the "access to and use of the Internet" beyond state jurisdiction. States are therefore under an international obligation to "ensure that their actions within their jurisdictions do

55 J. E. Savage and Bruce McConnell (2015) *Exploring Multi-Stakeholder Internet Governance*. EastWest Institute, https://www.eastwest.ngo/sites/default/files/Exploring%20Multi-Stakeholder%20Internet%20Governance_0.pdf (accessed 27.03.2019), 2.

not illegitimately interfere with access to content outside their territorial boundaries or negatively impact the transboundary flow of Internet traffic" with a failure to meet this obligation resulting in possible responsibility for a non-diligent state.

One of the significant elements of the international legal order that comes into play with reference to online threats is the international human rights law, obliging states to refrain from putting illegitimate, from an international point of view, limitations on individual rights, in particular the right to privacy or freedom of expression.[56] Effectively, any "blanket surveillance;" that is, a non-case-specific invasion of privacy or any other restriction of online communications may not be introduced as a preventive measure as it would go against the body of international human rights law in general and against the recommendations of the Human Rights Council in particular, including, for example, those referring to Article 17 of the International Covenant on Civil and Political Rights (ICCPR).[57]

Furthermore, the aforementioned CoE 2011 Declaration by the Committee of Ministers on internet governance principles includes "human rights, democracy and the rule of law". This principle reflects the close reliance of all internet-related policies and laws to the fundamental principles of human rights law. Internet governance arrangements must ensure the protection of all fundamental rights and freedoms and affirm their universality, indivisibility, interdependence and interrelation in accordance with international human rights law. They must also ensure full respect for democracy and the rule of law and should promote sustainable development. All public and private actors should recognise and uphold human rights and fundamental freedoms in their operations and activities, as well as in the design of new technologies, services and applications. They should be aware of developments leading to the enhancement of, as well as threats to, fundamental rights and freedoms, and fully participate in efforts aimed at recognising newly emerging rights.

Taking the seemingly established concept of human rights "sameness" on and offline, one could reflect on its practical application. Does the internet's transboundary nature, scale, speed of communication, automation, interconnectivity and invisibility change the way in which we view and protect fundamental rights (privacy, data protection, non-discrimination, due process, presumption of innocence and free speech)? Are human rights online exactly the same as offline or are they modified by the internet-specific circumstances, possibly impacting their very core. In light of the observations made previously, the latter seems to be true, in line with Dworkin's interpretative approach to the law. All documents cited previously imply the need to apply human rights online "accordingly;" that is, with reference to and respect for the very nature of online communications. Law, as a reflection of time, ethics and culture, is a living organism, adaptable to current and particular circumstances. As such, it must attempt to protect the fundamental, core legal good behind a particular legal provision in the specific circumstances where this is needed. The arguments presented in this chapter imply that human rights law making and its application are being subjected to change. States are no longer the only makers and addressees of human rights law. The role of private companies is increasing, but so is the role of private parties, with users often interacting directly with the service providers ("voting with their feet") to change company policies, as the rapidly

56 *CoE, Recommendation CM/Rec(2011)8 . . .*, para. 1.1.1.

57 United Nations (1966) International Covenant on Civil and Political Rights, G.A. res. 2200A (XXI), U.N. Doc. A/6316 (1966).

changing Facebook policies prove. Companies no longer wait for states to introduce relevant legislation, changing their company policies solely based on consumer satisfaction polls.

However, despite the multistakeholder dynamics and the changing norm-making paradigms, there is a line to be drawn and it stems directly from human rights law. Whatever the practical applications of human rights online, despite the actors interpreting the norms, their core must remain protected. This core – the fundamental value behind the individual legal provision – is described and elaborated upon by the theory and practice of international law. If we are then to ask what is, for example, the right to privacy – international law will offer a comprehensive answer, spanning across decades and jurisdictions, implying one's right to decide upon the information referring to them. Yet if we ask about the ways and means to protect this particular right online – the current practice, be it "lex Facebook" or the actual, unfolding (2018) implementation of the EU's General Data Protection Regulation, will provide us with guidance. Multistakeholderism implies a balance: one between the values enshrined in law and the "appropriate" current ways of protecting them. This aim is to be met with the active participation of all stakeholder groups and will very much be a practical, balancing exercise.[58]

Conclusion

The current internet governance landscape was originally designed to reflect bottom-up governance processes, rooted strongly in the technical community, such as the Internet Society (ISOC) or the Internet Engineering Task Force (IETF) with its "Requests for Comments" (RfCs), community-developed common standards voluntarily followed by its members (Internet service providers or software developers). While "security by design" or "privacy by design" remain common paradigms within both ISOC and IETF, there is no link between this extra-legal, community-based rule-making and hard norm-setting model of, for example, the UN. While states, international organisations as well as internet governance bodies, such as ICANN, ISOC, or the IETF have been attending to the issue, this communications gap holds crucial relevance for the development of any effective international internet policies and must be addressed by whatever model of global internet policy comes next. As with other areas of international law, the effective cooperation between states and private stakeholders is a necessary precondition for any successful regulation. While the most significant challenges to applying the multistakeholder principle are security and human rights, international law offers a vast array of tools and measures with which those challenges may be tackled.

Applying the existing human rights law principles, norms and procedures to the internet with due respect for its multistakeholder model and as applicable to this unique, transnational environment is a safe path to follow. As previously described in detail, the "rough consensus and running code" imply a very practical, utilitarian approach to this norm-setting exercise.

Originating in the technical community – the IETF – the internet is all about practical, effective networking. This is also the lesson to be learned for human rights: while human rights as such leave room for discussion and prove challenging to effectively enforce on the

58 For a comprehensive look at how human rights balance can be met online see: Mart Susi, *Internet Balancing Formula* in this volume.

global scale, the internet offers a unique ambience where this challenge may be tackled. With the participation of all stakeholders – states, internet service providers and users – a better understanding of the needs of each actor can be elaborated. The international community can consider one of the two following scenarios as a way forward for global multistakeholder governance:

- Traditional international law making through a treaty (e.g. an internet cybersecurity framework convention) effective against all signatories, necessitating its transposition onto national laws;
- A novel approach to international law-making, inclusive of non-state actors, in particular open to ICANN and RIRs, who could use the conventional framework as a point of departure for their contractual compliance mechanisms.

From among the existing venues useful for enhancing the internet governance debate, ICANN seems best equipped to fuel the discussion. Yet by its very design it lacks effective tools to make any compromise internationally binding. It can therefore serve as a discussion platform, but not a diplomatic venue for advancing intergovernmental dialogue in its traditional sense. The contemporary international landscape lacks one venue where pertinent issues of governing cyberspace, protecting human rights, protecting and securing the global network can be discussed. It is therefore to be recommended for the existing venues to continue their work, aiming to provide an updated model for multistakeholder governance, one that takes account of the lessons learned thus far. As has been the case with the law of the sea or, more recently, environmental law, the principles shared among all stakeholders and across different venues may serve as a foundation for a comprehensive customary framework for internet governance, cybersecurity or, more specifically, human rights online, later to be transposed onto an international contractual compromise.

9 Judicial balancing of human rights online

Oreste Pollicino and Oleg Soldatov[1]

Introduction

This chapter addresses questions regarding the judicial balancing of competing rights and values online. To set the stage, it introduces the conceptual framework of judicial balancing in the digital age, providing the necessary definitions, and exploring the nature of judicial framing and its importance for understanding why judicial balancing that involves the same rights can lead to different results. In the second part of this chapter, the authors explore the polynomial components of the "balancing equation" that courts must solve in the digital age: namely, the various conflicting human rights as well as public and private interests that courts attempt to reconcile. Before reaching a conclusion, the authors move on to an examination of several case studies, underlining the differences in the approaches of the Court of Justice of the European Union (CJEU), the European Court of Human Rights (ECtHR), and the US Supreme Court.

Conceptual framework

One should not underestimate the role of courts in formulating the current global agenda. Some researchers even speak of the "judicialisation" of legal regimes: that is, the feedback effect of judicial law-making, where states delegate significant rights to courts.[2] This effect is amplified by "judicial globalization", which is a "process of judicial interaction [across] borders, exchanging ideas and cooperating in cases involving national as much as international law".[3]

Barak sees judicial balancing as "a metaphor, which assumes the shape of a scale",[4] on one side of which are the goals to be achieved, while on the other side are the limitations on rights. Whenever courts attempt to solve the "balancing equation", they have to decide between the marginal benefit to the public good and the marginal limitation on human rights. The act of balancing may be either "definitional" – where courts apply specific methodologies to arrive at outcomes with a degree of predictability, or "procedural" – where such an activity can be sliced into distinct logical steps, which tend to transform the

1 Oreste Pollicino authored the Introduction, Case Studies section and Conclusion; Oleg Soldatov authored the Conceptual Framework and Human Rights & Contemporary Challenges Section.

2 A. Stone Sweet and T. L. Brunell (2013) Trustee Courts and the Judicialization of International Regimes. *Journal of Law and Courts,* Vol. 1, 62.

3 A. Slaughter (2000) Judicial Globalization. *Virginia Journal of Intenational Law,* Vol. 40, 1104.

4 A. Barak (2010) Proportionality and Principled Balancing. *Law and Ethics of Human Rights,* Vol. 4, No. 1, 7 with further references.

underlying legal reasoning from a prudential to a procedural kind of judgement activity.[5] According to Durante, "individual rights can be partially sacrificed only . . . through the judicial activity of the Courts".[6]

When it comes to balancing in the digital era, "the demands of a democratic society and its obligations towards protecting individual rights must be balanced against the need and appetite for electronic commerce and information technology".[7] The speed of cyberspace development so far provides evidence that "the technical ability leads the policy component, which in turn is ahead of the legal and wider political framework".[8] This predicament gives momentum to the various searches for solutions in areas lagging behind technical developments. As Sajo points out, "translation of a technology and its consequences into the legal frame is not automatic".[9] This is where courts play an important role through the judicial process of translating something new into the language of past legal models[10] by means of the judicial framing technique. In other words, whenever judges are confronted with issues requiring a certain amount of technical expertise not related specifically to the law domain, judicial decision-making processes are influenced by the contextualisation of a given issue, arising from real life, in a legal frame.[11] This framing activity shapes the legal argumentation, and is characterised by the recurrence of words, lemmas, or rhetoric formulas. Examples of the judicial framing approach include the use of the term "piracy" in copyright infringement disputes related to the peer-to-peer exchange of data, or the resort to the word "privacy" in data protection disputes.[12]

A second layer of complexity is the nature of the internet itself – borderless on the one hand and multi-jurisdictional[13] on the other. The globalisation of the information society "progressively erodes the traditional distinction between national and supranational spaces".[14]

A third layer of complexity relates to the fact that there are two different approaches to state cyber power: a more liberal "free Internet" approach, in which the proponents see the state as a mild regulator of the online domain, and a more restrictive "national cyber sovereignty" approach that accentuates the authority of states to strictly control

5 M. Durante (2013) Dealing with Legal Conflicts in the Information Society. An Informational Understanding of Balancing Competing Interests. *Philosophy & Technology*, Vol. 26, No. 4, 446–447.

6 See Ibid., 455.

7 A. Rengel (2014) Privacy in International Law Privacy as an International Human Right and the Right to Obscurity in Cyberspace. *Groningen Journal of International Law*, 2(2), 42.

8 A. Klimburg (2017) *The Darkening Web*. New York: Penguin Random House, 6.

9 A. Sajó and C. Ryan (2016) Judicial Reasoning and New Technologies: Framing, Newness, Fundamental Rights and the Internet. In: O. Pollicino and G. Romeo (Eds.), *The Internet and Constitutional Law: The Protection of Fundamental Rights and Constitutional Adjudication in Europe*. New York: Routledge, 7.

10 Ibid., 8.

11 C. Riley (2009) The Rite of Rhetoric: Cognitive Framing in Technology Law. *Nevada Law Journal*, Vol. 9, No. 3, 495–544.

12 O. Pollicino and G. Romeo (2016) Concluding Remarks: Internet Law, Protection of Fundamental Rights and the Role of Constitutional Adjudication. In: O. Pollicino and G. Romeo (Eds.), *The Internet and Constitutional Law: The Protection of Fundamental Rights and Constitutional Adjudication in Europe*. New York: Routledge, 237–238.

13 O. Pollicino and M. Bassini (2014) Free Speech, Defamation and the Limits to Freedom of Expression in the EU: A Comparative Analysis. In: A. Savin and J. Trzaskowski, (Eds.), *Research Handbook on EU Internet Law*, 1st ed. Cheltenham: Edward Elgar, 508–542; B. Maier (2010) How Has the Law Attempted to Tackle the Borderless Nature of the Internet? *International Journal of Law and Information Technology*, Vol. 18, No. 2, 142–175.

14 See Durante 437–457, with further references; O. Pollicino (2015) The European Judicial Dialogue and the Protection of Fundamental Rights in the New Digital Environment. In: S. Morando-Foadi (Ed.), *The Case of Freedom of Speech*, Fundamental Rights in the EU: *A Matter For Two Courts*. London: Hart, 112.

the information that flows within their borders. For example, the Russian authorities, together with like-minded states such as China and Iran, being proponents of the second direction, have repeatedly emphasised the point that information in all its forms is a weapon, most often employed by terrorists.[15] Essentially, their approach maintains and highlights the notion that information on the Web should be managed rather than free-flowing. In the international arena, the views of the "managed flow" group of states were manifested in the International Code of Conduct for Information Security,[16] which was submitted for consideration to the UN General Assembly in January 2015 by the founding Member States of the Shanghai Cooperation Organisation – China, Russia and the "-stan" countries.[17] The burden of keeping in check the often-conflicting wishes of legislators in different nation-states falls heavily on the shoulders of courts. Nowadays, courts occupy a "privileged position that enables them to identify the risk of potential collisions that may encroach upon the effective protection of fundamental rights between interconnected legal systems".[18]

Naturally, a question arises as to the qualification of the judges to tackle IT-related issues and to go deeply into technicalities.[19] Sajo notes that the new technology may generate decisional uncertainty owing to the fact that the applicable constitutional rights and norms are often deliberately vague; the implications of a new technology therefore may not be transparent to the judge.[20] Should the society or the professional community of judges be in search of multi-disciplinary court judges? Could a professional judicial dialogue between courts of different jurisdictions help to foster an exchange of experiences, avoid fragmentation, ensure coherence between legal systems and develop a single vision for judicial balancing online?[21] At the European level, this dialogue was recently demonstrated in the *SABAM v. Scarlet* string of cases concerning the obligations of Internet Service Providers.[22] The dialogue was maintained in two directions: horizontal (between the Court of Justice of the European Union and the European Court of Human Rights) and vertical – between the supranational and national courts.[23] However, when it comes to a wider judicial dialogue between courts on different sides of the Atlantic Ocean, the authors' view leans towards pessimistic.[24]

15 See Klimburg 105–110.

16 Letter dated 9 January 2015 from the Permanent Representatives of China, Kazakhstan, Kyrgyzstan, the Russian Federation, Tajikistan, and Uzbekistan to the United Nations addressed to the Secretary-General, ccdcoe.org/sites/default/files/documents/UN-150113-CodeOfConduct.pdf (accessed 17.12.2017).

17 This draft document was criticised for being "a fundamental challenge to the flourishing of global thought" – see S. McKune (2015) An Analysis of the International Code of Conduct for Information Security. *The Citizen Lab*, citizenlab.ca/2015/09/international-code-of-conduct/ (accessed 4.1.2018).

18 See Pollicino 94.

19 A. Brenden and J. Priester (2011) Judicial Use of The Internet. *American Judges Association*. aja.ncsc.dni.us/conferences/2011Annual/SpeakerMaterials/13%20-%20Brenden_Priester_Internet.pdf, visited 20 July 2018.

20 See Sajó 8.

21 O. Pollicino and G. Martinico (2012) *The Interaction between Europe's Legal Systems: Judicial Dialogue and the Creation of Supranational Laws*. Cheltenham: Edward Elgar Publishing.

22 Case C – 70/10 *Scarlet Extended SA v. SABAM* [2011] ECR I – 11959 and Case C – 360/10 *SABAM v. Netlog NV* [2012] ECR – 0000.

23 European Judicial Cooperation in The Fundamental Rights Practice of National Courts. *European University Institute*. www.eui.eu/Projects/CentreForJudicialCooperation/Documents/JUDCOOPdeliverables/FinalHandbookUseofJudicialInteractionTechniquesinthefieldofEFRs.pdf (accessed 3.7.2018).

24 See Pollicino 112.

Human rights and contemporary challenges

The recent trend in internet development is a "shift towards mass participation in content creation", extending participation and fostering novel means with regard to the exchange of knowledge.[25] People may prefer using the world wide web to prior forms of media and communication because the internet allows "multiway" simultaneous forms of communication.[26] The European Court of Human Rights Judge Robert Spano acknowledged that in its current state the internet is unique, as a rich variety of content is made immediately available to anyone who can afford the relatively minimal cost of access; individuals can communicate their views, ideas and thoughts to others; and individuals have equal opportunities for communication.[27] These developments have had serious implications for freedom of expression, which, since its inclusion in Article 19 of the Universal Declaration of Human Rights, has been part of all of the relevant international human rights treaties.[28] For instance, in Europe this fundamental right falls within the ambit of Article 10 of the European Convention on Human Rights. The Convention protects the freedom to hold opinions and to receive and impart information and ideas without interference by a public authority, and regardless of frontiers. However, the freedom of speech protection offered by the European Convention of Human Rights is not absolute, since this right often must be reconciled with conflicting policy objectives such as the fight against illegal or harmful content.[29] Similar limitations can be found in other international treaties and national legal instruments,[30] and the interpretation of such provisions has an impact on both the public and the private sector.[31] However, the self-directing or unguided reading of such restrictions may lead to unnecessary curbing of freedom of expression. Individuals seeking to exercise this right can encounter government-imposed limitations (introduced with goals such as combating defamation or hate speech online) where "targets of restrictions include journalists and bloggers, critics of government, dissenters from conventional line, provocateurs and minorities of all sorts".[32] Here, courts act as the last line of defence, deciding or defining whether the laws or administrative practices that, on the surface, have a legitimate purpose, are not "a pretext for blocking or censoring the Internet".[33]

25 D. Kilburn and J. Earley (2015) Disqus Website-based Commenting as an E-research Method: Engaging Doctoral and Early-Career Academic Learners in Educational Research. *International Journal of Research & Method in Education,* Vol. 38, No. 3) 288.

26 P. Ford (2014) Freedom of Expression through Technological Networks: Accessing the Internet as a Fundamental Human Right. *Wisconsin International Law Journal,* Vol. 32, No. 1, 144–145.

27 R. Spano (2016) The Internet and the ECHR – A Paradigm Shift? [video]. *European Court of Human Rights.* tv.coe.int/ECHR/video.php?v=ECHR_20160118_Spano (accessed 2.5.2018).

28 See, generally, E. Howie (2018) Protecting the Human Right to Freedom of Expression in International Law. *International Journal of Speech-Language Pathology,* Vol. 20, No. 1, 12–15.

29 Article 10, European Convention on Human Rights. It should be noted that Article 10 also applies to the various forms and means in which it is transmitted and received – see, Council of Europe (2015) *Internet: Case-Law of the European Court of Human Rights.* Strasbourg: Council of Europe, 40.

30 A. Stone Sweet (2011) The Comparative Constitutional Law of Freedom of Expression. In: T. Ginsburg and R. Dixon (Eds.), *Comparative Constitutional Law.* Cheltenham: Edward Elgar, 406–421.

31 Intermediary liability for third-party behaviour is a concept recently introduced into the discussion concerning freedom of expression on the Internet – see, *Delfi AS v. Estonia* (Grand Chamber) Application No. 64569/09 (ECtHR, 16 June 2015).

32 UN General Assembly (2016) Report of the Special Rapporteur on the promotion and protection of the right to freedom of opinion and expression, UN Doc. A/71/373, para. 55.

33 P. Ford (2014) Freedom of Expression through Technological Networks: Accessing the Internet as a Fundamental Human Right. *Wisconsin International Law Journal,* Vol. 32, No. 1, 170.

Moreover, issues such as public morality or national security are notoriously difficult to define precisely and often a case-by-case examination by competent courts may be the only way forward.[34]

The media's switch from offline to the digital world has happened simultaneously with the expansion of the scale on which modern journalism operates. Back in pre-internet times, the proliferation of media was limited by the constraints of the physical world: "the airwaves could handle only so many TV and radio programs, shops could stock only so many books and records".[35] These constraints (high costs and narrow distribution channels) are currently disappearing, as "the virtual shelves of the Internet can expand to accommodate everything".[36] Anybody who has internet access is now a journalist.[37] This situation has profound implications when it comes to media-related freedoms,[38] as it has been long acknowledged that the media perform an essential function in a democratic society, and play a vital role in the form of public watchdog[39] and purveyor of information.[40] At the same time, there is an elevated risk of "fake news" being spread by either uneducated or ill-intentioned individuals. Under this "umbrella term", the authors refer to information that has been deliberately twisted or fabricated, and disseminated with the intention of deceiving and misleading others into believing falsehoods or doubting verifiable facts.[41] All of the preceding means that when it comes to the internet as a form of media, the balancing exercise is an extremely precarious one, since universal rules are either almost or entirely impossible to define.[42] Courts should be careful in limiting forms of online expression while combating fake news.[43]

The dynamics of the internet becoming a prevalent platform for expressing opinions are already finding their way into judicial reasoning.[44] Several new dimensions still need to be explored in detail in this regard – in particular, net neutrality[45] and recognition of access to the internet as a universal human right.[46] The first idea, net

34 See, *Perrin v. UK* Application No. 5446/03 (ECtHR, 18 October 2005).

35 N. Carr (2008) *The Big Switch*. New York: W.W. Norton & Company, 149.

36 Ibid., 150.

37 Rephrased statement of Sandra Mims Rowe, an editor for the Portland Oregonian in 1999, cited from K. Mushohwe (2014) Everyone Is Now a Journalist, Thanks to the Internet. *The Herald*, www.herald.co.zw/everyone-is-now-a-journalist-thanks-to-the-Internet/, (accessed 7.6.2018)

38 Move of media online and the challenges of balancing freedom of expression with other human rights are further corroborated in several high-profile cases before international courts, such as *Delfi AS v. Estonia*.

39 *The Sunday Times v. The United Kingdom* Application No. 6538/74 (ECtHR, 26 April 1979).

40 *Barthold v. Germany* Application No. 8734/79 (ECtHR, 25 March 1985).

41 See, T. McGonagle (2017) "Fake news": False Fears or Real Concerns? *Netherlands Quarterly of Human Rights*, Vol. 35, No. 4, 203–209.

42 In Europe, for instance, false stories and conspiracy theories presented as news and that constitute racist expression, incitement to hatred, or denial of the Holocaust will not benefit from freedom of expression protection; while satire, however, does enjoy protection, as it is a form of artistic expression and social commentary. See McGonagle 204, with further references.

43 See McGonagle 204.

44 In 2003, the US Supreme Court stated that Internet access in public libraries was not a "'traditional' public forum like sidewalks, because the Internet did not exist until recent times". See *United States v American Library Assn* 539 U.S. 194 (2003). Fourteen years later, the majority of the same Court analogised access to the Internet to public streets and parks, finding that the Internet was no different from traditional public forums – see, *Packingham v. North Carolina* 582 U.S. ___ (2017), para. 1735.

45 D. Brouwer (2017) Zero-rating and Net Neutrality in the European Union. *Tilburg University*, arno.uvt.nl/show.cgi?fid=143432 (accessed 20.7.2018).

46 S. Edwards (2012) Is Internet Access A Human Right? *Amnesty International*, blog.amnestyusa.org/middle-east/is-Internet-access-a-human-right (accessed 4.7. 2018).

neutrality, has emerged at the intersection of commerce, antitrust law, and human rights. It means that a broadband internet provider should not block, slow, or otherwise discriminate unfairly against any website or online service.[47] In other words, the internet should be operated like a public "road" – carrying all traffic, with no discrimination against any traveller, no matter what size, shape, or type.[48] This aspiration often conflicts with the commercial interests of network owners, who "would be delighted to have a tiered Internet, where if you pay the most you get the top tier, hence, your services run faster then everybody else's".[49] As regards the second idea, while it appears that internet access is not yet considered a human right, this question is high on the agenda of the international courts.[50]

The private sector has its own incentives for monitoring and controlling thoughts and opinions online. One of the typical challenges posed by the nature of the internet arises from the ease of information dissemination and is compounded by the prevalence of anonymity/pseudonymity among internet users. In practice, these two characteristics translate into widespread copyright violations.[51] Once converted to digital files, many works of authorship, including text, music and videos can be copied flawlessly at no cost – "technology, therefore, makes it possible for anyone with a computer to become a global distributor of published works".[52] In addition, modern technologies have helped to establish "new forms of art that rely on reproduction"[53] (e.g. remixing). Here, courts play a role in drawing a demarcation line between the clearly illegal dissemination of information and "fair use" or "private copy" use.[54] A tangential issue is a shift to selling consumer goods online, given the ease with which a user can become an online vendor. As a result, the sale of counterfeit goods online[55] has become a serious problem, and courts can participate by adjudicating quickly to determine the trademark likelihood of confusion[56] while balancing the rights of involved parties to a peaceful enjoyment of property.[57]

47 L. Downes (2017) The Tangled Web of Net Neutrality and Regulation. *Harvard Business Review*, hbr.org/2017/03/the-tangled-web-of-net-neutrality-and-regulation (accessed 15.7.2018).

48 J. Wihbey (2014) The Net Neutrality Debate and Underlying Dynamics: Research Perspectives. *Journalist's Resource*, journalistsresource.org/studies/society/Internet/net-neutrality-debate-underlying-dynamics-research-perspectives (accessed 14.7.2018).

49 T. Wu (2003) Network Neutrality, Broadband Discrimination. *Journal of Telecommunications and High Technology Law*, Vol. 2, 141.

50 European Court of Human Rights (2018) Factsheet – Access to Internet and Freedom to Reveilve and Impart Information and Ideas. *European Court of Human Rights Press Unit*, www.echr.coe.int/Documents/FS_Access_Internet_ENG.pdf (accessed 20.7.2018).

51 See, among many other sources, *Fredrik Neij and Peter SundeKolmisoppi (The Pirate Bay) v. Sweden* Application No. 40397/12 (ECtHR, 19 February 2013).

52 R. Ku and J. Lipton (2010) *Cyberspace Law: Cases and Materials*, 3rd edition, New York: Wolters Kluwer, 356.

53 B. J. Jütte (2016) The Beginning of a (Happy?) Relationship: Copyright and Freedom of Expression in Europe. *European Intellectual Property Review*, Vol. 38, No. 1, 11.

54 For instance, as provided in the exceptions set forth by the Information Society Directive. See B. J. Jütte (2016) Coexisting Digital Exploitation for Creative Content and the Private Use Exception. *International Journal of Law & Information Technology*, Vol. 24, No. 1, 1–21.

55 J. M. Schaefer (2011) IP Infringement Online: the Dark Side of Digital. *WIPO Magazine*, Vol. 2, 19.

56 See, P. Maeyaert and J. Muyldermans (2013) Likelihood of Confusion in Trademark Law: A Practical Guide Based on the Case Law in Community Trade Mark Oppositions from 2002 to 2012. *The Trademark Reporter*, Vol. 103, No. 5, 1032–1115.

57 IP rights also qualify as "possessions" within the meaning of the European Convention on Human Rights. See A. Grgić et al. (2007) *The Right to Property under the European Convention on Human Rights*. Strasbourg: Council of Europe, 7.

Another area where courts make a difference has to do with global surveillance and data protection.[58] The demands of a democratic society and its obligations towards protecting individual rights must be balanced against the need and desire for electronic commerce and information technology. The right to a private life – that is, the right not to be "subjected to arbitrary interference with his privacy, family, home or correspondence" as per Article 12 of the Universal Declaration of Human Rights – is also one of the universally applicable human rights.[59] The post-9/11 era "can be characterized by the desire and ability of governments to develop a global mass surveillance system, largely unseen".[60] Recent times have witnessed an increase in international police activities to fight terrorism, supported by "an enormous exchange of information for law enforcement purposes".[61] Private companies jumped gleefully onto a surveillance and data-gathering bandwagon, collecting information on online users that could later be used for marketing purposes,[62] or even for more nefarious reasons, as the recent Cambridge Analytica scandal demonstrated.[63] In this sphere, court adjudication may be an effective way of keeping overzealous legislators in check, as well as making sure private actors do not overstep the boundaries set by human rights standards.

Case studies: a tale of three courts

In this section, the authors document different approaches to balancing, as well as discuss diverse judicial frames by examining the practice of several influential courts, each of which has had opportunities to proclaim its standpoint on internet-related issues: the Court of Justice of the European Union (CJEU), the European Court of Human Rights (ECtHR), and the US Supreme Court.

Tale One. In analysing the recent developments in CJEU case law, one might conclude that the Luxembourg Court is taking privacy seriously, maybe even too much so. When it comes to balancing these interests with other fundamental rights, there is an asymmetry in the extensive interpretation of the scope of the right to privacy and data protection.

This view was encountered in the *Google Spain* decision,[64] in particular with regard to two specific points.[65] The Court of Justice said that the rights protected, respectively, by

58 See, for general discussion, D. Eady (2015) Privacy: A Judicial Perspective. In: J. Lewis et al. (Eds.), *Media Law and Ethics in the 21st Century*. New York: Macmillan, 3–34.

59 A. Rengel (2014) Privacy in International Law Privacy as an International Human Right and the Right to Obscurity in Cyberspace. *Groningen Journal of International Law*, Vol. 2, No. 2, 37–42. This right is enshrined in Article 17 of the International Covenant on Civil and Political Rights, Article 16 of the United Nations Convention on the rights of the child, Article 8 of the European Convention on Human Rights and so on.

60 A. Vedaschi and V. Lubello (2015) Data Retention and its Implications for the Fundamental Right to Privacy. *Tilburg Law Review*, Vol. 20, 15.

61 Opinion of the European Data Protection Supervisor on the Communication from the Commission to the European Parliament, the Council, the Economic and Social Committee and the Committee of the Regions. A comprehensive approach on personal data protection in the European Union, OJ C 181/01, 22 June 2011, 1.

62 See, generally, E. Pariser (2011) *The Filter Biubble*. London: The Penguin Group.

63 Anonymous (2018) Fire and Fury for Facebook. *Interntational Financial Law Review*, www.iflr.com/Article/3803223/Fire-and-fury-for-Facebook.html (accessed 18.7.2018).

64 Case C-131/12 *Google Spain SL, Google Inc. v. Agencia Española de Protección de Datos, Mario Costeja González* (2014). As is well known, the *Google Spain* case concerned the enforceability of the rights set forth by the Data Protection Directive vis-á-vis Internet search engine service providers. Accordingly, the question raised before the Court also called for consideration of the impact on the freedom to conduct business that organisations enjoy pursuant to Article 16 of the Charter.

65 See also O. Pollicino and M. Bassini (2015) The Luxembourg Sense of the Internet: Towards a Right to Digital Privacy? In G. Ziccardi Capaldo (Ed.), *The Global Community Yearbook of International Law and Jurisprudence 2014*. Oxford: Oxford University Press, 223.

Article 7 and Article 8 of the Charter of Fundamental Rights of the European Union, should in principle prevail over the economic interests of search engine service providers. Such an underestimation of economic freedoms resulting from this approach seems inconsistent with the Charter, which does not appear to assign different priorities to the various fundamental rights within its scope.[66]

Additionally, in the reasoning of the Court, the same "data privacy-oriented" approach was confirmed by the lack of any reference to freedom of expression and information. In its judgement, the Court did not even mention Article 11 of the Charter, which was in contrast to the much more balanced approach of the Advocate General.[67] It is worth mentioning at least one passage contained in the opinion in which – contrary to the CJEU approach – the AG clearly considered the need to balance enforcement of the right to privacy on the internet with the need to secure the protection of freedom of expression online. Specifically, as regards the possible implementation of a notice and takedown procedure based upon individual complaints, the AG articulated that the imposition of such a system for the removal of the indexed content would undermine the freedom of expression of the websites' owners, as it would amount to private censorship. This radical privacy-based approach weakens protection of the rights that may conflict with the new digital right to privacy. The excessive protection of the right to be forgotten puts at risk the necessary protection afforded to the right of expression, and particularly to the right of each internet user to be properly and fully informed. [68]

Soon afterwards, the decision of the Court of Justice in *Schrems*[69] brought about a wave of judicial activism related to *Google Spain*. At the heart of this enthusiasm were efforts to strengthen enforcement of the digital right to privacy. The *Schrems* case can also be contextualised within the framework of the application of the principle of "equivalence" and the shift away from the principle of "adequacy" for the protection of fundamental rights in Europe. In *Schrems*, the Court of Justice had to confront the relationship between the EU legal order and the level of protection guaranteed to fundamental rights by a national legal order – that of the US.

The Court pointed out that the European Union is a union based on the rule of law, to clarify that "all acts of its institutions are subject to review of their compatibility with, in particular, the Treaties, general principles of law and fundamental rights", and that "a third country cannot be required to ensure a level of protection identical to that guaranteed in the EU legal order". With respect to other legal orders interacting with EU law, the protection of fundamental rights constitutes a distinguishing feature that may not be compromised by the European institutions when "opening" to any act of domestic or international law. If viewed through the lenses of relevant case law on the principle of equivalence, the *Schrems* decision introduces significant novelties: the Luxembourg Court seemed to have taken an approach that makes Europe, in an almost paradoxical way, a fortress of personal data without considering the political and legal impact of this decision in terms of the relationship with third countries.[70]

66 See Article 52, Charter of Fundamental Rights of the European Union.

67 Case C-131/12 *Google Spain SL, Google Inc. v. Agencia Española de Protección de Datos, Mario Costeja González* (2014), opinion of Attorney General Niilo Jääskinen, 25 June 2013.

68 M. Ronsenfeld, and A. Sajo (2006) Spreading Liberal Constitutionalism: An Inquiry Into the Fate of Free Speech in New Democracies. In: S. Choudhry (Ed.), *The Migration of Constitutional Ideas*. Cambridge: Cambridge University Press, 146.

69 Case C-362/14 *Maximillian Schrems v. Data Protection Commissioner* (2014).

70 See O. Pollicino and M. Bassini (2017) Bridge Is Down, Data Truck Can't Get Through … In: G. Ziccardi Capaldo (Ed.), *The Global Community Yearbook of International Law and Jurisprudence 2017*. Oxford: Oxford University Press, 245–265.

Tale Two. The Strasbourg-based European Court of Human Rights is not a newcomer to the balancing game. Even in the world of atoms it has had to deal with balancing issues that would later have repercussions in the world of bits. In *Handyside*,[71] the Court rejected a complaint by an editor who had been convicted for publishing a school textbook that contained sexually explicit content. The Court found that the restrictions imposed on freedom of expression, including seizure of the available copies of the book, met the criteria set forth under Article 10(2) of the Convention. However, the Court stressed that *freedom of expression* is applicable not only to "information" or "ideas" that are favourably received or regarded as inoffensive or as a matter of indifference, but also to those that offend, shock or disturb.

The ECtHR often acts within the frame of fear, as if risking the loss of control over the internet. In recent ECtHR decisions, the internet is seen as a medium posing new risks. This point emerged for the first time in the *Editorial Board of PravoyeDelo and Shtekel v. Ukraine*, a case concerning freedom of the press, as a specific segment relating to freedom of expression, where the ECtHR held that "the policies governing reproduction of material from the printed media and the Internet may differ".[72]

The assumption behind the Court's reasoning was that the internet is likely to generate new problems regarding the protection of fundamental rights, and that the measures applied to traditional media will be ineffective in the new digital environment. This means finding a new balance between freedom of expression and other human rights. In a nutshell, since the internet is giving rise to unprecedented legal issues, restrictions on freedom of expression should be accepted more broadly and vigorously. This remark alone is enough to illustrate how the ECtHR approach differs from that of the US Supreme Court, which expressed an opposite view in *Reno v. ACLU*, discussed in the following.

In *K.U. v. Finland*,[73] the ECtHR also emphasised the non-absolute nature of the protection of certain fundamental rights on the internet. The case concerned the dissemination of personal data related to a child by an anonymous individual who had posted an online advertisement in which he claimed to be looking for a sexual relationship. When the applicant lodged a complaint with the local court, no legal grounds were found under domestic law to force an ISP to disclose personal data in this type of criminal conduct case. In addition, domestic legislation failed to strike a balance between the right to data protection and other interests. Although the complaint was not based on Article 10 of the ECHR, the ECtHR made significant remarks concerning the exercise of free speech on the internet:

> Although freedom of expression and confidentiality of communications are primary considerations and users of . . . Internet services must have a guarantee that their own privacy and freedom of expression will be respected, such guarantee cannot be [absolute]. It is nonetheless the task of the legislator to provide the framework for reconciling the various claims which compete for protection in this context.[74]

It is only when limitations imposed on freedom of expression become excessive, compared with the aim pursued, that the Court will adopt a stricter approach. It did so for

71 *Handyside v. the United Kingdom* Application No. 5493/72 (EctHR, 7 December 1976).
72 *Editorial Board of Pravoye Delo and Shtekel v. Ukraine* Application No. 33014/05 (EctHR, 5 May 2011).
73 *K.U. v. Finland* Application No. 2872/02 (ECtHR, 2 September 2008).
74 Ibid., para. 49.

instance in *Ahmet Yildirim v. Turkey*,[75] where the ECtHR concluded that Turkey had violated Article 10 of the Convention by imposing a disproportionate restriction regarding internet access. In criminal proceedings against the owner of a website where expressions of opinion insulting Ataturk's memory had been posted, the Court made a note that the blocking of a website could be one of the legitimate restrictions that contracting states might adopt in accordance with Article 10(2) of the Convention, but only upon the condition that such a restriction would meet the requirement referenced in that provision. In that case, there was neither a strict legal framework as to the scope of the ban nor any provision for judicial review.

Ultimately, the ECtHR's approach has proved to be very cautious. Indeed, it has concluded that Article 10 of the ECHR would be violated if the restrictions on freedom of expression did not comply with the conditions set out in Article 10(2). Still, it has conceded that free speech is not an absolute right and does not enjoy greater protection compared with other fundamental rights; given the risks brought about by the internet, it is more likely that freedom of expression may be more limited online than it would be in a non-digital context.

The same thinking accompanied the decision in the *Pirate Bay*[76] case, in which the ECtHR rejected an application based on Article 10. The applicants were the owners of a famous online platform, where users were provided with links enabling the illegal downloading of copyrighted materials through peer-to-peer systems. The applicants had been convicted under the Swedish law forbidding copyright infringements; however, they made a complaint that their right to freedom of expression had been violated. The Court ruled the complaint inadmissible, as the restriction imposed on free speech complied with the conditions set out in Article 10(2) of the Convention, and was proportional to the legitimate aim pursued.[77]

Generally, the Court of Strasbourg supports the view that the advent of new technologies, and of the internet in particular, has not expanded the scope of freedom of expression. On the contrary, in the *Stoll* case,[78] the Court's reasoning relies on the assumption that new technologies have made the duties and responsibilities of journalists more demanding.

The application of the proportionality principle was at the heart of *Delfi v. Estonia*.[79] The ECtHR in this case had to consider whether a fine imposed on an internet news portal for defamatory comments posted by users, and that were not promptly removed by the provider, amounted to a restriction of freedom of expression. The Strasbourg Court confirmed that Article 10 of the Convention did not afford protection to freedom of expression in absolute terms and proclaimed that the national measure did not constitute a disproportionate restriction on the applicant company's right to freedom of expression. Accordingly, no violation of Article 10 of the Convention was determined. The Court reasoning simultaneously supports two opinions that sit uncomfortably together – one

75 *Ahmet Yildirim v. Turkey* Application No. 3111/10 (EctHR, 18 December 2012). In this case, an administrative authority had ordered that all Google sites be blocked to prevent access to the site in question, without ascertaining whether a less far-reaching measure could have been taken.

76 *Fredrik Neij and Peter SundeKolmisoppi (The Pirate Bay) v. Sweden* Application No. 40397/12 (ECtHR, 19 February 2013).

77 See also *Ashby Donald and Others v. France* Application No. 36769/08 (ECtHR, 10 January 2013).

78 *Stoll v. Switzerland (*Grand Chamber) Application No. 69698/01 (ECtHR, 10 December 2007).

79 See *Delfi AS v. Estonia*.

describes the internet as "an unprecedented platform for the exercise of freedom of expression", and the other characterises the internet as a medium posing "certain danger".[80] Overall, the "certain danger" perspective seems to prevail. Noteworthy is that the joint dissenting opinion of two Judges, Sajó and Tsotsoria, was focused critically on this issue, and it argued that the result of the case was influenced by the overall "technology-biased" frame of mind. The presumption of civil liability of the intermediary was grounded in the idea that the internet was uniquely dangerous. The two dissenting judges held the strong view that the internet was "a sphere of robust public discourse with novel opportunities for enhanced democracy".[81]

It appears that the ECtHR – in the process of resettlement from the world of atoms to the world of bits – has changed its approach to balancing freedom of expression with other rights. This also marked the decrease in the relative weight of freedom of expression whenever balanced with other fundamental rights.

Tale Three. In contrast, in the authors' view, the US Supreme Court acts within the frame of "digital trust". A landmark ruling by the US Supreme Court in the sphere of freedom of expression on the internet is *Reno v. ACLU*.[82] The Supreme Court found unconstitutional the provisions contained in the Communication Decency Act, which criminalised the online distribution of obscene or indecent materials to any person under the age of 18. In the view of the Court, the CDA posed restrictions that were too vague and lacked the precision required to limit free speech only to the extent necessary for the protection of minors, in particular by failing to properly define "indecent" and "patently offensive" content. The decision took expressly into account the difference between the nature of the internet and that of other media such as radio and television:

> radio and television, unlike the Internet, have . . . received the most limited First Amendment protection, . . . in large part because warnings could not adequately protect the listener from unexpected program content. . . . [On the Internet], the risk of encountering indecent material by accident is remote because a series of affirmative steps is required to access specific material.[83]

A similar ethos informed the attempt of the US government to regulate the protection of minors online. In 1998, after the US Supreme Court had struck down the relevant part of the Communication Decency Act, the Child Online Protection Act came into force with the same purposes in mind. The act was reviewed by the Supreme Court, which declared it to be contrary to the First Amendment. Specifically, the COPA defined "the material harmful to minors" as being any material that was obscene, or that – based on community standards – might be considered by the average person as being appealing to prurient interests. This definition, according to the Supreme Court,[84] failed to meet the standards required to circumscribe limitations regarding free speech.

Another decision on the protection of freedom of speech on the internet was taken in *Ashcroft v. Free Speech Coalition*.[85] Reinforcing efforts – by way of the Child Pornography

80 Ibid., para. 110.

81 Ibid., Joint dissenting opinion of Judges Sajó and Tsotsoria, para. 6.

82 *Reno v. American Civil Liberties Union* 521 U.S. 844 (1997).

83 Ibid.

84 *Ashcroft v. American Civil Liberties Union* 535 U.S. 564 (2002).

85 Ibid.

Prevention Act adopted in 1996 – to protect minors from the dissemination of explicit content, the judgement found disproportionate and overly broad the restrictions introduced by this act with regard to freedom of expression. Most notably, the decision was focused on the provisions that prohibited the diffusion of images of persons that appeared to be minors engaged in sexual activity, as well as any form of speech conveying the impression that the images reproduced minors involved in sexual behaviour. Free-speech activists complained that this type of regulation had chilling effects. The Supreme Court found that notwithstanding the fact that Congress had the authority to pass laws with the aim of preventing child pornography and the circulation of obscene material, the restrictions to freedom of speech were overly broad and in violation of the First Amendment.

Fifteen years later, judging from the reasoning in *Packingham v. North Carolina*, the US Supreme Court still found itself operating in the frame of digital trust. In 2008, the North Carolina General Assembly enacted legislation[86] that bans the use of commercial social networking websites by sex offenders. This law makes it a felony for any person on the state's registry of former sex offenders to "access" websites – including Facebook and YouTube – that allow minors to have accounts and enable communication. The law covers people who have completed all criminal justice supervision, and it applies without the requirement for the state to prove that the accused had contact with – or had gathered information about – a minor, or had accessed a website for any illicit or improper purpose. North Carolina is not the only state to pass a law banning access to social media for certain categories of sex offenders – similar statutory provisions can be found in Indiana, Louisiana and Nebraska.[87] In April 2010, the police identified Mr Packingham, who, despite being aware of the prohibition, had been making use of his Facebook account. The defendant was subsequently indicted. The North Carolina Supreme Court[88] sustained his conviction and upheld the constitutionality of the disputed provision, claiming the state had sufficient interest in "forestalling the illicit lurking and contact" of registered sex offenders and their potential future victims, thereby facilitating "the legitimate and important aim of the protection of minors". The dispute eventually reached the US Supreme Court, which determined the impugned law to be unconstitutional. It was further stated that the Court should exercise "extreme caution"[89] before limiting application of the First Amendment to the internet.

> While we now may be coming to the realization that the cyber age is a revolution of historic proportions. . . . The forces and directions of the Internet are so [new and far-reaching] that courts must be conscious that what they say today might be obsolete tomorrow.[90]

On reflection, the differences are very clear in terms of how the three selected courts approach a judicial balancing of human rights online. Regrettably, this disparity between judicial solutions does not promote optimism or hope with regard to a timely convergence

86 N.C.G.S. § 14–202.5.

87 J. Hitz (2014) Removing Disfavored Faces from Facebook: The Freedom of Speech Implications of Banning Sex Offenders from Social Media. *Indiana Law Journal*, Vol. 89, No. 3, 1239.

88 *State v. Packingham*, 368 N.C. 380 (2015).

89 *Packingham v. North Carolina* 582 U.S. ___ (2017).

90 Ibid.

in the balancing approaches. On the contrary, signs of divergence can be discerned in the way courts interpret fundamental rights online.

Conclusion

The courts play a major role in formulating the current global agenda, as states tend to delegate significant rights to courts, while the courts interact across borders, exchanging ideas with regard to cases that involve national and international law. In the process of adjudication, courts solve multiple "balancing equations", taking on the uneasy responsibility of deciding whether to limit certain fundamental rights with a view to protecting competing fundamental rights for the benefit of the public. The speed of cyberspace development means that courts, through the application of the judicial frame, must translate the language of technology into the language of past legal models, ensuring a transition from the world of atoms to the world of bits.

The nature of the internet – borderless, multi-jurisdictional, and, as of now, still mostly uncontrolled – adds an extra layer of complexity to the job of courts. A recent shift towards mass participation in content creation online – coupled with the fact that people prefer using the world wide web to prior forms of media – has threatened freedom of expression. Everyone is a journalist nowadays, playing what was formerly the media's role of public watchdog. This development makes many governments uncomfortable and calls for courts to act as the last line of defence, striking down those laws or practices that censor the internet. The reverse side of this coin – the darker face of the internet – features fake news, is full of IP-infringing content, and it is a tool in the network of global mass surveillance.

To conclude this analysis – a conclusion which must inevitably be approximate and will require further inquiry – if one considers the differences within the results arrived at by the US Supreme Court on the one hand and the ECtHR on the other hand in the area of freedom of expression, it must be confirmed that the use of a particular value frame is capable not only of influencing the argumentative structure of a decision and the balance struck by the courts, but also consequently of impinging upon the level of protection for the fundamental rights in play.

Let us return for a moment to the *Reno* judgment, in which the Supreme Court saw the internet as a "new free marketplace of ideas" and held that:

> As a matter of constitutional tradition, in the absence of evidence to the contrary, we presume that governmental regulation of the content of speech is more likely to interfere with the free exchange of ideas than to encourage it. The interest in encouraging freedom of expression in a democratic society outweighs any theoretical but unproven benefit of censorship.[91]

We shall now compare this passage with the findings reached in the decisions referred to previously in which the ECtHR has been called upon to rule on the compatibility with Article 10 of the Convention of limits imposed by the respondent state on the exercise of the applicant's freedom of expression on the internet. As this study has attempted to establish, it is possible to identify from this analysis a judicial frame that seeks to

91 Reno para. 49.

re-moderate and rein in the expansive scope of Article 10 protection compared to the very broad protection freedom of expression enjoys in the analogue domain. Perhaps, the most complete manifestation of this re-moderation and reining in may be found in 2011 when the ECtHR held that:

> the Internet is an information and communication tool particularly distinct from the printed media, especially as regards the capacity to store and transmit information. The electronic network, serving billions of users worldwide, [is not] subject to the same regulations and control. The risk of harm posed by content and communications on the Internet to the exercise and enjoyment of human rights and freedoms . . . is certainly higher than that posed by the press. Therefore, the policies governing reproduction of material from the printed media and the Internet may differ. The latter undeniably have to be adjusted according to technology's specific features.[92]

It is evident that the European Court placed the emphasis less on the benefits of further expansion of the exercise of freedom of expression online and more on the risks that such an expansion could have – through a technological instrument that, at least *prima facie*[93] falls beyond the control of states – on effective protection for rights and other freedoms.

The two courts appear to be working on the basis of opposite presumptions: in contrast to the digital distrust in the new technology apparent from the case law of the European courts, the frame underlying the case law referred to of the Supreme Court is one of unconditional faith in the instrument, which is considered to be capable of further expanding the reach of First Amendment freedoms.[94] For the purposes of this analysis the need to examine the new technology and compare it with traditional media takes on a different significance depending upon the frame of reference chosen.

For the Supreme Court, acting in accordance with that value frame defined by trust in the "novelty" of the web, the original nature of the technology is referred to in support of the need for reduced regulatory intrusion on the web compared to the regulatory framework applicable to television; for the European Court the same argument is drawn upon in order to justify greater encroachment by the states on freedom of expression when it is exercised online compared to when it is exercised, for example, through the printing press. This occurs in accordance with a frame that is characterised by substantial mistrust in the new technology.

Within the cases analysed, the choice of frame (of a value context of a highly figurative nature within which disputes may be resolved) cannot simply be described as the use of a rhetorical and argumentative contrivance to persuade the audience of the soundness of the decision reached. On the contrary, this choice has immediate repercussions on the way in which the courts engage with new technologies, and ultimately on the outcome to the balancing operation between the rights and freedoms that come into play online.

92 See *Editorial Board of Pravoye Delo* para. 63.

93 J. Goldsmith and T. Wu (2006) *Who Controls Internet? Illusions of a Borderless Worl.*, New York: Oxford University Press.

94 The First Amendment to the US Constitution states: "*Congress shall make no law respecting an establishment of religion, or prohibiting the free exercise thereof; or abridging the freedom of speech, or of the press; or the right of the people peaceably to assemble, and to petition the Government for a redress of grievances*".

However, metaphors such as those that describe the internet as a "new free marketplace of ideas" and the law of the web as a "Law of the Horse"[95] are, thanks to their imaginative capacity, capable of impinging significantly on the frame of reference, conditioning the scope of the value frame that is used by the courts or by the decision-making body in the particular case. If the reference to the "free marketplace of ideas" to define the expansive scope of digital technology reflects a vision of the Supreme Court amplifying the unbridled freedom of expression under the First Amendment beyond its scope in the real world, the provocative reference by Easterbrook to the law of the horse reveals an opposing attitude of incomplete acceptance of the new technology, typical of someone considering the internet from the point of view of the analogue reality. The freedom which the courts have within the digital domain in choosing the metaphorical universe that is capable of offering the decisive parameters to resolve the disputes that come before them gives rise to further grounds for discussion within the ongoing debate in North America and Europe concerning the institutional role of the courts.[96] Still, it cannot be denied that the courts nowadays occupy a privileged position within their respective legal systems in identifying the risks of constitutionally relevant collisions between rights, in particular in terms of the identification of the highest standard of protection for the particular rights in play, and consequently in intervening – through dialogue – to avoid the risk of an inter-constitutional "collision" and to improve the quality of interaction between legal systems.

All of this appears to be even more applicable to that specific interaction between courts that occurs in relation to the internet, where the risk of a collision is even higher for at least two reasons, one substantive and the other procedural. Regarding the first reason, on the one hand the continuous and dizzying change in the relevant technological scenario and on the other hand the transnational nature of the web considerably magnify the difficulties, which are already apparent in other areas, that national and supranational legislatures encounter in providing even minimum normative protection capable of addressing the most significant questions. It is evident that an immediate consequence of that inertia on the legislative side is the amplification of the creative, substitutive role of the courts. As regards the second, procedural, reason, this role – and, generally, the centrality of the jurisprudential "moment" – have been further expanded on the one hand by the fact that the questions relating to the relevant court perform a crucial role due to the cross-border nature of the web, and on the other hand by the fact that the issue as to the applicable law – a question logically related to that concerning the jurisdiction of the relevant court – has far-reaching implications for the standard of protection for the fundamental rights in play.

Do these factors indicate the pre-eminence of the judicial over political/representative bodies in identifying para-constitutional conflicts between fundamental rights (and systems) within the digital realm? Probably not.

The recovery of an institutional system that can guarantee sufficient standards of foreseeability for judicial decisions, and at the same time an articulation of powers that is consistent with the founding principles of contemporary constitutional democracies appears to be an objective that can realistically (and perhaps must) be achieved. The

95 F. Easterbrook (1996) Cyberspace and the Law of the Horse. *University of Chicago Legal Forum*, 207.

96 A. Rosas (2007) The European Court of Justice in Context: Forms and Patterns of Judicial Dialogue. *European Journal of Legal Studies*, Vol. 1, No. 2; R. Hirschl (2004) *Towards Juristocracy. The Origins and Consequences of the New Constitutionalism*. London: Harvard University Press; J. Allard and A. Garapon (2005) *Les juges dans le mondialisation. La nouvelle révolution du droit*. Paris: Seuil.

problem is how to achieve it: whether specifically by giving back a significant role to representative political institutions or through the adoption by the courts of an approach characterised by self-restraint, without the risk of the legislative inertia turning into more general inertia, immobility and stagnation.

These questions largely fall beyond the limits of this study. However, the point to stress upon conclusion of this inquiry is the importance of studying the argumentative paths followed by the courts in reaching their decisions, affording attention to the metaphors they use to provide an answer to the various questions of justice.

Metaphorical language structures narratives even in the world of the law; it is therefore necessary to analyses the strategies followed by the principal "narrators" of the web, to understand the dynamics within the development of the current legal reality and to verify its consistency – within new technological and globalised contexts – with the traditional paradigms of modern constitutionalism.

10 The role and practices of online stakeholders

Thomas Wischmeyer

Introduction

When the internet began to take off in the early 1990s, neither the legal concept nor the business model of an online intermediary truly existed.[1] Twenty years later, scholars call intermediaries the "governors"[2] or the "sovereigns of cyberspace"[3] and the experience provided by online intermediaries are what most users consider to be "the internet". Intermediaries such as social media platforms and search engines control large parts of the global information flows.[4] The companies have earned their powerful position, because they are the gatekeepers[5] of the online world and can charge all parties of a transaction for their matchmaking services: content providers pay with money in order to place their products in an attractive environment; consumers pay with personal data.[6] At the same time, intermediaries are largely exempted from liability for illegal activities committed through their services, because lawmakers across the globe have enacted safe-harbour laws in order to jump-start the digital economy. Economically and legally, online intermediaries seem to live in the best of all worlds.

However, these golden days are slowly coming to an end, not because the business model is failing – this might happen, if blockchain technology becomes commercially viable – but because governments are slowly re-tightening their regulatory grip. Various factors are responsible for this development. For one, the industry is now mature, which makes indirect subsidies in the form of liability exemptions more difficult to justify. More important, however, is the fact that the gatekeeping role of intermediaries turned out to be not just economically advantageous, but also a matter of great political salience. Despite their best efforts to remain neutral vis-à-vis the content created by their users, intermediaries could not avoid making decisions on which forms of speech are permissible on

1 On the rise of online intermediaries see Laura DeNardis (2014) *The Global War for Internet Governance*. New Haven, CT: Yale University Press, 153–172.

2 Frank A. Pasquale (2010) Beyond Innovation and Competition: The Need for Qualified Transparency in Internet Intermediaries. *Northwestern University Law Review*. Vol. 104, 105; Kate Klonick (2018) The New Governors: The People, Rules, and Processes Governing Online Speech. *Harvard Law Review*. Vol. 131, 1598.

3 Rebecca MacKinnon (2012) Consent of the Networked: The Worldwide Struggle for Internet Freedom. *Politique étrangère*, Vol. 50, No. 2, 115–168.

4 Cf. DeNardis 154.

5 Jonathan Zittrain (2006) A History of Online Gatekeeping. *Harvard Journal of Law & Technology*. Vol. 19, 253. See also Natasha Tusikov (2016) Chokepoints. *Global Private Regulation on the Internet*. Oakland, CA: University of California Press.

6 On the business model of intermediaries see David S. Evans and Richard Schmalensee (2016) *Matchmakers: The New Economics of Multisided Platforms*. Boston, MA: Harvard Business Review Press.

their platforms and what level of privacy protection their users enjoy.[7] For authoritarian states, which fear that they might lose influence in cyberspace, this power is a direct provocation. But democratic governments, too, are challenged, if the internal codes of conduct and the privacy policies of information and communications technology (ICT) companies supersede statutory law and become the *de facto* regime for online speech. Moreover, governments realised that because of their role as gatekeepers, online intermediaries naturally possess large troves of personal data, which can be used for intelligence and law-enforcement purposes. Intermediaries were therefore encouraged to join – or coerced into – partnerships with government agencies, which made them an integral part of the online surveillance architecture built up in many countries over the last decade.[8]

That intermediaries are not only "neutral" carriers of data became even more evident with the rise of social media, a type of intermediary which did not exist when the original liability exemptions for intermediaries were enacted. Social media build a unique space for meaningful debate and social connectivity. However, they also create new and exacerbate old problems for the public sphere: The proliferation of harmful content, including the incitement to terrorism, child pornography and hate speech, turned out to be the ugly underbelly of the social media revolution. And while the effects of social media-induced filter bubbles, echo chambers and fake news are still debated amongst social scientists, intermediaries are no longer able to convince the general public that their activities consist solely in providing an infrastructure for other people's content.[9]

Against this backdrop, we are currently observing that all over the globe intermediaries are struggling against what they frame as an overly zealous regulatory state and what regulators conceptualise as necessary and proportionate measures to bring the political, economic and social powers of intermediaries in line with public interests such as security, privacy, consumer protection and the respect for the fundamental rights of those affected by liability exemptions, e.g. the victims of online hate speech. In this debate, intermediaries are increasingly often described as quasi-public entities for the online world which must be held to the same standards of transparency, rights protection and legitimacy as state actors. This turn from limited liability to responsibility, which mirrors a broader development of the global internet from a societal playground to an essential infrastructure for markets, politics and public discourse, has received widespread attention in literature.[10]

While intermediaries will most likely not be able to evade the new wave of regulation completely, the wealth and the power they could acquire in the past and the crucial role they continue to play for the architecture of cyberspace will allow them to negotiate the terms of their deal. In this context, state actors will evaluate the need for enhanced regulation also in light of the activities and performance of major stakeholder-led initiatives currently underway both regionally and internationally. These initiatives, which include the Global Network Initiative (GNI) or the Manila Group, are mostly organised by or

7 Rebecca MacKinnon et al. (2014) *Fostering Freedom Online: The Role of Internet Intermediaries*. Paris: UNESCO Publishing.

8 Cf. Thomas Wischmeyer (2017) *Überwachung ohne Grenzen*. Baden-Baden: Nomos.

9 Karine Nahon (2015) Where There Is Social Media There Is Politics. In: A. Bruns et al. (Eds.), *The Routledge Companion to Social Media and Politics*. London: Routledge.

10 Urs Gasser and Wolfgang Schulz (2015) Governance of Online Intermediaries: Observations from a Series of National Case Studies. *Korea University Law Review*, Vol. 18, 79; Mariarosaria Taddeo and Luciano Floridi (2017) *The Responsibilities of Online Service Providers*. Berlin/Heidelberg: Springer; Giancarlo F. Frosio (2018) Why Keep a Dog and Bark Yourself? From Intermediary Liability to Responsibility. *International Journal of Law and Information Technology*, Vol. 26, (start page) 1.

around the business practices of large intermediaries. The better these *collective* instruments of horizontal governance operate, the greater the chances for intermediaries to avoid vertical intervention.[11]

Because the self-regulatory efforts of these stakeholder-led initiatives must be situated in the broader technological, legal and historical context of intermediary liability, this chapter on the role and practices of online stakeholders starts by analysing the recent discussions about intermediary responsibility. It then maps the global landscape of current stakeholder-led initiatives and evaluates whether we can observe the emergence of some common standards in intermediary self-regulation. Lastly, it will discuss the success of the initiatives in terms of horizontal governance.

Intermediaries: from limited liability to intermediary responsibility

The concept of an "intermediary" refers to a wide range of actors within the internet ecosystem. According to a 2010 definition of the Organisation for Economic Co-operation and Development (OECD), internet intermediaries provide "the Internet's basic infrastructure and platforms by enabling communications and transactions between third parties as well as applications and services" and, more specifically, by "giv[ing] access to, host[ing], transmit[ting] and index[ing] content, products and services originated by third parties on the Internet or provide Internet-based services to third parties".[12] This definition includes telecommunication and internet service providers, search engines, social networks, cloud service providers, platforms and many more.[13]

When governments first started to consider the rights and duties of online intermediaries in the early 1990s, they soon recognised that the question of intermediary liability was central for internet regulation. Now, building on the work of *Reinier Kraakman* on "gatekeepers", it would have been only natural to hold intermediaries responsible for the behaviour of primary infringers, even though there were mere "third parties", because they are "able to disrupt misconduct by withholding their cooperation from wrongdoers".[14] And indeed, some scholars argued that it would be "the best policy ... to hold the service provider liable. ... Service providers reap rewards for infringing activity. It is difficult to argue that they should not bear the responsibilities".[15]

Some Asian countries, most notably China and Thailand, decided to follow this approach and implemented strict liability regimes for intermediaries. Most countries, including the US and the EU Member States, however, went in the opposite direction and enacted laws which limit the liability of intermediaries, because they reasoned that doing otherwise might curb technological innovation.[16] In the US, section 230 of the Communications

11 Whether or not the self-regulatory efforts of ICT companies on an individual level are sufficient is a different question, which is not addressed in this chapter.

12 Karine Perset (2010) The Economic and Social Role of Internet Intermediaries. Paris, Organisation for Economic and Co-operation and Development (DSTI/ICCP(2009)9/FINAL), 6, 9, www.oecd.org/internet/ieconomy/44949023.pdf.

13 Cf. MacKinnon et al., 15.

14 Reinier H. Kraakman (1986) Gatekeepers: The Anatomy of a Third-Party Enforcement Strategy. *Journal of Law, Economics, and Organization*, Vol. 2, 53.

15 Bruce Lehman (1995) *Intellectual Property and the National Information Infrastructure: The Report of the Working Group on Intellectual Property Rights* 117–118. Darby, PA: Diane Publishing; cf. Frosio 3.

16 Cf. Frosio 3–12.

Decency Act of 1996 shields intermediaries from liability for any content provided by their users. In 1998, the Online Copyright Infringement Liability Limitation Act, which was part of the Digital Millennium Copyright Act, extended the safe harbour to copyright infringement and established a complex notice and takedown regime, according to which "Online Service Providers" are exempted from liability if they remove illegal content promptly upon receiving notice or block access to the data and inform the copyright holder of potential infringements which they have become aware of. Similarly, Articles 12 to 15 of the EU E-Commerce Directive of 2000 (ECD) oblige EU Member States to enact liability exemptions for access and host providers, and prohibit that Member States impose a general obligation on "Information Society Service Providers" to "monitor the information which they transmit or store" and "actively to seek facts or circumstances indicating illegal activity".[17] Shortly afterwards, the InfoSoc Directive and the Enforcement Directive paved the way for EU Member States to establish a notice-and-takedown-regime for intellectual property (IP) matters, too.[18]

Technically, intermediaries were thus never completely exempted from liability. In practice, however, they were largely shielded from any meaningful responsibility for the content which could be accessed through their services – as long as they had implemented internal enforcement mechanisms which allowed them to *react* quickly to complaints of IP rights-holders or other third parties whose rights were infringed. This situation was economically advantageous for intermediaries, because reactive measures to remove illegal content are relatively cheap and the right-holders or, respectively, the state and the victims bear the majority of enforcement costs.

As is well known, however, it is difficult not only for individuals, but also for law-enforcement agencies to identify the primary infringer and disrupt its illegal behaviour online, because of the "un-territoriality" of cyberspace, which conflicts with the territorial logic of law enforcement[19], the sheer quantity of online communications, and the speed with which illegal content can be moved and reposted. In many cases, it is therefore either the "gatekeeper" or nobody who will enforce the rules. For this reason, the content industry has been lobbying aggressively ever since the 1990s for mechanisms such as upload filters and a stricter liability regime for intermediaries in order to better protect IP rights. In recent years, similar concerns have been growing also with regard to non-IP related matters.

Especially the toxic culture of social media, which are increasingly used for terrorist recruitment, child pornography, and hate speech, harassment, bullying, etc., has led many political actors, including human rights activists and representatives of minority groups, to reconsider their attitude towards the obligation of platforms to introduce proactive measures for the removal of all illegal content. The idea that intermediaries "assume an

17 Directive 2000/31/EC of the European Parliament and of the Council of 8 June 2000 on certain legal aspects of information society services, in particular electronic commerce, in the Internal Market. OJ L 178, 17.7.2000, 1–16 [hereinafter E-Commerce Directive].

18 Directive 2001/29/EC of the European Parliament and of the Council of 22 May 2001 on the Harmonisation of Certain Aspects of Copyright and Related Rights in the Information Society, OJ L 167, 22.6.2001, 10–19 [hereinafter InfoSoc Directive]; Directive 2004/48/EC of the European Parliament and of the Council of 29 April 2000 on the Enforcement of Intellectual Property Rights, OJ L 195, 2.6.2004, 16–25 [hereinafter Enforcement Directive].

19 Jennifer Daskal (2015) The Un-Territoriality of Data. *Yale Law Journal*, Vol. 125, 326.

obligation as trustees of the greater good", which was still exotic in 2000,[20] has become commonplace in 2018. As Raphael Cohen-Almagor recently put it:

> Facebook and Google have more power than presidents and prime ministers. Power without responsibility is dangerous, corrosive and undermines our well-being. The internet's way should not be harmful. The internet's way should be enlightening, innovative, entertaining, productive, voicing the best of humanity. To ensure this, boundaries should be introduced, antisocial and violent activities should be curbed, and safe environments should be established.[21]

Similarly, Mariarosaria Taddeo and Luciano Floridi have advocated that intermediaries should now start to face their moral responsibilities towards their users and the society as a whole.[22]

These arguments have also started to resonate with lawmakers. In many countries, intermediary liability has become a major issue on the parliamentary agenda. Brazil's "Marco Civil da Internet" counts among the more prominent of these initiatives.[23] In the US, section 230 of the Communications Decency Act was amended in 2018 by the "Allow States and Victims to Fight Online Sex Trafficking Act – Stop Enabling Sex Traffickers Act", excluding the enforcement of sex-trafficking laws from its immunity. And when the European Commission emphasised in 2016 that "responsibility of online platforms is a key and cross-cutting issue" and a new goal of the Digital Single Market[24], Giancarlo Frosio is right in calling this "a substantial shift in intermediary liability theory that apparently would move away from a well-established utilitarian approach towards a moral approach by rejecting negligence-based intermediary liability arrangements".[25] Even if Frosio overlooks the fact that also the current "utilitarian" system expresses a certain moral standpoint, he is correct in pointing out that the change in semantics is probably the harbinger of a new wave of regulation. In 2017, the European Commission has reaffirmed its position that "the constantly rising influence of online platforms in society, which flows from their role as gatekeepers to content and information, increases their responsibilities towards their users and society at large".[26] Similarly, on an international level, the "Joint Declaration on Media Independence and Diversity in the Digital Age" by

20 See already Andrew Shapiro (2000) *The Control Revolution: How the Internet is Putting Individuals in Charge and Changing the World We Know*. New York: Perseus Books, 225.

21 Raphael Cohen-Almagor (2017) The Role of Internet Intermediaries in Tackling Terrorism Online. *Fordham Law Review*, Vol. 86, 425; see also Raphael Cohen-Almagor (2015) *Confronting the Internet's Dark Side: Moral and Social Responsibility on the Free Highway*. Cambridge: Cambridge University Press.

22 Mariarosaria Taddeo and Luciano Floridi (2016) The Debate on the Moral Responsibilities of Online Service Providers. *Science English Ethics*, Vol. 22, 1575; Mariarosaria Taddeo and Luciano Floridi (2017) New Civic Responsibilities for Online Service Providers. In: M. Taddeo and L. Floridi (Eds.) *The Responsibilities of Online Service Providers*. Berlin/Heidelberg: Springer. See also Marcelo Thompson (2016) Beyond Gatekeeping: The Normative Responsibility of Internet Intermediaries. *Vanderbilt Journal of Entertainment & Technology Law*, Vol. 18, 783.

23 For an overview see Corey Omer (2014) Intermediary Liability for Harmful Speech: Lessons from Abroad. *Harvard Journal of Law & Technology*, Vol. 28, 289; MacKinnon et al. For Brazil cf. Nicolo Zingales (2015) The Brazilian Approach to Internet Intermediary Liability: Blueprint for a Global Regime? *Internet Policy Review*, Vol. 4, 1.

24 European Commission (2016) Online Platforms and the Digital Single Market: Opportunities and Challenges for Europe (Communication). 25.5.2016, COM(2016) 288 final.

25 Frosio 32.

26 European Commission (2017) Tackling Illegal Content Online. Towards an enhanced responsibility of online platforms (Communication). 28.9.2017, COM(2017) 555 final.

the UN Rapporteur on Freedom of Opinion and Expression and others emphasises that "[m]edia outlets and online platforms, as (often) powerful corporate actors, should take seriously their responsibility to respect human rights".[27]

Intermediaries have reacted to this development by introducing or improving – with varying degrees of success – their internal rulebooks and the technical tools such as image-matching technology or digital fingerprinting, which they employ to proactively combat and delete illegal content such as terrorist propaganda or child pornography.[28] At the same time, they have started to engage or intensified their engagement in various stakeholder-led initiatives which deal with freedom of expression online, privacy and IP rights under the angle of intermediary responsibility. The question is, whether this engagement will convince lawmakers that everything is in order and prevent them from increasing regulatory pressure.

Mapping the landscape

Numerous stakeholder-led initiatives currently analyse the obligations of online intermediaries in protecting fundamental rights online and propose more or less detailed guidelines for its members and for politics. The initiatives have in common that they recognise the unique position of intermediaries in fighting the dark side of cyberspace, but generally advocate self-regulation rather than government intervention. While the initiatives all share a similar goal, they differ in their *territorial scope* – some operate primarily in a national context, some have regional ambitions, and some have a global reach; their *organisational structure* – some are primarily driven by one institution, some operate with a specific type of stakeholders, some are organised as multistakeholder initiatives; the *topics* they address – some focus exclusively on IP rights, some on free speech in general and some also address data protection; and in various other categories. The following analysis focuses on three paradigmatic initiatives, all global in reach, but with a different organisational structure, a different thematic focus, and a different understanding of what self-regulation means: the process-driven Global Network Initiative, the substance-oriented Manila Principles and the issue-oriented Google Advisory Council.

The Global Network Initiative

Mission and membership

The Global Network Initiative (GNI), which was launched in 2008 in order "to respond to government censorship and threats to privacy"[29], is still the most prominent

27 United Nations (UN) Special Rapporteur on Freedom of Opinion and Expression/Organization for Security and Co-operation in Europe (OSCE) Representative on Freedom of the Media/Organization of American States (OAS) Special Rapporteur on Freedom of Expression/African Commission on Human and Peoples' Rights (ACHPR) Special Rapporteur on Freedom of Expression and Access to Information [hereinafter: Joint Special Rapporteurs], Joint Declaration on Media Independence and Diversity in the Digital Age, 2.5.2018, www.ohchr.org/Documents/Issues/Opinion/JointDeclaration2May2018_EN.pdf

28 Cf. Cohen-Almagor 445–446.

29 GNI, Diverse Coalition Launches New Effort to Respond to Government Censorship and Threats to Privacy (PressRelease), 26.10.2008, https://web.archive.org/web/20090227023205/www.globalnetworkinitiative.org/newsandevents/Diverse_Coalition_Launches_New_Effort_To_Respond_to_Government_Censorship_and_Threats_to_Privacy.php

multistakeholder initiative, which concerns itself with the responsibilities of online intermediaries. Only recently, it was mentioned favourably in the 2018 Report of the Special Rapporteur on the promotion and protection of the right to freedom of opinion and expression.[30]

Since its founding, the membership of the GNI, which describes itself as a non-governmental organisation, consists of a diverse coalition of ICT companies (including Alphabet and Microsoft), human rights organisations (including Human Rights Watch), investors (including the Church of Sweden) and academic institutions (including the Berkman Center for Internet & Society at Harvard Law School). The most prominent member, which joined the GNI after its founding, was Facebook, in 2013. As of 2018, GNI members include six academic organisations, twelve individual academics, 20 civil society groups, eleven ICT companies, and seven investors. Two ICT companies have an observer status. However, several organisations have also left the GNI since 2008: Amnesty International, which had participated in the preparation of the GNI principles, walked out even before the GNI was formally launched citing concerns that the principles were "not yet strong enough" for Amnesty to support them.[31] The Electronic Frontier Foundation (EFF), which had been a member of the GNI since its formation in 2008, left the organisation in 2013, criticising the collaboration of several GNI corporate members with US government in surveillance matters.[32] And in 2016, the NYU Center for Business and Human Rights resigned its membership following an internal dispute about the long-term strategy of the GNI for reasons, which we will return to in a moment.

The self-ascribed mission of the GNI is "to protect and advance the human rights of freedom of expression and privacy when faced with pressures from governments to take actions that infringe upon these rights".[33] This understanding is spelled out in the GNI's three founding documents:

(i) The high-level GNI Principles, which affirm central commitments on freedom of expression and on privacy from various human rights treaties, including the Universal Declaration of Human Rights (UDHR), the International Covenant on Civil and Political Rights (ICCPR) and the International Covenant on Economic, Social and Cultural Rights (ICESCR).[34] The Principles, which are formulated in a very general manner, emphasise the "duty of governments to respect, protect, promote and fulfill human rights".[35] Correspondingly, ICT companies are said to have a responsibility "to respect and protect the freedom of expression and privacy rights of their users" by "seeking to avoid or minimize the impact of government restrictions" on these rights.[36] The document does not contain any specific proposals or strategies.
(ii) The GNI Implementation Guidelines, which describe, similarly in a rather abstract way, how companies can demonstrate compliance with the GNI principles, e.g., by

30 UN Human Rights Council, Report of the Special Rapporteur on the promotion and protection of the right to freedom of opinion and expression, 6.4.2018, A/HRC/38/35, para. 23.

31 Bobbie Johnson (2008) Amnesty Criticises Global Network Initiative for Online Freedom of Speech. *The Guardian* (30 October), www.theguardian.com/technology/2008/oct/30/amnesty-global-network-initiative

32 EFF, Resignation letter, 10.10.2013, www.eff.org/de/document/gni-resignation-letter

33 GNI, Frequently asked questions, https://globalnetworkinitiative.org/content/frequently-asked-questions

34 GNI, Principles, http://globalnetworkinitiative.org/principles/index.php

35 Ibid.

36 Ibid.

showing "responsible company decision making", by undertaking "human rights impact assessments", and by "encourage[ing] governments to be specific, transparent and consistent in the demands, laws and regulations" that are issued regarding privacy online and freedom of expression.[37]

(iii) The Governance, Accountability & Learning Framework, which "sets out a multi-stakeholder governance structure, goals for collaboration and a system of company accountability to support the Principles, maximize opportunities for learning and ensure the integrity and efficacy of the Initiative".[38]

The GNI principles

While the GNI locates itself within the "business and human rights" (BHR) movement and describes its founding documents as "informed by the U.N. Guiding Principles on Business and Human Rights" proposed by UN Special Representative on BHR *John Ruggie*, the GNI remains committed to a classical liberal concept of rights: Whereas the BHR Principles emphasise both the duty of states to "promote respect for human rights by business enterprises" and the "responsibility of business enterprises to respect human rights" thus recognising the adverse human rights impact businesses can cause through their "own activities"[39], the GNI focuses almost exclusively on governments. According to the GNI Principles, states have the "duty" to protect human rights. Therefore, every form of government intervention into the free flow of data and communications is considered to be potentially harmful and in need of a reasonable justification. At the same time, the responsibility of ICT companies to "advance and protect" human rights consists of – according to the GNI – mainly supporting the rights of their customers vis-à-vis the state. Potential violations of free speech or of privacy rights through the companies' "own activities" are addressed in the founding documents only in passing. A certain myopia with regard to their own activities can also be seen in the passages on privacy. Compared to the laws on informational privacy, which are already in place in many countries, the GNI Principles are much less ambitious and very vague, stating only that "participating companies will assess the human rights risks associated with the collection, storage, and retention of personal information in the jurisdictions where they operate and develop appropriate mitigation strategies to address these risks".

While the GNI Principles downplay the problems concerning privacy and freedom of expression created by ICT companies themselves and ignore the complicity by at least some ICT companies in government censorship and surveillance, the activities of the GNI reflect a broader understanding of its mission. The activities can be grouped into two major categories. First, the GNI hosts various workshops, discussion panels, etc. to foster multistakeholder dialogue on contentious issues such as extremist content, account deactivation or US surveillance law, partly in collaboration with other organisations, such as the

37 GNI, Implementation Guidelines, http://globalnetworkinitiative.org/implementation-guidelines

38 GNI, Accountability, Policy, and Learning Framework, https://globalnetworkinitiative.org/content/accountability-policy-and-learning-framework

39 UN (2011) Guiding Principles on Business and Human Rights, www.ohchr.org/Documents/Publications/GuidingPrinciplesBusinessHR_EN.pdf. For the original report see John Ruggie (2008) Protect, Respect and Remedy: A Framework for Business and Human Rights, Human Rights Council, A/HRC/8/5, 7.4.2008, www.reports-and-materials.org/Ruggie-report-7-Apr-2008.pdf

OECD or UNESCO.[40] More important, however, is the second type of activity, the assessment process, which the GNI offers for its members. According to the latest public report, the GNI conducted in 2015/16 assessments of five of its member companies – Facebook, Google, LinkedIn, Microsoft and Yahoo. For Google, Microsoft and Yahoo, three of the GNI's founding companies, this was the second assessment cycle, while Facebook and LinkedIn were participating for the first time.[41] The assessment process is conducted by independent "assessor organizations", which have to be accredited by GNI's multistakeholder Board, and include big auditing firms, such as KPMG or Ernst & Young LLP. The GNI assessment process itself is confidential. The results and recommendations to GNI members in general and to the audited companies in particular are presented to the public only in aggregated form. Most cases and examples referred to in the public report are anonymised. Therefore, the reasons presented in the report for a positive assessment are not really informative for the general public.

Outlook

The GNI could never really avoid the impression that its corporate members participated in the initiative mainly because they saw a voluntary code of conduct as a shield against government action. At least in the case of Facebook, a US senator had publicly indicated that the company might face regulation if it did not join the GNI. Whether or not regulatory avoidance is the main motivation for GNI members, the initiative itself, now at its tenth anniversary, has lost much of its initial momentum. Apart from its assessment process, the GNI has so far not developed into a prominent voice in the international discourse on privacy and free expression.

This is also felt at least by parts of the academic members of the GNI and summed up in a letter in which the NYU Center for Business and Human Rights resigned its membership in the GNI on 1 February 2016.[42] According to *Sarah Labowitz* and *Michael Posner*, who signed the letter, the current strategy of the GNI, which prioritises making the assessment process available to a much larger group of ICT companies, over a more ambitious strategy, is wrong-headed. Rather, the GNI should try to build up an organisational structure and a funding model to "meet the pressing human rights challenges it was established to address". Moreover, the critics argue that the GNI has watered down the assessment procedure in 2016 in order to make the GNI more attractive to ICT companies. While it was previously testing the "compliance" of a member company with the GNI principles, since 2016 it only assesses whether a "company has committed to the principles . . . and is making a good-faith effort to implement and apply them". As the NYU representatives write: "This is not a meaningful standard".

40 For an example see GNI (2016) Extremist Content and the ICT Sector A Global Network Initiative Policy Brief, https://globalnetworkinitiative.org/gin_tnetnoc/uploads/2016/12/Extremist-Content-and-ICT-Sector.pdf

41 GNI (July 2016) Public Report on the 2015/16 Independent Company Assessments, https://globalnetworkinitiative.org/2015-2016-company-assessments/

42 Sarah Labowitz and Michael Posner (2016) NYU Center for Business and Human Rights Resigns its Membership in the Global Network Initiative, 1 February, https://bhr.stern.nyu.edu/statement/cbhr-letter-of-resignation-gni

The Manila principles on intermediary liability

Mission and membership

On 24 March 2015, a global civil society initiative consisting of several human rights groups presented the "Manila Principles on Intermediary Liability" (MPIL), which are further described as "Best Practices Guidelines for Limiting Intermediary Liability for Content to Promote Freedom of Expression and Innovation". The MPIL differ from the GNI by focusing more on substance and less on institutions and process. The original drafters include the US-based Electronic Frontier Foundation (EFF), the British NGO Article 19, the Centre for Internet and Society (India), KICTANET from Kenya, Derechos Digitales (Chile), Asociación por los Derechos Civiles (Argentina) and Open Net (South Korea).[43] No major company was part of the steering group.

The key principles

Like the GNI principles the MPIL make ample reference to international human rights law, in particular to the UDHR and the ICCPR. But while the GNI covers freedom of expression and privacy rights, the MPIL are solely concerned "with the laws, policies, norms, and practices that relate to how intermediaries handle third-party Internet content that could raise criminal or civil liability issues for them or for their users".[44] Substance-wise, however, the MPIL are much more detailed than the GNI regime. Accompanied by a comparative study of intermediary liability rules[45] and a background paper[46], the MPIL core document proposes six key principles for intermediary liability:

1. Intermediaries should generally be shielded by law from liability for third-party content.
2. Content must not be required to be restricted without an order by a judicial authority.
3. Requests for restrictions of content must be clear and unambiguous.
4. Laws and content-restriction orders and practices must comply with the tests of necessity and proportionality.
5. Laws and content-restriction policies and practices must respect due process.
6. Transparency and accountability must be built into laws and content-restriction policies and practices.

Each of these principles is then spelled out in several sub-principles which address specific cases and situations, such as the CJEU's decision in the *Google Spain* case on the "right to be forgotten"[47], which is criticised for failing to take countervailing interests, in particular the freedom of expression, properly into account.[48]

43 The Manila Principles on Intermediary Liability Background Paper Version 1.0, 30 May 2015, www.eff.org/files/2015/07/08/manila_principles_background_paper.pdf

44 Ibid., 4.

45 J. Jyoti Panday, Carlos Lara, Kyun S. Park and Kelly Kim (2015) Jurisdictional Analysis Comparative Study of Intermediary Liability Regimes Chile, Canada, India, South Korea, UK and USA in support of the Manila Principles On Intermediary Liability, www.eff.org/files/2015/07/08/manila_principles_jurisdictional_analysis.pdf

46 See Manila Principles on Intermediary Liability Background Paper 2015.

47 CJEU, *Google Spain SL and Google Inc v. AEPD* (C-131/12).

48 The Manila Principles on Intermediary Liability Background Paper 22.

While the MPIL reflect a clear commitment towards extensive liability exemptions for intermediaries, the signatories recognise that intermediaries may bear some responsibility for content, especially certain classes of intermediaries, which are not only providing conduit services.[49] However, they also point to the fact that even in cases, where intermediary responsibility might be justified in principle, state regulators should not mandate proactive screening mechanisms, because this might incentivise intermediaries to over-block even legal content. They also make a balanced proposal on the problem of who should decide on what constitutes "illegal content". While the second Manila principle demands that, generally, court orders are necessary for content restrictions, the Manila group recognises that the judiciary with its limited resources is unable to review each case individually. For this reason, the Manila group proposes a regime which shares the financial and organisational burden of the review process between the state and intermediaries.

Outlook

Despite such innovative proposals, the momentum of the Manila group was limited. The principles were discussed at the Internet Governance Forum 2015 and are referred to from time to time in academic papers and human rights reports. However, because the group did not set up a process or an organisation which debates, updates, or refines the ground rules, the MPIL had no major impact either on the political processes of intermediary regulation or on the activities of intermediaries themselves.

Google Advisory Council

A third type of stakeholder-led initiative is the Advisory Council to Google on the Right to be Forgotten. The Council was initiated by one company, Google, in the wake of the previously mentioned CJEU decision on the "right to be forgotten".[50] In this decision, the CJEU, to the surprise of many observers, obliged search engine operators to remove from the list of search results certain links, if "the data subject has a right that the information in question relating to him personally should, at this point in time, no longer be linked to his name by a list of results displayed following a search made on the basis of his name".[51] In order to determine whether or not the data subject had such a right, the search engine operator had to balance the opposing rights and interests concerned, with special regard to the data subject's rights arising from Articles 7 and 8 of the Charter of Fundamental Rights of the European Union. The Court mentioned four criteria on which this balancing act might depend, namely "the nature of the information in question and its sensitivity for the data subject's private life and . . . the interest of the public in having that information, an interest which may vary, in particular, according to the role played by the data subject in public life".[52]

Such a complex balancing act is a daunting task even for a court of law. For a technology company, which has to set up processes to apply this formula to several hundred cases per day, it is an extreme challenge. In order to develop an internal policy on the judgment,

49 Ibid.
50 CJEU, *Google Spain SL and Google Inc v. AEPD* (C-131/12).
51 Ibid., para. 96.
52 Ibid., para. 81.

Google set up the Council, whose members were – besides the two Google-employed conveners – eight eminent persons from academia, media and politics, including the former Federal Minister of Justice of Germany, the UN Special Rapporteur on the Promotion and Protection of the Right to Freedom of Opinion and Expression and the Founder of the Wikimedia Foundation. The Council held seven public consultations in European capitals between September and November 2014 and published its final report in January 2015.[53] The short report elaborates on the balancing criteria mentioned by the CJEU and develops ideas for the procedural implementation of the judgment. An appendix to the report contains comments from individual Council members and transcripts of the public consultations.

The Google Advisory Council itself was never involved in making decisions on the removal of specific content.[54] It was set up as a temporary initiative which ceased to exist after its mission – the report – was accomplished.

Others

Besides these three initiatives, various other non-state actors have addressed intermediary liability from the perspective of free speech, privacy, or the protection of victims of harmful content over the past years. A special mention is deserved by the Dynamic Coalition for Platform Responsibility (DCPR), which acts within the framework of the United Nations Internet Governance Forum (IGF) and which comprises a multistakeholder group of members from civil society, NGOs, academia, ICT companies, and intergovernmental organisations. The DCPR has addressed many aspects of intermediary liability over the past years. The original goal of the group was to develop model contractual provisions for platform providers (Terms of Service), which ensure the protection of individual rights of their users. The recommendations, which the DCPR published in 2015, address privacy issues, due process rights of customers, freedom of expression on platforms (including monitoring obligations and government blocking and takedowns) and the protection of children and young people.[55] Since then, the DCPR has further explored the human rights dimension of the digital platform debate and published a series of analyses on platform regulation.[56] Currently, a DCPR Working Group has been set up to analyse alternative dispute resolution mechanisms provided by platforms. The DCPR operates largely by open calls for papers and for multistakeholder dialogues, which are organised by the two coordinators Luca Belli and Nicolo Zingales.

53 The Advisory Council to Google on the Right to be Forgotten (2015) Report, 6 February, https://static.googleusercontent.com/media/archive.google.com/de//advisorycouncil/advisement/advisory-report.pdf

54 This is dealt with by Google employees. Since 2014 there have been 702,590 removal requests (as of July 22, 2018), according to Google's latest transparency report available at https://transparencyreport.google.com/eu-privacy/overview

55 See L. Belli, P. De Filippi and N. Zingales (Eds.) (November 2015) Recommendations on Terms of Service & Human Rights, www.intgovforum.org/cms/documents/igf-meeting/igf-2016/830-dcpr-2015-output-document-1/file. See also Jamila Venturini et al. (2016) Terms of Service and Human Rights: Analysing Contracts of Online Platforms.

56 See, e.g., Luca Belli and Nicolo Zingales (2017) *Platform Regulations: How Platforms Are Regulated and How they Regulate Us*. Rio De Janeiro: FGV Direito Rio.

The emergence of common standards?

The diversity of the stakeholder-led initiatives and the very limited output, which especially the more prominent of these initiatives produce, make it difficult to identify the emergence of common standards or principles. Nevertheless, we find some common threads and ideas underlying most initiatives:

1. Most stakeholder initiatives, which are led by actors from the private sector and civil rights groups, emphasise that self-regulation is the most adequate form of regulation for intermediaries. In this sense, they are firmly committed to policies on internet regulation dating back to the 1990s. Now, with the increasing political pressure on ICT companies and the rise of the concept of "intermediary responsibility", the idea of company self-regulation is increasingly re-framed in terms of "corporate responsibility".[57] This helps to connect the initiatives with the BHR movement.[58] However, taking the idea of corporate responsibility seriously means that ICT companies themselves have to critically assess their activities and need to implement safeguards to protect their users and third parties from the harm they cause. The initiatives differ in how seriously this commitment is taken.
2. There is a growing, but limited consensus on what can count as illegal content. The obvious case is child pornography, for which it is generally recognised that intermediaries have a duty of removal. Following a report of the UN Special Rapporteur, the "direct and public incitement to commit genocide", the "advocacy of national, racial or religious hatred that constitutes incitement to discrimination, hostility or violence", and the "incitement to terrorism" are mostly recognised as grounds for removal, too.[59] However, the lack of an internationally agreed upon definition of "terrorism", limits the practical effects of any general commitment that intermediaries should restrict terrorist propaganda and recruitment online.[60]
3. There is even less clarity and consensus on what has emerged as probably the most corrosive type of online speech: hate speech and so-called fake news. As far as stakeholder initiatives have positioned themselves in this debate, they tend to emphasise that aggressive government intervention against fake news or hate speech constitutes itself a potential threat to the freedom of expression, because it incentivises intermediaries

57 See on this connection Emily B. Laidlaw (2015) *Regulating Speech in Cyberspace: Gatekeepers, Human Rights and Corporate Responsibility*. Cambridge: Cambridge University Press; Dennis Broeders and Linnet Taylor (2017) Does Great Power Come with Great Responsibility? The Need to Talk About Corporate Responsibility. In: M. Taddeo and L. Floridi (Eds.), *The Responsibilities of Online Service Providers*. Berlin/Heidelberg: Springer.

58 *See* the references in note 39, and Institute for Human Rights and Business/Shift (June 2013) ICT Sector Guide on Implementing the UN Guiding Principles on Business and Human Rights, Report for the European Commission, https://ec.europa.eu/anti-trafficking/sites/antitrafficking/files/information_and_communication_technology_0.pdf

59 Frank La Rue (2011) Report of the Special Rapporteur on the Promotion and Protection of the Right to Freedom of Opinion and Expression. United Nations, Human Rights Council, 16 May, paras. 42–43, 75, http://www2.ohchr.org/english/bodies/hrcouncil/docs/17session/A.HRC.17.27_en.pdf. Cf., e.g., the Manila Principles on Intermediary Liability Background Paper 41.

60 See on this issue GNI (2016) Extremist Content and the ICT Sector a Global Network Initiative Policy Brief, November, https://globalnetworkinitiative.org/wp-content/uploads/2016/12/Extremist-Content-and-ICT-Sector.pdf. Cf. also Cohen-Almagor (2017).

to over-block even legal content.[61] While this is certainly true, it remains unclear how the negative impact, which hate speech and fake news have on democratic politics, can be addressed in an effective way.

Horizontal versus vertical governance

The stakeholder initiatives analysed here show both the potential and the difficulties of intermediary self-regulation. Traditionally, international organisations, expert bodies and scholars considered horizontal governance or self-regulation as an "effective tool" in redressing harmful speech which "should be promoted".[62] Collective self-regulation is usually defined as "a group of firms or individuals exert[ing] control over their own membership and behaviour. Membership is voluntary and participants draw up their own rules using tools such as codes of conduct as well as technological solutions and standards. Members take full responsibility for monitoring and compliance without reference to a statutory regulatory authority".[63] In this sense, the stakeholder initiatives certainly qualify as self-regulation.

However, in regulatory theory, self-regulation is usually recommended for specific situations in which public interests can be realised through pursuing private interests. *Martin Eifert* describes the idea of self-regulation as characterised "by the emergence of collective order through the exercise of individual freedom, which uses diffuse knowledge, and typically wants to realize private interests. It originates in a normative claim for freedom . . . which is not conceptualized as an end in itself, but connected to macro-economic expectations concerning the increase in welfare for society as a whole and the superior innovative capacity of the decentralised experimentation and search processes thus made possible".[64]

Compared to these grand expectations, the results of over a decade of collective intermediary self-regulation are sobering. The efforts of ICT companies and other online stakeholders to develop codes of conduct and to set common technical standards can be called limited at best. Especially the GNI, whose architecture comes closest to the idea of self-regulation, lacks the vision and the will to address the pressing problems of the online world. Because ICT companies are failing to develop a collective approach, it is understandable that states are starting to increasingly rely on methods of vertical governance, especially on co-regulation, thus forcing stakeholders to "self-regulate". However, when doing so, regulators should not forget two things. First, despite the lack of success of self-regulation in the past, there are still major benefits of involving online stakeholders in the

61 Cf. the statement of the GNI on the German Network Enforcement Act of 2017: GNI (2017) Proposed German Legislation Threatens Free Expression Around the World (20 April), https://globalnetworkinitiative.org/proposed-german-legislation-threatens-free-expression-around-the-world/

62 Cf. already Joint Special Rapporteurs (2011) Declaration on Freedom of Expression and the Internet (1 June), www.osce.org/fom/78309. See also Council of Europe Committee of Ministers (2003) Declaration on Freedom of Communication on the Internet (Decl-28.05.2003E), 28 May, encouraging "self-regulation or co-regulation regarding content disseminated on the Internet".

63 Christopher T. Marsden (2011) Internet Co-Regulation: European Law, Regulatory Governance, and Legitimacy in Cyberspace, 54.

64 Martin Eifert (2012) Regulierungsstrategien. In: W. Hoffmann-Riem et al. (Eds.), *Grundlagen des Verwaltungsrechts*, Munich: C.H. Beck para. 145.

regulatory process: because of the sheer volume of user-generated content on the internet and the speed with which it is distributed, any liability regime that wants to organise the monitoring and the evaluation process without recourse to the knowledge and technical skills of intermediaries will fail. Second, while it seems inevitable that regulators start to make intermediaries more accountable, their interventions must always be balanced and justified in light of fundamental rights and the rule of law.[65]

65 Cf. The OSCE Representative on Freedom of the Media (2016) 3rd Communiqué on Open Journalism. Communiqué No.1, 29.1.2016, 2, www.osce.org/fom/219391

11 The jurisprudence of the ECJ and ECtHR regarding data protection in the internet

Carsten M. Wulff

Since the early 2000s, both the European Court of Human Rights (ECtHR) and European Court of Justice (ECJ) have seen a dramatic increase in the rise of internet-related case law. This chapter will address the role of data processing and the impacts on the protection of the right to privacy and freedom of expression within the case law of the Courts. The chapter will open with an overview of the development of legislation in the European Union (EU) and Council of Europe (CoE), proceed with an analysis of relevant cases of both Courts and conclude with an overview of where overlaps and differences in the approaches of the Strasbourg and Luxembourg Court can be found. This chapter will solely deal with case law regarding the rights of data subjects and the legality of mass surveillance mechanisms.

Development of internet-related legislation in the European context

Council of Europe

Already during the early stages of the internet, supranational organisations were considering the impacts of the world wide web and were drafting guidelines on how to ensure that fundamental rights could be protected.

In 1980, the Organization for Economic Cooperation and Development (OECD) issued Guidelines Governing the Protection of Privacy and Transborder Flows of Personal Data. These defined a data controller as a party which "is competent to decide about the contents and use of personal data regardless or not such data are collected, stored, processed or disseminated by that party or by an agent on its behalf".[1] Personal data was defined as "any information relating to an identified or identifiable individual".

The guidelines laid forth seven basic principles concerning the collection and use of data. There should be consent of the data subject and the data should be relevant for the purpose for which it is used. The reason for collection must be specified at the time of collection. The data may not be disclosed to third parties without consent. The data should be protected and an individual should be allowed to ask whether a controller has data

1 Recommendation of the Council concerning Guidelines governing the Protection of Privacy and Transborder Flows of Personal Data (23 September 1980), www.oecd.org/internet/ieconomy/oecdguidelinesontheprotectionofprivacyandtransborderflowsofpersonaldata.htm (accessed 26.11.2018).

relating to him. Furthermore, the individual should have the right to modify his data.[2] The guidelines were compiled by a group of experts commissioned by the OECD to review the legislation in the member states.

In 1981, the Council of Europe opened Convention 108 for signature. In this, a data controller or "controller of the file" defines, "the natural or legal person, public authority, agency or any other body that is competent according to the national law to decide what should be the purpose of the stored data, which categories of personal data should be stored and which operations should be applied to them".[3]

The Convention also provided similar thresholds regarding how data can be obtained as in the OECD guidelines from 1980.[4] Data which enables the identification of a subject should only be stored as long as is necessary for the processing of the data. Article 8 grants the data subject the right to determine whether personal data is stored and the right to have the stored data rectified or erased if the processing has been completed. In accordance with the OECD guidelines, the Convention explicitly allows for uninterrupted and secure transborder data flows with other countries which are a party to the Convention.[5] In order to monitor compliance with the Convention, a consultative committee was established with the powers to make proposals to facilitate or improve the application of the Convention, propose amendments and at the request of a party express opinions concerning the application of the Convention.[6]

In 2004, Protocol 181 to Convention 108 was opened for signature, with the aim to increase the protection of personal data of data subjects through the establishment of national supervisory authorities and placing restrictions on transborder data flows to third countries.[7] The transfer of personal data to third countries should only be allowed where the third country provides an, "adequate level of protection for the intended data transfer".[8]

In 2018, Protocol 223 was opened for signature. This Protocol will amend Convention 108 and add some provisions further strengthening the rights of the data subject. Article 5 will be amended to include the paragraph, "Data processing shall be proportionate in relation to the legitimate purpose pursued and reflect at all stages of the processing a fair balance between all interests concerned, whether public or private, and the rights and freedoms at stake".[9] The Protocol also clarifies under what circumstances a third country

2 Annex to the Recommendation of the Council of 23 September 1980, Art. 7–14.

3 Council of Europe, Convention for the Protection of Individuals with regard to Automatic Processing of Personal Data (01 October 1985), ETS No. 108.

4 Article 5 contains provisions on the quality of data. "Personal data undergoing automatic processing shall be: (a) obtained and processed fairly and lawfully; (b) stored for specified and legitimate purposes and not used in a way incompatible with those purposes; (c) adequate, relevant and not excessive in relation to the purposes for which they are stored; (d) accurate and, where necessary, kept up to date; (e) preserved in a form which permits identification of the data subjects for no longer than is required for the purpose for which those data are stored".

5 See Articles 15–17 of the annex to the recommendation of the Council of 23 September 1980 (OECD Guidelines) and Article 12 of Convention 108.

6 Convention for the Protection of Individuals with regard to Automatic Processing of Personal Data (01 October 1985), ETS No. 108, Articles 18–19.

7 Council of Europe, Additional Protocol to the Convention for the Protection of Individuals with regard to Automatic Processing of Personal Data, regarding supervisory authorities and transborder data flows (08 November, 2001), ETS No. 181.

8 Ibid., Art. 2.

9 Council of Europe, Protocol amending the Convention for the Protection of Individuals with regard to Automatic Processing of Personal Data (10.X.2018), ETS. No. 223, Article 7.

can be attributed an "appropriate level of protection"[10] and what powers the national supervisory authorities should at least have.[11] In case of a breach of data, which puts the fundamental rights of data subjects at risk, a data controller must at least notify the competent supervisory authority. The data controller himself furthermore needs to notify the data subjects of his or her identity and habitual residence or establishment, the legal basis and the purposes of the intended processing, the categories of personal data processed and the recipients or categories of recipients of the personal data.[12]

The European Convention on Human Rights also must be noted. Article 8 provides the right to respect for family and private life. Article 10 grants the right to freedom of expression. Both rights may only be infringed to the extent that is, "necessary in a democratic society in the interests of national security, public safety or the economic well-being of the country, for the prevention of disorder or crime, for the protection of health or morals, or for the protection of the rights and freedoms of others".[13] In the case of the right to freedom of expression, derogation is also possible on grounds of territorial integrity and, "for the protection of the reputation or rights of others, for preventing the disclosure of information received in confidence, or for maintaining the authority and impartiality of the judiciary".[14]

European Union

In 1995, the European Community passed Directive 95/46/EC on the protection of individuals with regard to the processing of personal data and the free movement of such data. Article 12 of the Directive granted data subjects the right to obtain the information of the data controller if data processing of his data is taking place and the right to have data rectified, erased or blocked if it is of an incomplete or inaccurate nature.[15] Restrictions could be laid forth by Member States transposing the Directive.[16]

Similar to Convention 108, the 1995 Directive also provided clear guidelines in regards to how data can be collected. There must be unambiguous consent of the data subject, or at the least the processing must be necessary on the grounds of a legal obligation of the

10 Article 17 (3) "An appropriate level of protection can be secured by: (a) the law of that State or international organization, including the applicable international treaties or agreements; or (b) ad hoc or approved standardized safeguards provided by legally-binding and enforceable instruments adopted and implemented by the persons involved in the transfer and further processing".

11 Article 19 provides that authorities: "(a) shall have the powers of investigation and intervention; (b) shall perform the functions relating to transfers of data provided for under Article 14, notably the approval of standardized safeguards; (c) shall have powers to issue decisions with respect to violations of the provisions of this Convention and may, in particular, impose administrative sanctions; (d) shall have the power to engage in legal proceedings or to bring to the attention of the competent judicial authorities violations of the provisions of this Convention".

12 Ibid., Article 10.

13 Council of Europe, Convention for the Protection of Human Rights and Fundamental Freedoms (November 4, 1950), ETS No.005, Article 8 (2).

14 Ibid., Article 10 (2).

15 European Parliament and Council Directive 95/46/EC of 24 October 1995 on the protection of individuals with regard to the processing of personal data and on the free movement of such data, OJ L281/23, Article 12

16 Article 13 provides for restrictions of the rights listed in Articles 6 (1), 10, 11 (1), 12 and 21 when necessary to safeguard, " (a) national security; (b) defense; (c) public security; (d) the prevention, investigation, detection and prosecution of criminal offences, or of breaches of ethics for regulated professions; (e) an important economic or financial interest of a Member State or of the European Union, including monetary, budgetary and taxation matters; . . . (g) the protection of the data subject or of the rights and freedoms of others".

controller, or protection of vital interests of the data subject.[17] The data subject was given the right to obtain the identity of the controller, the purposes of the processing of his data and a list of recipients or categories of recipients of the data.[18]

The 1997 Telecommunications Directive[19] and 2002 E-Privacy Directive further outlined how the principles of the 1995 Directive would be transposed in the telecommunications and online fields.

The E-Privacy Directive 2002/58/EC, also applies to legal persons. It did not apply to the second and third pillar, namely the common foreign and security policy and police and judicial cooperation in criminal matters. It condemns any forms of spyware, which are seen as a serious intrusion of privacy, but it sees cookies as a legitimate tool for obtaining relevant information. Clear and concise information on the use of cookies has to be given to the users.[20]

Restrictions on national security grounds are allowed for the confidentiality of transmission, traffic data and location data other than traffic data.[21] Retention of data for a limited amount of time explicitly is allowed,[22] but must be in accordance with the Treaty on European Union (TEU).[23]

Following the surge of terrorist attacks in the early 2000s, a Directive on data retention was released in 2006 which amended the 2002 Directive and placed an obligation on telecommunications networks to store certain categories of traffic for a period of at least six months. The data could only be accessed with the permission of the domestic Court, based on the procedures of the country.[24]

The Charter of Fundamental Rights entered into force with the Lisbon Treaty. The Charter reflects the principles of the European Convention on Human Rights, the European Social Charter and the case law of the Court of Justice. It includes the right to respect for private and family life, right to protection of personal data and freedom of expression, and information.[25]

In 2016 the General Data Protection Regulation (GDPR) was adopted and recently entered into force in May 2018. The Regulation supersedes the 1995 Directive. Some of the key improvements include data protection by design, changes to the right to

17 See further Article 7 on the Criteria for Data Processing to be legitimate.

18 Ibid., Article 10.

19 European Parliament and Council Directive 97/13/EC of 10 April 1997 on a common framework for general authorizations and individual licences in the field of telecommunications services, OJ L117/15.

20 European Parliament and Council Directive 2002/58/EC of 12 July 2002 concerning the processing of personal data and the protection of privacy in the electronic communications sector (Directive on privacy and electronic communications) Para 24–25 on cookies and Article 1 on the scope.

21 Ibid., Articles 5, 6 and 9.

22 Ibid., Art. 15 (1).

23 See further TEU, Article 6 (1 and 2) "The Union is founded on the principles of liberty, democracy, respect for human rights and fundamental freedoms, and the rule of law, principles which are common to the Member States. 2. The Union shall respect fundamental rights, as guaranteed by the European Convention for the Protection of Human Rights and Fundamental Freedoms signed in Rome on 4 November 1950 and as they result from the constitutional traditions common to the Member States, as general principles of Community law".

24 European Parliament and Council Directive 2006/24/EC of 15 March 2006 on the retention of data generated or processed in connection with the provision of publicly available electronic communications services or of public communications networks and amending Directive 2002/58/EC, OJ L105/54, Articles 3–6.

25 Charter of Fundamental Rights of the European Union (2012/C326/02) C-326/391, Article 7 provides for the Respect for private and family life, Article 8 for the Protection of Personal Data, Article 11 for the Freedom of expression and information.

erasure and high sanctions for non-compliance. Data protection has to be designed into the development of business processes for products and services. The controller has to implement measures to ensure that the personal data is only processed to the extent necessary for the specific purpose. Privacy settings, by default should be set to a high level.[26]

Reflecting recent case law, which will be addressed later in this chapter, the right to access known from the 1995 Directive was widened. Whereas the 1995 Directive allowed the data subject the right to rectification, erasure or blocking of data processing in the case of the incomplete or inaccurate nature of data,[27] the GDPR, in addition, grants a right to erasure when the personal data is no longer required for the purpose it was collected for, or if the user revokes his consent for the processing of the data. This right is not absolute – it has to be weighed against the freedoms of expression and information. Furthermore, if the processing is required for the compliance with a legal obligation, for the interest of public health, for archiving purposes in the public interest, or for the establishment, exercise or defence of legal claims, the request for erasure also may be denied.[28]

In order to enforce the provisions of the Regulation, it provides for high fines in case of non-compliance. Depending on the nature of the infringement, the maximum fine is either €20 million or 4% of the annual turnover – whichever is larger.[29]

In 2019, the ePrivacy Regulation is scheduled to be finalised. It will replace the 2002 E-Privacy Directive. In the most recent proposal of the Commission, it is expected to also apply to non-traditional electronic communications services, including WhatsApp, Facebook Messenger and Skype. Similar to the GDPR, through its direct applicability across the European Union, it will ensure the same level of protection across member states. Metadata which can be used to identify the time and location of a call must be anonymised or deleted, unless if users gave their consent or the data is required for billing.[30]

Consent for cookies will be simplified. Browser settings need to provide a simple way for users to either accept or refuse tracking cookies. In the case of non-privacy intrusive cookies, consent will not be required for every website anymore where consent has been set in the browser settings. To avoid spam, people will either have the option to not receive unsolicited electronic communications by default or be added to a do-not-call list to avoid marketing phone calls. In case of calls, marketers need to either display their phone number or a special prefix which indicates it is a marketing call. The data protection authorities will be responsible for the enforcement of the regulation.

26 Regulation (EU) 2016/679 of the European Parliament and of the Council of 27 April 2016 on the protection of natural persons with regard to the processing of personal data and on the free movement of such data, and repealing Directive 95/46/EC, OJ L 119. Article 25 on the implementation of data protection by design and default, Article 17 on the right to erasure which allows the data subject to request erasure of personal data on a number on grounds, including if the data is no longer relevant for the purposes of processing or if the data subject withdraws consent.

27 European Parliament and Council Directive 95/46/EC of 24 October 1995, Article 12.

28 Regulation (EU) 2016/679 of the European Parliament and of the Council of 27 April 2016, Article 17.

29 Ibid., Article 83.

30 Proposal for a Regulation of the European Parliament and of the Council concerning the respect for private life and the protection of personal data in electronic communications and repealing Directive 2002/58/EC (Regulation on Privacy and Electronic Communications) 2017/0003 (COD). For a summary see https://ec.europa.eu/digital-single-market/en/proposal-eprivacy-regulation (accessed 26.11.2018).

Internet-related case law of the European courts

As Advocate General (AG) Maduro has already pointed out in 2008:

> [T]he protection of fundamental rights in the Community legal order exists alongside other European systems of protection of fundamental rights. These include both systems developed within the national legal systems and those stemming from the ECHR. Each of those protection mechanisms certainly pursue objectives which are specific to it and the mechanisms are certainly constructed from legal instruments particular to them, but sometimes they apply none the less to the same facts. In such a context, it is important, for each existing protection system, while maintaining its independence, to seek to understand how the other systems interpret and develop those same fundamental rights in order not only to minimize the risk of conflicts, but also to begin a process of informal construction of a European area of protection of fundamental rights. The European area thus created will, largely, be the product of the various individual contributions from the different protection systems existing at European level.[31]

This section will explore to what extent recent jurisprudence of the ECJ and ECtHR is displaying a uniform application of the law in data processing related cases, or if the Courts are applying different standards in their judgments. The chosen cases focus on two aspects of internet-related case law, the individual right to privacy and data protection exercised through the rectification, erasure or deletion of inaccurate data and the legality of mass surveillance mechanisms, specifically where these allow for the transfer of data to third countries.

European Court of Justice

The landmark Google Spain case dealt with and expanded the scope of the 1995 Directive. A Spanish citizen requested that Google delete personal data which was stored from an auction of his repossessed home. As a legal basis, the applicant Mr. Costeja, referred to the 1995 Data Protection Directive. Three questions were referred to the Court. These can be summarised as:

1 Does the EU 1995 Data Protection Directive apply to search engines such as Google;
2 Does EU law apply to Google Spain, given that the company's data processing server was in the United States;
3 Does an individual have the right to request that his or her personal data be removed from accessibility via a search engine (the Right to be forgotten)?[32]

The Court ruled that Google can be regarded as a data controller in the meaning of the Directive. Here, the Court went against the interpretation of the AG who concurred that

31 Opinion of AG Maduro in Case C-465/07 *Elgafaji v. Staatssecretaris van Justitie*, available at: www.refworld.org/pdfid/501665e02.pdf (accessed 10.11.2018), para 22.

32 Case C-131/12, Google Spain SL and *Google Inc. v. Agencia Española de Protección de Datos* (AEPD) and Mario Costeja González, available at: http://curia.europa.eu/juris/document/document.jsf?docid=152065&doclang=EN (accessed 27.10.2018), abbreviated from para 20.

the business model of Google made them subject to the jurisdiction of the Directive, however not as a data controller in the meaning of the Directive.

Controversially, the Court upheld that individuals have the right to request personal data to be removed from accessibility, again going against the assessment of the AG. The AG held that freedom of information and expression take precedence over a right to erasure. He predicted that granting such a right would lead to the "automatic withdrawal of links to any objected contents or to an unmanageable number of requests handled by the most popular Internet search engine service providers".[33] The case played a role in the drafting of the General Data Protection, specifically Article 17.[34]

A few months before the Google Spain case strengthened a data subject's right to have his data delinked after a certain amount of time has passed, the Court delivered a judgment which dealt with the mass storage of data by communications networks. The judgment in *Digital Rights Ireland Ltd.*[35] voided Directive 2006/24 (the Data Retention Directive). Article 3 of the Directive placed an obligation on public communications networks to store all traffic and location data for a period from six months to two years. The data could only be accessed with the permission of the domestic Court, based on the procedures of the country.

Digital Rights Ireland and private citizens from Austria brought actions in the national Courts that the implementation of the Data Retention Directive violated fundamental rights. The highest Courts sent the case to the Luxembourg Court for a preliminary reference, where the Court decided to join the two proceedings. Although the Directive did not allow for the storage of content data, the Court ruled that it seriously infringed Articles 7 and 8 of the Charter of Fundamental Rights which respectively provide for the respect of private and family life and protection of personal data.[36]

In its judgment, the Court highlighted three reasons for its judgment. The Directive did not differentiate between the traffic data which was stored, or provide for any limitations or exceptions. It applied to all persons, regardless if there was any evidence linking them with a serious crime.[37] Furthermore, the Directive did not contain any substantive or procedural conditions outlining how data can be processed and be subsequently used by the national authorities. As the Directive did not outline what constitutes "serious crime", it failed to lay down objective criteria of what crimes justify such a serious infringement of the rights listed in the Charter.[38] Thirdly, the requirement to store data for at least six months makes the interference of fundamental rights go beyond what was strictly

33 Opinion of AG Jääskinen in Case C-131/12, Google Spain SL and *Google Inc. v. Agencia Española de Protección de Datos* (AEPD) and Mario Costeja González, available at: http://curia.europa.eu/juris/document/document.jsf?text=&docid=138782&pageIndex=0&doclang=EN&mode=lst&dir=&occ=first&part=1&cid=928931 (accessed 29.10.2018), para 133.

34 M. Ambrose and J. Ausloos (2013) The Right to Be Forgotten Across the Pond. *Journal of Information Policy*, Vol. 3.

35 Joined Cases C-293/12 and C-594/12 *Digital Rights Ireland Ltd v. Minister for Communications*, Marine and Natural Resources and Others and Kärntner Landesregierung and Others, http://curia.europa.eu/juris/document/document.jsf?docid=150642&doclang=EN (accessed 25.11.2018).

36 Ibid., para 34 and 38.

37 Ibid., para 56, "the Directive requires the retention of all traffic data concerning fixed telephony, mobile telephony, Internet access, Internet e-mail and Internet telephony".

38 Ibid., para 60, "Directive 2006/24 also fails to lay down any objective criterion by which to determine the limits of the access of the competent national authorities to the data and their subsequent use for the purposes of prevention, detection or criminal prosecutions concerning offences that, in view of the extent and seriousness of the interference with the fundamental rights enshrined in Articles 7 and 8 of the Charter, may be considered to be sufficiently serious to justify such an interference".

necessary. The Directive also failed to provide effective protection against the risk of abuse and unlawful access to the data retained.[39]

One year later, in *Schrems v. Data Protection Commissioner*,[40] the Court followed in the footsteps of the Digital Rights Ireland Ltd. case. In this case, the Austrian national, Mr. Schrems, filed a complaint to the Irish Data Protection Officer, stating that the storage of his personal data by Facebook Ireland Ltd. on US servers violated his fundamental rights. Under the 1995 Directive, transborder flows of data to third countries are in compliance as long as the third country provides an adequate standard of protection.

In order to ensure an adequate standard of protection of personal data in the United States, the safe harbour principles were developed. In these, the US agreed to comply with seven principles listed in the 1995 Directive. Individuals must be informed that their data is being collected and of how it will be used. There must be an option to opt out of the collection and transfer of data to third parties. In general, transfers may only occur to third parties that follow adequate data protection principles. Data controllers must make reasonable efforts to prevent the loss of collected information. Collected data must be relevant and reliable for the purpose it was collected. Individuals have the right to access information about them and the right to amend or delete it if inaccurate. Finally, the United States will ensure there are effective ways to enforce the rules.[41]

The Commission Decision 2000/520/EC ("Safe-Harbour" Decision) confirmed that the safe harbour principles provide for an adequate level of protection of personal data as required under Article 25 (2) of the 1995 Directive in regards to transborder flows of data to third countries.[42]

After the revelations of Edward Snowden, Schrems filed an application to the Irish data protection supervisory authority to investigate whether the transfer of data from Facebook Ireland Ltd. to servers located in the United States was in compliance with the 1995 Directive. The data protection authority declined to investigate the case. The case went to the Irish national Courts where it was referred for preliminary reference to the Luxembourg Court. The Court was asked to answer the questions:

1 Whether the supervisory authority is absolutely bound by Decision 2000/50 concerning whether the United States provide an adequate level of Protection;
2 Or, alternatively, may and/or must the office holder conduct his or her own investigation of the matter in the light of factual developments in the meantime since that Commission decision was first published?'[43]

The Court found that Article 3 (1) of the Commission Decision overstepped the competences granted to national data protection authorities in the 1995 Directive. This specific

39 Ibid., para 63, "Article 6 of Directive 2006/24 requires that those data be retained for a period of at least six months, without any distinction being made between the categories of data set out in Article 5 of that Directive on the basis of their possible usefulness for the purposes of the objective pursued".

40 Case C-362/14, *Maximillian Schrems v. Data Protection Commissioner*, http://curia.europa.eu/juris/document/document.jsf?docid=169195&doclang=en (accessed 26.11.2018).

41 Commission Decision of 26 July 2000 pursuant to Directive 95/46/EC of the European Parliament and of the Council on the adequacy of protection provided by the safe harbour privacy principles and related frequently asked questions issued by the US Department of Commerce, L 215/7, Annex 1.

42 Ibid., Art. 1.

43 Case C-362/14, *Maximillian Schrems v. Data Protection Commissioner*, para 36 (first question abbreviated by the author).

provision gave the authorities the power to suspend data flows where the relevant government body in the United States has found an organisation to not comply with the safe harbour principles, or where there is a substantial likelihood that the principles are being violated.[44] As the decision furthermore did not specifically state that the United States in fact "ensures" an adequate level of protection, the Court reached the conclusion that the Safe Harbour Decision was invalid.[45]

Recently, in *Unabhängiges Landeszentrum für Datenschutz Schleswig-Holstein v. Wirtschaftsakademie Schleswig-Holstein GmbH*[46], the Court ruled on issues which touch on the aspects of all three of the preceding cases. The defendant created a fan page on Facebook. This fan page collected anonymised cookies which were stored by Facebook for two years and could be used to obtain statistics on who viewed the fan page. Neither Facebook, nor Wirtschaftsakademie informed the user of the collection of these cookies. The data protection authority of Schleswig-Holstein ordered Wirtschaftsakademie to either shut down the fan page or face a fine. Wirtschaftsakademie argued that it was not a data controller as defined in Art. 2 (d) and therefore is not bound to national laws as defined in Art. 4 (a) of the 1995 Directive.[47]

Following the proceedings in the domestic Courts, the highest administrative Court referred the case for preliminary reference. In essence, the Court was asked to rule on three sets of questions:

- Can Wirtschaftsakademie be viewed as a data processor as defined in Art. 4 (a) despite not actively processing data but allowing Facebook to process data on its fan page?
- Is the national data protection authority competent to investigate where an organisation has subsidiaries in multiple member states and the domestic branch is not directly involved in the processing?
- Is a national data protection authority of one member state bound to the assessment of another member states' data protection authority where the processing is conducted within that member states' jurisdiction?[48]

The Court ruled that Wirtschaftsakademie can be viewed as a data processor and therefore is liable for the violations which occurred on its fan page. The main liability however rests in Facebook and therefore the fines may differ. Citing *Google Spain*,[49] the Court found that despite the processing not being carried out by Facebook Germany, it

44 Ibid., para 103–104.

45 Ibid., para 97 and 106.

46 Case C-210/16 Unabhängiges Landeszentrum für Datenschutz Schleswig-Holstein v. Wirtschaftsakademie Schleswig-Holstein GmbH, https://eur-lex.europa.eu/legal-content/EN/TXT/PDF/?uri=CELEX:62016CJ0210&from=EN (accessed 26.11.2018).

47 Each Member State shall apply the national provisions it adopts pursuant to this Directive to the processing of personal data where: (a) the processing is carried out in the context of the activities of an establishment of the controller on the territory of the Member State; when the same controller is established on the territory of several Member States, he must take the necessary measures to ensure that each of these establishments complies with the obligations laid down by the national law applicable.

48 Case C-210/16 *Unabhängiges Landeszentrum für Datenschutz Schleswig-Holstein v. Wirtschaftsakademie Schleswig-Holstein GmbH*, abbreviation of para 24.

49 Ibid., para 57, "it must be pointed out that Article 4(1)(a) of Directive 95/46 does not require that such processing be carried out 'by' the establishment concerned itself, but only that it be carried out 'in the context of the activities of' the establishment (judgment of 13 May 2014, Google Spain and Google, C-131/12, EU:C:2014:317, paragraph 52)".

nonetheless was carried out in the context of the activities of the establishment. Therefore, the German data protection authority had the jurisdiction to investigate. Thirdly, citing *Schrems*,[50] the Court found that data protection authorities are to act in complete independence in exercising their functions. The 1995 Directive does not place an obligation for one data protection authority to be bound by the assessment of another data protection authority.

European Court of Human Rights

In 2006, the ECtHR dealt with the case of *Weber and Saravia v. Germany* (no. 54934/00).[51] In this case, the Court had to rule on surveillance measures which included the interception of wireless telecommunication messages for crimes listed in the German law on restrictions on the secrecy of mail, post and telecommunications. ("G10 law"). Weber, a journalist researching matters which fell under the G10 law contested that certain provisions of the law violated, amidst others, her rights to privacy and freedom of expression. She contested that the provisions of the law were too vague and did not provide for effective remedies to contest the surveillance in front of the Courts.[52] Furthermore, in the applicants' view, the surveillance also affected the freedom of the press as provided in the German Basic law and the European Convention on Human Rights.[53]

In domestic proceedings, the German Court partially found a violation of the German law regarding the requirement to forward information to the federal authorities even if there only was a suspicion of a crime having been committed. Furthermore, the Court also ruled as unproportional a provision of the law which placed the obligation to forward collected information to multiple offices and services. It rejected the complaints of the second applicant on grounds of rationae personae (the applicant was not a German national and the alleged infringement did not occur within Germany's jurisdiction).

The applicants filed an application with the Strasbourg Court. The chamber considered three matters – whether the infringements were necessary for public safety, if the infringements were proportionate and provided proper safeguards and whether the infringements constituted an unproportionate interference with the freedom of the press.[54]

50 Ibid., para 68 "As provided for by the second subparagraph of Article 28(1) of that Directive, the supervisory authorities whose task it is to supervise the application, in the territory of their own Member States, of the provisions adopted by those States pursuant to the Directive are to act with complete independence in exercising the functions entrusted to them. (see, to that effect, judgment of 6 October 2015, Schrems, C-362/14)".

51 *Weber and Saravia v. Germany* (no. 54934/00) 29 June 2006, http://hudoc.echr.coe.int/eng?i=001-76586 (accessed 25.11.2018).

52 Ibid., para 9, "Numerous telecommunications could be monitored, in the absence of any concrete suspicions, with the aid of catchwords which remained secret. Strategic monitoring could then be used in respect of individuals, preventing the press from carrying out effective investigations into sensitive areas covered by the Act", and 154, "They complained, in particular, about the destruction of personal data (section 3(6) and (7) taken in conjunction with section 7(4) of the G 10 Act), the failure to receive notice of restrictions on the secrecy of telecommunications (section 3(8) of the G 10 Act), and the exclusion of judicial review of monitoring measures (section 9(6) taken in conjunction with section 3(1))".

53 Ibid., para 142, "The first applicant submitted, in particular, that the impugned monitoring powers under section 3(1) of the amended G 10 Act prejudiced the work of journalists investigating issues targeted by surveillance measures. She could no longer guarantee that information she received in the course of her journalistic activities remained confidential".

54 Ibid., para 63–65.

Regarding the nature of the infringements, the Court affirmed the position of the German government that the infringements were necessary in a democratic society. Data could only be stored for a maximum of three months and after a Court order outlining reasons for the surveillance.[55] Once the surveillance is over and it is clear that further surveillance will not be required, the authorities are obligated to inform the affected individuals that they have been subject to surveillance.[56] Finally, the Court found the essence of the law was not to target journalists, nor uncover journalistic sources. Therefore, the interference of the law with the freedom of expression was not found to be particularly serious. The Court concluded that the application was manifestly ill-founded.[57]

Recently, the Court in *Big Brother Watch v. UK* reached a different verdict in a case which affected the mass surveillance of European citizens.[58] The case addressed the nature of interception of electronic communications by the United Kingdom. Following the revelations of Snowden, the Government Communications Headquarters (GCHQ) was accused of running operation TEMPORA, which allowed it to tap into and draw data from bearers. Based on so-called simple selectors (i.e. an email address), data of targets was collected and stored. Other data was automatically discarded.[59] Following a "triage" process the GCHQ determined which data to actually open. The legal basis for the collection of data was the Intelligence Services Act and Security Services Act.

Big Brother Watch and other British non-profit organisations asked the government to deem these operations inadmissible with the ECHR.[60] Domestic proceedings (first and third joined cases) in front of the UK Investigatory Powers Tribunal (IPT) failed. The Court also had to deal with the PRISM and Upstream programmes of the United States, which allowed targeting non-US nationals located outside of the United States. Regarding UK citizens, the Regulation of Investigatory Powers Act (RIPA) set forth that, in the absence of a mutual legal assistance agreement, a warrant must first be issued by the RIPA, or in exceptional circumstances, by the secretary of state personally, in order to target a UK national. The IPT, in the third case found that data had been stored longer than necessary.[61]

The RIPA provides that an intercept warrant must first be issued before intercepting the communications of UK citizens[62] or, in the case of serious crime; the storage is

55 Ibid., para 116, "the Court notes, with regard to the implementation of surveillance measures and the processing of the data obtained, that safeguards against abuse were spelled out in detail".

56 Ibid., para 136.

57 Ibid., para 156.

58 Case of *Big Brother Watch and Others v. The United Kingdom* (nos. 58170/13, 62322/14 and 24960/15) 13 September 2018, available at: http://hudoc.echr.coe.int/eng?i=001-186048 (accessed 23.11.2018).

59 Ibid., para 10 and 12, "As communications flow across the targeted bearers, the system compares the traffic against a list of "simple selectors". These are specific identifiers (for example, an email address) relating to a known target".

60 Ibid., para 19.

61 Ibid., para 52, "However, the IPT was satisfied that the material had not been accessed after the expiry of the relevant retention time-limit and that the breach could be characterised as a technical one. It amounted nonetheless to a breach of Article 8 and GCHQ was ordered to destroy any of the communications which had been retained for longer than the relevant period and to deliver one hard copy of the documents within seven days to the Interception of Communications Commissioner to retain for five years in case they were needed for any further legal proceedings. nonetheless to a breach of Article 8".

62 Regulation of Investigatory Powers Act 2000, www.legislation.gov.uk/ukpga/2000/23/contents (accessed 26.11.2018), section 5 (1).

authorised directly by the secretary of state. Serious crime is defined as a crime which satisfies one of the following criteria.

(a) that the offence or one of the offences that is or would be constituted by the conduct is an offence for which a person who has attained the age of twenty-one and has no previous convictions could reasonably be expected to be sentenced to imprisonment for a term of three years or more;
(b) that the conduct involves the use of violence, results in substantial financial gain or is conduct by a large number of persons in pursuit of a common purpose.[63]

The RIPA also provides for the option of an Interception warrant – this can only be issued by the Secretary of State. Warrants issued on the grounds of economic well-being of the UK may only be authorised by the Secretary of State if there is a direct link with national security.[64] Non-judicial cooperation between counterpart agencies outside of the UK is allowed, but human rights standards of the UK must be upheld.[65]

The United Kingdom did not suggest that an interception of communications was taking place outside the United Kingdom's territorial jurisdiction. Furthermore, the government did not raise any objection under Article 1 of the Convention; nor did they suggest that the interception of communications under the section 8(4) regime was taking place outside the United Kingdom's territorial jurisdiction.[66]

The Court found the provisions of the RIPA did not provide clear enough definitions as to what constitutes "serious crime". On these grounds, it found that the current regime was in violation of Articles 8 and 10 of the Convention.

Although the Court ruled in favour of the applicants, two points have to be made which lessen the scope of victory. The Court explicitly sees bulk interception as, "a valuable means to achieve the legitimate aims pursued, particularly given the current threat level from both global terrorism and serious crime.[67] Second, the entire judgment only allocates two paragraphs to the proportionality of the interference. The Court deduced from its case law that States have a large margin of appreciation when taking measures against terrorism. As it found enough safeguards in the RIPA, the Court here upheld the view that the interference was kept to what is "necessary in a democratic society".[68]

Delfi AS v. Estonia[69] was the first case in which the Court had been called upon to examine a complaint concerning the liability of a company running an internet news portal because of comments posted on the portal by its users. The portal provided a platform, run on commercial lines, for user-generated comments on previously published content. In such cases some users – whether identified or anonymous – can post clearly unlawful comments which infringe the personality rights of others. The Court held that the commercial operator of an internet news portal may be held accountable for offensive comments posted on the portal by users.

63 Ibid., Section 81(2)(b).
64 Ibid., Section 5 (3)(c).
65 Ibid., Section 7.16 and 7.17.
66 *Case of Big Brother Watch and Others v. The United Kingdom*, para 271.
67 *Case of Big Brother Watch and Others v. The United Kingdom*, para 386.
68 Ibid., paras 445 and 446.
69 Case of Delfi AS v. Estonia (no. 64569/09), 16 June 2015, http://hudoc.echr.coe.int/eng?i=001-155105 (accessed 26.11.2018).

The applicant company, Delfi AS, complained that the domestic courts had found it liable for the offensive comments left by its users under one of its online news articles, about a ferry company. Delfi AS removed the offending comments, at the request of the lawyers of the owner of the ferry company, around six weeks after they were published. The question was not whether the rights of the authors of the comments to freedom of expression had been infringed, but whether finding Delfi AS liable for these third-party comments had infringed its right to freedom of expression.

The Grand Chamber laid down four criteria for determining whether or not the finding that Delfi AS was liable for comments posted by third parties had violated its freedom of expression. It took into account the nature of the comments in question which violated human dignity and were "clearly unlawful". The Court found an economic interest of Delfi AS increasing the amount of comments on its articles. Furthermore, it declared as insufficient the measures taken by Delfi AS to remove the comments in a timely manner. Finally, it found the moderate sanction imposed on Delfi AS by the domestic Court (€ 320) to be proportionate. Ultimately, the Court found no violation of the right of freedom of expression.

In *M.L. and W.W. v. Germany*,[70] the Strasbourg Court for the first time dealt with the possibility of a Right to be Forgotten to be deduced from Articles 8 and 10 of the Convention. In May 1993 the applicants were convicted of murdering a popular actor in 1991 and sentenced to life imprisonment. In August 2007 and January 2008, they were released on probation. The convictions were not deleted under German law.

In 2000 a radio station ran a report on the occasion of the anniversary of the murder, which named the applicants and made reference to the fact that they had been unsuccessful in a recent application to the Constitutional Court to have their case reopened. A transcript of the report remained online in the radio station's archive in 2007, at which point the applicants brought proceedings requesting the anonymisation of the personal data in the report.

On 29 February 2008 the Hamburg Regional Court granted the applicants' requests, placing particular weight on the fact that, prior to their release in 2007, their interest in no longer being confronted with their past actions having regard to their aim of reintegrating themselves into society. The public had been sufficiently well informed about the matter. The Court of Appeal upheld those judgments.

The Federal Court of Justice reached a different conclusion, mainly on the grounds that the Court of Appeal had not taken sufficient account of the radio station's right to freedom of expression and the public's interest in being informed. Among the factors referred by the court were the tone of the report, the fact that it could only be found by internet users searching for information about the applicants and the public interest in being able to do research on past events. Also significant was the concern that any requirement for publishers to check regularly their archives would have a chilling effect.

The Strasbourg Court in its analysis looked into four criteria in determining the scope of infringement:

- The contribution of the report to a debate of public interest.
- The notoriety of the applicants and the topic of the report

70 Case of M.L. and W.W. v. Germany (nos. 60798/10 and 65599/10), 28 June 2018, http://hudoc.echr.coe.int/eng?i=001-184438 (accessed 26.11.2018).

- The previous conduct of the applicants in regards to the media
- The form, content and consequences of the publication.[71]

The Court unanimously found that the anonymisation of the report would have a chilling effect on publishers who would be placed under an obligation to constantly review their archives. It also negatively weighed the fact that the applicants themselves have sought media attention during the original proceedings, which also made them more known to a wider public. Finally, it found that the thirteen-year-old pictures included in the report could not be realistically used to identify the applicants anymore. Therefore, the Court found no infringement of Article 8.[72]

A unified approach?

In 2010, Judge Bay Larsen of the ECJ and Judge Lorenzen of the ECtHR in two parallel articles confirmed that there is a "dialogue" between the Strasbourg and Luxembourg Courts. This dialogue has both a horizontal and vertical dimension. The ECtHR has in multiple cases informally reviewed EU law when deciding cases involving actions taken under EU law by Member States. This is the vertical dimension. The horizontal dimension refers to the cross-referencing taking place between the two courts in their judgments. Through doing so, they can either appraise or criticise the actions of the other court in their own case law.[73]

Walter van Gerven has pointed to, "mutual learning, which is typical of courts of law, both between the two European courts, the European Court of Human Rights (ECtHR) and the European Court of Justice (ECJ), and between the Member States' courts".[74]

The preceding sections have looked into the case law of the ECJ and ECtHR. This final section will provide an assessment as to whether the judgments of the Strasbourg and Luxembourg Courts reflect a unified or scattered approach regarding data protection in the European sphere.

One factor hinting at an active Strasbourg/Luxembourg dialogue is the cross-referencing of judgments. Such cross-referencing is present in some of the judgments. The case of *Digital Rights Ireland Ltd.* cited *Marper v. United Kingdom* while looking into the proportionality of the interference of fundamental rights of the Irish Data Protection Authority in choosing to not investigate Schrems case and also when establishing that, "EU legislation in question must lay down clear and precise rules governing the scope and application of the measure in question and imposing minimum safeguards so that the persons whose data have been retained have sufficient guarantees to effectively protect their personal data".[75]

71 For a commentary of the effects of the M.L. and W.W. v Germany Judgment, see H. Tomlinson and A. Wills, Case Law, Strasbourg: ML and WW v Germany, Article 8 Right to be Forgotten and the Media. https://inforrm.org/2018/07/04/case-law-strasbourg-ml-and-ww-v-germany-article-8-right-to-be-forgotten-and-the-media-hugh-tomlinson-qc-and-aidan-wills/ (accessed 29.11.2018).

72 Case of M.L. and W.W. v. Germany (nos. 60798/10 and 65599/10), para 116.

73 L. Hallestov Storgaard (2015) Composing Europe's Fundamental Rights Area: A Case for Discursive Pluralism. *Cambridge Yearbook of European Legal Studies*, Vol. 17, 210–246.

74 Walter Van Gerven (2008) The Open Method of Convergence. *Juridica International*, XIV, 36.

75 Case C-362/14, Maximillian Schrems v. Data Protection Commissioner, para 54.

The Strasbourg Court appears to have returned the favour in its Big Brother Watch Judgment where it devotes an entire section of its judgment towards the case law of the ECJ. In its judgment, the Court did not find mass surveillance itself to be in violation of the rights granted under the European Convention. As highlighted in the partly concurring and partly dissenting opinion of Judges Pardalos and Eicke, the Court has chosen to not follow the conclusions reached by the ECJ and instead rely on its own history of case law on deciding whether there has been a violation of the Right to Privacy. The Judges of the opinion hint that the case law of the ECJ reflects that the scope of protection granted by the Charter of Fundamental Rights is wider than the scope of the European Convention.[76]

A rejection of a wider scope of rights being applied can also be seen in the recent M.L. and W.W. judgment of the ECtHR. The Court found that leaving the article on the website online did not constitute a breach of a Right to Privacy; deleting it could in fact have a chilling effect on the freedom of expression. However, it should be noted that in contrast to Google Spain, this case dealt with deleting the actual article, not merely de-listing it in the search engines. The reasoning of the judgment also does not appear to hinder the Court from reaching a different conclusion in a case concerning the de-listing of results.[77]

Finally, despite the recent clash between the Strasbourg and Luxembourg Courts regarding mass surveillance, the recent development of legislation of the EU and the CoE shows signs of a conversion. The Charter of Fundamental Rights is based on the European Convention on Human Rights. Now, Protocol 223 of Convention 108, as one of its aims, is ensuring that the data protection standards of signatory states correspond to an adequate level of protection as outlined in the General Data Protection Regulation.[78]

To conclude, the recent case law of the Strasbourg and Luxembourg Court in regards to data protection displays two trends. On the one hand, there have been rather significant clashes, specifically regarding mass surveillance measures and an overall reluctance of the Strasbourg Court to judge in favour of widening the scope of the Convention rights. On the other hand, the cross-referencing of judgments and legislation between the two Courts is visible and appears to be increasing. The "mutual learning" of the two Courts is ongoing.

76 Case of Big Brother Watch and Others v. The United Kingdom, Joint Partly Dissenting and Partly Concurring Opinion of Judges Pardalos and Eicke, para 22.

77 H. Tomlinson and A. Wills, Case Law, Strasbourg: ML and WW v Germany, Article 8 Right to be Forgotten and the Media.

78 Explanatory Report to the Protocol amending the Convention for the Protection of Individuals with regard to Automatic Processing of Personal Data, https://rm.coe.int/cets-223-explanatory-report-to-the-protocol-amending-the-convention-fo/16808ac91a (accessed 29.11.2018).

12 The Internet Balancing Formula*

Mart Susi

Introduction

Balancing has swiftly emerged as the dominant discursive practice for reacting to conflicts of competing fundamental rights in the digital dimension. A discursive practice of stakeholders, endorsed by international courts and legislators and occasionally by academics, by itself is not sufficient to conclude that balancing is justifiable from ontic or epistemic perspectives. Without such justifications, balancing cannot claim correctness in the digital dimension of a modern society, as the arguments which have been raised against balancing in the offline dimension – the absence of morality and the impossibility of avoiding arbitrariness – can easily lead to the rejection of balancing as a universal tool applicable in horizontal internet relationships and having the potential to bring some element of order into the predominantly existentialist online realm. Such discursive practice may have developed independently from any theoretical considerations, being driven primarily by the political understanding of the need to provide a rational tool against abuses of fundamental rights on the internet, or, even more pragmatically, to provide a shield for private online companies against the claims that they are not concerned with the matter of fundamental rights protection. This chapter will explore the question of ontic and epistemic justifiability of balancing on the internet in horizontal relationships by private online companies, and thereafter propose a mathematical formula for balancing conflicting fundamental rights in the digital dimension. This chapter will demonstrate that the Internet Balancing Formula contains certain ontic and epistemic elements which minimise the strength of arguments usually raised against balancing as a general generic fundamental rights concept or balancing by private entities on the internet in particular. Therefore, this Internet Balancing Formula has the potential to decisively and globally influence the discursive practice of balancing on the internet, primarily raising confidence in private balancing by providing a tool to claim correctness. The chapter will claim that the Internet Balancing Formula will increase the rational element of balancing online.

Theoretical background

The rationality aspect

Objections against or acceptance of balancing performed by private online companies is inseparable from objections against or acceptance of content assessments of these companies in principle. This relates to the epistemic dimension of balancing, that is, how the

* A previous version of this article was first published in March 2019 in the European Law Journal 25 (2), 198–212. Susi, Mart (2019) The Internet Balancing Formula. *European Law Journal*, 25 (2), 198–212.

information about conflicting rights is obtained, how it is evaluated and how the outcome is formulated and then implemented in practical terms. There are two principal positions. The first position claims that private companies should not be given the task to assess online content, and the second, that these companies are best placed to do so. The first position is advocated, for example, by the UN Special Rapporteur Frank La Rue's categorical opinion: "The Special Rapporteur believes that censorship measures should never be delegated to a private entity . . . no State should use or force intermediaries to undertake censorship on its behalf".[1] The concept of a "safe haven" for internet intermediaries is based on similar recognition. The Council of Europe Committee of Minister's Draft Recommendation CM/Rec (2017x)xx to member states on the roles and responsibilities of internet intermediaries directs in paragraph 1.3.5. that "State authorities should not directly or indirectly impose a general obligation on intermediaries to monitor content which they merely give access to, or which they transmit or store, be it by automated means or not".[2] Most academic authors have the view that private internet companies should not be trusted with the task of protecting fundamental rights, which also means that they should not balance.[3] Such an absolutist position that internet companies should never be assigned the task of balancing conflicting rights may have political (private online companies can thereby influence public opinion), economic (if required to perform the task of balancing, private companies cannot rely on artificial intelligence only and would need to hire thousands of network administrators with the task of monitoring network traffic) and constitutional (private online companies have no constitutional authority to balance conflicting fundamental rights) justifications, but it does not have a justification for a rejection from the perspective of legal theory. This is so because balancing is an application of the principles theory, which defines principles as *optimisation requirements* demanding "that something be realized to the greatest extent possible given the legal and factual possibilities".[4] The conducting of balancing by private entities is *prima facie* not against the principles theory, as the digital realm and the necessity of performing balancing by private online entities can be viewed as such a concrete legal and factual possibility.

The second position, that internet intermediaries are well positioned to balance conflicting rights online, is gaining strength as a recognition of the inevitable. Academic writings are hesitant to accept this position as justifiable primarily due to the absence of constitutional legitimacy, but international courts, legislators and stakeholders do not exhibit the same

1 Report of the Special Rapporteur on the promotion and protection of the right to freedom of opinion and expression, Frank La Rue, adopted by the UN Human Rights Council on 16 May 2011, para 43.

2 Recommendation CM/Rec (2017x)xx of the Committee of Ministers to member states on the roles and responsibilities of internet intermediaries, available at https://rm.coe.int/recommendation-cm-rec-2017x-xx-of-the-committee-of-ministers-to-member/1680731980 (accessed 15.05.2019)

3 Coudert and Werkers are critical of the ability of Internet service providers to protect fundamental rights, since these are not binding upon private entities, and of the legitimacy of any balancing conducted by the private entities – Fanny Coudert and Evi Werkers (2008), In the Aftermath of the Promusicae Case: How to Strike the Balance? *International Journal of Law and Information Technology*, Vol. 18, No. 1, 50–71. Angepoulus has analysed the efficiency of the notice-and-action systems in the context of the practice of the European regional courts – which in his view support the doctrine of balancing – and concluded that the proper answer to the intermediary liability question must be in the vertical approach, where the states carry the burden of implementing fundamental rights protection formulas and not the private intermediaries – Christina Angelopoulos and Stijn Smet (2016) Notice-and-fair-balance: How to Reach a Compromise between Fundamental Rights in European Intermediary Liability. *Journal of Media Law*, Vol. 8, No. 2, 266–301, at 300–301.

4 Robert Alexy (2002) *A Theory of Constitutional Rights* (first publ. 1985), trans. Julian Rivers. Oxford: Oxford University Press, 47.

hesitancy. Both the European Court of Human Rights[5] with the statement that balancing by online news portals is an appropriate tool to react to hate speech in the *Delfi* case, and the Court of Justice of the EU[6] in the *Google* case with the statement that the data controller (Google as private online company) has itself to conduct the examination whether to end an intrusion into privacy when countering requests for data blocking – clearly stand behind this second position. The new EU Data Protection Regulation[7] includes an obligation for private entities to balance conflicting rights online. Therefore, the judicial task of balancing is trusted to private entities through the authority of the law or the courts, which means that the concern over the proliferation of constitutional adjudication[8] within horizontal online relationships is weakened. The third example is that of global internet corporations who have taken up the initiative to establish standards of their own for the purpose of balancing – like the Google Advisory Council[9] after the CJEU *Google* judgment.

Both positions claim that their conclusion is rational – both surprisingly relying on the matter of the immediate closeness of the private online companies to the content published through their platforms. The first position claims that because of such closeness balancing cannot be rational; the second claims the contrary, that because of such closeness balancing can be rational. Within the digital domain, it seems justified to speak of balancing vis-à-vis rationality not in absolute, but in relative terms. Those who state that balancing should never be trusted to private companies are saying that such balancing would be irrational. Consequently, it is a rational choice to deny irrational balancing online. Those who state that private entities can balance are saying that such balancing would lead to a rational outcome. The claim of rationality of balancing online depends on whether balancing can be justified from ontic and epistemic perspectives. If it can, then it is a rational method. If it cannot be justified from these perspectives, it remains irrational to balance. In principle, the element of rationality in online balancing is that of degree, where at one end the ideal rationality is based on no contestation of ontic and epistemic aspects or discursive practice under ideal conditions. At the other end, irrationality is due to the absence of ontic and epistemic justification or divergent discursive practices.

The ontic aspect relates to the relationship between the fundamental rights to be balanced, whereas the epistemic aspect relates to the question of whether in the online dimension these rights can be properly balanced. The latter is a matter of the capabilities of the actors in the online dimension to perform the balancing exercise. The proposed Internet Balancing Formula becomes central to increasing the degree of rationality in the online dimension when rights collide.

The ontic dimension

The balancing principle rests on the understanding that the rights to be balanced are of equal value; for example, the right to privacy and the freedom of expression. This is the

5 ECtHR judgment *Delfi v. Estonia* (Grand Chamber), no 64569/09, 16 June 2015, para 110.

6 *Google Spain SL, Google Inc. v. Agencia Española de Protección de Datos (AEPD), Mario Costeja Gonzáles* (Grand Chamber), C-131/12, judgment of 13 May 2014.

7 Regulation (EU) 2016/679 of the European Parliament and of the Council of 27 April 2016 on the protection of natural persons with regard to the processing of personal data and on the free movement of such data, and repealing Directive 95/46/EC (General Data Protection Regulation).

8 L. Besselink (2013) The Proliferation of Constitutional Law and Constitutional Adjudication, or How American Judicial Review Came to Europe After All. *Utrecht Law Review*, Vol. 9, 19.

9 The Advisory Council to Google in the Right to be Forgotten, published in 2014, http://docs.dpaq.de/8527-

ontic *status quo* of the offline world; in other words, the cornerstone of the balancing paradigm. There appears a rhetorical consensus by key players within the global human rights community that the rights online are the same as offline, which would mean that the ontic cornerstone remains the same. Under rhetorical consensus, I mean exactly what the term suggests – the statement of sameness of rights online and offline has not been profoundly and theoretically reasoned.

The UN Human Rights Committee has expressed in General Comment no 34 to the ICCPR Article 19 that paragraph 2[10] protects all forms of expression and the means of their dissemination, including internet-based modes of expression.[11] Michael O'Flaherty, as one of the key authors of General Comment no 34, has explained that the standards for online media are the same as standards for traditional media and that the UN Human Rights Committee clearly had this approach in mind.[12] O'Flaherty does not provide a reasoning for this approach. The Council of Europe's Committee of Ministers has expressed the view that rights on the internet are the same as offline.[13] This may suffice here to make the case of the sameness of rights, although this doctrine of the sameness of rights at this point seems vested upon the general idea of the universality of fundamental rights. The *Delfi* Grand Chamber judgment[14] and subsequent "Hungarian" case[15] of the Strasbourg court are built upon the opinion that the standards do not differ online and offline, the court expressing it as follows in the section of preliminary remarks:

> Defamatory and other types of clearly unlawful speech, including hate speech and speech inciting violence, can be disseminated like never before, worldwide, in a matter of seconds, and sometimes remain persistently available online. These two conflicting realities lie at the heart of this case. Bearing in mind the need to protect the values underlying the Convention, and considering that the rights under Article 10 and 8 of the Convention deserve equal respect, a balance must be struck that retains the essence of both rights.[16]

For the purposes of this chapter we consider that the doctrine of the sameness of rights online and offline can be justifiable. This does not mean, however, that in order to achieve the ontic *status quo* of sameness, one right may not deserve more protection than another. There are contestations from both sides to the idea that freedom of expression and the right to privacy deserve equal protection online: some think that freedom of expression online deserves more protection, others that the right to privacy does.

10 Paragraph 2 of Article 29 of the International Covenant on Civil and Political Rights guarantees the right to freedom of expression, without explicitly mentioning Internet, since it was adopted in 1966.

11 General comment no. 34 to Article 19 (Freedoms of opinion and expression), of the International Covenant on Civil and Political Rights, adopted by the Human Rights Committee on its 102nd session in Geneva on 12 September 2011, para 12.

12 Michael O'Flaherty (2012) Freedom of Expression: Article 19 of the International Covenant on Civil and Political Rights and the Human Rights Committee's General Comment No 34. *Human Rights Law Review*, Vol. 12, 627–654.

13 "Internet users have the right to freedom of expression, including the right to receive and impart information, by using services, applications and devices of their choice, in full compliance with Article 10 of the Convention" (para 1) – see Appendix to Recommendation CM/Rec(2016)1 of the Committee of Ministers to member States on protecting and promoting the right to freedom of expression and the right to private life with regard to network neutrality, adopted by the Committee of Ministers on 13 January 2016, at the 124th meeting of the Ministers' Deputies.

14 *Delfi v. Estonia* (Grand Chamber), no 64569/09, 16 June 2015.

15 *Magyar Tartalomszolgáltatók Egyesülete and Index.Hu ZRT v. Hungary*, no 22947/13, 02 February 2016 – further in this article *MTE v. Hungary*.

16 *Delfi v. Estonia* (Grand Chamber), para 110, *MTE v. Hungary*, para 59.

The example of the preponderant need to protect the freedom of expression more is evident from the UN General Assembly Resolution "The promotion, protection and enjoyment of human rights on the Internet",[17] which affirms in paragraph 1 that "the same rights that people have offline must also be protected online, in particular freedom of expression". It is argued in academic literature that the various legislative initiatives create a mechanism which amounts to private censorship,[18] meaning that such private censorship is a threat to freedom of expression. Pollicino and Romeo conclude that in the case law in most European courts, balancing is used to justify limiting the freedom of expression,[19] implying that freedom of expression should be protected more.

From the other perspective, La Rue warns that activities on the internet "can constitute a violation of the internet users' right to privacy and undermine people's confidence and security on the internet, thus impeding the free flow of information and ideas online".[20] Marsoof calls for privacy-specific legislation on the internet.[21] Land predicts that without consideration of international human rights law and values, governments and industry will drive towards standards on issues of privacy that are inconsistent with and even undermine international human rights.[22]

The arguments mapped briefly here do not relate to the ontic aspect of the conflicting rights on the internet but relate to the capabilities and discursive practice of the internet intermediaries when assessing content online. The distinction between the ontic and epistemic aspects is essential for clarity, and for concluding whether balancing is a justifiable method for resolving conflicts of fundamental rights online. The ontic aspect is related to the matter of whether the initial weight to the conflicting rights is the same or not, and the epistemic aspect is related to the matter of how the balancing is performed, that is also, whether during the balancing for some reason more weight is given by implication to either side of the balancing scale. In other words, whether during the process of balancing the internet intermediaries are capable of achieving a correct or biased relationship.

Convergence of these polarised viewpoints (e.g. freedom of expression deserves more protection vis-à-vis the right to privacy deserves) becomes possible if one develops a theory which sets the relationship between conflicting rights not on the same level but realises the internet vulnerability as an ontic condition that confronts anyone who enters the digital domain.[23] Internet vulnerability realises that the traditional means of protecting one's privacy, known from the offline world, cannot be effectively realised or are

17 UN Human Rights Council resolution A/HRC/32/L.20, adopted on 43rd meeting on 01 July 2016.

18 Aleksandra Kuczerawy (2015) Intermediary Liability and Freedom of Expression: Recent Developments in the EU Notice and Action Initiative. *Computer Law and Security Review*, Vol. 31, 46–56.

19 Oreste Pollicino and Graziella Romeo (2016) Concluding Remarks: Internet Law, Protection of Fundamental Rights and the Role of Constitutional Adjudication. In: Oreste Pollicino and Graziella Romeo (Eds.), *The Internet and Constitutional Law: The Protection of Fundamental Rights and Constitutional Adjudication in Europe*. Routledge Research in Constitutional Law, 234–251.

20 La Rue report, para 82.

21 Althaf Marsoof (2011) Online Social Networking and the Right to Privacy: The Conflicting Rights of Privacy and Expression. *International Journal of Law and Technology*, Vol. 19, No. 2, 110–133.

22 Molly Land (2013) Toward an International Law of the Internet. *Harvard International Law Jorunal*, Vol. 54, No 2, 393–458, at 394.

23 Martina Gillen states that the Internet vulnerability of users in cyberspace is an ontic condition, which has been downplayed but should allow to lead to the protection of privacy. Martina Gillen (2012) Human versus Inalienable Rights: Is there Still a Future for Online Protest in the Anonymous World? *European Journal for Law and Technology*, Vol. 3, No 1.

considerably weakened in the digital realm. This is so because any information published on the internet can stay online forever and the time to react to violations of privacy is non-existent after information is published. These factors by default diminish the protection of privacy online. The Internet Balancing Formula therefore proposes that internet vulnerability as an ontic condition will lead to a shift in the initial relationship between the conflicting rights before the balancing exercise starts; for example, the scale is set to protect privacy if the relative weight of other factors against one another would produce an ideal equilibrium.

The epistemic dimension

There are two main concerns related to the epistemic dimension of balancing online, which concern first, the way information is gathered, and second, how it is assessed.

The concern related to how information is gathered is online-specific; that is, this concern does not emerge in relation to the epistemic dimension of balancing offline. It is related to the element of time. Within any framework of judicial balancing the courts have the luxury of utilising time as long as needed to reach a correct assessment of conflicting rights and establish a proper balance. Conversely on the internet, such luxury to disregard the element of time is non-existent, as it would lead to non-effective, retrospective recognition that rights were violated and proper balance would not have been achieved. Effective balancing online depends on swift decisions about whether certain information published overrides someone else's concern about an intrusion into his or her private domain. Here time is a different concern from the understanding that with the passage of time the balance of interests may reverse; for example, when processing personal data.[24] The shortness of time for reasoned decision-making can easily lead ultimately to the rejection of the rationality of online balancing. Here the Internet Balancing Formula becomes central, since it is a mathematical formula with easily established input, leading to an immediate conclusion about which of the conflicting rights in the given circumstances should prevail. Currently, internet intermediaries use artificial intelligence to assess easier cases and human intelligence to assess more complex situations. The question of how these different intelligences actually assess the cases leads us to the second main concern – over arbitrariness.

The objection of arbitrariness raised against the balancing method in the offline dimension is formulated by Habermas: "Because there are no rational standards for this, weighing takes place either arbitrarily or unreflectively, according to customary standards and hierarchies".[25] Alexy's response is that the weight formula provides the rational standard. The objection of arbitrariness and the response to this objection via a mathematical formula are applicable towards balancing in the online dimension as well. Therefore, it is not necessary to address this more general matter here. The novel objection against balancing online via private entities, related to the objection of arbitrariness, is related to the lack of transparency. This objection involves the aspects of who is the decision maker (artificial or human intelligence), which standards are applied, and what is the argumentation.

24 Giovanni Sartor (2016) The Right to be Forgotten: Balancing Interests in the Flux of Time. *International Journal of Law and Information Technology*, Vol. 24, 72–98, at 72.

25 Jürgen Habermas (1996) *Between Facts and Norms. Contributions to a Discourse Theory of Law and Democracy* (first publ. 1992), trans. William Rehg. Cambridge: Polity Press, 259.

The Council of Europe has stated that "Internet service providers should put in place appropriate, clear, open and efficient procedures to respond within reasonable time limits to complaints from internet users alleging breaches of the principles included in the foregoing provisions".[26] The United Nations "*Calls upon* all States to consider formulating, through transparent and inclusive processes with all stakeholders, and adopting national internet-related public policies that have the objective of universal access and enjoyment of human rights at their core".[27] Similarly, La Rue "encourages corporations to establish clear and unambiguous terms of service in line with international human rights norms and principles".[28] These examples may suffice to demonstrate the concern about the arbitrariness and lack of transparency.

The current discursive practices among internet intermediaries when balancing conflicting fundamental rights are against the principle of transparency. It is an issue of capability – the online corporations simply are unable to provide reasoned decisions each time they have to balance conflicting rights; moreover, sometimes these arguments are not even in need of articulation. This limited capability to provide a transparent decision-making process is a factual reality. The practical response has been to make at least some information about the decision-making process publicly available – not in relation to individual cases but as a matter of principle. Two examples illustrate this. The Article 29 Data Protection Working Party adopted the guidelines on 26 November 2014[29] reflecting upon the CJEU *Google* judgment. The Working Party encourages search engines to publish their own-delisting criteria and make detailed statistics available.[30] The Google Advisory Council[31] was established to formulate guidelines for the practical realisation of the right to be forgotten. Although some experts suggested that Google should provide detailed explanations of its decisions, the recommendations limit the request for transparency for making guidelines publicly available and providing anonymised statistics.[32]

The Internet Balancing Formula can become a generic instrument for overcoming the objections related to arbitrariness and the lack of transparency in the private online balancing of fundamental rights. The application of this formula overcomes the objection related to arbitrariness due to the reliance on the same standard formula in all circumstances. The objection related to the lack of transparency is avoidable on the basis of the knowledge of the internet users that the outcome of the balancing exercise originated from the application of the formula. The assessment criteria are provided by the formula and the argumentation is a mathematical calculation. These replies to the objections justify the Internet Balancing Formula, which in turn means that the outcome of the solutions in individual cases can claim correctness.

26 Appendix to Recommendation CM/Rec(2016)1, para 6.1.

27 UN Human Rights Council resolution A/HRC/32/L.20, referred above, para 12.

28 La Rue report, para 48.

29 Available on the internet at: www.dataprotection.ro/servlet/ViewDocument?id=1080.

30 Ibid., 10.

31 The Advisory Council to Google in the Right to be Forgotten, 2014, http://docs.dpaq.de/8527-report_of_the_advisory_committee_to_google_on_the_right_to_be_forgotten.pdf.

32 Ibid., 21.

The Internet Balancing Formula

Assumptions

The Internet Balancing Formula (IBF) has to include a sufficient degree of flexibility, so that its input elements and their relation to one another can be altered in response to future changes in the digital environment. The capability to respond to the changes, which may not be known today, allow us to refer to the IBF as a living instrument of fundamental rights protection.

The current assumptions are the following. First, the mathematical formula of the IBF should not enable the blocking of information that is of vital importance for the whole nation. Second, the IBF is inspired by the Weight Formula developed by Robert Alexy,[33] especially since the Weight Formula has introduced mathematics as an ordering tool to the human rights adjudication framework. Third, the input elements of the IBF are based on criteria usually identified by the courts, especially the European Court of Human Rights, for balancing conflicting rights offline, and on the additional criteria due to the ontic and epistemic considerations inseparable from the online dimension of human rights. Fourth, the IBF should be applicable by everyone; in the other words, assigning concrete value to different input elements should not require any professional legal training and should be based on empirical experience.

The IBF is a quotient of the relative numerical value of two fundamental rights – the numerical value assigned as a result of input elements for the right to privacy divided by the numerical value assigned to the freedom of expression as a result of input elements. Some numerical values are on a scale from zero to one, some are on the scale from one to three, representing in the latter case the values of light (numerical value 1), moderate (numerical value 2) and intense (numerical value 3) interference. The explanation of the different scales will be provided in the following.

The current human rights global landscape has prohibited hate speech on the internet in absolute terms, including incitements to violence and any forms of hatred. It is sufficient to note for the purposes of this chapter that according to this established consensus, balancing is precluded when hate speech occurs. The availability or absence of concrete criteria to establish hate speech remains outside the focus of this chapter. Therefore, the IBF becomes applicable after the assertion of hate speech is excluded. In the other words, step 1 is to answer the question whether the matter concerns hate speech. If not, then we proceed to step 2.

The right to privacy

The following elements make up the right to privacy side of the equation.

First, the element of internet vulnerability, which has a constant numerical value of 1 – this element is represented by the capitol letter "V". The fact that the capabilities of the digital realm in the future might develop towards minimising the consistent threat to privacy cannot be ruled out, so that this numerical value can transform into one of degree, or be eliminated.

33 Robert Alexy (2007) The Weight Formula. In: Jerzy Stelmach, Bartosz Brożek, and Wojciech Załuski (Eds.), *Frontiers of the Economic Analysis of Law*. Krakow: Jagiellonian University Press, 25.

Second, the element of interference in privacy – there is no abstract weight, but its numerical value will depend on the intensity of the interference. A three-level scale will be used where the intensity of interference can be assessed as "light" (numerical value 1), "moderate" (numerical value 2), or "intense" (numerical value 3). The weight of the interference is therefore relative, dependent not on the subjective perception of the person who alleges or might allege a violation of privacy rights, but originates from the perception of a neutral onlooker. By means of this scale, the second element of interference in the right to privacy will be determined, represented by the capitol' letters "PR", while the level of intensity is represented by the small letter "x" – designated to measure more significant elements – having the numerical value 1, 2 or 3. So far, the right to privacy side has the following mathematical formula: V (1) + PR (x).

Third, the element of time. This element is based on the assumption, unchallenged by the courts[34] and academia,[35] that with the passage of time the interference of privacy by some information or opinion will diminish, since the relevance of the information or opinions decreases. The influence of time upon balancing is a matter of degree, which calls for, at first sight, the arbitrary assignment of a numerical value for the years that have passed. Time will be represented by the capitol letter "T", while the level of intensity is represented by the small letter "y" designated to measure less significant values 0.25 (passage of time more than 3 years and less than 7 years) and 0.5 (passage of time more than 7 years and less than 10 years) and 0.75 (passage of time more than 10 years and less than 13 years) and 1 (passage of time more than 13 years). If less than 3 years have passed from the event subject to balancing, the element of time will be 0. So far, the right to privacy side has the following mathematical formula: V (1) + PR (x) + T (y).

Freedom of expression

The following elements make up the freedom of expression side of the equation.

First, the level of public interest in the subject matter, which in the way it is published, raises someone's concern about an intrusion of privacy. The numerical value will depend on the level of public interest, which again is an objective criterion and not a subjective criterion through the eyes of the person who claims the realisation of the freedom of expression. Public interest level is related to the impact the respective information may have upon the recipients.

A three-level scale will be used, the element of public interest will be represented by the capital letters "PI", while the level of public interest is represented by the small letter "x" – designated to measure more significant elements – having the numerical value 1, 2 or 3. Minor public interest (1) is the level of interest for local community matters or for an issue where its importance is time-sensitive, connected to a particular event. In other

34 For example, the Google judgment of the CJEU introduced the element of time in understanding "the right", as time may change the relevance of information – *Google Spain SL, Google Inc. Vs Agencia Española de Protección de Datos (AEPD), Mario Costeja González,* judgment of the CJEU from 13 May 2014, case no C-131/12, para 93.

35 Korehof and colleagues have devoted an entire essay to the exploration of the element of time in the context of the right to be forgotten. They conclude by stating that "Taking the passing of time into consideration can help assess the information landscape at issue for the RTBF and account for the changing values of information as it ages, establishing the balance all rights must find with other interests". Paulan Korenhof, Jef Ausloos, Ivan Szekely, Meg Ambrose, Giovanni Sarto and Ronald Leenes (2014) *Timing the Right to be Forgotten: A Study into "Time" as a Factor in deciding About Retention or Erasure of Data.* Part of the Law, Governance and Technology book series (LGTS volume 20), Berlin/Heidelberg: Springer, 171–199, at 199.

words, the subject matter is limited by space and/or time. Medium public interest (2) concerns matters of interest for larger communities, which may not have an immediate direct impact upon the lives of the majority. Significant public interest (3) concerns matters which are important for the entire nation, or which may have a direct effect upon the lives of the majority. For example, whether to reconstruct a community centre has a public interest level of 1, the ranking of a nation's best public universities in international rankings has a public interest level of 2, but the government proposal to introduce tuition fees in public universities instead of free education has a public interest level of 3. The level of public interest may also be "0", when, for example, the publication of information or opinions serves the goal of simply satisfying curiosity.

Objections to the Internet Balancing Formula in terms of the justifiability of the numerical values of intensity (intrusion of privacy or level of public interest) in the context of Alexy's weight formula transforms in the digital domain due to the non-availability of the element of time, which is usually associated with the possibility to articulate reasons for deciding about intensity. In the context of the weight formula, Alexy has countered objections related to intuition[36], decisionism[37] and arbitrariness[38] with the "argumentation thesis", that the propositions about the intensity of interference and degrees of importance lend themselves to rational justification.[39] Rational justification offline implies articulation, but not online because of the element of time, which requires immediate reaction. Therefore, the meaning of rational justification regarding propositions about intensity and degrees of importance must be given a narrow interpretation online. This means, that the usage of the scale and numerical value to identify intensity is by itself a rational approach. The majority of neutral observers are likely to identify the level of the intensity of interference of privacy or the level of public interest on the three-level scale in the same way, given that they have the same information to start with. The Internet Balancing Formula thus assumes that the one who is making the assessment about the level of intensity belongs to this group of the majority. Even if she does not, it has to be assumed that the person's (either physical or artificial) overall approach is rational – the assessment of various situations can be described via a curve, be it platykurtic or normal or any other distribution, which means that the same curve would appear in the assessment of colliding elements in the IBF. In this case the potential bias from distribution would be cancelled out because it is applied in the same way on both sides of the formula.

A separate line of research, calling perhaps for a mixed methods approach using the quantitative and qualitative methods in combination, which is not possible in this chapter, is to study whether the results of rationality in the narrow and wide sense are by and large the same. Whether the assessment of the levels of intensity reached by the courts, formulated after the possibility to gain more information and take time for consideration, are comparable to those reached by human and/or artificial intelligence, which operate in the conditions of the non-availability of time. In the event of similarities, conclusions may be

36 Alexy (2002) 82–84; see also Robert Alexy, *A Theory of Legal Argumentation* (first publ. 1978), trans. Ruth Adler and Neil MacCormick. Oxford: Clarendon Press, 1989, 212–220.

37 Bernhard Schlink, Freiheit durch Eingriffsabwehr – Rekonstruktion der klassischen Grundrechtsfunktion. In: *Europäische GRUNDRECHTE-Zeitschrift* 11 (1984), 462.

38 Habermas 259.

39 Robert Alexy (2019) *A Non-Positivistic Concept of Constitutional Rights, in: Human Rights and Controversy About the Nature of Law.* Mart Susi, Massimo La Torre, and Leone Niglia (Eds.), Edward Elgar2019 (forthcoming).

drawn for the process of judicial assessment. The occurrence of the opposite – similarities are absent or non-significant – does not at the same time lead to the rejection of the IBF, since it does not claim overall correctness, but correctness at the given time when assessment had to be conducted. The element of the level of public interest on the freedom of the expression side is thus represented by PI (x).

The second element is whether the information concerns a public figure. The capital letters "PF" will be used to represent this element. This is a significant element in the offline balancing of the right to privacy against the freedom of expression according to established consensus; thereby, the level of the public figure is represented by the small letter "x" – an individual holding significant public power is given the numerical value "3", an individual who has voluntarily entered the public domain is given the numerical value "2" and an individual who involuntarily appears in the public domain is given the numerical value "1". The majority of people, when asked, would be able to assess that a government minister holds significant power, that a member of parliament has voluntarily entered the public domain, and the wife of a famous football player has involuntarily entered the public domain. Case law from the European Court of Human Rights regarding the status of a public figure can serve as a source of inspiration. The IBF on the side of the freedom of expression is so far: PI (x) + PF (x).

The third element is related to how information was obtained. The rationale for this element originates from the need for differentiation in the protection of the freedom of expression online depending on the origin of the information. This element is represented by the capital letters "OI". Since its significance for the overall assessment is lighter, a narrower scale of 0 to 0.75 will be used, therefore the small letter "y" is applicable. This element has a negative impact, and therefore illegally obtained information is represented by "−0.75", information obtained in a morally unacceptable yet legally acceptable way is represented by "−0.5", and information obtained in a morally questionable way is represented by "−0.25". The division between morally questionable and morally wrong criteria is that of degree and may change over time. The assessment regarding this division, which could be reached by the majority of the individuals in a group, represents the rational choice as a manifestation of societal values. The criterion of illegality in turn has an objective character, which does not depend on the opinion of the majority. The freedom of expression side so far is: PI (x) + PF (x) – OI (y).

The aspect of empathy

All the preceding elements in relation to the right to privacy and the freedom of expression can in principle be assessed by human or artificial intelligence. It has to be assumed that the majority of individual decisions regarding online content in the present and foreseeable future are made by artificial intelligence for major online companies. Smaller and medium online enterprises and citizen journalists make these decisions as humans. This does not mean that the outcome would be irrational. In order to retain the "human" touch in the assessment of online content, the element of empathy will be used in the IBF. While the other elements are in principle subject to rational argumentation, the numerical value of this element of "empathy" is the result of the moral evaluation of the colliding rights. As far as is known today, artificial intelligence is not yet capable of moral evaluation. This element of empathy will thus guarantee that the task of online assessment will not remain the exclusive domain of artificial intelligence.

The element of empathy is represented by the capital letter "E", and the relative maximum weight for the whole formula is 1, with numerical values 0.25; 0.5; 0.75 and 1. The small letter "z" is used to signify this value where the sum from both sides cannot exceed 1. This means, for example, that when the element of empathy for privacy is set at 0.25 and for freedom of expression 0.75, then the numerical value remaining from this element for privacy is 0.5.

The inclusion of empathy in the assessment of colliding online rights is not compulsory and may occur in two situations. First, when the quotient of the sum of elements of the right to privacy divided by the sum of the elements related to the freedom of expression is 1. Secondly, when the situation itself calls for distinguishing it from comparable situations for certain moral reasons, primarily when the principle of equality deserves derivation due to some specific contextual reasons which may not be connected to the collision at all.

The Internet Balancing Formula

The preceding input elements lead to the following formula:

$$IBF = \frac{V\ (1) + PR\ (x) + T\ (y) + E\ (z)}{PI\ (x) + PF\ (x) - OI\ (y) + E\ (z)}$$

When the quotient is larger than 1, the right to privacy prevails and the information in questions should not be published or should be blocked. When the quotient is smaller than one, the situation is the opposite – the freedom of expression prevails. This result produced by the formula is not open for future argumentation, as several input elements change over time and are dependent on how something is assessed in a given context. This means, that when applied after some time due to some new need, the IBF may produce a different result.

The interest in historical truth

The starting point for the application of the IBF, as explained previously, is after the matter of hate speech has been excluded. The application of the IBF ends at the gates of historic truth. In the other words, the IBF should not become, in principle, an instrument to block information about a matter which is at the relevant time in a given society defined as historic truth. What is defined as the interest in historical truth may change over time; that is, there exists a threshold that allows us to define the interest in some matter as interest in historical truth. La Rue has expressed the significance of historical truth in the context of the online realm as follows: "In the case of human rights, one of the fundamental principles to eradicate impunity is to establish the truth of human rights violations when they exist, and this is recognized as the right to truth of the victims and their families but also to society as a whole to reconstruct historical memory, to memorialize the victims of the past".[40] The purpose of this chapter is not to venture into the exploration of the concept of historical truth, or its contextual dependence on concrete time and space. It suffices to note that, for the purposes of the IBF, this formula becomes non-applicable once it has

40 Google Advisory Council report, La Rue opinion, page 31.

been established that the matter at hand concerns historical truth. One can state, therefore, that the IBF as a mathematical formula is bordering from one side on the concept of hate speech and from the other side on the concept of historical truth.

Testing the Internet Balancing Formula

In order to test the workability of the formula, the IBM is applied as follows in two real-life cases of the European Court of Human Rights: the Delfi case[41] and the Egill Einarsson case.[42] I will also apply this to two hypothetical cases.

The Delfi case

The case concerned anonymous comments posted on Estonia's largest online news portal Delfi concerning an article about the destruction – by the ferry company providing a monopoly service – of an ice road leading from the mainland to the largest island. About twenty comments were insulting towards the main owner of the ferry company; a few among these were categorised as hate speech by the ECtHR. On the basis of the comments constituting hate speech, the ECtHR established that there was no violation of the freedom of expression when the online company was found to be in breach of its obligation to safeguard privacy.

This is a situation where the IBF is not applicable due to the matter of hate speech. Had there been no hate speech comments, the Court would have upheld the freedom of expression.

The IBF would indicate the following regarding comments not constituting hate speech. From the privacy side:

- Internet vulnerability as a constant value: V = 1;
- Insult in relation to business operation – minor intrusion of privacy: PR = 1;
- There was no issue of time, since the comments followed immediately: T = 0;
- The owner of the enterprise would not most likely merit any empathy: E = 0.

From the freedom of expression side:

- The matter of the destruction of an ice road is significant for the whole state, but not essential for its well-being: PI = 2;
- The owner of a major enterprise is certainly a public figure: PF = 2;
- The information was obtained legally: OI = 0;
- And likely no empathy issue in relation to the matter from the side of expression as well: E = 0.

The outcome of the IBF for thde Delfi case without the matter of hate speech would be:

$$\text{IBF} = \frac{\text{V}\ (1) + \text{PR}\ (1) + \text{T}\ (0) + \text{E}(0) = 2}{\text{PI}\ (2) + \text{PF}\ (2) - \text{OI}(0) + \text{E}(0) = 4}$$

41 *Supra* note 13.

42 *Egill Einarsson v. Iceland*, no 24703/15, 7 November 2017.

The IBF is 0.5, which means that freedom of expression prevails. The conclusion of the IBF is the same that the ECtHR would have reached, had there been no issue of hate speech.

Egill Einarsson case

The matter concerned posting comments on Instagram towards Mr. Einarsson, alleging that he is guilty of rape, after he had been acquitted by the court just a few days before. Mr. Einarsson sought the protection of his privacy from the Icelandic courts but lost as these courts considered the comments to be value judgments towards an individual, who himself through his communication with the public at large had become a public figure. The IBF would produce the following result regarding the question of posting comments on Instagram.

From the privacy side:

- Internet vulnerability as a constant value: V = 1;
- Calling someone a rapist against the judicially established facts is a major intrusion of privacy with the value: PR = 3;
- There was no issue of time, since the comments followed immediately: T = 0;
- Mr. Einarsson would not most likely merit any empathy: E = 0.

From the side of freedom of expression:

- The public interest regarding matters of violent crimes has to be assumed. At the same time, it is significant for the whole state, but not essential for its well-being: PI = 2;
- Mr. Einarsson had actively communicated with the public on his own initiative; therefore, he was a public figure: PF = 2;
- The information was obtained legally: OI = 0;
- And likely no empathy issue in relation to the matter from the freedom of expression side means: E = 0.

The outcome of the IBF for the Einarsson case is:

$$IBF = \frac{V\ (1) + PR\ (3) + T\ (0) + E\ (0) = 4}{PI\ (2) + PF\ (2) - OI\ (0) + E\ (0) = 4}$$

The IBF is 1, which means that the freedom of expression and right to privacy are equally protected in the given situation. The European Court of Human Rights was not anonymous in the case: 5 out of 7 Chamber judges voted for the finding of the infringement of the right to privacy, while the other 2 expressed in a dissenting opinion that the freedom of expression deserved more protection.

Hypothetical case of fatally ill Prime Minister admitting the country will go bankrupt soon

This is a hypothetical case, where a fatally ill Prime Minister of country X discussed with his Cabinet the imminent perspective that the government will be unable to pay out public salaries and meet other financial commitments as of next month. After making the announcement, the PM instructs the members of the Cabinet to keep this information secret at least for another two weeks. During this instruction, the PM is hit by strong pain and he interrupts his instruction by mumbling "Here comes the pain from the cancer again which means that I have not more than a few months to live". The Cabinet meeting is recorded. Journalist Y obtains against a bribe this recording and an online media enterprise considers whether to make the whole recording public. If they cut out the part where the PM admits of having cancer and dying soon, the public may easily think that the media enterprise is concealing something. The main editor of the media enterprise now turns to the Internet Balancing Formula for guidance.

In terms of protecting the privacy of the Prime Minister:

- Internet vulnerability as a constant value: V = 1;
- Allowing the entire population to know that someone is dying of cancer is a major intrusion of privacy with the value: PR = 3;
- There was no issue of time, since the publication of the recording would follow immediately: T = 0;
- The Prime Minister is deeply respected by the majority in the country, he is widely seen as a person with high moral character, which could bring the empathy criterion to full: E = 1.

From the freedom of expression side in relation to the publication of the recording:

- The matter of the country's possible bankruptcy is without doubt significant for the entire population and essential for its well-being: PI = 3;
- The Prime Minister is a public figure of significant power: PF = 3;
- The information was obtained illegally: OI = – 0.75;
- The criterion of empathy is fully used for the privacy side: E = 0.

The outcome of the IBF for the hypothetical case is:

$$IBF = \frac{V\ (1) + PR\ (3) + T\ (0) + E\ (1) = 5}{PI\ (3) + PF\ (3) - OI\ (0{,}75) + E\ (0) = 5.25}$$

The IBF result is 0.95, which means that prime minister's privacy is less protected. This would remind the attentive reader of one of the assumptions presented previously regarding the IBF – namely, this formula should not become a tool to block information which is essentially important for the entire nation.

One can see that with passage of time the outcome may shift towards protecting privacy more. After eight years the element of T on the privacy side would be 0.5, leading to an outcome of 5.5 / 5.25 = 1.05, provided all other elements remain the same. Therefore, the online company would be precluded from publishing the information, unless there is a strong argument that the interest in the prime minister's illness is an interest in historic truth.

Case of who would be the new authoritarian leader?

In August 1991, a political coup to overthrow Mikhail Gorbachev, the president of the Soviet Union, failed. There was talk that plans were in place to put new figures into key positions in the Soviet republics who would be extremely loyal to the coup leaders and perhaps take repressive measures towards previous independence-minded local leaders and the intelligentsia. Mr. Arnold Rüütel was at that time one of the top leaders in Soviet Estonia, he was later also elected president in independent Estonia. It is believed that he knows who was supposed to become the new leader if the coup was to succeed. In this hypothetical case, Mr. Rüütel is giving an interview to an online media enterprise and when asked about this name, mentions Mrs. Z. This Mrs. Z. is unknown to the public, she is in her 70s and living peacefully in a small town. The main editor of the media enterprise now turns to the Internet Balancing Formula for guidance on whether to publish this name.

In terms of protecting the privacy of Mrs. Z:

- Internet vulnerability is a constant value: V = 1;
- Allowing the entire population to know that someone was supposed to become the new leader of an oppressive regime is a major intrusion of privacy with the value: PR = 3;
- The events referred to happened more than 25 years ago: T = 1;
- The aspect of empathy cannot be assessed for Z, since she is not known at all: E = 0.

From the freedom of expression side in relation to the publication of the information about Z:

- The matter is without doubt significant for the entire population: PI = 3;
- Z is not a public figure yet: PF = 0;
- The information was obtained legally: OI = 0;
- The criterion of empathy may be irrelevant: E = 0.

The outcome of the IBF for the hypothetical case is:

$$\text{IBF} = \frac{\text{V}(1) + \text{PR}(3) + \text{T}(1) + \text{E}(0) = 5}{\text{PI}(3) + \text{PF}(0) - \text{OI}(0) + \text{E}(0) = 3}$$

The outcome of the IBF for this hypothetical case is 1.67, which means that the privacy of Z clearly calls for more protection. However, if this matter is considered to concern historic truth, then the result of the IBF is not relevant.

Conclusion

The Internet Balancing Formula presented here is capable of maximising the element of transparency and minimising the element of arbitrariness in private online balancing. It is therefore a tool that brings optimised order to the online dimension of conflicting fundamental rights. The formula can be justified from ontic and epistemic perspectives, which means the ability to claim correctness in a given time-space related context. It is a rational, mathematical and living instrument.

The practical application of the formula will depend on the willingness of stakeholders to abide by the growing international consensus calling for clear standards and transparency in decisions regarding online content assessment.

Research into the question of whether the results reached by the formula would be close to the results of judicial balancing may be of interest, but not inevitable for the formula's application.

Part IV

Specific issues related to human rights and the internet

13 Human rights and the right to be forgotten

Ugo Pagallo and Massimo Durante

Introduction

The right to be forgotten, as defined in, for example, Article 17 of the EU General Data Protection Regulation No. 679 from 2016 (the "GDPR"), is not a new legal right.[1] In France, a *droit à l'oubli* – literally, the right to oblivion – has been recognised and enforced by the courts since the mid 1960s. In Italy, the protection of the right to be forgotten can be traced back to the late 1970s. In the US, this right has been acknowledged from time to time. For example, the *Briscoe v. Reader's Digest Association* court case from 1971 had to consider whether or not "the identification of the actor in reports of long past crimes" may serve the public interest, or simple curiosity. By quoting the *Restatement of Torts*, the conclusion of the Californian justices was that individuals should not satisfy the curiosity of the public, lest they re-attract "the public eye in some independent fashion".

The right to be forgotten appears in all these cases as a specification of the individual's right to privacy. The latter is enshrined in both Article 12 of the 1948 Universal Declaration of Human Rights (UDHR), and Article 8 of the 1950 European Convention on Human Rights (ECHR). As a subclass of this human right, namely, "privacy" and the respect for one's "private life", the right to be forgotten should thus be considered a relative, rather than an absolute human right.[2] Whereas an absolute human right, such as Art. 5 of the UDHR on the ban on torture, entails no balancing, relative human rights, such as the right to be forgotten, have to be balanced against further rights and freedoms protected by the legal system.[3] Among these rights and freedoms, it suffices to mention the right to information, freedom of speech or of the press. Likewise, in the legal framework of the ECHR, the right to privacy and hence the right to be forgotten are subject to several restrictions "in accordance with the law" and vis-à-vis what "is necessary in a democratic society in the interests of national security, public safety" and so forth.

One of our main contentions in the chapter will be that the digital revolution has impacted this traditional framework in two different, albeit intertwined ways. On the one hand, the use of information and communication technologies (ICTs), such as the internet, social networks and smartphones, has made much easier and even trivial "the

1 Ugo Pagallo and Massimo Durante (2014) Legal Memories and the Right to be Forgotten. In L. Floridi (Ed.), *Protection of Information and the Right to Privacy. A New Equilibrium?*, Dordrecht: Springer, 17–30.

2 Ugo Pagallo (2013) Online Security and the Protection of Civil Rights: A Legal Overview. *Philosophy & Technology*, Vol. 26, No. 4, 381–395.

3 Massimo Durante (2013) Dealing with Legal Conflicts in the Information Society: An Informational Understanding of Balancing Competing Interests. *Philosophy & Technology*, Vol. 26, No. 4, 437–457.

identification of the actor in reports of long past events", according to the phrasing of the *Briscoe* case. On the other hand, legal issues have increasingly turned into a matter of access to, and control and protection over, information in digital environments. Legislators and policymakers have accordingly complemented the canonical protection of the human right to privacy with a new right; that is, the right to the protection of personal data. Consider Art. 8 of the EU's Charter of Fundamental Rights from 2000, which aims to complement the safeguards of Art. 7 on the traditional and pre-digital respect for private life. Therefore, the right to be forgotten has also evolved in the digital age. As a specification of the individual's right to the protection of her personal data, most of the time, the right to be forgotten should be conceived of today as a right to the erasure – or de-listing – of personal data concerning that individual.

In light of these profound transformations, both social and legal, a number of critical issues follow as a result. The first problem concerns whether the rights to privacy and data protection may or may not overlap. Whereas the protection of privacy can entail no data processing at all; for example, the protection against cases of "unwanted fame" or "false light", the protection of the rights of the data subject may aim to safeguard the data as such, that is, regardless of any harm, prejudice, or privacy issue. In addition, the protection of personal data mostly revolves around the transparency with which such data are collected, processed and used, while the right to privacy mostly regards the protection of an individual's opaqueness, in accordance with the definition by Hannah Arendt.[4] Therefore, should the protection of personal data and hence, the individual's right to its erasure, or de-listing, be conceived of as a human right?

A second class of problems has to do with the protection of the right to be forgotten, or to the erasure of personal data, as a relative right. Much as occurs with the right to privacy, the protection of personal data shall be balanced against further rights and freedoms protected by the legal system. Key differences have been repeatedly stressed between the EU and US legal systems, as to how they have traditionally balanced such rights and freedoms, for example, the right to privacy and freedom of speech. Would those differences be broadened by the digital updating of the right to be forgotten? How should we manage such a right in an interconnected world? Would the only solution be the fragmentation of the internet?

In order to provide a hopefully comprehensive view of these issues, the chapter is divided into four parts. The next section focuses on the 2014 ruling of the EU Court of Justice (EUCoJ) in the *Google Spain* case, also known as the *Conejero González* case, in which an informational right to be forgotten was granted in the EU legal system, paving the way for the provisions of Art. 17 of the data protection regulation (GDPR). The third section dwells on the US legal system and how scholars have reacted to the developments of the EU law, both at procedural and substantive levels. The fourth section scrutinises the current state-of-the-art in Europe, in accordance with the conditions set up by Art. 17 of the GDPR, with its merits and drawbacks. The last section finally brings us back to the digital version of the traditional right to be forgotten as the individual right to the erasure of personal data. The overall aim of the analysis is to elucidate whether and to what extent this latter right is here to stay, and the reasons why it should be deemed under certain circumstances as a human right.

4 See Ugo Pagallo (2012) On the Principle of Privacy by Design and Its Limits: Technology, Ethics and the Rule of Law. In S. Gutwirth et al. (Eds.), *European Data Protection: In Good Health?* Dordrecht: Springer, 331–346.

The turning point

The *Google Spain* decision has been a turning point in the field of data protection. The ruling crucially establishes how to interpret four main legal issues, whose relevance transcends the field of the right to be forgotten. Let us explore those issues, in light of how they have been stressed and summarised by the 2014 Guidelines of the Article 29 Working Party (hereinafter doc. WP225):

1 The EUCoJ ruling establishes that search engine operators ("SEOs") process and control personal data. SEOs are indeed data controllers within the meaning of Article 2 of Directive 95/46/EC and nowadays, of Article 2 of the GDPR. This means that the processing of personal data; that is, the indexing of search results returned by an SEO, must be distinguished from – and is additional to – the processing of personal data accomplished by publishers of third-party websites. This differentiation is the main and long-lasting outcome of the *Google Spain* case.
2 The decision establishes that a data subject is entitled under Articles 7 and 8 of the EU Charter of Fundamental Rights to the right to be forgotten in the narrow sense of the right to a de-listing; that is, the right to request that information should no longer be made available to the general public through a list of results returned by a search made by reference to the data subject's name. It is important to stress that, on the basis of the *Google Spain* decision, it is unnecessary for the data subject to prove that the inclusion of the information in the list of the search results caused prejudice to him, or her. Furthermore, SEOs have no duty to prior notice; that is, to communicate to website editors the de-listing of specific links.
3 The *Google Spain* decision does not set up a data subject's right to erasure: no information is deleted from the original source. De-listing does not entail deletion of the link from the indexes of the search engine operator altogether, or deletion of the information through the chain of controllers processing the information. On the one hand, the original information can still be accessed by reference to other search terms, or by directly accessing the web page where the information was originally published. On the other hand, the SEO as a data controller, to which the de-listing request is addressed, may fulfil or refuse such request without necessarily involving the original publisher of the information in the decision-making process.
4 The ruling calls for a fair balance to be struck between the data subject's fundamental rights and the interests of the general public in having access to the information in question. This balance hinges on a number of relevant factors, such as the nature and sensitivity of the data processed, the timeliness or relevance of the information, the role played by the data subject in public life, etc. To the aforementioned list of interests and rights enshrined in Article 8 of the ECHR, such as the interests of national security, or public safety, the art of legal balancing shall thus take into account the protection of further human rights, such as freedom of expression and access to information.

Admittedly, we may still wonder about the nature of the "right to be forgotten". Claimants under the *Google Spain* case, after all, did not ask to be forgotten. Rather, their claim was not to be remembered inaccurately. The right to de-listing should not be confused with the *right to erasure*; that is, to remove information from the internet, or from a public record. As recently pointed out by the UK Royal Court of Justice in *NT1 & NT2 v. Google LLC*, "a successful de-listing request or order in respect of a specified URL will not prevent Google returning search results containing that URL; it only means that the URL must not be returned in response to a search on the claimant's name" (§ 38). Therefore, the new right set up by the Court properly entitles claimants to the right to dissociate their name from a list of search results related to one or more URLs.

The Art. 29 Working Party argues that once the EUCoJ 2014 decision is interpreted on such a strict legal basis, the impact of the ruling is not particularly relevant. According to their opinion, "in practice, the impact of the de-listing on individual rights to freedom of expression and access to information will prove to be very limited. When assessing the relevant circumstances, European Data Protection Authorities will systematically take into account the interests of the public in having access to the information. If the interests of the public overrides the rights of the data subject, de-listing will be not appropriate" (doc. WP225).

It seems fair to admit, however, that the impact of the de-listing will be – and already is – noticeable for a twofold reason. First, as a general rule, the de-listing process sets the limits for the enforcement of some crucial rights, such as the individual right to freedom of expression and access to information. More particularly, these latter rights have to be balanced against the right to dissociate our own name from a list of search results. Therefore, we may wonder whether the right to a de-listing should be grasped as a human right, much as occurs with such rights as, for example, freedom of expression. We return to this in section 5. Second, the systematic assessment of the interests of the public is, firstly, granted to Google – as the leading SEO – rather than the European Data Protection Authorities, or national courts. How the enforcement mechanism has worked since the ruling of the *Google Spain* case is highly instructive. According to *Google's Transparency Report*,[5] more than 673,000 de-listing requests have been filed (concerning about 2,500,000 URLs) after the 2014 case. Google has processed tens of thousands of requests each month: "In the first two months after Google began de-listing URLs under the RTBF, it took a median of 85 days to reach a decision from the time a requester first filed a request. This delay resulted from the reviewers establishing cases for what constituted inaccurate, inadequate, irrelevant, or excessive information. After 1 January 2017, a URL took a median of 4 days to process".[6] As claimed in the *Report*, the US company has so far rejected about 56% of de-listing requests. Out of this considerable amount of rejected requests, only a negligible percentage of them appealed to a National Authority, with very few appeals to a National Court. In the case of the right to be forgotten, it may be argued that, "the European Union has not only ordered Google to comply with European law; it has essentially handed off enforcement of the right in the first instance to Google".[7]

On 13 May 2014, the day the *Google Spain* ruling was released, Google headquarters, so goes the legend, toasted the decision. The enforcement of the right to de-listing is indeed very expensive, and suggests that most potential competitors will be kept off the market. Going back to the words of Balkin, "the large private enterprises that constitute the digital infrastructure have the technical and bureaucratic capacity to regulate and govern speech, through blocking, filtering, and removing content, through otherwise controlling access

5 Google's Transparency Report (2018) Google Europe Public Policy, https://transparencyreport.google.com/eu-privacy/overview.

6 Theo Bertram et al. (2018) Three Years of the Right to be Forgotten. *Google Europe Research Paper,* 1–17, 7.

7 Jack M. Balkin (2017) Free Speech in the Algorithmic Society: Big Data, Private Governance, and New School Speech Regulation (September 9, 2017). *Yale Law School, Public Law Research Paper No. 615,* 34.

to their facilities, and through digital surveillance".[8] As a result, companies like Google or Facebook "have also created private bureaucracies to govern their end-user communities in the interests of the community (and the company's profits)".[9] This inevitably raises crucial democratic concerns as to the enforcement of human rights in information societies.[10] What is at stake here does not only concern the balance of new and old human rights. The enforcement of human rights in an information society also regards the network of competences and institutions summarised by the idea of governance.[11] By taking into account the new role of ISPs in the European version of the "notice-and-takedown" mechanism, "companies that began as technology companies soon discover not only that they are actually media companies, but that they are also governance structures".[12]

The US reaction

Scholars have extensively debated whether the right to be forgotten, as enshrined in the *Google Spain* decision, might exist in the US legal framework or at least be implemented in accordance with the protection of further US constitutional rights. The first hurdle has to do with the First Amendment to the US Constitution. In particular,

> many U.S. commentators responded to the *Google Spain* decision by claiming that it was patently inconsistent with the First Amendment's free speech guarantee and could not withstand constitutional scrutiny in the United States. These commentators contend that if the U.S. passed a law granting individuals the right to demand that search engines remove links to web sites containing embarrassing, harmful, or offensive personal information about them, such a law would violate the First Amendment.[13]

The EU right to de-listing would in fact be inconsistent with the protection of free speech rights in America, which always outweigh and trump privacy rights that can be triggered – as occurs in the EU with the right to de-listing – regardless of any harm or prejudice caused by the inclusion of personal data and information in a list of search results. Eric Goldman pointed out that "the ECJ ruling shocked many Americans because American law would not permit a similar result".[14] Andrew Hughes tersely commented that both supporters and detractors of the EUCoJ ruling "agree that such a law is likely impossible in the United States".[15]

8 Ibid., 29.

9 Ibid., 35.

10 Ugo Pagallo (2017) The Broken Promises of Democracy in the Information Era. In C. Prins et al. (Eds.), *Digital Democracy in a Globalized World*, Elgar, Cheltenham, 365–378. See also Ugo Pagallo and Massimo Durante (2016) The Philosophy of Law in an Information Society. In L. Floridi (Ed.), *The Routledge Handbook of Philosophy of Information*, 396–407.

11 Ugo Pagallo (2016) Good Onlife Governance: On Law, Spontaneous Orders, and Design. In L. Floridi (Ed.), *The Onlife Manifesto*. Dordrecht: Springer, 161–177.

12 Balkin 36.

13 Dawn C. Nunziato (2017) Forget about It? Harmonizing European and American Protections for Privacy, Free Speech, and Due Process. *GWU Law School Public Law Research Paper No. 2017–52*, 2.

14 Eric Goldman (2014) Primer on European Union's Right to be Forgotten. *Technolgy & Marketing Law Blog* (21 August).

15 Andrew Hughes (2014) Does the U.S. Have an Answer to the European Right to be Forgotten?, *Landslide*, Vol. 7, 18, 19.

Still, more nuanced positions exist. Some ground an American way to the right to be forgotten: "The development of a right to be forgotten in the United States has not, as in Europe, derived from a balancing of two constitutionally recognised rights, but rather from a series of attempts by the various states to carve out for their citizens a sphere of individual privacy inviolable from the mass media".[16] Moreover, according to some other scholars, we should properly distinguish between a *substantive* and a *procedural* legal standpoint:

> The privacy protections recognized in the *Google Spain* decision are not necessarily incompatible with the *substantive* protections provided by U.S. free speech law and the balance U.S. courts have struck over time between privacy and free speech. Yet, as implemented, these privacy protections fail to comport with the *procedural* protections required under the U.S. Constitution.[17]

More particularly, from the standpoint of substantive law, there would then be no big difference between how the right to de-listing has been implemented in the EU after the *Google Spain* ruling, and how US Courts have so far struck a balance between the individual right to privacy and the protection of the First Amendment. "The balance struck by Google in responding to hundreds of thousands of de-listing requests after the *Google Spain* decision is not necessarily dissimilar to or inconsistent with the balance that has been struck by US courts in weighing privacy and free speech rights".[18]

On closer inspection, however, there is a procedural issue. The EU viewpoint can be summed up with the aforementioned opinion of the Art. 29 Working Party, according to which "search engines should not as a general practice inform the webmasters of the pages affected by de-listing of the fact that some web pages cannot be acceded from the search engine in response to a specific name-based query. There is no legal basis for such routine communication under EU data protection law" (WP225, 3). This is unacceptable from a US perspective, since the procedures of EU law would be inconsistent with the due process provisions of the US Constitution, according to which individuals should be accorded notice and "an opportunity to be heard to the affected content providers before their free speech rights are determined".[19]

Yet, providing no notice – or providing notice *after the fact* – to individuals or legal persons whose rights are directly affected by a de-listing request, does not only affect a basic tenet of the rule of law, such as the principle of due process. In addition, the ways in which the right to de-listing has been implemented in the EU may impinge on basic principles of EU law as well. Theoretically, "European Data Protection Authorities will systematically take into account the interest of the public in having access to the information" (WP225). Basically, this is not how the system works in practice, however. We have seen that in most of the cases how the right to be forgotten should be balanced against, say, freedom of speech and of information in Europe is decided by Google. Consequently, we may wonder whether the new right to erasure set up by Article 17 of the GDPR overcomes the

16 Franz Werro (2009) The Right to Inform vs. the Right to be Forgotten: A Transatlantic Clash, in Liability in the Third Millennium. In Ciacchi et al. (Eds.), *CTLS Colloquium, Georgetown University, Research Paper No. 2.* Nomos: Baden-Baden, 285–300, 292.

17 Nunziato 3.

18 Ibid., 13.

19 Ibid., 14.

problems brought about by the right to de-listing established by the EUCoJ 2014 ruling. Did legislators pay attention to such problems when discussing the new provisions of the GDPR? And if any, what changes should we expect in the EU legal framework?

The EU troubles

The right to erasure is not a new right in the EU legal framework. In the 1995 directive no. 46 on data protection, for instance, the notion appears five times, namely, in (a) Art. 2(b) on definitions of data processing; (b)–(c) Art. 12(b) and (c) on the processing of data "which does not comply with the provisions of this Directive" and the notification to third parties; (d) Art. 28(3) on the effective powers of intervention by the supervisory authorities; and, (e) Art. 32(2) on the obligations of Member States.

These provisions have been preserved and strengthened by Art. 17 of the GDPR on the right to erasure and, curiously, using single inverted commas, the "right to be forgotten" (we will return to this double title of Art. 17 in section 5). The critical points of this article can be summed up in accordance with three issues. First, as mentioned previously in Sections 2 and 3, it is up to the data controller to strike a balance between the request of the data subject – pursuant to Art. 17(1) – and the restrictions set up by Art. 17(3); for example, in regard to freedom of speech. The mechanism at work in the field of data protection in Europe since the ruling of the EUCoJ in 2014, is not new. This EU version of the "notice-and-takedown" procedure is well known in the field of intellectual property and liability of online service providers.[20] In both cases, interestingly, it is still an open issue whether this mechanism of "notice-and-takedown" is consistent with due process provisions in Europe; for example, in Article 6 of the ECHR on the "equality of arms", which is mentioned by Art. 6(2) of the EU Treaty as a source of fundamental rights in the European Union. Although data subjects can always challenge the decisions of data controllers before their national courts, it remains controversial whether this two step-procedure will guarantee both rights of data subjects and the public interest. After all, even in the US, pursuant to Section 512 of the Digital Millennium Copyright Act (DMCA), the notice-and-takedown procedure has now and then been used to censor legitimate criticism or to silence adversarial political speech. Besides, an empirical study on intermediary immunity under Section 230 of the *Communications Decency Act* argues that, while Section 230 largely protects intermediaries from liability for third-party speech, this provision does not represent the free pass that many of its critics lament. In a nutshell, "judges have been haphazard in their approach to its application".[21]

Second, the duty to inform pursuant to Art. 17(2) can be understood either as a toothless mechanism or as a powerful means to safeguard the data subjects. The wording of the regulation on "reasonable steps", "available technology", or "cost of implementation", allows either to be true. Admittedly, these rather vague provisions may represent a wise mechanism of legal flexibility with which to address the challenges posed by advancements in technology and to prevent over-frequent revisions so as to tackle such progress. Yet, it is hard to envisage how the entire chain of controllers of Art. 17(2) – triggered by the request of the data subject pursuant to Art. 17(1) – will end up erasing "any links to, or

20 Patrick Van Eecke (2011) Online Service Providers and Liability: A Plea for a Balanced Approach. *Common Market Law Review*, Vol. 48, No. 5, 1455–1502.

21 David S. Ardia (2010) Free Speech Savior or Shield for Scoundrels: An Empirical Study of Intermediary Immunity under Section 230 of the Communications Decency Act. *Loyola of Los Angeles Law Review*, Vol. 43, No. 2, 373–505.

copy and replication of, those personal data". After all, we are dealing with a technology, such as the internet's packet switching method, which hinges on copying and grouping data. How shall the EU legislators attain their purpose?

Third, the restrictions provided by Art. 17(3)(d) on archiving purposes in the public interest, scientific or historical research purposes, or statistical purposes, of course, make sense. However, pursuant to Art. 89(2) and (3), safeguards and conditions for the processing of personal data are delegated in such cases back to the national legal systems. This delegation may either entail a European form of experimental federalism, or trigger threats and risks of fragmentation. For instance, according to certain scholars, this mechanism "will certainly reduce the impact of the regulation as a harmonizing force of data protection regulation in Europe in the context of Big Data, and it will make life harder for companies and organizations operating not just in one but multiple Member States in Europe"[22]. Although Articles 60, 61, 75(4) and 97(2)(b) of the GDPR provide a number of ways to cope with the centrifugal forces of the system; that is, methods of coordination between multiple jurisdictions of national supervisory authorities, it seems fair to concede that the first data controller triggered by the data subject's request pursuant to Art. 17(1), may have a hard time in striking a fair balance between this request and the restrictions that shall be often evaluated on a national basis in accordance with Art. 17(3)(d).

As previously mentioned, in light of some rather vague provisions of the regulation, their substance will crucially depend on how courts and authorities will finally interpret such notions as the "reasonable steps" of Art. 17(2), or the exemption for statistical uses of personal data in Art. 17(3)(d). However, there is the even harder issue of how to tackle the new provisions of the GDPR's Art. 17. This harder issue brings us back to the double reference of Art. 17 to the right to erasure and the right to be forgotten. How should we grasp this double reference? Is there any meaning in the use of single inverted commas for this latter right –"the right to be forgotten"? Moreover, should we conceive the right to erasure as a human right, or as fundamental right, or as simple "qualified right" of the individual?

A new human right?

In order to determine whether and to what extent we should conceive the right to be forgotten and its digital counterparts, the right to de-listing and to erasure, as human rights, the first step is distinguishing from a strict legal viewpoint, human and fundamental rights. As to the first set of rights, we follow in this context that which one of the drafters of the 1948 Universal Declaration used to say: "We agree on the rights, providing we are not asked why. With the 'why', the dispute begins"[23]. On the basis of this assumption, three corollaries follow as a result. First, a right is here conceived of as a human right if, and only if, it has been recognised by an international human rights convention or declaration, such as the UDHR, or the ECHR; otherwise, we would need another chapter to argue the moral reasons why a certain right should be deemed a human right. Second, every particular application of a human right, such as the right to be forgotten under the legal umbrella of the protection of privacy rights, is grasped as a human right. Third, even

22 Viktor Mayer Schönberger and Yann Padova (2016) Regime Change? Enabling Big Data through Europe's New Data Protection Rregulation. *Columbia Science and Technology Law Review*, Vol. 17, 315–335.

23 Jacques Maritain (1951) *Man and the State*. Washington, DC: The Catholic University of America Press.

a fundamental or constitutional right (e.g. the right to data protection in the EU legal system) has to be considered a human right if (some specific aspects of) the former right are attributed to the latter, namely, once again, to the right to privacy. Consider how the European Court of Human Rights has dealt with issues concerning the protection of personal data pursuant to Art. 8 of the ECHR, in such cases as *Peters* (2003), *Ovey and White* (2006), *Meyer-Ladewig* (2006), *Marauhn* and *Meljnik* (2006), *Grabenwarter* (2009), and so forth. From this latter stance, the protection of personal data thus appears as a case of the protection of the right to privacy and hence, as a human right.

Against this framework, we can go back to our previous question: Whereas certain aspects of the right to be forgotten and the protection of personal data can properly be assumed as human rights safeguards, how about the status of such a new right as the right to erasure?

All in all, we reckon that the three hypotheses will increasingly draw the attention of experts and courts. The first scenario concerns cases in which the right to erasure represents the digital counterpart of the right to be forgotten as a particular kind of the respect for one's "private life" within the human rights. This is the case in which the use of single inverted commas – so as to refer to the right to be forgotten in the title of Art. 17 – may make sense. Obtaining from data controllers the erasure of their personal data without undue delay can indeed represent in the digital era the only way in which individuals may protect themselves against simple curiosity. In addition, consider the request of individuals to obtain the erasure of (some of) their personal data collected and processed when they were children, in accordance with the GDPR Art. 27(1)(f), or the California Eraser Law from 2015. In light of the 1989 UN Convention on the Rights of the Child – and more particularly, Art. 16 of the international agreement on privacy rights – we can infer that this particular case of the right to erasure should also be treated as a human right. (Embarrassingly, this conclusion could be inappropriate in the US, because the United States is the only country in the world that has not ratified the convention.)

The second hypothesis concerns the right to erasure as a simple qualified right of the individual – the withdrawal of consent pursuant to the GDPR Art. 17(1)(b). In such a case, our contention is that the right to erasure does not amount to the status of a human right, since the right is exercised at the will of the data subject, regardless of any protection against a specific harm. Here, the right to erasure has nothing to do with the traditional, pre-digital right to be forgotten (and this is, maybe, why the EU legislator makes the double reference in the title of Art. 17). Although for different motives, the same reasoning applies to further cases of the right to erasure, such as the GDPR Art. 17(1)(e) on legal obligations to which the data controller is subject. As occurs with cases of the withdrawal of consent, the erasure of personal data does not necessarily entail in this latter case of Art. 17(1)(e), any protection against simple curiosity, namely, any protection of the right to be forgotten as a specific case of the right to privacy in the digital age.

The third hypothesis is the trickiest. The right to erasure has to do with the protection against potential harms in the digital age and still, it may be difficult to trace this right back to recognised forms of the individual's privacy protection. For instance, contemplate the right to erasure pursuant to the GDPR Art. 17(1)(b); that is, cases in which personal data shall be deleted because they are no longer necessary in relation to the purposes for which such data were collected, or otherwise processed. Therefore, the right to erasure can be activated regardless of any harm or public curiosity involved, and moreover, the enforcement of such a right could even be fully automated through the means of the principle of privacy by design – Art. 25 of the GDPR. This scenario goes hand-in-hand with previous rulings of the EUCoJ, and of further MS Constitutional courts on data retention. By taking into account the legal constraints on data retention, data protection appears more like a social or collective right to be protected, than an individual right. As shown by the case on the 2006 EU data retention directive (joined cases C-293/12 and C-594/12), Justices in Luxembourg declared the latter invalid because D-2006/24/EC infringed the proportionality principle by generally affecting "all persons and all means of electronic communication as well as all traffic data without any differentiation, limitation or exception being made in light of the objective of fighting against serious crime" (*op. cit.*, § 56). From this stance, the right to erasure can thus be understood in accordance with the principle of proportionality, which sets limits to data retention in an information society.

The supervening of personal data beyond the purposes for which they were collected through the means of indiscriminate data retention periods can indeed impact people's lives. From getting insurance to landing credit, from going to college to finding a job, even down to the use of GPS for navigation and interaction with the voice recognition features on our smartphones, data processing is dramatically transforming and reshaping people's daily interaction with others and their environment through such techniques as data mining and profiling, AI predictive algorithms, facial recognition software, and more. Since any processing of personal data entails a risk, the GDPR is comprehensibly devoted to the regulation and prevention of such risks through old and new means. As a new individual right to erasure, rather than simply dissociating individual names from a list of search results related to one or more URLs, the provisions of Art. 17(1)(b) suggests two different ways in which we may interpret the legal approach to this risk. The provisions on legal deletion can either represent a new human right under the umbrella of the ECHR Article 8, or be a "simple" fundamental right of the EU legal system that should be restricted pursuant to other interests and rights listed by Article 17(3) of the GDPR. Both solutions are compatible with the legal text.

Yet, contrary to the opinion of the Art. 29 Working Party on the effects of the *Google Spain* ruling, we need no divinatory powers to suspect that the impact of Art. 17 of the GDPR will not be "very limited". Two sets of reasons suggest this forecast. They regard the drawbacks and potentialities of this new bunch of rights. On the one hand, attention should be drawn to the open problems of the EU regulation on data erasure; for example, the mechanism of legal balancing delegated to SEOs, rather than the EU data authorities. Such problems recommend conceiving the right to erasure as a specific and even controversial EU right that will be tested by further rights and principles of EU law (e.g. Art. 6(2) of the EU Treaty, which refers to Article 6 of the ECHR on the "equality of arms"). On the other hand, further rulings on data retention principles, and the protection of both individuals and collective rights in a Black Box Society,[24] suggest that the right to erasure may also be conceived of as a key component of novel forms of protection in the Big Data era (e.g. group privacy and collective data protection).[25] Whether or not the European Court of Human Rights will embrace this latter stance, remains of course an open issue on how the interpretation of Art. 8 of the ECHR will evolve over the next years. However, the ways in which the provisions of the GDPR will actually be understood and

24 Frank Pasquale (2015) *The Black Box Society: The Secret Algorithms that Control Money and Information*. Cambridge MA: Harvard University Press.

25 Ugo Pagallo (2017) The Group, the Private, and the Individual: A New Level of Data Protection?, In L. Taylor et al. (Eds.), *Group Privacy*. Dordrecht: Springer, 159–173.

enforced, in accordance with further principles of EU law, are going to clarify this point: could the right to erasure become a novel human right that protects groups and individuals against the new potential harms of the digital age?

Conclusion

This chapter has examined today's state-of-the-art on the right to be forgotten and the ways in which the information revolution has impacted on the pre-digital version of this right through the worldwide use of the internet, smartphones and social networks. Section 2 scrutinised the reasons why the 2014 decision of the EUCoJ represents a turning point in this sector of the law: the ruling introduced the right to dissociate our own name from a list of search results related to one or more URLs. Section 3 dwelt on the US views from both a substantive and a procedural stance, so as to determine whether and to what extent the protection of the First Amendment and due process provisions of the US Constitution are compatible with the EU approach. For one reason or another, most scholars think this is not the case. Section 4 scrutinised the provisions of Art. 17 of the GDPR on the right to erasure and, with inverted commas, the right to be forgotten, insisting on three sets of open issues that regard the European version of the "notice-and-takedown" procedure, the vagueness of some legal clauses, and risks of fragmentation. Section 5 explored whether the right to be forgotten and its counterpart in the digital era, the right to erasure, should be considered human rights. No one-size-fits-all answer was available. Some cases suggest that, under the label of the right to erasure, we are dealing with simple qualified rights of the individual, such as the withdrawal of consent pursuant to the GDPR Art. 17(1)(b). Here, the right is exercised at the will of the data subject, regardless of any protection against a specific harm. However, other provisions of the GDPR, such as Art. 27(1)(f), in accordance with the 1990 UN Convention on the Rights of the Child, illustrate cases in which the right to erasure should properly be conceived of as a human right, that is, as a new specification of such a well-known human right as that enshrined in the general formula of Art. 8 of the ECHR. While the right to erasure can also be understood as a key component for the protection of novel forms of privacy in information societies, what should our conclusion be?

At the end of the day, we suspect that traditional cases of the right to be forgotten will occur even in the digital era: still, this traditional right, as a specification of the right to the protection of our private life, will increasingly concern the right to erasure as its digital counterpart in the field of data protection. Depending on the specific aspect of the right we are looking at, the right to erasure can be grasped either as a simple qualified right, or as a new specification of the old human right to privacy, or as a novel form of collective right, or as entangled with the other side of the legal coin, namely, data retention. This chapter examined the many problems of EU law that may increase differences and misunderstandings with the US; for example, the EU version of the "notice-and-takedown" procedure and the Google-centred de-listing mechanism. Despite these problems and differences, we reckon that the EU right to erasure may however open up a new legal path. As shown by the provisions of Art. 17(1)(b) of the GDPR, the law provides for new ways in which groups and individuals can be protected against potential harms in the digital age. These ways either concern new dimensions of the right (e.g. data privacy as a collective right), or technological solutions (e.g. legal deletion by design). This set of new ways is as such in-between the protection of already established human and fundamental rights of data protection (e.g. Art. 17(1)(f) of the GDPR), and the protection of what we dubbed simple qualified rights of individuals (e.g. Art. 17(1)(b) and (e) of the GDPR; that is, where the right is exercised at the will of the data subject, regardless of any protection against a specific harm). How the provisions of Article 17 on, say, the mechanism of legal deletion by design will thus be implemented, appears a crucial test on whether the GDPR is effectively going to complement the traditional protection of individual rights with a new right to group privacy and collective data protection. The issue will increasingly draw the attention of courts in the coming years.

14 Finding a judicial definition of journalism

A challenging exercise in the digital age

Ellen Hovlid

Introduction

This chapter tries to tackle the question of what journalism essentially is. More precisely put, the problem under discussion is how the concept of journalism has been delimited and defined in European human rights law. This question is important because journalism enjoys a stronger human rights protection than other forms of publishing.

The primary focus of the chapter is on how The European Court of Human Rights (ECtHR) has delimited and defined journalism. Towards the end, the chapter also takes up how the European Court of Justice (ECJ) defined journalism in its judgement *Tietosuojavaltuutettu v. Satakunnan Markkinapörsi Oy and Satamedia Oy*. The definition ECJ used in this case will be compared with the ECtHR's definition. Prior to these considerations, I will discuss how the digitalisation challenges the boundaries of journalism. I will also explain more thoroughly how journalism enjoys a particular protection in European human rights law.

How the digitalisation challenges the boundaries of journalism

In the analogue age, when it was the established media companies that provided most of the production of information and publication in society, it was easier to determine what was journalism and what was not.[1] Technological and economic possibilities made sure that there existed a clear line of demarcation between the journalists and "the man in the street". The digitalisation has made this dividing line much fuzzier. The technological and economic barriers that used to keep the man in the street from reaching a larger public no longer exist. Today, everyone who wants to can produce information and publish it on the internet. This is described as a democratisation of the information ecosystem.[2] At the same time, journalism has become de-institutionalised.[3] In the previous century, journalism developed institutionalised norms and ideals, while roles and routines were professionalised. As a result of digitalisation, the boundaries of this institution have become fluid and unclear.

Does this development mean that we are all engaged in journalistic activities? Should all forms of production and publication of information be classified as journalism? Or

1 Cf. John Russial, Peter Laufer and Janet Wasko (2015) Journalism in Crisis?, *Javnost-The Public*, 299–312 and Tim Gleason (2015) If We Are All Journalists, Can Journalistic Privilege Survive?, *Javnost-The Public*, 375–386 (375).

2 Gleason 376.

3 Russial et al. 377.

must the production of information meet certain criteria for it to be defined as journalistic activity? And if so, what kinds of criteria are we talking about?

These overarching questions can be made more precise and be exemplified in a number of ways. In mainstream journalistic research, mention is often made of the development characterised as "citizen journalism".[4] Should citizen journalism be classified as journalism? The development of what is called whistle-blowing websites, with Wikileaks as the most prominent example, may also be mentioned as an instance of a development that makes the question of what journalism essentially is more urgent.[5] One may also point to the development of so-called "user-generated content".[6] This entails that the "traditional", "established" or "professional" press (hereafter to be referred to as the traditional press), has opened up for the reading public at large to comment on and otherwise contribute to the presentation of their cases in various ways. Furthermore, the evolution of the "blogosphere" is often mentioned as a development that challenges the traditional boundaries of journalism.[7] The question of "what is journalism" has also been raised in connection with phenomena such as "alternative media" and "fake news".[8] A final, but still very important, example in this area, is how one should classify the content of what is published by ordinary users on social media.[9]

The question of "what is journalism" has been frequently discussed in journalistic research in recent years.[10] Concepts that have traditionally been used in the social sciences, such as "boundaries" and "boundary work", have now also found their way into journalistic research. There seems to be a consensus that digitalisation does not entail that everyone *automatically* can be said to be engaged in journalistic activity.[11] Headlines like "we're all journalists now"[12] are usually taken to mean that everyone *may* be engaged in journalistic activity, which is certainly not something new. The really difficult question, which appears more frequently now than before, is what should be classified as journalism and what should not.[13] It is clear that the definitions of journalism and journalist in journalistic research have changed as a consequence of digitalisation. A majority of researchers now appear to base their work on a functional understanding of these concepts, as opposed to a professional or institutional one. A functional definition emphasises the nature and purpose of journalistic activities, while a professional or institutional emphasises the link

4 See Seth C. Lewis and Matt Carlson (2015) *Boundaries of Journalism: Professionalism, Practices and Participation*. London: Routledge, 1.

5 See for example Tarlach McGonagle (2013) How to Address Current Threats to Journalism?: The Role of the Council of Europe in Protecting Journalists and Other Media Actors, 2013.

6 See for example Anne Flanagan (2012) Defining "Journalism" in the Age of Evolving Social Media: A Questionable EU Legal Test. *International Journal of Law and Information Technolandy,* 1–30.

7 See for example David Domingo and Ari Heinonen (2008) Weblands and Journalism. *Nordicom Review*, 3–15 and Jason M. Shepard (2009) Blandgers After the Shield: Defining Journalism in Privilege Law. *University of Baltimore Journal of Media Law & Ethics,* 186.

8 See for example Oscar Westlund (2017) Journalistik och falska nyheter. *Norsk medietidsskrift,* 1–6.

9 See for example Alfred Hermida (2010) Twittering the News: The Emergence of Ambient Journalism. *Journalism Practice,* 297–308.

10 See for example Lewis and Carlson 2015.

11 See for example Gleason 375 and Russial et al. 301.

12 See for example P. Gant (2007) *We're All Journalists Now: The Transformation of the Press and Reshaping of the Law in the Internet Age*. New York: Free Press; Deirdre Dlugoleski (2013) We Are All Journalists Now: 140 Journos and Turkey's Counter-media Movement. *Columbia Journalism Review*. Available at: https://archives.cjr.org/behind_the_news/turkey_counter_media.php (accessed 27.03.2019).

13 Cf. Gant 201.

between the journalist and media institutions or membership in a professional association. A good example of this development is Kovach and Rosenstiel's change in their definition of a journalist in the most recent edition of their frequently quoted book, *The Elements of Journalism*. While they earlier operated with an "industrial journalism" definition, "describing a group of organized professionals", they introduced, in their 2014 edition, the more comprehensive definition "anyone who might find him- or herself producing news and who aspires to do it ethically and responsibly".[14]

However, journalistic researchers have not succeeded in finding a single definition of journalism that they can all agree on.[15] The challenge lies in delimitating the concept of journalism in such a way as to recognise the democratisation of the channels of information and to include new and untraditional publishers, while avoiding a definition so broad as to include just about everyone who publishes anything.[16] There are, in fact, several reasons why too broad a definition of journalism is problematic. In a judicial perspective, a particularly relevant point is the fact that the privileges that we under the next point will see are accorded to those who are engaged in journalistic activity, will become harder to defend if they are made to apply to too many people.[17]

The special protection of journalism in European human rights law

Journalism is all about the exercise of freedom of expression. The freedom of expression is anchored in Article 10 of the European Convention on Human Rights (ECHR) and in Article 11 of the Charter of Fundamental Rights of the European Union. In Article 10 of the ECHR, it is stated that "[e]veryone has the right to freedom of expression". In the wording of this provision, journalism is not given any special protection. It is, however, obvious that according to the ECtHR's practice, the court considers the press to be a particularly important user of the freedom of expression. The court often repeats its conviction that the press plays an "essential role" in a democratic society.[18] The ECtHR has stated that "[n]ot only do the media have the task of imparting such information and ideas: the public also has a right to receive them".[19] Because the press plays such a vital role in society, it is accorded "a higher level of protection of their freedom of expression under Article 10 than, for example, persons expressing themselves in a private dispute".[20] The principles laid down in Article 10 of the ECHR are "of particular importance as far as the press is concerned".[21] It is thus clear that the press enjoys a stronger protection than others who express themselves.

14 Kovach and Tom Rosenstiel (2014) *The Elements of Journalism: What Newspeople Should Know and the Public Should Expect*. New York: Three Rivers Press.

15 Cf. Russial et al. 2015.

16 Cf. Gleason 376.

17 Cf. Jörg Ukrow (2017) Basis and General Framework for Journalism and Media Privilege. *IRIS Special* No. 2. See also J. Oster (2016) *European and International Media Law*, 9.

18 See for example *Flinkkilä vs. Finland*, no. 25576/04, ECtHR 2010 § 73 and *Von Hannover vs. Germany (no.2)*, no. 40660/08 and 60641/08, ECtHR 2012 § 102.

19 For example, *Sunday Times vs. United Kingdom*, no. 6538/74, ECtHR 1979 § 65.

20 *Niskasaari and Otavamedia Oy vs. Finland*, no. 32297/10, ECtHR 2015 § 58.

21 *Lingens vs. Austria*, no. 9815/82, ECtHR 1986 § 41 and *Observer and Guardian vs. United Kingdom*, no. 13585/88, ECtHR 1991 § 59.

Article 11 on freedom of expression in the Charter of Fundamental Rights of the European Union contains the same general provision as what is expressed in Article 10 of the ECHR. In addition, the provision contains a second paragraph where it is stated that "[t]he freedom and pluralism of the media shall be respected". The Charter is to be interpreted in accordance with the ECHR.[22] The second paragraph of Article 11 must thus be read as a reinforcement of the strengthened protection enjoyed by the press that already follows from Article 10 of the ECHR.

This strengthened protection enjoyed by the press entails that journalists are granted certain *special rights* or *privileges* that are not given to other users of the freedom of expression.[23] This applies both to the collection and editing of information (what is called the production phase) and its publication (the publication phase). During the production phase, it is a central tenet that journalists can refuse to identify and comment on their sources in a criminal case, i.e., it is granted source protection.[24] During this phase, journalists also enjoy stronger protection than others in the form of extended rights of access.[25] Furthermore, journalists are not obliged to follow many of the rules that ordinarily apply to processing of personal data.[26] In addition, journalists are also given special protection against home and office searches, as well as against the seizure of materials.[27]

When it comes to the publication phase, journalists are given a great deal of freedom in their dissemination of information of general interest.[28] Article 10 of the ECHR does not only protect "the substance of ideas and information" that are published in the press, but also "the form in which they are conveyed".[29] In other words, the press is, as a starting point, accorded editorial freedom from the courts. The courts shall not "substitute their own views for those of the press as to what technique of reporting should be adopted by journalists".[30] This freedom entails that journalists may even allow themselves "a degree of exaggeration, or even provocation".[31] The ECtHR has also stated that the margin of appreciation afforded to the states is narrower in cases concerning the press than in other cases, because of "the strong interest of a democratic society in the press exercising its vital role as a public watchdog".[32]

As a reciprocal obligation incurred by such privileges, journalists have to live up to certain special responsibilities. This means that they have to act in keeping with the ethical principles of journalism. The ECtHR frequently repeats the following sentence:

> Article 10 protects journalists' right to divulge information on issues of general interest subject to the proviso that they are acting in good faith and on an accurate factual

22 See https://ec.europa.eu/info/aid-development-cooperation-fundamental-rights/your-rights-eu/eu-charter-fundamental-rights/why-do-we-need-charter_en#conventiononhumanrights

23 About this, see also for example McGonagle 22.

24 See for example *Goodwin vs. United Kingdom*, no. 17488/90, ECtHR 1996 § 39.

25 See for example *Társaság a Szabadságjandokért vs. Hungary*, no. 37374/05, ECtHR 2009 § 36.

26 This follows from article 9 in Directive 95/46/EC of the European Parliament and of the Council of 24 October 1995 on the protection of individuals with regard to the processing of personal data and on the free movement of such data.

27 See for example *De Haes and Gijsels vs. Belgium*, no. 19983/92, ECtHR 1997.

28 See for example *Bergens Tidende vs. Norway*, no. 26132/95, ECtHR 2000.

29 For example *Oberschlick vs. Austria*, no. 11662/85, ECtHR 1991 § 57.

30 For example *Jersild vs. Denmark*, no. 15890/89, ECtHR 1994 § 31.

31 For example *Prager and Oberschlick vs. Austria*, no. 15974/90, ECtHR 1995 § 38.

32 For example *Animal Defenders International vs. United Kingdom*, no. 48876/08, ECtHR 2013 § 102.

basis and that they provide "reliable and precise" information in accordance with the ethics of journalism.[33]

For journalists to avoid liability in a libel lawsuit, for example, they have to show that they have given accurate and reliable information "in accordance with the ethics of journalism". This means, among other things, that they have to observe the press ethics' demand for criticism and control of sources, as well as providing opportunities for immediate refutation.[34]

After this it is clear that inside both the ECHR and the EU the press is regarded as a particularly important user of the freedom of expression. The press is accorded certain special rights and obligations because of the central function it performs in a democratic society. The press produces journalism, and therefore we can also say that journalism is given special protection. But who can be said to constitute "the press" today? Who produces journalism? What is actually journalism?

The previous shows that not only journalists and journalism researchers have to deal with the challenges of defining journalism. Other institutions with whom journalists interact are also facing this issue. Amongst those outside journalism who are regularly required to deal with the changing definition of journalism are the judiciary, legislators and policymakers.[35] Journalistic researchers may discuss these questions and tentatively try out different definitions without creating any tangible consequences in the world around them. On the contrary, the conceptual delimitations laid down by the courts, legislators and policymakers will create immediate consequences for the legal status and rights a user of the freedom of expression is given.

The ECtHR's definition of journalism

A functional definition

The ECtHR has delivered a number of judgements where the question has been if a non-governmental organisation (NGO) can be considered equal to the traditional press and therefore be given the same, enhanced protection that professional journalists enjoy. The judgement in *Steel and Morris v. United Kingdom* from 2005 is the first of these judgements. The case involved a leaflet that two members of London Greenpeace had made and distributed in the mid-eighties. London Greenpeace was an NGO which worked on social and environmental protection cases. The leaflet was a part of an anti-McDonald's campaign and contained a number of negative allegations involving McDonald's operations. In the light of this leaflet, McDonald's filed a libel suit against two people who were responsible for making the leaflet. McDonald's won their case in the U.K., but the two defendants filed an appeal with the ECtHR. When the case came up before the court, the British government made a point of the fact that the two defendants were not journalists and could therefore not be given the same high degree of protection that the

33 For example *Couderc and Hachette Filipacchi Associés vs. France,* no. 40454/07, ECtHR 2015 § 131.

34 See or example *Bladet Tromso and Stensaas vs. Norway*, no. 21980/93, ECtHR 1999 §§ 65–66.

35 Cf. Jane Johnston and Anne Wallace (2017) Who Is a Journalist? Changing Legal Definitions in a De-territorialised Media Space. *Digital Journalism,* 850–867 (850).

press enjoys under Article 10 of the ECHR. In rebuttal, the ECtHR made the following pronouncement:

> The Court considers, however, that in a democratic society even small and informal campaign groups, such as London Greenpeace, must be able to carry on their activities effectively and that there exists a strong public interest in enabling such groups and individuals outside the mainstream to contribute to the public debate by disseminating information and ideas on matters of general public interest such as health and the environment.[36]

Here we can clearly see that the decisive fact for the plaintiffs being granted the same rights and obligations as the traditional press was that the organisation they were working for had the same function as the traditional press. The ECtHR described the function of the press as, "to contribute to the public debate by disseminating information and ideas on matters of general public interest".

The ECtHR has referred to its pronouncements in the *Steel and Morris* case in a number of subsequent judgements, for example in *Társaság a Szabadságjogokért v. Hungary* from 2009. This case concerned an NGO that had as its goal to further fundamental rights as well as to strengthen the civil society and due process protection in Hungary. It was also active in the field of drugs policy. In 2004 the organisation asked for the right of access in a complaints case lodged with the constitutional court that concerned new amendments to the Criminal Code regarding drug-related crimes. This access was denied, and the case eventually ended up in the ECtHR. The court stated that the collection of information is "an essential preparatory step in journalism as an inherent, protected part of press freedom". Then the court made the following pronouncement:

> The function of the press includes the creation of forums for public debate. However, the realisation of this function is not limited to the media or professional journalists.[37]

In this case the ECtHR explicitly stated that it is the *function* that decides whether a user of the freedom of expression can be regarded on a par with the journalists of the traditional press. In other words, the ECtHR now takes as its starting point a functional understanding of a journalist and journalism, as opposed to a professional or institutional understanding.[38] The court's definition has expanded as a result of new forms of media appearing in the digital age.[39] In the literature, this is called a "paradigm shift" in the case law of the ECtHR.[40]

A functional understanding of journalism and journalists is in line with the statements of the Commitee of Ministers of the Council of Europe. While the Committee

36 *Steel and Morris vs. United Kingdom* 2005, no. 68416/01, ECtHR 2005 § 89.

37 Case of *Társaság a Szabadságjandokért vs. Hungary,* no. 37374/05, ECtHR 2009 § 27.

38 Cf. McGonagle 27; Oster 12 and Arturs Kucs and Jukka Viljanen (2018) Updating Freedom of Expression Doctrines in the New Media Cases: Lessons from Strasbourg and Other Internation Treaty Bodies. In: Mart Susi, Jukka Viljanen and Eiríkur Jónsson (Ed.), *Human Rights Law and Regulating Freedom of Expression in New Media: Lessons from Nordic Approaches*. London: Routledge, 198.

39 Cf. Recommendation CM/Rec(2016)4 para. 4.

40 Oster 12.

earlier defined a journalist as "any natural or legal person who is regularly or professionally engaged in the collection and dissemination of information to the public via any means of mass communication",[41] it now recognises that a growing number and diversity of actors are contributing to journalism in different ways[42] and defines a journalist everyone who "contribute to public debate and who perform journalistic activities or fulfil public watchdog functions".[43] As shown earlier, a functional definition of journalist and journalism is also in line with the definitions laid down by most journalistic researchers.

What is the function of the press?

A question naturally following from the previous, is how the ECtHR describes the function of the press. We have seen that in the *Steel and Morris* case, the ECtHR described the function of the press as "[contributing] to the public debate by disseminating information and ideas on matters of general public interest". In other words, the court had a tripartite justification for recognising the organisation as performing the same function as the traditional press: First of all, the organisation disseminated "information and ideas". This will also be the case for a great many other users of the freedom of expression. Both "information" and "ideas" are quite comprehensive concepts that could apply to most utterances.

Secondly, the organisation had spread the information and ideas in order to contribute "to the public debate". This can be interpreted as a contrast to the putting forward of utterances in private discussions. It is not entirely clear what should be required for an utterance to become a part of "the public debate". Can, for instance, statements shared within a closed Facebook group of fifty members be said to be spread "to the public debate"? Still, even if such borderline cases may arise, it seems clear that a great deal of the publishing that takes place on the internet, must be considered to have been disseminated "to the public debate".

Thirdly, the information in question concerned "matters of general public interest". The ECtHR thus also assessed *the content* of the information and the ideas that were disseminated. This point we shall return to later.

In the *Steel and Morris* case, the ECtHR also repeated its opinion that journalists must act in keeping with "the ethics of journalism", before the court emphasised that "the same principle must apply to others who engage in public debate". Here, the court used a shorter definition of the function of the press. It shows that the essential to ECtHR was that the organisation engaged in and contributed to public debate. This pronouncement was interpreted to mean that the ethical demands made of the press could be given an analogical application to others who engage in public debate.[44] After stating this, the court evaluated the two plaintiffs in the same way as it would the traditional press and concluded that the sentencing of the plaintiffs implied a violation of Article 10 of the ECHR.

41 Recommendation No. R (2000) 7.

42 Recommendation CM/Rec (2011) 7.

43 Recommendation CM/Rec (2016) 4 para. 4.

44 David J. Harris, Colin Warbrick and M. O'Boyle (2014) *Law of the European Convention on Human Rights*. Oxford: Oxford University Press, 684.

In the *Társaság case,* the ECtHR formulated the function of the press as "the creation of forums for public debate". With a reference to the *Steel and Morris* judgement, the court then continued:

> The Court has repeatedly recognised civil society's important contribution to the discussion of public affairs. . . . The applicant is an association involved in human rights litigation with various objectives, including the protection of freedom of information. It may therefore be characterised, like the press, as a social "watchdog".

The ECtHR stated that the organisation, for this reason, "warrant[s] similar Convention protection to that afforded to the press". The court then concluded that the organisation should have been granted right of access, and that the defendants were in breach of Article 10 of the ECHR. In this quote, the ECtHR justified such parity with the press by arguing that the organisation was "involved in" cases of general interest.

We can thus see that the ECtHR in the *Társaság* case formulated its reasons for accepting that the organisation fulfilled the function of the press somewhat differently than in the *Steel and Morris* judgement. Still, the court's reference to this judgement suggests that these formulations are just alternative ways of expressing the same basic theme. The decisive factor was that the organisation contributed to a debate of general interest. It is interesting to note that the ECtHR seems to have made a point of the fact that the organisation *generally* did this (it was "involved in human rights litigation with various objectives"), and not just in the concrete instance that this case was all about.

In the *Társaság* case it is also worth noting that the ECtHR referred to the press as "one of society's 'watchdogs'", and not as *the* watchdog. This may be seen as an extension of the court's pronouncements in the *Steel and Morris* case regarding the desirability of getting more groups and individuals to contribute to the public debate. We also see that the ECtHR referred to the press and this organisation as "social" rather than "public" watchdogs, which was the description the court had used on earlier occasions.

In the judgement in the case of *Youth Initiative for Human Rights v. Serbia* from 2013, which also concerned the demand for right of access from an NGO, the ECtHR again argued for the organisations' similarity to the press by citing their being "involved in" matters of general interest. The case involved an organisation that works to defend human rights in Serbia. The organisation asked the country's intelligence service for a survey of how many people were the subject of electronic surveillance. The organisation was denied access to such a survey. Here, too, the ECtHR concluded that there was a violation of Article 10 of the ECHR. The court repeated that when an organisation "is involved in matters of public interest", they should enjoy the same protection as the press.[45] In this case, the ECtHR did not say anything about whether this should apply more generally or if it is sufficient that there exists such an engagement in a single case.

In their judgement in the case of *Österreichische Vereinigung zur Erhaltung, Stärkung und Schaffung v. Austria*, the ECtHR again returned to the theme of "contributing to the public debate". The case concerned an organisation that had as its goal to conduct research on the social consequences of changes in ownership in agricultural and woodland areas. The organisation also commented on draft legislation in this field. The organisation asked for access to all judgements made by the change-of-ownership

45 *Youth Initiative for Human Rights vs. Serbia,* no. 48135/06, ECtHR 2013 § 20.

commission in Tyrol during the last five years, but this request was denied. The ECtHR here repeated its opinion that organisations may be regarded as equal to the press, and went on to comment that this organisation was often engaged in "subjects of general interest". Then the court made a special note of the fact that the purpose of requesting access in this case was to comment on a piece of draft legislation, and "thereby contributing to public debate".[46]

In this judgement, too, the ECtHR assessed both the organisation's general activity and its activity in this concrete case, concluding that the organisation should enjoy the same protection as the traditional press. Consequently, the court ruled that there was a violation of Article 10 of the ECHR.

In a Grand Chamber judgement from 2013, *Animal Defenders International v. United Kingdom.*, the ECtHR used yet another formulation. The case concerned the showing of a campaign film on TVS. The film was made by an animal rights group. The ECtHR made the following pronouncement:

> In the present context, it must be noted that, when an NGO draws attention to matters of public interest, it is exercising a public watchdog role of similar importance to that of the press.[47]

The animal rights group was awarded the same protection as the press. The formulation "draws attention to matters of public interest", does not seem to entail anything else than that the organisation must contribute to a debate of general public interest. This formulation has been repeated in several subsequent judgements.[48]

Against this background, it seems clear that NGOs may be given parity with the traditional press and enjoy the same protection if they fulfil the same function as the traditional press. The ECtHR has expressed the theme of whether organisations fulfil such a function in various ways, but the decisive factor seems to be that the organisation in question contributes to the public debate about matters of general interest. In the judgements where the ECtHR has considered this in more detail, the court has emphasised the need for the organisation, both generally and in the case in question, to actually fulfil such a function. We cannot on this background conclude that the ECtHR *requires* that the organisation generally contributes to a debate of public interest and not only in a single or unique case. It is still interesting to note that the ECtHR has placed weight on the general activities of the relevant organisations.

Can only NGOs execute the same function as the traditional press?

The question then becomes if, according to the ECtHR's practice, it is only NGOs that can exercise the functions of the press and therefore enjoy the same protection as the traditional press, or if also other groups and individuals may be viewed in the same way. The ECtHR's statement in the *Steel and Morris* judgement that "there exists a strong public interest in enabling such groups and individuals outside the mainstream to contribute to

46 *Österreichische Vereinigung zur Erhaltung, Stärkung und Schaffung vs. Austria,* no. 39534/07, ECtHR 2013 §§ 35–36.

47 *Animal Defenders International vs. United Kingdom*, no. 48876/08, ECtHR 2013 § 103.

48 *Medžlis Islamske Zajednice Brčko and Others vs. Bosnia Herzegovina*, no. 17224/11, ECtHR 2017 § 86, *Gra Stiftung Gegen Rassismus Und Antisemitismus vs. Switzerland*, no. 18597/13, ECtHR 2018 § 57.

the public debate", would seem to indicate that the court is also open for treating others than NGOs as equal to the press.[49]

The judgement in *Guseva v. Bulgaria* from 2015, however, may be interpreted so as to indicate that the ECtHR is sceptical about treating other organisations than NGOs as equal to the press. The plaintiff in this case was a woman who worked for an animal rights group. She demanded access to several types of information about the municipality's treatment of homeless animals. The majority in the ECtHR appears to have attached a lot of importance to the fact that the woman's request for access was related to her work for this animal rights group, and that such organisations can be regarded as being equal to the press.[50] The dissenting judge, Wojtyczek, interpreted this to mean that the majority was creating a dividing line between journalists and NGOs on the one hand, and everyone else on the other. Such a division Wojtyczek would not accept. He pointed out that the court's practice when it came to the rights of journalists and the press had evolved at a time when the press had a quasi-monopoly on the collection and dissemination of information. He emphasised that this was different today, before going on:

> It is no exaggeration to say that today we, the citizens of European States, are all journalists. We (at least many of us) directly access different sources of information, collect or request information from public authorities, impart information to other persons and publicly comment on matters of public interest. We directly participate in public debate through various channels, mainly through the Internet. We are all social watchdogs who oversee the action of the public authorities. Democratic society is – inter alia – a community of social watchdogs. The old distinction between journalists and other citizens is now obsolete. In this context, the case-law hitherto on the functions of the press seems out of date in 2015 and should be adapted to the latest social developments.[51]

According to Judge Wojtyczek, the woman's belonging to the organisation was irrelevant; she could in any case be treated on a par with the press. Wojtyczek was of the opinion that all who "directly access different sources of information, collect or request information from public authorities, impart information to other persons and publicly comment on matters of public interest", are engaged in journalistic activity.

In the Grand Chamber judgement *Magyar Helsinki Bizottság v. Hungary* from 2016, the ECtHR issued a statement that clearly shows that other entities than NGOs may be given parity of status with the press. This case also involved an NGO that wanted access, more precisely access to the use of court-appointed defence lawyers in the judicial system. The ECtHR here repeated its pronouncements to the effect that NGOs can be treated on a par with the press, and then followed up with this statement:

> Thus, the Court considers that an important consideration is whether the person seeking access to the information in question does so with a view to informing the public in the capacity of a public "watchdog".[52]

49 Cf. McGonagle 27.

50 See *Guseva vs. Ungarn*, no. 6987/07, ECtHR 2015 §§ 37, 38, 53, 54 and 55.

51 Woytyczek's votum § 7.

52 *Magyar Helsinki Bizottság vs. Hungary*, no. 18030/11, ECtHR 2016 § 168.

The ECtHR appears to base its judgements on the view that everyone, not just NGOs, may fulfil such a "watchdog" function and thus be equal to ordinary journalists. The quote implies that it is *not* necessary that the person *generally* fulfil this function. It is enough that they do it in the relevant case.

Furthermore, the court made clear that this situation also applies to bloggers and users of social media:

> The Court would also note that given the important role played by the Internet in enhancing the public's access to news and facilitating the dissemination of information. . ., the function of bloggers and popular users of the social media may also be assimilated to that of "public watchdogs" in so far as the protection afforded by Article 10 is concerned.

This statement is in line with ECtHR's recognition of "citizen journalism" in the judgement *Cengiz m. fl. mot Tyrkia*. The case concerned publishing on YouTube, and the ECtHR stated that "political content ignored by the traditional media is often shared via YouTube, thus fostering the emergence of citizen journalism".[53] The court repeated the statement in the *Magyar* judgement in *Falzon v. Malta* in 2018.[54]

After this it appears clear that also other groups and individuals, such as bloggers and users of social media, can be regarded as equal with and be awarded the same enhanced protection as the traditional press, if they fulfil a "watchdog" function. In order for the relevant actors to fulfil such a function, they need to contribute to a public debate of general interest.

In the literature *Flanagan* asserts that the ECtHR, in addition to the general interest requirement, also establishes a "threshold requirement" for an activity to be accepted as journalism: It has to be about the "disclosure of accurate and reliable information published in good faith in conformity with journalistic ethics".[55] As shown earlier in this chapter, the ECtHR has stated that Article 10 protects the rights of journalists to publish information "subject to the proviso that they are acting in good faith and on an accurate factual basis and that they provide 'reliable and precise' information in accordance with the ethics of journalism". This opinion from the ECtHR has been expressed in connection with cases where journalists have been accused because of something they have published, e.g., in libel cases. For giving freedom of expression prevail in such cases, the court seems to require upholding of ethical principles. This requirement is referred to as "a trade-off" in return for the enhanced protection that the court awards the press and equal groups and individuals.[56] In *Pedersen and Baadsgaard v. Denmark* for example, the ECtHR found that the journalists lacked a sufficient factual basis for the allegation and the sentences imposed on them did not constitute a violation of Article 10 of the Convention.

The ECtHR has not, in the cases discussed here, made a requirement of living up to the ethical principles of journalism in the evaluation of whether a group or individual can be granted equality with the traditional press or not. The requirement of living up to such ethical principles appears to be a demand that the ECtHR puts up *after* the court has ascertained that the case concerns publication by the press or equal media actors, not *as*

53 *Cengiz and others vs. Turkey,* no. 48226/10 and 14027/11, ECtHR 2015 § 52.
54 *Falzon vs. Malta,* no. 45791/13, ECtHR 2018 § 57.
55 Flanagan 2012.
56 McGonagle 29.

a part of the assessment of whether it was the press or equal actors who were responsible for the publication. The question before the ECtHR seems to be who is a journalist and therefore has to follow the ethical principles of journalism,[57] and not who follows the ethical principles and therefore is a journalist.

Remarks to the ECtHR's definition

The preceding survey of cases has shown that the ECtHR bases its judgements on a functional understanding of journalism. Such an understanding has the advantage of being capable of including new and untraditional media actors.[58] The challenge inherent in such a definition is to formulate what the function of journalism essentially is. Studies show that the courts, legislators and policymakers are often struggling with this task.[59]

The ECtHR has defined this function as providing contributions to the public debate about matters of general interest. This definition may be criticised for at least two reasons: first of all, the definition may be criticised for being too wide. The ECtHR has based its reasoning on a wide-ranging understanding of what may be said to be matters of general interest.

Admittedly, the court has rejected the general interest in some cases. For instance, the court was of the opinion that information about Princess Caroline's everyday life in the case of *Von Hannover v. Germany* was without general interest.[60] The same assessment applied to the information provided in the case of *Standard Verlags GmbH v. Austria No. 2* about the rumours of infidelity and marital problems attributed to the president of Austria.[61] The ECtHR, furthermore, does not consider purely commercial advertising to be of general interest.[62] In *Satakunnan Markkinapörssi Oy and Satamedia Oy v. Finland* the court found that publishing tax information about 1,2 million people did not have general interest. The media companies tried to argue that the publication of their tax data made it possible for the general public to see the results of the taxation policies, for instance the significance that differences in income had for people's health, or differences between regions, professions and genders. The ECtHR was not convinced by these arguments, and instead pointed out that the publication had a sensationalist and voyeuristic character.[63] The ECtHR has been criticised for not valuating "big data journalism" in this judgement.[64] We will return to this case later in the chapter.

57 Cf. for example Ibid., 24 who asks what he calls "the thorny question" of who can be expected to adhere the similar ethical standards and values as the ECtHR requires from the professional press.

58 Ivor Shapiro (2014) Why Democracies need a Functional Definition of Journalism Now More than Ever. *Journalism Studies*, 555–565.

59 See for example Johnston and Wallace 2017 who have studied recent developments and key cases in New Zealand, the United States, the United Kingdom, Australia, Canada and Hong Kong and conclude that "the courts, legislators and policy makers rethink and reframe the answers to these questions, sometimes controversially so and often incorporating fundamental differences of opinion" (862).

60 *Von Hannover vs. Germany*, no. 59320/00, ECtHR 2004.

61 *Standard Verlags GmbH vs. Austria (no. 2)*, no. 21277/05, ECtHR 2009 § 52.

62 See for example *Markt Intern Verlag GmbH and Klaus Beermann vs. Germany*, no. 10572/83, ECtHR 1989.

63 *Satakunnan Markkinapörssi Oy and Satamedia Oy vs. Finland, no.* 931/13, ECtHR 2017 § 171.

64 Dirk Voorhoof (2017) No Journalism Exception for Massive Exposure of Personal Taxation Data. *Strasbourg Observers Bland.*

Even if the ECtHR has not considered *all* information to have general interest and in some cases has been criticised for accepting a too narrow application of the public interest requirement, many researchers are of the opinion that the threshold for fulfilling this requirement is generally quite low.[65] The court has itself explicitly said that it interprets the concept of "public interest" "rather widely".[66] A case that illustrates this fact is that of *Lillo-Stenberg and Sæther v. Norway*. This case concerned a news story in a tabloid Norwegian magazine (*Se og Hør*) about the wedding of a Norwegian recording artist and an actress. The story was all about how the bride was barefoot, the groom wore red shoes, that the couple had six bridesmaids, that a male choir sang, as well as who the guests were, and that many of them were crying. In spite of this, the ECtHR concluded that the news story did not have "the sole aim of satisfying public curiosity".[67] There was "an element of general interest" in the report because a wedding has a "public side", in the sense that it will have legal consequences in many areas.

With such a low threshold for when public utterances may be regarded as being of general interest, much work done by citizen journalists must undoubtedly be classified as journalism. This also goes for much of what is published by Wikileaks and alternative media. When the ECtHR seemingly does not require that the group or person generally must contribute to a debate of public interest, but instead focuses on the concrete situation, much of the user-generated content in the traditional press will also have to be classified as journalism. A number of blog postings and comments on social media may also concern matters of general interest, and will therefore have to be regarded as journalism according to the ECtHR's definition.

Furthermore, the ECtHR's definition can also be criticised for being unclear and therefore difficult to practise. This was pointed out by two dissenting judges in the *Magyar* case. They stated that the division between "public watchdogs" and others will be "exceedingly difficult to circumscribe in any sensible manner".[68] The assessment of the general interest of various utterances is clearly difficult,[69] and it is not always easy to understand what criteria the ECtHR uses in this assessment. For this reason, the classification of the legal status of any given media activity, i.e., whether or not it qualifies as journalism, may become quite unpredictable.

There is nothing that indicates that the ECtHR applies different definitions of journalism when it comes to digital and analogue media. A more interesting question to ask is whether the ECtHR will apply the same definition when assessing all journalistic privileges.[70] We have seen that most of the cases where the court has applied this definition have concerned access to information. The court has also used the definition in cases

65 Cf. Tarjei Bekkedal (2014) Avveiningen mellom ytringsfriheten og privatlivets fred – om EMDs balansetest (The balancing between freedom of expression and private life – about ECtHR's balancing exercise), *Lov og Rett,* 315–333 (327), Ellen Lexerød Hovlid (2015) *Vern av privatlivets fred (Protection of Private Life)*. Oslo: Gyldendal Juridisk, 267 and Vibeke Borberg, Thomas Riis and Henrik Udsen (2015) Mediernes ret til at offentliggøre billeder af offentligt kendte personer efter von Hannover nr. 2 (Media's right to publish photos of publicly known persons after von Hannover no. 2). *Juristen,* 8–18 (12).

66 *Couderc and Hachette Filipacchi Associés vs. France,* no. 40454/07, ECtHR 2015 § 58.

67 *Lillo-Stenberg and Sæther vs. Norway*, no. 13258/09, ECtHR 2014 § 37.

68 *Magyar Helsinki Bizottság vs. Hungary*, no. 18030/11, ECtHR 2016 § 46.

69 Sten Schaumburg-Müller (2013) Privacy and Publicity. In: Thomas Gammeltoft-Hansen Ida Elisabeth Koch, Bettina Lemann Kristiansen, Sten Schaumburg-Müller (red.), *Protecting the Rights of Others: festskrift til Jens Vedsted-Hansen*. København: DJOF Publishing, 389–405 (393).

70 Cf. Kucs and Viljanen 200.

concerning defamation[71] and political advertising[72]. However, the court has not yet decided whether a similar approach would apply to for example the protection of sources and protection against seizure of journalistic material.[73]

The European Court of Justice's definition of journalism in the *Satakunnan* judgement

The question of how journalism should be delimited and defined in EU law has been particularly discussed in connection with the case of *Tietosuojavaltuutettu v. Satakunnan Markkinapörssi Oy and Satamedia Oy.*[74] The case began when a Finnish media company (Satakunnan) in 1994 collected information about taxes and taxation and published them in the newspaper *Veropörssi*. The paper printed the full name and tax details for approximately 1.2 million unique persons, who had an annual income over a certain amount. In 2003 this media company began to send data to another company (Satamedia), which was owned by the same shareholder. This company started an sms service where anyone could access this information by sending a name to a telephone number. In 2004 the Data Protection Ombudsman demanded that the Data Protection Board should prohibit the companies' operations, but this demand was rejected. The Data Protection Ombudsman lodged an appeal with the administrative tribunal, but this appeal was dismissed because the court considered the information to be in the public domain and of public interest. In 2005 this decision was further appealed to the Supreme Administrative Court, which asked the ECJ for a preliminary ruling on the interpretation of the Data Protection Directive. One of the questions posed by the Supreme Court was whether the operations of these media companies in this case should be regarded as the processing of personal data "solely for journalistic purposes", within Article 9 in the Data Protection Directive.

The most interesting aspect of the ECJ's judgement can be found in the court's concluding statement:

> Article 9 of Directive 95/46 is to be interpreted as meaning that the activities ... must be considered as activities involving the processing of personal data carried out "solely for journalistic purposes", within the meaning of that provision, if the sole object of those activities is the disclosure to the public of information, opinions or ideas.[75]

The ECJ thus defined journalism as "disclosure to the public of information, opinions or ideas". We also see that the court made it a condition that the utterances had to be disseminated "to the public". This resembles the ECtHR's requirement that the utterances must have been disseminated to "the public debate" and not just be a part of a private discussion.

Beyond this requirement that the utterance has to be disseminated "to the public", the ECJ did not make any further demands of these utterances. The concepts of "information,

71 *Magyar Helsinki Bizottság vs. Hungary*, no. 18030/11, ECtHR 2016 and *Falzon vs. Malta*, no. 45791/13, ECtHR 2018.

72 *Animal Defenders International vs. United Kingdom*, no. 48876/08, ECtHR 2013.

73 Cf. Kucs and Viljanen 200.

74 Judgment of the Court (Grand Chamber) of 16 December 2008, Case C-73/07. Discussed by for example Flanagan 2012.

75 § 62.

opinions or ideas" are extremely wide concepts that will include the great majority of possible utterances. The court did not, unlike the ECtHR, make any requirement that the utterance should be of general interest, nor did it specify any other demands in terms of content.

The ECJ's definition of journalism is very wide, and it has been criticised for this reason.[76] It is easy to join in this criticism. Even blog postings and status updates on social media about what a person will have for dinner, for instance, must be presumed to be journalism according to this definition, because it involves "[the] disclosure to the public of information". The ECJ's definition in this case appears, on the whole, to make all information production into journalism and thus turn us all into journalists. As shown under the comment to the ECtHR's definition, such a too-wide definition of journalism is quite problematic. This is also recognised within the EU. The *High Level Group on Media Freedom and Pluralism*, established by the European Commission, emphasised that the journalistic privileges "become very difficult to defend, if the net is cast too wide and includes practically everybody who has an opinion to express or a fact to proclaim".[77]

The ECJ's definition of journalism is also problematic because it is even more comprehensive than the ECtHR's definition. When the Finnish Supreme Administrative Court was asked to decide whether the activities of the media companies in the Satakunnan case had "journalistic purposes" or not, the court had to pay attention to definitions from both the ECJ and the ECtHR. The Supreme Administrative Court formulated the theme to be assessed in the following way:

> The starting point is whether the aim of their activities was to disclose information, opinions or ideas to the public. In this assessment, account must be taken of whether or to what extent those activities can be seen as contributing to a debate in a democratic society rather than solely satisfying the curiosity of certain individuals.

This court, then, took as its starting point the ECJ's requirement that the purpose of the activity must be "to disclose information, opinions or ideas to the public". Then the court stated that in this assessment, it must be taken into account if the activity contributes to a debate of general interest. The Finnish Supreme Administrative Court here seems to delimit and narrow down the ECJ's definition in the light of the ECtHR's practice.

The Finnish Supreme Administrative Court arrived at the conclusion that to collect information about people's taxes and file it in the media companies' internal systems might be necessary as *background information* for publishing articles on taxation of general interest, and thus to have fulfilled the demand for "journalistic purposes". To *publish* all this background information, however, the court found not to be necessary. The media companies were banned from continuing their practice. The companies were of the opinion that this ban implied a violation of their right of expression according to Article 10 of the EMK, and they therefore appealed the decision to the ECtHR. As mentioned previously, the ECtHR accepted the dividing line that the Finnish Supreme Administrative Court

76 Flanagan 2012.

77 Vaira Vikefreiberga, Herta Däublergmelin, Ben Hammersley mfl., (2013) A Free and Pluralistic Media to Sustain European Democracy. The Report of the High Level Group on Media Freedom and Pluralism. *European Commission*, 34.

had drawn between the public interest inherent in the collection of tax information on the one hand and its publication on the other.[78]

In February 2019 the ECJ delivered a new judgement concerning the exemption for journalism in the data protection regulation. It is the case Sergejs Buivids vs. Datu valsts inspekcija. The case concerned a video posted on Youtube showing police officers at a police station in Latvia. Since the judgement was delivered after this article was written, it is not possible to go into detail about it here. However, it must be mentioned that the ECJ in this judgement, after quoting the Satakunnan judgement, found reason to comment that not "all information published on the internet, involving personal data, comes under the concept of 'journalistic activities'". When deciding whether publishing the video on internet was "journalistic activity" or not, the referring court could, in particular, take into consideration the fact that the video was published "to draw to the attention of society alleged police malpractice". In other words: The purpose of the publication was to contribute to a public debate on a matter of public interest (police malpractice). The ECJ thereby, in line with the ECtHR, in this case seems to attach great importance to the public interest of the information published.

Conclusion

This chapter shows that the ECtHR has based its recent judgements on a functional definition of journalism, as opposed to a professional or institutional understanding. This is important to notice for courts, legislators and policymakers in countries bound by the ECHR.

A challenge related to the functional definition is to formulate what the function of journalism essentially is. The definition of the ECtHR can be criticised for being too wide and unclear. The definition laid down by the ECJ in the case of *Tietosuojavaltuutettu v. Satakunnan Markkinapörssi Oy and Satamedia Oy* is also very wide. This creates problems since the privileges granted to those who are engaged in journalistic activity, which are seen as indispensable in a democratic society, become difficult to defend if they are granted to too many people.

As mentioned in the beginning of this chapter, it has been impossible for journalism scholars to agree on a definition of what journalism is. It is, therefore, not surprising that the courts are also struggling to formulate a definition that is wide enough to encompass new and non-traditional publicists, but at the same time narrow enough to keep journalism from becoming a hopelessly comprehensive concept. The discussion of how one may formulate a judicial definition that finds a good balance between these two competing considerations will need to continue.

78 *Satakunnan Markkinapörssi Oy and Satamedia Oy vs. Finland, no.* 931/13, ECtHR 2017 § 175.

15 Combating hate speech online

Jukka Viljanen

Introduction

In the field of free speech, technological innovations and digitalisation have developed new outlets for freedom of expression that avoid the filtering mechanisms of traditional print media or broadcasting. This obviously entails the fact that speech which is not within the scope of the freedom of expression is more widely disseminated. On digital platforms, hate speech has increased both in quantity and velocity. In addition, internet and social media platforms have introduced new forms of hate speech using the relative anonymity of social media by introducing fake accounts, spammers and bots. In addition, online hate speech does not just take the form of text but also pictures, internet memes and short videos.[1] An increasing form of hate speech is the dissemination of fake news and disinformation.[2] Often these are intended to influence democratic processes (elections), divide the political discourse and intimidate people from participating. Sometimes the aim is no more than to provoke a discourse and incite the opposing team. However, the background to the hate speech is occasionally more sinister and propagandist as a part of a wider political strategy.

The aim of disinformation is to challenge the role of the free press and the reliability of the news media. Tension and divisiveness have led to major digital platforms (Google, Apple, Facebook, Spotify) adopting new self-regulatory rules and supervising these more rigorously.[3] The problem with the effectiveness of online self-regulation is that it is always possible to find an alternative platform where the distribution of the same hate speech material can continue after it has been initially blocked. Some have also questioned whether these internal supervisory systems have the necessary interpretative skills required to examine the hate speech.

Online distribution means that hate speech can circulate the world in a matter of seconds. It also leaves a permanent mark on discussions because internet archives and search

1 E. Heinze (2017) *Hate Speech and Democratic Citizenship*. Oxford: Oxford University Press, 19, speaks about expression including oral and printed, including also pictorial or other non-verbal manifestations of ideas.

2 See Joint Declaration on Freedom of Expression and "Fake News", Disinformation and Propaganda the United Nations (UN) Special Rapporteur on Freedom of Opinion and Expression, the Organization for Security and Co-operation in Europe (OSCE) Representative on Freedom of the Media, the Organization of American States (OAS) Special Rapporteur on Freedom of Expression and the African Commission on Human and Peoples' Rights (ACHPR) Special Rapporteur on Freedom of Expression and Access to Information, www.osce.org/fom/302796?download=true

3 In August 2018 Apple, Facebook and YouTube removed the pages of Alex Jones (Infowars) for violating community guidelines. Earlier, Facebook, Apple and Spotify removed content due to violations of company policies regarding hate speech www.cnbc.com/2018/08/06/youtube-removes-alex-jones-account-following-earlier-bans.html

engines cause dangerous speech to appear over and over again. There is a growing tendency to use hate speech as a method to manipulate public discourse, silence experts and prevent genuine public discussion. Often this causes deep scars in society, distorting public debate and open dialogue. The results can polarise society, where the middle ground is vanishing. A large proportion of people might be afraid to express their opinion due to intimidation and pressure. This kind of climate is obviously in conflict with pluralism and tolerance. It can even prevent people from taking part in public debate and have a chilling effect on free speech.[4]

The landmark "right to be forgotten" case – Google Spain (C-131/12) before the European Court of Justice – provides a basic introduction to the problems caused by the very nature of the transformation of the media. Advocate General Jääskinen perfectly considered those elements that the internet magnifies, and how it facilitates the dissemination of information. Information can easily be accessed, consulted and disseminated through social media, as well as downloaded to various devices such as tablet computers, smartphones and laptops. However, it is clear that the development of the internet into a comprehensive global stock of information, which is universally accessible and searchable was not foreseen by the Community legislator.

Recent studies show that online hate speech is a widespread problem in many countries.[5] Digitalisation and online distribution produce a media world where the question of national jurisdiction is often irrelevant, and this is also so in the field of hate speech. In the global media market, it is much harder to prevent hateful attacks by taking actions through domestic courts. Solving a problem within one jurisdiction might just transfer the distribution channel to another.

The combating of hate speech online is not just a task for regional and national authorities or traditional media actors. Even international IT-giants must take into account hate speech, although the level of acceptable speech significantly varies globally. Much of the combating is done by community standards and increasing the awareness of those using social platforms. This chapter will examine several aspects of combating online hate speech and especially concentrates on international human rights instruments, relevant case law and the responsibility of intermediaries, and will then provide some examples of domestic pilots to combat online hate speech.

The international legal framework providing instruments to combat hate speech online

There are several international human rights instruments that provide a foundation for combating online hate speech. These are the Universal Declaration of Human Rights (General Assembly Resolution 217 A, 10.12.1948) Art. 19, the International Covenant on Civil and Political Rights (General Assembly Resolution 2200A, UNTS vol. 999, 19.12.1966, hereinafter CP-Covenant) art 19 (freedom of expression) and 20 (prohibition

4 This has been acknowledged in many community standards and rules. See Twitter rules that include under "Abusive behaviour" e.g. "We believe in freedom of expression and open dialogue, but that means little as an underlying philosophy if voices are silenced because people are afraid to speak up. In order to ensure that people feel safe expressing diverse opinions and beliefs, we prohibit behavior that crosses the line into abuse, including behavior that harasses, intimidates, or uses fear to silence another user's voice".

5 See country reports in Susi, Viljanen, Jonsson and Kucs (2018) *Human Rights Law and Regulating Freedom of Expression in New Media, Lessons from Nordic Approaches*. New York: Routledge.

of advocacy to hatred), the International Convention on the Elimination of All Forms of Racial Discrimination (General Assembly Resolution 2106, UNTS Vol. 666, 1965) Art. 4 and 5 and the European Convention on Human Rights (i.e. Convention for the Protection of Human Rights and Fundamental Freedoms, Council of Europe Treaty Series, CETS No. 5, 4.11.1950) Art. 17 (prohibition on abuse of rights) and 10 (freedom of expression). Other regional level human rights instruments are also relevant in the regulation of hate speech; for example, the Inter-American Convention on Human Rights (American Convention on Human Rights, OAS Treaty Series No. 36, 22.11.1969) Art. 13 and the EU Charter of Fundamental Rights (Official Journal of the European Union 2012/C 326/02) Art.11.

One of the other relevant international instruments is the Additional Protocol to the Convention on Cybercrime, concerning the criminalisation of acts of a racist and xenophobic nature committed through computer systems (CETS 189). It entered into force on 1 March 2006. It now has 29 ratifications. The Cybercrime Convention, also known as the Budapest Convention on Cybercrime, is supervised by the Cybercrime Convention Committee (T-CY), which has given several Guidance Notes. The Protocol concerning the criminalisation of racist actions provides a clear duty on states to provide the necessary legislation in order to prevent the dissemination of racial material, racially motivated threats and insults. It also requires states to take action against denial, gross minimisation, approval or justification of genocide or crimes against humanity.

The United Nations Educational, Scientific and Cultural Organisation (UNESCO) is a key organisation which has actively studied measures related to combating hate speech online. In a study (Countering Online Hate Speech) published in 2015, the research group provides some answers for the field of online hate speech. In this study, the concept of hate speech is relatively wide.[6]

The essential concept for understanding the limits of free speech is to recognise which kind of speech falls into the category of hate speech. The type of speech which is protected under human rights treaties also includes information and views that offend, shock or disturb the state or any sector of the population.[7] However, some scholars like Eric Heinze favour instead of free speech and hate speech the terms free expression and hateful expression including both verbal and non-verbal acts. But even those scholars use the term hate speech bans, because this is widely used.[8]

The UN human rights treaty bodies have also introduced general comments on the issue of hate speech. The UN Human Rights Committee, which supervises the CP-Covenant, described the key principles of hate speech in General Comment No. 34.[9] According to General Comment 34, Article 19 of the CP-Covenant and its paragraph 2 protect all forms of expression and the means of their dissemination. Such forms include spoken, written and sign language and such non-verbal expression as images and objects of art. Means of expression include books, newspapers, pamphlets, posters, banners, dress and legal submissions. They include all forms of audio-visual as well as electronic and internet-based modes of expression.[10]

6 See I. Gagliardone, D. Gal, T. Alves and G. Martinez (2015) *Countering Online Hate Speech*. Paris: Unesco.

7 See *Handyside v. the United Kingdom*, 7.12.1976, § 49.

8 See Heinze 18–19.

9 See the HRC, the General Comment 34, 12.9.2011, http://www2.ohchr.org/english/bodies/hrc/docs/gc34.pdf

10 See the General Comment 34, § 12 (*supra* note 9).

The Committee considered that the scope of paragraph 2 embraces even expressions that may be regarded as deeply offensive, although such expressions may be restricted in accordance with the provisions of Article 19, paragraph 3 and Article 20. In 2013, the Committee on the Elimination of Racial Discrimination (CERD) gave General recommendation No. 35 focusing on combating racist hate speech.[11]

What is obvious in all the new guiding principles is the change in the media environment, which provides faster and faster tools for spreading hate speech. This is especially due to deliberate strategies in recent years to distribute hatred. One of the additional principles suggested by the Committee on the Elimination of Racial Discrimination for qualifying what is punishable under the Convention is the reach of the speech, including the nature of the audience and the means of transmission: whether the speech was disseminated through mainstream media or the internet, and the frequency and extent of the communication, in particular when repetition suggests the existence of a deliberate strategy to engender hostility towards ethnic and racial groups.[12]

Hate speech case law and online media

The European Court of Human Rights has developed significant case law that provides basic principles regarding hate speech. For example, in the case of *Erbakan v. Turkey* the Court stated:

> [T]olerance and respect for the equal dignity of all human beings constitute the foundations of a democratic and pluralist society. That being so, as a matter of principle, it may be considered necessary in certain democratic societies to sanction or even prevent all forms of expression which spread, incite, promote or justify hatred based on intolerance. . ., provided that any "formalities", "conditions", "restrictions" or "penalties" imposed are proportionate to the legitimate aim pursued.[13]

One of the fundamental elements concerning the ECHR and understanding the case law related to hate speech is the abuse of the rights provision in Article 17 of the Convention. This means that any application of interference with a hateful expression is considered inadmissible because it is meant to distort the purpose of freedom of expression and considered to be contributing to the destruction of rights and freedoms guaranteed by the Convention.[14]

One landmark online hate speech judgment is *Delfi AS v. Estonia* (ECtHR, 16.6.2015 Grand Chamber). The Delfi case was about messages published in the comment section of the Estonian internet news portal. Those user-generated contents included hate speech and the ultimate human rights law question was whether the internet portal provider was liable for that content. The Court noted "at the outset that user-generated expressive activity on the internet provides an unprecedented platform for the exercise of freedom of expression. . . . However, alongside these benefits, certain dangers may also arise. Defamatory and other types of clearly unlawful speech, including hate speech and speech

11 General recommendation No. 35, Combating racist hate speech, CERD/C/GC/35, 26.9.2013.

12 CERD/C/GC/35, 26.9.2013. para. 15.

13 *Erbakan v. Turkey*, 2006 § 56.

14 See Article 17 e.g. Van Dijk, P. van Hoof, F. van Rijn, L. Zwaak (2006) *Theory and Practice of the European Convention on Human Rights*, 4th edition. Intersentia, 1083–1092.

inciting violence, can be disseminated as never before, worldwide, in a matter of seconds, and sometimes remain persistently available online". The Court also pointed out that "it is also mindful that liability for defamatory or other types of unlawful speech must, in principle, be retained and constitute an effective remedy for violations of personality rights".

The context of the Delfi case was an essential and specific part of the interpretation. The Court was clearly distinguishing the case from other ways of online discussion and discussion forums. This was a large professionally managed internet news portal run on a commercial basis which published news articles of its own and invited its readers to comment on them. The applicant had not removed the comments immediately after the request. The question was also about whether there was a necessary review system in place. According to the Court, there were certain measures taken against hate speech including an automatic system to delete certain comments, a notice-and-take-down system in place (clicking a notice button), and the administrators also removed inappropriate comments at their own initiative. The Court was aware of the measures but they were insufficient. The rights and interests of others and of society as a whole may entitle Contracting States to impose liability on internet news portals, without contravening Article 10 of the Convention, if they fail to take measures to remove clearly unlawful comments without delay, even without notice from the alleged victim or from third parties.

In the absence of the vast amount of online hate speech cases, there is a strong need to use an analogical interpretation from previous offline hate speech judgments and decisions. The main element in all hate speech cases is that hate speech is understood to be against the spirit of the human rights treaties that were founded in order to protect rights and freedoms. The European Court of Human Rights has especially recognised that there are attempts to deflect Article 10 of the Convention by using it to ends that are contrary to the text and spirit of the Convention. Therefore, hate speech includes, for example, statements denying the Holocaust, justifying a pro-Nazi policy, linking all Muslims with a grave act of terrorism, or portraying the Jews as the source of evil in Russia.[15]

Often Article 17 cases have been related to racist and xenophobic speech. These cases are similar in both the online or offline context in the sense that there is often some kind of conspiracy theory or other fabricated story. One of the clear categories within the case law is what is referred to as negationism. This includes Holocaust denials and other forms of the distortion of historical facts, so called historical revisionism (negationism). One of the questions is whether this should be punishable in criminal law. The internet and social media platforms are clearly increasing the dissemination of fake news and even they could provide ways of targeting certain groups during election campaigns as was widely reported in the Facebook-Cambridge Analytica scandal.[16]

In the case of *Garaudy v. France* (24.6.2003), the applicant had written texts that included the chapter "The Myth of the Nuremberg Trials and The Myth of the Holocaust" and he

15 See *Garaudy v. France* (dec.). General principles related to hate speech are collected to the case *Roj TV A/S v. Denmark*, paras. 26–38. The Court refers to an established continuum that includes cases *Witzsch v. Germany* (dec.), no. 4785/03, 13 December 2005*Hizb ut-Tahrir and Others v. Germany* (dec.) no. 31098/08, §§ 72–75 and 78, 12 June 2012, *Norwood v. the United Kingdom* (dec.), no. 23131/03, ECHR 2004 XI), and Pavel Ivanov v. Russia (dec.), no. 35222/04, 20 February 2007), *Kasymakhunov and Saybatalov v. Russia* (dec.) nos. 26261/05 and 26377/06, 14 March 2013) *Dieudonné M'Bala M'Bala v. France* (dec.), no 25239/13, §§ 34 to 42, 20 October 2015, *Belkacem v. Belgium* (dec.), no. 4367/14, 20 July 2017).

16 See www.nytimes.com/2018/04/04/us/politics/cambridge-analytica-scandal-fallout.html

was found guilty in several successive proceedings for the crime of the denial of crimes against humanity and the publication of racially defamatory statements and incitement to racial hatred.[17] This was also the situation in the case of Garaudy v. France (2003).

> There can be no doubt that denying the reality of clearly established historical facts, such as the Holocaust, as the applicant does in his book, does not constitute historical research akin to a quest for the truth. The aim and the result of that approach are completely different; the real purpose being to rehabilitate the National-Socialist regime and, as a consequence, accuse the victims themselves of falsifying history. Denying crimes against humanity is therefore one of the most serious forms of the racial defamation of Jews and of incitement to hatred of them. The denial or rewriting of this type of historical fact undermines the values on which the fight against racism and anti-Semitism are based and constitutes a serious threat to public order. Such acts are incompatible with democracy and human rights because they infringe the rights of others. Its proponents indisputably have designs that fall into the category of aims prohibited by Article 17 of the Convention.

The Court considers that the main content and general tenor of the applicant's book, and thus its aim, are markedly revisionist, and therefore run counter to the fundamental values of the Convention, as expressed in its Preamble, namely justice and peace. It considers that the applicant attempts to deflect Article 10 of the Convention from its real purpose by using his right to freedom of expression for ends which are contrary to the text and spirit of the Convention. Such ends, if admitted, would contribute to the destruction of the rights and freedoms guaranteed by the Convention.

Accordingly, the Court considers that, in accordance with Article 17 of the Convention, the applicant cannot rely on the provisions of Article 10 of the Convention regarding his conviction for denying crimes against humanity.

The universal system and European system have a similar approach to these problems. One of the leading holocaust deniers is Robert Faurisson, whose communication was decided under the UN Human Rights Committee supervising the CP-Covenant (Comm. 550/1993, 8 November 1996). The focus was on the Gayssot Act. On 13 July 1990, the French legislature passed the "Gayssot Act", which amends the law on the Freedom of the Press of 1881 by adding Article 24 bis; the latter makes it an offence to contest the existence of the category of crimes against humanity as defined in the London Charter

17 One of the more recent cases before the ECtHR was the *M'Bala M'Bala v. France*. Dieudonné M'Bala M'Bala had brought onto the stage an actor, dressed as a Jewish deportee in a concentration camp, for the purpose of awarding a prize to Robert Faurisson, one of the best-known French negationists, to honour him and give him a platform. In this promotion of negationism, through the key position given to Robert Faurisson's appearance and the degrading portrayal of Jewish deportation victims faced with a man who denied their extermination, the Court saw a demonstration of hatred and anti-Semitism and support for Holocaust denial. In the Court's view, this was not a performance which, even if satirical or provocative, fell within the protection of Article 10 of the Convention. In the circumstances of the case, it was an expression of an ideology which ran counter to the values of the Convention, namely justice and peace.

Accordingly, since the acts at issue were unmistakeably negationist and anti-Semitic in nature, the Court found that Dieudonné M'Bala M'Bala had sought to deflect Article 10 from its real purpose by using his right to freedom of expression for ends which were incompatible with the letter and spirit of the Convention and which, if admitted, would contribute to the destruction of Convention rights and freedoms.

of 8 August 1945, on the basis of which Nazi leaders were tried and convicted by the International Military Tribunal at Nuremberg in 1945–1946.

Applicant Mr. Faurisson was interviewed by the French monthly magazine Le Choc du Mois, and the conviction was based, inter alia, on the following Faurisson statements:

> No one will have me admit that two plus two make five, that the earth is flat, or that the Nuremberg Tribunal was infallible. I have excellent reasons not to believe in this policy of extermination of Jews or in the magic gas chamber. . . .
>
> I would wish to see that 100 per cent of all French citizens realize that the myth of the gas chambers is a dishonest fabrication ("est une gredinerie"), endorsed by the victorious powers of Nuremberg in 1945–46 and officialized on 14 July 1990 by the current French Government, with the approval of the "court historians".

The Human Rights Committee reviewed whether the conviction that was placed on Faurisson was in accordance with principles set out in the CP-Covenant and Committee case law. His conviction did not encroach upon his right to hold and express an opinion in general; rather the court convicted Mr. Faurisson for having violated the rights and reputation of others. For these reasons the Committee is satisfied that the Gayssot Act, as read, interpreted and applied to the author's case by the French courts, is in compliance with the provisions of the Covenant.

Since the statements made by the author, read in their full context, were of a nature as to raise or strengthen anti-semitic feeling, the restriction served the respect of the Jewish community to live free from fear of an atmosphere of anti-semitism; the Committee concluded that the restriction was permissible under Article 19.

The Human Rights Committee noted the state party's argument contending that the introduction of the Gayssot Act was intended to serve the struggle against racism and anti-semitism. It also noted the statement of a member of the French government, the then Minister of Justice, which characterised the denial of the existence of the Holocaust as the principal vehicle for anti-semitism. No other material countered this. The Committee was satisfied that the restriction was necessary.

The question of where to draw the line between hate speech and expression that should be considered as offensive speech is often revisited in Strasbourg case law. It is important to remember that the hate speech categorisation should not prevent people from protesting against institutions and giving their opinion on those who are in power. The case of *Stern Taulats and Roura Capellera v. Spain* (13.3.2018) is one of most recent additions to the line between Article 17 and Article 10. The applicants had been convicted for insulting the King of Spain. However, the Court considered that the conviction was disproportionate and the premise that you would be under prosecution when you offend a head of state is not in conformity with the spirit of the Convention (para. 35). What should be especially important in general terms is that the Court also noted the context where the insult was not aimed at the King himself but what he represents, as leader and symbol of state, and therefore corresponds to the expression of a rejection of the monarchy as an institution (36). Therefore, in the Stern Taulats and Roura Capellara case the Court correctly reminded that if hate speech should include also symbolic expressions and criticisms of institutions then excluding this kind of expression from the scope of freedom of expression would be an overly broad interpretation and be detrimental to pluralism, tolerance and transparency (para. 41).

Finally, a clear trend that can be deducted from recent case law is a stricter view of terrorism. In the recent inadmissibility decision in *Roj TV A/S v. Denmark* (17.4.2018), the company was prohibited from broadcasting because they had promoted the PKK (the Kurdish Workers Party), which was listed as a terrorist organisation. The domestic courts in Denmark had considered that the company had not distanced itself from incitements or other views, for example, posing critical questions. There was no independent and impartial journalist activity, so the licence to broadcast was revoked.

The Court found it decisive whether the speech is incompatible with the values proclaimed and guaranteed by the Convention. If statements are directed against the Convention's underlying values, meaning, for example, that they stir hatred or violence or that by making the statement the author attempted to rely on the Convention to engage in an activity or perform acts aimed at the destruction of the right and freedoms lain down in it (para 31).

In order to combat hate speech rigorously also on digital platforms, it is important to define the criteria for hate speech online based on similar factors that have been used for offline speech. As was rightly noted by the Court in the Roj TV case, the dissemination of hatred should be counterbalanced with fact checking, counter arguments and other forms of professional journalistic actions, which are an essential part of responsible free speech. It is also important to take into account what kind of online forum is in question. The ECtHR has even been cautious about introducing rules that would be generally applicable in all type of cases. In the Delfi AS case and cases since that time, there has been a quest for distinguishing features. Economic resources and other practical factors were relevant in the assessment of the proportionality of the obligations that can be imposed on the intermediary.

Responsibility of internet intermediaries in regard to hate speech online, developing community standards

In comparison to offline speech, the dialogue on hate speech is strongly connected to the question of how liability extends to internet intermediaries rather than public authorities. This category includes internet service providers, social media platforms and search engines. The UN Special Rapporteur on Freedom of Expression David Kaye has acknowledged in his 2016 report that intermediaries are increasingly required to assess the validity of state requests and private complaints against general legal criteria, and remove or delink such content based on such assessments.[18]

Critical comments have been made among legal scholars about whether the increased pressure on intermediaries and social platforms might ultimately lead to unnecessary censorship or at least to a public climate of debate which does not tolerate a wide range of opinions.[19] The problem with the intermediary's responsibility is also inadvertently linked to whether these mechanisms can sufficiently test the necessity of the restrictions that this type of responsibility places on online publishing. Even with the domestic courts it has been quite difficult to manage a proper balancing exercise that would make the final equation satisfactory. What is required from private companies and their supervisory

18 See Special Rapporteur David Kaye's Report 2016 https://documents-dds-ny.un.org/doc/UNDOC/GEN/G16/095/12/PDF/G1609512.pdf?OpenElement

19 See report 2016, paragraphs 40–44.

models in order to establish the right weight on the all the different factors that have to be considered.

In the changed media environment, it is also necessary to reconsider who has the responsibility to identify and respond to online hate speech. In traditional systems, the combating of hate speech is based on state authorities and especially on the criminal justice system. States have been obliged to offer the necessary provisions within the Criminal Code that could lead to the prosecution of those who are responsible for hate speech and who are distributing hate speech.

All the major internet intermediaries and social platforms have specific community standards or codes of conduct that are based on the idea of respecting human rights and combating hate speech.[20] Many social networking platforms use a reactive approach and use the community to report on hate speech. In recent research there are views that new approaches should clearly be taken which are more proactive especially in collecting data to facilitate analysing the dynamics of hate speech.[21] One of the most efficient methods has been very pragmatic and concentrates on shutting down business opportunities and, for example, pressuring advertisers to withdraw support from sites that disseminate hate speech.

The EU Commission has been actively involved in creating soft law instruments with major IT companies Facebook, Microsoft, Twitter and YouTube. One of the measures was to agree with them in 2016 on a Code of Conduct on countering illegal hate speech online[22]. Illegal hate speech is determined by EU law including both public incitement to hatred and violence against a group, but also denying or condoning crimes of genocide and crimes against humanity.[23] This is done in order to help users who are informing the authorities about illegal hate speech. The Code of Conduct places different obligations on the IT companies. This means, for example, having in place clear and effective procedures for reviewing notifications regarding illegal hate speech on their services so they can remove or disable access to such content. There is also a 24-hour target period. According to the Code of Conduct "The IT companies must review the majority of valid notifications for the removal of illegal hate speech in less than 24 hours and remove or disable access to such content, if necessary".

The results of the third monitoring exercise have revealed continuous progress on the removal of hate speech. The companies removed 70% of the hate speech they received notifications about and there is a steady increase in the removal of illegal hate speech. All the IT companies meet the target of reviewing the majority of the notifications within 24 hours reaching on average more than 81%. Overall, the IT companies removed 70% of the content notified to them. The purpose and the context of the expression form part of the relevant criteria for assessing whether it is hate speech.[24]

Assessing what could be illegal hate speech includes considering criteria such as the purpose and context of the expression. The expression "I hate you" would not appear to qualify as illegal hate speech, unless combined with other statements, for example, about

20 See Gagliardone and others 29–30. In more recent versions of these standards can be found from company web-sites e.g. www.google.com/+/policy/content.html and www.facebook.com/communitystandards/

21 Gagliardone and others 57.

22 See Code of Conduct http://ec.europa.eu/newsroom/document.cfm?doc_id=42985

23 See more precisely Framework decision on combating certain forms and expressions of racism and xenophobia by means of criminal law (2008/913/JHA, 28.11.2008).

24 See http://ec.europa.eu/newsroom/just/item-detail.cfm?item_id=612086

the threat of violence and referring to race, colour, religion, descent and national or ethnic origin, among others. However, it is difficult to give a very precise rule on what kinds of expressions qualify as illegal hate speech and what do not because policies can evolve and the context is relevant.

All the major actors in the social media scene have updated their community standards and given them more transparency by publishing them. Different social platforms have, by reason of their architecture, different ways of intervening in the case of hate speech. The most common methods are user flagging, reporting and counter-speaking. There is, however, quite a significant change of attitudes towards the phenomenon itself and how to tackle it. The companies have taken hate speech combating seriously only after the major scandals or pressure from national or EU level regulation.

Facebook introduced (24.4.2018) Community Standards in Six Parts (Violence and Criminal Behavior, Safety, Objectionable Content, Integrity and Authenticity, Respecting Intellectual Property, Content-Related Requests) giving detailed criteria for its users.[25] Under the third category (Objectionable Content) they have rules on Hate Speech. They define it as including direct attacks on people based on what they call protected characteristics – race, ethnicity, national origin, religious affiliation, sexual orientation, sex, gender, gender identity, and serious disability or disease. Some protection is also aimed at immigration status. An attack is defined as violent or dehumanising speech, statements of inferiority, or calls for exclusion or segregation. In addition, they have three tiers of attacks concerning severity.

The consequences for violating the Community Standards vary depending on the severity of the violation. First, there might be a warning; if they continue to violate policies, Facebook restricts the user's ability to post on Facebook or disables the profile. They can also report the user to the law-enforcement officials when there is a genuine risk of physical harm or a direct threat to public safety.

Another internet giant, Google, which includes YouTube, has also developed rules for combating online hate speech.[26] The list of characteristics that are protected are similar to that of Facebook, and includes formulated content that promotes or condones violence against individuals or groups based on these characteristics, or whose primary purpose is inciting hatred on the basis of these characteristics. The crossing of a line is linked to attacking a protected group. In addition, the Google rules prohibit harassment, bullying and threats and inciting others to these activities.

The microblog site Twitter has acknowledged rules against abusive behaviour. There are clear rules of conduct that prohibit hateful conduct.[27] The policy is explained as including promoting violence against or directly attacking or threatening other people on the basis of race, ethnicity, national origin, sexual orientation, gender, gender identity, religious affiliation, age, disability or serious disease. Twitter also does not allow accounts whose primary purpose is inciting harm towards others on the basis of those categories. Examples of what Twitter does not tolerate includes, but is not limited to, behaviour that harasses individuals or groups of people with: violent threats; wishes for the physical harm, death, or disease of individuals or groups; references to mass murder, violent events, or specific means of violence in which/with which such groups have

25 See Facebook community standards www.facebook.com/communitystandards/

26 See e.g. www.youtube.com/intl/eng/yt/about/policies/#community-guidelines

27 See https://help.twitter.com/en/rules-and-policies/hateful-conduct-policy

been the primary targets or victims; behaviour that incites fear about a protected group; repeated and/or non-consensual slurs, epithets, racist and sexist tropes, or other content that degrades someone.

The consequences for violating the Twitter rules vary depending on the severity of the violation and the person's previous record of violations. For example, the company may ask someone to remove the offending Tweet before they can Tweet again. For other cases, Twitter may suspend an account.[28]

One of the features of hate speech on the internet is that from the perspective of vulnerable minorities, attacks have become a permanent or semi-permanent part of their lives.[29] In the Google Spain case the right to be forgotten was established, but we also talk from the point of view of vulnerable groups that have the right to be protected from attacks in the form of hate speech. The storage and distribution of hate speech has expanded in comparison to the traditional forms like books or newspapers.

There are more interesting cases pending on the topic of online hate speech. Currently, the case of *Glawischnig-Piesczek* (Case C-18/18) is before the European Union Court of Justice. The Austrian Supreme Court (Oberster Gerichtshof, OGH) is asking for a preliminary ruling on a case where the applicant is Eva Glawischnig-Piesczek and the Defendant is Facebook Ireland Limited.[30] The Austrian Supreme Court has asked for a preliminary ruling on the admissible scope of control obligations of Facebook. The Austrian Supreme Court is requesting the ECJ to interpret Article 15 of the e-commerce Directive (Article 15 (1) of Directive 2000/31/EC). This concerns the question of whether Facebook (as a host service provider) can be obligated to search on the websites provided worldwide for content-related unlawful content (such as the concrete content incriminated) and also to block these.

On a Facebook page, an article consisting of a photograph of the plaintiff and an accompanying text was public ("Green: Guaranteed minimum for refugees to stay"). On this Facebook page, insulting statements were posted ("lousy traitors"). These posts were available to every Facebook user. Facebook did not meet the request for deletion in advance.

In the proceedings for infringement of the right on one's own image (§ 78 UrhG) and honour insult (§ 1330 ABGB), the question arose whether the obligation of the disseminator of such honour insults (Facebook), not only delete these specific contributions, but also delete content or to prevent similar contributions, is contrary to Article 15 (1) of Directive 2000/31/EC on electronic commerce. Under this provision, Host Providers may not be required to have a general obligation to monitor the information transmitted or stored or to actively investigate circumstances that indicate unlawful activity. However, Recital 48 of the Directive states that the Directive does not prejudice the possibility of applying reasonably expected due diligence in order to detect and prevent certain types of illegal activity.

The OGH considered that the line between the mere application of the law reserved for the courts of the Member States and the necessary European interpretation of the Directive exceeded the objective of the Directive (promotion of the free movement of services), and the effectiveness of personal protection requires uniform protection by a

28 See https://help.twitter.com/en/rules-and-policies/hateful-conduct-policy

29 J. Waldron (2014) *The Harm in Hate Speech*. Cambridge and London: Harvard University Press, 37.

30 The quest for preliminary ruling: www.ogh.gv.at/entscheidungen/vorabentscheidungsersuchen-eugh/vorabentscheidungsverfahren-zum-zulaessigen-umfang-der-kontrollverpflichtungen-von-facebook/

general legal interpretation based on an interpretation of Union law.[31] The role of intermediaries in removing the hate speech and developing standards has raised questions on whether those in charge of removing texts have the necessary interpretative skills. In the offline media, the responsibility of combating illegal hate speech is placed on the judiciary. They apply norms that have been drafted in the democratic process. However, the online standards are based on company regulations and supervised internally. The lack of judicial adjudication and a transparent legislative process casts a shadow of doubt on the legitimacy of combating online hate speech. Who will assure the proper discretion in these cases and review whether all relevant factors were taken into account while making a decision? These questions have been discussed in a German pilot legislation intended to combat online hate speech.

Experiment in combating online hate speech at the national level: Germany and the NetzDG (2017)

One of the most thought-provoking issues concerning hate speech online is what happens to the different national doctrines concerning hate speech and how they influence online hate speech doctrines. The diversity within the offline hate speech doctrine is founded on the country-specific historical background. The global nature of the online media indicates that national diversity should be changing towards global consensus. The US Supreme Court has traditionally been very cautious of anything that might restrict the First Amendment and freedom of speech. Instead of restraints on the First Amendment, the US system is based on the idea of a marketplace of ideas.[32]

The discussion on hate speech provides a fluctuating picture in European jurisdictions. It is obvious that particular national histories are influential in order to understand the interpretation and application of hate speech rules; for example, the severity of sanctions against different neo-Nazi groups and whether they should be understood to be within the scope of free speech. Previously, the discussion was on the French Gayssot Act that has been tested also before the ECtHR and the UN Human Rights Committee.

In the context of online hate speech one of the most comprehensive domestic laws in enforcing hate speech regulation for online media has been enacted in Germany. The Netwerkdurchsetzungsgesetz (NetzDG) came into force in early October 2017 and IT companies had until 1 January 2018 to prepare for the arrival of the new legislation.[33] The legislation creates a reporting system on illegal hate speech and requires that most material must be removed in 24 hours; however, in complex cases networks have a week to act.

31 The question before the EUCJ is how far does the E-Commerce directive obligation extend concerning identically worded information: a. worldwide? b. in the relevant Member State? c. of the relevant user worldwide? d. of the relevant user in the relevant Member State?

32 See R.L. Moore, M.D. Murray, J.M. Farrell and K.H. Youm (2018) *Media Law and Ethics*, 5th edition, Routledge, 604.

33 See Act to Improve Enforcement of the Law in Social Networks (Network Enforcement Act). Gesetz zur Verbesserung der Rechtsdurchsetzung in sozialen Netwerken, Bundesgesetzblatt Jahrgang 2017 Teil 1 Nr. 61, ausgeben zu Bonn am 7 September 2017, 3352–3355.

According to Section 3 of the Network Enforcement Act subsection 2, the procedure shall ensure that the provider of the social network:

1 Takes immediate note of the complaint and checks whether the content reported in the complaint is unlawful and subject to removal or whether access to the content must be blocked;
2 Removes or blocks access to content that is manifestly unlawful within 24 hours of receiving the complaint; this shall not apply if the social network has reached agreement with the competent law-enforcement authority on a longer period for deleting or blocking any manifestly unlawful content.

According to subsection 3, all material should be removed within 7 days of receiving the complaint. In certain circumstances there are conditions that can prolong this 7-day time limit. These are questions about factual issues where it is possible to give more time to respond or when there is reference in the complaint to a self-regulation institution.

The UN Special Rapporteur on Freedom of Expression David Kaye gave his views on the draft of the NetzDG. In his opinion, the premise is that there should be similar restrictions online as offline. One of the key positions is whether private companies are required to provide censorship or other steps that are disproportionately interfering with freedom of expression.

While it is recognised that business enterprises also have a responsibility to respect human rights, censorship measures should not be delegated to private entities (A/HRC/17/31). States should not require the private sector to take steps that unnecessarily or disproportionately interfere with freedom of expression, whether through laws, policies or extra-legal means (A/HRC/32/38).[34]

According to SR Kaye, the obligations placed upon private companies to regulate and take down content raises concern with respect to freedom of expression. He also noted that the high fines raise proportionality concerns, and may prompt social networks to remove content that may be lawful. Kaye has also pointed out the legitimate concern of whether private companies are equipped to use tools that require judicial discretion and especially might lead to measures that are not so much based on legal analysis as the application of principles with a strong incentive to be overcautious and in favour of censorship.

The same chilling effect of the NetzDG has been discussed in recent academic texts. This discussion is related to the question of whether the NetzDG will introduce overblocking; that is, an overly aggressive deletion policy.[35] According to Section 4, there is the option of introducing regulatory fines up to 500 000 euros or even 5 million euros. This is only possible in a case of systemic and persistent failure in the complaint procedure set up by NetzDG. Stefan Theil has considered that the NetzDG provides a more robust enforcement mechanism and he considers this as a goal in limiting the divide between online and offline world.

The German experiment should be examined carefully and a proper follow-up impact assessment should be conducted. It serves also as a good precedent for other countries

34 See David Kaye's opinion, www.ohchr.org/Documents/Issues/Opinion/Legislation/OL-DEU-1-2017.pdf
35 See Stefan Theil (2018) The German NetzDG: A Risk Worth Taking?, VerfBlog, (2 August), https://verfassungsblog.de/the-german-netzdg-a-risk-worth-taking/, DOI: https://dx.doi.org/10.17176/20180208-184652.

on whether similar regulatory frameworks are necessary or if these phenomena could be resolved without creating procedures that would disproportionally interfere with freedom of expression.

Conclusions

The ECtHR has noted (Times cases No. 1 and 2) in light of its accessibility and its capacity to store and communicate vast amounts of information, that the internet plays an important role in enhancing the public's access to news and facilitating the dissemination of information in general.[36] In principle, there should be a similar standard for respecting the right to freedom of expression, whether disseminated offline or online. At the same time, it is important to recognise that there are new and previously unidentified questions that have to be taken into account due to digitalisation and technological developments. The question is not just about geographical expansion, but also that novelties may exist in the quantitative expansion and side-effects that might be unexpected.

The case law has confirmed that certain basic principles in the online context need to be taken into account, despite the source and media neutrality principle, meaning that the same standards apply to online and offline speech. One of the essential elements seems to be removing online hate speech content without delay. Sufficient procedural safeguards need to be established in order to have harmful messages removed. Second, the key idea has been to extend the liability to private corporations. This development has raised profound questions on whether some kind of detrimental private censorship would develop and undermine the whole purpose of the internet – an unprecedented platform for the exercise of freedom of expression. The pending cases provoke new questions that should be answered. The main test for the courts will be to set out principles on how far the obligation of internet intermediaries will extend. What kind of obligation should exist for internet intermediaries to remove harmful content and does this extend beyond a particular jurisdiction?

The combat of online hate speech needs to include diverse and innovative methods. The global market in online media means that there is a huge variety in relation to measures taken against hate speech in different parts of the world. There is no emerging international consensus. The German NetzDG is the avant-garde of legislative responses to the problem. The big IT-companies have been pressured to remove hate speech messages without delay or significant fines would be imposed on them. Other countries are hesitant to take similar measures.

Those that produce and disseminate hate speech should be held accountable. In this century inciting hatred or harassing others has become a norm on online social media platforms. The deterioration of free speech has been accepted without too much criticism. In addition to recently adopted self-regulatory codes of conduct, there is an enormous need to educate people to use new media channels more responsibly. There is also a need to update research on the impacts of hate speech. The violence and discrimination of the last century started from the racial propaganda and demonising and dehumanising groups of people from Germany and continued later in the former Yugoslavia and Ruanda. This history of human rights violations and their undeniable link to hate speech requires vigilant measures on all levels to protect our democracies and the rule of law.

36 *Times Newspapers Ltd (Nos. 1 and 2) v. the United Kingdom*, 10.3.2009, para. 27.

16 European copyright and human rights in the digital sphere

Christina Angelopoulos[1]

Introduction

The interaction between copyright and human rights is not a new phenomenon,[2] but it is one that for a long time was ignored and undervalued. Until recently, the two areas of law appeared to develop in isolation from one another.[3] The reason for this can be found in the problems that preoccupied each in the post-war period. Evolutions at the international level are indicative. On the one hand, the human rights movement concentrated on elaborating and codifying legal norms, improving monitoring mechanisms and establishing international or regional court systems. On the other, international intellectual property ("IP") law was focused on the periodic revisions of the WIPO (World Intellectual Property Organisation) and other multilateral treaties and the development of a link between IP and trade.[4]

Moving into the 1990s however, the accretion of international IP treaties and institutions increased the pressure they impose beyond their own confined domains. The "upward harmonisation" approach taken by these initiatives, which sought more uniform IP norms across different countries in the proliferation of stronger intellectual property rights ("IPRs"), solidified the concerns to which this gave rise. In the particular area of copyright, the emergence of modern digital technologies played an additional role, both challenging the traditional inter-copyright balances and providing the tools for the expansion of rights and the strengthening of their enforcement.[5] In parallel, the end of the Cold War and widespread ratification of human rights treaties appeared to herald an "age of humanitarian intervention", increasing the perceived relevance of human rights, as well as efforts to rely on them as a means of controlling other areas of law.[6] As a result, in the last couple of decades, the previously unchartered interface between the human rights and IP has emerged into prominence.[7]

1 Christina Angelopoulos is Lecturer in Intellectual Property Law with the Centre for Intellectual Property and Information Law (CIPIL), University of Cambridge (cja58@cam.ac.uk).

2 Notably, the protection of the "moral and material interests resulting from any scientific, literary or artistic production" has been enshrined in Article 27 of the Universal Declaration of Human Rights since 1948. See UNGA, Universal Declaration of Human Rights (adopted 10 December 1948) Res 217 A (III).

3 P. Torremans (2007) Copyright as a Human Right. *Michigan State Law Review*, 271.

4 L. Helfer and G. Austin (2012) *Human Rights and Intellectual Property*. Cambridge: CUP, 1–2, 31–34.

5 For a discussion of some such expansions see J. Litman (2017) Fetishizing Copies. In R. Okediji (Ed.), *Copyright in An Age of Limitations and Exceptions*. Cambridge: CUP, 107.

6 Helfer and Austin 1–2, 34.

7 Ibid., 1–2.

A similar trajectory (on a somewhat delayed timeline) can be sketched out at the EU level.[8] This is particularly evident in copyright. The initial emergence of EU copyright law focused on the adoption of the copyright directives and the implications of copyright for the single market.[9] These early years are characterised by what has been called "a rejection and ignorance of human rights".[10] As the dust settled on EU copyright's foundational legal texts however, the Court of Justice of the EU (CJEU) turned its sights to the consolidation of early harmonising achievements. After its entry into force in 2009, strategic referrals to the Charter of Fundamental Rights of the EU ("the Charter")[11] provided useful constitutional underpinnings for the Court's copyright interpretations.[12]

Broadly speaking, the discussions on intellectual property and human rights tend to concentrate on two main questions: whether IPRs themselves qualify as human rights and what the consequences of protecting IPRs are for other human rights.[13] In the following, we shall briefly concentrate on the first, before moving on to a deeper examination of the second. As the analysis will show, the two issues are closely connected. A brief conclusion touching on current developments will be offered in the last section. Although situating the discussion in the broader international IP context, the analysis shall focus primarily on copyright in Europe.

Copyright as a human right

René Cassin, one of the fathers of the Human Rights framework, postulated that the creative impulse is common to all humankind. Consequently, it deserves the protection and respect granted through the human rights regime to all basic faculties of humanity.[14] Along similar lines, Goldsmith has observed that,

> [i]t is most fitting that intellectual property should be given universal recognition, since once an invention, literary, scientific or artistic work is revealed, it is "expansible over all space" – it leaps all national boundaries and pervades the ends of the earth.[15]

8 In the national law of the EU Member States, the situation is broadly the same. The German courts are outliers, having started to consider freedom of expression as a limitation to copyright in the 1960s. In most countries however, case law on the intersection between copyright and human rights did not begin to appear before the 1990s. See B. Hugenholtz (2000) Copyright and Freedom of Expression in Europe. In R. Dreyfuss et al. (Eds.), *Working within the Boundaries of Intellectual Property: Innovation Policy for the Knowledge Society*. Oxford: OUP.

9 T. Aplin and J. Davis (2017) *Intellectual Property Law – Text, Cases and Materials,* 3rd ed., Oxford: Oxford University Press, 36–48. For more detail see B. Hugenholtz (2013) Is Harmonisation a Good Thing? The Case of the Copyright *Acquis*. In: J. Pila and A. Ohly (Eds.), *The Europeanization of Intellectual Property Law: Towards a European Legal Methodology*. Oxford: OUP, 57, 58–64.

10 T. Mylly (2012) The Constitutionalization of the European Legal Order: Impact of Human Rights on Intellectual Property in the EU. In: C. Geiger (Ed.), *Constructing European IP: Achievements & New Perspectives*. New York: Edward Elgar, 107.

11 [2012] *OJ C 326/391.*

12 Mylly 107. See also J. Griffiths (2013) Constitutionalising or Harmonising? The Court of Justice, the Right to Property and European Copyright Law. *European Law Review*, Vol. 38, No. 1, 65.

13 Aplin and Davis 9.

14 R. Cassin (1960) L'intégration, parmi les droits fondamentaux de 1'homme, des droits des crgateurs des oeuvres de 1'esprit. In: *Études sur la propriété industrielle, littéraire, artistique: mélanges Marcel Plaisant*. Sirey, 225–229, as cited in Torremans 271.

15 H. Goldsmith (1969) Human Rights and Protection of Intellectual Property. *Patent, Trademark and Copyright Journal of Research and Education*, Vol. 12, 889.

Notwithstanding these evocative statements, the human rights status of copyright (and other IPRs) cannot be said to be immediately obvious.[16] Indeed, strong criticism has been levelled against the suggestion.[17] Indicatively, Yu has noted that,

> the inclusion in the human rights debate of a relatively trivial item like intellectual property protection would undermine the claim that human rights are of fundamental importance to humanity. Such inclusion may also revive the old, and somewhat lingering, debate about whether economic, social, and cultural rights should be considered as significant as civil and political rights, or the so-called "first generation" human rights.[18]

From a public advocacy perspective, the worry also arises that qualifying copyright as a human right may lead to a further "ratcheting up of the already very high protection" afforded under current intellectual property systems.[19] Yu also quotes Raustiala's concerns that

> the embrace of [intellectual property] by human rights advocates and entities . . . is likely to further entrench some dangerous ideas about property: in particular, that property rights as human rights ought to be inviolable and ought to receive extremely solicitous attention from the international community.[20]

These considerations aside, as a matter of positive law, the protection of (at least some aspects of) copyright under the current international and European human rights frameworks is a well-established fact. According to Article 27(2) of the Universal Declaration of Human Rights (UDHR),

> Everyone has the right to the protection of the moral and material interests resulting from any scientific, literary or artistic production of which he is the author.

The UDHR only has an aspirational or advisory nature, meaning that, initially at least, it conferred no obligation upon states to implement its admonitions. Nonetheless, over the course of time, it has acquired the authoritative status of customary international law. It is now considered the definitive global human rights blueprint.[21] Furthermore, Article 15(1)(c)

16 It is perhaps worth noting that the human rights justification for copyright, a right intrinsically tied up with personality and expression, is arguably more convincing than for other IPRs, such a parents or trade mark law. On this see R. Dreyfuss (2010) Patents and Human Rights: Where is the Paradox? In W. Grosheide (Ed.), *Intellectual Property and Human Rights – A Paradox*. New York: Edward Elgar, 72. See also L. Bently and B. Sherman (2014) *Intellectual Property*. 4th ed. Oxford: OUP, 815, talking about the relative weakness of creativity as a justification for the protection of trade marks.

17 Torremans 271.

18 P. Yu (2006–7) Ten Common Questions about Intellectual Property and Human Rights. *Georgia State University Law Review*, Vol. 23, 709, 714–715.

19 Ibid.

20 K. Raustiala (2007) Density and Conflict in International Intellectual Property Law. *U.C. Davis Law Review*, Vol. 40, 1021, 1032, as cited in Yu (2006–7) 714–715.

21 Torremans 271, citing A.R. Chapman (1998) A Human Rights Perspective on Intellectual Property, Scientific Progress, and Access to the Benefits of Science, www.wipo.int/edocs/mdocs/tk/en/wipo_unhchr_ip_pnl_98/wipo_unhchr_ip_pnl_98_5.pdf.

of the International Covenant on Economic, Social and Cultural Rights (ICESCR) repeats its wording verbatim.[22] Being a treaty, the ICESCR does impose legally binding obligations on Contracting Parties.[23]

The protection of copyright as a human right has also found confirmation at the highest level in European human rights law. Although the European Convention on Human Rights (ECHR)[24] does not expressly mention intellectual property, according to the European Court of Human Rights (ECtHR), the term "possessions", used in Article 1 of Protocol No. 1 to the ECHR on the right to property, is intended to cover any "assets, including claims, in respect of which the applicant can argue that he has at least a 'legitimate expectation' of obtaining effective enjoyment of a property right".[25] This indicates that the ECHR protects not only tangible, but also intangible property. Subsequent ECtHR case law confirms that the protection of Article 1 of Protocol No. 1 extends to IP. So, in *Anheuser-Busch Inc v. Portugal*, the Court stated that, "intellectual property as such incontestably enjoys the protection of Article 1 of Protocol No. 1".[26] That decision concerned trade marks, but the same conclusion has subsequently been repeated with regard to copyright.[27]

The Charter of Fundamental Rights of the European Union has gone one step further, enshrining the protection of intellectual property in its actual text. According to Article 17(2) of the Charter, "[i]ntellectual property shall be protected". This straightforward declaration masks considerable ambiguity, leading one commentator to dub it "mysterious".[28] Nevertheless, some interpretative guidance can be gleaned from its positioning within Article 17's general property clause.[29] Such a contextual reading would confirm that, as in the ECHR context, in the EU too, intellectual property is seen as covered by the right to property. The clear historical connection between Article 17(1) and Article 1 of Protocol No. 1 reinforces this interpretation.[30] The consequence is the qualification of Article 17(2) *mutatis mutandis* by the limitations foreseen in Article 17(1). According to this, exceptions

22 UNGA, International Covenant on Economic, Social and Cultural Rights (adopted 16 December 1966, entered into force 3 January 1976) 993 UNTS 3.

23 Torremans 271.

24 Council of Europe, European Convention for the Protection of Human Rights and Fundamental Freedoms, as amended by Protocols Nos. 11 and 14 (adopted 4 November 1950, entered into force 3 September 1953), ETS 5.

25 ECtHR (2001) *Prince Hans-Adam II of Liechtenstein v Germany,* application. no. 42527/9812, 12 July.

26 *Anheuser-Busch Inc. v. Portugal,* Application No. 73049/01, 11 October 2005, para. 43, confirmed by the Grand Chamber in *Anheuser-Busch Inc. v. Portugal* [GC], Application No. 73049/01, 11 January 2007 para. 72.

27 *Balan v Moldova,* Application No. 19247/03, 29 January 2008, para. 34.

28 C. Geiger (2009) Intellectual Property Shall be Protected?! Article 17(2) of the Charter of Fundamental Rights of the European Union: A Mysterious Provision with an Unclear Scope. *EIPR*, Vo. 31, No. 3, 113. Intriguingly, scholars have noted subtle linguistic inconsistencies. In French, the provision reads *'La propriété intellectuelle est protégée'* and in *German 'Geistiges Eigentum wird geschützt'*. These statements could perhaps be better translated into English as "intellectual property *is* protected", rather than 'intellectual property *shall be* protected'. This phrasing could be understood as a simple declaration that, as a matter of fact, intellectual property is a recognised area of law within the EU. See J. Griffiths and L. McDonagh (2012) Fundamental Rights and European Intellectual Property Law – The Case of Art. 17(2) of the EU Charter. In C. Geiger (Ed.), *Constructing European IP: Achievements & New Perspectives*. New York: Edward Elgar, 75.

Such ambiguities of translation serve only to heighten the mystery surrounding the provision.

29 D. Voorhoof (2016) Freedom of Expression and the Right to Information. In C. Geiger (Ed.), *Research Handbook on Human Rights and Intellectual Property*. New York: Edward Elgar, 343. See also Griffiths and McDonagh 75.

30 P. Torremans (2015) Copyright as a Human Right. In P Torremans (Ed.), *Intellectual Property Law and Human Rights,* 3rd (Ed.) Wolters Kluwer, 233.

to the right to property are possible "in the public interest and in the cases and under the conditions provided for by law, subject to fair compensation being paid in good time for their loss". Regulation of the right by law is also permitted "in so far as is necessary for the general interest".

Of course, the language of these international and regional documents does not in itself settle the matter. Naturalists object to the positivistic focus on legal texts. Instead, they regard the content of human rights as flowing from immutable values with universal validity that raise doubts over copyright's human rights credentials. That being said, from a pragmatic perspective, it is hard to argue against the normative consensus represented by widely ratified treaties.[31] In Europe in particular, the text of the Charter and the findings of the ECtHR have set the tone for the debate on copyright as a human right. The focus has shifted instead to the second big question raised by the intersection of copyright and human rights: the impact of copyright on other human rights.

Balancing copyright and other human rights

Whether or not intellectual property enjoys human rights protection in its own right, its implications for the effective protection of other human rights is a growing concern.

The academic literature in the area of international IP law has tended to conceptualise the relationship between IP and human rights in two primary ways. One approach is to conceive of the interaction as one of *conflict*. In its narrowest interpretation, this would understand human rights and intellectual property law as mutually incompatible, so that, in every interaction between them, compliance with one would result in the violation of the other. The conflict model suggests that, in such instances, the primacy of human rights should determine the outcome. In this way, human rights law is seen as setting a limit or ceiling to the protection and enforcement of IP. Alternatively, the two areas of law can be understood as seeking *coexistence*. According to this view, both legal regimes pursue the same fundamental objective: the encouragement of creativity and innovation, without stifling appropriate uses of intellectual creations by others. From this perspective, intellectual property law can be understood as a means of implementing human rights.[32]

A third conceptual framework attempts to merge the previous two. This rests on a more discerning approach to the human rights status of IPRs that attempts to distinguish between the attributes of IPRs that qualify for human rights protection and those that have no basis in human rights law.[33] The suggestion here is that human rights and intellectual property may both conflict or coexist, depending on whether the relevant aspect of intellectual property enjoys human rights recognition or not.[34] Where intellectual property does not attract human rights protection, the principle of human rights

31 Yu (2006–7) 715–718.

32 Helfer and Austin 65–81. See also Torremans 271; H. Grosse Ruse-Khan (2016) *The Protection of Intellectual Property in International Law*. Oxford: OUP, 211–212.

33 Examples of elements of intellectual property rights that have been argued to have no grounding in human rights law include those that protect the economic investments of institutional authors, see P. Yu (2007) Reconceptualizing Intellectual Property Interests in a Human Rights Framework. *UC Davis Law Review*, Vol. 40, 1039. See also Yu (2006–7) 738–739.

34 Yu (2007) 1075–1123. See also, Yu (2006–7) 710–713.

primacy resolves the conflict. Otherwise, more complicated solutions must be devised.[35] While this approach might be persuasive in the international context, as noted above, to date the European texts and case law have taken a less probing approach, mitigated only through the recognition of "exceptions". As a result, such subtle distinctions can have limited applicability in Europe. They do however indicate the way forward for the European copyright debate.

Indeed, as shall be shown below, a different type of "merged approach" has emerged in the European copyright case law. While the language employed by Europe's two highest courts in cases involving copyright and human rights evokes the imagery of a "conflict" (though not necessarily always using that terminology), the solution is sought in "coexistence": the concept of a "balance".[36] This raises the complicated and contested question of what is meant by "balancing".[37] Scholars have suggested that the relevant conflict – and hence the "balancing" that resolves it – may take two fundamental forms: "internal" and "external".[38] The first relates to the balance between competing interests inherent to copyright itself and the second to the balance that must be struck between copyright and other human rights.[39] The two are clearly connected, with the difference between them situated in the *locus* of the balancing exercise.[40] Traditionally, copyright law has been understood as absorbing potential clashes with opposing human rights, so as to provide balanced solutions incorporated within its own framework. At the same time, a system desirous of maintaining a proper balance in the face of evolving circumstances can never entirely dispose of external checks. Indeed, such checks become especially important in times of rapid technological advancement that strains old notions on the regulation of creative processes.[41] Further than that, how to strike the relevant balance remains the murkier matter.[42]

The following below consider the recent balancing case law of the ECtHR and CJEU in the area of copyright. First, the internal balance embedded in EU copyright law and its treatment by the courts is analysed. External balancing is then considered: how can

35 Yu (2007) 1039, 1075–1123. See also, Yu (2006–7) 710–713.

36 In the ECHR context, see e.g. ECtHR, *Ashby Donald and others v. France*, Application No. 36769/0810, 10 January 2013, para. 40 (*'intérêts éventuellement contradictoires des uns et des autres'*) and ECtHR, *Fredrik Neij and Sunde Kolmisoppi v. Sweden*, Application No. 40397/12, 19 February 2013 ('two competing interests which were both protected by the Convention'), 11. In the CJEU context, see e.g. Case C-70/10, *Scarlet Extended*, 24 November 2011, para. 45 ('affected by'); CJEU, Case C-314/12, *UPC Telekabel*, 27 March 2014, para. 46 ('in conflict with') and CJEU, Case C-484/14, *McFadden*, 15 September 2016 ('have highly restrictive consequences for').

37 C. Angelopoulos (2015) Sketching the Outline of a Ghost: The Fair Balance between Copyright and Fundamental Rights in Intermediary Third Party Liability. *Info*, Vol. 117, 87.

38 M. Birnhack (2003) Acknowledging the Conflict between Copyright Law and Freedom of Expression under the Human Rights Act. *Entertainment Law Review*, Vol. 14, No. 2, 24.

39 This use of the terms "internal" and "external" balance/conflict results from an intra-copyright perspective and should not be confused with the use of the terms as viewed from the perspective of human rights law. See e.g. Yu, who uses the term "external conflicts" to refer to conflicts at the intersection of the human rights and intellectual property regimes and "internal conflicts" to refer to conflicts between rights within the human rights regime: Yu (2007) 1039, 1044.

40 Torremans (2015), 231.

41 Birnhack 24.

42 On the resolution of clashes between conflicting fundamental rights more generally see S Smet (2016) *Resolving Conflicts between Human Rights: The Judge's Dilemma*. New York: Routledge. See also S. and E. Brems (2017) *When Human Rights Clash at the European Court of Human Rights: Conflict or Harmony?* Oxford: OUP.

clashes between copyright and other human rights be resolved? Finally, an emerging phenomenon is examined: the "internalisation" of balancing by the CJEU in to EU copyright law, i.e. the process through which the need for a balance between opposing fundamental rights[43] is currently being digested by the EU's highest court into new and surprising copyright doctrine read *ex post* into the directives.

The internal balance: copyright as a vehicle of human rights balancing

Balancing is at the core of copyright law. On the one hand, copyright has to guarantee authors a certain level of exclusivity over their work. On the other, it must also take care not to impinge upon the legitimate interests of others to access and use protected works, as well as the general interest in cultural participation and the free dissemination of information. This fundamental function is recognised by all justification theories for copyright, albeit in different ways.[44] In practice also, copyright statutes across the globe incorporate numerous mechanisms geared at integrating balance into their provisions.[45] Basic copyright principles, such as the idea/expression dichotomy, ensure that the right-holders' monopoly does not inhibit the free circulation of thoughts. The rules on protectable subject matter,[46] the requirement of originality,[47] the closed list of exclusive economic and moral rights,[48] the limited term of protection[49] and, most obviously, limitations and exceptions to copyright[50] form additional barriers to the overexpansion of copyright at the expense of users and society at large.[51]

43 It should be noted that whether the term "fundamental rights" or "human rights" is used depends on the relevant source: rights derived from international law are termed human rights, while rights derived from domestic national constitutional law, as well as from European law are termed fundamental rights. See Patrick Kinsch (2012) Human Rights and Fundamental Rights (ChFR and ECHR). In: Jürgen Basedow et al. (Eds.), *The Max Planck Encyclopedia of European Private Law*. Oxford: Oxford University Press, 839.

44 See Aplin and Davis 2–26.

45 Torremans 281–282.

46 According to the CJEU, copyright will only extend to subject matter which is original in the sense that it is its author's own intellectual creation (see CJEU, Case C-5/08, *Infopaq I*, 16 July 2009, para. 37). Certain Member States have traditionally adopted different thresholds. For example, the UK applies a "closed list" approach that limits copyright to literary, dramatic, musical or artistic works (see s. 1(1) of the UK's Copyright, Designs and Patents Act 1988).

47 Works are considered original in the EU where they are the author's own intellectual creation (ibid). According to the CJEU, "[a]n intellectual creation is an author's own if it reflects the author's personality. That is the case if the author was able to express his creative abilities in the production of the work by making free and creative choices", see CJEU, C-145/10, *Eva-Maria Painer,* 1 December 2011, para. 88–89.

48 The economic rights protected under EU copyright law cover the rights of reproduction, communication to the public and distribution (see Articles 2–4 of the InfoSoc Directive). Moral rights are not harmonised in the EU. In most EU countries, they will at least include the rights of paternity and integrity (see e.g. ss. 77 and 80 of the UK's Copyright, Designs and Patents Act 1988). Mere access to a work is not covered by either economic or moral rights.

49 In the EU, the normal term of protection is 70 years after the death of the author, as harmonised by the Term Directive (Directive 2006/116/EC of the European Parliament and of the Council of 12 December 2006 on the term of protection of copyright and certain related rights [2006] OJ L372/12 (codified version)).

50 In the EU, one mandatory exception and a exhaustive "shopping list" of possible exceptions and limitations to copyright that may be adopted by the Member States are set out in Article 5 of the InfoSoc Directive.

51 Hugenholtz 2000.

Occasionally, explicit references to this internal balance are also encountered. Recital 31 of the EU's InfoSoc Directive identifies balance as one of its core objectives:

> A fair balance of rights and interests between the different categories of rightholders, as well as between the different categories of rightholders and users of protected subject-matter must be safeguarded.[52]

Significantly, this internal balance of copyright law was for a long time understood as providing a defence against human rights-based analyses. The idea was that the intra-copyright concern for the interests of persons other than right-holders meant that potential clashes between copyright and other human rights had been successfully "internalised" by copyright law.[53] Commentators have noted the judicial deference to statute to which this has lead on the national level.[54] An initial disinclination to take fundamental rights seriously in the area of copyright can be observed the case law of the CJEU as well.[55]

For example, in *Metronome Musik*,[56] the CJEU concluded that the deviation from the principle of exhaustion with respect to the rental and lending right, as established in Article 1 of the Rental and Lending Directive,[57] was not incompatible with the freedom to pursue a trade or profession.[58] The reasoning provided in the decision was not well developed. The Court relied on the recitals to the Directive to find that the new right was aimed at harmonising the rental and lending right, as well as guaranteeing an appropriate income for right-holders in the face of rising piracy. On this basis, the Court concluded that the directive was in the general interest and did not represent an intolerable interference with competing rights – yet no substantive weighing was attempted. The Court also relied on the obligations of the EU under TRIPs,[59] though no explanation was given as to why that treaty should take precedence over international human rights obligations.[60]

Later on, in *Laserdisken*, the CJEU found that the exclusion of international exhaustion[61] by Article 4(2) of the InfoSoc Directive was not incompatible with the freedom of

52 See Directive 2001/29/EC of the European Parliament and of the Council of 22 May 2001 on the harmonisation of certain aspects of copyright and related rights in the information society [2001] OJ L167/10.

53 Hugenholtz 2000.

54 Birnhack 24. See also *supra*, note 7. A striking example is provided by the decision of the Vice-Chancellor in *Ashdown v. Telegraph* ([2001] R.P.C. 34), who stated that "The balance between the rights of the owner of the copyright and those of the public has been struck by the legislative organ of the democratic state itself, in the legislation it has enacted. There is no room for any further defences outside the code which establishes the particular species of intellectual property in question". A more nuanced decision was subsequently handed down by the Court of Appeal ([2002] R.P.C. 5).

55 Mylly 107–112.

56 CJEU, Case C-200/96, *Metronome Musik*, 28 April 1998.

57 Directive 2006/115/EC of the European Parliament and of the Council of 12 December 2006 on rental right and lending right and on certain rights related to copyright in the field of intellectual property (codified version) [2006] OJ L376/28 ("Rental and Lending Rights Directive") (at the time Council Directive 92/100/EEC of 19 November 1992 on rental right and lending right and on certain rights related to copyright in the field of intellectual property [1992] OJ L 346/61).

58 CJEU, Case C-200/96, *Metronome Musik*, 28 April 1998, para. 21–27.

59 See Articles 11 and 14, Agreement on Trade-Related Aspects of Intellectual Property Rights, Marrakesh Agreement Establishing the World Trade Organization, Annex 1C (adopted 15 April 1994, entered into force 1 January 1995) 1869 UNTS 299.

60 Mylly 108–109.

61 I.e. the principle according to which the first sale outside of the EU of a copy of the work does not deprive the right-holder of their right to control its distribution within the EU. The implication of this rule is that other

purchasers of a copy of a work to receive information.[62] The Court stated that the need to protect copyright justifies the alleged restriction. Again, this conclusion was supported by no real analysis – the primacy of copyright over freedom of expression was simply presumed.[63]

More recently, in *Renckhoff*,[64] the Court employed the concept of a "fair balance" to explain why the notion of communication to the public could not be narrowed to exclude the making available to the public on a school website of a protected image that had already been posted online with the permission of the right-holder. While the defendant had argued that the right to education, laid down in Article 14 of the Charter, meant that no infringement should be found, the Court observed that this right had already been taken into account by the EU legislator with Article 5(3)(a) of the InfoSoc Directive. This provision enables Member States to introduce exceptions for uses of works for the sole purpose of illustration for teaching or scientific research.[65] Whether further accommodation for Article 14 should be made by copyright law was not considered.

Of course, where a "fair balance" with other fundamental rights has been successfully embedded into copyright law, this should be validated. However, internal balancing mechanisms will sometimes prove insufficient. This will especially be the case in the face of fast-paced modern technological developments. Article 51 of the Charter makes clear that it is addressed to the institutions and bodies of the Union – including therefore to the CJEU. As a result, that institution should neither reflexively accept nor reject legislative balances: copyright law cannot be granted an *a priori* immunity to fundamental rights review. Instead, the use of fundamental rights as external correction mechanisms is required. As Chapman has put it:

> a human rights approach to intellectual property takes what is often an implicit balance between the rights of inventors and creators and the interests of the wider society within intellectual property paradigms and makes it far more explicit and exacting.[66]

In order to be safeguarded, a right must first be openly acknowledged. On top of the internal balance, one has to acknowledge that copyright as a human right exists in the context of other interests of equal weight. An external balance is also necessary.

The external balance: conflicts between copyright and other human rights

Before both the CJEU and the ECtHR, cases engaging in external balancing between copyright and human rights have so far focused primarily on enforcement: how far should measures to remedy or prevent copyright infringement go? As the following analysis shows, the ECtHR has been more cautious in its approach to this question than the CJEU. In view of the margin of appreciation that the former must respect, this is not surprising.

persons may not import into the EU copies of the work that have been sold outside of the EU without the consent of the copyright owner.

62 CJEU, Case C-479/04, *Laserdisken,* 12 September 2016, para. 64–65.

63 Mylly 110–111.

64 CJEU, Case C-161/17, *Renckhoff,* 7 August 2018.

65 Ibid., para. 41–43.

66 A. Chapman (1998) A Human Rights Perspective on Intellectual Property, Scientific Progress, and Access to the Benefits of Science, www.wipo.int/edocs/mdocs/tk/en/wipo_unhchr_ip_pnl_98/wipo_unhchr_ip_pnl_98_5.pdf

While the ECtHR is concerned with identifying cases of disproportionality, the CJEU must guide national courts on the interpretation of EU law. It can therefore be more proactive in the identification of the right "balance" in EU copyright rules.[67]

Before examining the relevant case law, it is important to note that the right to property (including intellectual property) is considered to be a *relative* right.[68] It should therefore not be understood as being inviolable and deserving of absolute protection.[69] As a general rule, the rights up against which it is likely to come are also relative rights. Accordingly, such rights deserve, in the language of the ECHR, "equal respect".[70]

Copyright and human rights in the case law of the ECtHR

While most of the ECtHR's early IP-related case law has concentrated on the protection of IPRs under the ECHR, later decisions have moved on to the balance between those rights and other human rights. One judgement and one decision delve into this issue.

In *Ashby Donald v. France*, three fashion photographers lodged a complaint against decisions by the French courts finding them liable for copyright infringement after they took and published online photographs of designer clothes without the consent of the rightholders.[71] The photographers claimed that the French courts had violated their rights under Article 10 of the ECHR on freedom of expression. Although it ultimately didn't find a violation, the Court did confirm that copyright enforcement can amount to an interference with the right to freedom of expression. A conflict in need of balancing thus exists. To assess whether the interference was lawful or not, the Court applied its usual test, as that is set out in Article 10(2) ECHR. This requires that interferences with freedom of expression be "prescribed by law", pursue a "legitimate aim" and be "necessary in a democratic society". As long as the plaintiff in the domestic proceedings enjoys an exclusive right under national copyright law, the first two conditions will usually be straightforward.[72] The third, however, opens up the possibility of future judgements finding copyright enforcement incompatible with Article 10. What *Ashby* thus indicates is that Contracting States cannot simply rely on the provisions of national copyright law. An external human rights perspective must be added to the internal copyright analysis.[73]

The modest impact of Article 10 in *Ashby* itself was due to the wide margin of appreciation recognised in that case to the national authorities in assessing necessity in a democratic society: "*une marge d'appréciation particulièrement importante*".[74] Decisive in this regard were two factors specific to the case.[75] For one thing, the fact that it concerned copyright

67 Grosse Ruse-Khan 245–246.

68 See Case C-70/10, *Scarlet Extended*, 24 November 2011, para. 43–44. See also CJEU, Case C-360/10, *Netlog*, 16 February 2012, para. 41–43.

69 Case C-70/10, *Scarlet Extended*, 24 November 2011, para. 43.

70 ECtHR, *Delfi v. Estonia* [2015] ECHR 586, para. 138–139. For more on hierarchies of human rights, see P. Ducoulombier (2016) Interaction between Human Rights: Are All Human Rights Equal? In C. Geiger (Ed.), *Research Handbook on Human Rights and Intellectual Property*. New York: Edward Elgar, 39.

71 ECtHR, *Ashby Donald and others v. France*, Application No. 36769/0810, 10 January 2013.

72 Ibid., para. 34–37.

73 D. Voorhoof and I. Høedt-Rasmussen, ECHR: Copyright vs. Freedom of Expression. Kluwer Copyright Blog, 25 January 2013, http://kluwercopyrightblog.com/2013/01/25/echr-copyright-vs-freedom-of-expression/ (accessed 23.10.2018).

74 ECtHR, *Ashby Donald and others v. France*, Application No. 36769/0810, 10 January 2013, para. 41.

75 Ibid.

was relevant, this being an interest which itself has been found by the ECtHR to enjoy human rights protection. According to standing ECtHR case law, in cases of clashes between rights covered by the Convention, states enjoy a broad margin of appreciation.[76] At the same time, the commercial nature of the photographers' expression was also emphasised by the Court. The fact that the photos were sold online for a profit was especially significant. Under ECtHR case law, states enjoy a broad margin of appreciation in the regulation of commercial speech.[77] As commentators have postulated, a case concerning the publication of copyright-protected material for the purposes of inciting public debate on women's rights in the fashion industry or the latter's contribution to anorexia in young girls might have met with a different treatment.[78] Likewise, cases of prior restraint (e.g. through website blocking), artistic or political speech, the use of official documents, use for educational or scientific purposes or cases concerning the media's public watchdog function would likely necessitate a more careful balancing between Article 10 and Article 1 of Protocol No 1.[79]

A later judgement confirmed the position taken in *Ashby*: in *Neij & Kolmisoppi v. Sweden*[80] the applicants were convicted by the Swedish courts for their involvement in the operation of the Pirate Bay, one of the world's largest file-sharing websites. The applicants complained that their convictions interfered with their right to freedom of expression. The Court confirmed that the Convention did extend protection to the applicants' activity, as they had "put in place the means for others to impart and receive information within the meaning of Article 10".[81] An interference had therefore occurred. Consequently, as in *Ashby*, the case turned on the lawfulness of that interference and, thus, on whether it was "necessary in a democratic society".[82] Once again, both the protection of copyright under Article 1 of Protocol No. 1 and the type of information at issue were seen as resulting in a "particularly wide" margin of appreciation.[83] With regard to the first point, the Court noted that, for the genuine protection of copyright, states must not only refrain from interference, but may also be required to take positive measures of protection, such as measures of enforcement. With regard to the second, while the Court agreed that material distributed through the Pirate Bay was protected by Article 10, it emphasised that this protection could not reach the same level as that afforded to political expression. On this basis, the interference was found to be "necessary in a democratic society", meaning that no violation of Article 10 had occurred.[84]

Importantly, a wide margin of appreciation does not give Contracting Parties free rein. Instead, as the ECtHR has emphasised, it "goes hand in hand with European

76 Voorhoof 342.

77 See e.g. ECtHR, *Mouvement Raëlien Suisse v. Switzerland*, Application No. 16354/06, 13 July 2012, para. 61.

78 Voorhoof and Høedt-Rasmussen.

79 Ibid., Writing in 2000, well in advance of the judgement, Hugenholtz predicted such outcomes for future ECtHR cases, see Hugenholtz 2000.

80 ECtHR, *Fredrik Neij and Sunde Kolmisoppi v. Sweden*, Application No. 40397/12, 19 February 2013.

81 The Court also made clear that "Article 10 applies not only to the content of the information but also to the means of transmission or reception", as well as that the internet plays and important role in "enhancing the public's access to news and facilitating the sharing and dissemination of information generally".

82 Ibid., 10.

83 ECtHR, *Fredrik Neij and Sunde Kolmisoppi v. Sweden*, Application No. 40397/12, 19 February 2013, 11.

84 Ibid., 11.

supervision".[85] Where it applies, the Court must determine whether the reasons given by the national authorities to justify the interference are "relevant and sufficient". As other judgements have explained, when the balancing exercise has been undertaken by the national authorities "in conformity with the criteria laid down in the Court's case-law", strong reasons will be needed for an interference to be found.[86] This approach presupposes, however, that pertinent criteria have in fact been established in the case law. In other areas, the ECtHR has been proactive in developing lists of factors to guide the balancing exercise. This has notably been the case for conflicts between Article 10 and Article 8 on the right to respect for private and family life.[87] Yet, neither *Ashby* nor *Neij & Kolmisoppi* elaborated on the criteria relevant in a clash between Article 10 and Article 1 of Protocol No. 1. Before these are clearly set out, uncertainty will pervade the area.[88]

Copyright and human rights in the case law of the CJEU

As with the ECtHR, the CJEU's decisions on balancing copyright against competing fundamental rights have also concentrated on enforcement, albeit of a particular type: that in which right-holders have demanded that internet intermediaries take action against third parties that have allegedly engaged in online infringement. Other cases have also examined the exceptions and limitations to copyright. Each of these two categories shall be examined in turn below.

Balancing and injunctions against intermediaries

The foundation for the first category of cases is Article 11 of the Enforcement Directive.[89] According to this, Member States must ensure that right-holders can apply for an injunction against intermediaries whose services are used by a third party to infringe an IPR.[90]

The leading CJEU judgement in the area is that of *Promusicae*.[91] Here, the CJEU was called upon to clarify whether EU law requires that Member States impose a duty on internet access providers to retain and communicate the personal data of users whose IP addresses are found to have been used to infringe copyright, so as to allow the copyright holders to bring proceedings against them. The Court found that, in principle, no such obligation exists. However, the directives do not prohibit national law from laying down an obligation to disclose such data either. Given this paucity of guidance in EU secondary law, the CJEU turned to the Charter of Fundamental Rights of the European Union. It interpreted the circumstances of the case as involving a clash between fundamental rights.

85 ECtHR, *Ashby Donald and others v. France*, Application No. 36769/0810, 10 January 2013, para. 34. See also ECtHR, *Axel Springer v. Germany*, Application No. 39954/08, 7 February 2012, para. 86.

86 See e.g. ECtHR, *Axel Springer v. Germany*, Application No. 39954/08, 7 February 2012, para. 88.

87 See e.g. ECtHR, *Axel Springer v. Germany*, Application No. 39954/08, 7 February 2012, para. 89–95.

88 Voorhoof and Høedt-Rasmussen. See also Voorhoof and I Høedt-Rasmussen, "ECHR: Copyright vs. Freedom of Expression II (The Pirate Bay)", Kluwer Copyright Blog, 20 March 2013, http://copyrightblog.kluweriplaw.com/2013/03/20/echr-copyright-vs-freedom-of-expression-ii-the-pirate-bay/ (accessed 23.10.2018).

89 Directive 2004/48/EC of the European Parliament and of the Council of 29 April 2004 on the enforcement of intellectual property rights (2004) OJ L 157/45.

90 Specificially for copyright, see also Article 8(3) of the InfoSoc Directive.

91 CJEU, Case C-275/06, *Promusicae*, 29 January 2008.

On this basis, the Court stated that, in transposing the directives and implementing the transposing measures:

> the Member States must . . . take care to rely on an interpretation of the directives which allows a fair balance to be struck between the various fundamental rights protected by the Community legal order.[92]

No input on how such a "fair balance" might be achieved was provided.

In subsequent case law, the CJEU has confirmed the "fair balance" approach. As a general rule, in cases of intermediary liability, the CJEU sets up a tripartite dynamic. This distinguishes between the fundamental rights of copyright holders, intermediaries and internet users. For the first, (a) the right to intellectual property (Article 17(2) Charter) is at stake, occasionally bolstered by (b) the right to effective judicial protection (Article 47 Charter). Depending on the particular circumstances of the case, this may collide with (c) the intermediaries' freedom to conduct a business (Article 16 Charter). The rights of end users to (d) the protection of their personal data (Article 8 Charter), (e) their private life (Article 7 Charter) and (f) their freedom to receive and impart information (Article 11 Charter) are also taken into account. This deconstruction has proved productive: while the application of the "fair balance" approach in *Promusicae* yielded no concrete guidance, the rulings that followed have offered increasingly useful insights.

So, in 2012, in *Bonnier Audio*,[93] the CJEU once again went down the "fair balance" route. The case concerned the same issue encountered in *Promusicae*, i.e. the legality of obligations on intermediaries to communicate end-users' personal data for the purposes of copyright enforcement. In this case, the national legislation in question required, *inter alia*, that clear evidence of copyright infringement exist, that the provision of the information be likely to facilitate investigation into that infringement and that the reasons for the disclosure outweigh any harm it might entail for others. The obligation was to be imposed by means of a court order. On this basis, the CJEU declared that the relevant national legislation enables a weighing of the conflicting interests involved, taking into account the facts of each case. It therefore "must be regarded as likely, in principle, to ensure a fair balance". Although remarkably non-committal, this decision sheds a bit more light into the balancing process envisaged by the CJEU. Aside from confirming the importance of judicial oversight, it also highlights the need for balancing to be grounded in a factor-based appraisal.

A further step forward was taken in *L'Oréal v. eBay*.[94] Although itself a trademark case, the decision provides useful guidance for copyright. While, as with *Promusicae*, the *L'Oréal* ruling gave no instructions on how to achieve a "fair balance" in injunctions against intermediaries, it did list two measures that would fit the bill: (a) the suspension of the primary perpetrator, so as to prevent future infringements of the same trademark by the same user; and (b) measures that make it easier to identify the intermediary's end users, as long as these persons are operating in the course of trade and not in a private matter. Although, as

92 See Ibid., para 68.

93 CJEU, C-461/10, *Bonnier Audio*, 19 April 2012.

94 See CJEU, Case C-324/09 *L'Oréal v eBay*, 12 July 2011.

before, no firm answers were provided, the decision advanced the case law by giving actual *examples* of potential balancing measures.

The subsequent twin *Sabam* cases, *Scarlet*[95] and *Netlog*,[96] achieved more concrete resolutions. The cases concerned injunctive orders, granted in national courts, imposing filtering obligations on intermediaries for the purposes of copyright enforcement. While *Scarlet* concerned an internet access provider, *Netlog* involved a hosting platform. In both cases, the requested filtering system was an exceptionally broad one, which would have applied for all the intermediary's customers, *in abstracto* and as a preventive measure, exclusively at the cost of that intermediary and for an unlimited period of time. The Court found that the requested systems would impose too complex, costly and permanent burdens on the intermediaries' business model, thus resulting in serious infringements of the operators' Article 16 rights. They would also require the systematic analysis of the personal data of all users, including non-infringing ones, in a manner incompatible with Article 8. Finally, they would run the risk, given the complicated nature of copyright law, of not distinguishing adequately between lawful and unlawful content. This would risk the blocking of legal communications, contrary to Article 11. On this basis, the Court rejected the contested measure as incapable of striking a fair balance. Although the Court's reasoning in the two decisions was opaque, with no elaboration of the factors that determined its conclusions, this was the first time balancing *results* were provided by the CJEU.

But the most concrete guidance to date on how to achieve a "fair balance" in injunctions against intermediaries is provided by *UPC Telekabel Wien*.[97] Here, the CJEU considered the imposition of an injunction ordering an internet access provider to block access to copyright-infringing content. Moving along by now well-trodden paths, the Luxembourg court held that blocking injunctions issued against an intermediary in the enforcement of copyright strike a "fair balance", provided that the intermediary is given the right to choose the measure it will apply and is able to avoid incurring coercive penalties for breach of the injunction, by showing that it has taken all reasonable measures. The measures taken must, moreover:

> (i) . . . not unnecessarily deprive internet users of the possibility of lawfully accessing the information available and (ii) . . . have the effect of preventing unauthorised access to the protected subject-matter or, at least, of making it difficult to achieve and of seriously discouraging internet users who are using the services of the addressee of that injunction from accessing the subject-matter that has been made available to them in breach of the intellectual property right, that being a matter for the national authorities and courts to establish.[98]

Satisfying all these goals simultaneously will obviously require delicate legal navigation. A way out of potential impasses was signalled when the Court explicitly recognised that measures capable of achieving a complete cessation of the copyright infringement while also respecting user rights might not exist.

95 Case C-70/10, *Scarlet Extended*, 24 November 2011.
96 CJEU, Case C-360/10, *Netlog*, 16 February 2012.
97 CJEU, Case C-314/12, *UPC Telekabel*, 27 March 2014.
98 Ibid., para 64.

But the most important contribution of *Telekabel* is the list of conditions itself. This provides some insight on how to achieve the coveted "fair balance" – if only with regard to blocking injunctions against access providers. After *Telekabel*, national courts have at least one set of balancing benchmarks, however case-specific these might be. That being said, the effect of this contribution was, disquietingly, somewhat diluted by the way it was framed: the CJEU appeared to envisage the necessary weighing as falling, not to the national authorities that are usually identified as the duty-bearers of human rights, but to the intermediaries themselves.[99]

In any case, in subsequence case law, the same broad analysis can be discerned. This is evident in *McFadden*,[100] in which the CJEU recapped the factors identified in *Telekabel*. Interestingly, a further twist can be discerned here. While previously the case law of the CJEU on injunctions against internet intermediaries limited itself to examining whether injunctions considered by the Member States were compatible with the principle of a "fair balance", in *McFadden* the Court concluded that at least one of the three measures proposed by the national court "must be considered to be necessary in order to ensure the effective protection of the fundamental right to the protection of intellectual property". The Court therefore seems to be moving beyond the negative conceptualisation of "fair balance" as a tool that only informs Member States when they have overstepped the boundaries set by fundamental rights – in other words, a tool that only clarifies what is permissible, not what is prescribed – towards the establishment of positively stated rules that require that certain measures *must* be adopted.

That being said, uncertainty continues to prevail. Though the CJEU case law has moved beyond the hands-off approach characterising the ECtHR balancing rulings in copyright, the factors governing the EU balance remain nebulous. Interestingly, the ECtHR case law on injunctions against intermediaries in other areas of law is better developed. Two recent decisions stand out in this regard: *Delfi v. Estonia*[101] and *MTE v. Hungary*.[102] Both cases concerned the liability of online hosts for allegedly defamatory content posted by anonymous users in the comment sections below news articles published by the platforms. For this purpose, the Court developed the following factors:

(a) The context and content of the comments;
(b) The measures applied by the platform in order to prevent or remove the comments;
(c) The liability of the actual authors of the comments as an alternative to the platform's liability;
(d) The consequences of the domestic proceedings for the platform; and
(e) The consequences of the comments for the victim.[103]

Potentially, the CJEU can seek inspiration here for a clearer elaboration of the balancing criteria applicable to injunctions against intermediaries in copyright.

99 C. Angelopoulos (2014) Are Blocking Injunctions against ISPs Allowed in Europe? Copyright Enforcement in the Post-Telekabel EU Legal Landscape. *Journal of Intellectual Property Law & Practice*, Vol. 9, No. 10, 812.

100 CJEU, Case C-484/14, *McFadden*, 15 September 2016.

101 ECtHR, *Delfi v. Estonia* [GC], Application No. 64569/09, 16 June 2015.

102 ECtHR, *Magyar Tartalomszolgáltatók Egyesülete and Index.hu Zrt v. Hungary*, Application No. 22947/13, 2 February 2016.

103 See *Delfi* at 142 and *MTE* at 68–69. The same factors were applied in the later case of *Pihl*, see ECtHR, *Pihl v. Sweden*, Application No. 74742/14, 7 February 2017, para. 28.

Balancing and exceptions and limitations

Aside from enforcement, "fair balance" as an external balancing tool has also been applied by the CJEU in the area of exceptions and limitations to copyright. A first reference to this was made in *FAPL*, where the Court considered the temporary copyright exception introduced by Article 5(1) of the InfoSoc Directive. It concluded that, "in accordance with its objective", that exception must "safeguard a fair balance between the rights and interests of right holders, on the one hand, and of users of protected works who wish to avail themselves of those new technologies, on the other".[104] No instructions on how this should be done were provided.

The Court revisited balancing in exceptions and limitations in 2013 in *Deckmyn*.[105] Under Article 5(3)(k) of the InfoSoc Directive, Member States can introduce an exception to copyright for uses of a work for the purpose of parody. *Deckmyn* concerned a political parody of a cartoon that added a discriminatory message to the original. The Court approached the issue as a matter of striking a "fair balance" between the rights of the author to the protection of their copyright and those of users to freedom of expression.[106] Noting that "all of the circumstances of the case" must be taken into account, the CJEU additionally brought into the mix the principle of non-discrimination (Article 21 of the Charter). The Court observed that right-holders have a legitimate interest in ensuring that their works are not associated with discriminatory messages.[107] Ultimately, the determination of where the correct balance was to be found was left to the national courts.[108]

The decision added a surprising touch of uncertainty to one of the most robust exceptions to copyright. As Mylly has worried, it established poorly defined, but powerful possibilities for right-holder control over expression.[109] It also revealed the complexity inserted into copyright law by the external balancing process. The painstaking progress made by the CJEU in its decisions on balancing in cases of injunctions against intermediaries does not aid the law on balancing in other parts of copyright. In exceptions and limitations, the case law has instead been forced to begin anew at the "*Promusicae* stage" of development, i.e. with vague admonitions. This perhaps indicates the need for something more than a mere lists of factors: what is additionally necessary is broader guidance on the appropriate *process for determining* the relevant factors: how should these factors be identified?

Internalising the external balance: shaping copyright law through human rights

The above analysis raises the question of the relationship between the internal and external balance. Which approach is preferable? The initial legal instinct in the face of external conflicts between copyright and other human rights is to re-internalise them: to make the correct balance a part of copyright law, rather than something that has to be managed on a case-by-case basis.[110] This instinct is appropriate, as long as it is not focused on superfi-

104 CJEU, Joined Cases C-403/08 and C-429/08, *FAPL*, 4 October 2011, para. 164.
105 CJEU, Case C-201/13, *Deckmyn*, 3 September 2014.
106 Ibid., para. 26.
107 Ibid., para. 30.
108 Ibid., para. 32.
109 Mylly 123.
110 Birnhack 24.

cial reconciliation, but on the improvement and modernisation of copyright law. At the same time, external balancing exercises should never be entirely abandoned. As long as technology and society do not remain static, the balance in the law must also be accepted as ever-shifting.

Attempts at internalising the fundamental rights balance are discernible in the CJEU's copyright case law. This time, the development has occurred in the area of hyperlinking. In a series of decisions, the CJEU has considered whether hyperlinks infringe the copyright owner's exclusive right of communication to the public.[111] Standing case law holds that an infringement of this right requires two cumulative elements: a) an "act of communication" that must b) be to a "public". Early on, in *Svensson*, the CJEU found that the first of these is satisfied for hyperlinks, as they afford users direct access to the linked-to works.[112] As a large, indeterminate number of people is reached, a "public" also exists. However, according to the CJEU, this public must be a "new" one, i.e. one not taken into account by the right-holder when they authorised the initial communication.[113] In *Svensson*, this requirement was used to safeguard from liability the providers of hyperlinks to content that had been uploaded with the consent of the right-holder.[114]

In the follow-up case of *GS Media*, the Court employed the "new public" criterion as a fundamental rights-balancing mechanism. The Court noted that the internet is of particular importance to freedom of expression and information. It also observed that hyperlinks contribute to the sound operation of the internet, as well as to the exchange of opinions online. The Court then acknowledged that considering all hyperlinks to be communications to the public,

> would have highly restrictive consequences for freedom of expression and of information and would not be consistent with the right balance which [the InfoSoc Directive] seeks to establish between that freedom and the public interest on the one hand, and the interests of copyright holders in an effective protection of their intellectual property, on the other.[115]

On this basis, the Court went on to introduce a new element to the act of communication to the public: that of knowledge of the infringing nature of the material. It thus found that, only where the provider of a hyperlink *knew or ought to have known* that the hyperlink leads to a work illegally placed online, will the hyperlink amount to a communication to the public.[116]

A concept of knowledge had previously been employed by the Court in communication to the public. Since *SGAE*, the Court has held that, in order for there to be a communication to the public, the user must "intervene in full knowledge of the consequences of his actions".[117] However, it is clear that these earlier references were to a different kind of knowledge. The wording suggests an attempt to exclude *inadvertent* behaviour, rather than to depend liability on knowledge of a prior infringement by another. This interpretation

111 See Article 3 of the InfoSoc Directive.
112 CJEU, Case C-466/12, *Svensson,* 13 February 2014, para. 18.
113 Ibid., para. 27.
114 Ibid., para. 25–28.
115 CJEU, Case C-160/15, *GS Media,* 8 September 2016, para. 44–45.
116 Ibid., para. 49.
117 CJEU, Case C-306/05, *SGAE,* 7 December 2006, para. 42.

accords with the "accessory" nature of the liability discussed in *GS Media*, that concerns not the behaviour of the uploader herself, but of a person further promoting already posted infringements.[118] This aspect of *GS Media* is especially interesting, given that accessory liability is an area previously understood to have been left to national law.

As the preceding reveals, the search for a "fair balance" in *GS Media* has led to a significant modification of established EU copyright law: the introduction of a novel condition for infringement by communication to the public. This development was solidified in subsequent CJEU case law. *Filmspeler*[119] expanded the reach of the new balance-based knowledge criterion to the manufacturers of multimedia players that provide links to infringing content. *Ziggo*[120] applied it to the operators of file-sharing websites.[121] In the same way, the Court also expanded EU harmonisation. Through the new balance-inspired interpretation, a new dimension was encrusted onto Article 3 of the InfoSoc Directive, collapsing the historical division between primary and accessory liability and transforming communication to the public into a hybrid notion.[122] In the end, the traditional notion of communication to the public was substantially altered.

The approach taken by the CJEU in the hyperlinking case law is remarkably different to both the internal and external balancing discussed previously. In *GS Media* and its progeny, the Court was not merely relying on the provisions of the copyright directives to decide where the legislator intended to place the balance between competing interests, under the assumption that this will satisfy human rights law (internal balance). Nor was it using human rights to interpret and guide the application of copyright to the circumstances of the case (external balance). Instead, human rights were relied upon as a means of changing the meaning of copyright terminology, expanding EU copyright harmonisation and, ultimately, updating copyright law to achieve a better balance for the digital age. In this setting, human rights emerge not as a mere review mechanism, but as a remodelling tool – a way to shape (and "Europeanise") the substance of copyright. The balance is struck during the remodelling process, after which its effect becomes invisible – there is no need to repeat and refine the balancing exercise for every case.[123] In this way, the search for a "fair balance" becomes simultaneously more concrete and more discrete.

The human rights internalisation will of course not be fully complete until reflected in the statutory provisions on copyright. An opportunity to embed the CJEU's case law on communication to the public in the EU directives was presented by the recent EU copyright reform. The new Directive on Copyright in the Single Digital Market[124]

118 Knowledge is traditionally a hallmark of accessory liability, while primary infringement in copyright (i.e. the direct violation of an exclusive right) has always been understood to be a strict liability tort. See, C. Angelopoulos and J. Quintais (2019) Fixing Copyright Reform: How to Address Online Infringement and Bridge the Value Gap. forthcoming 2019.

119 CJEU, C-527/15, *Filmspeler*, 26 April 2017.

120 CJEU, C-610/15, *Ziggo*, 14 June 2017.

121 C. Angelopoulos (2017), Hyperlinks and Copyright Infringement. *The Cambridge Law Journal*, Vol. 76, No. 1, 32; C Angelopoulos (2017), Communication to the Public and Accessory Copyright Infringement. *Cambridge Law Journal*, Vol. 76, No. 3, 499.

122 J. Ginsburg, The Court of Justice of the European Union Creates an EU Law of Liability for Facilitation of Copyright Infringement: Observations on *Brein v. Filmspeler* [C-527/15] (2017) and *Brein v. Ziggo* [C-610/15] (2017), https://ssrn.com/abstract=3024302 (accessed 23.10.2018).

123 Indeed, *Filmspeler* and *Ziggo* make no reference to balancing or fundamental rights at all, relying entirely on the Court's previous findings in *GS Media*.

124 See European Parliament legislative resolution of 26 March 2019 on the proposal for a directive of the European Parliament and of the Council on copyright in the Digital Single Market (COM(2016)0593 – C8-0383/2016 – 2016/0280(COD)).

includes a new Article 17 on the liability of certain online platforms for their users' infringing uploads. Unfortunately, this does not properly reflect the CJEU's new emphasis on knowledge in their approach to communication to the public. Instead, it limits itself to the usual admonitions that fundamental rights must be respected. Yet, as commentators have observed, the provision is badly designed to ensure a "fair balance" in practice.[125]

This raises questions regarding the interaction between the CJEU's case law and new directives: if a definition of communication to the public is adopted for a specific category of defendant that is incompatible with the edicts of the CJEU, which approach applies? The principle of *lex specialis derogat legi generali* might be said to offer the answer. On the other hand, if the knowledge element was superimposed on Article 3 of the InfoSoc Directive, it could just as easily be superimposed on Article 13 of the new directive.

Conclusion

For a long time, copyright and human rights took little account of each other. The emergence of digital technology, however, has forced a more intimate interaction. This interaction raises questions about both the nature of copyright and its relationship with other interests: is copyright a human right and, if so, how can its clashes with other human rights be resolved? In the European context, the answer to the first question has so far been "yes", raising the stakes with regard to the second.

Both the CJEU and ECtHR have approached the matter as one requiring a "balance". In this piece, three different balancing mechanisms were identified: the "internal balance" approach, the "external balance" approach and the "internalised balance" approach. The first defers to the balance struck by the legislator, in the hope that this reflects the requirements of human rights. The second returns the balance to the courts, which guide the application of copyright provisions to the facts of each case in view of human rights law. The third reintegrates the balancing process within the interpretation of copyright terminology.

All three have their purpose. Ideally, a proper balance between all relevant interests should be embedded within the statutory provisions. At the same time, external mechanisms should be maintained to keep those provisions in check. Where imbalances are detected, the reintegration of balance into the law should be pursued.

What has yet to be properly considered is the human rights obligations of legislators. While constraining the law is one of the basic functions of human rights, commentators have also worried that the "constitutionalisation" of copyright law through human rights review results in a "lock-in" effect that disables flexibility: if an interpretation of copyright is justified by reference to human rights norms, it becomes more difficult subsequently to change it.[126] This can box in both future courts and the legislator. In the recent EU

125 See e.g. Angelopoulos and Quintais forthcoming 2019. See also See e.g. S Stalla-Bourdillon et al., 'A Brief Exegesis of the Proposed Copyright Directive' (24 November 2016) <https://ssrn.com/abstract=2875296> accessed 26 April 2019; M Senftleben et al., 'The Recommendation on Measures to Safeguard Fundamental Rights and the Open Internet in the Framework of the EU Copyright Reform' 40(3) (2018) EIPR 149–163; C Angelopoulos, 'Study on Online Platforms and the Commission's New Proposal for a Directive on Copyright in the Digital Single Market' (January 2017) <https://ssrn.com/abstract=2947800> accessed 26 April 2019.

126 Mylly 127. See also Husovec, talking of the "petrification" of copyright law: M. Husovec (2016) Intellectual Property Rights and Integration by Conflict: The Past, Present and Future. Cambridge Yearbook of European Legal Studies, Vol. 18, 239–269.

copyright reform however, the EU legislator showed a remarkable lack of concern for the balances previously identified by CJEU case law. If a human rights review is to be undertaken, this should be seriously done by the courts and seriously taken by the legislator. As Article 51 makes clear, the Charter binds both institutions. The first should develop robust processes for human rights review, employ these responsibly and revisit them when necessary. The second should respect the outcomes to which the human rights review leads or adequately explain divergences.

17 Digital security and human rights

A plea for counter-infringement measures[1]

Mireille Hildebrandt

Introduction

We are often told that we must sacrifice some of our liberties to gain security. Though this is usually explained as a matter of balancing liberty against security, it actually refers to a trade-off, not a balance. The idea of balancing would imply that whenever we increase the security measures that violate our liberties, we must also increase the safeguards, to regain a balance. In this chapter, I focus on the fundamental rights infringements generated by digital security technologies and investigate what is meant when the image of the scale is invoked. The latter raises two questions. First, whether we must we necessarily trade liberty against security, including the question of whether giving up liberty necessarily results in more security. Second, what type of balancing is required whenever a trade-off is inevitable? Finally, I will argue that the balancing act requires checking for an adequate implementation of counter-infringement measures.

In the next section, I discuss the difference between security and safety and its relevance for digital security technologies (DSTs). After that, three types of DSTs will be discussed: those safeguarding access and confidentiality, those involved in monitoring, filtering and blocking of data and systems. I then discuss how privacy and other fundamental rights are impacted by the employment of DSTs, arguing that they require an assessment of the need for counter-infringement measures. This is followed an analysis of the image of the scale in terms of the trade-off that may be required between DSTs and fundamental rights, and the subsequent balancing act required by human rights law, notably the European Convention of Human Rights (ECHR). Finally, the conclusion sums up the findings regarding counter-infringement measures.

Digital security and human rights

Common sense easily confuses safety and security. In specialist discourse, safety is usually understood to refer to protection against physical or other harm, whereas security is taken to denote the prevention of or the resilience against deliberate attacks.[2] The concepts overlap. Safety can be increased if attacks can be prevented or withstood, but safety is also at stake beyond deliberate attacks, as in the case of natural disaster, harmful side-effects of human action and unintentional negligent causing of harm. Meanwhile, the concept of

1 This chapter is an abbreviated and revised version of Mireille Hildebrandt (2013a) Balance or Trade-off? Online Security Technologies and Fundamental Rights.

2 B. Schneier (2006) *Beyond Fear. Thinking Sensibly about Security in an Uncertain World*. Berlin: Springer, 12.

security is often used to refer to the reduction of foreseeable harm (thus hopefully increasing safety) and related to resilience against crime.[3]

Digital security concerns the confidentiality, integrity or availability (CIA) of data, computing systems or service provision – it does not necessarily involve safety.[4] Digital security is also a subdiscipline of computer science (focused on cryptography). Safety is thus both more and less than security and vice versa, and both safety and security overlap in part with digital security. Increased digital security does not imply increased safety, both because safety hazards exist beyond intentionally caused harm and because technical security also concerns issues that have no direct link with harm.

This chapter investigates how the legal framework of fundamental rights relates to issues of digital security. The focus is not an analysis of positive law but on the purposiveness, justice and legal certainty of legal protection in a constitutional democracy. With Radbruch,[5] these three dimensions of the law can be seen as antinomies; they direct the operations of the law even though they do not always work in concert.[6] This implies a balancing act. For instance, if the *purpose* of the law is to increase the safety of citizens or the availability of online services, while *justice* requires equal respect and concern for all, this implies that safety and security are distributed in a fair way and that infringements of rights and freedoms are complemented by adequate safeguards. Legal certainty means that citizens can base their own actions on the expectation that legal norms will be effective, creating trust that justice will be done while purposes are pursued. In relation to digital security, the construction of the legal framework determines the incentive structure for public and private investment in security measures that incorporate counter-infringement measures.[7]

Digital security: threats and vulnerabilities

The discipline of digital security thinks in terms of an "attacker model". Researchers develop so-called use-cases to foresee what types of attacks could compromise which types of digital systems, resulting in requirements to prevent such compromise at the level of hardware, operating systems, firmware, software, applications and organisation (social engineering) and in tools (both technical and social) to counter attacks and/or reduce the damage. Digital security can thus be defined in terms of threats from the side of attackers (e.g. attack toolkits) and in terms of vulnerabilities on the side of the systems, networks, services and infrastructure that may be under attack (e.g. buffer overflow and

3 L. Zedner (2009) *Security*. London: Routledge.

4 If a webshop, e.g. selling shoes, suffers an attack that causes a disruption of its services, this impacts its availability and may even cause financial damages; it does not impair anybody's safety. Also see K. M. M. de Leeuw and J. Bergstra (Eds.) (2007) *The History of Information Security: A Comprehensive Handbook*. Amsterdam: Elsevier.

5 G. Radbruch (1950) Legal Philosophy. In: E. Lask and C. Wilk (Eds.), *The Legal Philosophies of Lask, Radbruch and Dabin*. Cambridge: Harvard University Press.

6 M. Hildebrandt (2015a) Radbruch's Rechtsstaat and Schmitt's Legal Order: Legalism, Legality, and the Institution of Law. *Critical Analysis of Law*, Vol. 2, No. 1, http://cal.library.utoronto.ca/index.php/cal/article/view/22514 (accessed 17.07.2018).

7 For instance, product liability for security vulnerabilities in software would create an entirely different incentive structure than the current one. At a more basic level, tort law and criminal liability – including the applicable law of evidence and burden of proof – determine who will invest up to what level in security measures. As counter-infringement measures become a legal requirement, the market for security technologies will adapt, ensuring their economic feasibility.

SQL protocols). Vulnerabilities can be exploited by what is called malicious code (e.g. a virus, worm and Trojan horse) that is capable of destroying data or running destructive or intrusive programmes, for instance stealing sensitive information (of a person or a business). Other digital security issues concern spam that may be sent by remotely controlled spam zombies and fraud that may be conducted by phishing hosts or bot-infected computers.

As indicated previously, security in the technical sense is usually defined in terms of confidentiality, integrity and availability, and builds on the assumption of attackers trying to violate either one. Confidentiality concerns data (including databases and software) and nourishes the numerous narratives of Alice who want to send a confidential message to Bob, while Eve tries to figure out the content of the message. Eve is clearly the attacker here; she may be a person, a computer system, or a web bot. Integrity concerns either data or computer systems and here the attack aims to manipulate data or systems, which renders them incorrect or incomplete, and/or rewrites code thus compromising the programme (e.g. hacking the operating system of a smart car). Availability concerns a computing system or service whose resilience is broken, resulting in a loss of functionality. In addition, digital security also concerns the identification and authentication mechanisms that enable access or other control; attackers will for instance try to gain access to online services by spoofing (false identification) or phishing (collecting credentials for authentication). It is important to discriminate between the digital security of, first, individual transactions or communications, second, of public or private service providers and, third, that of critical infrastructure. The seriousness of a threat or vulnerability will depend on the probability that confidentiality, integrity and/or availability is compromised and the severity of its impact. Ranking the impact will depend on the number of individuals who will be affected, on the distribution of the impact, the invasiveness, duration and on potential secondary effects. Evidently, attacks on the availability of critical infrastructure, such as telecom providers, banks, the Smart Grid, the Internet, or public transport will impact a large number of individuals as well as the resilience of societies, compromising their safety and security in the broader sense.

Threats to digital security are not equivalent with the threats of cybercrime. In a broader sense, however, digital security may also refer to resilience against cybercrime, which entails criminal offences committed with or against interconnected computing systems.[8] The Cybercrime Convention[9] obligates states to criminalise threats to CIA (illegal access, illegal interception, unlawful data interference, system interference, misuse of devices (including passwords)), to criminalise computer-related offences (computer-related forgery and fraud), and to criminalise content-related offences (online child pornography and online copyright infringements). Cybercrime thus partly concerns existing criminal offences that are grouped under cybercrime insofar as cyberspace has transformed the nature of these offences due to the change in the scope, speed, distribution and distance of both the relevant conduct and its effects. As will be discussed in the next section, measures to fight cybercrime may paradoxically threaten online security.

8 S.W. Brenner (2007a) History of Computer Crime. In K. De Leeuw and J. Bergstra (Eds.), *The History of Information Security*. Amsterdam: Elsevier, 705–721.

9 M. Watney (2012) Cybercrime Regulation at a Cross-road: State and Transnational Laws versus Global Laws. In: *2012 International Conference on Information Society (i-Society)*, 71–75.

Digital security is also implicated in the notion of cyberwar. Though not the subject of this chapter, due to the issue of extraterritorial jurisdiction-to-enforce and the blurring of internal and external sovereignty, this topic looms in the background.[10]

Digital security technologies

To evaluate the balance or trade-off between digital security and human rights, we can think in terms of benefits generated by digital security measures on the one hand, and the costs of human rights on the other. Note that the measures themselves are not a benefit; whether they are depends on their effectiveness, which obviously cannot be presumed. Also, both costs and benefits involve distribution issues: who share the costs and who share the benefits?

DSTs can be divided in three types. First, technologies to ensure confidentiality of communication in digital environments (e.g. online, but also Internet of Things, connected cars, etc.). Second, technologies to detect and counter threats and vulnerabilities against availability or integrity of digital environments. Third, technologies to detect and counter cybercrime such as forgery, fraud, child pornography and copyright violations committed in digital environments.

The first type of DSTs means to ensure confidentiality. This involves encryption for identification (enabling to single out an individual user) and/or authentication (verifying access rights). Encryption is often seen as a guarantee of what some call data privacy or data confidentiality, while it may also protect against profiling based on content or metadata. The fundamental rights to privacy and data protection are often defined in terms of secrecy or data minimisation; though this covers only part of these rights it seems that encryption will not, in principle, violate fundamental rights.[11] However, encryption often depends on trusted third parties for key management and certification. To the extent that trust is intransitive and does not scale, this implies that encryption generates new vulnerabilities that require further DSTs to detect fraudulent third parties or attacks against trusted platforms. Similarly, DSTs which ensure authentication may seem neutral as to human rights, but this conclusion is again premature. Authentication allows access control and though this may be a benefit for individual citizens (to the extent that it prevents unauthorised access to personal data by others) it all depends on who is in control, how much transparency is built-in and what remedies individuals have against illegitimate access to their data. Authentication technologies allow to exclude people, they afford walled gardens on the web and within a secured environment these techniques may also afford the monitoring of individuals by means of re-recognition.[12]

10 M. Hildebrandt (2013b) Extraterritorial Jurisdiction to Enforce in Cyberspace. *Toronto Law Journal*, Vol. 63, No. 2, 196–224 (Focus Feature: Criminal Jurisdiction: Comparison, History, Theory) and M. Hildebrandt (2017) The Virtuality of Territorial Borders. *Utrecht Law Review*, Vol. 13, No. 2 (12 May), https://doi.org/10.18352/ulr.380 (accessed 17.07.2018).

11 S. Gürses, B. Berendt and T. Santen (2006) Multilateral Security Requirements Analysis for Preserving Privacy in Ubiquitous Environments. In *Proceedings of the UKDU Workshop*, 51–64.

12 C.J. Bennett and D. Lyon (2008) *Playing the Identity Card: Surveillance, Security and Identification in Global Perspective*. London: Routledge and O.H. Gandy, Jr. (2000) Exploring Identity and Identification in Cyberspace. *Notre Dame Journal of Law, Ethics & Public Policy*, Vol. 114, 1085.

The second type of DSTs mean to detect and counter threats and vulnerabilities in digital environments. They can be divided in monitoring, filtering and blocking technologies.[13] Monitoring may require analysing internet traffic (attack monitoring, detection of adversarial machine learning),[14] which means that volume, address, routing or even content of the packets that co-constitute the internet are inspected to detect various types of malware or illegal content. Filtering removes or diverts internet traffic, e.g. viruses, malicious users, child pornography, advertisements, or hate speech. Filtering is automated and based on code that may be either over-inclusive or under-inclusive (filtering more or less then intended). Note that child pornography, advertisements or hate speech do not threaten digital security, and advertisements are not necessarily illegal, but filtering that type of content is performed by using the same technology that protects against malware. Blocking entails preventing a specific IP address or set of IP addresses from uploading and/or downloading content to or from the Internet, for instance to prevent illegal file-sharing, to prevent malicious attacks or to prevent a computing system from controlling other computers by means of a botnet. Monitoring is connected with surveillance, and filtering and blocking is often considered to be a violation of so-called Net Neutrality. It should be clear that the eruption of the "fake news" scandals, the use of microtargeting to influence elections and more generally attempts to confuse constituencies as to the reliability of information has resulted in tech platforms running automated software to detect (monitor) and remove (filter) potentially unreliable content and/or to block websites that supposedly make it their business to spread misinformation. Even if human moderators are involved, content will first be flagged by algorithms as the volume of information that must be scrutinised is too big. Monitoring, filtering and blocking of content based on DSTs raises a number of human rights issues, especially due to the fact that they involve censure by private companies.

The third type of DSTs mean to detect and counter cybercrime. This concerns the powers of law-enforcement agencies, such as those imposed on states in the Cybercrime Convention: expedited preservation of stored computer data, production orders, search and seizure of stored computer data, real-time collection of computer data, and interception of content data. The most relevant technologies in relation to digital security are those that enable remote access to and remote control of computing systems (hacking), which includes disabling, disconnecting, or even destroying data and software running on a remote computing system (server). This includes decryption technologies to gain access to content, operating systems, cloud servers and social media profiles. Obviously, these technologies are precisely those that threaten the CIA of data, software, hardware and related services – thus compromising the digital security of the environment we

13 On monitoring based on deep packet inspection, see, e.g. R. Bendrath (2009) Global Technology Trends and National Regulation. Explaining Variation in the Governance of Deep Packet Inspection. Conference Paper at International Studies Annual Convention New York City, 15–18 February 2009, http://userpage.fu-berlin.de/bendrath/Paper_Ralf-Bendrath_DPI_v1-5.pdf (accessed 17.07.2018).

More generally on monitoring, filtering and blocking, see L. DeNardis (2007) A History of Internet Security. In: K. De Leeuw and J. Bergstra (Eds.), *The History of Information Security*. Amsterdam: Elsevier, 681–704.

14 Adversarial machine learning is a technique to disrupt the output of machine learning, for instance reducing the accuracy of image recognition techniques to prevent detection of child pornography or copyright infringements. Also see L. Chen, Y. Ye and T. Bourlai. (2017) Adversarial Machine Learning in Malware Detection: Arms Race between Evasion Attack and Defense. In 2017 European Intelligence and Security Informatics Conference (EISIC), 99–106, https://doi.org/10.1109/EISIC.2017.21 (accessed 17.07.2018).

increasingly depend on. Employment of these technologies will often fall within the scope of criminal offences, requiring specifically circumscribed and purpose-bound legal competences as a justification. In the case of law enforcement this is in the first place required by the criminal law legality principle that constrains the investigation and prosecution of criminal offences. The wave of so-called crypto wars highlights that decryption technologies, while potentially enabling a breakthrough in an individual case, may cause havoc at some of the deeper levels of our critical infrastructure, basically increasing the vulnerability of the system as a whole, potentially also endangering a series of human rights in the process.

Unsurprisingly, DSTs generate new digital security risks as well as violations of fundamental rights: encryption requires trusted third parties (certification authorities, key management) that can violate their duties; authentication allows monitoring and exclusion; monitoring is connected with surveillance which threatens confidentiality and privacy; surveillance also links with social sorting which threatens equal treatment; and finally filtering and blocking is often considered a violation of net neutrality that should guarantee equal access for all users, while filtering and blocking often grants unprecedented powers of censure to private companies with private interests that may not align with the human rights such filtering ultimately aims to protect.

DSTs and human rights

Security technologies have always generated new security risks. Guns can be used to defend against attacks or to enforce compliance with the law, providing trust and security between citizens. However, they can also be used to intimidate a population into submission. The monopoly of violence that grounds internal and external sovereignty has been tamed by the legal framework of the Rule of Law that binds those in power to the law, limiting their capability to bend the law to their own purposes. This is a historical artefact that cannot be taken for granted, necessitating a vigilant civil society and an independent judiciary to keep the system of checks and balances in operation. DSTs have a disruptive potential, like guns, and require reinstatement of the Rule of Law on the nexus of national and international jurisdiction, taking into account the new affordances of data- and code-driven infrastructures, compared to the previously prevalent text-driven ICTs (written regulations). This section discusses the affordances of DSTs with regard to fundamental rights, arguing their radical difference from traditional security technologies (guns, search and seizure, incarceration, interception of traditional communications such as letters and telephone).

Cybercrime differs from "ordinary" crime in terms of distance (e.g. remote hacking), scale (e.g. DDOS attack, spam), speed (e.g. dissemination of malware), automation (e.g. Web bots tracing and tracking vulnerabilities, DDOS attack), interconnectivity (e.g. peer-to-peer file-sharing of malicious software, remote hacking[15]) and invisibility (the backend systems are often intransparent due to their computational complexity, incomprehensibility and intellectual property rights). This provides the reasons for treating cybercrime differently from "ordinary" crime, resulting in the need for new types of investigative methods. These new methods (e.g. DSTs) in turn differ from previous technologies in terms of distance (e.g. remote search, notably extraterritorial reach), scale (e.g. easy access

15 Also see S.W. Brenner (2007b) *Law in an Era of "Smart" Technology*. New York: Oxford University Press.

to data on SNSs, blogs and publicly posted personal information), speed (e.g. deleting evidence of unlawful investigative methods), automation (e.g. profiling of online content and of online behaviours), interconnectivity (once data are disclosed, difficult to put back in Pandora's box due to the network effect), and, invisibility (law-enforcement agencies may work with proprietary software they cannot explain). While both cybercrime and DSTs have novel impacts on safety and security, the same goes for their impact on fundamental rights. One may expect that the impact of DSTs in terms of distance, scale, speed, automation, interconnectivity and invisibility change the mode of existence of fundamental rights such as privacy, data protection, non-discrimination, due process, presumption of innocence and free speech. I will briefly discuss how these novel security technologies reconfigure these rights to prepare for the central argument in the next section, which concerns the image of balance that permeates discussions on liberty and security.

The first type of DSTs may infringe privacy in the sense of control over one's personal data when key management or certification go awry, and data breaches occur. Attempts to prevent this may involve monitoring that could involve profiling with far more invasive privacy effects. Also, online authentication may – depending on whether this involves full identification or the management of credentials – allow for full-scale monitoring behind the access-point. This will, again, allow for invasive types of profiling with more complex and invasive impacts on privacy. The second type of DSTs requires monitoring of Internet traffic and thus links up with surveillance. Monitoring can consist of shallow or deep packet inspection to check on volume, routing, origin or destination, or even content. It affords eavesdropping, censorship and all kinds of statistical operations such as data mining, for instance for commercial purposes, law enforcement or intelligence. This easily results in privacy infringements and erosion of free speech, while it enables different types of discrimination and reduces rights of due process (due to the invisibility of online surveillance). The third type of DSTs provide extensive investigatory technologies for law enforcement, again infringing privacy, enabling invisible discrimination, generating a chilling effect on the freedom of expression, while also reducing the protection of the presumption of innocence as criminal investigation shifts to the pre-trial phase.

The notion of the scale: trade-off and balance?

Immediately after 9/11 the metaphor of the scale gained traction. It gives the impression of balance and reasonableness in times of emergency. The core idea seems to be that between security and liberty, we cannot have our cake and eat it too; choices will have to be made and if so, they had better be well balanced. The idea that some of our liberty must be given up to achieve security has a rhetorical ring that fits the political agenda of extended law-enforcement competences, as well as that of the security technologies' industry in the broad sense, including arms production for military purposes. That agenda also includes DSTs and we can imagine that companies developing and selling them have two strategies to enlarge their turnover: they can increase their market share or expand the market. This usage of the metaphor of the scale can be used to sell security technologies which may infringe fundamental rights: if we want online security, we must accept that privacy, data protection, non-discrimination, due process and free speech will have to be limited. Giving up a measure of privacy to gain a measure of security sounds reasonable to many people.

Preliminary observations

Before embarking on the intricacies of the image of the scale several caveats apply. First, the discourse of balance evokes the notion of weighing. On a scale, one can weigh different ingredients, assuming that all that matters is their weight. In the case of security technologies that infringe fundamental rights this raises the question of the nature of the ingredients, noting they are weighted in terms of a trade-off rather than a balance. Is the public good of security traded against the private good of privacy, or must we consider both to be public goods? Must these goods be qualified as rights or as interests?[16] Is the right to safety or that to security traded against the right to privacy or to non-discrimination? Is an individual right such as privacy traded against collective interests such as security? Or do we trade a private interest in privacy against a public interest in security? Obviously, such questions are related to traditional distinctions in moral philosophy. Kantian deontologists may vouch for a rights approach, whereby rights are trump cards that overrule interests. Benthamite utilitarians may vouch for an approach based on aggregate interests, though Millian liberals could restrict the utilitarian calculation by claiming a fundamental right to liberty that can only be overruled by security interests that serve to protect individual liberty. Pitting individual rights or interests in fundamental rights against a public good or a collective interest in online security is highly problematic. It assumes that fundamental rights and security are at the same level, whereas their relationship is more complicated as one may be conditional for the other. It also, wrongly, assumes that privacy is not a public good or a collective interest and security not a private good or individual right. For their realisation, private interests in privacy and security both depend on a legal framework that provides a minimum of legal certainty with regard to these interests, which explains that *individual privacy and individual security are also public goods.*

This brings to the fore the question whether legal certainty can be achieved without security in the broad sense of being safe against violent attacks. This relates to the question of whether security is, like privacy, a human right or rather a precondition for the legal framework on which effective human rights depend, which, in turn, raises the issue of power and authority.[17] These are hefty terms, often mistakenly used interchangeably. Authority is based on the power to command obedience, power is based on the economic or military ability to enforce submission. Under the Westphalian system of sovereign states, state authority depends on the monopoly on violence and implies the power to protect citizens against violence from other citizens (internal sovereignty depends on this) and from other states (external sovereignty). Social contract theory from Hobbes to Rousseau somehow assumes that the state is capable of providing the fundamental security required to go about one's daily business.[18] Once such security can no longer be provided, the social contract crumbles and states dissolve in civil war. Security in that broad sense,

16 On different theories concerning the difference between rights and interests. Also see W.A. Edmundson (2004) *An Introduction to Rights*. Cambridge: Cambridge University Press.

17 M. Hildebrandt (2010) The Indeterminacy of an Emergency: Challenges to Criminal Jurisdiction in Constitutional Democracy. *Criminal Law and Philosphy* Vol. 4, No. 2, 161–181 and M. Hildebrandt (2013b) Extraterritorial Jurisdiction to Enforce in Cyberspace. *Toronto Law Journal*, Vol. 63, No. 2, 196–224 (Focus Feature: Criminal Jurisdiction: Comparison, History, Theory).

18 This is related to the fact that contract theory concerns the institution of the monopoly of violence, that is only acceptable insofar as the state actually manages to protect its subjects from violent attack. On the complexities of, e.g. the right of resistance in Hobbes, Locke and Rousseau Also see J. C. Johari (1987) *Contemporary Political Theory: New Dimensions, Basic Concepts and Major Trends*. New York: Sterling, 388.

combining safety against attack and legal certainty, seems conditional for state authority. This means that authority works within the state but hardly between competing states and transnational corporations, where power is at stake rather than authority. This raises a number of questions as to how security technologies function across national borders, playing out across various jurisdictions, where the user may be unaware of the actual location of the data servers that are being accessed to wipe out botnets or other threats to cybersecurity. It is worthwhile to note here that the protection of human rights ultimately depends on a court of law and an administration that grants and executes the substance of the right, whereas at the level of extraterritorial jurisdiction such protection is not guaranteed. In that case, security may be provided without being complemented with the safeguards of fundamental rights.

Six caveats from Jeremy Waldron

Not long after 9/11, when criticising security measures in the USA was easily interpreted as unpatriotic behaviour, legal philosopher Jeremy Waldron spoke at a workshop on "Terrorism and the Liberal Conscience" at All Souls College, Oxford on the subject of "Security and Liberty: The Image of Balance".[19] In his topical paper, he develops six concerns regarding the idea that international terrorism requires states to strike a new balance between security and liberty. These concerns are relevant for similar calls to strike a new balance with regard to online security, based on the plethora of threats and vulnerabilities that endanger critical infrastructure, service providers and individual citizens.

First, the image suggests that by diminishing liberties we will achieve security. This, however, cannot be taken for granted, as it will depend on a number of empirical facts, many of which are simply not known when taking the measures. In other words, their effectiveness cannot be assumed but should be assessed. Whether DSTs achieve effective protection against threats and vulnerabilities of the ICT infrastructure and against various types of cybercrime does not depend on whether they infringe fundamental rights. In many instances alternative technologies that cause less or even no infringement could be equally or even more effective.

Second, the image suggests a measure of precision that is inherent in cost-benefit analyses; to increase security (benefit) we must decrease liberty (cost). Such precision is an illusion, due to various types of incertitude, for instance those discussed by Waldron, who discriminates between risk, uncertainty, ambiguity and ignorance. [20] The precision suggested reinforces a bias to quantifiable, machine readable criteria whose weighing depends on a tertium comparationis that may not be available: how does one weigh rights' infringements against security interests?

Third, the image suggests that liberties can be traded at will, though from the perspective of the Rule of Law these liberties are exclusionary reasons,[21] side constraints,[22]

19 J. Waldron (2003) Security and Liberty: The Image of Balance. *Journal of Political Philosophy*, Vol. 11, No. 2, 191–210. doi:10.1111/1467-9760.00174.

20 Andy Stirling (2008) Science, Precaution, and the Politics of Technological Risk. *Annals of the New York Academy of Sciences*, Vol. 1128 (Strategies for Risk Communication Evolution, Evidence, Experience), 95–110.

21 Joseph Raz (1999) *Practical Reason and Norms*. Oxford: Oxford University Press.

22 Robert Nozick (1988) Side Constraints. In Samuel Scheffler (Ed.), *Consequentialism and Its Critics*. Oxford: Oxford University Press.

or trump cards[23] that cannot simply be overruled by assumed security gains. The image thereby seems to privilege a utilitarian rather than a Kantian ethics.

Fourth, the image also suggests that one's liberty must be traded against one's security, whereas in practice there is a problem of distribution. Usually the liberties of specific groups (illegal immigrants, unemployed, convicted criminals, suspects, outliers in the case of profiling technologies) are traded against the security of other groups (those assumed to be law abiding citizens, those who remain "under the radar" in the case of profiling technologies). This raises the issue of distribution of costs and benefits.

Fifth, the image is not transparent about the fact that by diminishing liberties the powers of the state are increased and that this simple fact will entail security threats. Montesquieu's warning about the need to introduce countervailing powers regards precisely this point. DSTs may reduce citizens' security against state powers.

Sixth, the image may condone symbolic measures that have no real effect in terms of security, hoping to achieve a largely illusionary public sense of security. This has been coined "fact-free policies" and we should note that much of what is presented as evidence-based policies in fact engages a rhetoric that is entirely fact free.[24]

Limitation of fundamental rights

Constitutional and international human rights law employ various strategies to limit the scope of fundamental rights, while ensuring they do not lose their substance. Limitation is inevitable, either because they clash with public goods that are conditional for the effectiveness of fundamental rights or because various rights or liberties clash and must be aligned one way or another. Within the context of the European Convention of Human Rights which determines the human rights framework within the Council of Europe (52 states), the limitation of the rights to privacy, freedom of thought, conscience and religion, freedom of expression and freedom of assembly and association require a triple test to determine whether a security technology measure that violates one of these rights can be legally justified. This triple test can be used to exemplify how the trade-off and the balance that define the image of the scale can be related to the impact of DSTs on fundamental rights.

After attributing a right to privacy in the first paragraph of Art. 8 of the Convention, the second paragraph articulates three cumulative conditions to justify the infringement:[25] the infringing measures must be in accordance with the law, necessary in a democratic society and have a legitimate aim. The "legitimate aim" and the requirement that the measure is "necessary in a democratic society" imply that a trade-off *can be* justified, but only if the infringing measure is necessary and proportional to achieve public goods such as the protection of public order, health or morals or the protection of the rights and freedom of others. DSTs that cannot be expected to achieve one of the public goods enumerated in

23 Ronald Dworkin (1991) *Law's Empire*. Glasgow: Fontana.

24 In the context of anti-terrorism measures such as anti-money laundering. Also see N. Passas (2006) Fighting Terror with Error: The Counter-productive Regulation of Informal Value Transfers. *Crime, Law and Social Change*, 45(4–5), 315–336.

25 S. Sottiaux (2008) *Terrorism and the Limitation of Rights. The ECHR and the US Constitution*. Oxford: Oxford University Press and P. De Hert and S. Gutwirth (2009) Data Protection in the Case Law of Strasbourg and Luxembourg: Constitutionalism in Action. In: S. Gutwirth, Y. Poullet, P. De Hert, S. Nouwt, and C. de Terwangne (Eds.), *Reinventing Data Protection?* Dordrecht: Springer, 3–44.

Art. 8.2, cannot be justified. This implies at least a marginal test of the effectiveness of the infringing measure. The trade-off is a necessary – but not sufficient – condition. Justification is also conditional on the assessment that the infringing measures are "in accordance with the law". In the case law of the ECHR the requirement of lawfulness is detailed as demanding a basis in national law that is adequately accessible, sufficiently foreseeable and contains effective safeguards. Adequate accessibility and sufficient foreseeability means that citizens can anticipate what types of measures their government can take that might infringe their privacy and thus relates to their reasonable expectation of privacy. For instance, secret surveillance may be allowed, if citizens can foresee in what circumstances it might occur, even if the police will not notify them before wiretapping or requiring access to the personal data of a subscriber to an online service provider. Adequate and effective safeguards necessitate that secret surveillance is neither unlimited in scope (time and content) nor in scale (number of people, frequency of interception) and the condition of safeguards also entails that a warrant or permission from a judge is needed if the invasiveness, frequency or duration of the measure increases beyond a certain threshold. The most important safeguard has been that infringing measures are only allowed in specific cases, ruling out general monitoring of groups or individual citizens.[26]

In line with new approaches to "protection by design", the General Data Protection Regulation (GDPR) has articulated a legal obligation to implement "data protection by default and by design" (DPbD, Art. 25 GDPR), requiring that those responsible for respecting the fundamental right to data protection (Art. 8 Charter Fundamental Rights of the European Union) implement state of the art technical and organisational protection at the level of the sociotechnical architecture that may infringe various fundamental rights. I have argued elsewhere that this right to DPbD should be understood as an instance of a broader concept of legal protection by design that is meant to ensure that the protection of human rights in the era of data-driven environments remains effective. The point is that data- and code-driven human rights infringements require data- and code-driven protection, entailing a translation of text-driven legal protection into the architecture of data- and code-driven systems.[27]

DSTs that aim to detect and counter online security threats, vulnerabilities and various types of cybercrime may infringe privacy. Building on the triple test of European human rights law, such infringements should be justifiable in terms of a proportional trade-off that instigates a threshold before the employment of such technologies is allowed. If, however, that threshold is reached, the requirement of proportionality demands the implementation of *counter-infringement measures* that reduce potential infringements to what is reasonable in relation to expected benefits. In that case, the notion of proportionality becomes contingent upon the technical and economic state of the art in counter-infringement technologies. Next to that the employment of DSTs should be conditioned by the implementation

26 See e.g. on mass interception in the context of national security ECtHR, 19 June 2018, Application no. 35252/08, Case of *Centrum för Rättvisa v. Sweden*, finding that the abstract test requested by the applicant (who did not provide evidence of being a victim of an infringing measure) was not required, as the applicant was considered to have enough alternative legal remedies. For minimum safeguards see consideration 95 of ECtHR, 29 June 2006 Application No. 54934/00, Case of *Weber Saravia v. Germany*.
Seminal judgements can be found in the fact sheet on mass interception of the ECHR at www.echr.coe.int/Documents/FS_Mass_surveillance_ENG.pdf

27 Mireille Hildebrandt and Laura Tielemans (2013) Data Protection by Design and Technology Neutral Law. *Computer Law & Security Review* and M. Hildebrandt (2017) The Virtuality of Territorial Borders. *Utrecht Law Review*, Vol. 13, No. 2 (12 May), https://doi.org/10.18352/ulr.380 (accessed 17.07.2018).

of a set of safeguards that are proportional in relation to the expected scope of potential infringements (the more substantial the infringement, the more substantial the safeguards). These safeguards will require human intervention, for instance to judge whether the threshold for a justifiable trade-off is reached – while in an automated environment some of the safeguards should be automated,[28] for instance by flagging potential abuse of DSTs based on certain indicators.

In short, the issue of the trade-off means that if an DST is not effective in reaching a legitimate aim, it cannot be proportionate and must be prohibited in as far as it infringes privacy or other fundamental rights. To assess this, we need *freedom infringement impact assessments for DSTs*, resulting in evidence-based DSTs instead of fact free security policies. The issue of balance requires that the more serious the infringement may be, the more substantial the required counter-infringement technologies should be. This can be achieved, for instance, by developing smart security and data protection by design – as imposed by the proposed General Data Protection Regulation.

Concluding remarks: counter-infringement measures as necessary safeguard under human rights law

The reach, scope, speed, automation, interconnectivity and invisibility of threats and vulnerabilities of data- and code-driven systems have offset a growing demand for DSTs, both in the private and the public sector. Various types of DSTs can be distinguished, based on encryption technologies and key management, on monitoring, filtering and blocking and on (remote) hacking of computing systems. DSTs are meant to increase online security in the broad sense of safety from attacks against confidentiality, integrity and availability of personal data and critical infrastructure; resilience against fraud and forgery; and detection and prevention of child pornography and violations of copyright. At the same time, they afford violations of human rights, notably privacy. This chapter inquired into the nature of the metaphor of the scale, fleshing out the difference between a trade-off and a balance. A trade-off suggests that more digital security means less privacy. This cannot be assumed. A more effective level of digital security is a necessary but not a sufficient condition for giving up some privacy, also taking into account that the more privacy invasive a DST the higher the threshold should be for allowing it. If security threats and proportionate DSTs meet the threshold of a sufficient condition, a balance must be struck: the higher the infringement of human rights, the more effective safeguards must be implemented. In line with data protection by design and default, human rights law must develop the notion of counter-infringement measures as part of the necessary safeguards under human rights law. Like data protection by design this would be another instance of legal protection by design.

28 This involves Legal Protection by Design and/or Privacy by Design. Also see M. Hildebrandt (2011) Legal Protection by Design. *Legisprudence*, Vol. 5, No. 2, 223–248 and M. Langheinrich (2001) Privacy by Design – Principles of Privacy-Aware Ubiquitous Systems. In *Proceeding of 3rd Interntional Conference Ubquitous Computing*. Berlin: Springer, 273–291.

Part V

Data protection issues

18 The challenge of personal data protection in the digital era and global responses

Alexandros Varveris and Fereniki Panagopoulou[1]

Introduction

Undeniably, this is a revolutionary year for personal data protection – a momentous issue for the European Union (EU) over the last two decades. Recently, with the emergence of the General Data Protection Regulation (GDPR), the said issue was significantly elevated to an entirely new level. In addition to a new set of legal requirements demanding both organisational and technological responses, the GDPR became applicable to almost every global organisation that collects or processes data on EU residents, including permanent residents, visitors and expatriates. Compliance is therefore predicated on the geographical location of the individuals about which the organisation possesses personal data and not the organisation's country of registration.

Given that, internet and related technologies have the ability to revive the public sphere,[2] it must be noted that several aspects of these technologies simultaneously restrict and expand that ability. The data storage and retrieval capabilities of internet-based technologies infuse the political discussion with otherwise unavailable information, while at the same time, information access inequalities and new media literacy compromise the representativeness of the virtual sphere. In addition, internet-based technologies enable discussions between people on opposite sides of the globe, while they can also frequently fragmentize political discourse. Furthermore, with the patterns of global capitalism, it is possible that internet-based technologies might adapt themselves to the current political culture, rather than create a new one. In this way, the internet and related technologies have created a new public space for politically and technologically oriented conversation.

Giovanni Buttarelli, the European Data Protection Supervisor (EDPS), noted that

> Privacy and data protection matter more than ever to people. For the first time in a generation, the EU has an opportunity to modernize, harmonize, and simplify the rules on how personal information is handled. These rules must be relevant for the next generation of technologies. As part of my remit to be proactive and constructive, my recommendations aim to support the co-legislators to get a better deal for the individual, to make safeguards more effective in practice and enable them to benefit from technological innovation are still feasible. The GDPR is not the reform of my

1 Alexandros Varveris has authored the first part of this paper and Fereniki Panagopoulou the section on global responses.

2 Z. Papacharissi (2018) *SAGE Journals: Your Gateway to World-class Journal Research*. Journals.sagepub.com, http://journals.sagepub.com/doi/pdf/10.1177/14614440222226244 (accessed 18.7. 2018).

dreams but I thoroughly support "the institutions in the last mile to achieve the best possible outcome: improvements are still feasible".[3]

As expected, in several recent trade negotiations, the EU is under pressure to advocate for higher standards of data privacy so as to earn greater public trust within its domestic jurisdictions, noting that there is strong disagreement from the other side of the Atlantic.

When conforming with data localisation laws for companies, a fundamental problem one comes across is the difficulty of controlling which data categories are needed, so they can be locally stored before moving abroad.[4] Moreover, legal experts may have a problem in assessing the legal liability of foreign companies that do not have a business presence in a specific country, while they may be handling large quantities of client data for citizens during normal day-to-day business transactions in the global marketplace. In addition, when companies are forced to relocate their servers to jurisdictions that have low levels of internet security, concerns may arise regarding the possible breaches of consumer trust that may entail further legal liability. In conclusion, foreign companies are also concerned and worried when operating data centres in several demanding jurisdictions where state censorship and surveillance laws are over-encompassing and create significant liabilities for service providers. While these laws fail to satisfy their objective of providing adequate security and privacy for user data, they create several economic and technical drawbacks that can prejudice the resilience and utility of the internet as a platform for communication and trade.[5]

The rights to respect private life and personal data protection are closely related since both of them defend similar values.[6] Within the EU, however, an independent fundamental right to data protection has gradually emerged in addition to the right to privacy.[7] After its separate recognition in the EU Charter of Fundamental Rights, the right to data protection acquired a prominent position in the EU General Data Protection Regulation 2016/679 (GDPR). Article 1(2) of the GDPR unambiguously supports that it protects fundamental rights and in particular the right to data protection. This is in contrast to the current EU Data Protection Directive 95/46/EC, which protects in particular the right to privacy with respect to the processing of personal data.[8]

The main concern for the affected companies is how they will be able to identify and link all the data that they need to protect the new, updated rights[9] of the data subjects. This is essentially the fundamental pillar of data protection, which lies in the enhancement of the protection of data subjects and the corresponding strengthening of the duties of data controllers. Nevertheless, concerns that have been put forward suggest that the recognition of such reinforced rights may also end up being misused, thereby adversely affecting administrative efficiency. The main personal data challenges of the GDPR will be discussed in the upcoming sections.

3 Edps.europa.eu. (2018) *Opening a New Chapter for Data Protection*, https://edps.europa.eu/sites/edp/files/edpsweb_press_releases/edps-2015-06-edps_gdpr_en.pdf (accessed 18.7.2018).

4 W. Drake (2018) *Data Localization and Barriers to Transborder Data Flows*, www3.weforum.org, http://www3.weforum.org/docs/Background_Paper_Forum_workshop%2009.2016.pdf (accessed 20.7.2018).

5 N. Mishra (2018) *Data Localization Laws in a Digital World: Data Protection or Data Protectionism?*. Papers.ssrn.com., https://papers.ssrn.com/sol3/papers.cfm?abstract_id=2848022 (accessed 18.7.2018).

6 Handbook (2018) *Handbook on European Data Protection Law*. 1st ed. European Union Agency for Fundamental Rights and Council of Europe, 19.

7 G.G. Fuster (2014) *The Emergence of Personal Data Protection as a Fundamental Right of the EU*. Dordrecht: Springer, doi:10.1007/978-3-319-05023-2

8 M. Mostert, A. Bredenoord, B. van der Slootb and J. van Delden (2017) From Privacy to Data Protection in the EU: Implications for Big Data Health Research. *European Journal of Health Law*, Vol. 25, No. 1, 44–45.

9 Right to be forgotten, Right to access, Right to data portability, Right to rectification, Right to object.

Identity resolution

Identity resolution enables an organisation to analyse the identity of a particular individual or entity based on its available data records and attributes. The problem arises when one is called to manage numerous consents and correct personal data while informing the individual of the data a company holds, and how the said data is used. This is best achieved using an identity resolution, which is mostly a data management process where an individual is identified from different data sets and databases in order to resolve their identity. In other words, companies with different systems, databases and customer data entries need to identify the data of each individual and merge it into one central profile, displaying the most valid and up-to-date personal data.

An example of duplicated data[10] is when an individual has two separate customer profiles in different systems for the same company, while the said data must be removed and replaced into a single customer profile. This may sound like plain simplicity; however, it can be a tremendous challenge, as scattered systems and duplicate and/or incomplete customer profiles seem to be the norm rather than the exception in most companies.[11] If you cannot identify that single version of a customer, what will you be doing when someone asks you for an overview of their personal data?

Consent

Organisations will have to adapt to a new controlled consent procedure, allowing them to store and use individual personal data. Furthermore, consent from data subjects must be specific to distinct purposes. Later on, there is a need to link each profile to the various processes that the individual has agreed to, such as newsletter subscriptions, online purchase histories, etc.

At this point, it must be noted that there is a need to provide an overview showing a list of all the business processes and/or services that an individual has consented to.

To begin with, if securing consent is burdensome, the data controller must seek a different legal basis. At the same time, the receipt of consent must coincide with the identification of options for the data subject, with genuine consent essentially putting individuals in charge, building customer trust and engagement, while also enhancing reputation. Furthermore, consent must be refreshed if it does not meet the strict requirements of the GDPR: for this reason, care must be taken to ensure that all consents should be granted on the basis of a positive/opt-in choice, hence pre-ticked boxes or any other method of default consent should be avoided. It is also very important to ensure that consent is clearly distinguishable for each act of processing, as well as that there must be an option for

10 Techopedia.com. (2018) *What is Identity Resolution? – Definition from Techopedia*. www.techopedia.com/definition/29011/identity-resolution (accessed 18.7.2018).

11 A recent Royal Mail Data Services study concludes "Over half of all businesses have missing, incomplete or out-of-date customer data. According to the research, 63.3% of UK businesses reported out-of-date customer information, while 62.8% reported that their customer data was incomplete with gaps in certain data fields, with a further 60.1% admitting to having hardly any data for certain customers". Poor data quality is one of the modern marketer's most pressing concerns, with 66% of those polled citing data accuracy as a "top priority". And little wonder, when you consider the importance of clean and accurate data, with successful customer relationships depending on having the right information to personalise communications. Furthermore, digital and physical customer communications that either don't reach the intended recipient or contain inaccurate information may not only represent cost for no return, but could also damage a brand's reputation.

its withdrawal. Moreover, the granting of consent to process data should be well recorded, while it should not be a precondition for a service. Lastly, public authorities and employers will need to take extra care to show that consent is freely given, while they should also avoid over-reliance on consent.

Indeed, as it transpires from the preceding, the issue of consent, as set forth in the GDPR, involves a notably high standard, requiring regular reviews of consent practices and existing consents, as well as regular reviews and refreshing of consents whenever this is necessary in order to ensure compliance with the GDPR. In the interest of achieving this, it is highly recommended that companies should secure explicit consents. This, in turn, requires a very clear and concise statement of consent, with consent requests kept separate from other terms and conditions. In this respect, it helps a lot if one is as specific and "granular" as possible, in order to ensure that separate consents are in place for separate issues, as well as that information will be provided with regard to third-party controllers who will be relying on such consent. To this effect, it is also important to keep evidence of consents granted, including but not limited to who, when, how and what you said to people. When it comes to consent withdrawal, data subjects should be assisted in terms of withdrawing such consent, and therefore there should be clear instructions to facilitate them as to how they can do this.

To begin with, if an organisation has already created records of processing in order to meet Article 30 requirements, these records can be consulted as a first point of identifying which processing activities rely on consent. These records are not only required under Article 30, but they can also serve as a tool when working toward meeting other requirements; therefore, it is recommended to consider expanding the scope of these records so as to include information on their legal basis and consent.

Upon identifying where consent is being relied on, ask the question: "Is this consent really the most appropriate legal basis for this processing activity?" It should be taken into consideration that consent may not be the best choice in the following situations: (a) when the organisation would still process the data under a different legal basis, even if consent is refused or withdrawn; (b) where consent cannot be refused or withdrawn without detriment to the data subject; (c) where the organisation is in a position of power over the data subject; and (d) where a processing activity is necessary for the performance of a contract.

As stated by the Working Party 29 (WP29), "a controller must always consider whether consent is the appropriate lawful grounds for the envisaged processing or whether other grounds should be chosen instead".[12] If one is struggling to obtain or manage valid consent for a particular activity, this may mean that another legal basis may be more appropriate.

The GDPR also includes requirements for making a valid request for consent. For example, under Article 7(2), it is noted that "the data subject's consent is given in the context of a written declaration which also concerns other matters, the request for consent shall be presented in a manner which is clearly distinguishable from the other matters, in an intelligible and easily accessible form, using clear and plain language".

12 WP29 (2018) *Guidelines on Consent under Regulation 2016/679*. Ec.europa.eu. https://ec.europa.eu/newsroom/just/document.cfm?doc_id=48849 (accessed 20.7.2018).

Therefore, it is important to ensure that consent requests are kept separate from other terms and conditions, as well as that the request is prominent and clearly visible to the data subject, while also being user-friendly.

One of the essential elements of valid consent under the GDPR is to be informed. Informing data subjects about the processing of their personal data is vital to their understanding of what it is that they are consenting to, but also in order to ensure that real choice is provided to them.

According to the WP29, the following information should be provided to the data subject as a minimum: the controller's identity, the purpose of each of the processing operations for which consent is sought, the types of data that will be collected and used, the existence of the right to withdraw consent, information about the use of the data for decisions based solely on automated processing, including profiling, in accordance with Article 22(2), and if the consent relates to transfers, information regarding the possible risks of data transfers to third countries in the absence of an adequacy decision and appropriate safeguards (Article 49(1)(a)).

To ensure this information is conveyed in a manner that remains clear, concise and not unnecessarily disruptive, the use of layered and just-in-time notices should be favoured. It is important to note, however, that the initial layer contains all of the key information needed so as to render this an informed choice.

Record consents

Another requirement of the GDPR, set out in Article 7, is that controllers should "be able to demonstrate that the data subject has consented to the processing of his/her personal data".[13] One way of doing this, according to the WP29, is to "keep a record of consent statements received, so (the controller) can show how consent was obtained, when consent was obtained and the information provided to the data subject at the time and also be able to show that the data subject was informed and the controller's workflow met all relevant criteria for a valid consent".

With this guidance in mind, and from a practical standpoint, the controller should consider keeping records that will include, as a minimum, the name or other identifier of the data subject that has granted consent and make sure to also have in place the dated document and a time stamp or note of when an oral consent was granted. At the same time, thee controller should also keep the version of the consent request and privacy policy existing at the time of the consent, and the document or data capture form on the basis of which the data subject submitted his/her data. Consent receipt mechanisms can be especially helpful in generating such records automatically.

While the GDPR does not specify a time limit for how long these consents shall last, it is assumed by many that the validity of consent may degrade over time, while the WP29 has recommended "as a best practice that consent should be refreshed at appropriate intervals".

According to this recommendation, we may consider using tools that provide visibility of an organisation's various processing activities and how they change over time, allow for

13 A. Clearwater and B. Philbrook (2018) *Practical Tips for Consent under the GDPR*. Iapp.org., https://iapp.org/news/a/practical-tips-for-consent-under-the-gdpr/ (accessed 18.7.2018).

reminders to be set to refresh consent at regular intervals, and provide data subjects with the ability to directly control their consent preferences.

Data quality – data profiling

Data quality has three main components,[14] which include: data profiling, data correction, and data monitoring. Data profiling is the act of analysing your data contents, data correction is the act of correcting your data contents when it falls below your standards, while data monitoring is the ongoing act of establishing data quality standards in a set of metrics meaningful to the business, reviewing the results in a re-occurring fashion, and taking corrective action whenever the acceptable thresholds of quality are not met.

The field of data quality and data management has now become an important and currently active research domain. Numerous researchers[15] have attempted to define data quality and identify its dimensions. Traditionally, data quality has been described from the perspective of accuracy.[16] Nevertheless, much of the research has indicated that data quality should be defined beyond simple accuracy, hence researchers have identified it as encompassing multiple dimensions.

Some properties pertaining to the quality of data include that it should be correct and consistent with real data, that it should be unambiguous (i.e. it should contain only one meaning), as well as that it should be complete, in the sense that it should have no null value or missing values.

Data profiling is the systematic up-front analysis of the content of a data source, all the way from counting bytes and checking up on the most thoughtful diagnosis of whether the data can meet the high-level goals of the data warehouse.[17]

Data profiling is the process of analysing data and assessing its meaning and implications, as well as its structure, which is often considered a fundamental process for any data quality assessment initiatives. Additionally, data profiling quantifies the current data quality issues and helps establish a solid understanding of the critical areas. Furthermore, practising data profiling on an ongoing basis allows an organisation to continuously monitor its data quality performance.

Data profiling methods are classified into four categories[18], namely attribute domain constraints (column profiling), relational integrity rules, rules for historical data, and rules for state-dependent objects.

Data governance

Another necessary element is to set up a data governance agenda and business rules for the data flow. Data governance is defined as "a system of decision rights and account

14 Search Data Management (2018) *What Is Data Profiling? – Definition from WhatIs.com*. https://searchdatamanagement.techtarget.com/definition/data-profiling (accessed 18.7.2018).

15 J. Gao, P. Woodall, A. Koronios and A. Kumar Parlikad (2018) *Data Profiling Challenges in Engineering Asset Management Data – Conceptual Design for Next Generation Data Profiling Software. CUED Publications Database*. Publications.eng.cam.ac.uk., http://publications.eng.cam.ac.uk/634543/ (accessed 18.7.2018).

16 R. Wang (1998) A Product Perspective on Total Data Quality Management. *Communications of the ACM*, Vol. 41, No. 2, 58–65.

17 R. Kimball (2004) *Surprising Value of Data Profiling*. Kimballgroup.com., www.kimballgroup.com/wp-content/uploads/2012/05/DT59SurprisingValue.pdf (accessed 20.7.2018).

18 A. Maydanchik (2007) *Data Quality Assessment*. Bradley Beach, NJ: Technics Publications, 14.

abilities for information-related processes, executed according to agreed-upon models, which describe who can take what actions with what information, and when, under what circumstances, using what methods".[19] Stated more simply, data governance includes the processes and framework involved in managing data assets; for example, if organisations need to know how to define their data by understanding what "customer" means within different departments and how this should be managed overall. Because customers can have multiple touch points within an organisation, managing those interactions becomes important to ensure.[20]

With regard to the question of how long this data will be valid, you need to identify the sustainability of the data in order to set up a validity period. This is necessary since the GDPR's new storage limitation requirement means that you can only store data for as long as it is necessary for the purpose it was collected.

In answer to the question of who can access the data, there is a need to limit who can see and use consumer data to people within an organisation for whom this access is critical. For instance, social media handles might only be relevant to certain marketing and sales people, whereas the finance department does not need to have access to them. In this process, there is also a need to define certain terms, such as, what is contact data to you? Is it, for instance, only email, or is it name, email, address and phone number, or is it some third option? All these are policy decisions that a company is called to make as we move to implement the GDPR.

There is not one simple GDPR solution that can make someone compliant. Currently, there are several "black box" solutions and "magic" software packages in the market trying to address the regulation, but it must be admitted that compliance with the regulation needs to be tailor made for each company and each market.

Transforming your data and data processes is a major task, and what needs to be done is to break down data silos and integrate your personal master data into a single, complete source of trusted data, as well as apply a data governance framework.[21]

Increased fines and sanctions

The GDPR can have a substantial impact on companies that fail to comply with it. The supervisory authorities can take one or more measures listed in the GDPR, such as (a) to issue a warning or impose a temporary and/or definitive ban on the processing of personal data, and/or (b) impose a fine.

There will be two levels of fines based on the GDPR. The first fine is up to 10 million euros or 2% of the company's global annual turnover in the previous financial year, whichever is higher. The second fine is up to 20 million euros or 4% of the company's global annual turnover in the previous financial year, whichever is higher.[22] The potential fines are substantial and this is a good reason for companies to ensure compliance.

19 G. Thomas (2018) *Defining Data Governance – The Data Governance Institute*. The Data Governance Institute, www.datagovernance.com/defining-data-governance/ (accessed 20.7.2018).

20 L. Wise (2016) Understanding Data Governance. *CIO*. www.cio.com/article/3116812/business-intelligence/understanding-data-governance.html (accessed 20.7.2018).

21 D. Andersen (2018) *Solved! 4 Biggest Personal Data Challenges of the General Data Protection Regulation*. Blog.stibosystems.com, http://blog.stibosystems.com/the-four-biggest-personal-data-challenges-of-the-general-data-protection-regulation (accessed 18.7.2018).

22 See Article 83 GDPR.

The European Parliament had requested for fines to reach 100 million euros or 5% of the company's global annual turnover. The agreed fines are the compromise that was reached.

Fines for infringements will be considered on a case-by-case basis and will take a number of criteria into consideration, such as the intentional nature of the infringement, how many subjects were affected and any previous infringements by the controller or processor.

The lower level fines, up to 10 million euros or 2% of the company's global annual turnover, will be considered for infringements listed in Article 83(4) of the General Data Protection Regulation.

The following includes infringements relating to integrating data protection by design and by default; records of processing activities; cooperation with the supervising authority; security of processing data; notification of a personal data breach to the supervisory authority; communication of a personal data breach to the data subject; data protection impact assessment; prior consultation; designation, position or tasks of the data protection officer; and certification.

The higher-level fines, up to 20 million euros or 4% of the company's global annual turnover, will be considered for infringements listed in Article 83(5) of the General Data Protection Regulation.

This includes infringements relating to the basic principle for processing, including conditions for consent, lawfulness of processing, and processing of special categories of personal data, but also the rights of the data subject, as well as transfers of personal data to a recipient in a third country or an international organisation.

When determining whether to impose a fine and/or the amount to be paid as a fine, a number of factors should be taken into consideration for each individual case. These include the nature, gravity and the duration of the infringement, taking into account the nature, scope or purpose of the processing concerned, as well as the number of data subjects affected, and the level of damage suffered by them; the intentional or negligent character of the infringement; any action taken by the controller or processor to mitigate the damage suffered by data subjects, and the degree of responsibility of the controller or processor, taking into account technical and organisational measures implemented by them. Moreover, any relevant previous infringements by the controller or processor and the degree of cooperation with the supervisory authority should also be considered in order to remedy the infringement and mitigate the possible adverse effects of the infringement. The categories of personal data affected by the infringement are also relevant, as is the manner in which the infringement became known to the supervisory authority and, in particular, to what extent the controller or processor notified them of the infringement.

Where measures referred to in Article 58(2) have previously been ordered against the controller or the processor concerned regarding the same subject matter, compliance with those measures would also be a matter to take into account. Finally, adherence to approved codes of conduct pursuant to Article 40 or approved certification mechanisms pursuant to Article 42, and any other aggravating or mitigating factor applicable to the circumstances of the case, such as financial benefits gained, or losses avoided, directly or indirectly, from the infringement, are all matters that should be borne in mind.

If a controller or processor makes several infringements, the total amount of the administrative fine will not exceed the fine applicable for the most serious infringement for the same or linked processing operations.

Member States will also have the ability to apply penalties for infringements to the GDPR. Each Member State will be responsible for implementing such penalties, which must be effective, proportionate and dissuasive. In addition, and independently of these fines and penalties, individuals will have the right to claim compensation for any damage suffered as a result of violating the GDPR.

Data breach

A personal data breach means a breach of security leading to the accidental or unlawful destruction, loss, alteration and unauthorised disclosure of or access to personal data. This includes breaches that are the consequence of both accidental and deliberate causes. It also means that a breach is more than just about losing personal data.[23]

A personal data breach can be generally defined as a security incident that has affected the confidentiality, integrity and/or availability of personal data. In short, there will be a personal data breach whenever any personal data is lost, destroyed, corrupted, and/or disclosed; if someone accesses the data or passes it on without proper authorisation or if the data is made unavailable, for example, when it has been encrypted by ransomware, or accidentally lost or destroyed. The GDPR recital 87 makes it clear that when a security incident takes place, you should quickly establish whether a personal data breach has occurred and, if so, to promptly take steps to address it.

When a personal data breach has occurred, you need to establish the likelihood and severity of the resulting risk to people's rights and freedoms. If it's likely that there will be a risk then you must notify the DPA; if it is unlikely, you do not have to report it. If, however, you decide that you do not need to report the breach, you need to be able to justify this decision, so you should document it.

In assessing the risk to rights and freedoms, it is important to focus on the potential negative consequences for the individuals involved. Recital 85 of the GDPR explains that:

> A personal data breach may, if not addressed in an appropriate and timely manner, result in physical, material or non-material damage to natural persons such as loss of control over their personal data or limitation of their rights, discrimination, identity theft or fraud, financial loss, unauthorized reversal of pseudonymisation, damage to reputation, loss of confidentiality of personal data protected by professional secrecy or any other significant economic or social disadvantage to the natural person concerned.[24]

This means that a breach can have a range of adverse effects on individuals, which include emotional distress, along with physical and material damage. Some personal data breaches will not lead to risks beyond a possible inconvenience to those who need the data to do their job. Other breaches can significantly affect individuals whose personal data has been compromised, and this needs to be assessed case by case, looking at all relevant factors.

23 P. Lambert (2018) *Understanding the New European Data Protection Rules*. Boca Raton, FL: RC Press, 66.
24 See Article 85 GDPR.

If a breach is likely to result in a high risk to the rights and freedoms of individuals, the GDPR instructs you to inform those concerned directly and without undue delay, in other words, this should take place as soon as possible.

"High risk" means the threshold for informing individuals is higher than for notifying the DPA. Again, one will need to assess both the severity of the potential or actual impact on individuals as a result of a breach and the likelihood of this occurring. If the impact of the breach is more severe, the risk is higher; if the likelihood of the consequences is greater, then, again the risk is higher. In such cases, you will need to promptly inform those affected, particularly if there is a need to mitigate an immediate risk of damage to them. One of the main reasons for informing individuals is to help them take steps to protect themselves from the effects of a breach.[25]

Specifically, Article 33 of the GDPR stipulates that:

1 In the case of a personal data breach, the controller shall, without undue delay, no later than 72 hours after being aware of the incident, notify the personal data breach to the supervisory authority competent in accordance to Article 55, unless the personal data breach is unlikely to result in a risk to the rights and freedoms of natural persons. However, if the notification to the supervisory authority is not made within 72 hours, it shall be accompanied by reasons for the delay.
2 The processor shall notify the controller without undue delay after becoming aware of a personal data breach.

The notification referred to in paragraph 1 shall at least:

(a) Describe the nature of the personal data breach, including where possible, the categories and approximate number of data subjects concerned, and the categories and approximate number of personal data records concerned.
(b) Communicate the name and contact details of the data protection officer or to other contact point where more information can be obtained.
(c) Describe the likely consequences of the personal data breach.
(d) Describe the measures taken or proposed to be taken by the controller to address the personal data breach, including, where appropriate, measures to mitigate its possible adverse effects.

3 Where, and in so far as, it is not possible to provide the information at the same time, the information may be provided in phases without undue further delay.
4 The controller shall document any personal data breaches, comprising the facts relating to the personal data breach, its effects and the remedial action taken. That documentation shall enable the supervisory authority to verify compliance with this Article.[26]

Global responses

It is hoped that the new regime will take the lead not only on a European, but also on a global level,[27] and affect a change of culture when it comes to personal data protection.

25 ICO (2018) *Personal Data Breaches*. Ico.org.uk., https://ico.org.uk/for-organisations/guide-to-the-general-data-protection-regulation-gdpr/personal-data-breaches/ (accessed 20.7.2018).

26 See Article 33 GDPR.

27 In accordance with article 3 of the GDPR, the territorial scope of the Regulation applies to the activities of an establishment of a controller or a processor that takes place in the EU, but also to the activities of an establishment.

Companies will have far more awareness and sensitivity in relation to data processing, while data subjects will be more careful in terms of what information they share, for which purposes and in the context of what legal basis. At the same time, data processors will no longer find themselves in a state of quasi-immunity and will be responsible for any leakage of data that takes place under their responsibility. All of these, however, should it fall into the right hands, may – indeed – a summer make for the purposes of personal data protection. If, on the other hand, the matter is handled in a wrongful manner, this may well lead to the stifling of development. A pessimistic version of events would suggest that citizens will do little more than block processes, employees will refuse everything through their trade unions that will be receiving advice from specialist data protection lawyers, while customers will persistently seek the fulfilment of their rights, at times with the assistance of NGOs.[28] Imagine if a company were to be faced with a thousand requests for the erasure of data, coupled with corresponding requests for portability, access and correction. In this case, the company will end up having to exhaust its resources in order to deal with these requests, in fear of disproportionate fines, thus neglecting its main mission – which is development. Therefore, could it be that what we are actually currently faced with is a maximalist piece of legislation? Is there a lurking danger of paralysing the entire system? Is it not somewhat contradictory to seek something far beyond Directive 95/46/EC, even though its main objectives appear to have failed?

But what has happened so far? A sense of concern is being spread, at times, in fact, with great zeal and in the wrong direction. A characteristic example can be seen in the panic that overtook companies when they sent out a message to their entire user list regarding the granting of consent in the context of the new regulatory framework, which is something that was not, to a large extent, actually required.[29] More than a few companies spent a considerable amount of money sending such messages, rather than investing in ensuring that they are compliant with the new rules. Indeed, quite a number of companies erased a large number of their contacts, without good reason, thus losing a significant part of their clientele, and consequently, of their business activity.

Nevertheless, the new regulatory framework extends beyond the EU as a kind of quasi-global law. It is true that the period of mockery and irony on the part of American companies was followed by a period of concern and compliance. Companies outside the EU have complied or are at a stage of achieving compliance with the new regulatory framework. Japan has taken a further step by incorporating a large part of the GDPR into its national legislation. On 25 April 2018, Japan's data protection authority published draft guidelines relating to adequacy findings for international personal data transfers from Europe to Japan (Guidelines). If the Guidelines come into force in their current form, subject to the EU's adequacy decision, they will allow for personal data to be transferred from the EEA (which includes the EU, Iceland, Liechtenstein and Norway) to Japan without measures such as specific data subject consent or standard contractual clauses. These Guidelines form part of a broader effort to recognise "mutual adequacy" between the EU and Japan respectively under the incoming EU General Data Protection Regulation (GDPR) and Japan's Act on the Protection of Personal Information (APPI).

---

of a controller or a processor outside the EU, when the processing concerns data subjects who are in the EU (such as, for example, in cases of e-commerce and profiling).

28 See article 60 GDPR.

29 C. Gottlieb (2017) *The GDPR Soft Opt-In Opt-Out*. Linked in. www.linkedin.com/pulse/gdpr-soft-opt-in-opt-out-carl-gottlieb/ (accessed 20.7.2018).

But how will extraterritoriality be enforced? How will a European institution impose sanctions on a non-European entity with regard to legislation that the latter has not become a party to? Are there adequate mechanisms in existence? These questions also concern the writers of the present chapter and they will, no doubt, find their answer in practice, given that we find ourselves faced with a piece of legislation of monumental extraterritoriality.

At the same time, a new entrepreneurial activity is blossoming not only within the EU, but all around the world. The compliance of data controllers and processors constitutes an expensive developmental procedure, which has as its main aim the changing of the mentality pertaining to personal data protection. The institution of the data protection officer, as well as the need to train all those who exercise this profession, has led to the rekindling of activity amongst lawyers in that area. Data processors have begun to conclude agreements with data controllers relating to the limits of each of their responsibilities, which also stipulate that employers must inform employees regarding the management of their data and to bind them, as well as their associates, in relation to the confidentiality of data. Information on the processing of personal data has also started to become more transparent, without this necessarily meaning, however, that it satisfies all the requirements set out in the GDPR adequately.

Furthermore, there is concern that our enthusiasm for personal data protection has led to the neglect of other constitutional rights. The imperative need for the protection of personal data that has now emerged has led to a global refusal toward the provision of information. The non-protection of information is not protected equivalently to the necessity of providing the said information. There are quite a few cases where personal data protection is used in an abusive manner, as an obstacle to the fulfilment of the right to information. This is because non-protection is punishable, whereas the lack of provision of information is mostly left unchallenged. Additionally, an independent supervisory authority may impose the protection of personal data, but it cannot do so with the same ease and access to information. This is because, in the majority of cases, no such single administrative authority for the protection of personal data, as well as for the freedom of information, has been established.[30] In the spirit of what has been discussed previously, it is concluded that national authorities are not doing all that they ought to and they only do so when they change and become data protection and access to information authorities.

Lastly, concerns have been raised to the effect that the text of the GDPR itself has already started to become obsolete, due to technological progress. A characteristic example can be seen in Article 22 of the GDPR on automated individual decision-making, including profiling, which expressly stipulates that in the event of automated processing, the data subject has the right of securing human intervention on the part of the data controller, the right to express an opinion and to question the decision taken. At the same time, the right of an individual to receive information on the logic involved in the making of such a decision in the context of the assessment in question is also recognised, and it is set out, in practice, in the context of the information duties enshrined in Articles 13(2)(f) and 14(2)(g). This reasoning is not always possible, however, as the manner in

30 A classic example of authorities that carry out a dual protection function is the German supervisory authority and the corresponding one in the United Kingdom (Der Bundesbeauftragte für den Datenschutz und die Informationsfreiheit and the Information Commissioner's Officer, respectively). See F. Panagopoulou-Koutnatzi (2017) The Constitutionally Enshrined Protection Relating to Decisions on Authorizations Issued by the Hellenic Data Protection Authority (DPA) for the Granting of Data. *Administrative Trial Legal Journal*, Vol. 29, No. 3, 340–341.

which decisions are made through artificial intelligence is no longer technically known and verifiable.[31] In fact, it is often argued that the text of the Regulation is characterised by a marked disaffection toward the making of automated decisions, without making any reference to the advantages offered by the use of artificial intelligence in the decision-making process.[32] Additionally, there has been severe criticism regarding the fact that the text of the Regulation only offers protection against the making of decisions on the basis of automated processing, while it does not adequately address the issue of profiling.[33]

The all-conquering time shall be the main judge of all this. As it will pass, enthusiasm will abate and maturity will ensue. Independent authorities will also, no doubt, be decisive co-players in this journey of personal data protection. Depending on the stance that they will take, but also on how strict they will be in terms of imposing sanctions and, mainly, depending on the severity of the fines that they will issue, protection will either be intensified or eased up.

31 W. Knight (2018) There's a Big Problem with AI: Even its Creators Can't Explain How it Works. *MIT Technology Review*, www.technologyreview.com/s/604087/the-dark-secret-at-the-heart-of-ai (accessed 20.7.2018).

32 P. Gola, C. Eichler, L. Franck, and C. Klug (2017) *Datenschutz-Grundverordnung*. München: C.H. Beck.

33 See S. Schulz (2017) Art. 22, section 2. "Kapitel III. Rechte der betroffenen Person". In: P. Gola (Ed.), *Datenschutz-Grundverordnung Kommentar*. Munich: C.H. Beck. See also P. Gola (2017) Einleiting. In: P. Gola (Ed.), *Datenschutz-Grundverordnung Kommentar*. Munich: C.H. Beck.

19 Data protection in the private sector

Convergence or localisation of rights and expectations?

W. Scott Blackmer

Introduction

Twenty years ago, in the dawn of the commercial internet, Sun Microsystems cofounder Scott McNealy provocatively declared, "You have zero privacy anyway. Get over it".[1]

The quotation is famous, or notorious, but what is often forgotten is the context: McNealy's comments came just hours after rival Intel announced that it was disabling identification features of its forthcoming Pentium III chip, reacting to a storm of criticism over privacy and security risks. After McNealy's session with reporters, the director of the Bureau of Consumer Protection at the United States Federal Trade Commission promptly denounced McNealy's statement, asserting that "millions of American consumers" had expressed concerns about their privacy online and suggesting that both industry and the government meant to do something about that, on both sides of the Atlantic.

In fact, at that time the 1995 European Union's Data Protection Directive[2] had just reached its implementation date of December 1998 (although many Member States missed that deadline), with the objective of firmly establishing personal data protection as a modern human right:

> Whereas data-processing systems are designed to serve man; whereas they must, whatever the nationality or residence of natural persons, respect their fundamental rights and freedoms, notably the right to privacy, and contribute to economic and social progress, trade expansion and the well-being of individuals.
>
> (Recital 2)

The EU Data Protection Directive (Recital 1) cited the 1950 European Convention for the Protection of Human Rights and Fundamental Freedoms,[3] which commits signatories to respect the individual's "private and family life, his home and his correspondence"

1 As quoted in Wired Magazine (1999), 26 January 1999, www.wired.com/1999/01/sun-on-privacy-get-over-it/ (accessed 02.12.2018).

2 Directive 95/46/EC of the European Parliament and of the Council of 24 October 1995 on the protection of individuals with regard to the processing of personal data and on the free movement of such data, https://eur-lex.europa.eu/legal-content/EN/TXT/?uri=CELEX%3A31995L0046 (accessed 02.12.2018).

3 Convention for the Protection of Human Rights and Fundamental Freedoms, Council of Europe, as amended, CETS No. 194, www.echr.coe.int/Documents/Convention_ENG.pdf (accessed 02.12.2018).

(Article 8). This statement paralleled a provision of the Universal Declaration of Human Rights adopted by the General Assembly of the United Nations in 1948[4]:

> No one shall be subjected to arbitrary interference with his privacy, family, home or correspondence, nor to attacks upon his honour and reputation. Everyone has the right to the protection of the law against such interference or attacks.
>
> (Article 12)

The Directive was meant to safeguard this human right in the digital world, but in a manner that avoided "obstacles to flows of personal data" arising from national differences in data protection regulation, by ensuring an "equivalent" level of protection across the EU (Recital 8). As described elsewhere in this volume, that Directive has now been supplanted by the EU General Data Protection Regulation ("GDPR")[5], promising an even greater degree of uniformity across the EU and, by treaty, the European Economic Area ("EEA").

At almost the same time, the largest US state has enacted the California Consumer Privacy Act of 2018 ("California CPA" or "A.B. 375"),[6] similar to GDPR but somewhat more limited in scope. This law will take effect on 1 January 2020 and inevitably impact national business practices in the US, as have California's earlier measures regarding data breach notification[7], personal information security,[8] online privacy[9] and disclosure of third-party data sharing.[10] Other major trading nations, from China[11] to Brazil,[12] have also recently enacted sweeping data protection measures.

Thus, two decades after Mr. McNealy's "zero privacy" remark, it is fair to ask who got it right: Is information privacy becoming irrelevant, or is it an imperative for businesses and other organisations to manage data protection successfully? And is data protection an

4 Available online at www.un.org/en/universal-declaration-human-rights/ (accessed 02.12.2018).

5 Regulation (EU) 2016/679 of the European Parliament and of the Council of 27 April 2016 on the protection of natural persons with regard to the processing of personal data and on the free movement of such data, and repealing Directive 95/46/EC, https://eur-lex.europa.eu/legal-content/EN/ALL/?uri=celex%3A32016R0679 (accessed 02.12.2018).

6 Available online at https://leginfo.legislature.ca.gov/faces/billTextClient.xhtml?bill_id=201720180AB375 (accessed 02.12.2018).

7 California Civil Code sections 1798.29 and 1798.82. The California Data Breach Notification Act, originally enacted in 2002 and effective July 1, 2003, became a model for breach notification acts in all 50 US states (with some variations) by 2018.

8 California Personal Information Security law (AB 1950), Civil Code sec. 1798.81.5 (2004) (security obligations to protect the data covered by the Data Breach Notification Act, as well as health information not covered by the federal HIPAA act or other laws).

9 California Online Privacy Protection Act of 2003 (requires a website privacy policy with certain disclosures) (California Business and Professions Code sections 22575–22579).

10 California "Shine the Light" law, Civil Code sections 1798.83–1798.84, requires disclosure of third-party data sharing on request.

11 People's Republic of China, National Information Security Technology – Personal Information Security Specification, May 1, 2018, www.tc260.org.cn/upload/2018-01-24/1516799764389090333.pdf (accessed 02.12.2018); Cybersecurity Law (2016), 6 November 2016, effective 1 June 2017, Articles 40–44, www.tc260.org.cn/upload/2018-01-24/1516799764389090333.pdf (accessed 02.12.2018), (unofficial English translation available at www.newamerica.org/cybersecurity-initiative/digichina/blog/translation-cybersecurity-law-peoples-republic-china) (accessed 02.12.2018).

12 Brazil, Lei General de Proteção de Dados (Law No. 13,709 of August 14, 2018), www.dataprivacy.com.br/protecao_de_dados_pessoais.docx (accessed 02.12.2018).

example of convergence around fundamental principles of fair and lawful information practices or is it inevitably entangled in local culture and politics?

This chapter approaches these questions from the perspective of a legal practitioner advising global organisations, both businesses and nonprofits, over more than three decades and across most borders. As an advisor to general counsel and data protection officers, the author is well aware that global enterprises struggle with the diverse and changing compliance issues in this field. The challenge is to find solutions that are meaningful and understandable to the affected individuals and also workable for the organisations that must implement them. In most cases, those solutions should presumably not differ greatly from one country to another, if information privacy is really a human right and not a first-world luxury. And yet, in practice, there is considerable variation and resulting confusion, especially in cross-border applications. There is a price to pay for this complexity, both for companies and consumers. Could we do better?

Why data protection in the private sector matters

For all of our legitimate concerns about setting appropriate controls on the uses of personal information by government authorities, it remains true that most of the collection, use and sharing of personal information is not by "Big Brother" but by an assortment of "little brothers", largely in the private sector. They are the ones who deal with individuals in a wide variety of everyday transactions. More than two-thirds of the world's population carry mobile devices; that share is projected to rise to three-quarters by 2020.[13] It is estimated that just over half of the world's population is connected to the Internet.[14] As our communications, personal relationships, work, study, entertainment, browsing, movements, comments, purchases, reading, photos, music, videos, preferences, health and habits are increasingly recorded, shared and tracked online, an array of enterprises and organisations gradually build up profiles of us with more or less sophistication. These are reflected in mailing lists and transactional databases, in marketing analytics shared by software-driven advertising networks, and ultimately in deep pools of "big data" plumbed by artificial intelligence.

Commercial advertisers are not alone in seeking information about us, in their quest to find the most likely audience and optimise their marketing efforts. Our profiles are of interest as well to potential employers and business partners, political parties and candidates, advocacy groups, charities and other nonprofits, sometimes to fraudsters and other criminals.

Our dilemma as individuals is that, with the exception of the last category, we typically *want* to have some contact with at least some of these parties, but we want also to have some control over the type and frequency of messages we receive and the kinds of information these people have about us and what they are allowed to do with it. For that to happen, we need some information about who they are and how they operate, and we need to understand the rules that apply and how to enforce those rules.

The "zero privacy" conclusion accepts that this is impracticable: it posits that we need to get accustomed to swimming in an ocean of big data, where we cannot know all the possible data users and their purposes, much less police them. But an alternative is convergence around accepted norms of respect for information privacy, with accountability

13 R. Hollander (2017) Two-Thirds of the World's Population Are Now Connected by Mobile Devices. *Business Insider*, 19 September, www.businessinsider.com/world-population-mobile-devices-2017-9 (accessed 02.12.2018).

14 Miniwatts Marketing Group (2018) Internet World Stats, Usage and Population Statistics (June 30), www.internetworldstats.com/stats.htm (accessed 02.12.2018).

for abuses in both the private and public sectors. Convergence is important as well for the organisations that operate online or in multiple jurisdictions, as it quickly becomes impractical to segregate data, notices, options and procedures in multiple fashions based on the residence on the individual and the location of the database.

The case for convergence

The UN and Council of Europe declarations cited previously reflect a post-war interest in privacy as a human right following the spread of totalitarian governments in the twentieth century and the horrors of the Second World War and military occupation of many countries. Notably, both documents refer to privacy of "correspondence". As early as 1789, the Fourth Amendment to the United States Constitution declared the people's right "to be secure in their persons, houses, papers, and effects", laying the foundation for later legislation and jurisprudence concerning electronic records and messages. This fundamental (but not absolute) right required definition, however, and it has taken time to develop consensus views of what it entails.

In the 1890s, American lawyers Samuel Warren and Louis Brandeis (the future Supreme Court justice) articulated an Anglo-American privacy tort and defined privacy most simply as a person's "right to be left alone".[15] Columbia University Professor Alan Westin was an early advocate for what came to be called "information self-determination", arguing in 1967 that privacy includes the concept that individuals may choose freely "under what circumstances and to what extent they will expose themselves, their attitude and their behaviour to others".[16] He participated in Congressional hearings that led to one of the first major legal efforts in the US to tackle digital privacy, the 1970 Fair Credit Reporting Act ("FCRA"),[17] amending US federal consumer protection law to regulate the consumer reporting industry. FCRA, which has been amended several times over the decades, was a response to inadequate transparency into commercial databases affecting individuals' ability to obtain consumer credit, home mortgages, or employment. FCRA establishes standards for the purposes of collection, data quality, data sharing, and security, and it requires notices to individuals when information from a consumer reporting agency is used in making an adverse determination, giving individuals rights to access the information and submit corrections and objections. It has served as a model for consumer reporting regulation in other countries.

Such principles also soon found their way into the "Code of Fair Information Practice" included in the US Privacy Act of 1974.[18] This landmark act regulated the collection, storage, use and sharing of personally identifiable information by US federal government agencies. It became a model for legislation at the state level and in other countries, often as part of a "freedom of information act" defining public access to government data.

Also in 1970, the German state of Hesse adopted the first comprehensive data protection act in the world,[19] followed by other German states and ultimately the German federal legislature in 1977.[20] These acts incorporated principles similar to those in the US sectoral

15 Samuel Warren and Louis Brandeis (1890) The Right to Privacy. *Harvard Law Review*, Vol. 4, 193–220.

16 Alan F. Westin 1967. *Privacy and Freedom*. New York: Atheneum, 7.

17 15 U.S. Code sec. 1681.

18 5 U.S. Code sec. 552a.

19 Datenschutzgesetz (7 October 1970), Hessiches Gesetz-und Verordnungsblatt 1.

20 Gesetz zum Missbrauch personenbezogener Daten bei der Datenverarbeitung (27 January 1977), BGBL I at 201.

data privacy legislation such as purpose limitation, data quality, transparency, security and accountability. Sweden's Data Act of 1973[21] gained the distinction of becoming the earliest *national* data protection law, with similar principles but a more bureaucratic approach than the German acts, initially requiring the licencing of databases by a national Data Inspectorate. France enacted a comprehensive data protection law in 1978[22] along similar principles, with a system of full or simplified declarations. Other European countries followed in the course of the next few years. But persistent national differences resulted in compliance difficulties for international business. The author recalls the pre-Directive era when the French data protection authority CNIL, for example, routinely required prior authorisations to transfer data to the United Kingdom, because CNIL did not recognise equivalent protection in the UK under the Data Protection Act 1984.[23]

The movement toward information privacy protections on both sides of the Atlantic, and accompanying concerns arising from variations in national legislation, prompted the Organisation for Economic Cooperation and Development ("OECD") to draft the 1980 Guidelines on the Protection of Privacy and Transborder Flows of Personal Data[24] (revised in 2013) (the "OECD Guidelines"),[25] reflecting an international consensus on fundamental data protection principles as well as the value of promoting transborder information flows. The Guidelines have been influential in the drafting of national and sub-national legislation, given the composition of the OECD (thirty-four developed countries, with participation by the European Commission as well). The principles can be summarised as follows:

- **Collection limitation** (data should be limited, obtained by fair and lawful means, and, where appropriate, with "the knowledge or consent of the data subject");
- **Data quality** (data should be relevant to the purposes for which they are used, accurate, complete and up to date);
- **Purpose specification** (purposes should be specified when collected and when changed);
- **Use limitation** (data should not be used or disclosed for other purposes except with consent or legal authority);
- **Security measures** should reasonably safeguard personal data;
- **Openness principle**: a general policy of openness should apply, disclosing data practices and policies as well as the identity and location of the data controller;
- **Individual participation**: individuals should have the right to confirm whether the data controller has data relating to him or her, to have the data communicated in a reasonable time at a reasonable charge, in an intelligible form, to challenge data, and to have successfully challenged data erased or rectified; and
- **Accountability**: a data controller should be accountable for complying with measures to give effect to these principles.

21 Datalag (1973), https://open.karnovgroup.se/yttrandefrihet-mm/SFS1973-0289, p.289 (accessed 02.12.2018).

22 Loi informatique et libertés, Act. No. 78–17 of 6 January 1978, (English) www.cnil.fr/sites/default/files/typo/document/Act78-17VA.pdf (accessed 02.12.2018).

23 www.legislation.gov.uk/ukpga/1984/35/pdfs/ukpga_19840035_en.pdf (accessed 02.12.2018) See P. Schwartz (1995) European Data Protection Law and Restrictions on International Data Flows. *Iowa Law Review*, Vol. 80, 471, https://scholarship.law.berkeley.edu/cgi/viewcontent.cgi?article=2571&context=facpubs (accessed 02.12.2018).

24 Available online at www.oecd.org/internet/ieconomy/oecdguidelinesontheprotectionofprivacyandtransborderflowsofpersonaldata.htm (accessed 02.12.2018).

25 Available online at www.oecd.org/internet/ieconomy/privacy-guidelines.htm (accessed 02.12.2018).

The OECD Guidelines also recommend that Member countries "avoid creating, in the name of privacy protection, unjustified obstacles to transborder flows of personal data".

The 2013 revision adds a section for data controllers on "implementing accountability" including a privacy management programme with a privacy risk assessment, oversight mechanisms, plans for responding to inquiries and incidents, ongoing monitoring, and notice of security breaches to relevant authorities and affected data subjects.

Shortly after the publication of the OECD Guidelines, the Council of Europe promulgated the 1981 Convention for the Protection of Individuals with regard to Automatic Processing of Personal Data ("Convention 108").[26] The Convention is consistent with the principles of the OECD Guidelines, but it is a more detailed instrument and binding on signatories. It also has since been amended, most recently in May 2018.[27] Convention 108 remains the only data protection convention open to any country for accession by ratifying and adopting national legislation. According to the Council of Europe, some fifty-four countries have done so to date.[28] The "Modernized Convention" resulting from recent amendments was deliberately designed to be consistent with the EU GDPR. The GDPR is more detailed and prescriptive, and the Convention still simply articulates principles that the signatories are responsible for implementing in their national legal regimes. But the Modernised Convention adds or emphasises principles tracking those of the GDPR, such as privacy by design, legal bases for processing, additional criteria for consent, the principle of proportionality, the addition of genetic and biometric data to the list of sensitive data categories, notification of security breaches, data subject rights parallel to those under GDPR, and privacy impact assessments.

Convention 108 is a strong example of convergence. A country should be able to ratify the Convention, especially in its modernised form, with implementing legislation that would meet the EU "adequacy test" under GDPR Article 45(1). Indeed, a country could adopt separate pieces of legislation drawing on both Convention 108 and the EU Directive or GDPR with overlapping coverage but without obvious conflicts (Russia is an example).[29]

The EU moved toward even greater harmonisation within the internal market by adopting the EU Data Protection Directive in 1995, as mentioned previously. At the same time, the Federal Trade Commission ("FTC") assumed the role of policing privacy abuses in the digital economy in the US, asserting its enforcement powers under the Federal Trade Commission Act[30] to impose substantial fines and orders on companies that violated their own privacy terms, engaged in abusive data practices, or failed to secure personal information against significant data breaches. State authorities in the US have also imposed sanctions under similar state legislation against "unfair or deceptive practices".

26 COE ETS 108, available online at www.coe.int/en/web/conventions/full-list/-/conventions/treaty/108. (accessed 02.12.2018).

27 Protocol amending the Convention for the Protection of Individuals with regard to the Automated Processing of Personal Data, CM(2018)2-final (18 May 2018), https://search.coe.int/cm/Pages/result_details.aspx?ObjectId=090000168089ff4e (accessed 02.12.2018).

28 See table at www.coe.int/en/web/conventions/full-list/-/conventions/treaty/108/signatures?desktop=true (accessed 02.12.2018).

29 See Federal Law No. 149-FZ on Information, Information Technologies and Data Protection 2006 (Data Protection Act) (English version, www.wipo.int/wipolex/en/text.jsp?file_id=371388) (accessed 02.12.2018) and Federal Law No. 152-FZ on Personal Data 2006 (Personal Data Protection Act) (English version, https://iapp.org/media/pdf/knowledge_center/Russian_Federal_Law_on_Personal_Data.pdf) (accessed 02.12.2018).

30 Section 5(a) of the Federal Trade Commission Act (15 USC sec. 45) broadly prohibits "unfair or deceptive acts or practices in or affecting commerce".

In 1998, the FTC issued Privacy Online: A Report to Congress,[31] synthesising five "fair information practice principles" from earlier US legislation, the OECD Guidelines, and its own enforcement policies. These principles were formulated as notice/awareness, choice/consent, access/participation, integrity/security, and enforcement/redress. These principles have guided the FTC and other federal and state agencies in privacy enforcement actions, and they have been used in drafting privacy legislation and in negotiations over international instruments.

The US continued to adopt more sectoral privacy measures, prominently covering personal health information[32] and financial data[33]. These are highly detailed regulatory regimes, and although each shows the influence of the FTC's fair information practice principles, they each have a different scope and substantially different procedures, and even different terminology, to the extent that practitioners tend to specialise in one or the other but not both. Clearly, lawmakers and regulators were reacting to specific problems in highly regulated industries; there is little sense of a coherent approach to information privacy as the FTC conceived or on the European model, and as a result it may be questioned whether consumers grasp the often obscure and technical privacy notices they routinely receive under these laws.[34]

While the US and some other countries have taken a sectoral approach to information privacy (perhaps California's new Personal Privacy Act signals a change in that tradition in the US), the trend in much of the world has been to follow the European path toward comprehensive data protection legislation. Some countries (like Switzerland[35] and Argentina[36]) heavily modelled their laws on the EU Directive, while others (like Canada[37] and Japan[38]) based theirs on the OECD Guidelines but were influenced by the Directive. Since the adoption of the GDPR, many of these countries are considering updating their laws to conform more closely to the current EU model. Many overseas territories and dependencies of EU members have already done so or have implementing bills in process, and several countries in and near Europe (such as Switzerland, Andorra, Monaco, Israel and Morocco) have adopted or are debating amendments. Thus, while the GDPR

31 Available online at www.ftc.gov/sites/default/files/documents/reports/privacy-online-report-congress/priv-23a.pdf (accessed 02.12.2018).

32 US Department of Health and Human Services (HHS) privacy regulations under the Health Insurance Portability and Accountability Act (HIPAA), 45 CFR Parts 160, 162, and 164, www.hhs.gov/sites/default/files/ocr/privacy/hipaa/administrative/combined/hipaa-simplification-201303.pdf (accessed 02.12.2018).

33 US Gramm-Leach-Bliley Financial Modernization Act ("GLBA"), 15 U.S. Code sections 6801–6809, and the privacy and security regulations promulgated under GLBA by the US federal financial supervisory bodies and the Federal Trade Commission, including provisions designed to curtail identity theft (see FTC Financial Information Safeguards Rule at www.ftc.gov/tips-advice/business-center/privacy-and-security/gramm-leach-bliley-act) (accessed 02.12.2018).

34 *See, e.g.*, the Electronic Information Privacy Center article on GLBA posted at www.epic.org/privacy/glba/ (accessed 02.12.2018).

35 Switzerland, Federal Data Protection Act, www.admin.ch/opc/de/classified-compilation/19920153/index.html (accessed 02.12.2018).

36 Argentina, Personal Data Protection Act (2000), English version, http://unpan1.un.org/intradoc/groups/public/documents/un-dpadm/unpan044147.pdf (accessed 02.12.2018)

37 Canada, Personal Information Privacy and Electronic Documents Act ("PIPEDA") (2000), https://laws-lois.justice.gc.ca/eng/acts/P-8.6/index.html (accessed 02.12.2018).

38 Japan, Act on the Protection of Personal Information (2003); Amended Act on the Protection of Personal Information (2016, effective May 30, 2017), English version, www.ppc.go.jp/files/pdf/Act_on_the_Protection_of_Personal_Information.pdf (accessed 02.12.2018).

applies directly to the twenty-eight EU Member States and three additional EEA countries, retailers and shippers at the time of this writing often display the GDPR version of their websites and forms to consumers in as many as forty-eight jurisdictions, on the assumption that substantially the same rules apply (or soon will). Other countries even farther afield, including Russia, Canada, Mexico and Argentina, are openly considering GDPR-inspired amendments.

Clearly, the nation-state is not withering on the vine when it comes to privacy regulation online. However, while the European model of a comprehensive rather than sectoral approach to personal information protection has become dominant, it is notable that some of the features of European data protection have not been universally emulated. Other countries have not adopted the model of registering data controllers or databases (but this has now also disappeared in Europe with GDPR, except for "prior consultation" in the case of particularly sensitive operations). Outside Europe it is also rare to see special treatment of "automated decision making", and many countries do not make a distinction as the EU does for defined classes of "sensitive" data. Many jurisdictions outside Europe make pragmatic exceptions for business contact details and publicly available information, while the EU does not. And it remains to be seen whether the newer features of the GDPR, such as the right of erasure, data protection officers and data protection impact assessments, and security breach notifications, will become standard in newer data protection laws outside Europe.

The European model has been closely followed in many African and Latin American countries, especially those with close trade ties to Europe,[39] but it is less influential in the Asia-Pacific region. The data privacy laws of China, Australia, New Zealand, Japan, Taiwan, Singapore and the Republic of Korea, to take leading examples, all differ markedly from each other and from the EU model in scope, rights, obligations, procedures and remedies, even though they are based on some of the same basic principles.

The twenty-one member economies of the Asia-Pacific Economic Cooperation group ("APEC") produced a 2005 APEC Privacy Framework, updated in 2015,[40] based on the OECD Guidelines but "with due consideration for the different legal features and context of the APEC region". There is, for example, more emphasis on proportionality (giving weight to the burden on the controller, information already made public, obstructions to data flows and trade, and derogations to protect national interests) and the principle of preventing any misuse of data that could harm the individual. The APEC Framework is a voluntary model for national legislation, and the 2015 version includes a system for national and corporate participation in Cross-Border Privacy Rules ("CBPRs"), under which participating companies can be assessed as compliant and subject to a dispute resolution procedure, similar to the US-EU Privacy Shield programme under the EU Data Protection Directive and now GDPR.[41] The US, Canada, Mexico, Japan, Singapore and the Republic of Korea are already participating. This is a potentially useful solution for

39 *See, e.g.,* Mexico (2010) Ley Federal de Protección de Datos Personales en Posesión de los Particulares (5 July), www.diputados.gob.mx/LeyesBiblio/pdf/LFPDPPP.pdf (accessed 02.12.2018); Morocco, Law No. 09–08 of 18 February 2009 relating to the protection of individuals with respect to the processing of personal data, www.egov.ma/sites/default/files/Loi%20n%C2%B009-08_Protection%20Donn%C3%A9es%20Personnelles.pdf (accessed 02.12.2018).

40 APEC Privacy Framework (2015), www.apec.org/Publications/2017/08/APEC-Privacy-Framework-(2015) (accessed 02.12.2018).

41 See GDPR Art. 45(9); Commission Implementing Decision (EU) 2016/1250 of 12 July 2016, https://eur-lex.europa.eu/legal-content/EN/TXT/?uri=uriserv%3AOJ.L_.2016.207.01.0001.01.ENG&toc=OJ%3AL%3A2016%3A207%3AFULL. (accessed 02.12.2018).

companies doing business regionally, where privacy laws are likely to remain diverse but a corporate group can offer a single, comprehensible privacy promise backed by an independent dispute resolution service.

Persistent divergence

As is evident from the preceding discussion, data protection laws are proliferating, but they are not all the same. There is substantial convergence around some fundamental principles, but there is enough variation in coverage and detail to create real problems for global operators and to keep consumers from feeling confident about the rules that apply in cross-border transactions.

Even the assumption that the GDPR brings uniformity in Europe is not wholly accurate. Recital 10 states that the Regulation "provides a margin of manoeuvre for Member States to specify its rules". Member States can specify additional rules for employee data, for example, as discussed further below (Article 88), and select the age for parental consent to process data about children, between ages thirteen and sixteen (Article 8). Member States can control how their official identifiers are used (Article 87) and introduce additional conditions for handling biometric, genetic, or health data (Article 9(4)) and background checks relating to criminal history and related security measures (Article 10). The national governments or data protection supervisory authorities are developing their own lists of activities that do or do not require data protection impact assessments or prior consultation (Articles 35 and 36), and of course those lists differ from one authority to another. There will certainly be other areas of potentially problematic differences in rules and interpretation, as there were under the Directive. GDPR provides, fortunately, for a lead supervisory authority in the case of operations in multiple EU countries (Article 60), and a "consistency mechanism" that may help avoid intractable differences that prove to be a real obstacle to cross-border operations over time (Article 63). These are thoughtful provisions, and it is to be hoped that they will be effective in practice. But it is clear that even GDPR will not produce a single, uniform data protection regime in the EU/EEA and in the other jurisdictions that echo GDPR; differences will persist.

Outside Europe, of course, the differences are more pronounced. A common question in practice is how to word a website privacy policy and structure an email marketing campaign, a website form, a mobile app, a subscription, or a purchase transaction when users from multiple countries can be anticipated. They often bring with them different rules and expectations. We have to answer a whole string of questions, and the answers may differ by country. Are we subject to the jurisdiction of their country's laws? Must we communicate with them in their native language? How are we required to ascertain their age and obtain parental consent? What disclosures must be made to them, where and when? What options must be presented, and how? How must we document the notices and choices? Is there anything special we have to do to safeguard their data? Is there a time limit to their consent or our ability to communicate with them? Are there limitations on the content of our communications with them? What information can we share with third parties? How do we handle (and document) subsequent requests from the individuals for access, corrections, deletion, etc.? How long can we keep the individual's data if we don't hear from them again? And do we really want to handle each of those issues differently for different subsets of customers or prospective customers?

These issues demonstrate the value of convergence, and the burden of divergence, to a global enterprise. The cost of complying with an additional regime may prove to be a barrier to entry into a new market, or an incentive to leave a market where a firm is not well established. As GDPR raised the bar for data protection compliance (with stricter requirements, for example, for consent, breach notification, data protection impact assessments, and the right of erasure), some non-European companies chose to leave the European market or not to enter it.[42] Others firmly entrenched in Europe, decided to apply GDPR procedures across the board rather than maintain parallel systems or explain to non-European customers why, for example, they could not honour their requests to delete data. This is an example of how convergence may occur within a global enterprise, for efficiency or to enhance its reputation, even when the various legal regimes in which it operates remain different. Still others, however, chose to maintain separate databases or tag data by origin, because they did not want to assume the burden of complying with GDPR rules for a majority of their customers who did not reside in the EU/EEA. For many of these clients the decisive factors were the uncertainly over new and still-evolving GDPR rules, as well as the possibility of litigation over promises to meet GDPR standards that were not imposed by law.

Workplace privacy

There is arguably even less uniformity in the application of data protection principles to individuals as employees than as consumers. Employment law is still strongly localised, even though a growing number of people work online or travel across borders in their employment. Employment law, anti-discrimination laws, immigration regulations, tax laws, occupational health and safety regulations, and other regulatory regimes often impose requirements or conditions for the collection and reporting of personal data concerning employees. In a federal system such as the United States, India, Brazil or Australia, such laws exist at federal, state and local levels and thus vary somewhat from one workplace to another within the same country. In addition, collective bargaining agreements or works council opinions sometimes address data privacy issues such as outsourcing or centralising certain human resources functions, the content of personnel directories and performance evaluations, automated performance monitoring, email surveillance, business use of personal smartphones, the deployment of closed-circuit television security cameras, geolocation using RFID tags in security badges, and acceptable use policies for personal use of company computers and telephones. Some labour agreements may apply by default across an entire industry sector or job category in a given country.

In Europe, Article 88 of the GDPR expressly allows Member States to provide "more specific rules to ensure the protection of the rights and freedoms in respect of the processing of employees' personal data in the employment context", mentioning in particular data processing for the purposes of recruitment, the performance of employment contracts, obligations under collective bargaining agreements, business management and planning, equality and diversity, health and safety, the protection of employer's and customer's property, employment benefits, and termination – a fairly inclusive list of employment-related issues! Article 88 directs Member States to adopt rules with safeguards that protect the data subject and ensure "transparency of processing", particularly with respect to data transfers within a group of undertakings and monitoring systems at the workplace. It also requires Member States to notify the European Commission concerning the "more

42 *See, e.g.,* I. Kottosová (2018) These Companies Are Getting Killed by GDPR. *CNN Business* (11 May), https://money.cnn.com/2018/05/11/technology/gdpr-tech-companies-losers/index.html (accessed 02.12.2018).

specific rules" that govern employee personal data. Recital 155 points out that these rules might derive from collective agreements or "works agreements" as well as from legislation. It is not at all clear in practice how thoroughly such agreements will be identified and notified to the European Commission as "more specific rules"; the Member States are still struggling to complete their official GDPR implementing measures.

Notably, the Canadian federal PIPEDA legislation does not apply to employee information except in federally regulated organisations such as banks, airlines, and telecommunications and broadcasting companies.[43] Thus, employee information protection issues are generally left to the provinces and territories to regulate. Some have done so comprehensively (Alberta, British Columbia, Quebec), while others have done so only for health information.[44]

Global enterprises continue to look for management efficiency and cost savings by centralising or outsourcing recruiting, payroll, benefits and certain human resources functions, and today much of that can be done online in a cloud-computing environment. That is especially efficient for smaller offices or branches. For such applications it is problematic to deal with divergent privacy and security requirements, so wherever possible the employer should standardise on a minimum set of data and a strong security protocol that satisfies all relevant privacy regimes. It is also usually possible to draft general employee privacy notices that cover all of the employer's legal requirements and legitimate interests for data, leaving consent for specific forms related to optional programmes such as employee benefits for which the individual employee is qualified. The other issue for employers, which is not faced in the consumer context, is the need to consult in some instances with employee representatives (a works council or trade union) before implementing a new data processing operation that affects employees. There may be sensitivities about losing local jobs, but there may also simply be mistrust about seeing personal data sent to another country for processing. If management cannot allay those misgivings, it may decide to accept the higher cost of localising processing.

Security, leaks and remedies

One aspect of convergence in data protection law is a trend toward more prescriptive security provisions, particularly for security breach notification, and for more emphasis on remedies. On the whole, this tends to cause data protection to be taken more seriously, although there is still great variety in procedures and remedies and therefore little predictability.

An unprotected right is largely meaningless, and there are unfortunately many instances, in the long history of privacy law, of solemn pronouncements in charters and constitutions followed by long periods of silence, with no implementing laws or jurisprudence, and of legislation without effective remedies. Perhaps this is partly because privacy intrusions often cause anxiety or embarrassment rather than measurable economic injury. It is usually difficult for individuals to prove, for example, that they suffered losses as a result of a particular data breach. The hackers are seldom caught; fraudulent charges are usually reversed. In a serious US incident, the merchant or card company might offer the victims a new bankcard and free credit monitoring service for a period of time, to protect against renewed fraudulent charges. The incidents are costly to the merchants and financial

43 PIPEDA Part 1, sec. 4(1)(b); sec. 2(1) ("federal work, undertaking or business" defined).

44 *See* Office of the Privacy Commissioner of Canada website, www.priv.gc.ca/en/about-the-opc/what-we-do/provincial-and-territorial-collaboration/provincial-and-territorial-privacy-laws-and-oversight/ (accessed 02.12.2018).

institutions involved,[45] and they presumably pass the costs on in the marketplace as best they can. The individuals are frustrated but often unable to point to specific losses.

The FTC has attracted attention to privacy and security best practices in the US by regularly bringing enforcement actions for "unfair and deceptive practices", including poor security as well as broken promises and covert practices, and imposing not only fines but "consent orders" involving detailed security requirements and multi-year supervision of corporate privacy practices. According to the FTC's Privacy and Data Security Update: 2017,[46] the FTC has brought over 500 consumer privacy enforcement actions. Similar actions are brought as well by authorities at the state level, sometimes coordinated with each other or with the FTC. These have probably had an effect on focusing management in many companies on privacy and security governance priorities.

The US HIPAA and GLBA laws, covering health and financial records, respectively, generated detailed security as well as privacy regulations, and the FCRA (covering consumer reports) is also accompanied by security requirements including quite detailed instructions on how to thoroughly dispose of storage media when data are no longer needed. GDPR has more to say about security than the Directive did (see Article 32), and it is also likely that the European Data Protection Board may approve more detailed security codes or guidelines over time (see Article 40). Some of the newer data protection measures in other jurisdictions are also more prescriptive and standards-based and similarly contemplate further guidance.[47] This is in some ways helpful, but of course if the prescriptions differ it will be difficult to comply with all of them simultaneously.

Perhaps the best advice for a global enterprise for security planning is to make use of global security standards such as ISO 27001 if possible, as these are likely to be broadly accepted and also meet the criteria of "reasonable and appropriate" safeguards under older or more loosely drafted privacy instruments or general negligence tests.

Fines and orders may be imposed when organisations fail to abide by their obligations under the applicable laws, but remedies for affected individuals remain difficult. In the case of some sectoral privacy laws, such as the US Fair Credit Reporting Act and the HIPAA law governing the privacy of health records, both mentioned previously, the law avoids the difficulty of proving compensatory damages by providing for statutory damages. This is typically a fixed amount per violation, with a cap per incident, so that a prohibited marketing mailing to an entire customer list, for example, could add up to a costly mistake for the company. Combined with the class action option in US litigation, these can be powerful incentives. California also has a law providing statutory damages for the "willful and knowing release of confidential information"[48] or for the "negligent release of confidential information".[49]

45 *See, e.g.*, T. Armerding (2018) The 17 Biggest Data Breaches of the 21st Century. *CSO* (January 26), www.csoonline.com/article/2130877/data-breach/the-biggest-data-breaches-of-the-21st-century.html (accessed 02.12.2018).

46 Available at www.ftc.gov/system/files/documents/reports/privacy-data-security-update-2017-overview-commissions-enforcement-policy-initiatives-consumer/privacy_and_data_security_update_2017.pdf (accessed 02.12.2018).

47 *See, e.g.*, India, the Information Technology (Reasonable Security Practices and Procedures and Sensitive Personal Data or Information) Rules, 2011, www.wipo.int/edocs/lexdocs/laws/en/in/in098en.pdf (accessed 02.12.2018), which mandate the use of ISO 27001 or other widely accepted international security standards to protect biometrics, passwords, and other specified "sensitive" categories of personal data; and Mexico, where the Mexican federal data protection law, cited previously, contemplates further guidance on security issues from a federal agency, the Institute for Access to Information and Data Protection.

48 California, Lanterman Petris Short Act, Welfare & Institutions Code sec. 5330(a) (USD 10,000 or three times actual damages).

49 Ibid., sec. 5330(b) (USD 1,000 plus actual damages).

In Europe, after enduring decades of criticism for anaemic enforcement in many countries under the Directive, data protection supervisory authorities suddenly have teeth. As detailed elsewhere in this volume, GDPR expands their investigative powers as well as the potential sanctions for violations, including penalties of up to 4% of gross worldwide turnover or EUR 20 million, whichever is higher (Article 83). For individuals, GDPR offers the right to pursue administrative or judicial remedies in the country where he or she resides, including claims for compensation for "material or non-material damage" (Article 82), and optionally to be represented by a non-profit advocacy organisation (Article 80)(1). Member States can choose to allow such groups to bring complaints on their own before the supervisory authority (Article 80(2)); Germany, for example, has done so in its GDPR implementing legislation.[50]

As the stakes rise, in Europe, in the US, and elsewhere, presumably organisations should view data protection as an important element of reputation and risk management, as well as an opportunity to distinguish themselves among peer enterprises in an area that matters more and more to consumers.

GDPR has also, for the first time, provided procedures for security breach notification to the authorities (within 72 hours!) if there is a likely risk to data subjects and, in consultation with the authorities, determine whether to notify the affected individuals (Articles 33–34). As noted previously, security breach notification for certain categories of personal data has long been a requirement in the US, starting with California and expanding to the other states since 2003. The GDPR approach is more similar, however, to breach notification amendments that came into effect in Canada[51] and Australia[52] in 2018, because of their broader application to personally identifiable information and the requirement to notify the privacy authorities (where there is a risk of "significant harm" [Canada] or "serious harm" [Australia]). The Mexican federal data protection law, cited previously, similarly requires prompt notice to affected individuals if a breach "materially" affects them.

For a multinational enterprise it is clearly important to have a security incident response team pre-designated, with an action plan and an understanding of what must be done in each jurisdiction, as the standards and requirements vary but the fuse is short. This is the aspect of data protection compliance that is highly visible, requires the quickest response, and also will not likely converge to a single solution.

Data localisation

A disturbing trend, from the perspective of international businesses and nonprofits, is the advent of data localisation laws requiring the local processing and storage of personal data or making it difficult to transfer data abroad.

The EU GDPR restrictions on transborder data flows (which are essentially unchanged from those of the Directive) are discussed elsewhere, but they do not force data localisation. Data controllers in the EU/EEA are able to transfer data abroad based on an

50 Gesetz zur Anpassung des Datenschutzrechts an die Verordnung (EU) 2016/679 und zur Umsetzung der Richtlinie (EU) 2016/680, www.bundesrat.de/SharedDocs/beratungsvorgaenge/2018/0401-0500/0430-18.html (accessed 02.12.2018).

51 Canada, Digital Privacy Act (2015), https://laws-lois.justice.gc.ca/eng/annualstatutes/2015_32/page-1.html (accessed 02.12.2018).

52 Australia, Privacy Amendment (Notifiable Data Breaches) Act 2017, Notifiable Data Breaches Scheme, www.oaic.gov.au/privacy-law/privacy-act/notifiable-data-breaches-scheme. (accessed 02.12.2018).

adequacy decision or subject to appropriate safeguards (such as approved contract clauses) or a derogation (such as consent, contract fulfilment, or an emergency) (Articles 45–49).

Of greater concern is the Russian Data Protection Act, Act No. 152 FZ, as amended in 2014 (effective September 2015) to require personal data operators to store and process personal data of Russian individuals in Russia, with some exceptions. The federal communications agency Roskomnadzor is authorised to keep a list of those in breach of this obligation and block their websites that handle Russian data. LinkedIn, owned by Microsoft and with six million Russian users, was blocked under this law in 2017. It appears that it is acceptable to record a copy of the data abroad, as long as the operator complies with transborder data transfer rules (which generally require consent).

China's Cybersecurity Law, mentioned previously, which came into effect in June 2017, requires "critical information infrastructure" ("CII") providers to store personal information and "important data" in China, unless their business requires them to store the data abroad and they have obtained a security assessment by regulators. The law defines critical information infrastructure as services that may endanger national security or the public interest if they fail or if their data leaks. Draft implementation regulations list twenty-seven types of data under this category, including financial, infrastructure-related, and health data. Unofficially, there are also indications that the data transfer restrictions may be extended to "network operators", which have been defined so broadly as to include private networks within a corporate group. This is an area where uncertainty continues to seriously affect business planning by foreign companies.

Other personal data localisation laws are more limited in scope, covering, for example, health records (Australia[53]), telecommunications metadata (Germany[54]), or online services (Vietnam[55]), or public services (Indonesia[56]).

Data localisation laws are often presented as efforts to protect citizens' privacy from foreign criminals and spies. But they are largely ineffective for those purposes, because security measures can be deployed wherever the data reside, and local data centres can just as easily be compromised by poor security. Critics speculate that the motivation for such laws is more likely trade protectionism (to bring technology jobs and investment to the country), or, more ominously, to make it easier for the local government to access the data itself.[57] In any case, forced data localisation runs counter to economic and technical efficiency in allowing organisations to find the most economical and technically viable way to structure their data processing and use distributed or cloud computing where there

53 Australia, Personally Controlled Electronic Health Records Act 2012, www.legislation.gov.au/Details/C2012A00063 (accessed 02.12.2018).

54 Germany, amendments to telecommunications act, www.gesetze-im-internet.de/tkg_2004/__113b.html (accessed 02.12.2018).

55 Vietnam, *e.g.*, Cybersecurity Law (2018, effective 1 January 2019) (online service providers must open office in Vietnam and store customer information there); see article on the law and draft implementing decree at https://blogs.duanemorris.com/vietnam/tag/data-localization/ (accessed 02.12.2018).

56 Indonesia, Regulation 82 of 2012 on Electronic System and Transaction Operation (electronic systems for public service providers are required to process protected private data only in data centers and disaster recovery centers located in Indonesia; a proposed amendment would limit this to "strategic data"), available online in English at www.flevin.com/id/lgso/translations/JICA%20Mirror/english/4902_PP_82_2012_e.html (accessed 02.12.2018).

57 *See, e.g.*, J. Panday (2017) Rising Demands for Data Localization a Response to Weak Data Protection Mechanisms. Electronic Frontier Foundation (14 August), www.eff.org/deeplinks/2017/08/rising-demands-data-localization-response-weak-data-protection-mechanisms (accessed 02.12.2018).

are compelling reasons to do so.[58] There are better ways to ensure cross-border privacy: maintain accountability for the data controller for both privacy and security, and employ mechanisms such as contracts and mutually recognised standards and dispute resolution programmes such as Privacy Shield or APEC's CPBRs.

Conclusion

The Internet, mobility and social media have turbocharged the collection and use of personal data, both in the range and quantity of data, since twenty years ago when a technology pioneer remarked that we have "zero privacy". And yet, for all that consumers seem eager to share information about themselves in exchange for convenience, interpersonal connections, and new services, it is clear by now that a majority in the "digital society" have personal limits and feel strongly enough about them that they still want enterprises to offer choices and lawmakers to enforce socially responsible behaviour.

And so there are many more laws, in more countries, with sharper teeth than there were twenty years ago. They are not identical. They reflect some cultural differences and perhaps some economic and political ambitions. But they also reflect a surprising degree of convergence around fundamental principles of fair information practices, with some changes over time that take account of what we have learned from experience about the kinds of disclosures and forms of regulation that are most likely to be meaningful to individuals and both motivating and practicable for organisations. Those of us who practice, teach, or debate in this field should be working to avoid its fragmentation into hostile islands and promote the willing adoption of best practices across the globe.

Some techniques of fair information practice have proven effective, for example, and are now broadly accepted. A good example is the principle of "notice", "transparency", or "openness", which goes hand in hand with the principles of data quality and subject access. It arises from the common sense insight that the person most likely to identify data errors and objectionable processing is the individual who is the subject of the processing. Surprisingly, the 1970 US Fair Credit Reporting Act was unusual among early information privacy laws in detailing requirements for individual notices to consumers and establishing enforceable subject access procedures and timelines for making corrections and acting on objections. That approach worked, in the sense that it fostered awareness among consumers, businesses and legal practitioners and a compliance environment where there were both legal and reputational consequences for non-compliance. Specific requirements for individual notice, subject access, and related data subject rights now regularly appear in comprehensive data protection instruments such as the EU GDPR and the Mexican, Brazilian, and recently amended Japanese data protection laws, with provisions for enforcement and remedies.

In fact, the GDPR expands data subject rights to include new rights of erasure and portability, and several countries outside Europe (such as Brazil) have followed suit or are considering amendments to add similar provisions. As those specific rights become better defined in law and practice, they may become global standards, perhaps learning from the GDPR experience in terms of balancing the relevant burdens and interests. These new GDPR requirements are already affecting the design of databases and information

58 *See, e.g.,* D. Reisman (2017) Where Is Your Data, Really?: The Technical Case Against Data Localization. *Lawfare* (22 May).

practices within enterprises, because it is costly and time-consuming to fulfil requests for data erasure from European data subjects on a manual, ad hoc basis. And once the systems are engineered and automated to accomplish data erasure on request, it is more feasible to do so for customers from other regions. Indeed, the author is aware of enterprises that already receive, and act on, requests for erasure from outside the EU without a legal or contractual obligation to do so, simply in the interest of good customer relations.

Similarly, the GDPR and several of the newer data protection laws and amendments outside Europe mentioned in this chapter have borrowed from the US experience with mandatory data breach notification laws. Those are sometimes criticised for resulting in consumer "fatigue" over frequent notices of data leaks, particularly if every breach must be publicised without standards for significance, but they have certainly had the effect of highlighting the importance of security hygiene for retailers, financial institutions, and employers. The GDPR raises the stakes with obligations for prompt reporting to the authorities and higher levels of potential fines. This is an aspect of data protection that attracts media attention and quickly raises public awareness, with the potential for prompting cooperation between business and law enforcement in reducing cybercrime. Here again, even before the new GDPR requirement, many international enterprises were routinely notifying EU authorities and data subjects at the same time they notified affected US data subjects, both because they were arguably obliged to do so under general principles of transparency and because they considered that it made for better customer and public relations over the long term.

These specific examples of the spread of privacy "best practices", and the more general influence of the EU Directive and now the GDPR in standardising data protection terminology and principles, are offset to some extent by persistent legal and cultural differences, especially in employment practices, in dealing with children, and in the balancing of privacy interests with political interests and academic, journalistic and artistic freedom. In these areas, the APEC Privacy Framework accepts that countries will differ in approach, and even the GDPR does not attempt to impose too much uniformity within the EU. (It will be interesting to see how far the GDPR "consistency mechanism" will go toward promoting convergence in these areas in Europe.) Recent laws requiring data localisation are likely to backfire economically and technologically, with little gain for privacy rights.

There must always be a balancing of competing rights and interests in a democratic society, and every country will not reach the same conclusions about that balance at any given time. There are obvious temptations for governments to rely on national security as an unquestionable excuse for intruding on privacy, even while insisting on transparency in the private sector. Individual corporate and government officials and political candidates will also be motivated to avoid journalistic scrutiny by pleading their privacy rights. Privacy is not an absolute right, and data protection will not look precisely the same even across the internet, although global enterprises will continue to try to reduce their information practices and options to a manageably small set of operating rules for the sake of efficiency. This is why, for example, it generally makes sense for the industry to promote convergence on such issues as information security management standards and codes of conduct for internet advertising, because it is costly and inefficient to manage compliance to multiple standards in multiple contexts.

Consumers, too, should benefit from a greater degree of standardisation and simplification. They may not be aware of basic data protection rights that apply even if they are dealing online with foreign providers of goods and services. Where they have choices, the privacy notices and options are often presented in such a dense and obscure fashion that they are never read. There is scope for cooperation between industry and government to establish standards, codes, trust seals, and public awareness campaigns to avoid such confusion and make data protection and cybersecurity more transparent and effective in the daily life of citizens.

In data protection, there has been progress, but we are still at the stage where consumers would walk into a grocery store and have little idea what was meant by an "organic" label on produce. In the EU, the US, Japan, Brazil and other countries, a combination of regulations and industry certification and marketing standards eventually defined terms and standards for the benefit of local consumers and export markets. It will require a greater degree of legal convergence and expansion of internet best practices for online data protection to be as well understood as organic bananas.

20 The protection of personal data in a digital society

The role of the GDPR

Tiina Pajuste

Introduction

The protection of privacy in the digital era is increasingly difficult. People publish personal data (both their own and of their friends and acquaintances) through social media and internet services on a daily basis. The methods of data collection and processing have been changing rapidly. The fast-paced technological developments have substantially increased the scope and extent of the collection and sharing of personal data. This has led to the necessity of changing how data is protected, as old methods do not match new realities.

Since most human activities leave behind some form of digital data trail, monitoring the behaviour of private persons has been made increasingly easy.[1] Often people do not understand how easy it is to utilise personal data for criminal or commercial purposes. This involves using personal data in ways not anticipated at the time of collection. The economic value of personal data is steadily increasing, making personal data the cornerstone for different business models both online and offline.[2] In addition, the cross-border data flows have increased significantly and to ensure the functioning of the EU internal market also in this area, it was considered necessary to regulate cooperation between Member States and the nuances of sharing data across borders. There were significant differences in the rules regarding the protection of personal data in the various EU Member States.[3] To protect private persons from the misuse of their data and to unify the legal regulation of this area, measures had to been taken on the regional level.

This resulted in the European data protection reform, which culminated in the adoption of the General Data Protection Regulation [GDPR] that came to force on 25 May 2018.[4] Even before the adoption of the GDPR, the right to the protection of

1 OECD, *The OECD Privacy Framework* (2013), Chapter 2, Supplementary Explanatory Memorandum to the Revised Recommendation of the Council Concerning Guidelines Governing the Protection of Privacy and Transborder Flows of Personal Data, 20.

2 Milda Macenaite (2017) The "Riskification" of European Data Protection Law through a Two-fold Shift. *European Journal of Risk Regulation*, Vol. 8, No. 1, 506. For a detailed consideration of the data collection market, see Beate Roessler (2015) Should Personal Data be a Tradable Good? On the Moral Limits of Markets in Privacy. In Beate Roessler and Dorota Mokrosinska (Eds.), *Social Dimensions of Privacy: Interdisciplinary Perspectives*. Cambridge: CUP.

3 A detailed example the differences between member states in relation to data protection is provided by the comprehensive analysis of data protection and media expression: David Erdos (2016) European Union Data Protection and Media Expression: Fundamentally Off Balance. *ICLQ*, Vol. 65, 139.

4 Regulation (EU) 2016/679 of the European Parliament and of the Council of 27 April 2016 on the protection of natural persons with regard to the processing of personal data and on the free movement of such data, and repealing Directive 95/46/EC, OJ L 119, 4.5.2016.

personal data was protected in the EU both as an independent right, but also as part of respect for private and family life, home and communications. The Article 29 Data Protection Working Party has affirmed that "[p]ersonal data (which includes metadata) may not be treated solely as an object of trade, an economic asset or a common good", yet at the same time they recognised that "[d]ata protection rights must be balanced with other fundamental rights, including non-discrimination and freedom of expression, which are of equal value in a democratic society".[5]

Recital 4 of the GDPR mentions "freedom to conduct a business" as one freedom that the right to the protection of personal data has to be balanced against, in accordance with the principle of proportionality. Whether an equilibrium was reached with the GDPR will be one of the aspects studied in this chapter.

This chapter will look at some of the changes made by the GDPR and what impact they will have on the regional and global levels. Both the positive contribution and the practical and theoretical problems posed by the Regulation will be addressed, to provide a balanced overview of the changes made to personal data protection in the EU. Although the focus is on Europe, the global reach of EU data protection rules makes this chapter also relevant for non-European readers.

Protection of personal data in the EU

The GDPR defines "personal data" as "any information relating to an identified or identifiable natural person".[6] A 2013 OECD report clarifies that personal data includes, among other things, the following types of data: user-generated content like blogs and photos, activity or behavioural data (e.g. what people search for and look at on the internet), social data (e.g. contacts and friends on social networking sites), locational data, demographic data, and official identifying data.[7] Thus, personal data derives from a range of sources and can be of differing levels of sensitivity. It can reveal very intimate details about a person's character, lifestyle and choices. This is one of the reasons why it merits protection.

The first instrument on the European (and also international) level, which directly addressed the protection of personal data, was the Convention for the Protection of Individuals with Regard to Automatic Processing of Personal Data, which already in 1981 recognised the need to "reconcile the fundamental values of respect for privacy and the free flow of information between peoples".[8] The aim of the Convention was to secure for every individual "respect for his rights and fundamental freedoms, and in particular his right to privacy, with regard to automatic processing of personal data relating to him".[9] The Convention was a response to technological advances and it constitutes a key international instrument in this area, as it establishes many of the principles of EU data protection law that were later written into the Directive and confirmed in

5 Joint Statement of the European Data Protection Authorities Assembled in the Article 29 Working Party, WP 227 (2014), 26 November 2014, 2.

6 Article 4(1).

7 OECD, Report on Exploring the Economics of Personal Data: A Survey of Methodologies for Measuring Monetary Value, Doc. DSTI/ICCP/IE/REG(2011)2/FINAL, 2 April 2013, 7.

8 28 January 1981, ETS No. 108, Preamble.

9 Article 1.

the GDPR.[10] The aim of the 1995 Data Protection Directive[11] was to elaborate on and expand the content of the principles regarding the right to privacy laid down in the aforementioned convention. But as the Directive was enacted at a time when the internet was at a nascent stage of its development and the so-called digital revolution was just beginning, in the coming decades it became inadequate to respond to the developments in the field.[12]

The legal bases for EU actions in the area of data protection are laid down in the founding treaties of the EU. Article 39 of the Treaty on European Union authorises the EU to legislate in the area of the protection and free movement of personal data –

> the Council shall adopt a decision laying down the rules relating to the protection of individuals with regard to the processing of personal data by the Member States when carrying out activities which fall within the scope of this Chapter, and the rules relating to the free movement of such data.[13]

Article 16 of the Treaty on the Functioning of the EU reaffirms that everyone has the right to the protection of their data and clarifies that the European Parliament and the Council should

> lay down the rules relating to the protection of individuals with regard to the processing of personal data by Union institutions, bodies, offices and agencies, and by the Member States when carrying out activities which fall within the scope of Union law, and the rules relating to the free movement of such data.[14]

The protection of persons in relation to the processing of their data is also a fundamental right established in the EU Charter of Fundamental Rights. Articles 7 and 8 of the Charter recognise respect for private life and the protection of personal data as connected, yet standalone rights.[15] The right to respect for private and family life, home and correspondence encompasses a right to be protected against the collection and use of personal data. And claims regarding breaches of data protection law can at times also include assertions regarding the violation of the right to privacy.[16] Even before the adoption of the Charter, the protection of personal data was recognised as an element of the right to privacy as laid down in the European Convention on Human Rights. This was recognised by the European Court of Human Rights in several cases

10 Sahar Bhaimia (2018) The General Data Protection Regulation: The Next Generation of EU Data Protection. *Legal Information Management*, Vol. 18, 22.

11 European Parliament and Council Directive 95/46/EC of 24 October 1995 on the protection of individuals with regard to the processing of personal data and on the free movement of such data [1995] OJ L281/23.

12 Orla Lynskey (2017) The "Europeanisation" of Data Protection Law. *Cambridge Yearbook of European Legal Studies*, Vol. 19, 252, 252.

13 Consolidated Version of the Treaty on European Union, 26 October 2012, OJ C 326, Article 39.

14 Consolidated Version of the Treaty on the Functioning of the European Union, 13 December 2007, 2008 OJ C 115/47, Article 16.

15 Charter of Fundamental Rights of the European Union, 26 October 2012, O.J. C 364/01, Articles 7 and 8.

16 See further European Union Agency for Fundamental Rights and Council of Europe (2018) *Handbook on European Data Protection Law*. Luxembourg: Publications Office of the European Union, 18–21.

that tried to restrict national data collection activities.[17] Also the Court of Justice of the EU affirmed that there is a right to the protection of personal data before the Charter came into force.[18] Although this right has been elevated to the status of a "fundamental right" in the EU, through its incorporation into the EU Charter of Fundamental Rights as a standalone right, on the global level it is not recognised as a distinct human right. Instead, it is seen and approached as a part of respect for private and family life, home and correspondence.

What is noteworthy about personal data protection law is that it is an area of law that is built on legal principles, instead of distinct and detailed legal rules. This should accommodate changes in circumstances and technological advances, without the need to make legislative changes. Article 8 of the Charter also mentions some of the main data protection principles. Paragraph 2 states that data "must be processed fairly for specified purposes and on the basis of the consent of the person concerned or some other legitimate basis laid down by law. Everyone has a right of access to data which has been collected concerning him or her, and the right to have it rectified". The cornerstone of EU data protection law (both under the Directive and the GDPR) is the principle that a company or an organisation cannot do anything with the personal data of an individual unless it is permitted by the law. The permissions are known as lawful bases for processing and they are included in EU data protection law in the form of an exhaustive list.[19] Thus, the presumption is a prohibition. And the burden is on the data controller, not on the individual.

As the aim of this chapter is not to give a full overview of all the relevant personal data protection rules, the focus will be on some of the main changes implemented with the GDPR.

Fundamental changes made with the GDPR

"Riskification"

Although the GDPR tries to achieve the same two goals as the directive that preceded it, i.e. to guarantee the functioning of the internal market through free personal data flows and to protect the right to privacy and personal data protection, the GDPR introduces a new methodology. It relies extensively on risk and constructs a number of the new provisions around the concept of risk. Although the Data Protection Directive also included five references to risk, in the GDPR risk is given a new prominent position and the term can be found throughout the whole text. In particular, risk is a core element of the accountability principle (introduced with the GDPR) and risk management is at the centre of the data protection impact assessments, a new tool that helps to achieve and demonstrate compliance with the Regulation. As Macenaite has noted, "risk has become a new boundary in the data protection field and a key indicator in deciding whether additional legal and procedural safeguards are required in a particular context in order to

17 E.g., *Rotaru v. Romania*, Application No. 28341/95, ECtHR (2000) and *Weber & Saravia v. Germany*, Application No. 54934/00, ECtHR (2006).

18 E.g. Case C-275/06, *Promusicae v. Telefónica de España*, 2008 ECR I-271, para 63. See further Ralf Poscher (2017) Right to Data Protection. In: Russell A. Miller (Ed.), *Privacy and Power: A Transatlantic Dialogue in the Shadow of the NSA-Affair*. Cambridge: CUP, 130.

19 GDPR, Article 6.

shield data subjects from potential negative impacts stemming from specific data processing activities".[20]

The obligation to conduct a data protection impact assessment [DPIA] is laid down in Article 35. It is mandatory when processing is "likely to result in a high risk" to the rights of natural persons. If that is the case, the controller must, before the processing, carry out an assessment of the impact of the planned processing operations on the protection of personal data. The assessment has to include (a) a description and the purposes of the processing operations; (b) an evaluation of the necessity and proportionality of the processing operations in relation to the purposes; (c) an assessment of the risks to people's rights and freedoms; and (d) the measures envisaged to address the risks, including safeguards, security measures and mechanisms to ensure the protection of personal data and to demonstrate compliance with the GDPR. The same article also obliges the controller to seek the views of data subjects or their representatives on the intended processing, if that is appropriate, considering the protection of commercial and security interests. These are wide-ranging obligations that are imposed on the data controller. Yet such obligations have been created with the aim of providing more flexibility and decreasing bureaucracy.

Risk-based data protection has been welcomed by different stakeholders because of several reasons. Firstly, relying on risk is seen as a more effective and adaptable method of data protection, when compared with a detailed framework of strict rules. It allows adjusting obligations for data controllers according to the risk involved. Secondly, there is the hope that a risk-based approach would improve transparency, accountability and lay the basis for a culture of data protection amongst data controllers.[21] The Article 29 Data Protection Working Party [Art 29 WP] considers the DPIAs to be "important tools for accountability", since they should assist data controllers with complying with requirements of the GDPR and, importantly, also with demonstrating that the controller has taken appropriate measures to ensure compliance with the Regulation. A DPIA is meant to be "a process for building and demonstrating compliance".[22] Its adaptable nature also makes this risk-based approach suitable in relation to technological advancements that happen at a fast pace in the field of data processing. Traditional rule-based systems tend to be too rigid to accommodate rapid changes in circumstances.

But there are also problematic aspects to the "riskification" of data protection. It is unclear what the impact of the risk-based provisions will be, since the rights of the data subject "should be respected regardless of the level of the risks" and the "fundamental principles applicable to the controllers . . . should remain the same, whatever the processing and the risks for the data subjects".[23] On the other hand, the same document states that "[i]mplementation of controllers' obligations through accountability tools and measures (i.e. legitimacy, data minimization, purpose limitation, transparency, data integrity, data accuracy) can and should be varied according to the type of processing and the

20 Milda Macenaite (2017) The "Riskification" of European Data Protection Law through a Two-fold Shift. *European Journal of Risk Regulation*, Vol. 8, No. 1, 506, 524.

21 Ibid., 515.

22 Article 29 Data Protection Working Party, Guidelines on Data Protection Impact Assessment (DPIA) and determining whether processing is "likely to result in a high risk" for the purposes of Regulation 2016/679, WP 248 rev.01, 4 April 2017, revised 4 October 2017, 4.

23 Article 29 Data Protection Working Party, Statement on the Role of a Risk-based Approach in Data Protection Legal Frameworks, WP 218, 30 May 2014, paras 2, 4.

privacy risks for data subjects".[24] There seems to be a contradiction between those statements and it remains to be seen what the effect of this approach on the relevant obligations will be.

Another difficulty is reconciling the rights-based approach to data protection with "riskification". The utilisation of risk assessments as a regulatory tool partially shifts the responsibility for the protection of fundamental rights to data controllers. But data controllers are not necessarily in the best position to assess risks and may not be motivated to limit their data processing.[25] For some data controllers the risk assessments may end up being just about following the formal procedure for the sake of it, instead engaging in a meaningful way with the risks and impact of their data processing activities.

Extending the reach of EU data protection law

The second major change that the GDPR brought with it is the expansion of the reach of the EU's data protection rules. Already prior to the GDPR, Europe was leading the way in relation to the protection of personal data. The rules that the EU policymakers have created since the mid-1990s have been adopted as global standards in many countries around the world. But the GDPR goes further than the Data Protection Directive did. The general rule regarding the territorial scope of the GDPR is laid down in Article 3, which states that it applies to "the processing of personal data in the context of the activities of an establishment of a controller or a processor in the Union, regardless of whether the processing takes place in the Union or not". This is similar to what was stated in the Directive.[26] But the innovation of the GDPR is contained in the second paragraph:

> This Regulation applies to the processing of personal data of data subjects who are in the Union by a controller or processor not established in the Union, where the processing activities are related to:
>
> (a) the offering of goods or services, irrespective of whether a payment of the data subject is required, to such data subjects in the Union; or
> (b) the monitoring of their behaviour as far as their behaviour takes place within the Union.

This provision widens the reach of EU data protection rules far beyond the borders of the Union.[27] Paragraph (a) applies to all data controllers and processors that provide goods or services to individuals in the European Union. Commentators have noted that stopping providing services to people in the EU and ending commercial ties with the world's largest trading bloc is unthinkable to most companies.[28] The GDPR explains that for the

24 Ibid., para 5.

25 See further Macenaite 540.

26 Data Protection Directive, Article 4(1)(a).

27 For a more detailed consideration of this issue, see Paul de Hert and Michal Czerniawski (2016) Expanding the European Data Protection Scope beyond Territory: Article 3 of the General Data Protection Regulation in its Wider Context. *International Data Privacy Law*, Vol. 6, No. 3, 230; and Jan Philipp Albrecht (2016) How the GDPR Will Change the World. *European Data Protection Law Review*, Vol. 2, 287.

28 See, for example, Mark Scott and Laurens Cerulus (2018) Europe's New Data Protection Rules Export Privacy Standards Worldwide. *Politico* (31 January), www.politico.eu/article/europe-data-protection-privacy-standards-gdpr-general-protection-data-regulation/ (accessed 1.9.2018).

determination of whether a data controller is offering goods or services to data subjects who are in the EU, it is necessary to establish whether that controller "envisages offering services to data subjects in one or more Member States in the Union". For this determination it is not enough that the controller's website or contact details are accessible in the EU. But factors like the use of a language or a currency generally used in one or more Member States, the ability to place orders in that other language and references to EU users or customers may lead to the determination that the controller envisages offering goods or services to data subjects in the Union.[29]

Paragraph (b) of Article 3(2) extends the territorial scope of the GDPR even further, as monitoring of individuals in the EU is also covered, if their behaviour takes place within the Union. "Monitoring" covers, among other activities, the tracking of individuals online to create profiles, including where this is used to take decisions to analyse personal preferences, behaviours and attitudes.[30] The recital of the GDPR clarifies that the determination of whether a processing activity is considered "monitoring", "it should be ascertained whether natural persons are tracked on the internet including potential subsequent use of personal data processing techniques which consist of profiling a natural person, particularly in order to take decisions concerning her or him or for analysing or predicting her or his personal preferences, behaviours and attitudes".[31] The expansion of the territorial scope of the GDPR is understandable from the European perspective as the aim is to guarantee the protection of personal data as comprehensively as possible for the people living in the EU.

However, one should also contemplate what would happen if other regions or states would start taking a similar approach. It has been questioned whether it is legitimate to apply "territorially delimited law to the global internet" and whether European data protection rules should be applied to global online activity, as the European stance on data protection is not universally shared around the world (e.g. the different approaches of the US and China).[32] It remains to be seen what the repercussions of this enlargement of the territorial scope of the EU data protection rules will be – whether the rules will become global standards or whether rival approaches to data protection will challenge the position of European norms.

Changes to data protection principles and rules

The GDPR updates existing EU data protection law, in an effort to address some of the shortcomings of the preceding Data Protection Directive. Many of the principles and rules of the Directive are maintained in the GDPR. But several developments have taken place, some that improve the position of the data subject and others that may bring with them complications.

Firstly, the principle of transparency under the GDPR mandates that an individual should be told the lawful ground for processing his or her personal data. The GDPR also significantly expands the list of information that must be provided to the individual

29 GDPR, Recital 23.

30 Bird & Bird (2017) *Guide to the General Data Protection Regulation*, www.twobirds.com/~/media/pdfs/gdpr-pdfs/bird–bird–guide-to-the-general-data-protection-regulation.pdf (accessed 1.9.2018), 2.

31 GDPR, Recital 24.

32 Uta Kohl and Diane Rowland (2017) *Censorship and Cyberborders through EU Data Protection Law*. Cambridge: Cambridge University Press, 540.

when collecting personal data. Among the new items of information are: (a) information on the data protection officer (where applicable); (b) the legal basis for the processing (e.g. consent or legitimate interest); (c) whether the controller intends to transfer data to third countries; (d) the storage period of the data; (e) if consent is used as the legal basis, information on the right to withdraw consent and its legal consequences; and (f) if automated decision-making is utilised, meaningful information on the mechanisms and the logic involved in the decision-making process.[33] The lists of information that needs to be provided at different instances take up six pages of the GDPR, thus there is a real risk that individuals may be overloaded with information, which may even worsen their situation when compared with prior regulation of the area. This is especially so as studies show that most people are not aware of the basic tenets of data protection and often lack knowledge about even the most basic functions and processes of the internet. Accordingly, it is highly unlikely that individuals will understand the complex processes involving their personal data.[34] Thus the utility of making it obligatory to provide them with such information can be questioned. The more information you give to people, the less likely it is that they will substantially engage with such information.

To alleviate this problem, the GDPR now includes rules on how information should be presented, although the terms are not elucidated in the Regulation. Article 12(1) states that the information should be presented "in a concise, transparent, intelligible and easily accessible form, using clear and plain language". This is a somewhat contradictory goal in relation to the obligation to provide such a wide range of information to data subjects, as an extensive amount of information, even if presented in clear language, will deter people from actually reading and processing the material. Connected to this is a phenomenon called the "privacy paradox". It describes, on the one hand, how individuals report that they highly value data protection but, on the other hand, it shows that they do not act accordingly. The underlying reason for this is the combination of a lack of knowledge of the complex processes involved and individuals' cognitive problems.[35]

Secondly, the conditions for obtaining consent have become stricter under the GDPR. Consent must be freely given, specific, informed and unambiguous. Consent must be a statement or other clear affirmative action demonstrating agreement to the processing. Thus, silence, pre-ticked boxes or inactivity are not valid ways of providing consent. Importantly, people now have a right to withdraw their consent at any time and it should be as easy to withdraw as to give consent. Controllers have a corresponding duty to keep a verifiable record of the consent.[36] This may prove problematic in situations where consent is asked in oral form.

There is a presumption that consent will not be valid unless separate consents are obtained for different processing activities and there is a presumption that forced consent mechanisms (where there is no actual choice involved) will not be valid. Accordingly, many organisations need to review existing consent mechanisms, to ensure they present a

33 GDPR, Articles 13, 14. See further Bhaimia 24.

34 For more details on the relevant studies in the EU and the US, see Christopher F. Mondschein (2016) Some Iconoclastic Thoughts on the Effectiveness of Simplified Notices and Icons for Informing Individuals as Proposed in Article 12(1) and (7) GDPR. *European Data Protection Law Review* Vol. 2, 507, 510–511.

35 Ibid., 513.

36 GDPR, recital 32 and Article 7.

genuine and granular choice.[37] The Article 29 Working Party has concluded that the condition of free consent is only met "if the data subject is able to exercise a real choice, and there is no risk of deception, intimidation, coercion or significant negative consequences (e.g. substantial extra costs) if he/she does not consent".[38] Moreover, the data subject must have sufficient information before exercising his or her choice, so "a precise and easily understandable description of the subject matter requiring consent" has to be presented to the data subject.[39] These new conditions for consent led to the barrage of emails most people received just prior to the entry into force of the GDPR – many companies realised that they had not asked for consent in a manner that is compatible with the Regulation.

Thirdly, the GDPR includes a new principle of accountability, which makes controllers responsible for demonstrating compliance with the data protection principles. The essence of accountability is the controller's dual obligation to: (a) put in place measures which should in normal circumstances ensure that data protection rules are adhered to during the processing operations; and (b) have documentation ready which demonstrates (to both data subjects and supervisory authorities) what are the measures that have been taken to achieve compliance with the rules.[40] In order to be able to demonstrate their compliance with the GDPR's principles, organisations should, among other things, ensure "data protection by design and by default" and implement modalities and procedures for the exercise of the rights of the data subjects. The principle of accountability demands that controllers actively demonstrate compliance and not just wait until data subjects or supervisory authorities point out shortcomings.[41] This may require organisations to adopt significant new technical and organisational measures as current mechanisms may not be sufficient to be able to prove their GDPR compliance. The changes to consent bring tangible benefits to a large amount of data subjects, by reducing the amount of unsolicited calls and emails that everyone has been bombarded with to differing degrees thus far.

Fourthly, the GDPR introduces several new rights for individuals in respect of their personal data. These include the right to erasure, the right to data portability, the right to object to certain processing activities and also to decisions taken solely based on automated processing.[42] The right to erasure is a right that corresponds to the principle of data minimisation (personal data must be limited to what is necessary for the purposes for which those data are processed). Article 17 of the GDPR gives data subjects the right to have their personal data erased without undue delay where, e.g. the personal data is no longer necessary regarding the purposes for which it was collected, where consent is withdrawn or data has been unlawfully processed. Often there is no actual need for the right to erasure, if the data controller abides by all its obligations. As an example, as was noted previously, the right to erasure applies when the personal data is no longer required for the purpose for which it was collected. But in that situation the data minimisation principle also dictates that this data can no longer be processed and should be deleted. Thus,

37 Bird & Bird, 6. For a overview of what the changes mean to US companies due to the extended reach of the GDPR, see Beata A. Safari (2017) Intangible Privacy Rights: How Europe's GDPR Will Set a New Global Standard for Personal Data Protection. *Seton Hall Law Review*, Vol. 47, 809, 826.

38 Article 29 Data Protection Working Party, Guidelines on Consent under Regulation 2016/679, WP 259, 28 November 2017, 8.

39 European Union Agency for Fundamental Rights and Council of Europe (2018) *Handbook on European Data Protection Law*. Luxembourg: Publications Office of the European Union, 146.

40 Article 29 Working Party, Opinion 3/2010 on the principle of accountability, WP 173, 13 July 2010.

41 European Union Agency for Fundamental Rights and Council of Europe (2018), 135, 137.

42 GDPR, Articles 17, 20, 21 and 22.

the right of erasure is an additional guarantee for the data subject that should facilitate demanding that their data is properly handled.

Under the GDPR, data subjects have the right to data portability in situations where the personal data is processed by automated means on the basis of consent or where the processing is necessary for the performance of a contract and is carried out by automated means.[43] If the right to data portability is applicable, individuals can have their personal data transmitted directly from one controller to another if this is technically possible. To facilitate this, the controller should develop interoperable formats that would make data portability technically possible.[44] Although the aim is to achieve interoperability, the GDPR does not impose particular rules or recommendations on the specific format to be provided as formats may differ across sectors. According to the Article 29 Working Party guidelines, the right to data portability "supports user choice, user control and user empowerment", aiming to give data subjects control over their own personal data.[45] Data portability should also have a positive effect on competition as changing service providers becomes easier for individuals.

And, fifth, the GDPR includes the role of the Data Protection Officer [DPO]. DPOs are persons who give advice regarding data protection rules in organisations that undertake data processing. They have been called "a cornerstone of accountability" since they should help ensure that organisations comply with the GDPR and they also act as intermediaries between the data subjects, supervisory authorities and the organisation that appointed them.[46] The GDPR foresees a mandatory appointment of a DPO in three instances: (a) where a public authority carries out the processing; (b) where the data controllers core activities consist of processing operations which require the regular and systematic monitoring of data subjects on a large scale, and (c) where the core activities consist of large-scale processing of special categories of data or personal data relating to criminal convictions and offences.[47]

The DPOs must be independent and provided with the necessary resources, including financial resources, infrastructure and equipment. Additional requirements include providing DPOs with sufficient time to fulfil their functions and continuous training to enable them to develop their expertise and stay up to date with all developments in data protection law.[48]

This change has led to a wide range of training events and courses being created both by law firms and academic institutions, to train the future DPOs and meet the demand currently on the employment market for DPOs. The position of the DPO will no doubt be of great assistance in ensuring that the GDPR is implemented, since it will guarantee that at least one person in the organisation is continually raising data protection issues and providing relevant guidance. Nonetheless, as assigning a DPO is not mandatory in relation to all organisations, this will not have a universal impact.

43 Ibid., Article 20.

44 European Union Agency for Fundamental Rights and Council of Europe (2018), 228; GDPR, Recital 68.

45 Article 29 Working Party, Guidelines on the Right to Data Portability, WP 242, 13 December 2016 and revised on 5 April 2017, 13.

46 European Union Agency for Fundamental Rights and Council of Europe (2018), 175.

47 GDPR, Article 37(1).

48 Article 29 Working Party, Guidelines on Data Protection Officers, WP 243 rev.01, last revised and adopted 5 April 2017, para. 3.1.

Of course, there is a range of other changes that came with the GDPR, but the previously mentioned aspects constitute some of the alterations that are likely to make the greatest impact or require specific action by data controllers.

Overarching problems connected to the GDPR

It is important to be aware of some of the theoretical and practical problems that are associated with the GDPR. On a theoretical level, the concept of individual control of data has been criticised. Fairfield and Engel assert that "[i]ndividual control of data is a fundamentally flawed concept because individuals cannot know what the data they reveal means when aggregated with billions of other data points".[49] They emphasise that when a person consents to information gathering, they often also become a conduit for gathering information about his or her entire social network, whether or not those other individuals have consented to it. They highlight that despite the fact that the US and EU rules on data protection are based on differing foundations – the US focusing on liberty and the EU on human dignity – both philosophies look at "privacy as a matter best resolved by informing and empowering individuals". In both Europe and the US, the aim of data protection law is for fully informed individuals to consent to the use of their individual data. Fairfield and Engel note that this does not solve the fundamental problem that the data does not exclusively impact that individual.[50] This is exemplified by "big data" and the increasing role of decisions that are based on aggregated data.

Another conceptual issue that has been raised is about the essence of the right to data protection. As was mentioned before, this right has been recognised as a "fundamental right" in the EU (although this approach has yet to spread to the global level). But questions have been raised about what this right actually protects, as fundamental rights usually have the aim of protecting a general or specific liberty or equality interest. Poscher notes that this question has haunted the right to data protection since its conception and has been at the centre of academic criticism directed against the right.[51] Roessler raises a connected issue and highlights the fact that the "collection and trade in personal data causes uneasiness and seems to constitute a harm that is not easy to analyse" as the harm does not seem reducible to violations of privacy or of property rights.[52] The fact that the value that the right to data protection aims to defend is unclear has led some scholars to conclude that this right is not an independent fundamental right, but instead more of a systematic enhancement of other fundamental rights. As an example of an enhanced right, Poscher gives the right to privacy. He explains how the body scanner showing an image of the person naked would be a traditional issue of privacy, but not an issue of data protection. But data protection is involved in the storage of the scanner's raw data, which gives rise to the risk that someone could access such images and thus also infringe the traditional right to privacy.[53] Thus, the main argument is that the right to data protection is a corollary to traditional rights and not a distinct right on its own.

49 Joshua Fairfield and Christoph Engel (2017) Privacy as a Public Good. In Russell A. Miller (Ed.), *Privacy and Power: A Transatlantic Dialogue in the Shadow of the NSA-Affair*. Cambridge: CUP, 98.

50 Ibid., 105–106.

51 Ralf Poscher (2017) Right to Data Protection. In Russell A. Miller (Ed.), *Privacy and Power: A Transatlantic Dialogue in the Shadow of the NSA-Affair*. Cambridge: CUP, 131.

52 Roessler 146.

53 Poscher 133–134.

There are also difficulties on a practical level. One of the aims of the GDPR was to end the "fragmentation in the implementation of data protection across the Union" which may "constitute an obstacle to the pursuit of economic activities at the level of the Union, distort competition and impede authorities in the discharge of their responsibilities under Union law".[54] Yet there are concerns that the problem of inconsistency may continue. Despite being a Regulation, the GDPR allows Member States to legislate in many areas. For example, this is possible if the processing of personal data is required to comply with a legal obligation, if it relates to a public interest task or is carried out by an entity with official authority.[55]

Several articles of the GDPR also state that their provisions may be further specified or restricted by Member State law.[56] Another significant area where Member States are allowed to take differing approaches is the processing of employee data.[57] As a step to ensure the consistent application of the GDPR, the Article 29 Working Party becomes the European Data Protection Board that is given a lengthy list of tasks, including issuing guidance, recommendations and best practices and issuing binding decisions in cross-border enforcement cases.[58] Although the extent of the inconsistencies will be reduced with the GDPR (especially as court decisions start providing guidance about how to interpret the often vaguely phrased articles of the GDPR) and the creation of the European Data Protection Board, this problem is not completely eliminated.

Conclusion

The protection of personal data has long been a prominent issue in the EU. On a global level, the EU has been leading the way in protecting individuals from abuses connected to their personal data. The GDPR is another example of the EU trying to create international standards and taking a somewhat aggressive approach in ensuring this through the expansion of the territorial scope of the GDPR beyond Europe's borders.

Although there are conceptual problems connected with both the "riskification" of data protection, the essence of the right and, additionally, the fundamental basis of EU's data protection law – reliance on individual control of data – has been questioned, the overall impact of the GDPR from the perspective of the data subject is a positive one. Individuals have been provided with additional rights and more control over their data. For example, the right to erasure and the right to data portability are among the rights that constituted innovations in comparison with the old Data Protection Directive. The changes to consent have perhaps had the most immediate effects as the amount of unsolicited emails and phone calls have decreased noticeably. And, as pre-ticked boxes and muddled wording on consent forms have become unacceptable, people will hopefully no longer inadvertently consent to data processing merely because they did not pay enough attention to the wording. Although transparency and providing information to data subjects is a commendable goal, it remains to be seen whether a balance will be found between providing enough information and making sure it does not overwhelm the reader by its sheer quantity. But the larger question remains of whether individuals will actually utilise those rights, as

54 GDPR, Recital 9.
55 Bird & Bird 3.
56 E.g. GDPR, Article 36(5), Article 49(5), Article 80(2).
57 Ibid., Article 88.
58 See further Bhaimia 23.

despite the increase in awareness, the overall level of knowledge of data protection issues of the general population is regrettably low.

The main objectives of the GDPR were to protect the fundamental rights and freedoms of natural persons (in particular their right to the protection of personal data) and to ensure the free movement of personal data within the Union. One can conclude that the GDPR has both improved the protection of the rights of individuals and expanded the substance of those rights. But living in a digital society means that often there is no choice but to consent to the processing of your personal data, and this does not change no matter how many procedural rights you are provided with.

From the point of view of the data controller, the GDPR tends to bring more obligations (e.g. reviewing and improving policies and administrative arrangements, conducting impact assessments, updating data security) and the concrete benefits tend to be limited to international companies that before had to navigate the differences in the various domestic systems of the EU Member States. The GDPR does indeed remove some pre-existing obstacles in the free movement of personal data and unify regulation of this area in the Member States (and beyond). Part of the goals of the GDPR was to find a balance between the "freedom to conduct a business" and the protection of the rights of data subjects. Although the details of implementation are yet unclear, the balance seems to be tipped in the favour of the data subjects.

Part VI

Global perspective

21 Africa, the internet and human rights

CH Powell and Tobias Schonwetter[1]

Introduction

On 12 February 2015, then President Jacob Zuma was due to open the South African Parliament with an address on the State of the Nation (the annual "SONA" address). At that time, South Africa was still embroiled in the long-standing "Nkandla" scandal,[2] and one of the opposition parties had threatened to disrupt the proceedings unless Zuma "paid back the money" spent unlawfully on upgrading his "Nkandla" home at state expense.[3] Before the proceedings began, members of Parliament and journalists in Parliament discovered that they had no telecommunications signal on their cell phones and other electronic devices, and were therefore prevented from reporting on the events of that evening in real time. It took vigorous objections from the opposition parties to get the Speaker of Parliament to look into the matter, after which the signal was restored.[4] It was subsequently discovered that the State Security Agency (SSA) had employed a device which disrupted or "jammed" such signals, ostensibly without seeking the approval of Parliament. The Speaker of Parliament, for her part, claimed that she had been unaware that the jamming device would be used but that she had consented to the provision of security arrangements by the SSA, and that this device formed part of these arrangements. According to both the Speaker and the SSA, the use of the jamming device by security forces, without the express permission of Parliament, was lawful.[5] South Africa's Supreme Court of Appeal subsequently held, however, that the jamming of the telecommunications signal was unlawful, on the basis that it interfered with the ordinary functioning of Parliament.[6]

Generally, the most obvious human rights-related concerns around the internet are that censorship of the internet violates freedom of expression, and internet surveillance violates the right to privacy. However, we take the signal-jamming incident as a good demonstration of how the internet impacts on the very governance structure which is meant to support and sustain the full panoply of rights in a constitutional democracy. It is not the only example. Elsewhere in Africa, the internet has played a vital role in the *setting*

1 We are deeply grateful to Tanveer Jeewa for her research support for this chapter.

2 Brewing since 2011, this scandal involved the use of public funds to make upgrades to the President's private home. In May 2014, the Public Protector (South Africa's Ombudsperson) had found that Zuma had benefitted from these unlawful improvements and had decided, amongst other measures, that he should repay a portion of the costs. Zuma had not carried out her recommendations at the time of this SONA incident.

3 See SA's Parliament of Paranoia, https://mg.co.za/article/2015-02-19-sas-parliament-of-paranoia.

4 See Signal Jamming and EFF Expulsion at SONA: Full Transcript, www.politicsweb.co.za/documents/signal-jamming-and-eff-expulsion-at-sona-full-tran

5 *Primedia Broadcasting v. Speaker* (784/2015) [2016] ZASCA 142 (29 September 2016), paras 56 and 62.

6 Ibid., paras 63–64.

up of government, as is evident in the intensive use of social media during the Arab Spring, and state censorship of social media around election periods across the continent.[7] But in the South African example, we see the importance of the internet in the very functioning of a constitutional structure.

We have chosen the signal-jamming incident as our starting point because it highlights some central themes which run through every aspect of the relationship between the internet and human rights in Africa. The first, as stated previously, is that the internet is not simply a forum in which rights may be threatened and must be protected. It is, instead, an essential medium for the protection of those rights, in two ways. The first, discussed previously, relates to governance. The internet ensures the communication that is a prerequisite for governance structures to fulfil their mandate of running the state in a democratic manner. More particularly, it provides the means for accountability between the elected branches of government, the organs they set up and the electorate, thereby supporting the government's capacity to fulfil any human rights obligations at all. The second reason is that the internet is itself a medium for the protection of rights because it can serve as the (only) portal through which a range of social and economic rights are realised. The internet is often the first, and sometimes only, tool for Africa's inhabitants to access education, information and employment. From this perspective, we might argue that the internet, or at least access to it, should itself be viewed as a human right – a perspective taken up by the African Declaration on Internet Rights and Freedoms,[8] discussed further as follows.

The second theme to emerge from the signal-jamming incident is the role of the executive in restricting or protecting rights. In this incident, the executive unilaterally assumed the right to block communication between the elected branch of government (the legislature) and the electorate. The problem with executive interference of this nature is that it is often covert, carried out beyond the powers bestowed by inadequate legislative authorisation or simply without any legislative basis at all. Given its invisibility, this type of interference cannot be tackled unless it is noted, investigated and, ideally, brought to a court of law. In the signal-jamming case, the executive overreach was noted and resisted on the day, brought before a court of law and declared unlawful. Even in this case, however, the SCA did not interrogate what had actually happened, accepting an explanation from the executive branch of government that the jamming had been an accidental result of a security measure to protect the president.[9] The covert nature of executive interference means that there will be little legislation and even less case law to illuminate the position on the ground. As a result, the true impact of a government on the internet and human rights will be impossible to ascertain without an empirical study. While such a study is not possible here, we note some examples of potential executive overreach and briefly touch on the relationship between the restriction of rights in the internet and counter-terrorism. Proponents of interference with the internet often broadly rely on security as their justification. Recall that the majority of the Western Cape High Court accepted that the Speaker of Parliament did not even need to know what measures the executive had set up on Parliament's own precincts,

7 G. Razzano (2016) Human Rights and Information in Africa. *FesMedia Africa Series 2016*, Friedrich Ebert Stiftung, 22.

8 See African Declaration on Internet Rights and Freedoms, http://africaninternetrights.org/declaration/ (accessed 02.12.2018).

9 This is problematic, because the explanation offered by the executive, and set out without comment in the judgments, conflicts with the evidence offered by journalists and other persons involved in the incident; *supra* note 5.

much less consent to them, because the Court accepted that only the executive can decide what measures are necessary for security.[10] We suggest that the level of scrutiny to which a state subjects claims by the executive that particular measures are needed for security will be a reliable indicator of how seriously it will take its obligations to protect the freedoms of the internet.

However, there is one important aspect of the relationship between the internet and human rights which the signal-jamming incident does not bring into focus, and that is that states cannot fulfil their duties to protect human rights in cyberspace simply by staying out of the way. It is not enough for the state to withdraw, that is, not to censor, surveil or block the internet. It also has positive duties related to cyberspace. We suggested previously that it may bear an obligation to give people access to the internet. However, it also has the obligation to prevent the harm that the internet can do, when it is used by criminals to defraud, steal and coerce.[11]

This chapter thus considers both the positive and negative duties borne by African states to protect human rights in relation to the internet, and provide a preliminary assessment of the extent to which states are fulfilling their obligations. It does so, first, by setting out the normative framework specific to Africa as a region. The focus of the second part of the chapter is on identifying the most relevant international and regional human rights instruments, including soft law instruments. In the third part, we tease out this framework in more detail, exploring states' fulfilment or neglect of the applicable norms. We divide the third part into three main sections: *control*, *accountability* and *access*. *Control* covers the extent to which African states impose restrictions on cyberspace, including the level of executive discretion exercised over internet access and freedom. The focus in this section is on control which the state should *not* be exercising over the internet, in particular, by censoring, surveilling or blocking access to it. The second section of the third part, *accountability*, considers the forms of control which the state *should* be exercising over the internet. The questions we are looking at here are whether the state has any measures in place to ensure that the internet is not misused to cause harm. The final section of the third part, *access*, briefly examines whether states have taken any practical measures to ensure that their people can, in fact, use the internet.

We must, at the outset, note particular challenges that bedevilled this chapter, and explain how we have attempted to resolve them. The challenges consisted of a vast topic, a vast continent, a dearth of empirical and legal research on many of the issues we needed to cover, missing or inaccessible primary sources, particularly legislation, and a modest word limit. We exacerbated this already difficult situation by extending the scope of our discussion beyond the traditional "internet freedom" concerns to how the internet impacts on governance structures and development, because we consider these factors particularly important in the African context. As a result of all these challenges, it was not possible to provide a comprehensive survey of all the domestic legislation or even all the issues implicated in the internet's relationship with human rights. We do, however, highlight what we consider the most significant issues in the region and provide examples that flesh out the general trends we have identified.

10 *Supra* note 5 at paras 52–53.

11 A phenomenon that we will not be addressing for reasons of space is "fake news", which is also starting to pose a problem in Africa; see, How Kenya Became the Latest Victim of "fake news", www.aljazeera.com/indepth/opinion/2017/08/kenya-latest-victim-fake-news-170816121455181.html (accessed 02.12.2018).

Human rights and the internet: Africa's normative framework

There is a rich body of international and regional human rights instruments which are formally binding as treaty law and protect most of the rights addressed in this chapter.[12] Of the 54 African states,[13] only South Sudan and Comoros[14] have not ratified the International Covenant on Civil and Political Rights (ICCPR).[15] Furthermore, only Botswana, Comoros, Mozambique and South Sudan[16] have not ratified the International Covenant on Economic, Social and Cultural Rights (ICESCR).[17] Most African states have also ratified the African Charter on Human and Peoples' Rights (ACHPR).[18] Only South Sudan and Morocco are not parties to the instrument.[19]

The ICCPR and the African Charter on Human & Peoples Rights (Banjul Charter) protect the right to equality[20] and freedom of expression[21] while the ICCPR protects the right to privacy.[22] The ICESCR and Banjul Charter both guarantee a range of socio-economic rights, including health,[23] education,[24] and economic, social and cultural development.[25] Privacy is threatened by surveillance of the internet, and freedom of expression and information by government censorship, as well as some forms of control over digital communication exercised by non-state actors. The relationship of equality and socio-economic rights to the internet is more complex; but we will develop our argument below that lack of access to the internet frustrates the realisation of this range of rights.

A range of soft law instruments, produced by intergovernmental bodies and other stakeholders, supplement the hard law sources. Under the auspices of UNESCO, newspaper journalists produced the Windhoek Declaration on Promoting an Independent and Pluralistic African Press of 1991, followed ten years later by the African Charter on Broadcasting of 2001. The African Commission, for its part, has produced the Declaration of Principles on Freedom of Expression in Africa of 2002, as well as the African Platform on

12 The Universal Declaration of Human Rights (UDHR) arguably provides a source of customary international law, partly because it has been internationally recognised for 70 years, and partly because its provisions have been taken up by states in other, formally binding instruments. However, our focus in this chapter is on legally binding treaty law. For further discussion of the UDHR; M. Robbins (2005) Powerful States, Customary Law and the Erosion of Human Rights Through Regional Enforcement. *California Western International Law Journal*, Vol. 35, 275, 280–281.

13 This number rises to 55 if we include Western Sahara, see, All Africa: Countries, https://allafrica.com/misc/sitemap/countries.html. For the purposes of this study, we will not be treating Western Sahara as a state. As it lacks a functioning legislative and executive authority, it is not in a position either to infringe or promote human rights through the types of measures that we are exploring here.

14 Comoros has signed but not yet ratified the instrument; See Status of Ratification: Ratification of 18 International Human Rights Treaties, http://indicators.ohchr.org (accessed 02.12.2018).

15 UN General Assembly (1966) International Covenant on Civil and Political Rights. United Nations (16 December 1966).

16 *Supra* note 14.

17 UN General Assembly (1966) International Covenant on Economic, Social and Cultural Rights. United Nations (16 December 1966).

18 Organization of African Unity (OAU). African Charter on Human and Peoples' Rights ("Banjul Charter"). CAB/LEG/67/3 rev. (27 June 1981), 5, 21 I.L.M. 58, 1982.

19 Morocco withdrew following the admission of the disputed state of Western Sahara.

20 Article 26 of the ICCPR and article 3 of the Banjul Charter.

21 Article 19 of the ICCPR and article 9 of the Banjul Charter.

22 Article 17 of the ICCPR. Interestingly, the Banjul Charter does not mention privacy.

23 Article 11 of the ICESCR and article 16 of the Banjul Charter.

24 Ibid.

25 Article 22 of the Banjul Charter. Article 9 and 11 of the ICESCR guarantee the rights to social security and an adequate standard of living, respectively. The latter includes the rights to food, housing and clothing.

Access to Information Declaration of 2011. While these declarations focus on freedom of the press and access to information more broadly, our focus for the purposes of this chapter is a declaration which deals directly with the internet and human rights in Africa. The African Declaration on Internet Rights and Freedoms,[26] drawn up by a group of 23 civil society organisations in 2014, was "intended to elaborate on the principles which are necessary to uphold human and people's rights on the internet, and to cultivate an internet environment that can best meet Africa's social and economic development needs and goals".[27] It therefore mentions, but moves beyond, the "first generation" rights of opinion, thought, conscience and religion, expression and information, and freedom of assembly and association. It adds a range of developmental rights, such as the right of ethnic, religious or linguistic minorities to enjoy their own culture, and to use their own language. Most significantly, the Declaration expressly acknowledges economic, social and cultural rights, noting that marginalised groups do not enjoy equal access to the internet and that special measures should be taken to ensure that the rights secured through the internet are available to all without discrimination. This Declaration includes an obligation that states make the internet accessible and affordable.[28]

African states and the internet: control, accountability and access

Control

As explained in the introduction, we are looking here at forms of state control that the state should, from a human rights perspective, *not* be exercising; that is, control that results in the infringement of such rights. The main forms of such control can broadly be grouped into three (overlapping) categories: surveillance (monitoring and interception of communication), blocking (removing access to parts or the entire internet) and censorship (restricting the content of the information on the internet).

The main multilateral instrument covering these issues is the 2014 AU Convention on Cyber Security and Personal Data Protection (the AU Convention). This Convention is not yet in force, but states are beginning to put some of its provisions into their domestic legislation.[29] The AU Convention addresses internet surveillance and censorship, but does not allow for blocking of the internet.

Notably, the AU Convention makes specific mention of human rights protection, particularly in its sections on cybersecurity. According to Article 25(3), state parties to the Convention must ensure legal measures adopted in the area of cybersecurity do "not infringe on the rights of citizens guaranteed under the national constitution and internal laws, and protected by international conventions, particularly the African Charter on Human and Peoples' Rights, and other basic rights such as freedom of expression, the right to privacy and the right to a fair hearing, among others".

The AU Convention contains several provisions that allow states some leeway in monitoring or sharing internet communications. Chapter Two, while generally prohibiting the

26 *Supra* note 8.

27 See, African Declaration on Internet Rights and Freedoms: About the Initiative, http://africaninternetrights.org/about/ (accessed 02.12.2018).

28 *Supra* note 8.

29 Further details are provided in part C.2 below.

processing of personal or sensitive data, allows for exceptions in the "public interest"[30] or in the "exercise of official authority".[31] The Convention does, however, not define either of these terms. It also specifically requires that states control the internet through the mechanism of a national cybersecurity authority "with a view to conferring on [the cybersecurity body] a statutory authority and legal capacity to act in all aspects of cyber security application, including but not limited to response to cyber security incidents, and coordination and cooperation in the field of restorative justice, forensic investigations, prosecution, etc [sic]".[32] The provision does not stipulate any limits to this cybersecurity regulator's power.

The grey areas in this regional framework would not in themselves seem to accommodate widespread and overbroad surveillance, particularly in the light of the general provision that states may not infringe on the constitutional and human rights of their citizens. But recent research reveals "dense sociotechnical arrangements of registration, monitoring, and spying" in Africa.[33]

One of the most pervasive tools for digital surveillance arises from the registration of prepaid subscriber identity module (SIM) cards, which is mandatory in almost all African states.[34] This measure, ostensibly aimed at reducing cybercrime and terrorism,[35] has been rejected as ineffective and an infringement of privacy in a number of other jurisdictions.[36] Through SIM registration, states force service providers to establish and keep on record the identity of every SIM card holder. Once a person can be connected to a specific number, that person's movements and communication can then be tracked. Such a population registry lowers the barriers for all forms of digital surveillance, which states such as Benin,[37] Ethiopia, Nigeria, South Africa,[38] Zambia[39] and Zimbabwe have been shown to conduct.[40]

30 Articles 13(1)(b) and 14(2)(f) of the AU Convention, the former setting out exceptions to the requirement of consent to share data, and the latter setting out exceptions to the prohibition of the collection of data "revealing racial, ethnic and regional origin, parental filiation, political opinions, religious or philosophical beliefs, trade union membership, sex life and genetic information or, more generally, data on the state of health of the data subject".

31 Article 13(1)(b) of the AU Convention, which sets out some exceptions to the requirement that the data subject's consent must be obtained before data can be shared.

32 Article 25(3) of the AU Convention.

33 K.P. Donovan, P.M. Frowd, and A.K. Martin (2016) African Studies Review on Surveillance in Africa: Politics, Histories, Techniques: Introduction. *African Studies Review*, Vol. 59, No. 2, 31–37.

34 In 2014, Kevin Donovan and Aaron Martin calculated that 49 African states either required, or were introducing, mandatory SIM card registration; K.P. Donovan and A.K. Martin, (2014) The Rise of African SIM Registration: The Emerging Dynamics of Regulatory Change. *First Monday*, Vol. 19, Nos. 2–3, http://firstmonday.org/ojs/index.php/fm/article/view/4351/3820

35 Al-Shabaab was alleged to have used unregistered cell phones during its attack on Nairobi; See, Radical Changes Planned for Kenya's SIM Registration Process, www.itwebafrica.com/mobilex/309-kenya/231733-radical-changes-planned-for-kenyas-sim-registration-process

36 These include Canada, the Czech Republic, Greece, Ireland, the Netherlands, and Poland; see C.M. Hemeson, (2012) Directive on Consumer Data for SIM Card Registration in the Telecommunications Sector: An African Perspective, http://papers.ssrn.com/sol3/papers.cfm?abstract_id=1982033 (accessed 02.12.2018).

37 P.M. Frowd (2013) President of Benin Alleged to be at Center of Surveillance Scandal. *Privacy International*, https://privacyinternational.org/blog/1205/president-benin-alleged-be-center-surveillance-controversy (accessed 02.12.2018).

38 For reports on these three states, see M. Marquis-Boire, B. Marczak, C. Guarnieri, and J. Scott-Railton (2013) For their Eyes Only: The Commercialization of Digital Spying. *Citizen Lab*, https://citizenlab.org/2013/04/for-their-eyes-only-2/ (accessed 02.12.2018).

39 R. Bendrath and M. Mueller (2011) The End of the Net as We Know It? Deep Packet Inspection and Internet Governance. *New Media & Society*, Vol. 13, No. 7, 1142–1160, available at http://dx.doi.org/10.1177/1461444811398031 (accessed 02.12.2018); J. Reed (2013) Africa's Big Brother Lives in Beijing. *Foreign Policy*, www.foreignpolicy.com/articles/2013/07/30/africas_big_brother_lives_in_beijing_huawei_china_surveillance (accessed 02.12.2018).

40 *Supra* note 34.

Surveillance is, by its nature, covert, which increases the possibility that states may act beyond what surveillance powers they have under domestic legislation. For example, South Africa's main surveillance law is currently the Regulation of Interception of Communications and Provision of Communication Related Information Act 70 of 2002 (RICA). Among other things, RICA places an obligation on communication service providers to assist the state in intercepting communications.[41] RICA requires judicial approval for the interception of communications;[42] however, NGO's and journalists report that this approval is frequently bypassed in practice.[43]

This covert action by the executive reminds us that legislation specific to cybercrime or even the internet does not give us the full picture of how a state is controlling the internet. A state's anti-terrorism regime may provide a better indication of how seriously the government takes the freedom of the internet and the rights of those who use it. Terrorism legitimately presents instances in which some rights may need to be limited for the common good, but the threat to individual rights and freedoms arises when the decision as to when, and to what extent, rights may be limited are left to the discretion of the executive.

Vaguely worded provisions in the internet-related legislation are therefore problematic, firstly because the very text of the legislation gives the executive a level of discretion which may threaten the rule of law, and secondly because the other branches of government may be hesitant to call the executive to account for its use of such discretion in the context of counter-terrorism. One examples of an overbroad and vague provision could be found in Kenya's 2017 Computer and Cybercrimes Bill.[44] Under clause 24 (1) of the Bill, "a police officer may, in special circumstances enter, without a warrant any premises in or on which the police officer suspects an offence under this Act has been or is likely to be committed, and take possession of such computer system". In light of such far-reaching authorisation for searches and seizures without a warrant, it was highly problematic that the Bill did not define the term "special circumstances". Notably, however, the final 2018 Computer Misuse and Cybercrimes Act [45] no longer contains such a broad provision.[46] In South Africa, the proposed Cybercrimes and Cybersecurity Bill of 2017 has been criticised for, among other things,[47] stipulating grounds for the issuing of a

41 See, for instance, section 28 of RICA.

42 Sections 16 and 17 of RICA. Sections 5 and 6 allow approval to be obtained after the event in case of emergencies.

43 See, Stop the Surveillance! Activist Guide to RICA & State Surveillance in SA, www.r2k.org.za/wp-content/uploads/R2K-Handbook-Rica-Surveilance-2017.pdf (accessed 02.12.2018); see Final Report to the Minister to the Intelligent Services, r2k.org.za/matthews-commission, and see, Interception of Communications in SA – You Should be Worried, https://mybroadband.co.za/news/security/119280-interception-of-communications-in-sa-you-should-be-worried.html (accessed 02.12.2018).

44 The Computer and Cybercrimes Bill, 2017, http://kenyalaw.org/kl/fileadmin/pdfdownloads/bills/2017/ComputerandCybercrimesBill_2017.pdf (accessed 02.12.2018).

45 Act No. 5 of 2018, http://kenyalaw.org/lex/rest//db/kenyalex/Kenya/Legislation/English/Acts%20and%20Regulations/C/Computer%20Misuse%20and%20Cybercrimes%20Act%20-%20No.%2015%20of%202018/docs/ComputerMisuseandCybercrimesAct5of2018.pdf (accessed 02.12.2018).

46 The Bloggers Association of Kenya (BAKE) obtained, however, in May 2018 a conservatory order from the Constitutional and Human Rights Division of the High Court of Kenya at Nairobi suspending the Act on the basis that they threatened freedom of opinion, freedom of expression, freedom of the media and the right to privacy. See the petition against the Act as well as a scanned version of the court order at www.blog.bake.co.ke/wp-content/uploads/2018/05/BAKE-petition-Cybercrimes-act.pdf (accessed 02.12.2018).

47 Concerns with regards to privacy, freedom of expression and freedom from surveillance were, for instance, raised in the Right2Know Campaign submission on the Cybercrimes and Cybersecurity Bill in 2017; see, Right-2Know, Cybercrimes, Cybersecurity and Internet Freedom, www.r2k.org.za/wp-content/uploads/170810-R2K-Cybercrimes-Submission.pdf (accessed 02.12.2018).

search warrant which are even vaguer than RICA's already vague grounds for the issuing of interception directions.[48]

The signal-jamming incident presents an occasion on which both the South African Parliament and (initially) the courts refused to exercise oversight over the executive when it claimed to be acting in the interests of national security.[49] Some scholars strongly resist the argument that there is any arena of public power that should not be subject to the law and review, even in states of emergency, but the thinking that law can somehow "hamper" an effective response to terrorism is found in both scholarship and legislation.[50] Sometimes anti-terrorism legislation expressly authorises the surveillance of electronic communication of a terrorist suspect without judicial or parliamentary oversight.[51] However, we suggest that there is a link beyond the express reference to the internet in anti-terrorism legislation. It will be found where-ever the executive is given wide discretion to prevent attacks (whether by surveilling or banning suspects, "listing" individuals as terrorist, blocking terrorist suspects from travelling, or seizing their assets),[52] and particularly where such discretion is not scrutinised by another branch of government.

As with surveillance, we see that blocking of the internet by government is generally justified as a security measure, although we noted that there is no normative basis for it in the AU Convention. And, indeed, when it takes place, its domestic legal basis is often tenuous or absent, too. In practical terms, Internet Service Providers (ISPs) play a key role in both the blocking of individual websites or the entire internet in a country by manipulating their so-called Border Gateway Protocols. Technically, shutting down the internet becomes more difficult when there is a higher number of ISPs involved and virtual personal network (VPN) software may help more sophisticated users to work around technically imposed blackouts. But it is still possible. Thus, what determines whether government can, practically, shut down the internet domestically or not is the factual control which it exercises over ISPs in the country. Such control may generally be higher in authoritarian regimes with only one or a few ISPs, but even in more democratic countries

48 See, for instance, Media Policy and Democracy Project Report (2015) *An Analysis of the Communications Surveillance Legislative Framework in South Africa*, Vol. 17, www.mediaanddemocracy.com/uploads/1/6/5/7/16577624/comms-surveillance-framework_mare2.pdf (accessed 02.12.2018).

49 The Minister of Safety and Security claimed to be acting under the authorisation of the National Strategic Intelligence Act 39 of 1994, which authorises the State Security Agency to take counter-intelligence measures ("measures and activities conducted, instituted, or taken to impede and to neutralise the effectiveness of foreign or hostile intelligence operations, to protect intelligence and any classified information, to conduct vetting investigations and to counter any threat or potential threat to national security"); *supra* note 5 at para 55.

50 For the academic debate on the role of law in states of emergencies, see D. Dyzenhaus (2005) The State of Emergency in Legal Theory. In: V. Ramraj, M. Hor and K. Roach, (Eds.), *Global Anti-Terrorism Law and Policy*. Cambridge: Cambridge University Press, 65; D. Dyzenhaus (2006) *The Constitution of Legality: Law in a Time of Emergency*. Cambridge: Cambridge University Press; Balasubramaniam, R.R. (2008) Indefinite Detention: Rule by Law or Rule of Law? In Victor V. Ramraj (Ed.), *Emergencies and the Limits of Legality*. Cambridge: Cambridge University Press, 118; Nardin, T. (2008) Emergency Logic: Prudence, Morality and the Rule of Law. In Victor V. Ramraj (Ed.), *Emergencies and the Limits of Legality*. Cambridge: Cambridge University Press, 97. For executive-leaning trends of anti-terrorism law generally, see C. Forcese (2007) Hegemonic Federalism: The Democratic Implications of the UN Security Council's "Legislative Phase". *Victoria University of Wellington Law Review*, Vol. 38, 175; R. Kent (2011) *The 9/11 Effect: Comparative Counter-Terrorism*. Cambridge: Cambridge University Press; Report of the United Nations Special Rapporteur on the Promotion and Protection of Human Rights and Fundamental Freedoms While Countering Terrorism (UN Doc A/67/396), especially para 34.

51 See, for example, sections 18–19 of Uganda's Anti-Terrorism Act of 2002.

52 From the anti-terrorism legislation that we were able to access for this chapter, we noted such measures in Botswana, Cameroon, Egypt, Ethiopia, Ghana, Gambia, Kenya, Mauritius, Namibia, Nigeria, Seychelles and Tanzania.

contractual obligations or the prospect of losing the licence to operate may make ISPs consider succumbing to government pressure.[53]

In Africa, planned government-directed internet disruptions, or full-fledged shutdowns through technological means,[54] are on the increase. A 2017 brief published by the Collaboration on International ICT Policy for East and Southern Africa (CIPESA) stated that at least 12 countries in Sub-Saharan Africa have had recent shutdowns, including Burundi, Cameroon, the Democratic Republic of Congo, Ethiopia, Gabon, the Gambia, Niger, the Republic of Congo, Togo and Uganda.[55] Of the 183 global internet shutdowns recorded for 2016 and 2017 by digital rights group Access Now, 29 occurred in Africa – making the continent the second most affected region in the world.[56] And already in 2012, a study found that most countries in Africa are at either severe or significant risk of internet disconnection.[57]

The third form of control which we wish to discuss in this section is censorship. Although security provides a common justification for this practice as well, governments also draw on a wider range of justifications, such as preventing defamation, indecency, public disorder, or the distribution of obscene content, or preserving the culture of the nation. A recent example to garner international attention was the arrest of a Swahili rapper in Tanzania – popularly known as Diamond Platinumz – after he had posted a clip of himself kissing a woman.[58] His arrest was based on the new Electronic and Postal Communications (Online Content) Regulations 2017.[59]

Censorship predates the internet by many years. We will not be able to address the phenomenon in full in this chapter, merely touching briefly on the crime of hate speech in the final section. Where the internet is concerned, we note that governments have begun expressly to impose censorship on electronic communication. The preceding Tanzanian example was based on a law regulating only online content. Rwanda also introduced a new law in 2016 that made it illegal to use a public electronic communication network for purposes of causing "annoyance, inconvenience, or needless anxiety".[60] A Freedom House Survey of 2015 found internet censorship in Sudan, Uganda, Zambia, Zimbabwe,

53 Governments also coerce ISP's into deleting content; See, Internet Censorship in Africa Threatens Democracy, Economy, https://mg.co.za/article/2018-08-06-internet-censorship-in-africa-threatens-democracy-economy

54 Definitions for internet shutdown differ and can be as broad as the definition suggested by the #KeepItOn Coalition: "An intentional disruption of internet or electronic communications rendering them inaccessible or effectively unusable, for a specific population or within a location, often to exert control over the flow of information". Such broad definition would include the shutdown of digital communication platforms such as WhatsApp.

55 See The Economic Impact of Internet Disruptions in Sub-Saharan Africa, https://cipesa.org/?wpfb_dl=249 (accessed 02.12.2018).

56 See What is an Internet Shutdown?, www.accessnow.org/keepiton/ (accessed 02.12.2018).

57 See Could It Happen in your Country?, https://dyn.com/blog/could-it-happen-in-your-countr/ (accessed 02.12.2018).

58 See How African Governments Try to Control What Is Said Online, www.economist.com/middle-east-and-africa/2018/04/19/how-african-governments-try-to-control-what-is-said-online

59 See Analysis of Tanzania's Electronic and Postal Communications (Online Content) Regulations 2017, https://cipesa.org/2017/11/analysis-of-tanzanias-electronic-and-postal-communications-online-content-regulations-2017/ (accessed 02.12.2018) and the Electronic and Postal Communications (Online Content) 2018, www.tcra.go.tz/images/documents/regulations/SUPP_GN_NO_133_16_03_2018_EPOCA_ONLINE_CONTENT_REGULATIONS_2018.pdf

60 Articles 60 of Law N°24/2016 of 18/06/2016 Governing Information and Communication Technologies, www.mitec.gov.rw/fileadmin/Documents/Policies_and_Rugulations/ICT_laws/ICT_LAW.pdf (accessed 02.12.2018).

Ethiopia, the Gambia, Kenya, Malawi, Nigeria and Rwanda. All of these states imposed some form of censorship on criticism of the authorities.[61]

The Gambian example demonstrates a link between censorship and counter-terrorism. The Information and Communication Amendment Act of 2013 imposes prison terms for spreading "false news" about government or public officials, making derogatory statements about such people, and inciting dissatisfaction with, or instigating violence against, the government.[62] Expression is also treated as a source of danger to the state when journalists report on terrorism.[63] Examples include the arrest of the "Zone 9" bloggers in Ethiopia[64] and the conviction in Cameroon of a journalist for "non-denunciation" of terrorism.[65] Other forms of censorship are directed more openly against opposition parties, without express reference to terrorism, such as the closing down of opposition-owned radio stations in the DRC.[66]

Another strategy that effectively results in censorship, particularly in Africa, is the imposition of taxes and licencing fees to limit the use of social media. For instance, the Ugandan government is considering a tax on use of social media platforms[67] and Tanzania's Electronic and Postal Communications (Online Content) Regulations,[68] set out here, require "any person who wishes to provide online content services" to apply for a licence and pay a prescribed fee.[69] This applies to online radio, online television, online blogs and other online services. Taken together, the application fee, initial licencing fee and annual licencing fees required from online content services (including bloggers, online forums and possibly even social media users) come to more than US $900.[70] This amount corresponds broadly with the country's GDP per capita.[71] At the same time, the Regulations allow for licences to be revoked with relative ease.[72]

Accountability

In this section and the following section, we are looking at positive measures that the state should be taking to protect human rights in the digital domain, and the extent to which its obligations are established and enforced. The focus for the current section is on the

61 See Freedom on the Net 2015, https://freedomhouse.org/report/freedom-net/freedom-net-2015 (accessed 02.12.2018) Other topics censored in some states included mobilisation for public causes, ethnic and religious minorities, corruption, political opposition and LGBTI issues.

62 *Supra* note 7 at p. 6.

63 For examples, see, Somali Authorities Detain Journalist Accused of Spreading False News, https://cpj.org/2018/09/somali-authorities-detain-journalist-accused-of-sp.php (accessed 02.12.2018); see, Journalists Not Terrorists, https://cpj.org/reports/2017/09/journalists-not-terrorists-cameroon-ahmed-abba-anti-terror-imprisoned.php (accessed 02.12.2018).

64 *Supra* note 7 at p. 7.

65 See, Journalists Not Terrorists.

66 The official reason for the closing of the stations was the radio had incited civil disobedience; see, DRC Authorities Close Two Opposition Radio Stations, https://cpj.org/2018/10/drc-authorities-close-two-opposition-radio-station.php (accessed 02.12.2018)

67 See Anger at Uganda's Tax on Social Media, www.bbc.com/news/world-africa-44682345.

68 *Supra* note 59.

69 Section 14 of the Regulations.

70 See the Second Schedule of the Regulations.

71 According to World Bank Data, see World Bank Data: GDP Per Capita, https://data.worldbank.org/indicator/NY.GDP.PCAP.CD?locations=TZ (accessed 02.12.2018).

72 See section 15 of the Regulations.

damage that the internet can do, and the obligations that each state may bear to prevent or minimise such damage. The third section focuses on the benefits of the internet and states' obligations to ensure that their citizens can claim those benefits.

What harm can the internet do? The most obvious dangers arise from the use of the internet to commit fraud, extortion, money-laundering and terrorism. However, cyber-crime is becoming increasingly inventive and sophisticated; a 2016 study by the African Union and Symantec revealed a range of methods for misappropriating and using digital information stored on electronic devices, including malware for mobile phones and computers,[73] ransomware, which has spiked in recent years;[74] hijacking of social media accounts; email threats and other scams.[75] While these offences are generally covered by the generic descriptions of acts proscribed in the relevant instruments (see the later discussion), there are other harmful activities which may not fall under the criminal codes. One example is the manipulation of information on social media for purposes of propaganda and financial gain, and another is the attempt by telecommunications companies to undercut voice-over IP services (VOIP), which enables internet users to speak to one another without the use of a telephone.[76]

While there are a number of regional instruments on the topic of cybercrime, there is currently a negligible body of legally binding norms regulating cyber security across all of Africa. The most recent and comprehensive instrument is the aforementioned African Union Convention on Cyber Security and Personal Data Protection of 2014. The Economic Community of West African States (ECOWAS) has produced a series of directives and acts[77] binding on the geographical region. Beyond this, two further, localised instruments, the Common Market for East and Southern Africa (COMESA) Model Cyber-crime Bill and the Southern African Development Community (SADC) Model Law on Computer Crime and Cybercrime, do not create binding obligations but suggest a template for domestic legislation.

Our focus in this chapter is the AU Convention. This treaty consists of three main chapters, of which two are relevant specifically to the issue of state accountability for internet use and harm: Chapter Two, on the protection of personal data, and Chapter Three, on cyber security and cybercrime.

Chapter Two aims to ensure the protection of personal data in every member state, requiring each state to establish a legal framework or mechanism[78] to strengthen fundamental rights and public freedoms and punish violations of privacy "without prejudice to the principle of the free flow of personal data".[79] The Convention requires all processing of personal data to be declared to the protection authority,[80] which has then to authorise that processing if the information relates to a number of categories, such as genetic

73 The study estimates that one in seven smartphones in Nigeria is infected with malware. See Symantec's Report (2016) Cyber Security Trends and Government Responses in Africa, 8.

74 Ibid., 10.

75 Ibid., 12.

76 *Supra* note 7, at p. 24.

77 Supplementary Act on Electronic Transactions available at www.tit.comm.ecowas.int/wp-content/uploads/2015/11/SIGNED-Electronic-Transaction-Act.pdf, Supplementary Act on Personal Data Protection and Directive on Fighting against Cybercrime available at www.ccdcoe.org/sites/default/files/documents/ECOWAS-110819-FightingCybercrime.pdf

78 The terms are used interchangeably; see article 8(1) and (2).

79 Ibid., Article 8(1).

80 Ibid., Article 10(2).

information, offences or security measures, and biometric data.[81] The "National Personal Data Protection Authority" has to be an independent administrative body staffed by people who are not members of government and not involved in the information and communications business sector.[82] It has the mandate of approving requests for the processing of information and ensuring that data controllers respect the principles of the Convention.[83] These principles require that the data subjects give their consent for processing of personal data,[84] and that data processing be carried out lawfully, fairly, accurately, transparently and confidentially.[85] The consent requirement may be waived in specific cases, including, problematically, the performance of a task "in the public interest or in the exercise of official authority vested in the controller or in a third party to whom the data are disclosed".[86] A similar provision exempts states from the requirement that they prohibit data collection and processing which reveals racial, ethnic and regional origin, parental affiliation, political opinions, beliefs and trade union membership, amongst other things.[87] The term "public interest" is not defined in the Convention.

The Convention spells out a number of rights held by the data subjects, including the right to information about the processing of their data,[88] the right to object,[89] and the right to demand rectification or erasure of the data.[90] The personal data controller, on the other hand, is obliged to maintain the confidentiality of the data,[91] keep it secure against unauthorised third parties,[92] and not to maintain the data once the purpose for which it was collected is fulfilled.[93]

Chapter Three of the Convention attaches criminal consequences to the failure to respect the principles set out in Chapter Two,[94] and also requires that specific authorities (pre-existing or new) bear responsibility for cyber security breaches and prosecution.[95] It requires states to criminalise the full range of activities which "affect the confidentiality, integrity, availability and survival of information and communication technology systems, the data they process and the underlying network infrastructure".[96] These crimes are spelt out in more detail in a separate section on criminal provisions, which cover offences specific to ICT (attacks on computer systems and interception of data)[97] and well as content-related offences[98] and offences relating to property (such as theft, fraud and extortion).[99]

81 Ibid., Article 10(4).
82 Ibid., Article 11(6).
83 Ibid., Article 12 (2). Enforcement mechanisms set out in article 12(3) and (4) range from issuing a warning to withdrawing the data controller's authorisation.
84 Ibid., Article 13(1).
85 Ibid., Article 13(2) to (6).
86 Ibid., Article 13 (1)(b).
87 Ibid., Article 14, with the relevant exception in article 14(2)(i).
88 Ibid., Articles 16–17.
89 Ibid., Article 18.
90 Ibid., Article 19.
91 Ibid., Article 20.
92 Ibid., Article 21.
93 Ibid., Article 22.
94 Ibid., Article 25(1).
95 Ibid., Article 25(2).
96 Ibid., Article 25(1).
97 Ibid., Article 29(1) and (2).
98 Ibid., Article 29(3).
99 Ibid., Article 30.

Of the content-related offences, Article 29(3)(f)–(h) deserve closer attention, because they present a potential threat to freedom of speech. While they might colloquially be referred to as the "hate speech" provisions, they in fact criminalise a far broader range of speech acts than generally encapsulated by the (admittedly contentious) term of "hate speech". Thus, the ICCPR[100] and the Banjul Charter[101] describe hate speech as *advocacy* of hatred against national, ethnic or religious groups[102] which constitutes incitement to cause some form of *harm*. In the case of the ICCPR, the harm is "discrimination, hostility or violence"; in the Banjul Charter the harm is described as "lawless violence or . . . any other similar illegal action". Thus two central elements of the crime are incitement and some form of harm.[103]

By contrast, Article 29(3)(g) criminalises the mere *insulting* of a person on the basis of his or her membership of a such groups or a political group. While the element of "harm" in the ICCPR and Banjul Charter may include psychological as well as physical harm, reducing the hate speech threshold to mere insult does raise the risk of particularly intrusive interference with free expression. This insult-based approach to hate speech is not unique to Africa[104] but we argue that it is dangerous in societies subject to growing government control over cyberspace. There is no theoretical engagement with the concept of hate speech in regional African human rights fora, so we do not yet know how the term will be interpreted. The African Commission on Human and People's Rights does seem still to require at least the potential of physical harm before hate speech is present.[105]

A separate article of the AU Convention is devoted to the establishment of an institution specifically to maintain cyber security. Although this section requires states parties to "establish clear accountability", there is no detail on how this cyber security institution should be constituted, what it should look like, to whom it should account and how.

Only two states have hitherto ratified the AU Convention,[106] which means that it is not yet in force.[107] States have nonetheless legislated on the matters covered by the Convention, but its implementation has been patchy. By September 2018, twenty-seven of Africa's

100 Article 20(2) of the ICCPR.

101 Article 13(5) of the Banjul Charter.

102 Article 20(2) of the ICCPR; the Banjul Charter adds groups distinguished by colour, language or national origin.

103 For further discussion on the balancing of the right to dignity and equality with the freedom of expression, see J. Waldron (2012) *The Harm in Hate Speech*. Harvard: Harvard University Press; T. Mendel (2010) Hate Speech Rules under International Law. *Centre for Law and Democracy*, Vol. 14, www.law-democracy.org/wp-content/uploads/2010/07/10.02.hate-speech.Macedonia-book.pdf (accessed 02.12.2018); A. Oboler (2014) Legal Doctrines Applied to Online Hate Speech. *Computers and the Law*, www.austlii.edu.au/au/journals/ANZComPuLawJl/2014/4.pdf.

104 For examples of "insult"-based hate speech elsewhere, see the review of international and Australian provisions in Oboler (2014).

105 The African Commission describes hate speech as: "any form of speech which degrades others, promotes hatred *and* encourages violence against a group on the basis of criteria including race, colour, religion, national origin, gender, disability or a number of other traits" (our emphasis). See 362: Resolution on the Right to Freedom of Information and Expression on the Internet in Africa, www.achpr.org/sessions/59th/resolutions/362/

106 As of October 2018.

107 According to Art. 36 of the AU Convention, the Convention will enter into force 30 days after the 15th instrument of ratification is received. As of October 2018, only Mauritius and Senegal have ratified the AU Convention (and a further ten have signed but not yet ratified the treaty). See, List of Countries Which Have Signed, Ratified/Acceded to the African Union Convention on Cybersecurity and Personal Data Protection, www.tralac.org/documents/resources/african-union/1661-au-convention-on-cyber-security-and-personal-data-protection-status-1-june-2016.html (accessed 02.12.2018).

fifty-four states had enacted data protection laws.[108] A further seven states were drafting or reviewing legislation in this regard.[109] While some states could be argued to provide limited data protection through their constitutional rights,[110] eleven states did not deal with the issue at all in their legislative framework.[111]

The patchwork nature of both the legislative schemes and the implementation of data protection laws across Africa has led to much uncertainty for companies wishing to use the internet for their businesses.[112] Amongst the variations identified between legislative schemes are whether they put a data protection authority (DPA), or a data protection officer (DPO), or neither, in place, the requirements and mechanisms for cross-border transfers, and whether companies are required to alert data subjects of a data breach.[113] However, the states which have enacted legislation in this area all require that individuals be notified if their personal data is collected or stored,[114] and that organisations which process or disclose personal data take reasonable security precautions to prevent loss, misuse and other forms of harm and maintain the integrity of the data.[115] All the states require registration of data processing and most of them restrict cross-border transfers of data, although to differing extents.[116]

The regulation required for smooth operation of these legislative schemes is often missing. Thus, for example, cross-border transfers of data to countries with inadequate data protection generally require some form of consent-based legal mechanism in the absence of specific authorisation by the DPA. However, Cynthia Rich notes that almost none of the DPAs which have been established have specified what must be contained in the relevant legal mechanisms which establish consent; nor have they produced lists of states which have inadequate data protection.[117]

Enforcement of data protection regimes by DPAs is also uneven, but is generally growing across the region. A 2017 survey describes the data protection programmes of Mauritius and Morocco as "well established" and notes increasing activity by the DPAs in Benin, Ghana, Mali, Senegal and Tunisia.[118] Furthermore, 2016 saw the creation of the African Network of Personal Data Protection Authorities (RAPDP) by Cape Verde, Benin, Burkina Faso, Cote d'Ivoire, Mali, Morocco and Tunisia. This inter-state body aims to ensure close cooperation between its members in the drafting of data protection laws, the formulation of opinions on specific issues and the promotion of African data protection instruments.[119]

In the area of cyber security, many African states have not yet enacted legislation to counter cybercrime. According to an UNCTAD survey of April 2018, twenty-eight African states (52%) have legislation against cybercrime, eleven are in the process of drafting

108 Deloitte (2017) Privacy is Paramount: Personal Data Protection in Africa, 6–7.
109 Ibid.
110 Ibid.
111 Ibid.
112 Ibid.
113 C. Rich (2017) A Look at New Trends in 2017: Privacy Laws in Africa and the Near East. *Privacy and Security Law Report*, 6–7; see also, Bloomberg BNA World Data Protection Report, 2.
114 Ibid.
115 Ibid.
116 Ibid.
117 Ibid.
118 Ibid., 1–2.
119 Ibid.

such legislation, and fifteen have no legislation in the area at all.[120] Other states have opted to include provisions concerning cybersecurity in more general legislation such as their criminal codes or laws that broadly deal with electronic transactions.[121] Of course, all the legislation that is expressly directed at the internet is complemented by the more general criminal laws that address traditionally offline activities which can now also be executed in cyberspace; such as fraud, extortion, money-laundering and terrorism.

Nonetheless, by international standards, the continent is vulnerable to cybercrime, and, indeed, some research claims that cybercrime is growing faster in Africa than on any other continent.[122] It is clear that Africa does present particular vulnerabilities, partly because of the gaps in its legislation against cybercrime, and partly because cyber security generally relies on an informed and alert public. Education generally lags behind in many regions of Africa,[123] and much of the electronic equipment and software in use is outdated or unlicensed, which means it is not protected against modern forms of hacking and malware.[124]

We need to add a caveat, however, as Africa's vulnerability to cyberattacks is not revealed only by treaty membership, legislation and enforcement mechanisms. A state may lack all three of these but nonetheless enjoy "cyber resilience", that is, the capacity "to withstand negative impacts due to known, unpredictable, uncertain, and unexpected threats from activities in cyberspace".[125] Iginio Gagliardone and Nanjira Sambuli point to the example of the territories of Somalia and Somaliland. Here, the collapse of government institutions in many areas and the lack of regulation have not thwarted a strong digital network, in which 26% of people pay bills from their mobile telephones – the highest rate in the world.[126] The network is run by private companies and supported by systems of customary law, as "complex relations among courts, clan-based governance and companies have been able to regulate and resolve conflicts (fraud, mistaken transfers or disputes over the amount of the transfer) over mobile money".[127]

Where commercial attacks are concerned, recent research suggests that only a small percentage target Africa specifically, and an even smaller fraction originate from the continent.[128] However, politically and ideologically motivated groups pose a separate and ongoing threat to the African region. A good example can be seen in areas controlled by Al-Shabaab. This organisation bans internet use on the one hand (thus also restricting the

120 See the UNCTAD survey of April 2018, https://unctad.org/en/Pages/DTL/STI_and_ICTs/ICT4D-Legislation/eCom-Cybercrime-Laws.aspx (accessed 02.12.2018) Our own survey in September 2018 found no cybercrime legislation enacted in Benin, Cabo Verde, the Central African Republic, Chad, Comoros, the Democratic Republic of Congo, Djibouti, Equatorial Guinea, Eritrea, Gabon, Guinea, Kenya, Lesotho, Liberia, Libya, Mali, Mozambique, Rwanda, Sierra Leone, Swaziland, Togo and Tunisia.

121 Countries with specific draft or enacted cybersecurity legislation include Angola, Benin, Botswana, Burkina Faso, Cameroon, Congo, Cote d'Ivoire, Ethiopia, Gabon, Kenya, Madagascar, Mauritius, Nigeria, Senegal, South Africa, Togo, Tunisia, Uganda, Tanzania and Zimbabwe.

122 F. Cassim (2011) Addressing the Growing Spectre of Cyber Crime in Africa: Evaluating Measures Adopted by South Africa and Other Regional Role Players. *Comparative and International Law Journal of Southern Africa*, Vol. 44, 123–126, https://issafrica.s3.amazonaws.com/site/uploads/PolBrief73_cybercrime.pdf (accessed 02.12.2018).

123 Razzano cites sub-Saharan Africa as one of the most undeveloped regions in the world, supra note 7 at p. 26. See also E. Ondari Okemwa (2004) Impediments to Promoting Access to Global Knowledge in Sub-Saharan Africa. *Library Management*, Vol. 25, No. 8/9, 361–375, https://doi.org/10.1108/01435120410562853.

124 *Supra* note 73 at p. 18.

125 I. Gagliardone and N. Sambuli (2014) Cyber Security and Cyber Resilience in East Africa 5. Citing ISACA.

126 Ibid., citing Stremlau and Osman (2015) and Penicaud and McGrath (2014).

127 Ibid.

128 *Supra* note 73 at pp. 24 and 33. See also the general survey from pp. 31 to 43.

networks which help to ensure cyber resilience) and uses social media for its propaganda on the other.[129]

Access

We conclude with some brief comments on access to the internet. As set out previously, almost all African states are parties to the International Covenant on Civil and Political Rights (ICCPR)[130] and the African Charter on Human and People's Rights (the Banjul Charter).[131] Furthermore, a strong majority have ratified the International Covenant on Economic, Social and Cultural Rights (ICESCR).[132] The ICCPR and the Banjul Charter protect the right to equality,[133] while the ICESCR and Banjul Charter both guarantee a range of socio-economic rights, such as health[134] and education.[135]

However, both equality and social development are intricately connected to the internet, which makes access to the internet itself a human rights issue. As then Secretary-General Kofi Annan commented in 1999:

> For [many inhabitants of development countries], the great scientific and technical achievements of our era might as well be taking place on another planet. . . . The capacity to receive, download and share information through electronic networks, the freedom to communicate freely across national boundaries – these must become realities for all people. . . . These people lack many things: jobs, shelter, food, healthcare and drinkable water. Today, being cut off from basic telecommunications services is a hardship almost as acute as these deprivations, and may indeed reduce the chances of finding remedies to them.[136]

The well-established link between poverty and "information poverty"[137] is not addressed in the binding regional human rights instruments we considered in the second section. It is only the soft law African Declaration on Internet Rights and Freedoms[138] which posits that individuals have a right to access the internet and that states therefore bear the corresponding duty to facilitate internet access. None of the other instruments place on the state the duty to put nationals who do not have the resources to connect to the internet

129 See, Somalia: Prevalence of Cell Phones and Internet Cafes in Mogadishu, Including the Ability to Use Cell Phones for Financial Transfers (2012–February 2015). *SOM105092.E* (5 March 2015), www.refworld.org/docid/550c35904.html (accessed 02.12.2018); see also, Kenya: Shabaab Attacks Cripple Phone Services in Parts of Garissa, https://allafrica.com/stories/201807230740.html (accessed 02.12.2018)

130 See *supra* note 13 on the position of Western Sahara.

131 See, Ratification Table: African Charter on Human and People's Rights, www.achpr.org/instruments/achpr/ratification/ (accessed 02.12.2018). See *supra* note 13 on the position of Western Sahara. Morocco had been a party but withdrew when Western Sahara was admitted as a member of the Charter.

132 *Supra* note 17.

133 Article 26 of the ICCPR and article 3 of the Banjul Charter.

134 Article 11 of the ICESCR and article 16 of the Banjul Charter.

135 Article 11 of the ICESCR and article 16 of the Banjul Charter.

136 *Supra* note 7 at p. 26, citing C. Fuchs and E. Horak (2008) Africa and the Digital Divide. *Telematics and Informatics*, Vol. 25, 99.

137 C.J. Kenny (2000) Expanding Internet Sccess to the Rural Poor in Africa. *Information Technology for Development*, Vol. 19, 25; C.U. Ngini, S.M. Furnell, and B.V. Ghita (2002) Assessing the Global Accessibility of the Internet. *Internet Research*, 329–330, https://doi.org/10.1108/10662240210438399 (accessed 02.12.2018).

138 *Supra* note 8.

in a position to do so. Similarly, our survey of African legislation did not uncover a legal obligation on the part of the state to connect its inhabitants to the internet.[139]

Nonetheless, in the case of *Retrofit (Private Limited) v. Posts and Telecommunications*, Zimbabwe's Supreme Court declared the monopoly of Zimbabwe's Posts and Telecommunications Service unconstitutional, in effect forcing the state to licence a private company to set up a mobile telephone network.[140] The decision was based primarily on the private company's own right to freedom of expression, but the Court also emphasised the rights of the people of Zimbabwe to receive and impart ideas:

> In my view, it is axiomatic that for the Corporation to monopolise telecommunication services in Zimbabwe, and then to furnish a public switched telephone network of dubious worth, available to but a small percentage of the populace, manifestly interferes with the constitutional right of every person in the country to receive and impart ideas and information by means of this "pervasive two-way communications system. . . . A public monopoly which fails to fulfil that essential role [of communicating ideas and information] imposes a severe restraint upon the constitutionally protected freedom of expression".[141]

Retrofit deals with communication and access to information, not digitalisation and the internet per se. But it is not a coincidence that the form of communication at the centre of the case was mobile telephones. Mobile phones are not only the main medium for communication in Africa (in 2016, the World Bank estimated that 60% of the inhabitants of sub-Saharan Africa had these devices,[142] far outstripping the provision of traditional telephone lines) but mobile phones are also the main medium through which communication is being linked to the internet.[143] The growing use of mobile phones also demonstrates that the internet itself has become an indispensable resource for socio-economic development. Commenting on broadband in particular (the provision of constant, high-speed internet) Natalija Gelvanovska et al. comment:

> There is growing consensus that broadband is an essential general purpose technology (GPT) that has pervasive productivity impact on multiple sectors of the economy (e.g., energy, water, industrial production, services, transport, and so on). Broadband has a similar impact on the transformation of the economy as previous GPTs had in the past, including the printing press, steam engines, and electricity.[144]

139 South Africa's Electronic Communications and Transactions (ECT) Act 25 of 2002, www.gov.za/sites/default/files/a25-02.pdf (accessed 02.12.2018) mentions "promoting universal access to electronic communications and transactions and the use of electronic transactions by SMMEs".

140 *Retrofit (Pvt) Ltd v. PTC* and another 1995(2) ZLR 199 (S).

141 Ibid., paras 218–219.

142 See, Media (R)evolutions: Convergence around Mobile Phones in Sub-Saharan Africa, https://blogs.worldbank.org/category/tags/mobile-phone-penetration (accessed 02.12.2018). Note that not all these phones were connected to the internet, however.

143 See, The AU's Cybercrime Response: A Positive Start, but Substantial Challenges Ahead, https://issafrica.s3.amazonaws.com/site/uploads/PolBrief73_cybercrime.pdf (accessed 02.12.2018); See also, Assessing the Global Accessibility of the Internet, note 136.

144 N. Gelvanovska, M. Rogy, and C.M. Rossotto (2014) Broadband networks in the Middle East and North Africa: Accelerating High-Speed Internet Access. World Bank Group E-Library, chapter 1 at 20, https://doi.org/10.1596/978-1-4648-0112-9 (accessed 02.12.2018).

Research groups, intergovernmental bodies and states themselves are gradually identifying how state practices and policies can hinder or improve access to the internet. But the primary factors that have been identified are the high cost of internet access, lack of infrastructure and the physical unavailability of the mechanisms which connect to the internet. [145] For this range of obstacles, a pro-competition regulatory system, which allows for non-state actors to provide internet services, combined with some forms of government subsidy where necessary, has been proposed as a solution.[146] African states have, unfortunately, shown themselves reluctant to institute either of these measures.

Where subsidy of internet infrastructure and access is concerned, a study in March 2018 revealed that, although 68% of African states have some form of Universal Service and Access Fund (USAF) to promote connectivity to the internet, these are largely untapped, and Africa remains the region with one of the lowest internet penetration rates in the world (22%).[147] And from the discussion in this chapter, we can see that the second suggested measure – a pro-competition regulatory system – will not have strong support in many African states, as it reduces government control over the internet. The chapter has provided regulatory and practical examples whereby states exert control over registration, use and content of the internet, including by imposing licence requirements and setting high licence fees. Indeed, and ironically, much of the funds of the USAFs are provided by mandatory contributions from telecommunications providers.[148]

We end, therefore, with the same phenomenon that introduced this chapter: unaccountable, non-transparent state control over the internet. In our opening anecdote, such control led to the breakdown of democratic governance. In the course of our discussion, it emerged as the main facilitator of the infringement of the right to privacy (through surveillance), the right to information and freedom of expression (through censorship and blocking) and, finally, the right to equality and development. While we have discussed areas where the state *should* control the internet – to ensure that private parties do not misuse it – we have found that empowering the state to do so can also serve to boost state power without preventing the harm which the state is meant to prevent. Here, too, accountability and transparency are key. Our final conclusion seems too obvious to state: that the protection of human rights in the internet is part and parcel of the promotion of democratic, accountable governance. But we hope that our discussion has teased out why this is so, and helped to establish the indispensable position that an open, free and accessible internet needs to play in Africa's future.

145 *Supra* note 137 on the need for incentives to build up the infrastructure for broadband (accessed 5.10.2018).

146 *Supra* note 137; see also, Broadband Internet Coming to Africa, http://blogs.worldbank.org/ic4d/broadband-internet-coming-to-africa on the need for incentives to build up the infrastructure for broadband (accessed 02.12.2018).

147 See, Universal Service and Access Funds: An Untapped Resource to Close the Gender Digital Divide, http://webfoundation.org/docs/2018/03/Using-USAFs-to-Close-the-Gender-Digital-Divide-in-Africa.pdf (accessed 06.03.2019)

148 Ibid.

22 The approach of North American courts towards the internet

David P. Stewart[1]

Introduction

Significant advancements in technology have always presented legal challenges, but perhaps none as difficult as those created by the rapid revolution in information technology and data sharing on the internet. Domestic legislatures and courts are increasingly challenged to respond by adapting traditional principles to new situations. This chapter provides an overview of recent developments in Canadian and US jurisprudence, initially with a particular focus on law-enforcement access to personal data on the internet. Although the examples are only illustrative, the broader aim is to identify some salient similarities and differences in the two countries' approach to "Internet Law".

As used here, "Internet Law" refers broadly to the legal issues related to the regulation and use of the internet for a wide variety of purposes – private, commercial, governmental. By definition, it encompasses fundamental questions of individual rights. It is also highly dynamic, adapting constantly in response to changes in information technology. In the United States and Canada, however, it has to date mostly involved the application of rules drawn from other areas (for example, government regulation, law enforcement, contract, tort, intellectual property, etc.) rather than the articulation of new rules specifically tailored to new technologies.

In both jurisdictions, the process of adaptation has been carried out largely by the courts against the backdrop of existing constitutional principles and prior decisional law. While legislation clearly plays a role (more in Canada than in the United States), it too must conform to constitutional requirements. In this sense, both legal systems implicitly adopt the "sameness of rights" doctrine.

As a point of departure, consider the following concrete illustrations, which examine these issues at the intersection of personal freedom and law-enforcement investigations.

Cell phones, texting and internet use

Mobile devices offer both unprecedented ease of communication and unique challenges to individual privacy due to their portability, wide range of sensors and constant presence near their owners. They give government authorities both access to personal communications and ways to track user location and behaviour.

In 2014, the Supreme Court of Canada addressed the question whether police conducting a search incident to an arrest may examine the contents of a cell phone seized

1 Professor from Practice, Georgetown University Law Center. Email: *stewartd@law.georgetown.edu*

during that search. In *R. v. Fearon*,[2] the accused was arrested on suspicion of committing armed robbery. During the "pat-down" search, the police found and searched an unlocked mobile phone in the accused's pocket. They discovered incriminating photographs and an unsent (draft) text message. The accused sought to exclude that evidence on the basis that the search had been conducted without a judicially issued warrant and therefore violated his privacy and his right under section 8 of the Canadian Charter of Rights and Freedoms against unreasonable search and seizure.[3]

A majority of the Court disagreed, holding that the authority of the police under common law to conduct a warrantless search incident to a lawful arrest permits the search of mobile phones and similar devices found on the suspect, if certain conditions are met. While acknowledging that "the searches of cell phones, like the search of computers, implicate important privacy interests which are different in both nature and extent from the search of other 'places'" and have "the potential to be a much more significant invasion of privacy than the typical search incident to arrest", the Court rejected a "categorical" approach in favour of a contextual test requiring "reasonable and probable grounds" in order to satisfy the Charter's requirements.[4]

Specifically, it said, the arrest itself must be lawful and the search must be "truly incidental" to the arrest, conducted reasonably and performed for an objectively reasonable law-enforcement purpose (i.e., protecting the safety of the police and the public, preserving and discovering evidence). Moreover, the nature and extent of the search must be tailored to the particular arrest for the particular offence (e.g., only recently sent or drafted messages, photos and call log, rather than all data), and the police must make detailed notes of the search indicating, inter alia, the extent of the search and the time, purpose and duration of the search. These conditions applied, the majority said, regardless of the nature or capacities of the device and whether or not it is password-protected.

The dissenting justices argued for a more stringent standard requiring judicial pre-authorisation. Stressing that "[a] private inner life is essential to the autonomous individual that forms the basis of a free and democratic society as envisioned by the Charter", they contended that "[c]ell phones cannot be treated like other types of physical evidence that may be found on an arrestee" because they are "fastidious record keepers", quantitatively and qualitatively different from other physical items traditionally subject to searches incident to arrest.[5] In consequence, a warrantless search of a mobile device incident to arrest can only be lawful in exigent circumstances, that is, when there is a reasonable basis to suspect that a search may prevent an imminent threat to safety or that the search may prevent the imminent loss or destruction of evidence.[6]

Some eight months earlier, the U.S. Supreme Court had confronted the same question in similar circumstances. In *Riley v. California*, [7] the police had stopped an individual for a traffic violation and, after an ensuing (lawful) search of the vehicle, had arrested him for

2 *R. v. Fearon*, 2014 SCC 77, 2014 CSC 77 (Dec. 11, 2014).

3 Section 8 provides that "[e]veryone has the right to be secure against unreasonable search or seizure". It applies when a person has a "reasonable privacy interest in the object or subject matter of the state action and the information to which it gives access". *R. v. Cole*, 2012 SCC 53, [2012] 3 S.C.R. 34 (S.C.C.) at para. 34. The judicially-articulated test is whether the individual's "subjective" expectation of privacy was "objectively reasonable" in light of the "totality of the circumstances". *R. v. Edwards*, [1996] 1 S.C.R. 128.

4 *Fearon*, paras. 51, 58 and 68.

5 *Fearon*, paras. 115, 127, 129, and 134.

6 Ibid. at para. 137.

7 *Riley v. California*, --- U.S. ---, 134 S.Ct. 2473 (2014).

possession of a concealed weapon. They seized and accessed his cell phone, discovered evidence linking him to an attempted murder and charged him accordingly. He sought to suppress the evidence on the ground that the search, while conducted pursuant to a lawful arrest, had been performed in violation of his rights under the Fourth Amendment to the U.S. Constitution.[8]

The Court agreed, holding that officers must generally secure a warrant before conducting such searches. Writing for a unanimous Court, Chief Justice Roberts noted that cell phones contain "vast quantities of personal information" and have become "such a pervasive and insistent part of daily life that the proverbial visitor from Mars might conclude they were an important part of human anatomy".[9] Because such devices are not themselves weapons and there is no intrinsic reason to fear that evidence seized by police will ordinarily be destroyed once in police possession, the typical justifications for allowing a search incident to an arrest do not apply.

The Chief Justice observed that "[m]odern cell phones are not just another technological convenience. . . [but] hold for many Americans 'the privacies of life'".[10] "The fact that technology now allows an individual to carry such information in his hand does not make the information any less worthy of the protection for which the Founders fought".[11] Cell phones are fundamentally different "in both a quantitative and a qualitative sense" from other objects traditionally covered by the "search incident to arrest" exception, like the wallets, bags, address books and diaries; their "immense storage capacity" puts an enormous array of potentially sensitive personal information at risk of exposure.[12] Thus, investigators must generally obtain a warrant to search the data contained on a cell phone, even if investigators seized the phone incident to an arrest.[13]

More recently, in late 2017, the Supreme Court of Canada determined that Canadians can reasonably expect the text messages they have sent to remain private, even after they have been sent and received by another individual.[14] The ruling in *R. v. Marakah* arose in the context of the criminal prosecution of several individuals for illegal transactions in firearms. After obtaining a judicial warrant to search their homes, the police seized their cell phones and discovered incriminating messages thereon, both sent and received. They sought to use those messages as evidence against the defendants, who argued that the messages had been obtained in violation of their rights against unreasonable searches and seizure as protected by Charter section 8.[15]

Writing for the majority, Chief Justice McLachlin noted that "depending on the totality of the circumstances, text messages that have been sent and received may in some

8 The Fourth Amendment provides "[t]he right of the people to be secure in their persons, houses, papers and effects, against unreasonable searches and seizures, shall not be violated." Searches conducted without prior judicial approval are *per se* unreasonable, subject only to a few exceptions, one of which encompasses searches incident to a lawful arrest. Prior to *Riley,* courts had generally upheld warrantless searches of mobile devices.

9 134 S.Ct. at 2484, 2485.

10 Ibid. at 2494–2495.

11 Ibid. at 2495. In *Commonwealth v. Mauricio*, 477 Mass. 588, 80 N.E.3d 318 (Sup. Jud. Ct. Mass. 2017), the *Riley* rationale was applied to exclude images recorded on a digital camera from the reach of the "search incident to lawful arrest" exception.

12 Ibid. at 2489, 2498.

13 Interestingly, the dissent in *Fearon* referred to (and the majority rejected) the categorical approach adopted in *Riley*.

14 *R. v. Marakah*, 2017 SCC 59, [2017] 2 CSC 59 (Dec. 8, 2017).

15 The decision itself does not indicate whether the warrant specifically authorised seizure of the cell phones or permitted the police to access the information thereon; one may assume it was not a relevant factor.

cases be protected under s.8".[16] In this case, the Chief Justice concluded, the sender had a reasonable expectation of privacy in his "electronic conversation" with his co-conspirator, considering such factors as the place of the search, the private nature of the information, and the measure of control the defendant retained over the information. "Control is not an absolute indicator of a reasonable expectation of privacy, nor is lack of control fatal to a privacy interest".[17]

Two Justices dissented, arguing that in the circumstances, the one defendant did not have sufficient control over (and therefore lacked standing to challenge the search and seizure of) text messages sent to the other and discovered on that other's telephone.[18] Privacy, they contended, is "context driven" and a total lack of control is a "compelling indicator" of the absence of a reasonable expectation of privacy. The rule propounded by the Chief Justice, they argued, was overbroad and threatened to impede legitimate law-enforcement interests.

Yet in *R. v. Jones*,[19] rendered the same day as *Marakah*, the Court held that, at least in some circumstances, the police may lawfully obtain the contents of "historical" text messages sent between individuals. In distinction to *Marakah* (where police searched the home pursuant to a warrant), in *Jones* the police had obtained a statutorily authorised "production order" for copies of messages sent between individuals accused of various firearms and drug trafficking offences. Writing for the majority, Judge Côté agreed that it was "objectively reasonable" for the sender of such messages to expect that a service provider will maintain privacy over those messages (which constitute an "electronic conversation") stored in its infrastructure even though the defendant had clearly relinquished direct control over them.[20] Nonetheless, while authorisation might not have been available under the relevant statute for the interception of future messages (not yet sent), a different rule applied to production of those which had already been sent.[21]

By contrast, the prevailing rule in the United States is that once a text message has been sent, any privacy interest in the message is lost, at least with respect to interception or acquisition by law-enforcement authorities.[22] Under the so-called "third party" rule, once individuals have voluntarily revealed information to others, they lose any reasonable expectation of privacy.[23] Courts have routinely analogised text messages (and other forms of electronic communication such as Twitter) to conventional mail, as to which (once received) there is no reasonable expectation of privacy, since the sender has given up control over the content of the messages.[24] Thus, persons who create an unrestricted-access website, post to an open social networking site, place an advertisement, post files for

16 *R. v. Marakah*, 2017 SCC 59 at para. 4.

17 Ibid. at para. 38.

18 Justices Moldver and Côté, see paras. 91–200.

19 *R. v. Jones*, 2017 SCC 60, 2017 CSC 60 (Dec. 8, 2017).

20 *Jones*, paras. 9, 45.

21 Ibid. para. 59.

22 See, e.g., *State v. Tentoni*, 365 Wisc.2d 211, 871 N.W.2d 285 (Ct. App. Wisc. 2015), but see *State v. Hinton*, 179 Wash.2d 862 (Sup. Ct. Wash. 2014).

23 *Smith v. Maryland*, 442 U.S. 735 (1979) (an individual can claim no legitimate expectation of privacy in information voluntarily given to a third party).

24 Some authority exists for the proposition that a user who sends communications through an Internet service provider retains an expectation of privacy while the communication is in transit. See Love v. State of Texas, 543 S.W.3d 835 (Texas Ct. Crim. App. 2017).

peer-to-peer file-sharing, or participate in a chat room have no reasonable expectation of privacy with regard to those electronic communications.

A similarly restrictive approach has applied to the external indicia ("metadata") of electronic communications. In 1979, for instance, the U.S. Supreme Court held that individuals have no expectation of privacy in numbers dialed on their telephones (as distinct from the content of an ensuing conversation), any more than they can properly assert that information on the outsider of an envelope is private in the same way as the enclosed communication.[25] Some have extended the rule to text messages as well.[26]

Along the same lines, US courts have held repeatedly that individuals have no reasonable expectation of privacy in the internet protocol (IP) addresses used in their online activity. Many such decisions have arisen in the context of government investigations into child pornography services using a specific type of "networking investigation technique" authorised by the courts pursuant to the relevant rule of criminal procedure. In rejecting Fourth Amendment challenges to the admissibility of the information thus obtained, the courts have held that individuals lose their privacy expectations when they voluntarily and routinely convey their IP addresses to third parties either by a website or by using third-party (ISP) equipment.[27] In that sense, an IP address is analogised to a telephone number or the address on the outside of an envelope.[28] Because individuals routinely share that information with others in using the internet, they cannot reasonably expect it to remain private.

In contrast, in *R. v. Spencer*,[29] the Canadian Supreme Court applied the concept of "privacy as anonymity" in finding that an internet user *does* have a reasonable expectation of privacy in his IP address and associated subscriber information (such as identification of accessed sites). In that case, the police had obtained the subscriber's identity from his ISP without a warrant[30] and determined that the computer in question was used to access child pornography by means of a file-sharing programme. They then obtained a warrant and discovered substantial amounts of pornography on the defendant's computer. Charged with a crime, the defendant sought to exclude the evidence as an unreasonable search contrary to s.8 of the Charter.

The Court agreed that the search had been a violation of the defendant's reasonable expectation of privacy. It said that "the mere fact that someone leaves the privacy of their home and enters a public space does not mean that the person abandons all of his or her privacy rights, despite the fact that as a practical matter, such a person may not be able to control who observes him or her in public".[31] Internet users, it said, have privacy interests extending beyond their names, addresses and telephone numbers found in the subscriber information, since the disclosure of such information "will often amount to the identification of a user with intimate or sensitive activities being carried out online, usually with the expectation that these activities would be anonymous".[32]

25 *Smith v. Maryland*, 442 U.S. 735 (1979).
26 See *United States v. Warshak,* 631 F.3d 266, 288 (6th Cir. 2010).
27 See, e.g., *United States v. Matish*, 193 F.Supp.3d 585 (E.D.Va. 2016).
28 Cf. *United States v. Ulbricht*, 858 F.3d 71 (2d Cir. 2017).
29 *R. v. Spencer*, 2014 SCC 43, 2014 CSC 43 (2014).
30 But pursuant to s. 7(3)(c.1)(ii) of the Personal Information Protection and Electronic Documents Act.
31 Ibid. at para. 44.
32 Ibid. at paras. 47, 66.

Most recently, the U.S. Supreme Court determined that individuals do have legitimate expectations of privacy in the records of their physical movements as captured through cell tower locational information (CSLI). In *United States v. Carpenter*,[33] two individuals had been convicted of participating in a series of armed robberies, in part on the basis of historical CSLI obtained from their wireless carriers. The government obtained that information pursuant to a court order issued under the Stored Communications Act,[34] which required the government to show "reasonable grounds" for believing that the records were "relevant and material to an ongoing investigation". The defendants claimed that the government had violated their Fourth Amendment rights by failing to obtain a judicially issued search warrant pursuant to a showing of "probable cause" that they had committed a crime.

The appellate court rejected that argument on the ground that the Fourth Amendment protects the content of a communication but not the external "routing" information necessary to convey it. That information was characterised as business records created and maintained by the defendants' wireless carriers, and the court noted the long-recognised distinction between the content of personal communications (which is private) and the information necessary to get those communications from point A to point B (which is not).[35]

The Supreme Court reversed, holding that to access historical CSLI records covering a week or more the government must obtain a judicial warrant based upon probable cause. Writing for the majority, the Chief Justice noted that the case required the Court to "apply the Fourth Amendment to a new phenomenon: the ability to chronicle a person's past movements through the record of his cell phone signals".[36] Modern cell phones, he noted, "generate increasingly vast amounts of increasingly precise CSLI", and "much like GPS tracking of a vehicle, cell phone location information is detailed, encyclopedic, and effortlessly compiled".[37] Individuals continue to have a reasonable anticipation of privacy in their physical location and "the whole of their movements", despite the "seismic shifts in digital technology" that make precise tracking possible through CSLI.

Moreover, "[w]hen the Government tracks the location of a cell phone it achieves near perfect surveillance, as if it had attached an ankle monitor to the phone's user".[38] The "third party doctrine" does not apply to "the qualitatively different category of cell-site records" because an individual cannot truly be said to have voluntarily shared CSLI.[39] "In light of the deeply revealing nature of CSLI, its depth, breadth and comprehensive reach, and the inescapable and automatic nature of its collection, the fact that such information is gathered by a third party does not make it any less deserving of Fourth Amendment protection".[40]

As these decisions illustrate, courts in Canada and the United States have been actively engaged in balancing (a) the need for effective law enforcement with (b) the obligation to

33 *United States v. Carpenter*, --- S.Ct. ---, 2018 WL 3073916 (June 22, 2018).

34 Stored Communications Act, codified at 18 U.S.C. §§ 2701–2712, addresses disclosure of "stored wire and electronic communications and transactional records" held by third-party ISPs.

35 *United States v. Carpenter*, 819 F.3d 880 at 886 (6th Cir. 2016).

36 Carpenter, 2018 WL 3073916 *9.

37 Ibid. at *4, 8.

38 Ibid. *10.

39 Ibid. at *9.

40 Ibid. at *15.

respect everyone's rights to privacy and to be free of unreasonable searches and seizures, by applying traditional (and broad) concepts of constitutional law to evolving technological contexts. In so doing they have reached different conclusions.

The domestic legal structures

The Canadian and US legal systems differ markedly in a number of ways. Both of course are federal structures founded on constitutional principles, and (to varying degrees) rely on principles of common law, but in respect of privacy and data protection, Canada depends much more heavily on codified legislation.

Canada

Without question, the Canadian legal system has been the more ambitious in promoting and protecting privacy interests. Although no explicit constitutional right to privacy exists, the Charter of Rights and Freedoms guarantees "freedom of thought, belief, opinion and expression, including freedom of the press and other media of communication" (section 2), the right to life, liberty and security (section 7), and protection against unreasonable search and seizure (section 8), all of which are directly related to privacy rights. Moreover, an array of provincial and territorial privacy statutes governs the protection of personal information in the private, public and health sectors.[41] Together with several overarching federal laws, they set out a comprehensive regime for the collection, use and disclosure of personal information not dissimilar to those found in EU law. This body of legislation has been recognised by the courts as having "quasi-constitutional" status.[42]

At the national level, the Privacy Act limits the collection, use and disclosure of personal information by government entities.[43] It grants individuals a legal right of access to personal information about them held by the federal government. It also imposes "fair information" obligations on the federal government in how it collects, maintains, uses and discloses personal information under its control. Importantly, it created an independent ombudsman (the Privacy Commissioner, who is an Officer of Parliament and reports to the House of Commons and the Senate) to oversee compliance with the legislation.

The Personal Information Protection and Electronic Documents Act (PIPEDA), enacted in 2000, addresses the collection, storage and use of personal information by organisations in the private sector.[44] PIPEDA was aimed at striking an appropriate balance between an individual's right to privacy and the reasonable needs of organisations to collect, use and disclose information for economic purposes. It is considered substantively similar to the EU Privacy Directive (indeed, the law was intended to conform Canada's

41 Quebec currently has the most stringent privacy regime, including its own Charter of Human Rights and Freedoms and an Act respecting the Protection of Personal Information in the Private Sector, CQLR c C-12, art. 35 of which provides that every person has "a right to the respect of his reputation and privacy".

42 See, e.g., *Douez v. Facebook, Inc.*, 2017 SCC 33, [2017] 1 S.C.R. 751, at paras. 59 and 105. As the Supreme Court has noted, "[t]he ability of individuals to control their personal information is intimately connected to their individual autonomy, dignity and privacy. These are fundamental values that lie at the heart of a democracy". *UFCW, Local 401 v. Alberta* (Information and Privacy Commissioner), 2013 SCC 62 (2013).

43 The Federal Privacy Act can be found at www.justice.gc.ca.

44 PIPEDA and additional information can be found at the Office of the Privacy Commissioner of Canada's website at www.priv.gc.ca.

law to the EU's adequacy standards).[45] Like the Privacy Act, PIPEDA has been afforded quasi-constitutional status by the Canadian courts.

Under PIPEDA, some types of "personally identifiable information" are considered sensitive and are therefore explicitly protected: (a) age, name, ID numbers, income, ethnic origin, or blood type; (b) opinions, evaluations, comments, social status, or disciplinary actions; and (c) employee files, credit records, loan records, medical records, existence of a dispute between a consumer and a merchant, intentions (for example, to acquire goods or services, or change jobs).

PIPEDA is enforced by the Privacy Commissioner, who may initiate an investigation on her own initiative or in response to a complaint. Depending on the findings, either the Commissioner or the complainant can take the matter to the Federal Court, which can issue a binding order to enforce compliance with PIPEDA or an award of damages.

However, PIPEDA itself did not address its application to electronic commerce. It was amended in 2015 by the Digital Privacy Act, which (among other things) added mandatory breach notification requirements.[46] Regulations implementing those requirements are due to come into force in November 2018.They include a requirement for organisations to give notice as soon as possible to affected individuals (and to the Privacy Commissioner) when it is reasonable to believe that the breach creates a "real risk of significant harm to the individual".

Canada's 2014 anti-spam law ("CASL")[47] created a comprehensive regime of offences and enforcement mechanisms designed to prohibit unsolicited or misleading "commercial electronic messages" and deter other forms of online fraud (such as identity theft and phishing). It also prohibits the unauthorised installation and use of computer programmes on other person's computer systems, which in general terms prohibits sending a commercial electronic message unless the person to whom the message is sent has consented (explicitly or implicitly) to receiving it, the message contains information.[48]

Every Canadian province and territory has laws that govern how its government agencies handle personal information. Québec, Alberta and British Columbia each have legislation substantially similar to PIPEDA, enforced by their own privacy commissioners. In addition, provincial laws impose privacy obligations on public bodies, private sector organisations and specific areas of particular sensitivity (for example, the health sector). The provincial statutes in British Columbia, Manitoba, Saskatchewan and Newfoundland permit individuals to bring damage suits for breach of privacy; others have recognised a common law tort for "intrusion on seclusion".

United States

No explicit right of privacy exists in the U.S. Constitution, nor has the United States enacted a national privacy statute similar to PIPEDA, much less one regulating the internet or (more generally) the collection, storage and use of personal data online.[49]

45 In fact the European Commission declared in 2001 that PIPEDA provided an "adequate" level of data protection for purposes of Directive 95/46/EC.

46 Canadian Digital Privacy Act, S.C. 2015, c. 32, at http://laws-lois.justice.gc.ca/eng/AnnualStatutes/2015_32.

47 See www.parl.gc.ca/content/hoc/Bills/403/Government/C-28/C-28_4/C-28_4.PDF.

48 Generally see www.crtc.gc.ca/eng/casl-lcap.htm and www.fightspam.gc.ca.

49 Ten state constitutions expressly recognise some form of privacy rights (Alaska, Arizona, California, Florida, Hawaii, Illinois, Louisiana, Montana, South Carolina and Washington).

Neither is there a privacy commissioner or other central governmental mechanism for independent oversight of privacy issues. Instead, the broad legal framework is provided by (a) constitutional requirements and (b) a patchwork of (largely sectoral) federal and state laws and regulations, adopted over time and in response to differing problems.

The First Amendment to the U.S. Constitution protects freedom of speech and expression,[50] and the Fourth Amendment protects against unreasonable searches and seizures.[51] Both were written in the eighteenth century and apply primarily to government action; their application to access and use of the internet is a difficult exercise in interpretation.

At the national level, a complex set of federal privacy-related laws regulates the collection and use of personal data in discrete (sectoral) areas. Some statutes apply specifically to activities that use personal information, such as telemarketing and commercial email.[52] Others protect particular categories of information, such as financial or health information.[53] In addition, various "consumer protection" laws prohibit specific types of unfair or deceptive practices involving the disclosure of, and security procedures for protecting, personal information.[54]

No single federal department or agency exercises overall supervision over the field. The Federal Trade Commission (FTC), an independent administrative agency with authority over "unfair or deceptive acts or practices in or affecting commerce", issues regulations and brings administrative enforcement actions concerning privacy and data protection and enforces certain statutory prohibitions.[55] It also investigates and prosecutes violations of privacy rights under other laws and provides guidance regarding best practices with respect to companies' collection, storage, use and protection of consumers' personal information. The Federal Communications Commission regulates telecommunication carriers and services to protect the privacy of customer proprietary network information, including personally identifying information that can track a customer's behaviour. [56]

Regulation of service providers has to date been minimal compared to Canada. Three federal statutes are particularly relevant to internet developments. The Electronic

50 U.S. Const. amdt. I provides: "Congress shall make no law respecting an establishment of religion, or prohibiting the free exercise thereof; or abridging the freedom of speech, or of the press; or the right of the people peaceably to assemble, and to petition the Government for a redress of grievances".

51 U.S. Const. amdt. IV provides: "The right of the people to be secure in their persons, houses, papers, and effects, against unreasonable searches and seizures, shall not be violated, and no Warrants shall issue, but upon probable cause . . . particularly describing the place to be searched, and the persons or things to be seized".

52 E.g., Federal Privacy Act, 5 U.S.C. § 552a; Video Privacy Protection Act, 18 U.S.C. § 2710; Computer Fraud and Abuse Act, 18 U.S.C. § 1030; Health Insurance Portability and Accountability Act, 42 U.S.C. § 300gg, 29 U.S.C. § 1181 *et seq.*, 42 U.S.C. § 1320d *et seq.*); Controlling the Assault of Non-Solicited Pornography and Marketing Act, 15 U.S.C. §§ 7701–7713 and 18 U.S.C. § 1037; Telephone Consumer Protection Act, 47 U.S.C. § 227 *et seq.*

53 For example, the Financial Services Modernization Act of 1999, 15 U.S.C. §§ 6801–6827, regulates the collection, use and disclosure of financial information collected by financial institutions.

54 The Right to Financial Privacy Act, 12 U.S.C. § 3401 *et seq.*, prohibits (with certain exceptions) the non-consensual disclosure to government authorities of a financial-institution customer's records.

55 The Federal Trade Commission Act, 15 U.S.C. §§ 41–58, prohibits unfair or deceptive practices that fail to safeguard consumers' personal information. It does not regulate specific categories of data but has been applied to offline and online privacy and data security policies. The FTC is also the primary enforcer of the Children's Online Privacy Protection Act, 15 U.S.C. §§ 6501–6506).

56 Under the Communications Act, 47 U.S.C. § 222; 47 C.F.R. § 64.2001 to 64.2011.

Communications Privacy Act[57] protects wire, oral and electronic communications while those communications are being made, are in transit, and when they are stored on computers. The Stored Communications Act[58] protects the privacy of the contents of files stored by service providers and records held by those providers about individual subscribers, such as subscriber name, billing records, IP addresses, etc. The Communications Decency Act[59] broadly immunises internet service providers from claims stemming from their publication of information created by third parties. In particular, it states that "[n]o provider or user of an interactive computer service shall be treated as the publisher or speaker of any information provided by another information content provider".[60] As a result, an individual or entity claiming to have been defamed on the internet can sue the original speaker but not the messenger.

The laws in the fifty states (as well as Puerto Rico, Guam, the Virgin Islands, etc.) address aspects of internet usage and information security. Most states have enacted some form of privacy legislation. Some provide similar protection to those under federal laws, for example "mini-FTC Acts" prohibiting companies from committing deceptive business practices (including inappropriate or undisclosed consumer tracking); others address areas not addressed at the federal level, such as data breach statutes requiring notification of unauthorised disclosures of personal information.[61]

California's privacy and data security laws are among the most protective. Its Online Privacy Protection Act requires operators of commercial Website or online services that collect personally identifiable information about individual consumers residing in California must conspicuously post its privacy policy on its Website;[62] its Electronic Communications Privacy Act sharply limited the ability of government authorities to seek electronic communication information for law-enforcement purposes;[63] and its data breach law requires any person or business that owns or licences computerised data that includes personal information to disclose any breach of the security of the system to all California residents whose unencrypted personal information was acquired by an unauthorised person.[64] Its new Consumer Privacy Act[65] has been referred to as "California's GDPR;" it provides consumers with greater transparency and access to their personal information, deletion rights, disclosures and opt-out rights. It gives consumers the right to seek disclosure of any personal information (broadly defined) that a business has collected about them and requires the business to delete such information upon request (subject to some exceptions). It also prohibits a business from selling the personal information of a consumer under sixteen years of age unless the sale is affirmatively authorised.

57 Pub. L. 99–508, Oct. 21, 1986, 100 Stat. 1848, 18 U.S.C. §§ 2510–2522, together with the Computer Fraud and Abuse Act, 18 U.S.C. § 1030, regulates the interception of electronic communications and computer tampering.

58 Stored Wire and Electronic Communications and Transactional Records Access Act, 18 U.S.C. §§ 2701–2712.

59 Communications Decency Act of 1996, PL 104–104, Feb. 8, 1996, 110 Stat 56.

60 47 U.S.C.A. § 230(c)(1).

61 See www.ncsl.org/research/telecommunications-and-information-technology/state-laws-related-to-internet-privacy.aspx

62 Cal. Bus. & Prof. Code § 22575.

63 Cal. Penal Code § 1546.1(b).

64 Cal. Civil Code § 1798.82.

65 Enacted in June 2018, effective January 1, 2020. Generally see www.caprivacy.org/.

Access to the internet

Free and equal access to high-speed broadband internet is recognised in principle in both countries. Under the Canadian Telecommunications Act, internet service providers are treated like utilities and precluded from giving "undue or unreasonable preference" to one application or online service over another and from influencing the content transmitted over their networks. A recent report to the House of Commons recommends the explicit incorporation of the principle of "net neutrality" in the statute.[66]

In the United States, the issue of net neutrality has proved contentious. The term refers to the principle that internet service providers may not discriminate based on user or content but must instead treat all online traffic and data equally. In 2005, the Federal Communications Commission adopted the principle in order to preserve a vibrant and competitive free market and to promote the continued development of the internet as well as advanced broadband capability.

In 2015, the FCC classified internet access as a "common carrier telecommunications service" (in other words, a public utility), subjecting ISPs to FCC oversight and prohibiting them from speeding up (or slowing down) traffic from specific websites and apps. In December 2017, however, in accordance with the policies of the new Administration, that "open internet" approach was reversed in favour of classifying ISP's as "information services" and thereby giving them control over the information flowing over their networks.[67]

Both legal systems recognise that government restrictions on an individual's internet access should be authorised only in the most compelling circumstances. In *R. v. Brar*,[68] the Ontario Court of Appeal described a "virtually unconditional prohibition on any Internet use . . . for a period of 20 years" as "demonstrably unfit and unreasonable under the circumstances" and modified it to permit limited usage, since "[i]n modern life", the court observed, at least some form of access to the Internet is simply unavoidable for "innocent purposes". The court in *R. v. A.C.*[69] relied on that decision in declining to impose an internet prohibition order on an individual convicted of online-posting intimate images of his former lover without her permission. In *Barr v. Canada*,[70] however, the Federal Court decided that it was reasonable for Canada's Parole Board to preclude an individual convicted *inter alia* of sexual assault from owning, using or possessing a computer or other device allowing him to access the internet given the nature of his offences, repeated use of the internet to "troll for relationships", and violations of previously imposed restrictions.

US courts have similarly resisted broad access restrictions for convicted individuals. For instance, the U.S. Supreme Court recently struck down a North Carolina statute that prohibited convicted sex offenders – including those no longer on probation, parole, or supervised release – from accessing social media sites on the internet. The statute made it a felony for a registered sex offender to access a commercial social networking Website when the sex offender knows that the site permits minor children to become members or

66 See May 2018 Report of the House of Commons Standing Committee on Access to Information, Privacy and Ethics entitled "Protection of Net Neutrality in Canada", available at www.ourcommons.ca/content/Committee/421/ETHI/Reports/RP9840575/421_ETHI_Rpt14_PDF/421_ETHI_Rpt14-e.pdf.

67 On May 16, 2018, the U.S. Senate approved a measure overturning that decision, but approval by the House of Representatives and signature by the President appears unlikely.

68 *R. v. Brar*, 2016 ONCA 724 (Ontario Ct. App. 2016), paras. 24, 26.

69 *R. v. A.C.*, 2017 ONCJ 317 (Ontario Ct. Justice, May 16, 2017).

70 *Barr v. Canada* (Attorney General), 2018 FC 217 (Fed. Ct. Feb. 26, 2018).

to create or maintain personal Web pages. The Court held that the law violated the First Amendment because it was "not narrowly tailored to serve the State's legitimate interest in protecting minors from sexual abuse".[71]

Relying on that decision, a federal court struck down a Kentucky statute prohibiting convicted sex offenders from using any social networking sites that might be used by individuals under age eighteen. To ensure compliance, one such offender had been required to provide his probation officer with all of his email and other internet name identities. His challenge succeeded because (the court said) it effectively prohibited sex offenders from engaging in "any speech whatever on a social media website, as innocent as that speech may be".[72] Similarly, a parole board's decision to impose a lifetime ban on a convicted sex offender's access to a computer and the internet was held "overbroad" and "a form of banishment", since "access to the Internet is considered to be a basic need and one of the most meaningful ways to participate in the essentials of everyday life".[73]

By distinction, a federal court declined to overrule a decision by authorities in a state hospital to deny internet access to a convicted "sexually violent predator" deemed likely to engage in violent behaviour if released. Acknowledging that convicted prisoners do not forfeit all constitutional protections, the court said the exercise of First Amendment rights by prisoners can nonetheless be limited by the fact of confinement and the needs of the penal institution. Citing significant safety concerns about the sharing and storage of child pornography, it found no precedent for a constitutionally protected right to access the internet in such circumstances.[74]

Freedom of speech and expression

Fundamental guarantees of freedom of speech and expression of course apply to the internet. In 1997, the U.S. Supreme Court held that the government can no more restrict a person's access to words or images on the internet than it can snatch a book out of someone's hands or cover up a nude statue in a museum.[75] Yet such protections do not preclude all restrictions or limitations.[76] In both legal systems, injured parties can recover for common law torts (such as libel and slander, defamation, trespass, invasion of privacy)[77] and in both criminal libel is recognised in certain circumstances, including online.[78]

Canada has considerably stronger restrictions against defamatory libel and "anti-hate" laws.[79] Section 13 of the Canadian Human Rights Act makes it an offence to communicate any matter that is likely to expose anyone to hatred or contempt, including by means of the internet. The Criminal Code prohibits the promotion of genocide or incitement of hatred in public and was amended in 2014 to prohibit publishing an intimate image

71 *Packingham v. North Carolina*, 137 S.Ct. 1730 at 1734–1735 (June 19, 2017).

72 *Doe v. Kentucky* ex rel. Tilley, --- F.Supp.3d – 2017 WL 4767143 at *4 (E.D. Ky. Oct. 20, 2017).

73 *J.I. v. New Jersey State Parole Board,* 228 N.J. 204, 220 (N.J. Sup. Ct. 2017).

74 *Johanneck v. Ahlin*, 2018 WL 1014454 *12–13 (E.D. Cal. Feb. 21, 2018).

75 *Reno v. American Civil Liberties Union*, 521 U.S. 844 (1997).

76 Cf. *Sandvig v. Sessions*, 2018 WL 1568881 (D.D.C. Mar. 18, 2018), on challenges to the constitutionality of the "Access Provision" of the Computer Fraud and Abuse Act, 18 U.S.C. §1030(a)(2)(C), which provides punishment for anyone who "intentionally accesses a computer without authorization or exceeds authorized access, and thereby obtains . . . information from any protected computer".

77 Cf. Restatement (Second), Law of Torts §652; Shiho Seki v. Groupon, Inc., 333 Ga. App. 319 (Ga. Ct. App. 2105).

78 Cf. Trout Point Lodge Ltd. v. Handshoe, 2014 NSSC 62, and Sagman v. Politi, 2014 ONSC 4183.

79 Cf. *R. v. Keegstra,* [1990], 3 S.C.R. 697.

without consent.[80] The offence (sometimes called "revenge porn") applies if a person "knowingly or recklessly publishes, distributes, transmits, sells, makes available or advertises an 'intimate image' of another person knowing that the person depicted in the image did not give their consent".[81] The law also authorises the removal of such images from the internet and the recovery of expenses incurred to obtain the removal of such images.

When US jurisdictions have enacted similar statutes, they have encountered First Amendment challenges.[82] For example, Texas's highest criminal court[83] and one federal court of appeals[84] have held that statutes criminalising non-obscene sexually related electronic communications with minors made with an intent to arouse impermissibly prohibit a substantial amount of protected speech. In contrast, other courts have upheld similar content-based restrictions on speech as meeting constitutional requirements.[85] In *Scott v. State*,[86] the defendant was indicted under a Georgia state statute prohibiting "obscene Internet contact with a child . . . that is intended to arouse or satisfy the sexual desire of either the child or the person". The Supreme Court of Georgia rejected his constitutional challenge because, properly construed, the statute prohibited only specific categories of online contact made with the specific intent to arouse or satisfy the sexual desires of the accused or the child victim, and thus did not prohibit a real and substantial amount of expression protected under the First Amendment.

To the same effect, a Texas court recently rejected a constitutional challenge brought by an individual who had been indicted for the felony offence of online solicitation of a minor under a Texas statute proscribing solicitation of minor via electronic messaging with intent that the minor would engage in sexual conduct.[87]

US courts have also considered the permissible limits on "cyber-bullying".[88] A North Carolina statute made it unlawful for any person to use a computer or computer network to post (or to encourage others to post) on the internet private, personal, or sexual information pertaining to a minor "with the intent to intimidate or torment a minor". The statute was invalidated on First Amendment grounds because it restricted some kinds of speech and not others (which, the court said, makes it impossible to determine whether the accused has committed a crime without examining the content of his communication) and because the restriction was "not narrowly tailored to the State's asserted interest in protecting children from the harms of online bullying".[89]

Uniquely, in the United States, ISP's are insulated by statute from liability arising from publication of information created by third parties. The Communications Decency Act states that "no provider or user of an interactive computer service shall be treated as

80 Crim. Code §§ 318 and 319; Protecting Canadians from Online Crime Act, S.C. 2014, c. 31, sec. 162.1. How the *Fearon* and *Spencer* decisions will affect its implementation and enforcement remains to be seen. For a related decision based on the common law tort of "breach of confidence", see Jane Doe 464533 v. D. (N.), 2016 ONSC 541.

81 *R. v. J.S.*, 2018 ONCJ 82 (Jan. 30, 2018).

82 On revenge porn, see, e.g., *People v. Iniguez*, 247 Cal.App.4th Supp. 1 (Sup. Ct. LA Cnty. 2016).

83 Ex Parte Lo, 424 S.W.3d 10 (Tex. Crim. App. 2013).

84 *Powell's Books, Inc. v. Kroger*, 622 F.3d 1202 (9th Cir. 2010).

85 *State v. Muccio*, 890 N.W.2d 914 (Sup. Ct. Minn. 2017).

86 *Scott v. State*, 299 Ga. 568, 788 S.E.2d 468 (Sup. Ct. Georgia 2016).

87 Ex parte Moy, 523 S.W.3d 830 (Texas Ct. Apps. 2017).

88 All U.S. states (and the District of Columbia) now have some form of statutory cyberbullying prohibition, many of which include criminal penalties, and half also cover "sexting". See http://cyberbullying.org.

89 *State v. Bishop*, 368 N.C. 869, 876, 787 S.E.2d 814, 819 (N. Car. Sup. Ct. 2016); cf. People v. Relerford, 2017 WL 5894178 (Sup. Ct. Ill. Nov. 30, 2017).

the publisher or speaker of any information provided by another information content provider".[90] The statute has presented some interesting questions. For instance, in 2017, a federal appellate court considered (and rejected) claims brought against Facebook alleging that Palestinian terrorists had used its services to incite, enlist, organise and dispatch would-be killers to commit acts of violence and that Facebook had failed to take action to prevent such use.[91] Even if the comments were not protected by the First Amendment because they involved hate speech against the plaintiff's African ethnicity, falsely accused plaintiff of being a criminal, or used fighting words, the court said, Facebook was entitled to immunity. The statute was recently amended, however, to remove that immunity when providers knowingly assist, support or facilitate third-party advertising that violates federal or state sex-trafficking laws.[92]

Emergent issues

Use of geo-locational information

Some years ago, the U.S. Supreme Court held that the attachment of a GPS device to a private vehicle and subsequent monitoring of its movements on public streets was a "search" requiring judicial permission based on "probable cause". [93] In the years since, more than a thousand judicial decisions have addressed GPS issues in diverse contexts, exploring various applications of the general rule and adopting differing approaches.[94] Most US courts have held that individuals have a reasonable expectation of privacy in their real-time phone locations, so as to require agents to obtain a warrant or otherwise meet constitutional probable cause standards before using cell-site simulators (IMSI catchers).[95]

Facial recognition and biometric tracking

The increasing sophistication of facial recognition and other biometric technology (such as gait motion analysis) presents particularly significant privacy challenges, particularly when implemented in public places. Neither country has addressed these developments in national law or regulation, although in Canada biometrics fall under PIPEDA. Some US states have begun to address the issue by statute.[96] Under Illinois' Biometric Information Privacy Act, for instance, no private entity can gather or obtain an individual's biometric identifiers without obtaining the person's written consent.[97] Users relied on that statute to

90 47 USC § 230(c)(1).

91 *Cohen v. Facebook, Inc.*, 252 F.Supp.3d 140 (E.D.N.Y. 2017).

92 Fight Online Sex Trafficking Act (FOSTA), Pub. L. 115–164 (Apr. 11, 2018), amending 47 U.S.C. § 230(e), specifically in respect of conduct violating 18 U.S.C. §§ 1591 or 2421A.

93 *United States v. Jones*, 565 U.S. 400 (2012); see also *Jones v. United States*, 168 A.3d 703 (D.C. Ct. App. 2017) (use of cell-site simulator to locate defendant's cell phone invaded a reasonable expectation of privacy).

94 See, e.g., *State v. Jenkins*, 294 Neb. 684 (Sup. Ct. Nebr. 2016), *State v. Muldrow*, 377 Wisc.2d 223 (Ct. App. Wisc. 2017). *United States v. Ponce*, 2017 WL 3251494 (M.D. Fla. July 31, 2017); *State v. Jean*, 243 Ariz. 331 (Sup. Ct. Az. 2018).

95 See, e.g., *Loomis v. Temple*, 2017 W 77988103 (E.D. Mo. Oct. 16, 2017).

96 For instance, Illinois' Biometric Information Privacy Act, 740 Ill. Comp. Stat. § 14/1 (2008), prohibits non-consensual collection and storage of certain types of biometric data. Texas and Washington have similar if weaker laws.

97 740 Ill. Comp. Stat. 14/15(b).

challenge Facebook's collection, retention and use of information about the geometry of their faces (from their uploaded photographs) without prior notice or informed consent.[98]

Right to be forgotten

Neither jurisdiction has yet recognised a clear right of individuals to prevent internet search engines from processing requests from third parties for information about them, as the European Union does.[99] It appears that Canada may be heading in that direction: in early 2018, the federal Privacy Commissioner published a report on the topic of "online reputation" and "source takedown" calling for consideration of several measures to recognise the right to ask search engines to de-index web pages and removing information at the source, which he claimed would be consistent with several provisions of the PIPEDA statute.[100] That report has occasioned substantial discussion.

To date, no similar initiatives have been undertaken at the federal level in the United States. In 2013, California adopted a statute[101] (the "online eraser law") requiring operators of websites directed to minors to permit users to request removal of content or information posted by them, subject to some exceptions, but even that has proven controversial. More recently, its new Consumer Privacy Act[102] requires businesses to delete certain information about consumers upon request. Of course, federal and state laws do impose restrictions on disclosure of certain types of information.[103]

Overall, most commentators see the First Amendment as an obstacle to a genuine "right to be forgotten" along the lines of *Google Spain*.[104] The First Amendment has been interpreted to prevent restrictions on the right of newspapers to publish lawfully obtained information about matters of public significance absent "a need to further a state interest of the highest order".[105] Under the common law of tort, individuals may have a basis for seeking damages for invasion of privacy when a publisher reveals secrets about his or her private life if it would be highly offensive to a reasonable person and is not of legitimate concern to the public.[106]

Interconnectivity

The advent of digital interconnectivity (the "Internet of Things") poses still-to-be resolved privacy challenges. What should be the rules regarding so-called "smart" devices that

98 In re Facebook Biometric Information Privacy Litigation, 185 F.Supp.3d 1155 (N.D. Cal. 2016). See also *Rivera v. Google Inc.*, 238 F.Supp.3d 1088 (N.D. Ill. 2017).

99 Cf. Case C – 131/12, *Google Spain SL v. Agencia Española de Protección de Datos* (May 13, 2014).

100 See www.priv.gc.ca/en/about-the-opc/what-we-do/consultations/consultation-on-online-reputation/pos_or_201801/.

101 Cal. Bus. & Prof. Code §§ 22580–22582, entitled "Privacy Rights for California Minors in the Digital World", came into effect in 2015.

102 Enacted in June 2018, effective January 1, 2020. Generally see www.caprivacy.org/

103 For example, Mississippi criminalises disclosure of information related to abortions. Miss. Code Annot. § 41–41–77 (2017). Other state statutes protect against disclosure of records relating to criminal convictions of juveniles (and sometimes adults) and adoption records. Under federal law, no report of bankruptcy can appear on an individual's credit report after a decade has passed. See 15 U.S.C. § 1681c(a)(1).

104 Generally, see Amy Gajda, Privacy, Press, and the Right to Be Forgotten in the United States, 93 Wash. L. Rev. 201 (2018).

105 *Smith v. Daily Mail Publishing Co.*, 443 U.S. 97 (1979).

106 Restatement (Second) of Torts § 652D (1977).

collect IP addresses, zip codes, product model numbers, hardware and software versions, chipset IDs, region and language settings, browsing and content-viewing histories (and even conversations) and share that information with manufacturers, advertisers and media content providers? Like website tracking, "device fingerprinting" via the internet poses real (and as yet unresolved) challenges.

International coordination

The digital world may be borderless but absent international oversight, regulation remains at the domestic or regional level. With the GDPR now in force, confronting the extraterritorial application of data privacy and protection rules is unavoidable. The legal systems of Canada and the United States have already had occasion to consider the question. In the *Equustek* case, involving a trademark infringement claim between two Canadian parties, the Canadian Supreme Court upheld an injunction forcing Google to delete search results about infringing products everywhere in the world.107 Reacting to the extraterritorial effect of this global deindexing order, a federal court in California enjoined its enforcement.108

The U.S. Supreme Court was poised to consider a similar question in the *Microsoft/Ireland* case, in which US prosecutors sought to compel Microsoft to turn over a US customer's data (including emails) hosted in an Irish storage facility. Microsoft refused, the trial court ruled in favour of the government, but the appellate court reversed, holding the statute did not apply abroad.[109] Before the U.S. Supreme Court could decide the issue, the U.S. Congress resolved the issue by enacting the so-called "Cloud Act" requiring ISP's to comply with relevant obligations "regardless of whether such communication, record, or other information is located within or outside of the United States".[110]

Conclusion

Courts in both Canada and the United States embrace the right to privacy as a fundamental value essential to their respective democratic systems. In an effort to adapt their traditional doctrines to the rapidly evolving digital environment, they have engaged in balancing principles of free speech and access to information with those protecting privacy and propriety.[111] Both have employed a "contextual" (rather than doctrinaire) approach emphasising an individual's "reasonable expectation" of privacy. Rather than creating new principles for the internet context, they have generally sought to ensure the "sameness of rights" as exist in non-internet situations.[112]

107 *Google Inc. v. Equustek Solutions Inc.*, 2017 SCC 34 (June 28, 2017).

108 *Google LLC v. Equustek Solutions Inc.*, 2017 WL 5000834 (N.D. Cal. Nov. 2, 2017).

109 In the Matter of a Warrant to Search a Certain Email Account Controlled and Maintained by Microsoft Corp., 15 F.Supp.3d 466 (S.D.N.Y. 2014), rev'd 829 F.3d 197 (2d Cir. 2016), cert. granted, 138 S.Ct. 356 (Mem) (2017), vacated and remanded, 138 S.Ct. 1186 (Apr. 17, 2018).

110 Clarifying Lawful Overseas Use of Data Act, part of Consolidated Appropriations Act, 2018, Pub. L. 115–141, amending the Stored Communications Act, 18 U.S.C. § 2701 et seq.

111 UNGA Res. 68/167(2013), entitled "The right to privacy in the digital age".

112 See, e.g., UN Human Rights Council Res. 34/7, para. 4, affirming that "the same rights that people have offline must also be protected online, including the right to privacy". UN Doc. A/72/153, 23 Mar. 2017 (UN GAOR 27nd sess. 53).

Because the relevant domestic statutory and regulatory framework in the United States is comparatively thin, US courts have to date tended to play a larger role in this process than their Canadian counterparts. Their approach is largely dictated by the requirements of the First and Fourth Amendments, both of which focus on constraining governmental intrusions. Privacy is thus conceived more in terms of limits on state action (a right not to be interfered with) than an articulation of individual autonomy or a right to anonymity (thus, the "third party" rule, the focus on free speech rather than data retention, etc.).

By comparison, the Canadian approach is more codified at both the federal and provincial levels and frames privacy issues more in terms of autonomy (individual control) over personal information. Where US law tends to focus on the private vs. public distinction, Canadian courts give greater weight to broader community (Charter) values, such as inclusion and equality of treatment, multiculturalism and respect for group identity, and "the inherent dignity owed to all human beings".[113] In this respect, Canadian doctrine is closer to the continental European notions of individual honour, a "general personality right" and the concept of "privacy in public".[114]

One thing is clear: the rapidity with which technology evolves guarantees that the courts will continue to be faced with new and novel circumstances in which to apply traditional doctrines, and legislatures will continue to be challenged to articulate new rules to govern and manage the internet. The law in this area is far from being settled.

113 See *Whatcott v. Saskatchewan Human Rights Tribunal*, 2013 SCC 11, paras. 66, 71, 79, noting that "hate speech" aims to marginalise individuals based on group membership and "to delegitimize group members in the eyes of the majority", contravening Charter rights and "other values essential to a free and democratic society", including the "commitment to equality and respect for group identity and the inherent dignity owed to all human beings" and "the objective of eliminating discrimination and substantive inequality".

114 See, e.g., *R. v. Spencer*, 2014 SCC 43, at paras. 38, 43, articulating "three conceptually distinct although overlapping understandings" of "privacy as secrecy, privacy as control and privacy as anonymity", the last of which "permits individuals to act in public places but to preserve freedom from identification and surveillance".

23 Asian human rights law, jurisprudence and practices toward the internet

Satoshi Yokodaido[1]

Introduction

What is Asia? What countries are categorised as Asia? Do Asian countries have common characteristics? Before discussing Asian human rights law on the internet, we need to consider these questions.

Based on the broadest definition used by the United Nations Statistics Division Geo-scheme (UNSD), 50 countries and regions[2] – about a quarter of all countries in the world – belong to Asia. Asia's size is bigger than any other macro-geographical region, four and a half times the size of Europe, and one and a half times Africa. It extends from the extreme north to the equatorial belt, and there are various climates such as tundra, taiga, desert, steppe and tropical rainforest. The UNSD divides Asia into five sub-regions: Central Asia, Eastern Asia, South-eastern Asia, Southern Asia and Western Asia. Another definition of Asia utilises these sub-regions. The Ministry of Foreign Affairs of Japan, for example, excludes Central Asia and Western Asia as their definition of Asia.[3] However, sub-regions of Asian countries also vary according to the political and legal system, economic system and conditions, the degree of development, race, religion, culture, custom and so on. As the UNSD has said, "the assignment of countries or areas to specific groupings is for statistical convenience and does not imply any assumption regarding political or other affiliations of countries or territories by the United Nations".[4]

Therefore, it is unrealistic to imagine a common Asian culture, and there is no such thing as "Asian Law" as a legal system comparable to "civil law" or "common law" in Europe. Asian countries think very differently about human rights and human dignity. Accordingly, this chapter cannot discuss common "Asian human rights law, jurisprudence, and practices toward the internet". Instead, the first part of this chapter will discuss how possible and difficult it is to treat freedom of internet access as a human right. Part II will divide attitudes toward the internet into three categories and describes the characteristics of each category and typical legal systems. Part III will show two prominent novel internet regulations among Asian countries: the Real-Name system, and anti-fake news laws.

1 Keio University Law School, Japan, professor of constitutional law.

2 USND, the online version of the United Nations publication, Standard Country or Area Codes for Statistical Use, https://unstats.un.org/unsd/methodology/m49/

3 *See* Figure 23.1 at the end of the chapter. It treats these countries as Asia: Bangladesh, Bhutan, Brunei, Cambodia, China, India, Indonesia, Japan, Republic of Korea (South Korea), Laos, Malaysia, Maldives, Mongolia, Myanmar, Nepal, Pakistan, Philippines, Singapore, Sri Lanka, Thailand, Timor-Leste, Vietnam, North Korea, and Taiwan. This chapter will use this narrow definition of Asia.

4 USND, *supra* note 2.

Figure 23.1 Scope of Asia

Source: http: //www.freemap.jp/

Source: Ministry of Foreign Affairs of Japan, www.mofa.go.jp/region/asia-paci/index.html

Internet access as a human right

The internet penetration rate in Asia

The internet has not yet become a universal service in Asia. The Internet Usage and World Population Statistics estimated the internet penetration rate by geographic regions on 31 December 2017, which showed the rate in Asia to be 48.1%. This is the second lowest in the world (the worst region is Africa where the rate is 35.1%), and lower than the world average of 54.4%.[5] Only about half of the Asian population can access the internet. Based on the statistics that estimate the internet penetration rate inside Asian countries, although a few countries have more than 90% internet penetration (Japan, South Korea, and Brunei), many countries only have about 30% (India, Laos, Myanmar, Pakistan, Sri Lanka, Timor-Leste) (see Figure 23.2).

5 Internet World Stats, www.internetworldstats.com/stats.htm

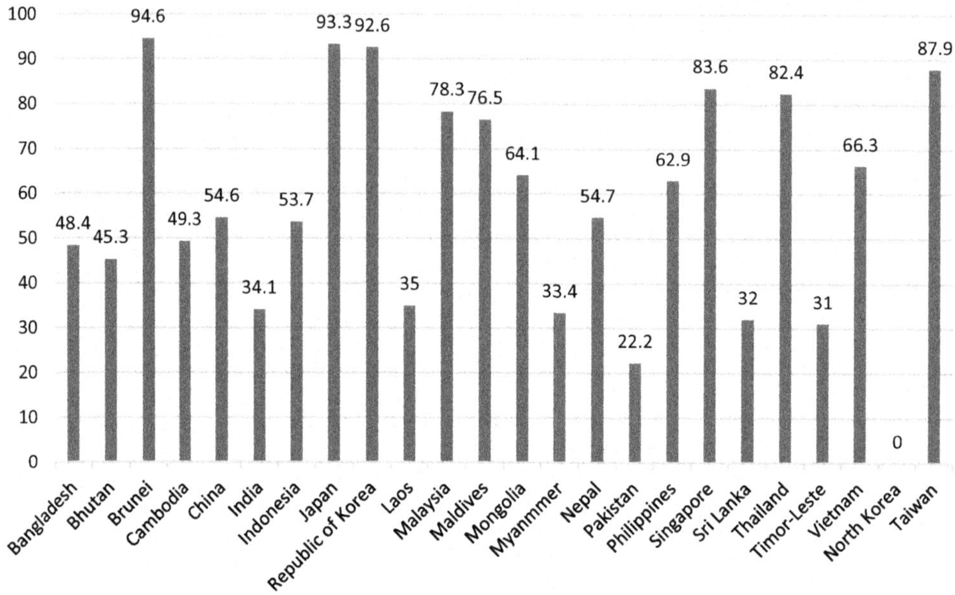

Figure 23.2 Internet penetration rate (% pop.) in Asian countries (2017)

Source: Data from Internet World Stats, World Internet Usage and Population Statistics, Dec. 31, 2017-Update, www.internetworldstats.com/Internet World Stats

The possibility of access to the internet as a human right

International law has gradually recognised internet access as a fundamental human right.[6] For instance, in 2012, the report by the transatlantic security body Organisation for Security and Co-operation in Europe (OSCE) claimed that access to the internet should be seen as a fundamental human right and respected as much as freedom of expression.[7] It concluded that

> everyone should have a right to participate in the information society, and states have a responsibility to ensure citizens' access to the internet is guaranteed. Furthermore, internet access policies, defined by governments, should be in line with the requirements of Article 19 of the Universal Declaration of Human Rights as well as Article 19 of the International Covenant on Civil and Political Rights.[8]

6 *See, e.g.,* Patrick Ford (2014) Freedom of Expression through Technological Networks: Accessing the Internet as a Fundamental Human Right. *Wisconsin International Law Journal*, Vol. 32, 142, 161–164. Philip Chwee (2015) Bringing in a New Scale: Proposing a Global Metric of Internet. *Fordham International Law Journal,* Vol. 38, 825, 830–836. *See also* Molly Land (2013) Toward an International Law of the Internet. *Harvard International Law Journal*, Vol. 54, 393.

7 OSCE, *Freedom of Expression on the Internet: A Study of Legal Provisions and Practices Related to Freedom of Expression, the Free Flow of Information and Media Pluralism on the Internet in OSCE Participating States,* Ed. Ženet Mujić, Deniz Yazici and Mike Stone, 2012, www.osce.org/fom/105522?download=true. *See also* United Nations, Human Rights Council (2016) The Promotion, Protection and Enjoyed of Human Rights on the Internet, A/HRC/32/L.20 (27 June), www.article19.org/data/files/Internet_Statement_Adopted.pdf. On the resolution, *see* Natalie Holland (2018) Freedom of Expression and Opinion in Wartime: Assessing Ukraine's Ban on Citizen Access to Russian-owned Website. *American University International Law Review,* Vol. 33, 943 (2018).

8 OSCE, *supra* note 7, at 15. Article 19 of the Universal Declaration of Human Rights provides that "everyone has the right to freedom of opinion and expression; this right includes freedom to hold opinions without interference

It is an important step to secure internet access as a human right, but the efficacy of international human rights is usually lower than their domestic counterparts because international law usually does not have any means to force states to observe it.

The difficulty of internet access as a human right

However, it is not an easy task to guarantee the right to access the internet as a human right domestically. First of all, Asian domestic constitutions do not treat the right to internet access as a human right. Even Japan, which has a 93.3% internet penetration rate, does not guarantee internet access as constitutional right. Although many Asian countries have tried to improve the accessibility of the internet, these efforts have not been based on the understanding that it is a human rights issue but one of state policy. For example, the Philippines enacted the Act Establishing the Free Internet Access Program in Public Places in the Country on 2 August 2017, and appropriated the relevant funds,[9] because "the State hereby recognizes the vital role of information and communications technology in nation-building, and declares its policy to promote an environment for the development of structures that would ensure the availability and accessibility of reliable and secure internet access suitable to the needs and aspirations of the nation".[10] These laws are to improve the penetration rate of internet usage as a policy goal, not as implementation of constitutional obligation.[11]

Second, even if the right to internet access is included in freedom of speech, domestic constitutional laws also allow restrictions of them in some circumstances for many reasons.[12] For example, Asian countries that have a clause on freedom of expression in their constitution can exercise content-based restrictions which would not be accepted in the United States or other liberal countries. Figure 23.3 indicates what types of expression have been restricted in Asian countries. Even the least protective country such as China guarantees freedom of speech in Article 35 of Constitution of the People's Republic of China.[13] In these countries, state action that restricts or blocks its citizens from accessing the internet would be constitutional because as real-world expression can also be constitutionally restricted, it is justified by other interests; not only national security or public order, but also other people's rights or dignity in their constitutional structure.[14]

---

and to seek, receive and impart information and ideas through any media and regardless of frontiers". Article 19 clause 1, 2 of the International Covenant on Civil and Political Rights provides in some detail that everyone shall have "the right to hold opinions without interference", "the right to freedom of expression" and "this right shall include freedom to seek, receive and impart information and ideas of all kinds, regardless of frontiers, either orally, in writing or in print, in the form of art, or through any other media of his choice".

9 Republic Act (RA) 10929 (Philippines).

10 Article 2 of RA 10929 (Philippines).

11 Japan's Basic Act on the Formation of an Advanced Information and Telecommunications Network Society (Act No. 144 of December 6, 2000) is also based on policy reason.

12 International law also indicates that these rights have "special duties and responsibilities" and "it may, therefore, be subject to certain restrictions", "for respect of the rights or reputations of others" and "for the protection of national security or of public order (ordre public), or of public health or morals". See article 19 clause 3 of ICCPR.

13 Democratic People's Republic of Korea, known as North Korea, one of the most dictatorial countries in the world also guarantees freedom of speech in article 67 of their constitution, states "Citizens are guaranteed freedom of speech, of the press, of assembly, demonstration and association. The State shall guarantee conditions for the free *activity* of democratic political parties and social organizations".

14 *See, e.g.*, Article 51 of Chinese Constitution.

	Bangladesh	*Cambodia*	*China*	*India*	*Indonesia*	*Japan*	*Malaysia*	*Myanmar*	*Pakistan*	*Philippines*	*Singapore*	*South Korea*	*Sri Lanka*	*Thailand*	*Vietnam*
Mobilisation for Public Causes			○											○	○
Ethnic and Religious Minorities			○		○				○						○
Criticism of Authorities	○	○	○	○	○		○	○	○		○		○	○	○
Conflict	○		○	○	○			○							○
Corruption	○		○		○		○	○						○	○
Political Opposition		○	○				○		○				○	○	○
Social Commentary			○	○	○		○	○	○		○			○	○
Blasphemy	○		○	○	○		○	○	○		○				
LGBTI Issues			○		○				○						
Satire	○		○	○			○	○	○		○			○	○

Figure 23.3 Topics censored by some Asian countries

Source: data from Freedom House, *Freedom on the Net 2017: Manipulating Social Media to Undermine Democracy*, 14, available at https://freedomhouse.org/sites/default/files/FOTN_2017_Final.pdf

Their way to balancing is remarkably different to western liberal countries.[15] Furthermore, as we will see in the next part, many Asian countries have seen the internet as something dangerous and have tried to restrict it.

The general attitude toward the internet among Asian countries

The impact of the internet

The internet has the characteristics of being ubiquitous, borderless and global. We use the word "cyberspace" interchangeably with the internet; that word implies a distinction between conventional geographic boundaries and the borderless virtual sphere. Because of these qualities, in the early years of the internet, many advocates claimed that it should not be regulated by any sovereign states, for it is an independent virtual world that does not belong to any countries. John Perry Barlow's article, "A Declaration of the Independence of Cyberspace"[16] is a typical example.

However, until now, this principle has not been endorsed by any other countries. Instead, Asian countries, like other countries in the world, seem to have endorsed the "illegal offline is also illegal online" principle. Furthermore, some Asian countries have a more hostile attitude toward internet freedoms than freedoms in the real world and seem willing to restrict free access to the internet. Although the reason for this attitude is purportedly to protect human rights or human dignity on the internet, the main reason is often a fear of the power of the internet threatening the legitimacy of the government. One report by Dubai's governmental think tank, which analysed the impact of Facebook and Twitter, concluded that "[o]ne thing that is certain is that given the region's young population and increasing penetration rates, social media will continue to play a growing role in political, societal and economic developments in the Arab region".[17] The internet empowers people to change the political system and to threaten the very foundations of the current government. Then it is a reasonable reaction for not only autocratic states but also democratic countries to try to regulate internet access or censor its content.[18]

The attitude toward the internet varies by country. Freedom House, an independent watchdog organisation dedicated to the expansion of freedom and democracy around the world, categorises net freedom into three categories: Free, Not Free and Partly Free.[19] Under these categories, Asian countries are categorised as follows. Free: Japan and the Philippines. Partly Free: Bangladesh, Cambodia, India, Indonesia, Republic of Korea (South Korea), Malaysia, Singapore and Sri Lanka. Not Free: China, Myanmar, Pakistan, Thailand and Vietnam.[20] Because

15 *See generally* Guosong Shao (2012) *Internet Law in China*, ch. 3. Even in Western liberal democracies, the contours of the freedom of speech vary from country to country. *See* Frederick Schauer (2005) The Exceptional First Amendment. In Michael Ignatieff (Ed.), *American Exceptionalism and Human Rights,* 43.

16 John Perry Barlow (1996) A Declaration of the Independence of Cyberspace (8 February), www.eff.org/ja/cyberspace-independence

17 Dubai School of Government (2011) Civil Movements: The Impact of Facebook and Twitter. *Arab Social Media Report*, Vol. 1, 2, https://journalistsresource.org/wp-content/uploads/2011/08/DSG_Arab_Social_Media_Report_No_2.pdf

18 As Justice Oliver Wendell Holmes, Jr. said "Persecution for the expression of opinions seems to me perfectly logical". *Abrams v. U.S.*, 250 U.S. 616, 630 (1919) (Holmes J., dissenting).

19 https://freedomhouse.org/report/freedom-net/freedom-net-2017

20 No data countries are as follow: Bhutan, Brunei, Laos, Maldives, Mongolia, Nepal, Timor-Leste, North Korea and Taiwan. Among these countries, we can categorise with confidence Taiwan as "Free" and North Korea as "Not Free".

we could not view the legal environment and policy on the internet for every Asian country, we will examine only some typical countries in each category.

"Not Free" countries: China and North Korea

Generally speaking, despotic governments or authoritarian countries tend to restrict internet freedom. China, which has the largest number of internet users in the world,[21] is one of the most internet restrictive countries in the world.[22] China has claimed the "internet sovereignty" or "cyberspace sovereignty" principle, namely, within Chinese jurisdiction the internet is under the sovereignty of China and could be controlled by the absolute power and right of the Chinese government's sovereign authority.[23] The Chinese government put this principle into practice by deploying a virtual border, known as the Great Firewall,[24] otherwise known as the Golden Shield Project, which has effectively facilitated the filtering and blocking of foreign online content, such as Facebook, YouTube and Twitter.[25] In the Cybersecurity Law of the People's Republic of China,[26] which is the first comprehensive internet regulation Act in China, adopted by the National People's Congress in November 2016 and came into effect on 1 June 2017, explicitly indicates the Chinese stance toward the internet.[27] The purpose of this law is "guaranteeing cybersecurity, safeguarding cyberspace sovereignty, national security and public interest, protecting the lawful rights and interests of citizens, legal persons, and other organizations, and promoting the sound development of economic and social informatization".[28] The concept of cybersecurity in the law is obviously broader than its usual meaning. It provides a broad range of content regulations; the user of the internet

> shall comply with the Constitution and laws, follow public order and respect social morality, shall not endanger cybersecurity, and shall not use the network to conduct any activity that endangers national security, honor, and interests, incites to subvert the

21 China's online population has touched 772 million at the end of 2017. *See* Internet World Stats, *supra* note 5.

22 China Open Net Initiative (2011), http://access.opennet.net/wp-content/uploads/2011/12/accesscontested-china.pdf

23 *See, e.g.,* Jyh-An Lee (2018) Hacking into China's Cybersecurity Law. *Wake Forest Law Review,* Vol. 53, 57, 67–70; Liudmyla Balke (2018) China's New Cybersecurity Law and U.S.-China Cybersecurity Issues. *Santa Clara Law Review,* Vol. 58, 137; Lucy Hornby (2017) China Defends State Control Over Internet at Technology Forum. *The Financial Times* (December 3).

24 *See* Jyh-An Lee and Ching-Yi Liu (2012) Forbidden City Enclosed by the Great Firewall: The Law and Power of the Internet Filtering in China. *Minnesota Journal of Law, Science & Technology,* Vol. 13, 125, 133. The ward is considered to be coined at Geremie R. Barme and Sang Ye (1997) The Great Firewall of China. *WIRED* (1 January), www.wired.com/1997/06/china-3/

25 *See generally* Human Rights Watch, How Censorship Works in China: A Brief Overview, www.hrw.org/reports/2006/china0806/3.htm (accessed 30.6.2018). *See also* Jeffrey (Chien-Fei) Li (2013) Internet Control or Internet Censorship? Comparing the Control Models of China, Singapore, and the United States to Guide Taiwan's Choice. *Pittsburgh Journal of Technology Law & Policy,* Vol. 14, 1, 21–26; Jyh-An Lee, Ching-Yi Liu, and Weiping Li (2013) Searching for Internet Freedom in China: A Case Study on Google's China Experience. *Cardozo Arts & Entertainment Law Journal,* Vol. 31, 40.

26 CLI.1.283838. English version is, www.lawinfochina.com/display.aspx?id=22826&lib=law

27 *See generally* Lee et al. 2013.

28 Article 1 of Cybersecurity Law (China). The concept of "cyberspace sovereignty" is introduced in this clause, and it is the most prominent concept created by the Act. *See* Vincent X. Wang and William W. Hellmuth (2016) What Does China's New Cyberspace Sovereignty Mean, and is Your Company Ready. *Davis Wright Tremaine LLP* (June 6), www.dwt.com/hat-Does-Chinas-New-Cyberspace-Sovereignty-Mean-and-is-Your-Company-Ready-12-06-2016

> state power or overthrow the socialist system, incites to split the country or undermine national unity, advocates terrorism or extremism, propagates ethnic hatred or discrimination, spreads violent or pornographic information, fabricates or disseminates false information to disrupt the economic and social order, or infringes upon the reputation, privacy, intellectual property rights or other lawful rights and interests of any other person.[29]

It is remarkable that one of the reasons for restricting content on the internet is other person's rights.

North Korea is the least internet-friendly country on Earth. North Korea uses an intranet system called "Kwangmyong" (Bright Star), which is accessible from within North Korea's major cities through libraries, universities and other organisations but goes no further than the country's borders. Only a few high-ranking officials and others can access the global internet,[30] but many sites such as Facebook, YouTube and Twitter are blocked. Accessing news sites in South Korea is also blocked.[31]

"Free" countries: Japan and the Philippines

By contrast, liberal democratic countries tend to respect internet freedom. In "Free" countries such as Japan and the Philippines,[32] there is no systematic, comprehensive government censorship of online content, and internet users enjoy unrestricted access to both domestic and international sources of information. It is true that these countries ban some online expressions which are also illegal when they are expressed in the physical world, and have many laws according to the internet's characteristics, but in principle, these countries guarantee the free flow of information on the internet without censorship.

However, the Philippines once tried to restrict expression on the internet. On 12 September 2012, the Congress of the Philippines enacted an act providing for prevention, investigation, suppression and the imposition of penalties and other purposes,[33] known as the Cybercrime Prevention Act. The Act dealt with content-related offences such as cybersex, child pornography, unsolicited commercial communications, and libel,[34] and when computer data was prima facie found to violate the provisions of this Act, the Department of Justice had the authority to issue an order to restrict or block access to such computer data.[35] Among other provisions, the constitutionality of this "take down" clause (section 19) was considered by the Supreme Court of the Philippines.

On 12 February 2014, the Supreme Court removed the "take down" clause because it violates constitutional guarantees to freedom of expression and is against unreasonable searches and seizures.[36] The Court pointed out: (1) that the clause in effect allows the government to seize and place the computer data under its control and disposition without

29 Article 12 of Cybersecurity Law (China).
30 Eric Talmadge (2017) North Korea's Digital Divide: Online Elites, Isolated Masses. *Chicago Tribune* (11 November).
31 *See* Internet Censorship in North Korea, www.le-vpn.com/internet-censorship-north-korea/. North Korea's Internet Usage penetration rate is only 0.1%.
32 Freedom House, Freedom on the Net 2017: Philippines Country Profile, https://freedomhouse.org/report/freedom-net/2017/philippines
33 Republic Act (RA) No. 10175 (Philippines).
34 Section 4(3) of Cybercrime Prevention Act (Philippines).
35 Section 19 of Cybercrime Prevention Act (Philippines).
36 SC Decision, G.R. No. 203335, 11 February 2014, http://bit.ly/1EZnzAA

a warrant. It violates Section 2, Article III of the 1987 Constitution. (2) Section 19 of the Act operates as a restriction on the freedom of expression over cyberspace because the content of the computer data can also constitute speech. It disregards jurisprudential guidelines established to determine the validity of restrictions on speech.[37] Because the Cybercrime Prevention Act has provisions that restrict freedom of speech other than Section 19, some legislators proposed The Magna Carta for Philippine Internet Freedom[38] as an alternative to the Act, but this has not become law.

Japan does not have any comprehensive law regulating the internet but does have many laws which are designed to cope with the problems that the internet will cause. For example, on 27 November 2014, Japan passed the Revenge Porn Prevention Act.[39] Article 175 of the Criminal Code[40] bans the sale or distribution of obscene material, but there are some images that do not fall within the meaning of "obscene material" but nevertheless infringe on a subject's rights. The Act on the Regulation and Punishment of Acts Relating to Child Prostitution and Child Pornography, and the Protection of Children[41] does not apply to people over 18 years, and defamation laws also have some limit on the application of revenge porn. Because of these limits of the current legal system to protect a victim's dignity, the Revenge Porn Prevention Act was passed. The Act criminalises the provision of private sexual images through a telecommunications line to unspecified or many persons in a way that a third party could identify the person depicted.[42]

How to apply the "illegal offline is also illegal online" principle in practice also became a problem in Japan; defamation laws are one of these problems. In the Japanese legal system, defamation (Japanese law does not distinguish libel and slander) gives rise to criminal and/or civil liability, but there is an exception in Article 203–2 of the Japanese Criminal Code: only when the person who performed the act can prove with reliable materials and evidence, that (a) the statement relates to public concern, (b) the motive of the statement is for advancing the public interests, and (c) the statement is true or there are reasonable grounds to erroneously believe the facts that he/she alleged to be true, can the defendant receive immunity from these liabilities.[43] This immunity was introduced in the Criminal Code after the enactment of the Japanese Constitution in 1946 with a mind to the media, who can collect information and access many information sources. When everyone can be a speaker as powerful as the media due to the power of the internet, should the same immunity rule also apply to the individual who usually does not have the ability to gather information to the same extent as the media? Tokyo district court holds that in consideration of the changes in the environment affecting acts of expression along with the development of the internet, the defendant, as a citizen, performed the act of expression

37 *Chavez v. Gonzales*, 569 Phil. 155 (2008) indicated that restraints on free speech are generally evaluated on one of or a combination of three tests: the dangerous tendency doctrine, the balancing of interest test, and the clear and present danger rule.

38 Senate Bill No. 53, Senate Bill No. 1091 and House Bill No. 1086. *See* Jillian York (2013) A Brief Analysis of the Magna Carta for Philippine Internet Freedom. *Electronic Frontier Foundation* (8 July), www.eff.org/deeplinks/2013/07/brief-analysis-magna-carta-philippine-internet-freedom

39 Act No. 126 of Nov. 27, 2014 (Japan). *See generally* Shigenori Matsui (2015) The Criminalization of Revenge Porn in Japan. *Pacific Rim Law & Policy Journal*, Vol. 24, 289 (2015).

40 Act No. 45 of April 24, 1907 (Japan).

41 Act No. 52 of May 26, 1999 (Japan).

42 Article 3(1) of the Revenge Porn Prevention Act (Japan).

43 *See* Supreme Court, grand bench, 25 June 1969, 23 Keishu 975. *See* Shigenori Matsui (2011) The Constitution of Japan. A Contextual Analysis 202.

after carrying out an investigation that meets the standards required as an individual internet user should be deemed to have had reasonable grounds for believing the facts that he/she alleged to be true, and therefore the crime of defamation cannot be established against the accused, because information published on the internet by individual users is regarded as less reliable information among the audience.[44] However, Tokyo High Court and Supreme Court held that in the case of an act of expression performed by an individual internet user, the establishment of defamation should not be denied by applying less strict requirements than the usual conditions of immunity.[45] This case illustrates the difficulty of adopting laws which are enacted in mind in the real world and applied to occasions on the internet.

"Partly Free" countries: Singapore and India

There are many Asian countries between the two poles of, on the one hand, restricting internet freedom comprehensively and, on the other hand, respecting the free flow of information on the internet generally.[46]

For example, Singapore, which according to the report by the World Economic Forum is the country that has the most potent capacity in the world to leverage ICTs for increased competitiveness and well-being,[47] has a licencing system for internet providers and the online media. Singapore does not restrict the internet directly, as China is doing. Under the Broadcasting Act,[48] internet content providers (ICPs) and internet service providers (ISPs) are automatically given a licence but subject to the Broadcasting (Class License) Conditions[49] and the Internet Code of Practice[50] issued by Infocomm Media Development Authority (IMDA). The Broadcasting Act makes it the duty of IMDA "to ensure that nothing is included in any broadcasting service which is against public interest or order, national harmony or which offends good taste or decency".[51] Both ICPs and ISPs must deny access to sites containing "prohibited content", which is defined as "material that is objectionable on the grounds of public interest, public morality, public order, public security, national harmony, or is otherwise prohibited by applicable Singapore laws".[52] Furthermore, ICPs are required to refrain from subscribing to any newsgroup if, in his/her opinion, it is likely to contain prohibited material and unsubscribes from any newsgroups that the Authority may direct.[53]

44 Tokyo District Court, 29 February 2008, *Keisyu* Vol. 2, No. 64, 59. Supreme Court, first petty bench, 15 March 2009, *Keisyu* Vol. 2, No. 64, 1.

45 Tokyo High Court, 30 January 2009, *Keisyu* Vol. 2, No. 64, 93.

46 Internet Law 8–9, Matsui et al. (Ed.) (in Japanese).

47 World Economic Forum, The Global Information Technology Report 2016: Innovating in the Digital Economy, http://www3.weforum.org/docs/GITR2016/WEF_GITR_Full_Report.pdf

48 Broadcasting Act (Cap. 28, 2012 Rev. Ed) (Singapore).

49 Broadcasting (Class License) Notification (Cap. 28, Sec. 9, 2004 Rev. Ed) Para. 4 (Conditions of Class License) (Singapore).

50 Internet Code of Practice, issued by IMDA, in the exercise of the powers conferred by section 6 of the Broadcasting Act (Cap. 28), with effect from 1st November 1997. *Available at* www.imda.gov.sg/-/media/imda/files/regulation-licensing-and-consultations/codes-of-practice-and-guidelines/acts-codes/19-policiesandcontent-guidelinesinternetinternecodeofpractice.pdf?la=en

51 Internet Code of Practice, Para. 1(1) (Singapore).

52 Ibid. at Para. 4(1).

53 Ibid. at Para. 3(2).

In India, the government has introduced a surveillance programme, formally called the Central Monitoring System (CMS), which since April 2013 allows government agencies to access any online communications directly.[54] The CMS could pose a serious threat to privacy and freedom of expression. As for freedom of expression, section 66A of the Information Technology Act provides punishment for sending offensive messages through a communication service. Among the prescribed offensive messages, it prohibits anything that is "grossly offensive or has menacing character".[55] Using the CMS and Section 66A of the Act, which could be used to prosecute any communication with little to no legal restraint,[56] the Indian government prosecuted citizens for their expression. However, in *Shreya Singhal v. Union of India*[57] in 2005, the Supreme Court of India struck down the Section 66A of the Act in violation of Article 19(1)(a) of the Constitution of India[58] and not saved under Article 19(2) of it,[59] declaring the law unconstitutionally vague and overbroad which is to be used in such a way as to have a chilling effect on freedom of speech.[60]

Some unique regulations or topics on the internet in Asian countries

As discussed earlier, the treatment of the internet in Asian countries varies markedly between countries. In this section, we will explore two different regulations on the internet in Asian countries: the internet Real-Name system and the Fake News regulation.

Internet anonymity in free countries

"Free" countries usually guarantee anonymity on the internet (even if not completely).[61] It is true that ISPs hold user identifiable information, but there are strict conditions via laws or regulations on using the information at will. For instance, information on the internet that infringes someone's rights, such as defamatory remarks, raise unique problems: what responsibility do Hosting Service Providers (HSPs) have, and how can a victim identify an offender? Article 21 section 2 of the Constitution of Japan provides freedom of speech and "the secrecy of any means of communication", and the Telecommunications Business Act[62] guarantees that "the secrecy of communications being handled by a telecommunications carrier shall not be violated".[63]

54 *See* Addison Litton (2015) The State of Surveillance in India: The Central Monitoring System's Chilling effect on Self-Expression. *Washington University Global Studies Law Review*, Vol. 14, 799, 799–804; Melody Party (2013) India: Digital Freedom under Threat? Surveillance, Privacy and Government's Access to Individuals' Online Data (21 November), www.indexoncensorship.org/2013/11/india-online-report-freedom-expression-digital-freedom-3/

55 Article 66A(a) of the Information Technology Act, No. 21 of 2000 (India). This Section came into force by virtue of an Amendment Act of 2009 with effect from October 27, 2009.

56 Litton 809.

57 *Shreya Singhal v. Union of India*, Writ Petition (Criminal) No.167 of 2012 (24 March 2015).

58 Article 19(1)(a) of the Constitution of India guarantees "freedom of speech and expression".

59 Article 19(2) of the Constitution of India provides reasonable restrictions on freedom of speech.

60 *See* Jason Burke (2015) India Supreme Court Strikes down Internet Censorship Law. *The Guardian* (24 March).

61 *See* Jason A. Martin and Anthony L. Fargo (2015) Anonymity as a Legal Right: Where and Why It Matters. *North Carolina Journal of Law & Technology*, Vol. 16, 311.

62 Act No. 86 of 25 December 1984 (Japan).

63 Article 4(1) of the Telecommunications Business Act (Japan).

If ISPs reveal a speaker's identity on the internet, the speaker can seek tort damages from the ISP under Article 709 of the Civil Code.[64] On the other hand, when someone has suffered damages from some anonymous form of online information such as defamatory remarks or a breach of privacy, the identity of the speaker on the internet is required in order to pursue a damages investigation. To reconcile both demands, Japan passed the Providers Liability Limitation Act, in 2001.[65] The Providers Liability Limitation Act "sets forth the limitation of liability for damages of specified telecommunications service providers and the right to demand disclosure of the sender's identification information in cases of an infringement of rights through the distribution of information by specified telecommunications services".[66]

Under the Act, any person alleging that his or her rights were infringed by the distribution of information via specified telecommunications may demand the provider of the disclosure-related service to disclose information identifying the sender pertaining to the said infringement of the rights possessed by the said provider of the disclosure-related service, when (a) there is evidence that the rights of the person demanding the said disclosure were infringed by the distribution of the infringing information, and (b) the information identifying the sender is necessary for the person demanding the said disclosure to exercise his or her rights to claim damages, and where there is justifiable grounds for said person to receive the disclosed identification information of the sender.[67]

The internet real-name system in South Korea

On the other hand, South Korea had introduced the real-name system; because false and defamatory online comments sometimes drive celebrities to suicide, preventing these tragedies and securing people's dignity was required.[68] An Act on the Promotion of Information and Communications Network Utilisation and Information Protection,[69] known as the Information Communications Network Act, Article 44–5 and Article 29 and 30 section 1 of the Enforcement Ordinance of the Act introduced an "identity verification system". It imposes duties on the ISPs who install and operate open message boards where the average number of users reaches or exceeds 100,000 per day to adopt methods of confirming the identity of the message board users and maintaining the identity information of those users such as Resident Registration Numbers. The purpose of this system is to promote a sound and healthy internet culture by restraining illegal acts such as defamation on message boards, and securing basic data in order to identify users committing such illegal acts for cases where harm and damages are caused by such illegal posting.

64 Act No. 89 of 27 April 1896 (Japan). Article 709 provides "a person who has intentionally or negligently infringed any right of others, or legally protected interest of others, shall be liable to compensate any damages resulting in consequence".

65 Act No. 137 of 30 November 2001 (Japan).

66 Article 1 of Providers Liability Limitation Act (Japan).

67 Article 4(1) of Providers Liability Limitation Act (Japan). ISPs and website operators will be held liable for information only if ISPs or website operator knew the rights of others were infringed by the information it hosted, or when there is a reasonable basis to believe that it should have known that the rights of others might be infringed by the information it hosted. Article 3 of the Act.

68 Choe Sang-Hun (2012) South Korean Court Rejects Online Name Verification Law. *New York Times* (24 August).

69 Revised by Act No. 9119 on June 13, 2008 (South Korea). The current version of this act is Act No. 11322, 17 Feb. 2012 (South Korea).

A petition was filed by an online media company (and others) in 2010, asserting that such an identity verification system infringes on the freedom of speech of information and communication service providers and users. The Constitutional Court unanimously (one seat was vacant) ruled[70] on 23 August 2012 that although the purpose of this system is legitimate, the system violated freedom of speech.[71]

The Constitutional Court pointed out that because the remedy for victims of illegal information such as defamatory remarks can be substantially obtained by blocking the distribution or diffusion of illegal information, tracing their IP addresses, compensation for the crime or criminal punishment, it is not the "least restrictive" means. Although limiting freedom of speech is only allowed when the public interests that would be achieved by that restriction are apparent, there is no evidence that the number of illegal acts such as defamatory remarks posted on internet sites has meaningfully decreased since the implementation of the identity verification scheme. Rather, it is hard to see that the system has actually achieved the public interests it was initially aiming at: domestic internet users have been fleeing overseas; there have been difficulties in implementing the system evenhandedly between domestic and foreign business entities; with the advent of new means of communication including mobile message boards and SNS, the public interests sought by the identity verification scheme can be achieved in a very limited range of internet space.

On the contrary, worried about regulations or punishment due to the disclosure of their identities under the identity verification scheme, domestic internet users are more likely to give up their freedom of expression. There is also a high possibility that the private information of message board users is stolen and exploited.

For the foregoing reasons, the Constitutional Court concluded that the identity verification system has a chilling effect on people's expression of opinions, and consequently becomes a restriction on the freedom of expression guaranteed by the Constitution, which amounts to an obstacle to the free formation of public opinion.

Internet real-name system in China, Vietnam and Mongolia

China's newly introduced real-name system requires the disclosure of the speaker's identity by the Cybersecurity Law mentioned in previously. The Chinese government expressed interest in establishing this system as early as 2003 and introduced many policies,[72] but the law is the first comprehensive one to address this issue.[73] This Law means network operators must "require users to provide true identity information when signing agreements or confirming the provision of services. If any user fails to provide his or her true identify information, the network operator shall not provide him or her with the relevant services".[74] Network operators shall monitor content published by users and when and

70 24–2(A) KCCR 590, 2010Hun-Ma47, 252 (consolidated), August 23, 2012. *See generally* Kim Kwangsuk (2013) Network Real Identity Requirements in Constitutional Law(1) (2): with special reference to the Election Act and the Information and Communications Network Act of South Korea. *The Nagoya Journal of Law and Politics*, Vol. 243, 1–45 (2012) (in Japanese) and Vol. 251, 193–235 (2013) (in Japanese).

71 Article 21 of The Constitution of the Republic of Korea guarantees freedom of speech.

72 *See generally* Jyh-An Lee and Ching-Yi Liu (2016) Real-Name Registration Rules and the Fading Digital Anonymity in China. Pacific Rim *Law & Policy Journal*, Vol. 25, 1, 10–17.

73 Charlotte Gao (2017) China's New Wave of Internet Censorship: Name Verification for Online Commenting. *The Diplomat* (26 August), http://thediplomat.com/2017/08/chinas-new-wave-of-internet-censorship-name-verification-for-online-commenting/

74 Article 24 of Cybersecurity Law (China).

upon discovering that a user has transmitted "unlawful" information, the operator must stop the transmission and delete it from the public, keep relevant records, and report the user to the authorities.[75]

Other countries in Asia are also trying to end online anonymity. On 15 July 2013, Vietnam, which is categorised as a "Not Free" country,[76] adopted Decree No. 72 on the management, provision, and use of internet services and online information.[77] The Decree provides comprehensive regulations for the internet,[78] and among these, it requires internet users to provide their real names online.[79] In Mongolia,[80] there was no state regulation to restrict internet users from accessing any domestic or foreign websites or joining social media sites. However, since 2011, the Communications Regulatory Committee (CRC) has adopted many internal regulations, including Resolution No. 1 "A Unified System for Website Comments"[81] adopted on 1 January 2013, which tasked government agencies with developing unified software and technical solutions to regulate the content of online comments on Mongolian online media. ISPs and mobile operators are obliged to install this software, and

> it was the government's intention to use this new software to identify netizens and thereby end online anonymity. Once the netizen was identified, he/she would be held accountable for posting comments that were considered, under Mongolian laws, to be potentially criminal in nature, libelous, insulting, threatening, or in breach of the obscenity laws.[82]

Fake news regulations in Malaysia and other countries

The phrase "fake news" has attracted attention since the 2016 presidential election in the United States in which falsehoods were spread online by both sides as well as a specific foreign state.[83] The Cambridge English Dictionary has recently added this phrase and defines it as "false stories that appear to be news, spread on the internet or using other media, usually created to influence political views or as a joke". Its definition indicates that the internet and SNS is the main reason for spreading fake news. Since fake news may

75 Article 47 and 48 of Cybersecurity Law (China).

76 Freedom House, *Freedom on the Net 2017: Vietnam Country Profile,* https://freedomhouse.org/report/freedom-net/2017/vietnam

77 Decree No. 72/2013/ND-CP of July 15, 2013, on the management, provision and use of Internet services and online information (Vietnam).

78 See Article 5(1) of the Decree.

79 Vietnam Internet Restrictions Come into Effect, *BBC News* (September 1, 2013), www.bbc.co.uk/news/world-asia-23920541. Article 20(4) of the Decree also prohibit Private websites from providing "aggregated information" which is defined in Article 3(19) of the Decree. The official said the purpose of this prohibition is to prevent the spread of false information online and help users find correct and clean information on the internet. In this sense, it can be seen as anti-fake news regulation.

80 *See* Globe International Center, Media Freedom Report 2012–2014 to UNESCO Beijing Office, www.globeinter.org.mn/images/upld/Hevleliinerhcholoo2015english.pdf

81 www.legalinfo.mn/law/details/8939 (in Russian).

82 Kh. Naranjargal (2018) Internet Freedom in Mongolia. *Focus*, 91. Asia-Pacific, Newsletter of the Asia-Pacific Human Rights Information Center, *Hurights Osaka*, Vol. 16, 7. See also Journalism for Development, *Freedoms of Opinion and Expression*, http://en.journalism.mn/content/57524.shtml. Because of these, Mongolia could be categorised in "Party Free" or "Not Free" country.

83 Hunt Allcott and Matthew Gentzkow (2017) Social Media and Fake News in the 2016, *Journal of Economic Perspectives*, Vol. 31, No. 2, 211.

provoke serious political and economic outcomes, many countries are trying to regulate it,[84] and Malaysia is the front-runner in this movement.

On 11 April 2018, Malaysia enacted the Anti-Fake News Act 2018.[85] The Act defines "fake news" very broadly, saying that it "includes any news, information, data and reports, which is or are wholly or partly false, whether in the form of features, visuals or audio recordings or in any other form capable of suggesting words or ideas".[86] Under this Act, someone who "maliciously creates, offers, publishes, prints, distributes, circulates or disseminates any fake news", and provides financial assistance for the purposes of committing or facilitating the commission of these offences is subject to punishment.[87] Furthermore, intermediaries or social media networks "having in his possession, custody or control any publication containing fake news" must immediately remove it after "knowing or having reasonable grounds to believe that such publication contains fake news".[88] Any person who failed to carry out the duty is also subject to punishment.[89] The Act applies to offences committed outside Malaysia so long as the fake news concerns Malaysia or affects a Malaysian citizen.[90] Moreover, any person affected by fake news can require *ex parte* a court order for the removal of the publication containing fake news.[91] It is true that someone who disseminates false information will be punishable in many countries if it causes defamation, damage to credit or obstruction of business in the real world,[92] but the Anti-Fake News Act 2018 is different.

The Act had been harshly criticised for impeding free speech and for its loose definition of fake news. The reason why the act was enacted just before the general election in May 2018 was said that the then Prime Minister Najib Razak tried to fend off criticism over scandal of state-owned investment fund 1 Malaysia Development Berhad (1MDB). Prime Minister Najib also tried to use this act to suppress opposition alliance reader Mahathir Mohamad, former prime minister in 1983–2003, who had promised to repeal the act.[93] After Najib lost the election, the new government led by Mahathir has repealed the act.[94]

84 *See* Sholto Byrnes (2018) Anti-Fake News Laws to Counter Disinformation. *The Independent* (8 April), 2018.

85 ACT 803, Anti-Fake News Act 2018, 11 April 2018 (Malaysia).

86 Section 2 of the Anti-Fake News Act 2018 (Malaysia).

87 Section 4(1) and 5 of the Anti-Fake News Act 2018 (Malaysia). Section 4 illustration (a) to (h) of this Act explain seven occasions where this clause will apply.

88 Section 6(1) of the Anti-Fake News Act 2018 (Malaysia).

89 Section 6(2) of the Anti-Fake News Act 2018.

90 Section 3 of the Anti-Fake News Act 2018 (Malaysia).

91 Section 7 of the Anti-Fake News Act 2018 (Malaysia).

92 For example, although Germany's Act to Improve Enforcement of the Law in Social Networks (vol 1. 9. 2017, BGBl I S. 3352) is sometimes called Anti-Fake News law, a target of the law is limited to the "unlawful content" which is also punishable by the Criminal Law (article 1(3)). *See* Hidemi Suzuki (2018) Act to Improve Enforcement of the Law in Social Networks in Germany and Freedom of Speech. *Keio Media Communication*, Vol. 60, 1 (in Japanese).

93 C. K. Tan, Mahathir Hit with 'fake news' Investigation Over Sabotage Claim: Malaysia's Ex-PM Alleges Jet was Tampered with to Prevent Election Registration. *Nikkei Asian Review* (3 May), https://asia.nikkei.com/Politics/Malaysia-in-transition/Mahathir-hit-with-fake-news-investigation-over-sabotage-claim

94 Praveen Menon (2018) Malaysian Parliament Throws Out Law Against "Fake News", *Reuters* (August 16), www.reuters.com/article/us-malaysia-politics-fakenews/malaysian-parliament-throws-out-law-against-fake-news-idUSKBN1L113P

Already One Person First Person Convicted under Malaysia's Fake News Law. *The Guardian* (30 April 2018), www.theguardian.com/world/2018/apr/30/first-person-convicted-under-malaysias-fake-news-law

Other Asian countries are considering enacting an anti-fake news law. For example, in Singapore, the Ministry of Communications and Information and the Ministry of Law presented a Green Paper entitled "Deliberate Online Falsehoods: Challenges and Implications"[95] to Parliament on 5 January 2018. This Green Paper showed some recent incidents involving online falsehoods in various countries, some of the risks that fake news could pose to Singapore and required the Parliament to appoint a Select Committee to examine and report on the problem of fake news and to examine "any specific measures, including legislation, that should be taken" to prevent and combat online falsehoods. In responding to the recommendation, a ten-member parliamentary committee was set up, and it held eight days of public hearings. At the hearings, sixty-five individuals and organisations from diverse backgrounds appeared to present their views, and the committee received a total of 170 written representations.[96] In India, the broadcasting and information ministry announced on 3 April 2018, that journalists responsible for creating or spreading fake news would lose their reporters' credentials.[97] But only a day after its announcement, Prime Minister Narendra Modi ordered that policy to be withdrawn due to an outcry by journalists and opposition politicians that the rules undermine the freedom of the press.[98] In the Philippines, many lawmakers have been actively proposing laws against fake news. [99] Indonesia and Cambodia also are considering to regulate fake news.[100]

Conclusion

The regulation of the internet has a dual nature: on the one hand, it restricts human rights such as the freedom of speech or free access to the internet, while on the one hand, it protects human rights such as privacy and dignity. Balancing these competing interests is not an easy task, and as we have seen, Asian countries are trying to tackle this task in their own way. It is true that discussing general Asian human rights law, jurisprudence, and practices toward the internet is difficult, but we can grasp some tendencies or characteristics in Asia. Many countries that emphasise the regulation of the internet assert the importance of securing not only human rights or dignity but also national security and social order.

95 www.mlaw.gov.sg/content/dam/minlaw/corp/News/Annexe%20A%20-%20Green%20Paper%20on%20Deliberate%20Online%20Falsehoods.pdf

96 Tang See Kit (2018) Select Committee Concludes Hearings on Fake News After 8 Sessions Marked by Tense Exchanges. *Channel News Asia* (29 March).

97 *See, e.g.,* Michael Safi (2018) India Backs Down Over Plan to Ban Journalists For "fake news". *The Guardian* (3 April).

98 Manoj Kumar (2018) India Drops Plan to Punish Journalists for 'fake news' Following Outcry. *Reuters* (4 April).

99 *See* Senate Bill No. 1942 and House Bill No. 6022 in 2017, Senate Bill No. 1680 in 2018 (Philippines). Despite these proposals, President Rodrigo Duterte has said he believed that a law against fake news would not be passed by Congress, saying that lawmakers should instead focus on increasing the punishment for defamation. CNN Philippines Staff, Duterte: Law Against Fake News Won't Be Passed. *CNN Philippines* (4 October 2017).

100 *See, e.g.,* Not Just in Malaysia: (Proposed) Fake News Laws around the World. *Malaymail* (26 March 2018), www.malaymail.com/s/1607547/not-just-in-malaysia-proposed-fake-news-laws-around-the-world; Shotaro Tani (2018) Asia's War on "Fake News" Raises Real Fears for Free Speech. *Nikkei Asian Review* (22 May).

However, the general state of affairs could change toward the latter even in "Free" countries, due to increased infringements of human rights on the internet.[101] If "Free" countries or western liberal countries begin to consider restrictions on the internet, then they should make sure they are aware of the laws and practices in the Asian countries described as "Not Free", such as the real-name system or Anti-Fake News regulations discussed in this chapter.

101 United Nations' Human Rights Council resolution, *supra* note 7, which emphasised free access to the internet as a human right also underscored that "by all human rights violations and abuses committed against persons for exercising their human rights and fundamental freedoms on the internet, and by the impunity for these violations and abuses".

24 Latin American human rights law jurisprudence and practices towards the internet

Oscar Raúl Puccinelli

Introduction

In Latin American countries there are still very few laws and constitutional clauses relating to the protection and development of human rights in cyberspace and most of them deal only partially with the issue or do not give enough consideration of the main ones involved in the problem under study. This is most likely because, in general terms, it has been accepted – both doctrinally and jurisprudentially – that rights should apply equally both online and in the physical world as a consequence of the principle of the sameness of online and offline human rights.

As Bertoni indicates, the countries of Latin America have taken some tentative steps towards the regulation of the internet. Initiatives in that arena have looked towards the United States and Europe, where the internet is more regulated and where legislative and public debates on the subject reflect the discussions that take place at the international level. Answers are being sought to some relevant questions: What policies should the region adopt to promote access to the internet? What level of liability should internet service providers (ISPs) have in monitoring and preventing illegal acts committed through the internet? How should copyright and rights related to new publishing practices and access to content on the internet be dealt with? To what extent should criminal law be adjusted to include behaviour on the internet? How do government and private policies originating in other countries affect internet access, online privacy and economic development in Latin America? A few Latin American countries have begun to address these questions, introducing laws in the areas of minority protection, discrimination, intellectual property, telecommunications, defamation, protection of personal data, net neutrality, regulation of content on the internet, regulation of spaces for internet access and responsibility of ISPs, among others.[1]

The existence of so few laws and the lack of constitutional rules force us to analyse the issue from the international perspective because, at the regional level, there is no treaty or other imperative rule regulating these specific aspects yet. Following the idea that human rights should apply both in the physical and in the digital world, the American Convention on Human Rights (ACHR)[2] is the principal treatise in this field. However, it is not adequate in covering digital-age problems: it was drawn up in 1969, long before the appearance of the internet and barely a month after the first message transmitted by Arpanet, so clearly aspects related to the virtual world could not be foreseen.

1 Eduardo Bertoni (2012) Towards an Internet Free of Censorship: Proposals for Latin America, www.palermo.edu/cele/libertad-de-expresion/publicaciones.html

2 Available at: www.cidh.oas.org/basicos/english/basic3.american%20convention.htm

Of course, since this Convention is a general treaty on human rights, several of its rules do apply to the internet, especially those related to the freedom of expression (Article 13); the rights to privacy, honour and dignity (Article 11); the right to property (Article 21); and the right to the judicial protection of rights and freedoms (Article 25). There are other relevant provisions such as the ones that oblige state parties to that treaty to respect and guarantee the free and full exercise of the human rights and freedoms contained in the Convention "without any discrimination for reasons of reasons of race, colour, sex, language, religion, political or other opinion, national or social origin, economic status, birth, or any other social condition" (Article 1.1) and to adopt, in accordance with their constitutional processes and the provisions of this Convention, "such legislative or other measures as may be necessary to give effect to those rights and freedoms" (Article 2), always noting that all persons "are entitled, without discrimination, to equal protection of the law" (Article 24).

As the Inter-American Court of Human Rights has repeatedly indicated, according to these rights state parties are obliged to refrain from discriminating in the exercise and guarantee of rights and to take positive measures, allowing every person under their jurisdiction to effectively enjoy and exercise their rights under equal conditions.[3]

The Inter-American Human Rights System comprises other rules of differing hierarchies related to aspects essentially linked to the development of human rights in the network, such as the "Inter-American Convention on the Rights of the Author in Literary, Scientific and Artistic Works", several resolutions from the OAS General Assembly and the Inter-American Commission on Human Rights (IACHR) and its Special Rapporteur for Freedom of Expression (RFOE), in particular those committed to the development of telecommunications and ITC[4] and to address freedom of expression peculiarities, access to public information and protection of personal data.[5] The key documents resulting from their work are the "Declaration of Principles on Freedom of Expression" adopted in 2000 by the IACHR, in support of the RFOE;[6] the "Model Inter-American Law on Access to Information", adopted in 2010 by the General Assembly of the OAS;[7] and the "OAS Principles on privacy and personal data protection", adopted by the Inter-American Juridical Committee in 2015.[8] The latter is a very brief document that has

3 *Yatama v. Nicaragua*, Preliminary Objections, Merits, Reparations and Costs, InterAm. Ct. H.R. (ser. C) No. 127, 124(20) (June 23, 2005).

4 Such as the AG/RES. 2702 (XLII-O/12) "Use of Telecommunications/Information and Communication Technologies to Build an Inclusive Information Society".

5 In fact, in relation to access to public information and personal data protection, several resolutions were approved throughout this period, by the General Assembly of the OAS and by its Inter-American legal committee, *e.g.*: AG/RES. 1395 (XXVI-O/96); AG/RES. 1932 (XXXIII-O/03); AG/RES. 2057 (XXXIVO/04); AG/RES. 2058 (XXXIVO/04); AG/RES. 2121 (XXXV-O/05); AG/RES. 2252 (XXXVI-O/06); AG/RES. 2288 (XXXVIIO/07); CJI/RES. 123 (LXX-O/07); CJI/RES. 130 (LXXI-O/07); AG/RES. 2418 (XXXVIII-O/08); AG/RES. 2514 (XXXIX-O/09); AG/RES. 2607 (XL-O/10); AG/RES. 2661 (XLI-O/11); CJI/RES. 186 (LXXX-O/12) AG/RES. 2727 (XLII-O/12); AG/RES. 2811 (XLIII-O/13).

6 Available at www.oas.org/en/iachr/expression/showarticle.asp?artID=26

7 Approved by the Resolution AG/RES 2607 (XL-O/10), available at: www.oas.org/dil/AG-RES_2607-2010_eng.pdf, currently being updated to consider the problems resulting from Internet development.

8 The OAS Assembly, in June 2014, through resolution AG/RES. 2811 (XLIII-O/13), instructed the Inter-American Juridical Committee to prepare proposals for the Committee on Juridical and Political Affairs on the different ways in which the protection of personal data can be regulated, including a draft model law on personal data protection, taking into account international standards in that area. The Standards are available at: www.oas.org/en/sla/dil/docs/CJI-doc_474-15_rev2.pdf.

been widely superseded by those issued by the Ibero-American Network for Data Protection ("*Red Iberoamericana de Protección de Datos*", RIPD), among which the publication "Standards for personal data protection for Ibero-American States"[9] stands out for its up-to-date parallels with the most recent European Community regulations, and especially for being aligned with the General Data Protection Regulation, which came into force in mid-2018.[10]

Besides the aforementioned rules, and always within the Inter-American System of Human Rights sphere, there are many other relevant documents adopted by the RFOE of the IACHR, which are specifically related to internet regulation. Among them, the "Report on Freedom of Expression and Internet"[11] and the "Standards for a Free, Open and Inclusive Internet"[12] stand out, both being extremely important because they establish the most relevant principles relating to human rights included in internet regulations in accordance with several previous documents, some of which have been adopted in a joint statement with other Rapporteurs for Freedom of Expression.[13]

As stated, there are very few constitutions and laws adopted in the region and none provides comprehensive coverage of the most relevant issues related to the protection and development of human rights on the web. It must also be said that there is no overriding jurisprudence either at national level or within the scope of the Inter-American Court of Human Rights. Therefore, and though they will be mentioned in this chapter, we will focus on the regional soft law principles in order to set the framework within which future laws (or any amendments of laws in force today) should be passed for them to conform to Latin American conventional parameters. We will take into particular consideration the content of the aforementioned Special Rapporteur's report as to the unprecedented potential of the internet for the right to freedom of expression, which is mainly due to "its multidirectional and interactive nature, its speed and its global scope at a relatively low cost as well as its decentralized and open design". The report also says that the internet is a platform for fulfilling other human rights such as the right to participate in cultural life and enjoy the benefits of scientific and technological progress, the right to education, the right to assembly and association, political rights, and the right to health, among other rights recognised by the ACHR and the Protocol of San Salvador.

9 The "Data Protection Standards of the Ibero-American States" constitute a set of guidelines that may contribute to the issuance of regulatory initiatives for the protection of personal data in the Ibero-American region, which encompasses those countries that do not yet have these regulations; or, if relevant, they may act as reference for the modernisation and updating of existing legislation. They were unanimously approved by the Ibero-American Data Protection Network members (the control authorities of the Ibero-American States) in the closed session of the Meeting of Cartagena de Indias at the XV Ibero-American Data Protection Meeting, held from June 20 to 22, 2017 in Santiago, Chile, www.redipd.es/documentacion/common/Estandares_eng_Con_logo_RIPD.pdf

10 Regulation (EU) 2016/679, adopted on 2016 and became enforceable on 25 May 2018, https://eur-lex.europa.eu/legal-content/EN/TXT/?uri=CELEX%3A32016R0679

11 Freedom of Expression and the Internet. Office of the Special Rapporteur for Freedom of Expression. Inter-American Commission on Human Rights, 31 December 2013, OEA/Ser.L/V/II. CIDH/RELE/INF. 11/13, www.oas.org/en/iachr/expression/docs/reports/2014_04_08_internet_eng%20_web.pdf

12 Office of the Special Rapporteur for Freedom of Expression of the Inter-American Commission on Human Rights, Standards for a Free, Open and Inclusive Internet. OEA/Ser.L/V/II CIDH/RELE/INF.17/17, www.oas.org/en/iachr/expression/docs/publications/internet_2016_eng.pdf

13 After the first "Freedom of Expression as a Fundamental Human Right" (1999) the joint declarations addressed different matters. Since 2010 they have addressed more specific issues of the Internet, such as the Wikileaks affair, Freedom of Expression and Free Speech, Surveillance Programs, Fake News, Disinformation and Propaganda, and media independence and diversity in the digital age.

Following the same rationale, but stated in the Standards, the Special Rapporteur notes that the internet is a platform for the enjoyment and exercise of human rights, characteristics directly linked to the architecture of the network and to the principles governing it, including those of openness, decentralisation and neutrality. It also highlights that it is a primordial means for the increasingly democratic, open, plural and expansive exercise of freedom of expression, the development of public policies and the actions of individuals in the digital environment. Accordingly, it must observe several guiding principles including access thereto under equal conditions, pluralism, non-discrimination and privacy, as well as neutrality of the network and multisectoral governance as transversal components of these principles. In that regard, the Special Rapporteur addresses the main issues involved in the deployment of rights and freedoms on the internet, from the right *to access* the web to the rights resulting therefrom *inside* the internet.

Because this is the most specific and relevant inter-American document and, as it is based on the Inter-American human rights regulations, including the criteria and the Inter-American Court of the Inter-American Commission on Human Rights, our analysis will start from its contents as a basis for the development of the main regulatory aspects of the internet in the region. The legal references will be limited to South American countries with the brief inclusion of some Mexican regulations, due to the critical influence of this document in other regulations.

The principles of internet regulation in the "RFOE Standards" and in Latin American national laws and jurisprudence

The RFOE Standards first address the guiding principles (free and open internet; access; multistakeholder governance; equality and non-discrimination) and then focus on three issues that are central axes of discussion on the internet: the right to freedom of thought and expression; the right to access information; and the right to privacy and protection of personal data.

What follows is our analysis as to the main regulatory framework that should govern local rules addressing the main issues related to the internet pursuant to the principles of the inter-American human rights system, mentioning the applicable laws in force and the local jurisprudence.

Universal access

This principle is, in common with the right to life, a prerequisite both for the full enjoyment of the benefits offered by the internet and for the defence of the rights that may be violated in the network. It implies the need to guarantee connectivity and universal, ubiquitous, equitable and truly affordable access, of adequate quality, to the internet infrastructure and ICT services and has a great impact on several emerging duties linked to the objective of closing the "digital divide" ("the gap between people with effective access to digital and information technologies, in particular the Internet, and those with very limited or no access at all"[14]). Said duties are, specifically: progressive access fostering both

14 Frank La Rue (2011) Report of the Special Rapporteur on the promotion and protection of the right to freedom of opinion and expression, Report to the Human Rights Council, 17th session, UN Doc A/HRC/17/27, 17.

internet infrastructure and the necessary technology enabling its use and also access to the greatest possible amount of information available in the network; elimination of arbitrary barriers to accessing online infrastructure, technology and information; and adoption of positive differentiation measures to allow the effective enjoyment of this right to persons or communities such as is necessary due to circumstances of their marginalisation or discrimination.

Universal access to the internet must comply with minimum standards regarding speed, stability, affordability, quality, integrity, multilingualism, "digital literacy", the inclusion of local content and accessibility by disabled people. Accordingly, states must apply long-term plans and public policies in order to avoid the arbitrary exclusion of certain sectors. They must also develop the necessary physical infrastructure and take any necessary measures enabling the development of the mobile internet. At the same time they must guarantee the quality and integrity of the service, preventing any blockages whatsoever, interferences or arbitrary slowdowns, disproportionate private barriers and access denials except when there are no less restrictive measures and, as long as those sanctions comply with the requirements of legality, proportionality and necessity in a democratic society, have been ordered by a competent jurisdictional authority, and have never been applied exclusively to certain sectors of populations.

Many countries and international organisations already regulate access to the internet as a basic right. We consider the most relevant cases are Estonia (since 2000), Greece (since 2001 and as a constitutional right), the European Union (since 2002), Spain and Finland (since 2003), Germany (since 2004), Turkey (since 2010) and the Organization for Security and Co-operation in Europe (OSCE) (since 2011). Finland (in 2009 and 2015) and Spain (in 2011) went one step further by stating the right to internet access should be granted through a broadband network, that is, at high speed and with a minimum speed required in the downstream direction.

At a constitutional level in the Latin American region, Mexico reformed its Magna Carta in 2013. In Article 6 (on freedom of expression and access to information) it sets out that the state will guarantee the right of access to information and communication technologies as well as to broadcasting and telecommunications services, including broadband and internet services. Moreover, Article 6 sets out that, to that end, the state will set conditions of effective competitiveness as to the provision of said services. Furthermore, and in order to protect the right to disseminate opinions, Article 7 sets out that information and ideas through any media include a prohibition to restricting this right by means of indirect measures "such as the abuse of government or private controls over . . . equipment used for information dissemination or any other means whatsoever and information and communications technologies aiming at avoiding communication and circulation of ideas and opinions".

At the legal level, Chile amended the General Telecommunications Law in 2010 through Law 20,453,[15] which "enshrines the principle of net neutrality for consumers and users of the Internet" and which has subsequently been reformed by Law 21,046,[16] adopted in 2017, where this principle is included in Article 24.

15 Law 20,453, amending the General Telecommunications Law. August 20, 2010. Available at: www.leychile.cl/Navegar?idLey=20453

16 Available at www.leychile.cl/Navegar?idNorma=1111298

Colombia adopted Law 1450[17] in 2011, whereby the "National Development Plan, 2010–2014" was issued, recognising this principle in Article 55, and also referring to a "social internet" in Article 58. This law was further replaced by Law 1753[18] in 2015, which regulates a new National Development Plan (2014–2018) where the principle is recognised in Article 194.

In 2014, Brazil approved Law 12,965,[19] which "Establishes the principles, guarantees, rights and for the use of Internet in Brazil" known as the "Civil Internet Framework" ("*Marco Civil da Internet*"), expressly including this principle in Articles 4 and 7.

Also in 2014, Argentina adopted Law 27,078[20] "Digital Argentina" ("*Argentina Digital*"), where this principle is specifically mentioned in Articles 1 and 2.

Finally, at the jurisprudential level of the highest local courts, and following the historic precedent of the French Constitutional Council issued in sentence number 2009–580 DC[21] on 10 June 2009, which recognised access to the internet as a basic right, the Constitutional Chamber of the Supreme Court of Justice of Costa Rica, in sentence number 12790–2010,[22] went even further by recognising access to the internet as a fundamental right. At the same time, Finland passed a law that came into effect on 1 July 2010, which recognised internet access as a right.[23]

Openness and accessibility

As is set out in the RFOE Standards, openness is a crucial principle that is achieved through certain technical standards, such as interoperability and open application interfaces and the absence of limitations that could otherwise be imposed through exclusive regimes of licences or protectionist limitations of the provision of services that artificially favour monopolies or archaic technological platforms. Accessibility is complementary and makes internet access ubiquitous, affordable, non-discriminatory, of adequate quality and available at low cost, and deems internet users as recipients or beneficiaries of information and contents and as producers thereof and of related services and applications. Accordingly, users' capabilities as to multilingualism and digital literacy should be promoted, fostering both "sustainable and reliable business models able to fund universal access and to grant accessibility through the maintenance of a diverse range of contents and services", such as trusted access, based, for example, on safe and authentic data.

Chile included these principles in Article 24 H of the General Telecommunications Law, amended by Law 20,453. Brazil included this principle in Articles 2 and 4 of the "Civil Internet Framework". Argentina recognised said principles in Articles 18 and 19 of Law 27,078.

17 Available at www.procuraduria.gov.co/portal/media/file/docs/ddr/CompiladoNormativo_Parte3.pdf

18 Available at www.mincit.gov.co/loader.php?lServicio=Documentos&lFuncion=verPdf&id=78676&name=LEY_1753_DE_2015.pdf&prefijo=file

19 Law 12,965. April 23, 2014. Available at: www.planalto.gov.br/ccivil_03/_ato2011-2014/2014/lei/l12965.htm 33

20 Available at http://cdh.defensoria.org.ar/2017/12/15/ley-27-078-argentina-digital-tecnologias-de-la-informacion-y-las-comunicaciones/

21 Available at www.conseil-constitutionnel.fr/sites/default/files/as/root/bank_mm/espagnol/es2009_580dc.pdf

22 Available at www.poder-judicial.go.cr/salaconstitucional/index.php/servicios-publicos/759-10-012790

23 www.itu.int/net/itunews/issues/2010/06/pdf/201006_34.pdf

Pluralism and diversity

Since pluralism and diversity are considered essential conditions for public deliberation processes and for the simple exercise of freedom of expression that must be specially preserved in the digital environment, this principle also aims to ensure that private actors do not impose disproportionate or arbitrary barriers to internet access or to the use of its main services. To that end, no changes must be introduced that could imply the reduction of voices and contents on the web or the promotion of platforms interfering with the search and dissemination of any kind of information and ideas, regardless of borders, as required in Article 13 of the ACHR.

Colombian Law 1450[24] recognised this principle in Article 55 and also refers to a "social internet" in Article 58. The new frame established by Law 1753 passed in 2015 included these principles in Article 194. The Brazilian "Civil Internet Framework" expressly includes this principle in Articles 2 and 4. In Argentinian Law 27,078, this principle is mentioned in Articles 2 and 62.

Non-discrimination

This principle applies both to the right to internet access (as seen before) and to the exercise of rights *inside* the internet; it rules that the states are obliged to grant the exercise of individual human rights on the internet under equal conditions, and individuals have the right to exercise their rights to assembly, association, freedom of expression, access to information, freedom of religion, and so on, without discrimination. In particular, States must guarantee that all persons may disseminate content and opinions on equal terms – especially those who belong to vulnerable groups or who express critical views on matters of public interest – and that they have access to public information while their right to privacy is respected.

In that regard, and since the internet is an essential tool for vulnerable communities and communities that were historically subject to discrimination relating to information access, asserted grievances, making their voices heard, participating actively in public debates, the states must adopt measures to avoid instances of online discrimination against particularly vulnerable groups, including women, children, the LGBTI community, migrants and disabled persons, among others. Moreover, and following the same rationale, privacy on the net today shows five main challenges generated or magnified by the internet phenomenon: personal data protection; surveillance, monitoring and interception; encryption and anonymity; "Big Data"; and the "Internet of Things".

At the regional level, the Inter-American Commission and the Inter-American Court on Human Rights highlight the duty of the states in the fight against any obstruction regarding ideas dissemination because it implies a violation of the right to freedom of expression in its individual and social dimension, since freedom of expression also includes and protects any wrongful or fake statement, without prejudice to subsequent responsibilities resulting therefrom. Consequently, states have a primary obligation to remain neutral with respect to the content disclosed, guaranteeing that there are no people, groups, ideas or means of expression *a priori* excluded from public debate.

24 Available at www.procuraduria.gov.co/portal/media/file/docs/ddr/CompiladoNormativo_Parte3.pdf

The inter-American jurisprudence, based on the relevance of the exercise of other human rights or for the consolidation, functioning and preservation of democracy, protects in particular:

a) any political discourse and on matters of public interest;
b) any discourse by public officials in the exercise of their functions and by candidates for public office; and
c) any discourse being an integral element of the personal identity or dignity of the person stating it.

Consequently, liabilities arising therefrom, such as abusive exercise of freedom of expression must always be adjudged (considering the "tripartite test" of legality, necessity and proportionality) by an independent and impartial judicial authority, always respecting the guarantees of due process, which cannot be discriminatory or discriminate, nor can they constitute censorship through indirect measures, specifically prohibited by Article 13.3 of the ACHR.

At a constitutional level, most of the Latin American constitutions recognise the three rights mentioned previously: freedom of expression, access to public information and personal data protection. In relation to the latter, every constitution amended since 1988 included the "right of habeas data" (a common heritage of inter-American Constitutional Law, recognised either in its substantive or in its procedural modality, a right that is useful to fight arbitrary interferences by the states or individuals in people's private lives) and several countries inf the region adopted data protection laws based on the European model, and are currently amending them owing to the recent approval of the General Data Protection Regulation and also based on, in general terms, the RIPD Standards.

Related to freedom of expression on the internet, Brazil approved a specific regulation in Articles 2 and 3 of the Civil Internet Framework and Argentina adopted, in 2005, Law 26,032, about "Internet service"[25] recognising in Article 1 that the search, reception and dissemination of information and ideas through the internet service is considered within the constitutional guarantee that protects freedom of expression. Further, the Supreme Court, in the case "Rodríguez c/Google"[26] held that freedom of expression includes the right to transmit ideas, facts and opinions disseminated through the internet, because it has been recognised in Law 26,032, which deems that, at the individual level, the internet substantiates the personal right to make public, to transmit, to disseminate and to externalise – or not – ideas, opinions, beliefs, criticisms, etc., and that, at a collective level, it constitutes an instrument for guaranteeing freedom of information and formation of public opinion.

Finally, there are several useful laws in the region regulating the right to access public information, based on the inter-American standards contained in the OAS Law model and in the jurisprudence of the Inter-American Human Rights Court, most precisely contained in the cases *Claude Reyes et al v. Chile*[27] and *Gomes Lund et al. v. Brazil*[28], but they don't specifically refer to the internet.

25 Available at www.bnm.me.gov.ar/giga1/normas/11096.pdf

26 Available at www.saij.gob.ar/corte-suprema-justicia-nacion-federal-ciudad-autonoma-buenos-aires-rodriguez-maria-belen-google-inc-otro-danos-perjuicios-fa14000161-2014-10-28/123456789-161-0004-1ots-eupmocsollaf#

27 Available at www.corteidh.or.cr/docs/casos/articulos/seriec_151_ing.pdf

28 Available at www.corteidh.or.cr/docs/casos/articulos/seriec_219_ing.pdf

Net neutrality

This design principle of the internet means that there should be no discrimination in the treatment of internet data and traffic, based on the device, content, author, origin and/or destination of the content, service or application involved and it is recognised in the Standards as "a necessary condition for exercising freedom of expression on the Internet pursuant to the terms of Article 13 of the American Convention" and as "a transversal component of the guiding principles".

Its main goal is to ensure that users are free to access and choose to use, send, receive or offer any lawful content, application or service through an internet not being subject to conditions, whether directed or restricted, through any blocking, filtering, or interference, so it requires all "data packages" to be treated equally and without distinctions, as a "dumb network".

As a direct consequence, states must guarantee the validity of this principle through appropriate legislation including exceptions, but only in cases that are "strictly necessary and proportional in order to preserve the integrity and safety of the network; to prevent the transmission of online content at the express request – free and not incentivized – of the user; and to temporarily and exceptionally manage network congestion".

This principle was adopted by several countries in the region. Chilean Law 20,453 recognised the principle by adding paragraph H to Article 24. Colombian Law 1450[29] recognised the principle of net neutrality in Article 56 and, in its final paragraph, ordered the Communications Regulation Commission (CRC) to regulate the terms and conditions of application of the provisions of this article within six months of the law coming into force. That regulation was given the same year in Resolution 3502 of the CRC but it was strongly criticised, especially because it did not clarify the exceptions to the principle of neutrality, listing a series of possibilities available for operators to justify the interference in datagram traffic, and opening a wide range of interpretations.

Argentinian Law 27,078 specifically includes this principle in Articles 1, 56 and 57. Brazilian Law 12,965 recognised the principle of net neutrality in Article 9. Paraguay recognised the principle through Resolution 190/2009 issued on 11 March 2009, by the National Telecommunications Commission ("*Comisión Nacional de Telecomunicaciones*"),[30] specifically in Article 26.

Finally, Mexico included the net neutrality principle in the Federal Telecommunications and Broadcasting Law (*Ley Federal de Telecomunicaciones y Radiodifusión*) adopted on 14 July 2014.[31] The law was subject to several amendments, and now the principle is included in Chapter VI ("Of the Neutrality of Networks"), specifically in Articles 145 and 146 of the legislation. This apparently sacred and consolidated principle recently and unexpectedly received setbacks.

The first issue that generated a great division among experts was the jurisprudential recognition, in 2014, of the right to be forgotten online ("RTBF 2.0"), ruled by the Court of Justice of the European Union (CJEU) in the case of "Google Spain S.L., *Google Inc. v. Agencia Española de Protección de Datos*, Mario Costeja González".[32] The CJEU interpreted

29 Available at www.procuraduria.gov.co/portal/media/file/docs/ddr/CompiladoNormativo_Parte3.pdf

30 National Telecommunications Commission. Resolution 190/2009, March 11, 2009, www.leyes.com.py/todas_disposiciones/2009/resoluciones/resolucion_190_09.php

31 Federal Telecommunications and Broadcasting Law, www.diputados.gob.mx/LeyesBiblio/pdf/LFTR_311017.pdf

32 Available at http://curia.europa.eu/juris/document/document_print.jsf?doclang=EN&docid=152065

that, under Directive 95/46/CE, individuals can request that their personal data be de-indexed from internet browsers or search engines, based on the protection of personal data on the internet, in this case ordering Google to de-index content due to the time elapsed and the loss of public relevance of the information published in a digital newspaper. The ruling is highly controversial in Latin America, where diametrically different judgments have been made in the highest local Courts[33] and in recent data protection laws and several reform projects.[34]

In addition, the RFOE "Standards" questions the compatibility of such measures (the removal and de-indexation of internet contents adopted by private companies as well as those requested by states), particularly because of the negative impact on the exercise of the right to freedom of expression in its individual and collective dimension. This rationale also leads us to consider that government limitations on internet content must be decided by a competent, independent and impartial judge or court granting due process guarantees as established in Article 8 of the ACHR.[35]

33 *E.g.* "Gloria vs. El Tiempo" (Colombian Constitutional Court decision T-277/2015); "Aida Curi" & "Chacina de Candelaria" (Brazilian Supreme Court, 2008); "XX vs. El Mercurio" (Supreme Court of Chile, 2016).

34 *E.g.* Article 10 of Decree No. 3755 of 2012 (which regulates the Costa Rican law on data protection) which recognises the right to be forgotten through the regulation of a period of 10 years of expiration of the data from the occurrence of the relevant event. Also, article 10 of Nicaraguan Law 787, passed in 2012, expressly provides for the right to be digitally forgotten by social networks, servers and search engines. More generally, article 47 of the Mexican "General law of protection of personal data in possession of obliged subjects" provides the right to object to processing of personal data even though the treatment is lawful, providing it must cease to prevent its persistence from causing damage or prejudice to the data subject. Current data protection law reforms projects in Argentina and Chile provide similar articles, but do not directly recognise the right to be forgotten even though it is included in the European GDPR.

35 The Standards set out that information that has been removed should no longer circulate, and the de-indexing of content causes a similar effect, affecting the right of individuals to express themselves and disseminate their opinions and ideas and the right of the community to receive information and ideas of all kinds. And according to the regional standards, prior censorship is prohibited except for the protection of minors at public events, and any restriction must be established by law, . . . suitable, proportionate, and necessary for the accomplishment of a legitimate aim in a democratic society . . . it must be the least restrictive one. The protection of personal data is a legitimate aim for the establishment of restrictions to the right to freedom of expression. Nevertheless, any limitation . . . must respect the three-part test . . . it must be legally established in a law, both substantively and procedurally; . . . necessary and suitable, . . . proportionate. Limitations . . . – must also be ordered by a competent, independent, and impartial judge or court, with all due process guarantees . . ." "If a State decides to adopt personal data protection systems that acknowledge the deindexing that is referred to as the 'right to be forgotten' should do so on an absolutely exceptional basis . . . laws on deindexing or the opposition of indexing should be designed in a clear, specific, and limited manner. . . . They should distinguish between informationand personal data, establishing those cases in which the action is inadmissible, particularly . . . on matters of public interest, and protecting lawful and legitimate speech . . . public officials are subject to greater scrutiny by society . . . a strong presumption should be put in place against content removal and deindexing requests lodged by a public official, public person or a candidate to public office. . . "This is particularly relevant in relation to the information produced and disseminated by media outlets that use the Internet as a platform. Media digital platforms cannot be understood as personal data controllers. They are public sources of information and platforms for the dissemination of opinions and ideas on matters of public interest, and therefore cannot be subject to a de-indexing order nor to the suppression of online content regarding matters of public interest . . . De-indexing laws should be restricted to those cases in which the petitioner demonstrates a substantive harm. . . . The de-indexing measures should always be enforced through a court order – . . . where affected parties can be heard, including the speaker, the publisher of media outlet and the intermediaries. . . . Transparency with respect to content de-indexing policies applied by private and public entities (including oversight bodies and the judicial branch) is fundamentally important. The law should subject intermediaries, government authorities, and courts to active transparency obligations, whereby information on the nature, volume, and outcomes of deindexingrequests received is regularly published".

On the other hand, since 2015 there has been a great debate around the "zero-rating" plans, which allow ISPs to provide costless access to specific applications (such as YouTube or WhatsApp) in the end user's data plan. These kinds of plans appeared in different countries in the region – including Argentina, Chile, Colombia, Brazil, Ecuador, Panama, Perú, México and Paraguay – but they are strongly criticised from the perspective of the principle of neutrality. As a matter of fact, the Standards highlight the fact that scholarly opinion is divided as to their impact on net neutrality and they also emphasise the fact that, regardless of the policy adopted by each state in relation to this issue, it is worth noting that in no case will states be able to replace their policies of universal access to the internet with zero-rating plans or policies.

As if this were not enough, and based on the ideas of supporters of net neutrality elimination (who consider that it will lead to higher competitiveness among service providers, which will result in cheaper and faster internet services for consumers), on 21 November 2017, the US Federal Communications Commission (FCC) voted to begin the rollback of Obama-era net neutrality regulations, so now cable and phone companies could divide the internet into fast and slow lanes: an internet service provider could slow down competitor content or block political opinions it disagrees with. This process seems not to be reversible and the impact on Latin American regulations is difficult to predict.

Multisectoral governance of the internet

This principle has particular relevance and must be implemented through a multipartite and democratic process in internet governance: the principle of enhanced cooperation prevails and therefore all relevant points of view can be considered and no actor can be attributed exclusively to its regulation. In addition, such multisectoral governance guarantees active. participation of the representatives of the different stakeholders involved in the development and regulation of the internet, including states, the private sector, the technological sector, civil society, the academic sector and, fundamentally, the users.

Multisectoral internet governance is crucial and it must be exercised under the principles of public resources and not simply as a matter of private contracts. Accordingly, states must guarantee the equitable participation of all relevant stakeholders, promote enhanced cooperation among competent authorities, academia, civil society, the technical community and the private sector, among others, both at national and international level, and within a framework of open debates and democratic participation. Other key elements of success are: inclusion, transparency, accountability, legitimacy, effectiveness, equality and non-discrimination (ensuring the full participation of women in the knowledge society, and promoting tolerance through social programmes, training and education and prohibiting illicit contents or unguarded discourses for the right to freedom of expression such as hate speech that constitutes incitement to violence, propaganda of war, direct and public incitement to genocide and child pornography).

Obviously, this multisectoral governance involves several issues that must be taken into account. The RFOE has noted with concern how some countries in the region have resorted to the blocking of websites or specific applications for different reasons and even under judicial order, with little or no consideration of the consequences of such measures on the right to freedom of online expression. It also added that internet content blocking and filtering systems have frequently generated the blocking of internet sites and legitimate content, and that some governments have used this ability to prevent the public from having access to fundamental information of public interest that governments are interested in hiding. Therefore, content blocking measures must not be used to control or limit the dissemination of specially protected speech or that have a presumption of protection when said presumption has not been invalidated by a competent authority that offers sufficient guarantees of independence, autonomy and impartiality.

An additional and linked issue is the impact of intellectual property on network contents. The RFOE states that governments must "recognize and reward creativity, human rights and innovation and, at the same time, guarantee public access to the results of these efforts", so that "the achievement of an adequate balance between these two objectives is the main challenge of both regimes". Consequently, material interests cannot be used to defend patent laws that do not sufficiently respect several rights (such as to participate in cultural life, to enjoy the benefits of scientific progress and its applications, to scientific freedom, to food and health, and the rights of indigenous peoples and local communities). In that regard, actions taken to promote open licencing and the adoption of exceptions in existing copyright regimes are welcome, such as the adoption of doctrines of "fair use" and open licences such as *Creative Commons*.

The RFOE Standards emphasise that transparency regarding policies for removing the content of intermediaries is of fundamental importance, so they must provide clear information on the type of content that could be removed from the platform according to the relevant terms of service or community guidelines, as well as the manner in which the removal could take place and if there is any form of appeal available to the user who feels that their content has been unduly removed.

In regard to the liability of intermediaries (including among them any entity enabling communication of information from one party to another), the Standards state that, since they have become key players in the protection of the rights to freedom of expression and privacy, the applicable liability regime on third-party content should be cautious, following the tripartite test, and be adjudged under the principle of mere transmission (deeming intermediaries not liable for any content generated by third parties and disseminated to third parties) and that any subsequent liability therefrom is to be enforced against the authors of the expression.

This further accentuates that different laws and initiatives at regional level must take account of the different frameworks within which the liability of intermediaries is regulated: laws covering protection of privacy and personal data, copyrights, or rights to reputation and good name that also regulate liability of intermediaries, and objective liability, which deems intermediaries liable for any content considered illegal on their platform, something that contradicts the ACHR, since it promotes in a democratic society the monitoring and censorship of intermediaries in a disproportionate and unnecessary fashion to protect their own users, a situation that is also contrary to the Manila Principles on Intermediary Liability.[36]

Finally, it postulates that when it comes to deciding questions of liability, judges with the "closest" contact with the case in question are the competent ones, depending on the

36 www.manilaprinciples.org/

victim's place of residence, where the content has originated, or where the author resides in order to avoid so-called "defamation tourism" or "forum-shopping".

In regard to the regulations approved in the region, the Brazilian "Internet Civil Framework" has specific rules in "Section III Liability for any damages arising from content generated by third parties" where it is stated that:

a) "The provider of connection to internet shall not be liable for civil damages resulting from content generated by third parties" (Article 18);
b) "In order to ensure freedom of expression and prevent censorship, the provider of internet applications can only be subject to civil liability for damages resulting from content generated by third parties if, under a specific court order, it does not take any steps to, within the framework of their service and within the time stated in the order, make unavailable the content that was identified as being unlawful, unless otherwise provided by law" (Article 19);
c) When an ISP executes a court order, it must provide the user "with information allowing them to legally contest and submit a defense in court unless otherwise provided by law or in a court order" (Article 20); and
d) The ISP "that makes third-party generated content available shall be held liable for the breach of privacy arising from the disclosure of images, videos and other material containing nudity or sexual activities of a private nature, without the consent of the relevant participants, when, after having been so noticed by said participants or their legal representative, refrains from removing, in a diligent manner and within its own technical limitations, such content" (Article 21).

At the jurisprudential level, in the case "Rodríguez c/ Google",[37] the Supreme Court of Argentina, applying the "notice and take down" liability system, held that court decisions on the activities of "search engines" should not be based on objective liability, but rather on subjective liability, as said "search engines" do not have a general obligation to monitor the contents that are uploaded thereto and that are provided by those liable for each web page shown thereon, and thus engines are not liable for contents they have not created.

Conclusion

We have tried to provide a comprehensive view of the status of the most relevant issues related to internet-linked human rights in Latin American countries. Many questions have been specifically addressed in general or partial laws, or even at a jurisprudential level, but a large proportion of them still remain unresolved, in part because they still depend on the interpretation of treaties that were not specifically designed to tackle internet issues. Obviously, for reasons of editorial space, many issues have not been addressed, but we hope that our contribution may be useful for interested parties seeking a general view of what has happened so far in the region about those main issues since the internet was created.

37 Available at www.saij.gob.ar/corte-suprema-justicia-nacion-federal-ciudad-autonoma-buenos-aires-rodriguez-maria-belen-google-inc-otro-danos-perjuicios-fa14000161-2014-10-28/123456789-161-0004-1ots-eupmocsollaf#

25 The Russian perspective on human rights protection online

Dmitry Dedov

Problems

Freedom in cyberspace has become almost unlimited. This makes the Russian authorities worried about the lack of security control. Conflict between all kinds of internet freedoms and public security has triggered numerous reforms in this sphere. However, the Russian expert community is very sensitive to the provision and development of a legal basis for the protection of personal data online, which covers all relevant areas including the automatic processing of personal data and the right to privacy, intellectual property, freedom of expression, journalism and access to information, and surveillance. The legal debates were therefore intense and revealed two major problems: (a) the absence of a theoretical vision for balancing between conflicting interests such as freedom of access to the internet and cybercrime, and (b) discrepancies between the law and practice in connection with interfering with individual rights and freedoms for the purpose of public security, prevention of crime and the protection of the rights of victims.

The internet plays an important role in Russian society. It spread across the country with a very high dynamic, and now internet coverage has reached almost 70% of the population. This result was inevitable due to the absence of any censorship or restrictions. However, since the authorities declared their plans to enhance the regulation of the internet, the issue became the subject of public debate. The most popular idea, first raised by Mikhail Fedotov, Chairman of the Presidential Council for Human Rights, was that the internet is a transnational phenomenon, and therefore it requires regulation by an international treaty on the basis of internationally recognised principles, including the confidentiality of personal data and respect of private life, rule of law and proportionality, adequacy and necessity. In his view, the same safeguards should apply both offline and online.[1]

Another problem under discussion is that the anonymity of internet users and their IP addresses facilitates the committing of offences. Anonymity then creates obstacles to bringing those responsible to justice. In the practice of the European Court of Human Rights ("the Court") this problem has been identified in the case *Delfi AS v. Estonia* [GC] (no. 64569/09, § 127, 16 June 2015), where a mass media operator was found guilty of not implementing a system to protect against defamation and insulting remarks posted by anonymous users. The Court noted that anonymity makes it impossible to find the perpetrators. This problem, according to the Russian authorities, could be resolved through transparency in regard to all users and their IP addresses, so that any user can be identified. Such a solution requires more control over the internet, more transparency and

1 Mikhail Fedotov (2017) Internet Is a Habitat, Not a Means of Interference. *Ogonyok* (6 November).

less anonymity. Granting anonymity becomes possible (and lawful) only if it is necessary to protect the user's right to privacy.

This also raises difficulties with how to regulate in order to achieve the transparency of users. For example, before the creation of a new IP address or the purchase of a SIM card, every user should disclose his/her personal data so it can be entered into a register held by the relevant telecoms operator and accessible to the authorities pursuing a legitimate aim. If the user loses the SIM card or even voluntarily gives it to another person, he/she remains responsible for any offence made with the help of the SIM card or IP address, unless proven otherwise. Therefore, such a regulation would be based on a presumption of guilt rather than of innocence, which is not in compliance with international standards. For example, Article 4 of the Budapest Convention on Cybercrime provides that the domestic law should define criminal offences relating to damaging, deterioration or suppression of computer data without right as offences committed intentionally. The same applies to other articles of the Cybercrime Convention (e.g. Articles 2–11); in particular, the distribution of a device designed or adapted primarily for the purpose of committing any cybercrime (Article 6).

In the Russian internet zone, social networks have been used for various types of criminal activity, such as the incitement of adolescents to commit suicide, paedophilia, fraud and extortion. One example could be taken from the Court's case law. In the case of *Premininy v. Russia* (no. 44973/04, 10 February 2011), the appellants were two Russian nationals who were tried and convicted in Russia on suspicion of hacking into the online security system of an American bank, "Green Point Bank", in 2001 and stealing its database of clients and extorting money in exchange for promising not to publish that database on the internet. It appears that Russian hackers were and are very active. There are a lot of publications in the global media that they are also involved in political matters, in particular, influencing the democratic elections in the United States of America, Germany and some other European countries.[2] In this context, experts have criticised the decision of the Russian authorities not to sign the Cybercrime Convention, the first international treaty on crimes committed via the internet, dealing particularly with infringements of copyright, computer-related fraud, child pornography and violations of network security. Those types of cybercrime are very common in Russia today. Moreover, the Cybercrime Convention contains procedures for searching computer networks and connections, which could also help resolve the anonymity problem. The decision of the Russian authorities creates the impression that they are not willing to combat cybercrime for political reasons.

Instead, the opposite seems to be the trend – to localise internet facilities for reasons of state security and sovereignty of the state. In contrary, the international providers explain the localisation shift by individual privacy and security and the improvement of the quality of their services.[3]

The Cybercrime Convention does not satisfy the Russian authorities because of Article 32, which allows transborder access to stored computer data. Such access could be dangerous, in the view of the Russian authorities, to the sovereignty of the state. The message is clear: it is important for the authorities to have unrestricted access to the personal data of their citizens, including for the purpose of mass surveillance. Since the international social networks traditionally store all personal data on their servers outside the national territory

2 See, for example, How We Deserted Common Ground. *TIME* (11 December 2017).

3 Gerry Shih, Paul Carsten (2014) Apple Begins Storing Users' Personal Data on Servers in China. *Reuters* (15 August).

of the states, this creates a problem for the domestic authorities. For these reasons, the Russian authorities proposed a draft alternative international treaty, similar to the Cybercrime Convention, intended to be adopted at UN level.[4] If the national personal data does not automatically transfer outside the national territory then the protection of the right to personal life remains on the national level which brings more clarity.

According to experts, international cooperation and mutual assistance is necessary because national measures alone are insufficient. In the case of blocking a site with child pornography at the national level, all foreign users of the site will retain access to the content. The blocking itself is not enough. The creators of such sites should be identified and punished. On the other hand, interference by the state agency should be supported by telecoms operators who should self-regulate and therefore react immediately to information received from users about cybercrimes.[5]

In my view, the decision not to sign the Cybercrime Convention was caused by Article 24, which permits the extradition of offenders to another Party to the Convention. The extradition of Russian citizens is prohibited by the Russian Constitution. This has both legal and political implications since the authorities are accused of allowing hackers to act under the control of those authorities. Unfortunately, this idea is only speculation and it cannot be impartially assessed without any relevant factual information. Mikhail Fedotov raised a similar problem linked to the organic transborder nature of the internet – the jurisdiction of national authorities over cybercrimes. Since no criteria for establishing jurisdiction are described by the Member-States of the Cybercrime Convention, the legal risks related to the competence of national courts remain.

Personal data

Nevertheless, Russia is a party to the Council of Europe Convention of 1981 for the protection of individuals with regard to the automatic processing of personal data. The Russian parliament has implemented the principles and guarantees envisaged by the Convention in its Personal Data Law no. 152-FZ[6] enacted on 27 July 2006. For example, the Personal Data Law provides that the processing of personal data is allowed only for explicit legitimate purposes. The scope of personal data subject to automatic processing should be limited to the particular legitimate purpose. The operators should ascertain that the personal data stored in a register remains accurate and relevant in connection with the purpose of it being processed. The limits and conditions of the storage of personal data also depend on the purpose of the processing. For example, personal data should not be stored longer than necessary for that legitimate purpose, unless the time limit is defined by the parties in a private contract. After the expiration of the time limit the personal data should be destroyed or become anonymous.

The collection and storage of personal data by operators (private companies, providers of services and suppliers of goods) is strictly regulated and controlled by the state agency Goskomnadzor. Operators are obliged to establish a corporate policy for the processing of personal data, including the types of data that are necessary to be collected, confidentiality measures, nominating the person or people who are responsible for the protection of the

4 Interfax: The Russian Ministry of Foreign Affairs proposed changing the rules of combat against global cybercrime. 14 April 2017.

5 Fedotov 2017.

6 "FZ" means "federal law" ("*federalnyy zakon*").

personal data, and obligatory instructions for the operator's personnel. The clients should have access to the policy before giving consent for their personal information to be processed. In general, the safeguards under Law no. 152-FZ are equal to the EU General Data Protection Regulation, in particular, to the provisions of Article 15, which provides the user the right to receive information regarding the processing of his or her personal data, including the recipients to whom the personal data has been disclosed.

The collection, processing, use and storage of the personal data by the provider of services is forbidden without written consent from the clients of the company or operator. Any breach of the preceding requirements is considered an administrative offence and could be punished under Russian administrative law. Processing personal data without consent is permitted only for a limited list of purposes established by the Personal Data Law including the execution of a court order, participation in civil or administrative proceedings or in a criminal trial, professional journalist activity or if the personal information could be received from public sources. In principle, the Personal Data Law prohibits the automatic processing of personal data concerning the nationality, race, religious beliefs, political or philosophical preferences, state of health and sexual life of individuals.

Yarovaya Law

The Yarovaya Law (Federal laws nos. 374-FZ and 375-FZ), enacted in 2016, relates to requirements for data collection and mandatory deciphering in the telecommunications industry. The Law is known to the public under the name of Irina Yarovaya, one the most influential members of the Parliament and the ruling party United Russia, Deputy Chairman of the state Duma and Head of the Security Committee. The Law requires telecom operators to store recordings of phone conversations, text messages and internet traffic for up to 6 months, and also to store all metadata for three years in the interests of public security. Internet and telecom companies are required to disclose these communications and metadata, as well as "all other information necessary" to the authorities on request and without a court order.

The Law was heavily criticised by local and foreign experts because of the extreme quantity of data storage technology needed to fulfil the requirements. The implementation of the Law has been described as impossible and extremely expensive because of the unprecedented data storage requirements, according to experts and the telecom operators. The Russian Post estimated that the implementation of the Law would cost the organisation 500 billion rubles for the initial purchases of equipment and 100 billion rubles annually. Implementation of the Law by other logistics, delivery and freight services was estimated to cost around 180 billion rubles, which is projected to cause a 30–40% drop in online purchases. Cell service operators need to find an additional 2.2 trillion rubles to comply, which may cause a two- or threefold rise in the cost of mobile services for the consumer. Edward Snowden estimated the combined cost of implementation to be 33 billion US dollars and predicted that the overall security levels will be unaffected, despite the huge affiliated costs. It appeared that the necessary equipment required to store all the data does not exist in Russia or anywhere else in the world.

Another part of the criticism relates to the way it interferes with fundamental human rights, including the right to have one's private life respected, as online services such as messaging services, email and social networks that use encrypted data are required to permit the Federal Security Service (FSB) to access and read their encrypted communications. In other words, the Law makes cryptographic backdoors mandatory in all messaging applications even if many messengers do not hold encryption keys. The Yarovaya Law also casts its eye on the freedom of expression on the internet, establishing punishment for incitement to hostility against an ethnic, social or religious group. It was not the first attempt to take control of the internet. Earlier, the state Duma (the Russian parliament) adopted the "Bloggers Law" (Federal Law no. 97-FZ, 5 May, 2014), which requires bloggers with over 3,000 daily readers to register as part of the mass media, and they can no longer remain anonymous online. Organisations that provide platforms for their work, such as search engines, social networks and other forums must maintain computer records on Russian soil of everything posted over the last six months. Major service providers including Facebook, Skype, Gmail and Twitter are also required to comply.

Russia's largest telecommunication and internet companies expressed their concerns regarding the negative impact of the law on their businesses and on the Russian economy as a whole. A *change.org* petition to completely cancel Yarovaya's Law collected over 600,000 signatures. A Russian Public Initiative petition has been signed more than 100,000 times. A number of protests were organised in the major Russian cities, including Novosibirsk, Yekaterinburg, Ufa, Kazan and Volgograd. A protest organised in Moscow on 9 August 2016, saw over 2,000 participants. The Electronic Frontier Foundation, a non-profit group that aims to defend civil liberties in the digital world, opposed the Yarovaya package, noting that "opposition to the Yarovaya package has come from many quarters". Technical experts have been united in opposing the law. Mikhail Fedotov and Russia's government internet ombudsman called upon senators to reject the draft law. Because messaging services and social media platforms

> cannot reasonably comply with all the demands of the Yarovaya package – they become de facto criminals whatever their actions. And that, in turn, gives the Russian state the leverage to extract from them any other concession it desires. The impossibility of full compliance is not a bug, it's an essential feature.[7]

The experts noted the lack of judicial oversight and stated that these provisions would ultimately jeopardise security, while being ineffective at preventing terrorists from using encryption, as well as unjustifiably expanding surveillance while undermining human rights and cybersecurity.

Public internet

As of August 2014, operators of public Wi-Fi networks in Russia have to identify users by their ID numbers, and the data is to be stored for at least six months. In Resolution no. 801 of 12 August 2014, the Russian government has given instructions to require public Wi-Fi user identification. The directive was published in the official regulatory database. Currently, free Wi-Fi networks are widely available in cafes, restaurants, other public places, at public transport stops and in the metro systems of large cities. The regulation does not specify why the internet users must be identified. However, it was publicly announced (and debated) that this was to avoid anonymity in the internet. Network operators are required to identify users by their passports or by their user numbers, if any, which they can receive

7 Eva Galperin and Danny O'Brien (2016) Russia Asks for the Impossible with Its New Surveillance Laws. *Electronic Frontier Foundation* (19 July).

after registering at the Unified portal of state services. This portal was organised as part of the project "Electronic State" designed to provide public services. It is very popular in Russia and many Russian citizens have registered. Apart from standard services (provision of various certificates and documents), the portal also provides information about minor administrative offences like breaches of traffic rules, and it makes it possible to participate in direct democracy by initiating draft laws and public debate in the state Duma.

Control over the dissemination of information

Law no. 149-FZ "On Information, Information Technologies and the protection of Information" (hereinafter, "the Information Act") is an important piece of the regulation of the internet in Russia. Under the Law, any network operators who are engaged in the delivery and processing of electronic messages are considered an organiser of the dissemination of information (OSP). This activity is subject to control exercised by Roskomnadzor, and all such operators should inform this state agency that they are involved in such operations. A special registry of such "organizers" is held by Roskomnadzor. That means that the dissemination of information in the internet is now under the control of the state. In particular, operators are obliged to store any processed information within 6 months. The Law also obliges operators to provide access to such information (data) to the state bodies responsible for public safety if their request is made in accordance with the Russian legislation (Article 10.1 of the Law). This rule does not refer to the court's authorisation as a condition enabling the authorities to make such a request, so human rights activists immediately concluded that the court's authorisation is not required. However, this conclusion is not entirely correct because this issue is quite complex, and it has been examined in depth by the European Court of Human Rights in the case *Roman Zakharov v. Russia* [GC], no. 47143/06, 4 December 2015. Nevertheless, the Law requires the authorisation of the court if, in the view of Roskomnadzor, the "organizer" does not comply with the Law and its activity should be suspended.

In practice, the authorities rely on the court decisions. It should further be established whether the court decision is a formality that leads to a miscarriage of justice or not; whether the Law gives access to the current exchange of information or to the archives only. In October 2017, a judge established that the Russian messenger Telegram has failed to exercise its duties to provide the Federal Security Service with secret codes necessary to gain access to the encrypted data. In March 2018 Roskomnadzor informed Telegram that the service would be blocked if the messenger refused to comply with its obligations set out in Article 10.1. It is worth noting that the request was not made in connection with an individual criminal case, but for the purpose of mass surveillance. It seems that the Russian authorities are reluctant to follow international tendencies based on the individual approach to data for public security purposes after the Digital Rights Ireland case[8] or the Apple cases,[9] where the request was made in respect to personalised information

8 Court of Justice of the European Union case C-293/12 *Digital Rights Ireland Ltd v. Minister for Communications, Marine and Natural Resources*; Judgment of 8 April 2014.

9 General overview can be taken from L. Grossman (2016) Inside Apple CEO Tim Cook's Fight With the FBI. *Time* (17 March). *Legal documents:* for example, the order of the US District Court for the Central District of California of February 16, 2016, compelling Apple Inc. To assist agents in search of a cellular telephone pursuant to an application of the All Writs Act, 28 U.S.C. 1651.

in connection with access to the iPhone of the perpetrator killed by law-enforcement agents. In the Telegram case, the management ultimately provided the secret codes to the authorities, although having informed them that the codes are to be regularly changed by the system within a short period. Fortunately, since then no social network, either international or local, has been blocked by Russian authorities.

Under domestic law, "organizers" are subject to control by Roskomnadzor in relation to the content of the information hosted by them. Roskomnadzor can request that any information in violation of copyright laws or information of an extremist nature be removed. In general, the operator of the website is not personally responsible for the violation of the copyright or anti-extremist requirements. Under Article 1253.1 of the Russian Civil Code, the hosting company is not responsible for the content of information disseminated by a third person if the operator does not know or should not know about the violation and the operator removed the content without delay after receipt of a request made by the copyright holder. The operator, however, can be involved in court proceedings (civil or criminal) as a third party or a witness without any possibility to compensate their expenses.

Moreover, about 260,000 websites were blocked unlawfully only because they shared the same addresses with the offenders. Internet experts believe that such excessive pressure is based on sporadic, extra-judicial, non-proportional and arbitrary interference in the freedom of the dissemination of information on the internet. Many holders of existing websites decided to emigrate from the Russian internet zone, and some new internet projects prefer not to register their domain names in the. ru zone.[10] Such operators can provide the storage of personal data outside the jurisdiction of the Russian authorities. However, this could create another problem because the website operator may not be allowed to provide any telecom services in Russia. In such a situation, the websites using "external" domain names become passive providers of information accessible solely at the request of the users seeking such information, and the information would not be actively disseminated through social networks. The impact of such information stored outside the Russian internet zone becomes less significant. In regard to personal data belonging to Russian citizens, this should be stored exclusively in the Russian internet zone due to the requirements of Law no. 242-FZ on the processing of personal data in information networks. Those requirements were partially caused by Edward Snowden's disclosure of the mass surveillance organised by the US National Security Agency. Law no. 242 required the establishing of the state register of offenders of personal data on the internet to be held by Roskomnadzor on the basis of court decisions that have entered into force. Within one day, the hosting providers are obliged to inform the owners of the websites in order to remove the unlawful information from the websites at the request of Roskomnadzor.

Extremist material

In many cases the authorities restrict the dissemination of information on the basis that it has been classified as extremist material. All the applications described in the following

10 See, for example, M. Habr. *Lawful Hosting in the context of localisation of personal data*. http://m.habr.com/post/293568 (accessed 16.07.2018); A. Zdolnikov, *Russia's State Censor Blocks Hundreds of Thousands of IP Addresses*. https://meduza.io/en/news/2018/04/16/russia-s-state-censor-blocks-hundreds-of-thousands-of-ip-addresses-owned-by-amazon (accessed 16.07.2018).

have been lodged with the European Court of Human Rights and communicated to the Russian government.

In December 2011, the elections to the state Duma of the Russian Federation were to be held. A forum of opposition parties and civil activists joined forces to call voters "to vote for any party, except United Russia" because the ruling political party has not fulfilled their promises. They uploaded a two-minute video on a YouTube account which featured a sequence of static frames, each of them showing one of the campaign promises from United Russia's manifesto printed in the 23 December 2002 issue of the Nezavisimaya Gazeta newspaper. Around that time Alsu Garapova and Yevgeniy Aronson copied a link to the video to the My Videos folder in their vk.com (VKontakte) accounts. VKontakte is the largest Russian social networking service, similar to Facebook.

In 2013, a district prosecutor in Novosibirsk applied to a court seeking a declaration of the extremist nature of seven videos found on the account of another VKontakte user. He relied on the findings of a linguistic study carried out by the Investigations Committee of the Novosibirsk Region to the effect that

> the video contains statements giving a negative assessment of a group of persons on account of their membership of the United Russia party. It also contains an incentivizing statement calling for hostile actions by one group against another group united by their membership of the United Russia party.

On 21 June 2013, the Kirovskiy District Court in Novosibirsk held an ex parte hearing and granted the prosecutor's application. Following the court's decision, the video was added to the Federal List of Extremist Materials under number 2066.

Later in 2013, the Tatarstan department of the Federal Security Service identified the Vkontakte users who had copied links to the video to their accounts and requested the social network administrator and a local internet service provider, on the basis of the Operational Search Activities Act, to submit information on the number of logins into their accounts by the applicants. The collected information was sent to a deputy prosecutor in Kazan who, on 11 June and 30 May 2014 respectively, instituted administrative proceedings against the applicants on the charge of mass dissemination and storage of extremist materials, an offence under Article 20.29 of the Code of Administrative Offences. Both applicants immediately deleted the videos from their saved links but the case was referred for trial to the Vakhitovskiy District Court in Kazan. On the basis of judgments on the 8 and 18 July 2014, the District Court found both applicants guilty as charged and sentenced them to a fine of 1,000 Russian roubles (21.5 euros). The finding of guilt rested on the fact that since 2011, the video had been publicly accessible on the applicants' VKontakte profiles and that it was identical to the video that had been declared to be extremist material and included in the Federal List of Extremist Materials.[11]

Authorities acted on the basis of Section 8(2) of the Operational Search Activities Act, which requires that the operational search measures involving interference with the constitutional right to the privacy of postal, telegraphic and other communications transmitted by means of a telecommunications network or mail services or within the privacy of a home – such as an inspection of premises or buildings, an interception of postal,

11 See http://minjust.ru/ru/node/221412 (accessed 16.07.2018).

telegraphic, telephone and other forms of communication or a collection of data from technical channels of communication – require prior judicial authorisation (for further details, see §§ 34–43 of the *Roman Zakharov* judgment).

In March 2014, under Section 15.3 of the Information Act ("calls for mass disorders, extremist activities, participation in unauthorized mass gatherings"), the office of the Russian Prosecutor issued an order to block access to three major opposition websites – Grani.ru, Eg.ru (the Ezhednevniy Zhurnal online newspaper), and Kasparov.ru. They posted materials relating to unauthorised meetings and accumulated articles and publications about protests held in Russia in support of the defendants in the criminal proceedings relating to clashes between protesters and the police in Bolotnaya Square during an authorised demonstration in Moscow in May 2012. Prosecutors submitted the blocking order directly to Roskomnadzor, who in turn sent a notice to the hosting providers of the previously mentioned websites identifying the information or web page to be deleted. The hosting providers immediately blocked access to the web pages and within twenty-four hours notified the owners.

The owners applied for a judicial review of the blocking order. They submitted that the indiscriminate blocking of access to the entire website, without giving notice of the specific offending publications, was in breach of the established procedure in so far as it prevented the applicants from restoring access to their websites by removing the offending material. They claimed that the indiscriminate blocking substantially restricted their right to impart information not declared unlawful. The courts rejected the claims referring to the lawfulness of the actions made by the authorities and concluded that the blocking order had had no effect on the applicants' rights or freedoms. They also removed the offending materials and asked Roskomnadzor to stop blocking access but received no response.

In December 2012, access to the website belonging to Vladimir Kharitonov was blocked because the IP address of another, unrelated website, which it shared with the applicant's website, had been blacklisted on the grounds that it contained propaganda about narcotics. The users from various Russian regions reported to the applicant that access to his website was blocked by their internet providers referring to "a decision by the competent Russian authority". He checked the register of websites blacklisted by Roskomnadzor and found that the IP address of his website had been entered into the blacklist according to a decision by the Federal Drug Control Service. The decision was intended to block access to another website, The Rastafari Tales (www.rastaman.tales.ru), featuring a collection of fictional stories about the use of cannabis, which was also hosted by the same operator, Dreamhost, with the same IP address as the applicant's website. The applicant complained to the court that the decision to block the entire IP address had the effect of blocking access to his website, which did not contain any illegal information. The court rejected the applicant's complaint, holding that Roskomnadzor had acted within its competence, in accordance with the Law, and for the purpose of protecting children from harmful information relating to the use of drugs. It did not assess the impact of the contested measure on the applicant's website.

I ought to mention that outside the political context, the Russian authorities are very effective in protecting fundamental rights on the internet, including copyright in the sphere of audio-visual productions. They usually act promptly and proportionately, targeting only those who violate the copyright laws and without blocking entire websites.

Means of mass surveillance

Russian law-enforcement authorities apply various technologies for surveillance. In order to monitor open sources and the internet, including the blogosphere and social networks within the Commonwealth of Independent States (CIS), they use a special analytical search system designed by the Russian firm Analytic Business Solutions called "Semantic Archive". The advertised features of Semantic Archive are as follows:

- Automated collecting and processing of information obtained from heterogeneous sources, both internal (file documents, proprietary databases, emails) and external (online databases, news media, blogs, forums, social networks).
- Single uniform storage for all types of collecting documents.
- Knowledge extraction, i.e. automatic and semi-automatic extraction of objects, events and relationships from documents.
- Maintaining knowledge bases and collecting dossiers on particular projects, investigations, partners, competitors, clients, etc.
- Revealing hidden or implicit relationships between objects.
- Visual presentation of knowledge in the form of semantic networks.
- Use of a variety of reports to present the results of research.

Another tool, the Russian System of Operational-Investigatory Measures (SORM) aims to provide the interception of any type of fixed or mobile communication, including telephone conversations and electronic messages. The telecommunications operators are required to install hardware provided by the Federal Security Service (FSB), which allows the agency to monitor user communication metadata and content, including phone calls, email traffic and web browsing activity. The SORM-1 system (implemented in 1995) captures telephone communications; SORM-2 (implemented in 1999) intercepts internet traffic, and SORM-3 collects information from all forms of communication, providing the long-term storage of all information and data on subscribers, including actual recordings and locations. In 2014, the system was expanded to include social media platforms. In 2016, SORM-3 added additional classified regulations that apply to all internet service providers in Russia.

The FSB is required to obtain a post-collection court warrant to access these records. Surveillance can begin before the warrant is granted or requested, the warrant need not be shown to the telecom operator, and it is only required for the retrieval of collected communications content, not for the metadata. In the *Roman Zakharov* judgment, the Court found that the Russian SORM legislation does not provide sufficient guarantees required by the European Convention on Human Rights. The equipment used by operators should be compatible with the surveillance equipment used by the authorities (including SORM). In addition, the operators are obliged to keep secret any information about the surveillance tactics and methods which become available to the staff of the operator.

The Russian law-enforcement agencies enjoy unrestricted interception of communications to conduct operational search activities. The technical requirements of the system of technical facilities enabling the conduct of operational search activities are regulated by Order no. 70 issued by the Russian Ministry of Communications and Information Technologies in 1999. The Order was not officially published and became available to the public only after the expansion of the internet on Russian territory. The Order specifies that the interception of communications is performed by law-enforcement agencies from a remote-control terminal connected to the interception equipment installed by the mobile network operators. The equipment must be capable, inter alia, of (a) creating databases of interception subjects to be managed from the remote-control terminal; (b) intercepting communications and transmitting the data thereby obtained to the remote-control terminal; (c) protecting the data from unauthorised access, including by the employees of the mobile network operator; and (d) providing access to databases containing subscriber addresses.

More precisely, the equipment must ensure (a) the interception of all the incoming and outgoing calls of the interception subject; (b) access to information about his or her whereabouts; (c) the maintenance of interception capability where an ongoing connection is transferred between the networks of different mobile network operators; (d) the maintenance of interception capability in cases involving supplementary services, such as call forwarding, call transfer or conference calls, with the possibility of registering the number or numbers to which the call is routed; (e) the collection of communications data concerning all types of connections, including fax, short messaging (SMS) or other; and (f) access to information about the services provided to the interception subject.

The remote-control terminal receives a password from the mobile network operator giving it full access to SORM. The remote-control terminal then changes the password so that unauthorised persons cannot gain access to SORM. From the remote-control terminal, SORM can be commanded, among others, to start an interception of a subscriber, interrupt or discontinue the interception, intercept a subscriber's ongoing communication, and submit specified information about a subscriber.

Surveillance (Roman Zakharov judgment)

In the *Roman Zakharov* judgment, the European Court of Human Rights examined the Russian legislation regulating surveillance from different perspectives. The Court reiterated that any interference can only be justified if it is in accordance with the law, pursues a legitimate aim and is necessary in a democratic society in order to achieve any such aim. The law must thus meet quality requirements: it must be accessible to the person concerned and foreseeable as to its effects. Consequently, the law must indicate the scope of any such discretion conferred on the competent authorities and the manner of its exercise with sufficient clarity to give the individual adequate protection against arbitrary interference. In its case law on secret measures of surveillance, the Court developed the following minimum safeguards that should be set out in law in order to avoid abuses of power: the nature of offences which may give rise to an interception order; a definition of the categories of people liable to have their telephones tapped; a limit on the duration of telephone tapping; the procedure to be followed for examining, using and storing the data obtained; the precautions to be taken when communicating the data to other parties; and the circumstances in which recordings may or must be erased or destroyed.

The Court noted that the Operational Search Activities Act (OSAA) does not give any indication of the circumstances under which an individual's communications may be intercepted on account of events or activities endangering Russia's national, military, economic or ecological security. It leaves the authorities almost unlimited discretion in determining which events or acts constitute such a threat and whether that threat is serious enough to justify secret surveillance, thereby creating possibilities for abuse.

The Court also noted that prior judicial authorisation for interceptions is required in Russia. Such judicial authorisation may serve to limit the discretion of the law-enforcement authorities in interpreting the broad terms of "a person who may have information about a criminal offence", "a person who may have information relevant to the criminal case", and "events or activities endangering Russia's national, military, economic or ecological security" by following an established judicial interpretation of the terms or an established practice to verify whether sufficient reasons for intercepting a specific individual's communications exist in each case. The Court accepted that the requirement of prior judicial authorisation constitutes an important safeguard against arbitrariness. However, the Court has found that the requirement to discontinue interception when no longer necessary is not specifically mentioned in OSAA, and therefore goes beyond judicial control. In regard to the procedures for storing, accessing, examining, using, communicating and destroying the intercepted data, the Court considered the six-month storage time limit set out in Russian law for such data reasonable. At the same time, it deplored the lack of a requirement to immediately destroy any data that is not relevant to the purpose for which they have been obtained. The automatic storage for six months of clearly irrelevant data cannot be considered sufficiently justified.

The Court concluded that Russian legal provisions governing interceptions of communications do not provide for adequate and effective guarantees against arbitrariness and the risk of abuse, which is inherent in any system of secret surveillance, and which is particularly high in a system where the secret services and the police have direct access, by technical means, to all internet and mobile telephone communications. In particular, the circumstances in which the public authorities are empowered to resort to secret surveillance measures are not defined with sufficient clarity. Provisions on the discontinuation of secret surveillance measures do not provide sufficient guarantees against arbitrary interference. The domestic law permits the automatic storage of clearly irrelevant data and is not sufficiently clear as to the circumstances in which the intercept material will be stored and destroyed after the end of a trial. The authorisation procedures are not capable of ensuring that secret surveillance measures are ordered only when "necessary in a democratic society". The supervision of interceptions, as it is currently organised, does not comply with the requirements of independence, power and competence, which are sufficient to exercise an effective and continuous control, public scrutiny and effectiveness in practice. The effectiveness of the remedies is undermined by the absence of notifications at any point of the interceptions, or adequate access to documents relating to the interceptions.

It is significant that the shortcomings in the legal framework as identified here appear to have an impact on the actual operation of the system of secret surveillance, which exists in Russia. The Court was not convinced by the government's assertion that all interceptions in Russia have been performed lawfully on the basis of a proper judicial authorisation. The examples submitted by the applicant in the domestic proceedings and in the proceedings before the Court indicate the existence of arbitrary and abusive surveillance practices, which appear to be due to the inadequate safeguards provided by law. In view of these shortcomings, the Court has found that the Russian law does not meet the "quality of law" requirement and is incapable of keeping the "interference" to what is "necessary in a democratic society". The Russian authorities are now debating whether to propose measures in order to implement the judgment.

Since the judgment is not implemented, one important problem arises in connection with the court's order to block Telegram messenger: whether or not the authorities have the right (legally and morally) to request unlimited and unrestricted access to the big data generated by new operators. The authorities cannot ensure Telegram users that they will apply conventional guarantees and safeguards. Pavel Durov, the Telegram founder, believes that the attempt by the authorities to block Telegram constitutes interference with the fundamental freedoms of the users. He was supported by twenty-six international human rights, media and internet freedom organisations who requested the blocking of Telegram be stopped.[12] In addition, there is an additional problem: if Telegram successfully managed to avoid the blocking by changing the IP addresses, does it mean that the interference really took place?[13]

Conclusion

Russia is a rapidly developing society characterised by a high penetration of the internet and widespread internet services and all kinds of negative consequences, such as internet fraud and other types of criminal activity online. There are no effective safeguards against the abuse of power by the law-enforcement authorities, and so the personal data used by public authorities and recordings of intercepted private conversations could be leaked to the public without any proper authorisation. Russian society is actively integrating with the international community, where fundamental rights and freedoms are respected. However, the isolation tendencies pursued by law-enforcement authorities in order to control personal data remain strong.

12 Russia: Telegram blocks leads to Widespread assault on freedom of expression online. https://twitter.com/durov (accessed 16.07.2018). https://twitter.com/AmnestyEECA/status/991281853763072000 (accessed 16.07.2018).

13 Matt Burgess (2018) This Is Why Russia's Attempts to Block Telegram Have Failed. 28 April, www.wired.co.uk/article/telegram-in-russia-blocked-web-app-ban-facebook-twitter-google (accessed 16.07.2018).

Index

access to internet: case studies 41–43; net neutrality 36–37, 136–137, 263–264, 347, 379–381; as a new human right 29; as a public good 30, 33; threats and challenges 35–37
African Union: African Charter on Human and Peoples' Rights 322–323; Convention on Cyber Security and Personal Data Protection 311, 329
American Convention on Human Rights 227, 371
Anti–Fake News Act (Malaysia) 368
Asia–Pacific Economic Cooperation Privacy Framework (2015) 293

balancing of rights 110, 132–134, 158–159, 178, 300–301, 342, 359–362, 372

Cambridge Analytica/Facebook scandal 49, 118, 138, 229
Central Monitoring System (India) 364
Code of Conduct on countering illegal hate speech online 233
Computer and Cybercrimes Bill (Kenya) 325
copyright as a human right 240–243
Council of Europe: Budapest Convention on Cybercrime 227, 385; Convention 108, 164, 291; Declaration of the Committee of Ministers on internet governance principles 122; European Convention on Human Rights 63, 68, 135, 165–166, 197, 211, 227, 242, 305, 393
Criminal Code (Canada) 348
Cybercrime Prevention Act (Philippines) 361–362
cybersecurity 91, 124–128, 299, 323–325, 360
Cybersecurity Law (China) 93, 299, 360–361, 366

data localization 274–275, 300
data protection: private sector 53–55, 135–137, 288–289, 301; workplace 295–296
Denmark: Criminal Code 115; Media Liability Act 115; Penal Code 114
diagonality of human rights obligations 82–84
Digital Divide 21–24, 33, 42–43, 374
digitalisation 75–76, 82–86, 209–210, 225–226
digital security technologies: confidentiality of communications 140; detection of cybercrime 261–265, 329, 333, 385–386; detection of threats 91–93, 99–101, 125, 260–262, 267–268; impacts on human rights 21–24, 76–77, 79–82, 84, 90–93, 259–260, 264–265; six caveats 267–268; threats and vulnerabilities 260–261, 270
distributed governance 121

European Court of Human Rights: *Animal Defenders International v. United Kingdom* 217; *Appleby et Al v. UK* 112–113; *Ashby Donald v. France* 248–250; *Big Brother Watch v. UK* 173–174, 177; *Delfi v. Estonia* 71–74, 108–110, 141, 174–175, 180–181, 190, 229, 253, 384; *Editorial Board of Pravoye Delo and Shtekel v. Ukraine* 140, 145; *Egill Einarsson v. Iceland* 107, 191; *Erbakan v. Turkey* 228; *Falzon v. Malta* 219; *Neij and Kolmisoppi (The Pirate Bay) v. Sweden* 141; *Garaudy v. France* 229–230; *Guseva v. Bulgaria* 218; *Handyside v. UK* 140; *Jersild v. Denmark* 111; *K.U. v. Finland* 107, 140; *Lillo–Stenberg and Sæther v. Norway* 221; *Magyar Helsinki Bizottság v. Hungary* 214, 218–219; *M.L. and W.W. v. Germany* 175–177; *Melnychuk v. Ukraine* 113; *MTE v. Hungary* 72, 253; *Österreichische Vereinigung zur Erhaltung, Stärkung und Schaffung v. Austria* 216; *Özgür Gündem v. Turkey* 112; *Pedersen and Baadsgaard v. Denmark* 219; *Premininy v. Russia* 385; *Reno v. ACLU* 140–142, 144; *Roj TV A/S v. Denmark* 232; *Roman Zakharov v. Russia* 389, 394; *S.A.S. v. France* 110; *Satakunnan Markkinapörssi Oy and Satamedia Oy v. Finland* 209, 220, 222; *Standard Verlags GmbH v. Austria No. 2* 220; *Steel and Morris v. United Kingdom* 213–216; *Stoll v. Switzerland* 66, 73, 141; *Társaság a* Szabadságjogokért v. Hungary 214, 216; *Taulats and Capellera v. Spain* 231; *Von Hannover v.*

Germany 107, 220; *Weber and Saravia v. Germany* 172; *X and Y v. Netherlands* 106; *Yildirim v. Turkey* 62, 65, 73, 141; *Youth Initiative for Human Rights v. Serbia* 216
European Court of Justice: Bonnier Audio 251; Digital Rights Ireland Ltd. 52, 169–170, 389; Filmspeler 256; Glawischnig–Piesczek 235; Google Spain 54, 56, 138–139, 157, 168–169, 177, 199–202, 226, 235, 351, 379; GS Media 255–256; Laserdisken 246; L'Oréal v eBay 251; McFadden 253; Metronome Musik 246; Promusicae 250–251; Renckhoff 247; Sabam 71, 134, 252; Schrems v Data Protection Commissioner 139, 170; Svensson 255; Tietosuojavaltuutettu v Satakunnan Markkinapörssi Oy and Satamedia Oy 222; Unabhängiges Landeszentrum für Datenschutz Schleswig–Holstein v Wirtschaftsakademie Schleswig–Holstein GmbH 171; UPC Telekabel Wien 252–253, Ziggo 256
European Union: Charter of Fundamental Rights 139, 158, 166, 177, 198–199, 211–212, 240, 242, 305–306; Data Protection Directive (95/46/EC) (Article 29 Working Party 199, 311–312; Data Protection Supervisor 273); E–Commerce Directive 71, 108–109, 151, 225; E–Privacy Directive (2002/58/EC) 166–167; ePrivacy Regulation 167; General Data Protection Regulation (Consent 275–277; Data Breach 281–282; Data Governance 278–279; Data Protection Officer; Data Protection Principles 309–312; Data Quality 278; Fines and Sanctions 279–280, 298; Global Responses 282–285; Global Standards 300, 309; Privacy by Design 269–270; Riskification 306–308); InfoSoc Directive 151, 246–247, 254; Telecommunications Directive (97/13/EC) 166

Federal Trade Commission: Federal Trade Commission Act 55, 291; Privacy and Data Security Update 297
Freedom House: net freedom status ("Free" countries 361–363; "Not Free" countries 360–361; "Partly Free" countries 363–364)
freedom of expression: intermediary liability exemptions 71–72; Internet Balancing Formula 186; journalists 211; legal basis 60; limitations 64–66, 268; net neutrality 379; scope 112–113; standard–setting 66; tools of repression 24; UNHRC discussions 20

Gayssot Act (France) 230–231, 236
Global Administrative Law 120
Global Conference on Cyber Space 101
Global Network Initiative: mission 153–155; principles 155–156
global surveillance 138
Google Advisory Council 158–159, 184

hate speech: case law 228–232; international framework 226–228; internet intermediaries 232–236
horizontal *vs.* vertical governance 161–162
hostile non–state groups 99
human rights online: balancing 132–134, 183; case law 138–143; contextualisation 133
human rights violations: human wrongs (aggregation of wrongs 79–83); normal accident theory 77–79

identity resolution 275
Information and Communication Amendment Act (Gambia) 328
information communication technology 23–24, 32, 42, 154–156, 160, 327–328, 374
Inter–American Commission on Human Rights 372, 378
Inter–American Court of Human Rights 372–374
International Telecommunications Union: Tunis Agenda 32, 39, 59, 122; World Summit on Information Society 31
Internet Balancing Formula: aspect of empathy 188–189; case studies 190–193; element of time 187; epistemic dimension 183–184; historical truth 189–190; interference into privacy 186; ontic dimension 180–183; rationality aspect 178–180; vulnerability 188
Internet Corporation for Assigned Names and Numbers: Bylaws 123–124; Internet Engineering Task Force 123, 130; Regional Internet Registries 123, 131
internet governance: International Telecommunications Union 121; multistakeholderism 123–124; second order internet governance (internet as a public resource 127–128; privatization of governance 126–127)
internet liability: intermediary 71, 150–152, 157; liability regimes 103–104; online private life violations 106–109
internet regulation: above 90, 92–94; access 334; accountability 290, 307, 312, 328; below 90, 94–96; beyond 90, 96–99; censorship 26, 144, 179, 182, 237, 274; control 323, 389–390; multisectoral governance 374, 381; net neutrality 36–37, 263–264, 347, 379–381; non–discrimination 16, 254, 265–266, 304, 377; openness and accessibility 376; pluralism and diversity 377; universal access 21–22, 374–376

Japan: Act on the Protection of Personal Information 283; Criminal Code 362; Revenge Porn Act 362 journalist: citizen journalist 59; definition (CJEU 222–223; ECtHR 213–214); function of the press 215–217; special protection 211; traditional press 218–219

Manila Principles on Intermediary Liability 157, 382

Netzwerkdurchsetzungsgesetz (Germany) 70

OECD Guidelines on the Protection of Privacy and Transborder Flows of Personal Data 164, 290–293

Retrofit (Private Limited) v. Posts and Telecommunications (Supreme Court of Zimbabwe) 335
right to be forgotten 54, 81, 121, 139, 157–158, 168, 175, 184, 197–199, 201–205
right to privacy: chilling effects 51, 55, 143; convergence of American and European Values 52–55, 289–291; four categories of legal rules 50; personal dignity 53; privacy bridges 54; privacy fatalism 45–47, 52; right to solitude 49
Russian Federation: Data Protection Act 299; Information Act 389; Law no. 152–FZ (Personal Data Law) 386–387; Law no. 242–FZ on the processing of personal data in the information networks 390; Russian System of Operational–Investigatory Measures 393; Yarovaya Law 387–388

Singapore: Broadcasting Act 363; Green Paper 369; Internet Code of Practice 363
South Africa: Cybercrimes and Cybersecurity Bill 325; State Security Agency 319
South Korea: Constitution 93; Information Communications Network Act 365–366; Personal Information Protection Act 98
Strasbourg Luxembourg dialogue 134, 176

treaty inflation: humanist perspective 39–40; rights as trumps 41; welfarist alternative 38

United Nations: Human Rights Committee 20, 61, 181, 227, 231; International Covenant on Civil and Political Rights 20–21, 41, 60, 129, 154, 226, 322, 334, 356; Millennium Development Goals 32–34; Special Rapporteur on the Promotion and Protection of the Right to Freedom of Opinion and Expression 20, 25, 32, 58, 61, 67, 95, 126, 154, 159–160, 179, 232, 237, 372–374; Statistics Division 354; Universal Declaration of Human Rights 21, 31–32, 38, 41, 60, 104–105, 135, 154, 197, 226, 241, 287, 356
United States: California Consumer Privacy Act (2018) 287, 351; Digital Millennium Copyright Act 151, 203; Fair Credit Reporting Act (1970) 289, 297, 300; Illinois' Biometric Information Privacy Act 350; US Privacy Act (1974) 289
United States Supreme Court: Ashcroft v Free Speech Coalition 142; Packingham v North Carolina 143

World Intellectual Property Organisation 239